INDIA VISION 2020

THE REPORT + BACKGROUND PAPERS

INDIA Vision 2020

THE REPORT

REPORT OF THE COMMITTEE ON INDIA VISION 2020,
PLANNING COMMISSION, GOVERNMENT OF INDIA

Chairman : **S.P. Gupta**

plus

BACKGROUND PAPERS

सत्यमेव जयते

Planning Commission
GOVERNMENT OF INDIA
NEW DELHI

Published by
Academic Foundation
NEW DELHI

Published in 2004 by
ACADEMIC FOUNDATION
4772-73 / 23 Bharat Ram Road,
(23 Ansari Road), Darya Ganj,
New Delhi - 110 002. INDIA.

Phones : 23245001, 02, 03, 04.
Fax : +91-11-23245005.
e-mail : academic@vsnl.com
www : academicfoundation.com

India Vision 2020 : The Report plus Background Papers
Planning Commission, Government of India

ISBN 81-7188-350-8

Printed and Bound in India.

CONTENTS

CONTENTS — PART ONE

REPORT OF THE COMMITTEE ON **INDIA VISION 2020**

Planning Commission, Govt. of India
Chairman: S.P. Gupta

CONTENTS — PART TWO

BACKGROUND PAPERS

India Vision 2020 Committee

S. P. Gupta

Chairman, Committee on India Vision 2020;
Member, Planning Commision. Government of India, New Delhi;
Former Adviser, Global Modelling, The World Bank, Washington D.C.

Amit S. Ray

Member Secretary, Committee on India Vision 2020;
Professor of Economics, School of International Studies,
Jawaharlal Nehru University, New Delhi.

Members and Contributors

Manas Bhattacharyya

Deputy Director General (Finance),
Department of Telecommunications, Ministry of Communication and IT, Government of India, New Delhi.

Ashish Bose

Former Professor, Institute of
Economic Growth, Delhi.

P. Chaturvedi

Chairman, The Institute of Engineering,
New Delhi.

Sarala Gopalan

Former Secretary to Government of India, Women and
Child Development, Ministry of Human Resource
Development, New Delhi.

M.C. Gupta

Director, Indian Institute of Public Administration,
New Delhi.

Anwar ul-Hoda
Professor, Indian Council for Research on International Economic Relations (ICRIER), Delhi.

P. V. Indiresan
Professor, Centre for Policy Research, New Delhi;
Former Director, Indian Institute of Technology, Madras (Chennai)

Ramaswamy R. Iyer
Professor, Centre for Policy Research, New Delhi.

Garry Jacobs
The Mother's Service Society, Pondicherry.

Mahesh Kapoor
Former Consultant, The World Bank, New Delhi.

G.N. Kathpalia
Alternative Futures : Development Research and Communication Group, New Delhi.

Nagesh Kumar
Director General, Research and Information System for the Non-Aligned and Other Developing Countries (RIS), New Delhi.

Amitabh Kundu
Professor, Centre for Studies in Regional Development, School of Social Sciences, Jawaharlal Nehru University, New Delhi.

P. N. Mari Bhat
Professor, Population Research Centre, Institute of Economic Growth, Delhi.

R K. Pachauri
Director General,
Tata Energy Research Institute (TERI), New Delhi.

V. A. Pai Panandiker
Former Director, Centre for Policy Research, New Delhi.

V. R. Panchamukhi
Chairman, Indian Council of
Social Science Research (ICSSR). New Delhi

R. Radhakrishna
Director, Indira Gandhi Institute of Development Research (IGIDR), Mumbai.

J.S. Rajput
Director General, National Council of Educational Research & Training (NCERT), New Delhi.

H. Ramachandran
Director, Institute of Applied Manpower Research (IAMR), New Delhi.

Prema Ramachandran
Adviser (Health), Planning Commission, Government of India, New Delhi.

C.P. Ramaswamy
Professor, Centre for Policy Research, New Delhi.

Shovan Ray
Former Consultant, Planning Commission, Government of India, New Delhi.

H.S. Saksena
Editor, The Eastern Anthropologist, Lucknow.

S.S. Sandhu
Major General, New Delhi.

Rohit Sarkar
Special Consultant, Planning Commission, Government of India, New Delhi.

Pronab Sen
Adviser (PP), Planning Commission, Government of India, New Delhi.

Shailendra Sharma
Adviser, Labour, Employment and Manpower, Planning Commission, Government of India, New Delhi.

Hira Singh
Former Director, National Institute of Social Defence, New Delhi

Jasjit Singh
Director, Centre for Strategic and International Studies (CSS), New Delhi;
Former Director, Institute for Defence Studies and Analysis, New Delhi.

Padam Singh
Additional Director General, Indian Council of
Medical Research (ICMR), New Delhi.

Panjab Singh
Director General, Indian Agricultural
Research Institute (IARI), New Delhi.

K.C. Sivaramakrishnan
Professor, Centre for Policy Research,
New Delhi.

Krishan Sondhi
New Delhi.

K. Srinivasan
Former Director, Population Foundation of India,
New Delhi.

R. Srinivasan
Member, Independent Commission on
Health in India; Former Secretary to Government of India,
Ministry of Health and Family Welfare, New Delhi.

K.L. Thapar
Director, Asian Institute of Transport Development,
New Delhi

M.C. Verma
Adviser to Minister of Labour,
Shram Shakti Bhavan, New Delhi.

Pravin Visaria
Late Professor and Former Director,
Institute of Economic Growth, Delhi

Introduction

S. P. GUPTA

The report on "India: Vision 2020" reproduced in Part One of this volume, has been the outcome of many detailed deliberations among all the Committee members comprising selected top scholars and experts in their respective fields under my chairmanship. The Committee had been constituted by the Planning Commission, Government of India in the year 2000 as a part of the exercise on Tenth Plan to develop a long-term twenty year vision for helping to work out a medium-term programme for India's development strategy. The Committee took more than two years to have an integrated and consistent view of how the countrymen would like to see India in the year 2020. The Committee's deliberations were further enriched by nearly 20 written contributions received from among the Committee members. The contributors represent a wide spectrum of the society and from different parts of India.

In the final report, we have not necessarily adopted and accepted all the views and assessments of each individual author. But an integrated view is taken from a broad consensus emerging from the views of the different Members. These papers provided broad guidelines and pointers to formulate our understanding of Vision for India in 2020 and providing often detailed rationales for taking these views. Indeed in preparing the final report we have benefitted enormously from the inputs received from the background papers. The Report, however, is unable to do full justice to the rich and detailed analysis contained in the various papers. The final report also draws valuable inputs from experts within and outside the Planning Commission. The Committee gained from the vision of Dr. A.P.J. Abdul Kalam's book "India 2020: A Vision for the New Millennium".

Dr. S.P. Gupta is Member, Planning Commission, Government of India and Chairman, India Vision 2020 Committee.

Given the complexity and vast scope of research and issues covered by individual papers, it is now felt that the papers will be a sources of great 'knowledge' value on their own, over and above their contribution to the final report on India Vision 2020. This prompted us to put together a volume with select background papers (with necessary editing) submitted to the Planning Commission for the India Vision 2020. Needless to mention, the view presented in these papers are that of the authors and not necessarily that of the Planning Commission.

A Brief Overview of the Background Papers

AMIT S. RAY

The final report of *India Vision 2020* (presented in Part One of this volume) draws largely, but not exclusively, upon the background papers submitted by distinguished scholars and experts. However, it would be wrong to presume that the Vision 2020 report is merely an executive summary of these selected background papers. Each paper has its own distinct view-point, approach and analytical structure, at times divergent from each other, to visualize India in 2020. It was indeed difficult to weave a coherent and consistent document from these diverse, sometimes contradictory, set of views adopted in the background papers. The final Vision 2020 report, therefore, stands out in some respects as distinct and independent from the set of papers commissioned by the Planning Commission. However, the background papers will be of academic interest to the readers.

In Part Two of this volume, we present the background papers as submitted by the authors. The final report covers several dimensions of the Indian economy, polity and society in a particular thematic order. We have deliberately kept the same order in presenting the papers in this volume according to their thematic focus.

Human development constitutes the first and most important area of concern for India in 2020. Human development includes issues of demography, food security and nutritions, employment, education, health and vulnerabilities. The first twelve chapters cover different aspects of the above themes broadly within the rubric of human development. P.N. Mari Bhatt (chapter 1), based on his demographic

---

Amit S. Ray is Professor, Jawaharlal Nehru University and Member-Secretary, India Vision 2020 Committee.

projections, suggests that India's population is expected to reach 1.3 billion by 2020. His paper also presents detailed projections of the age, spatial and gender-wise distribution of India's population for the next two decades with an analysis of their socio-economic implications. The immediate question that arises from this demographic profile is whether the country's agricultural sector will be able to meet the growing food requirements for its expanding population. Panjab Singh (chapter 2) addresses this question in a larger context of agriculture and agricultural policy for India in 2020. R. Radhakrishnan and K. Venkata Reddy (chapter 3) analyses the issue of food security and nutrition, concluding that elimination of food insecurity and malnutrition can not be achieved merely through the process of economic growth without active and effective policy intervention towards poverty reduction.

Employment generation can act as a key factor in poverty reduction. Shailendra Sharma's paper (chapter 4) contains a detailed perspective on the employment structure for India in years to come. The next two chapters by J.S. Rajput (chapter 5) and by Garry Jacobs and N. Asokan (chapter 6) focus on education and the role of knowledge. Both papers emphasize on the importance of knowledge revolution and knowledge society in building a more prosperous India by 2020 by tapping the enormous untapped human potential that exist in the country. Health is another key area of India's developmental concern for 2020. R. Srinivasan (chapter 7) presents the issues and prospects for India's health care in 2020. Prema Ramachandran (chapter 8) adopts a more holistic perspective covering issues of health, nutrition and population.

The final set of papers on human development (chapter 9-12) focus on different aspects of the problems of vulnerable sections of our society. Sarla Gopalan (chapter 9) presents a profile of the empowered Indian woman in 2020. Hira Singh (chapter 10) raises the issues of social defence in combating crime in society and emphasises on social justice and human rights. H.S. Saxena (chapter 11) presents a perspective on the vulnerable groups in Indian society, namely the scheduled castes, the scheduled tribes, the socially and educationally backward classes (OBC) and the religious minorities. M.C. Verma (chapter 12) synthesises the various social dimensions of long term growth and development.

Chapters 13-16 deal with infrastructural concerns in the process of India's development in the next couple of decades. The paper by Amitabh Kundu (chapter 13) focuses on problems of urbanisation and infrastructure financing, while P.V. Indiresan (chapter 14) looks at rural development. The vision for India's telecom sector in 2020 is discussed by Manas Bhattacharya (chapter 15). Mahesh Kapoor (chapter 16) presents a profile of transport sector for 2020.

Natural resources, energy and associated environmental concerns are covered in chapter 17 and 18. G.N. Kathpalia and R. Kapoor (chapter 17) focuses only on water policy and charts out a plan of action for 2020. R.K. Pachauri and P. Mehrotra (chapter 18) present comprehensive projections of all types of resource requirements and utilisation (energy, water, land) for India in 2020 under alternative scenarios. Their paper contains a detailed technical analysis of the issue of sustainability of India's material resources.

The next two chapters focus on economic aspects. Nagesh Kumar (chapter 19) analyses the international trade scenario for India in 2020. Rohit Sarkar (chapter 20) presents a profile of the financial sector in 2020.

Jasjit Singh (chapter 21) constructs a comprehensive vision of peace for India in 2020, with a goal to establish durable peace, both internally and in the external environment. The final chapter by H. Ramachandran (chapter 22) focuses on the issue of good governance to build a strong and prosperous India by 2020. He emphasises on the role of people's participation in ensuring good and responsible governance.

The set of 22 papers included in this volume will make an interesting reading for all who are interested in India. It contains a rich blend of various schools of thought and approaches of analysis cutting across different disciplinary perspectives.

Part One

India Vision : 2020

Report of the Committee on
India: Vision 2020

Chairman : S.P. Gupta

December 2002
PLANNING COMMISSION, GOVERNMENT OF INDIA

Contents : See Pages 7-8

Foreword

Every country needs a vision statement which stirs the imagination and motivates all segments of society to greater effort. It is an essential step in building a political consensus on a broad national development strategy, which encompasses, inter-alia, the roles and responsibilities of different agents in the economy, such as Central, State and local government, the private corporate sector, the small and tiny sector, people's organisations etc. It must identify the potential risks and bottlenecks and their possible solutions in order to mobilise efforts in a focussed manner. It is clear, therefore, that to meet these objectives, a vision statement has to operate at several levels of generality and specificity.

In order to address these issues, among others, the Planning Commission constituted a Committee on Vision 2020 for India in June 2000 under the chairmanship of Dr. S.P. Gupta, Member, Planning Commission. This initiative brought together over 30 experts from different fields. Their deliberations, extending over a period of more than two years, has helped to throw up a range of interesting possibilities, critical issues and crucial decision-points for government and private bodies for future action.

The Report of the Committee examines many important issues, but the ones that stand out most powerfully are employment and education. In order to ensure access to food and other essentials of a healthy life for all citizens, India faces the challenge of generating 200 million new employment opportunities over the next two decades. This report calls for raising employment generation to the top of the nation's development agenda and marshalling all available resources to create employment opportunities for all job-seekers. It goes even further by identifying the sectors which offer the greatest potential for job creation as well as critical policy issues that need to be addressed in order to fully tap that potential.

Education is the second main thrust area of this document. Greater coverage and better quality education at all levels from basic literacy to hi-tech science and technology is the essential prerequisite for raising agricultural productivity and industrial quality, spurring growth of India's budding IT and biotechnology sectors, stimulating growth of manufactured and service exports, improving health and nutrition, domestic stability and quality of governance. The report calls for concerted efforts to abolish illiteracy, achieve 100 per cent enrolment at primary and secondary levels, and broaden access to higher education and vocational training through both traditional and non-traditional delivery systems.

The document also examines issues related to population growth, food production, health, vulnerable sections of the population, transport, communication, energy self-sufficiency, water conservation and air quality, trade investment, peace, security and governance. It gives projections of India in 2020 in business as usual and in the best case scenario in various important sectors and also identifies nodal points of Indian prosperity. Its central conclusion is that India has the opportunity to emerge as one of the world's leading economies over the next two decades, provided her citizens have the self-confidence, the self-reliance, the will and the determination to realise their individual and collective potentials.

The turn of a century, and most especially the beginning of a new millennium, is an appropriate time for reflecting on the unfinished tasks of nation-building and the country's future possibilities, and placing the present Tenth Plan in tune with a Vision document. I commend the Vision 2020 Committee and especially Dr. S.P. Gupta for preparing this document that will provide a framework and perspective for those in government and the private sector who are tasked with formulating initiatives for national prosperity. I hope that this document will arouse public interest and debate which will help us to refine it further in the years to come.

— **K.C. Pant**

December 16, 2002

Deputy Chairman,
Planning Commission,
Government of India,
New Delhi.

Acknowledgement

The Committee on Vision 2020 had been constituted by the Planning Commission in June, 2000, under my chairmanship, for crystallising the country's vision for the future in the year 2020. The vision will reflect people's aspirations, the full potentials of growth and development, and lay out the efforts needed to fulfill this vision. The details of the terms of reference of this Committee and their composition have been given in the Annexure.

The Committee comprised more than 30 members and invitees from different walks of life, all experts in their respective areas, and they spent nearly two years to deliberate upon and assess the vision of the people by producing many notes and papers which have now become the basis of this Report. The details of most of the papers are yet to be finalised and edited. Once done, it is proposed to place them in the Planning Commission website prior to final publication, as background papers for this vision document.

I am indebted very much to all the Members of the Committee, the invitees and the many distinguished participants in all the meetings over which the Report has been deliberated. Their inputs were very valuable for designing and formulating this vision document. Besides, we also benefited from other innumerable sources covering many books, published and unpublished papers, and views and comments given by a large number of academics and policy makers. We got the benefit of several other vision 2020 documents pertaining to other countries and policies of different states in India. We have also gained from the vision of Dr. A.P.J. Abdul Kalam's book, *India 2020: A Vision for the New Millennium.*

Among the Members and invitees, we received special help in formulating and preparing this vision from Professor Gary Jacobs, Mother's Service Society, Pondicherry, Dr. H. Ramachandran, Director,

I.A.M.R., Shri Mahesh Kapoor, Dr. Manas Bhattacharrya, DDG, Department of Telecommunications, Shri R.P. Sinha, former Principal Adviser, Planning Commission, Professor Mari Bhat, Institute of Economic Growth, to mention only a few. In preparing this document, I have been helped enormously by Dr. Amit S. Ray, Member-Secretary of the Committee, and Professor Gary Jacobs and Dr. Nandita Khadria, members of the editorial group. I have also been fortunate to have very valuable inputs, help and suggestions from all the Principal Advisers and Advisers of the Planning Commission, including Shri Lakshmi Ratan, Dr. (Mrs.) Prema Ramachandran, Dr. (Mrs.) Rohini Nayyar, Mrs. T.K. Sarojini, Dr. Pronab Sen, Shri Shailendra Sharma, Mr. Rohit Sarkar, Shri A. Sekhar, Shri B.N. Puri, and Shri L.P. Sonkar, to mention only a few. My special thanks goes to all the Members of the Planning Commission for their support and advice and especially to Dr. D.N. Tewari, who helped me always whenever needed.

I wish also to place on record the excellent secretarial help provided by Shri Ashok Kumar Sharda, Shri P. Sankar, Shri Hemant Gaba, Ms. Neelam Khanduri and Shri P.R. Chatterjee of my office.

Before I end, I must express my respect to late Shri J.N. Maggo, who was the Member-Secretary at the outset of this project, and my thanks to Dr. Shovan Ray who later on succeeded him until he left the Planning Commission and joined IGIDR, Mumbai.

Lastly, but above all, my gratitude goes to Shri K.C. Pant, Deputy Chairman, Planning Commission, for giving me the opportunity to undertake the study reflecting the longer term perspective of the country's plan outlook amidst constant encouragement and guidance.

— **S.P. Gupta**

December 5, 2002

Member,
Planning Commission,
Government of India,
New Delhi.

Summary and Overview

Our vision of India's future should be both comprehensive and harmonious. It must encompass all the myriad aspects that constitute the life of the country and its people. It must balance and synthesise all the divergent views and forces that compete in the pursuit of self-fulfilment. It must be based on an objective assessment of facts and a realistic appraisal of possibilities, yet it must rise beyond the limitations of past trends, immediate preoccupations and pressing challenges to perceive the emerging opportunities and concealed potentials.

Most of all, our vision of India's future should serve to awaken in all of us a greater awareness of our cultural and spiritual strengths – which formed the bedrock of our past achievements and should form the foundation of our future accomplishments. Some of our traditions must change, but knowledge, in essence, is our greatest endowment. The vision should awaken in us an unswerving confidence in ourselves, a complete reliance on our own capacity as a nation and an unshakeable determination to realise our full potential. A true vision cannot be a static written statement. It must emerge as a living a dynamic reality in the minds and hearts of the people and their leaders.

This vision statement of India 2020 may not fulfill all these criteria to our full satisfaction, but it can serve as a useful starting point and foundation for contemplating future possibilities and our destiny as a nation. It can serve to indicate the board lines of policy and strategy by which India can emerage as a far stronger, more prosperous and more equitable nation in the coming years. This document draws upon many ideas and proposals contained in more than thirty background papers presented to the Committee over the last two years, which have been presented in the main body. The vast scope and complexity of the issues prevent us from doing full justice to them in this summary.

This vision statement is neither a prediction of what will actually occur, not simply a wish list of desirable but unattainable ends. Rather, it is a statement of what we belive is possible for our nation to achieve, provided we are able to fully mobilise all the available resources – human, organisational, technological and financial – generate the requisite will and make the required effort. In formulating our vision of the future India, it is important to see beyond the limits of the immediate past to rediscover the greatness that is India. Although the present Republic of India is a young developing nation, our people have a rich and illustrious history as one of the longest living civilisations in the world. In 1835, even Lord Macaulay, the British historian politician had to admit before the British Parliament: "I have travelled across the length and breadth of India and I have not seen one person who is a beggar, who is a thief. Such wealth I have seen in this country, such high moral values, people of such caliber.... the very backbone of this nation, which is her spiritual and cultural heritage...." *Thus, it would be wrong to state that in 1947 India started to construct a modern nation from scratch. Rather, it began the process of rediscovering its rich cultural and spiritual values that had formed the foundation of India in the past. It is on this foundation that we seek to formulate our vision of India 2020.*

An essential requirement for envisioning India's future in the new century is to recognise that the parameters which determine national development have changed in recent years and will change further in future. This will open up greater possibilities than ever before. A powerful set of catalytic forces is accelerating the speed of social change throughout the world. They include a rapid rise in levels of education, high rates of technological innovation and application, ever faster and cheaper communication that dissolves physical and social barriers both within countries and internationally, greater availability and easier access to information, and the further opening up of global markets. These trends are representative of a relative shift in the engines that drive development from manufacturing to the services sector and from capital resources to human and knowledge resources. Technology, organisation, information, education and productive skills will, therefore, play a critically decisive role in governing the future course of development.

The growing influence of these factors, acting on the foundation of India's increasingly dynamic and vibrant economic base, lend credence to the view that India can achieve and sustain higher than historical rates of economic growth in the coming decades. The compounded effect of achieving the targeted annual GDP growth rate of 8.5 to 9 per cent over the next 20 years would result in a quadrupling of the real per capita income and almost eliminating the percentage of Indians living below the poverty line. This will raise India's rank from around 11th today to 4th from the top in 2020 among 207 countries given in the World Development Report in terms of GDP. Further, in terms of per capita GDP measured in ppp India's rank will rise by a minimum of 53 ranks from the present 153 to 100. This will mean, India will move from a low income country to an upper middle income country. This is a very real possibility for us to seize upon and realise.

What will India be like 20 years from now? While in some areas we can confidently estimate quantitatively the outcome with a fair degree of accuracy, in some others we only know the broad direction. In still others we are unable to say with confidence the direction that future trends will take. We can only indicate what would be most desirable and signal the opportunities and obstacles that will arise along the way.

By 2020, the people of India will be more numerous, better educated, healthier and more prosperous than at any time in our long history.

In spite of the declining fertility rates, falling infant mortality and increasing life expectancy will spur an increase of at least 300 million people. The result: Total population of India will exceed 1.3 billion in 2020. A marked slowdown in birth rates will leave the under-15 population at roughly the same size as it is today (i.e., increase by 0.2 per cent per annum). This means that the pressure for expansion of the educational system will come only from increasing enrolment and efforts to reduce drop-out rates. The population over 60 years of age will double from 60 to 120 million people (i.e., around 3.5 per cent per annum). This will necessitate the adoption of special measures to support this vulnerable group, which will include a high percentage of illiterates and who are especially susceptible to both malnutrition and health-related problems. Unequal rates of population and economic growth are likely to further aggravate regional disparities within the country.

Well before 2020, India will have the capacity to produce more than sufficient quantities of food to provide a healthy diet to its entire population and become a major food exporter. Even by maintaining the moderate rates of productivity growth achieved during the 1990s, the country will be able to meet the projected demand in all major food categories and generate a substantial surplus of food grains and dairy products. Rising productivity and rapid diversification into value-added crops could spur another Green Revolution in Indian agriculture.

Production of surplus food will not, however, ensure the eradication of under-nutrition. In spite of enormous progress in the food production, nearly half the country's population still suffers from chronic under-nutrition and malnutrition. The most vulnerable are children, women and the elderly among the lower income groups. Eradication of this scourge will require the generation of sufficient employment opportunities so that all households have the purchasing power needed for assured economic access to food. Employment or livelihood security is an essential and inseparable element of a comprehensive strategy for national food security. Conversely, food security is an essential requirement for raising the productivity of India's workforce to international levels.

As population growth slows to replacement levels over the next two decades, India's greatest challenge will be to provide employment opportunities for all job-seekers. The working age population will expand by about 45 per cent, spurring rapid growth of the labour force and the number of job-seekers. Major changes in economic policy and strategy will be needed to eliminate the current backlog of more than 34 million unemployed job-seekers and assure employment opportunities for all additions to the labour force. India needs to generate around 200 million additional employment opportunities over the next 20 years. At the same time, the total proportion of the workforce involved in agriculture is likely to decline from 56 per cent to 40 per cent or even lower, thus increasing the pressure for rapid multiplication of non-farm employment opportunities.

Access to gainful employment is an essential condition for citizens to exercise their economic rights in a market democracy. The capacity to pay is the economic equivalent of the right to vote. India's vision for 2020 must be founded on the premise of Jobs for All. Employment must be considered a constitutional right of every citizen, backed by the full commitment of the Government. Granted that the requisite political will is forthcoming, the goal of full employment is certainly achievable. This will require a reorientation of national priorities, technology policy and government action. Formerly separate lines of sectoral planning need to be integrated around a central vision and set of goals, of which full employment must be one.

How and in which fields will these additional job opportunities be created? There are abundant opportunities and ample means available to the nation to achieve the objective of creating additional employment opportunities. The public organised sector however cannot be the target area, since it will continue to shed jobs for quite some time. Although the growth of the private organised sector will contribute significantly to the growth of the economy, its contribution to employment generation will be quite modest, since total employment in this sector at present represents only 2.5 per cent of all jobs. The largest number of new jobs will be created by small and medium enterprises (SMEs), which contribute the vast majority of private sector jobs in more advanced economies such as the USA, Japan and Korea. International experience confirms that SMEs are better insulated from the external shocks, more resistant to the stresses, and more responsive to the demands of the fast-chaning technology adoption, globalisation and entrepreneurial development. Employment has nearly tripled in India's small and medium sector over the past 20 years. A repetition of this performance would generate an additional 150-200 million jobs by 2020. A comprehensive package of venture capital, credit, liberalisation of controls, technology, training, marketing and management measures is needed to ensure continous expansion of this sector.

The vision document identifies a number of high employment potential sectors, including commercial agriculture, agro-industry and agri-business; forestation for pulp, fuel and power; retail and wholesale trade; tourism, housing and construction; IT and IT-enabled services; transport and communications; education, health and financial services. While all these sectors are already expanding, a wide range of strategies and policies are available to stimulate more rapid development. Induction of advanced crop technology will reduce production costs and expand the market for important commercial crops. Linkages to down-stream agro-industries can dramatically reduce waste and spoilage of perishable commodities, while broadening the range of marketable products. Adoption of an agriculture-based energy policy focusing on production of fuel oil and biomass power could generate millions of additional on-farm jobs and lucrative alternative markets for farm produce, while reducing the country's dependence on imported fuels. Tourism-related occupations presently employ only 5.6 per cent of the Indian workforce, compared to 10.8 per cent globally. Development of India's tourism infrastructure, combined with modifications in air transport, hotel rates and tax policies could generate an additional 25 million employment opportunities in this sector. Outsourcing of services by OECD countries will fuel a rapid expansion of IT and IT-enabled services, generating millions of jobs within the country. The country will also require millions of additional teachers and medical professionals to meet the surging demand for education and health services.

While it is difficult to project unemployment rates 20 years into the future, rising levels of education and growth of the over-60 age group will mitigate, to some extent, the growth of the labour force. Combined with the enormous opportunities for creation of new employment opportunities, the incidence of unemployment could be almost eliminated by 2020.

Successful education policy forms the bedrock of all fields of national development — political, economic, technical, scientific, social and environmental. Education is the foundation for a vibrant democracy, growth of productivity and income and employment opportunities. Literacy must be considered the minimum right and equirement of every Indian citizen. Presently, the country has about 300 million illiterate adults. The Government's goal is to achieve 75 per cent literacy within the next five years. A 100 per cent literate India is of paramount importance for realising the greater vision presented in this document.

Literacy is an indispensable minimum condition for development, but it is far from sufficient. In this increasingly complex and technologically sophisticated world, 10 years of school education must also be considered an essential prerequisite for citizens to adapt and succeed economically, avail of social opportunities and develop their individual potentials. The current enrolment rate for primary education is around 77 per cent and for secondary education about 60 per cent. Achieving 100 per cent enrolment of all children in the 6 to 14 year age group is an ambitious but achievable goal for 2020 that should be pursued as a top priority.

Increasing enrolment to cover the entire school-age population needs to be combined with efforts to increase the quality and relevance of school curriculum to equip students with not only academic knowledge, but also values and life-knowledge. A qualitative shift is needed from routine memorisation to development of children's capacity for critical thinking and from methods that emphasise teaching and passive learning to those that foster active interest and the ability of children to learn on their own.

Concentrated efforts are needed to tap the potentials of alternative methods of knowledge delivery for both school going and non-school going children and adults, including television, computerised self-learning and Internet-based courses. Given the huge number of young students that will quest for all levels of higher education and a severe shortage of qualified instructors, and given India's outstanding expertise in the IT industry, the country should embark on a massive programme to convert progressively the higher educational curriculum into a multi-media, web-based format and to establish accredited standards for recognition of courses taught under distance education programmes.

Our vision of India in 2020 is predicated on the belief that human resources are the most important determinant of overall development. A more than doubling of investment in education from the current level of 3.2-4.4 per cent of GNP is the soundest policy for quadrupling the country's GNP per capita.

The knowledge and skill of our workforce will be a major determinant of India's future rate of economic growth as well as the type and number of jobs we create. Currently, only five per cent of the country's labour force in the 20-24 age category have undergone formal vocational training, compared to levels ranging from 28 per cent in Mexico to 96 per cent in Korea. A comprehensive strategy is needed to enhance the nation's employable skills, including a cataloging of the entire range of vocational skills required to support development, expansion of the nation's system of vocational training institutes, widening of the range of vocational skills taught, and active involvement of the private sector in skill delivery. A national network of 50,000 or more computerised vocational centres run by private self-employed businesses, similar to the STD booths and Internet cafes, can deliver low-cost, high-quality training to 10 million workers every year — more than five times the total number covered by existing programmes. A parallel effort is required to upgrade the skills of Indian farmers, who represent 56 per cent of the total workforce. The existing system of 300 Krishi Vignan Kendras needs to be expanded and supplemented by a national network consisting of thousands of farm schools offering practical demonstration and training on lands leased from farmers in the local community.

The health of a nation is a product of many factors and forces that combine and interact. Economic growth, per capita income, employment, literacy, education, age at marriage, birth rates, availability of information regarding health care and nutrition, access to safe drinking water, public and private health care infrastructure, access to preventive health and medical care, and health insurance are among the contributing factors. Measued in terms of infant mortality rates, maternal mortality, life expectancy and nutrition, the health of the Indian population has improved dramatically over the past 50 years. Yet, despite these achievements, wide disparities exist between different income groups, between rural and urban communities, between different states and even districts within states, and a big gap from the level attained by the high middle income and advanced developed country.

Communicable diseases remain the major cause of illness. During the next 5 to 10 years, existing programmes are likely to eliminate polio and leprosy and substantially reduce the prevalence of kalaazar and filariasis. However, TB, malaria and AIDS will remain major public health problems. Improved diagnostic services and treatment can reduce the prevalance and incidence of TB by 2020. Restructuring the workforce and strengthening health care infrastructure can reduce the incidence of malaria by 50 per cent or more within a decade. Childhood diarrhea, another major cause of illness, can be largely prevented through community action and public education. Childhood under-nutrition can be addressed by targeting children of low birth weight and utilising low-cost screening procedures. Given the projected improvement in living standards, food security, educational levels and access to health care among all levels of the population, dramatic progress can be achieved in reducing the prevalance of severe under-nutrition in children substantially by 2020. Although private expenditure on health care is expected to rise sharply, the level of public expenditure needs to rise about four-fold from present levels in order to support a more equitable and effective health care system, providing universal access, fair distribution of financial costs, and special attention to vulnerable groups such as women, children, the aged and disabled. Health insurance can also play an invaluable role in improving the health care system.

Literacy and general education form the base of the knowledge pyramid which is essential for a rapid and sustained development of the society in the 21st Century. The continuous advancement of science and the application of improved technology constitute the middle rung. Social ideals and values form the apex. Technical education, both vocational and professional, provide the foundation for development of science and technology. A large number of the country's engineering colleges need to be upgraded to quality standards nearer to those of India's world-class IITs. India's expenditure on R&D, which is currently 1/60th that of Korea, needs to be considerably enhanced. Another essential requirement is to improve the linkage between technology development and technology application by fostering close ties between basic research and business.

India's urban population is expected to rise from 28 per cent to 40 per cent of the total population by 2020, placing increasing strain on the country's urban infrastructure. Future growth is likely to concentrate in and around 60 to 70 large cities having a population of one million or more. Decentralisation of municipal governance and greater reliance on institutional financing and capital markets for resource mobilisation are likely to increase the disparity between the larger and smaller urban centres. A satisfying outcome will depend on the formulation of effective public policies to accelerate all-round development of smaller urban centres and to refashion the role of the state as an effective facilitator to compensate for the deficiencies of market mechanisms in the delivery of public goods.

Simultaneous efforts are needed to strengthen the rural infrastructure relating to education, health care, transport, telecom, power and water. Unless bold steps are taken to promote a geographically more dispersed and equitable development paradigm, widening disparities between rural and urban centres will accelerate the migration to cities and the rapid expansion of urban slum areas. One promising alternative approach is to link clusters of villages together by high speed circular highways, thereby bringing 100,000 or more people into a circular community that can be crossed within 30 minutes of travel time, and promoting a balanced and distributed development of urban services along the periphery of the ring road.

Rapid flow of information is a catalyst for social development. Vision 2020 conceives of India evolving into an information society and knowledge economy built on the edifice of information and communication technology (ICT), of which telecommunications is the springboard. Rapid expansion and extension of the country's fixed and mobile telecom infrastructure is essential for stimulating growth of both the ICT sector and the economy as a whole. The number of fixed telephone line services will multiply another seven-fold in the next 18 years. As the fixed line market matures, more and more users will cross over to mobile communications as well, spurring a mobile revolution in India. Mobile telecommunications and the Internet will set the contours of technological progress over the next two decades. The third generation mobile devices with access to mobile data and voice should be within reach of wide sections of the population by 2020.

Development involves a continuous increase in the number of physical transactions and the speed with which they occur, both of which are highly dependent on the size and quality of the nation's transport system. Efforts to achieve higher GDP growth rates in future years cannot be sustained without correspondingly greater efforts to strengthen the nation's transport system. Based on the projected GDP growth of 8 per cent per annum, the total freight traffic is likely to reach five times the level in 2000. Passenger traffic is expected to increase more than four-fold over the next 20 years.

Increasing population combined with continued urbanisation will fuel the explosive growth of personal vehicle movement in cities, which can only be curtailed by massive investment in mass transport services. Specific plans need to be formulated by each urban authority, starting with the provision of bus services, developing intermediate public transport and identifying corridors for future growth, including reserving land for such activity. In the long run, rail-based mass transport systems appear to be the only viable solution to the problems of urban transport in India's major metropolitan areas.

A key component for rural development is the provision of roads for connectivity, access being essential for social and economic well-being. Families residing alongside roads benefit from better health and greater educational opportunities compared to the families living in remote villages. Based on current plans, all villages with more than 500 inhabitants will be connected by all-weather roads within the next decade.

Our vision of India 2020 is of a country having a well-developed network of roads and railways, with adequate capacity to handle the growth in transport demand. The volume of road traffic will multiply about five-fold, carried on a 70,000 km. network of national highways. State highways with at least two way lanes will link most districts. Rural roads will provide access to the furthest outlying villages. Technological progress is working towards generation of vehicles that are pollution free and fuel efficient. An efficient public transport system will lead to a reduction in the population of two-wheelers in major urban areas. We also envisage that connection of several major rivers through a network of interlinking canals will provide impetus to rapid growth of low-cost, inland water transport.

Total investment requirements to meet these needs will increase to levels three to four times higher than present levels in real terms. While the government will continue to be a major source of funds for infrastructure, internal generation of resources by the transport services will have to increase, supported by more realistic pricing of transport services, reduction in operating costs, and active involvement of the private sector in the development and operation of transport systems.

Economic growth is driven by energy that powers the nation's industries, vehicles, homes and offices. For future growth to be both rapid and sustainable, the energy source needs to be as resource-efficient and environmentally benign as possible. Total demand for power is expected to increase by another 3.5 times or more in the next two decades, which will necessitate a tripling of installed generation capacity from 101,000 to 292,000 MW by 2020. 'Business as usual' will result in a spiralling cost for imported fuels and a surge in emission of environmental pollutants.

The overall growth in demand for all forms of fuel will mirror the growth in the power sector. Total coal demand will nearly double, and both oil and gas demand will triple. Expanding domestic production capacity will require substantial investments, while increasing dependence on imported forms of energy will increase vulnerability to fluctuations in global energy prices. Surging demand will also place increased burden on the physical and social environment. Enhanced adoption by the public and private sector, of best-practices and environment-friendly technologies, more efficient use of energy, promoting private sector investment, and greater efforts to protect the environment will be required to cope effectively with the nation's growing energy appetite.

Greater reliance on renewable energy sources offers enormous economic social and environmental benefits. India is already the world's fifth largest producer of wind power, with more than 95 per cent of the investment coming from the private sector. Other renewable energy technologies, including solar photovoltaic, solar thermal, small hydro, biomass power and bio-fuels are also spreading. A concerted effort to implement a more visionary approach to alternative energy generation could significantly reduce India's dependence on imported fuels while also reducing the strain on the environment. Biomass power production, ethanol motor fuel and jatropa fuel oil can generate millions of rural employment opportunities and contribute to higher rural incomes, at the same time reducing the outflow of foreign exchange. Tapping this potential will require conducive national policies and programmes designed to attract strong participation from the private sector.

India possesses 16 per cent of the world's population but just 4 per cent of its water resources. At the national level, current water resources are more than sufficient to meet the demand, but future projections show that the supply situation could become difficult over the next half century. Total water consumption is expected to rise by 20-40 per cent over the next 20 years. India is not poor in water resources. What it lacks is the ability to efficiently capture and effectively utilise the available resources for maximum benefit. The government policy needs to be revised to provide incentives for efficient use of water, including appropriate water pricing and more effective institutional mechanisms for water management. Enormous potential exists for increasing the productivity of water in agriculture by methods to raise crop productivity combined with better water management. Both urban and rural water resources can be substantially enhanced by widespread adoption of rain-water harvesting techniques, designed to capture run-off water during the monsoon season and channel it to recharge both surface water and underground aquifers. These methods need to be applied throughout the country on a massive scale, both in rural and urban areas.

Proposals to link some of the major rivers together could channel surpluses from flood-prone areas into drought-prone regions, create millions of hectares of additional irrigated land, provide an inexpensive system of inland water transport, and generate millions of additional employment opportunities in construction, agriculture, trade and industrial development. Despite the high cost of such a system, the potential benefits to the nation are so vast that pragmatic proposals demand serious consideration. Given the vision and political will, India can convert the present water problem into a huge opportunity.

India's wide range of agro-climatic regions, vast extent of land and forest, and rich variety of biodiversity rank it among the most naturally endowed nations of the world, but its huge and still expanding human and animal populations and its urge for industrialisation tax these resources to the limit. The potential however exists for dramatically reversing the pattern of degradation that has taken place in recent decades by a systematic effort to halt soil erosion, restore precious nutrients and organic material to crop lands, recharge groundwater tables, and re-establish depleted forest lands. A combination of measures would make it possible to increase the land under forest and tree cover from the current level of 71 million hectares to 83 million hectares.

India's progress over the next 20 years will be intimately linked to events within the region and around the world. The World Bank estimates that India will become the fourth largest economy in the world by 2020. Liberalisation of trade will open up new opportunities for export of goods, while increasing pressures on domestic industry to cope with competition from imports. The global market for textiles, clothing and agricultural products will expand dramatically, but India's ability to export will depend on its capacity to keep pace with rising international standards of price, quality, productivity, and service.

The emerging global scenario will open up greater opportunities for countries with a surplus of well-educated, highly skilled labour that can provide an attractive commercial environment for the outsourcing of manufacturing and service businesses from high and even middle income countries. Export of services is a field in which India can excel. India's recent boom in outsourcing of IT services is only the tip of a rich vein of economic opportunity that could extend to a wide range of manufacturing and service businesses.

Computerisation, coupled with low cost global telecommunications are generating rapid growth of trade in service businesses, such as software and IT enabled services. This trend will accelerate, opening up vast opportunities for countries with the capacity to deliver low-cost, high-quality service. At the same time, the pressure for export of the highly educated and highly skilled individuals will also increase, so that a significant migration of scientific, engineering and medical talent is likely to continue.

Growth in the size of the international capital market will open up increasing opportunities for India to attract foreign direct and institutional investment, but a substantial improvement in infrastructure and elimination of most of the bureaucratic barriers will help India in attracting a greater share of FDI flows. Mobilisation of India's expatriate population could have momentous impact on the inflow of FDI in 2020.

India's technology policy needs to be reformulated in the light of the emerging international economic environment to capitalise on the accelerated global development and diffusion of technologies and keep pace with more demanding international standards for cost, quality and productivity. We will need to be far more aggressive in acquiring and applying advanced technologies in a wide range of fields, including agriculture, information technology, energy, health and education. At the same time, we can also aspire to become an important contributor to the expansion of global frontiers of technology by building upon and leveraging our already significant achievements in fields such as pharmaceuticals, biotechnology, software, space and energy.

India is in the midst of transforming an agrarian economy into a modern multi-dimensional economic enterprise and a traditional stratified society into an egalitarian society, while simultaneously fashioning and transforming itself into a modern democracy through consultative politics. It is inevitable that such a rapid social, economic, technological and political development of one billion people should generate turbulence. Yet it is essential that this turbulence be managed and confined within limits that preserve the social fabric and permit the nation's transformation to continue.

Underlying all our plans and hopes for a better future, underpinning all our efforts to evolve into a prosperous democratic nation is the shared aspiration of all Indian people for peace. Peace is not merely the absence or avoidance of conflict. It is the essential prerequisite for all human and social development, for which we can strive to increase our knowledge, develop our productive skills, strengthen our physical infrastructure, and integrate our multitudinous communities into a strong, united nation.

The challenges to peace are numerous and they come from all directions — from outside our borders and within, as well as from within our minds. Our capacity to preserve and build a lasting peace for all Indians will depend on the strength of our military to defend our borders, the strength of our economy to generate increasing employment and income opportunities for our citizens, the strength of our educational system to cultivate the knowledge and skills of our youth, the strength of our legal and judicial system to safeguard the rights of individuals and communities, the strength of our scientists and engineers to both develop and harness technologies for the benefit of the people, as well as the wisdom and determination of our political leaders to remove injustices and to direct the collective energies of the nation for greater achievement in every field of endeavour.

Development tends to reduce the extent of these disparities in some ways while aggravating them in others. Economic disparities aggravate perceptions of difference between sub-national, linguistic and communal groups, fostering ethnicity and communalism. A positive strategy for national security will depend on the secular and democratic values of the Indian nation deriving its strength from our culture, civilisation and freedom.

External security depends on national power. It requires a continuous enhancement of the country's capacity to use its tangible and intangible resources in such a manner as to affect the behaviour of other nations. While power is often conceived in narrow terms as military power, in the world that is emerging it must be much more broadly conceived to include political, economic, technological, social and intellectual dimensions. A vibrant economy and a leading role in international affairs may be as important as a strong military to the preservation and development of national power. Internationally, we must gravitate from a state-centered, egocentric and competitive security paradigm to a co-operative security paradigm that enhances the security of each nation by reducing potential threats to all nations. Human development in all its dimensions is and will remain our highest strategic priority.

India's economic and technological transition will be accompanied by a multifaceted political transformation that will have profound impact on the functioning of government. This transformation will foster decentralisation and devolution of power to local bodies, including financial devolution and financial responsibility; increasing direct participation of people in setting grass root priorities for distribution of resources, and building and managing local projects; and greater efficiency, transparency, and accountability in government agencies at all levels. E-governance has the potential, if fully harnessed and rightly utilised, to radically improve the speed, convenience, quality and transparency of public administrative services, while enhancing the ability of individual citizens to express and exercise their democratic rights.

Our vision of India in 2020 is of a nation bustling with energy, entrepreneurship and innovation. The country's people will be better fed, dressed and housed, taller and healthier, more educated and longer living than any generation in the country's long history. India

1

Introduction

> A Vision is not a project report or a plan target. It is an articulation of the desired end results in broader terms.
>
> — A.P.J. Abdul Kalam

This document is neither a plan nor a projection of what India will be in 2020. Twenty years is too long a period for one or the other. Even our demographic projections, based on the most reliable data and well-documented trends, are only able to estimate the country's population two decades hence and within a range of 100 million people. How then shall we hazard a projection of the harder to measure eventualities?

The second decade of the 21st Century lies behind a barrier that is impenetrable by statistical probes. Looking backwards, we become aware of how limited our horizon of certitude really is. In the mid-1960s, when India was confronted with the threat of widespread famine and was perennially dependent on foreign food aid to feed its people, who among the most visionary of us could have imagined that within such a short period food grain production would double and the country would be having significant surpluses? Who could have anticipated the sheer speed of Japan's rise in the 1970s and 1980s or its equally surprising stagnation during the 1990s? In 1980, who could anticipate the Personal Computers revolution that was to follow just two years later? In 1983, when India's total software exports were only $12 million, who could imagine that they would multiply 500 times in 17 years and the country would be recognised around the world as a major IT power? In early 1989, who could foresee that the fall of the Berlin Wall, the end of the Cold War, the break up of the USSR and the entire Eastern Bloc would all occur within 24 months? Even a visionary like Microsoft's founder Bill Gates admits that he was unable to grasp the enormous potential of the Internet until it had already spawned a global revolution. The growth rate of our cities, which mirrors global trends of urbanisation, is 25 per cent lower today than what we predicted just five years ago.

Planning and prediction over such long time horizons as two decades are beyond our capacity, but we do possess a still greater human endowment that can enable us to envision the real possibilities and to perceive the necessary actions we need to take to convert those possibilities into realities. Call it vision or imagination, or aspiration, or anything else, it is this faculty that most differentiates us from other species and constantly drives the evolutionary progress of humanity. Vision requires a subtle blend of humility and the courage to dare.

For a vision to be realisable, it must bring into view the untapped potentials and unutilised opportunities that await exploitation both domestically and internationally, as well as the problems and challenges that impede our progress. Indeed, it is the forces which oppose our progress that generate the necessary pressure compelling us to strive harder. They may even prove to be the best indices of what will be achieved.

In envisioning a better future, we should not make the mistake of dwelling on what we lack rather than on what we possess, for India today possesses both the capacities and the opportunities to achieve a state of super-abundance. The effective strategy should focus on fully utilising the material, human, technological and social resources that we possess in the most rapid, efficient and organised manner.

A realisable vision must identify the catalytic forces that can be harnessed to accelerate the nation's development, as well as the obstacles that must be overcome, and anachronisms and out-dated attitudes done away with, in order to advance rapidly. It must frankly own past errors and troublesome propensities, but with faith in our capacity to learn from the past and change – as indeed we are now changing – with ever increasing speed. In a realisable vision, there is no room for lofty optimism based on the premise that everything will turn out for the best regardless of what we decide or how we act. But, equally, there can be no scope for extreme pessimism based on ideas that deprive us of the freedom and power to determine our own future. Our vision must express the nation's aspirations, determination and commitment for self-realisation.

We begin our visioning exercise by cataloguing the untapped potentials and under-utilised resources that are available to the nation, and then turn our attention to the present problems and emerging opportunities which constitute the raw materials from which we must fashion a better future for our country and its people.

A Vision for India

In formulating our vision of the future India, it is important to see beyond the limits of the immediate past to rediscover the greatness that is India. Although the present Republic of India is a young developing nation, our people have a rich and illustrious history as one of the longest living civilizations in the world. In 1835, even the British historian and politician, Lord Macaulay, admitted before the British Parliament: "I have travelled across the length and breadth of India and I have not seen one person who is a beggar, who is a thief. Such wealth I have seen in this country, such high moral values, people of such caliber... the very backbone of this nation, which is her spiritual and cultural heritage..."[1] Thus, it would be wrong to state that in 1947 India started to construct a modern nation from scratch. Rather, it began the process of rediscovering its rich cultural and spiritual values that had formed the foundation of India in the past. It is on this foundation that we seek to formulate our vision of India 2020.

It is indeed a challenge to formulate a cohesive vision for India in 2020. Therefore, we thought it appropriate to seek inspiration from one who had a clear vision and possessed the gift to articulate it in a manner that has inspired the hearts and minds of countless Indians. The vision articulated by Rabindranath Tagore is all encompassing in every sense. In Annexure I, we identify eight components of the vision reflected in the following poem and attempt to translate them in operational terms for India Vision 2020.

1. *The Awakening Ray*, Vol. 4, No. 5, The Gnostic Centre.

Where the mind is without fear and the head is held high.
Where knowledge is free.
Where the world has not been broken up into fragments
By narrow domestic walls.
Where words come out from the depth of truth.
Where tireless striving stretches its arms towards perfection.
Where the clear stream of reason has not lost its way
Into the dreary desert sand of dead habit.
Where the mind is led forward by Thee
Into ever-widening thought and action.
Into that heaven of freedom, my Father, let my country awake.

Rabindranath Tagore

The Challenges Ahead

India's per capita income has doubled over the past 20 years. With population growth slowing now to about 1.6 per cent per annum, a growth rate of the gross domestic product (GDP) of around 9 per cent per annum would be sufficient to quadruple the per capita income by 2020.

Opinions on achievable rates of economic growth have a tendency to swing along with the short-term economic performances. Two years ago, the global boom, the IT revolution and the all-round optimism led many to believe that in the coming decade India could mimic the 9-10 per cent growth rates that China achieved over a twenty year period. Such optimism is out of fashion today. But there is ample evidence showing that if we can adopt a longer term perspective that is not blinded by immediate circumstances and fluctuating moods, higher rates of growth should be achievable for India in the coming years. This is not a prediction — it is a potential. The reality will depend on how effectively we seize the opportunity to do so.

From a historical perspective, global rates of development have been increasing for more than a century. The dramatic rise of Japan and the East Asian tigers, and most recently China, are illustrative of this point. An objective assessment reveals that all the major engines of economic growth that have accelerated growth up till now, will be present in greater abundance in the coming years than they had been in the past.

Engines of Economic Growth

- Educational levels are rising rapidly.
- Rates of technological innovation and application are accelerating.
- Cheaper and faster communication is dissolving physical and social barriers, both within the country and internationally.
- Information is being made available in greater quantity and quality than ever before.
- Globalisation is opening up new markets.

A vision is a statement of aspirations and intentions, and therefore, it is essential that we fully recognise the need for determined effort to transform all these potentials into realities. Ultimately, it is not our capacity for prediction but our action that will determine the outcome. That action needs to be based on proper appreciation of the forces available for accelerating our progress.

Assuming that India achieves this quadrupling of per capita income by 2020, it would attain a level of development far higher than where China is today, and on par with upper-middle income countries (UMA) such as Argentina, Chile, Hungary, Malaysia, Mexico and South Africa. One day India will rise higher still, and having achieved such a target, will know HOW she achieved it. But such knowledge could be acquired even now from the experiences of the many nations that have already passed through these stages of development. From their experiences India should endeavour to acquire the underlying principles and theoretical knowledge that can then be applied appropriately to our own specific case. Therefore, we refer to the average performance of this group of UMI countries as a benchmark for our development challenges and achievable goals by 2020. Table 1 compares India's current status on some key parameters of development with the average level achieved by a group of UMI countries. It may be noted that we are not holding up the UMI countries as the goal for India in 2020, but merely using them as a reference point to indicate the magnitude of progress India needs to make in different fields. Our vision is not only to reach these reference levels but to surpass them in many cases.

Table – 1

Developmental Parameters at a Glance India Present vs. UMI Reference for India 2020

Developmental Parameters	*India Present*	*UMI Reference for India 2020*
Poverty as % of population below poverty line	26.0	13.0
Income distribution (gini index 100=equality)	37.8	48.5
Unemployment rate (% of labour force)	7.3	6.8
Male adult literacy rate (%)	68.0	96.0
Female adult literacy rate (%)	44.0	94.0
Net primary school enrolment ratio	77.2	99.9
Public expenditure on education as % GNP	3.2	4.9
Life expectancy at birth in years	64.0	69.0
Infant mortality rate per 1000 live births	71.0	22.5
Child malnutrition as % of children under 5 years based on weight for age	45.0	8.0
Public expenditure on health as % GNP	0.8	3.4
Commercial energy consumption per capita (kg of oil equiv.)	486.0	2002.0
Electric power consumption per capita (kwh)	384.0	2460.0
Telephones per 1000 population	34.0	203.0
Personal computers per 1000 population	3.3	52.3
Scientists & engineers in R&D per million population	149.0	590.0
Sectoral Composition of GDP in %		
Agriculture	28.0	6.0
Industry	26.0	34.0
Services	46.0	60.0
International trade in goods as % of ppp GDP	3.6	35.0
Foreign direct investment as % of gross capital formation	2.1	24.5
Gross FDI as % of ppp GDP	0.1	3.5

Source: Based on *World Development Indicators, 2001*, The World Bank.

Striving to achieve these reference levels and surpass them in some cases will present very significant challenges insofar as the determination and resourcefulness of the country is concerned.

Major Challenges for India

- A targeted approach to bring millions of families above the poverty line.
- Generation of nearly ten millions of new employment opportunities per annum, especially for those in the lower income groups.
- Eradication of illiteracy.
- A concerted effort to raise primary and secondary enrolment rates and minimise drop-outs.
- Improved public health to reduce infant mortality and child malnutrition.
- Massive investment in power generation, telecommunications and other physical and social infrastructure.
- Accelerated acquisition of technology capabilities to raise productivity in agriculture, industry and services.
- Becoming a more important player in the world economy in terms of both trade and investments.

We are confident that we can and will meet these challenges. We also feel that we have the knowledge and the capacity as a nation to achieve food for all, health for all, and jobs for all. What we do not know for sure however is, how long it will take us to accomplish them. We need, therefore, to affirm the will and the determination to do it rapidly and achieve it now rather than sometime later.

2

Uncommon Opportunities

Knowledge and Information Technology

An essential requirement for envisioning India's future is to recognise that the equations which determine national development have changed in recent years, opening up greater possibilities than before. The same factors continue to be at work, but their relative contribution and importance is rapidly shifting along several dimensions as shown in the figure.

Shifting Determinants of Development
Manufacturing →→ Services
Capital resources →→ Knowledge resources

The sectoral composition of the GDP changes with economic development. The predominance of agriculture in the least developed economies is reduced by the increasing importance of manufacturing, and subsequently, services, as they move up the ladder of development. As this occurs, the rates of economic growth tend to increase. This transition is now occurring globally and is reflected in the explosive growth of the services sector, especially in the fields of financial services, information and communication technology (ICT), insurance, education and health.

India's services sector has already become the dominant contributor to GDP, accounting for 46 per cent of the total, but its share is still far below the UMI reference level of 60 per cent. The country very soon will get the opportunity to skip the long slow phase of industrialisation that the most developed nations have passed through, and transit rapidly into a predominantly service economy by 2020, creating services that meet human needs, generate employment covering the large unorganised segment of the economy, raise incomes and increase purchasing power. Even our notion of services may need to evolve further to recognise the importance of the emerging knowledge-intensive services.

Knowledge has replaced capital as the most important determinant of development. In a path breaking study in mid-1950s, Nobel laureate economist Robert Solow showed that seven-eighth of the growth of US from 1900 to 1950 was accounted for by technical progress, while only one-eighth was driven by capital. A study by Denison, of factors contributing to the growth of the US economy from 1929 to 1982, attributes 94 per cent of that growth to factors relating to knowledge generation and dissemination: 64 per cent of this is linked to advances in knowledge generation (i.e. R&D) and another 30 per cent to advances in education. Better resource management, which is an application of knowledge, is also identified as a more important factor than capital. This fact bodes well for countries whose economic planners are able to escape from their earlier faith in capital and fully tap the enormous productive potential of non-material, knowledge resources.

India's Green Revolution is a dramatic example of how the input of greater knowledge in the form of improved production technologies can rapidly increase the productivity of scarce land resources. India's IT Revolution is a striking instance of how the importance of human capital has come to acquire a higher position than that of material plant and machinery.

All efforts to project India's future progress get at times blinded by the question of resources, more specifically, the financial resources needed for all plan activities. We start with the conviction that financial (capital) resources will not be the key factor that decides the course of our future progress. If we fail, it will be mainly for want of a vision of what is possible, knowledge of how to realise it, belief in ourselves, commitment to achieve, will for the effort or skill in implementation — and not for lack of finance.

The knowledge revolution is not just a short-term blip on the radar screen which peaked in 2000 with the boom in dot com companies. It is a real and profound opportunity for countries around the world to increase the pace and scope of the benefits of development. It marks a significant shift in the relative importance of different resources or factors of production in the development process.

> *Knowledge Revolution*
>
> - By one recent estimate, 50-60 per cent of all industrial output is based on information.
> - Modern manufacturing industries depend as much for their success on the management of information relating to quality, cost and scheduling, as they do on the management of materials and production processes.
> - The services sector, which has the great potential for creating new employment opportunities and economic growth in the world economy, is essentially knowledge-based.
> - The phenomenal growth of employment potential in this century has been mostly driven by the rapid expansion of small and medium, technology intensive sectors and services.

This shift from material to knowledge-based resources opens up vast opportunities for the developing countries to accelerate the pace of development. India's rate of economic growth can be substantially increased if the country becomes a superpower in knowledge and if the potentials of information and information technology are fully understood and exploited.

Thus far, the potentials have been narrowly focused on the export potentials of the IT sector. But far greater potential lies in the extension and application of IT to stimulate the development of other sectors of the domestic economy. Information is a revolutionary force in bridging the digital divide that currently separates the advantaged and the disadvantaged of our nation. Apart from generating new employment opportunities, the application of IT can vastly extend access to education, health care, markets, financial services, vocational skills, administrative services and other aspects of modern society, to many more people at far lower cost. It can dramatically reduce the cost of communications, improve access to technology and marketing capabilities for the rural poor, eliminate intermediary exploitation in the production and distribution chains, increase government accountability and stimulate democratic participation. Therefore, rather than addressing IT as a specific sector, in this report, we have chosen to highlight its significant contributions under different headings, like employment, education, infrastructure and governance.

Knowledge Resources

There are a host of non-material, knowledge-based human resources that we possess in abundance and can apply to achieve far greater results.

Knowledge Resources

- Technology
- Organisation
- Information
- Education
- Skills

Technology: Knowledge in the form of information technology (IT) has opened up the opportunity for India to become the premier, low-cost provider of computer software and IT-enabled services to the industrialised world. It can not only provide high paying jobs and rising exports, but also transform the way we educate our youth — increasing the speed, quality and efficiency of learning manifold. In addition, it can and is already transforming the way we communicate among ourselves and with the rest of the world, shrinking the distances between hemispheres, providing instantaneous access to the whole world's knowledge base and customer base. Knowledge in the form of biotechnology offers not only a lucrative field for employment and economic growth, but a means for improving the health of our people and the productivity of our fields. In the form of agricultural technology, knowledge can increase crop yields from the present level, which is far below world averages, to levels two, three or four times higher. Pioneering Indian farmers have already achieved it for a variety of crops. What they have done individually, we can do as a nation. Finally, knowledge in the form of manufacturing technology will raise the competitiveness of the Indian manufactures to international standards of costs and quality.

Organisation: Technology is not the only knowledge resource now abundantly at our disposal. Today we have access to the whole world's experience in organisation. Organisation is nothing but the know-how for carrying out work most efficiently and expeditiously. India's highly successful Green Revolution and White Revolution were the results of organisational innovations as much as technology. We have the opportunity to fashion new and better forms of organisation to carry out the tasks of education, health-delivery, governance, commerce, industry and social welfare.

Information: Physical and biological reactions require the presence of catalytic agents to set them in motion and speed completion. Human social processes depend on a catalytic agent too and that catalyst is information. Free movement of information releases society from fear of uncertainties. Information about prices and market potentials spurs an entrepreneur into commercial activity. Information about scientific and technological discovery prompts a scientist or an engineer to adopt new innovations and practical applications. Widely disseminated public information about proper health care and nutrition contributes more powerfully to the general health of the community than does a hospital or medical innovation. Information about government policies enables individuals and communities to fully exercise their rights and take advantage of public programmes. Information about distant places spurs tourism and trade. Information in all forms and all fields — administration, commerce, education, finance, health, science and technology — is the very source from which we shape our dreams, plans, decisions and actions. The more and better the quality of that information, the more enlightened, expansive, productive and effective will be our efforts at individual and social advancement.

Today, the average Indian citizen has access to a wider range of timely and reliable information than had the government leaders in the world's most advanced nations a few decades ago. The fairly easy access to computers and the Internet has placed the world at our fingertips. Spread of information is further facilitated by the advancement of telecommunications technology, rapid expansion of cellular telephone networks, as well as the recent legalisation of Internet telephony, that makes live voice communication possible at a fraction of the cost, both within the country and internationally.

Education: What is true of information is true of education as well. Dissemination of useful information can be said to constitute the so-called unorganised sector of public education. The formal educational system is its organised counterpart. Education is the process whereby society passes on the accumulated knowledge and experience of past generations to its youth in a systematic and abridged form, so that the next generation can start off where past generations have ended and move on from there. Today, through education we have access not only to the knowledge of our own direct ancestors but to the accumulated experience and wisdom of people the world over. With the development of modern media that brings sound and video images into every household, and with the advent of the Internet that enables us to reach out to sources of knowledge around the world, education offers both unprecedented richness of content and the capacity to deliver it. If only we could break free from the limitations of out-dated curriculum and out-moded delivery systems, we could utilise the opportunity to close the education gap that separates the world's most prosperous communities from their poorer cousins.

Skills: Productive skills form another component of the precious human resource that we can and must fully utilise as leverage for national development. Skill is the ability to direct human energy efficiently to achieve desirable goals. A large reserve of unskilled people may be perceived as a problem, but a large population of skilled workers is a huge asset. It takes both knowledge and skill to train people and we have these in abundance. Imparting employable skills to our entire workforce is not only highly desirable but highly achievable as well.

All the resources that we have enumerated — technology, organisation, information, education and skill — are knowledge-based resources. Knowledge-based resources differ significantly in character from material resources. While material resources are consumed when they are utilised, knowledge resources increase when shared. Material resources are costly to transport and store, whereas knowledge resources are easily transportable at rapid speed and can be stored at negligible cost.

Historically, development has occurred under conditions in which access to critical resources was restricted to a relatively small portion of the population. The distinct characteristic of knowledge as a resource makes it possible, for the first time, to spread and share a resource among the entire population. The pace of India's future progress will depend to a large extent on its ability to make available the latest and most useful knowledge to vast sections of the population.

3

Human Development

The People

Human beings are distinguished among all living species by their capacity to develop and think. Though development is often measured in terms of so many miles of roads, number of tall buildings, airports, cars, TVs, computers etc., it is not things and places alone that define development. Development must be people centric. Twenty years hence, the people of India will be more numerous, better educated, healthier and more prosperous than at any other time in our long history. Having eradicated the scourge of famine that plagued the country for centuries, we still confront the challenging tasks of providing a nutritious diet to all our children, educating our teeming masses, abolishing epidemic diseases and creating employment opportunities for all our citizens.

Today India is the second most populous country in the world, with about 1.04 billion people, home to a-sixth of humanity. Although it is difficult to accurately predict population growth rates 20 years to the future, we expect this number to rise by another 300-350 million, in spite of continuous efforts to reduce fertility rates. This would raise the total population to about 1330 million by 2020.

India is in the process of a demographic transition from high fertility, high mortality and stable population to low fertility, low mortality and stable population. This transition is a global phenomenon generated by the improved availability and access to modern health care that sharply reduced mortality rates and increased life expectancy. The Crude death rate has declined to one-third of its level in 1941 and the expectation of life at birth has nearly doubled during this period. Falling mortality rates have been followed by a steady decline in birth rates, but this decline has not been as steep as the fall in death rate; even after reaching the replacement fertility rates, the population will continue to grow because of large numbers of young persons entering reproductive age.

While assessing future prospects, it is necessary to take into account the vast regional differences in demographic parameters. Population growth has recently decelerated below 2 per cent for the first time in four decades, but not uniformly across the length and breadth of the country. Several states in south India have already reached, or are about to attain, the replacement level of fertility that would ensure a zero growth rate of population in the long run. On the other hand, in many states in north India, characterised by high fertility rates, it may take several decades to reach the replacement level of fertility. There are also similar differentials in levels of mortality, especially in infant and child mortality.

At the national level, two alternate scenarios for achieving population stabilisation have been considered. In the optimistic scenario, which is based on achieving the demographic goals of the National Population Policy 2000, life expectancy is assumed to rise to 71 for males and 74 for females by 2020. Under the realistic scenario, life expectancy is assumed to reach 65 for males and 69 for females by 2020. Under either scenario India's population would exceed 1.3 billion in the year 2020.

In both cases the sex ratio of population (females per 1000 males) would marginally increase from 932 in 2000 to 950 in 2020; reversing the historical trend of falling sex ratio is expected in the 21st Century.

We can be more certain of the changes in the age structure of the population as given in Table 2.

Actually, the population under-15 years is expected to increase only marginally over the next 20 years. This means that pressure for expansion of the educational system will come only from increasing enrolment and efforts to reduce drop-out rates.

The largest growth of population will be in the 15-64 year age group, which will expand by about 46 per cent by 2020 (i.e., annually by 1.9 per cent as against the population growth of much lower, at 1.4 per cent). As shown in Table 2, it is expected to rise from 604 million in 2000 to 883 million in 2020, i.e., from 60 to

66 per cent of the total population. This rise will accentuate the need for challenge of reducing fertility and increasing employment opportunities, so that the family size comes down and incomes rise.

Table – 2

Population Projections (millions)

Year	*2000*	*2005*	*2010*	*2015*	*2020*
Total	1010	1093	1175	1256	1331
Under 15	361	368	370	372	373
15-64	604	673	747	819	882
65+	45	51	58	65	76

Source: Based on P.N. Mari Bhatt, "Indian Demographic Scenario 2025", Institute of Economic Growth, New Delhi, Discussion Paper No. 27/2001.

The elderly population is also expected to rise sharply from 45 to 76 million, (i.e., by 2.6 per cent per annum) and their share in the total population would rise from 4.5 to 5.7 per cent. As a consequence of these age structural changes, the age-dependency ratio (ratio of non-working age population to working age population) is expected to fall from 67 per cent in 2000 to 46 per cent in 2020, although the percentage of elderly people to population will increase.

Food Security

The single most important implication of India's rapid population growth during the second half of the twentieth century was the threat it posed to national food security. That threat reached dangerous proportions in the mid-1960s, leading to the launching of the Green Revolution, achievement of food self-sufficiency, and subsequently, a growing stock of surplus food grains by the mid-1970s. Happily, such a threat no longer exists for the country. Growth of food production has exceeded population growth for each of the past three decades.

Statistics present a confusing picture of India's progress on food security. Both per capita food grain consumption and total calorific intake have declined slightly in recent years among all levels of the population. At the same time, grain surpluses have reached peak levels and real per capita expenditure on food is rising among all income groups. The factors influencing this trend are numerous and complex, however, it can be primarily attributed to:

- Reduction in calorie requirement due to a more sedentary life style among both the rural and urban population. Bicycle and bus travel, mechanised pumps and equipments, access to telephones and newspapers have reduced the physical work to a greater or lesser extent for most Indians.
- Diversification of the Indian diet to include a larger intake of fruits, vegetables, dairy products, sugar, oil and pulses, eggs, fish and meat products, thereby reducing the required intake of calories from cereals.

However, the challenge of achieving food security for all our people remains a real one even today, and will continue to demand our attention in the coming decades. Food security depends on both availability of food and access to it. Long-term food security requires not only producing sufficient food to meet the market demand, but also ensuring that all citizens have the required purchasing power to obtain the food they need for a nutritious and healthy life. India has won the first battle, but the second still looms large. By best estimates, nearly half of the population still suffers from chronic under-nutrition. The most vulnerable are children, women and the elderly, specially among the lower income groups. While the number of children suffering from severe malnutrition declined significantly in the 1990s, the prevalence of mild and moderate under-nutrition, especially among those in the lower 30 per cent income group, is still high. Prevalence of micro nutrient deficiencies such as anaemia is also very high.

The problem of chronic macro and micro nutrient under-nutrition cannot be addressed simply by increases in food production or the accumulation of larger food buffer stocks. Nor has the public distribution system been able to effectively target the most needy in an effective manner. Targeted food for work programmes and targeted nutrition programmes can alleviate the problem temporarily. But in the long run, the solution is to ensure employment opportunities for all citizens so that they acquire the purchasing power to meet their nutritional requirements. Thus, employment or livelihood security becomes an essential and inseparable component of a comprehensive strategy for national food security and must be considered as one of the nation's highest priorities.

Increasing food consumption alone is not a sufficient condition for overcoming malnutrition in India. It is also necessary to address the factors responsible for the high incidence of gastrointestinal and respiratory infections as well as cultural factors responsible for faulty child feeding and weaning practices. Assured provision of safe drinking water, improved health care and education for all women are necessary elements of a comprehensive strategy to eliminate malnutrition and achieve the goal of Food for All before 2020.

India's population is still rapidly expanding. Living standards are rising and slated to rise faster than in the past. As they rise, both calorific intake and diversification of diet will increase significantly. Although a portion of this increase can and will be obtained from abroad, a fulfilling vision of India 2020 depicts this nation — with its conducive and varied climate, the largest irrigated area in the world and a vast farming population — as a major food exporter. Both as a challenge and as an opportunity, India can and must do much more to modernise and diversify its agriculture to meet the increased domestic and international demand for a wide variety of food products.

Continued growth of the agriculture sector is particularly important because it plays such a vital role in generating purchasing power among the rural population. Therefore, it is essential that agricultural development strategies for the 21st Century focus on generating both higher incomes and greater on-farm and off-farm employment opportunities.

India is now entering the fourth stage of agricultural transformation. The Green Revolution phase spread in the north-western and southern states from the mid-1960s to the mid-1980s. From the early 1980s, it spread rapidly in the central, and to a lesser extent the eastern states. This, coupled with a further growth of productivity in the north-western and southern states, enabled India to achieve a 3.77 per cent annual growth rate in agricultural production during the 1980s. The overall growth slowed to 2.72 per cent in the 1990s, which was associated with a reduction in public investment in both agriculture and agricultural research, slower growth of fertilizer consumption and the area under high yielding varieties, and degradation of soils.

Stages of Agricultural Development

1. Pre-Green Revolution	Boost in productivity growth of coarse grains and pulses per unit of land.
2. Green Revolution	Expansion of area and rapid growth in productivity of wheat and rice, made possible by widespread adoption of improved varieties, expansion of agricultural research, demonstration and education, and investment in irrigation, supported by establishment of a national infrastructure to produce and supply inputs and to warehouse, distribute and market outputs.
3. Post-Green Revolution	Continued growth in productivity through intensification of chemical and labour inputs, followed by a gradual deceleration in productivity growth. Expansion of area under maize, cotton, sugarcane, and oilseeds.
4. Commercialisation	Further diversification of cropping patterns from low value to high value crops such as fruits, vegetables, flowers and other horticulture crops for domestic consumption, processing and export.

There is enormous scope for accelerating growth in agriculture, through improved soil nutrition and pest management, diversification into higher value-added crops, expansion and more efficient use of irrigation potential, rainwater harvesting, and infrastructure development for agro-processing industries. India's productivity on major crops ranks far below the world average. This low productivity contributes to low farm incomes and wages, lower on-farm employment generation, and relatively high food prices for all Indians. Average yields from tomato cultivation, for example, are 76 per cent higher in Mexico and more than four times higher in the USA, while average yields on seed cotton are more than four times higher in Mexico and three times higher in USA. Even within India, some progressive farmers have achieved yields comparable to their foreign counterparts till recently; but these high achievers are a rare exception. Progressive farming must become the rule and the standard. Raising the productivity of our soil and water resources is an effective way to increase the profit margins of farmers, while at the same time reducing the cost of farm produce, so that it is more affordable to the masses. A minimum target should be to double or triple the average yields of major commercial crops. This will reduce pressure on scarce land and water resources as well as enable the country to utilise less fertile areas for other purposes.

Tapping the full potential of Indian agriculture to meet the rising domestic demand and to take advantage of the liberalisation of international trade will require, first and foremost, the recognition of the vital role that agriculture can continue to play in national development. The other necessary conditions are: greater public investment in research; expansion and development of rural infrastructure including roads, storage capacity and organised markets; improved farmer education; effective involvement of the private sector to provide technology, investment and organisational expertise for commercialisation; and modification of land regulations to achieve greater production efficiency. A suitable land use pattern will also need to be implemented, based on the principle that each region would focus on crops best suited to their agro-climatic characteristics, soil types and water resources. Strong measures will also be needed to address the problem of land degradation that affects an estimated 45 per cent of total land area. India's objective for 2020 must not only be to produce the food its population requires but also to fully exploit the comparative advantages it possesses — agro-climatic variety, irrigation, scientific capabilities and low labour cost — to become a low cost, high profit producer for the world market.

Figure 1 depicts the projected food production under two scenarios, together with estimates of food demand in 2020. Business-as-usual (BAU) assumes that growth of production continues at the same rates as during the 1990s. The Best-case scenario (BCS) assumes that production grows at the higher rates achieved during the 1980s. Even under the BAU, India will be able to meet the projected demand in all five food categories. This indicates that more emphasis can be placed on diversifying production to other value added agricultural products.

FIGURE 1

Current & Projected Food Production vs. Demand in 2020

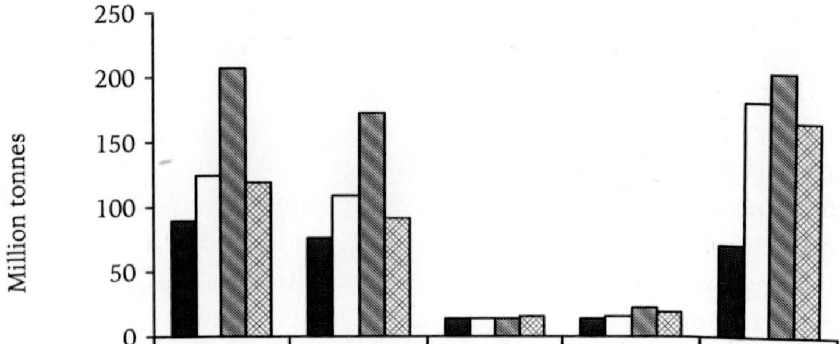

	Rice	Wheat	Coarse Cereals	Pulses	Milk
■ 2000	89	76	13.6	13.5	71
□ 2020 BAU	125	108	13	16	181
▧ 2020 BCS	207	173	14	23	203
⊠ 2020 Demand	119	92	15.6	19.5	166

Source: Based on R. Radhakrishnan and K. Venkata Reddy, "Vision 2020: Food Security and Nutrition", paper prepared for Planning Commission.

India needs to sustain an agricultural growth rate of 4.0 to 4.5 per cent in order to reduce food insecurity and poverty, while increasing rural purchasing power. At this growth rate, agricultural development could more rapidly diversify into horticulture, fishery, dairying, animal husbandry and other areas. It would also spur the growth of agro-processing industries in rural areas. Such an achievement is well within reach, provided there is the requisite commitment to raising crop productivity through dissemination of advanced technologies; increasing investment in irrigation, research and training; water harvesting and improved access to credit.

While food production should be able to comfortably meet the total domestic demand, there will still be sections of the population that require assistance in order to meet their nutritional requirements. In view of the high cost and inefficiency of the public food distribution system, reform should directly target the most vulnerable sections, which can be more effectively accomplished through programmes such as food vouchers or food stamps. For the vast majority of the population, food security can best be achieved by ensuring creation of gainful employment opportunities for all job seekers.

Employment

Population, food security, education and remunerative employment opportunities are closely interconnected. Rising levels of education and rising living standards are powerful levers for reducing birth and mortality rates. As population growth slows to replacement levels over the next two decades, India's greatest challenge will be to expand the opportunities for the growing labour force, to enrich their knowledge and skills through education, raise their living standards through gainful employment and make provisions for ensuring a good life for the aged. India has met the challenge of producing sufficient food to feed everyone, but it has yet to meet the challenge of generating sufficient employment opportunities to ensure that all its people have the purchasing power to obtain the food they require. Gainful employment is one of the most essential conditions for food security and economic security. Conversely, food security is an essential requirement for raising the productivity of India's workforce to international levels.

India's labour force has reached 375 million approximately in 2002, and it will continue to expand over the next two decades. The actual rate of that expansion will depend on several factors including population growth, growth of the working age population, labour force participation rates, educational enrolment at higher levels and school drop-out rates. Projections based on these parameters indicate that India's labour force will expand by 7 to 8.5 million per year during the first decade of this century, and will increase by a total of about 160-170 million by 2020, i.e., 2.0 per cent per annum.

Total unemployment in India has been estimated to be about 35 million persons in 2002. This figure takes into account the significant level of underemployment and seasonal variations in the availability of work. It also reflects wide variations in the rate of unemployment among different age groups and regions of the country. Approximately three-fourth of the unemployed are in rural areas and three-fifth among them are educated. The recent trends towards shedding excess labour to improve competitiveness and increasing capital intensity have further aggravated the situation. A clear consensus is now emerging that major changes in economic policy and strategy will be needed to meet the country's employment needs.

Future rates of unemployment will depend on a range of factors, including the growth rate of the labour force and changes in the structure of employment between different sectors, as well as the growth rate of the economy. Adopting the higher number takes us closer to understanding the full magnitude of the challenge the country faces for providing employment opportunities for all its people. India needs to generate on the order of 200 million additional employment opportunities over the next 20 years.

The first question that inevitably arises is whether generating nine or ten million jobs a year is feasible, and that naturally begets the question of what rates of economic growth would be required for achieving this. However logical and inevitable it may sound, we believe this is the wrong way to approach the problem. The right question to ask is: How important is it to us as a nation to create employment opportunities for all? The answer here is simple. It is extremely important. It is as important to create job opportunities for all citizens in a market economy as it is to provide universal suffrage to all adults in a democracy. Access to employment is an essential component of freedom of economic choice. Absence of such opportunity means depriving our young not only of economic freedom but of hope as well. India's vision for 2020 must be founded on the premise of gainful Jobs for All. Access to employment should not only be a top priority of the government but a constitutionally guaranteed fundamental human right.

But can we possibly achieve such an ambitious goal and that too within the framework of a non-subsidised market economy? In order to answer this question, first of all we need to recognise that the economy we build over the next two decades and the jobs we create will be products of the decisions we make, not some irreversible logic of economic science. It is we, the nation, that have to decide what we want to accomplish and how serious we are about doing it, how willing we are to change our attitudes and to alter our policies to achieve this desirable goal. We conclude that if the will and determination are present, the goal is achievable.

Achieving full employment will require a reorientation of national priorities, technology policy and government action. Until now, planning to achieve national goals has been largely done on a sector-wise basis by respective ministries assigned with the responsibility. These parallel lines of planning need to be integrated around a central vision and set of goals, of which full employment must be one. As we have incorporated an environmental analysis into all our planning, every plan initiative needs also to be re-evaluated to consider its impact on employment.

Despite a persistent tendency to associate employment with large industry in the organised sector, an in-depth examination of employment potentials makes it evident that the largest share of new jobs will come from the unorganised sector. In evaluating the importance of developing each sector, we must include an assessment of its potential contribution to employment. Such an assessment will have to be made for the unorganised sector, which currently contributes 92 per cent of the country's employment and generates seven times greater labour intensity per unit of production, as compared to the organised sector. The public organised sector has been and will continue to shed jobs. Although the private organised sector will contribute significantly to the growth of the economy, its contribution to the overall employment generation will be quite modest, since total employment in this sector currently represents only 2.5 per cent of all jobs. Even if this sector grows by 30 per cent per annum, over five years it will contribute less than one per cent to the growth of the workforce.

International comparisons reveal that small and medium enterprises (SMEs) create the majority of jobs. In the USA, nearly half of the private workforce is employed in small firms, of which three-fifth have less than five employees. In Japan, 78 per cent of jobs are generated by small and medium enterprises. The small and medium manufacturing enterprises in Korea account for 99 per cent of all manufacturing enterprises and 69 per cent of employment in this sector. Therefore, the unorganised sector, including small and medium enterprises, must play a central role in the country's employment strategy. This will require modification of policies and programmes to level the playing field, improve availability of credit, increase productivity, raise quality consciousness and competitiveness, and enhance job quality.

Recent experiences of different countries in the context of globalisation also demonstrate that SMEs are better insulated from the pressures generated by the volatility of world trade and capital markets. They are more resistant to the stresses, and more responsive to the demands of the fast-changing technologies and entrepreneurial responses. Indeed, they are observed to be a very important vehicle for new technology adoption and entrepreneurial development. What is true of the most developed countries today will be true for India in 2020. SMEs will play a crucial role in ensuring India's international competitiveness and its rapid assimilation of new technologies.

An assessment of the different sectors reveals a vast untapped employment potential in a wide range of fields for unskilled, semi-skilled, skilled and professionally educated workers. Table 3 provides a list of specific sectors with the largest gross employment potential per unit of output.

The growth of food grain production may not lead to a significant growth in on-farm employment opportunities. However, there is substantial scope for creating new jobs through watershed development programmes, expansion of the area under irrigated cultivation, raising crop yields which increases labour intensity, and diversification of cropping patterns into cash crops — especially vegetables and horticultural crops. Together, these could generate upwards of 20 to 30 million new on-farm employment opportunities during the next decade.

India processes less than 2 per cent of its fruit and vegetable products, as compared with 70 to 80 per cent in countries such as Brazil, Malaysia and Philippines. The development of downstream processing, packaging and distribution activities can generate millions of additional off-farm jobs. Policies are needed to attract greater private sector participation in terms of land development, production and processing technologies, investment, management and marketing. A concerted effort to fully develop the potentials of agri-business could generate millions of additional jobs.

Table – 3

High Employment Potential Sectors

- Commercial agriculture
- Agro-industry & agri-business
- Afforestation for pulp, fuel & power
- Retail and wholesale trade
- Tourism
- Housing
- Construction
- Garment industry
- Other small scale & medium industries
- IT & IT enabled services
- Education
- Health
- Financial services
- Transport
- Communications
- Community services

Source: Compiled from Planning Commission documents.

The recorded forest area constitutes about 23 per cent of the geographical area (about 71 million hectares) of the country, but half of this area is degraded. Hence, it is unable to play an important role in environmental sustainability and in meeting the forest produce needs of the people, the industry and other sectors. India has more than 50 million hectares of degraded wasteland that lie outside the national forests, in addition to 30 million hectares within protected areas. In spite of this huge expanse, the country is a net importer of forest products to the extent of $2.5 billion annually. Afforestation of India's vast expanse of wastelands and depleted forest areas for production of wood pulp, timber, fuel, fodder, biomass power, edible and fuel soil, fuel, herbs and medicinal plants for exports can create millions of jobs, while reversing environmental degradation and supporting industrial development. Every two hectares of additional area placed under plantation of forest crop such as bamboo, casuarina, eucalyptus or oil-bearing plants can generate year-round employment for one person. Development of forests can generate 10 to 15 million additional employment opportunities over the next five year plan period and increase the livelihood opportunities of low income families during the transition period, while educational levels are rising and other sectors of the economy are developing.

The contribution of primary sector employment to the total workforce has been coming down very slowly, to 56-57 per cent in 1999-2000, and should decrease to about 51 per cent by 2006-2007. This slow rate of decline is likely to continue for at least a decade, because of the hidden under-employment in the agriculture sector, partly compensated for by the vast potential for additional job creation by crop diversification and afforestation. Increasing prosperity in agriculture will naturally lead to the growth of non-farm jobs in agri-industries, agro-business and other occupations required to meet the needs of an increasingly prosperous farming community. During the second decade of the 21st Century, increasing domestic demand for manufactured products and services, coupled with more rapid mechanisation of agriculture will draw in more and more people to non-farm occupations. By 2020, total employment in agriculture may fall to less than 45 per cent, while the share of the services sector increases proportionately.

The small scale industries (SSI) sector accounts for 95 per cent of industrial units, 40 per cent of value addition, 35 per cent of exports, and 80 per cent of manufacturing employment. Registered SSI units provide nearly 18 million jobs in the country at this time. Among manufacturing sectors, the single largest employment potential is in textiles, which is slated to generate 7 million jobs over the next five years alone. More than 40 per cent of these jobs are in garment production units in the SSI sector. A healthy and rapidly expanding small sector is essential for a vibrant growth of the Indian economy as a whole. This sector serves as the field for entrepreneurship to flourish, as an entry point for new entrepreneurs who can start small and then grow, as a vehicle for extending the regional spread of industry, as a laboratory for development of innovative products and services, and as an essential support to attract large manufacturing assembling industries from overseas. Since SSIs are generally more employment intensive per unit of capital than large scale industry, they are also a source of much needed employment. Employment in the registered SSI sector has nearly tripled over the past 20 years. A repetition of this performance would generate an additional 36 million jobs over the next 20 years. A comprehensive package of venture capital, credit, liberalisation of controls, technical training, marketing and management measures is needed to ensure the continuous expansion of this sector.

By far, the largest number of new jobs will be in the services sector. Over the past 100 years, the US economy has more than quadrupled the total number of those employed, yet the percentage of the US workforce engaged in manufacturing is now back to the same level as it was in 1850, while agricultural employment has shrunk to less than 3 per cent of the US workforce. Today, the fastest growing job categories in the USA are in services industries such as financial services, insurance, education, health, construction and real estate. Rapid growth is slated for a wide range of services in India, including professional, computer-related research and development, real estate, leasing, advertising, printing and packaging, marketing, telecommunications, postal and courier, audiovisual, engineering and construction, wholesale and retail distribution, all levels and types of education, environment, banking, insurance, health, travel, sports and recreation, and all categories of transport services. By the year 2020 more than 120 million jobs will come from the services sector alone.

Tourism-related occupations, including hotels and restaurants, employ 10.8 per cent of workers globally, compared to only 5.6 per cent in India. Domestic tourism will rise rapidly as living standards increase. India's domestic tourist sector is the fastest growing in the world, but with the lowest level of investment. The potential for international tourism too has not yet been exploited properly. China currently attracts more than five times as many foreign tourists, excluding visitors from Hong Kong. Thailand, Malaysia, and Turkey attract three to four times as many. By one estimate, development of India's tourism infrastructure such as roads, airports and medium priced hotels, combined with modifications in air and hotel pricing and tax policies, could generate more than 20 million additional employment opportunities in tourist related businesses within a decade.

Numerous studies have been undertaken to assess the potentials of the IT industry and to identify specific strategies needed to accelerate development of this sector. The NASSCOM-McKinsey study in 1999 projected creation of a $ 70 billion IT industry, employing more than two million persons within 10 years. The worldwide market for IT services is expected to exceed $900 billion by 2010.

The recent growth of IT-enabled service businesses in India — call centres, medical transcription, technical support and back office processing, engineering and design, geographic information services, payroll and other human resource services, insurance claim processing, legal databases — is powerful evidence that the potential of IT technology and knowledge based industries extends far beyond the development of software and hardware. The US experience shows that, as the application of information technology spreads and encompasses traditional industries, it can generate new employment opportunities ten times greater in number than those directly involved in core IT industries.

IT is also a stimulant to the growth of home-based employment opportunities, especially suitable for women. The trend towards tele-working, which is growing rapidly in USA and some other countries, is just beginning in India. The lower cost and greater convenience of home-based employment is bound to open up greater job opportunities for educated women with children.

IT services will be a powerful engine of job growth, but the term 'Knowledge-based industries' includes a much wider range of commercial opportunities. It encompasses all fields in which the application of mind, judgment and skill, rather than the application of mechanised production technology is the core resource. Education, health services, biotechnology, pharmaceuticals, insurance and financial services are among the leading industries in this category. They are also among the fastest growing industries in the world. Added to these, there is enormous scope for other knowledge intensive activities such as clinical drug trials and many other types of scientific research.

The management of all types of information is emerging as a major growth industry worldwide and India is well poised to become a global leader in this field. Increasing demand for education within the country and worldwide will create tremendous demand for qualified teachers with adequate language skills. An estimated two million additional teachers will be needed in India to support 100 per cent primary school enrolment and to reduce the teacher-student ratio for improved quality of teaching. Another two million or more will be required to support higher rates of upper primary and secondary school education and to reduce teacher-student ratios at those levels. Teaching staff for vocational training and higher education need to be expanded as well.

Demand for health services is increasing worldwide. Already nurses and medical technicians are in short supply. The USA has a doctor-nurse ratio of about twice that of India. Yet the US currently faces a shortfall of nurses, that is more than three times India's total annual production of new nurses. Physicians, nurses, medical technicians and other scientific occupations will become growth industries to rival the IT sector within the next decade. Creation of new jobs in existing industries can and should be supplemented by creation of new services industries that will in turn stimulate increased employment opportunities.

It is extremely difficult to project unemployment rates 20 years into the future, when so much doubt exists even about current levels of unemployment and underemployment. However, it is clear that rising levels of education and growth of the 60 plus age group will mitigate to some extent the growth of the labour force. Combined with the enormous opportunities for creation of new employment opportunities, the incidence of unemployment should be almost eliminated during the second decade of the century.

Education

Successful population policy is directly linked to successful education policy. Success in raising literacy rates and school enrolment rates while reducing drop-out rates, especially for women, are closely correlated with the delayed onset of marriage and child birth, improved mortality for both mothers and children, and reduction in family size. In fact, a successful education policy forms the bedrock of all fields of national development — political, economic, technical, scientific, social, and environmental. Education is the foundation for a vibrant democracy in which informed citizens exercise their franchise to support the internal growth of the nation and its constructive role in the world community. It is the foundation for growth in productivity, incomes and employment opportunities and for the development, application and adaptation of science and technology to enhance the quality of life. Education is the foundation for access to the benefits of the information revolution that is opening up vistas on the whole world. Education is also the foundation for improved health care and nutrition.

Literacy, the basis of all education, is as essential to survival and development in modern society as food is to survival and development of the human body. Literacy rates in India have arisen dramatically from 18 per cent in 1951 to 65 per cent in 2001, but these rates are still far from the UMI reference level of 95 per cent. Literacy must be considered the minimum right and requirement of every Indian citizen. Vast differences also remain among different sections of the population. Literacy among males is nearly 50 per cent higher than females, and it is about 50 per cent higher in urban areas as compared to the rural areas. Literacy rates range from as high as 96 per cent in some districts of Kerala to below 30 per cent in some parts of Madhya Pradesh. Rates are also significantly lower among scheduled castes and tribes than among other communities.

These differential rates of progress leave approximately 300 million illiterate adults in the country, the largest number of illiterates in the world. For these people, the traditional avenues of knowledge dissemination through education and printed information are ruled out. These are the people who are most vulnerable to the challenges of development, because they are least equipped to rapidly expand their knowledge base. Since many of them are relatively young adults who will still be active in 2020, the country cannot afford to ignore them or leave them behind. The Government has already set a goal to achieve 75 per cent literacy by the end of the Tenth Five Year Plan. A 100 per cent literate India is of paramount importance for realising the vision for the country in 2020 as presented in this document. Even when this goal is achieved, innovative approaches will be needed to increase knowledge dissemination through TV and other means, to literate adults with little or no formal education.

Literacy is an indispensable minimum condition for development, but it is not sufficient. In this increasingly complex and technologically sophisticated world, ten years of school education must also be considered as an essential prerequisite for citizens to adapt and succeed economically, avail of the social opportunities and develop their individual potentials. Education is the primary and most effective means so far evolved for transmitting practically useful knowledge from one generation to another.

India's education system has expanded exponentially over the past five decades, but its current achievements are grossly inadequate for the nation to realise its potential greatness. The net enrolment rate in primary schools is around 77 per cent and in secondary schools it is around 60 per cent. These compare with the 99.9 per cent primary and 69 per cent secondary enrolment for the UMI reference level. The drop out rate was 40 per cent at the primary level and 55 per cent at the upper primary level in 1999-2000. These high drop out rates from both primary and secondary school, combined with low enrolment rates at the higher levels deprive tens of millions of children of their full rights as citizens. Out of approximately 200 million children in the age group 6-14 years, only 120 million are in schools and net attendance in the primary level is only 66 per cent of the enrolment. Further, less than 7 per cent of the children ever pass the 10th standard public examination.

Apart from addressing the needs of a large illiterate population, India's knowledge strategy must also develop innovative approaches to enhance knowledge acquisition among the large community of school drop-outs. Unless something is done to drastically reduce drop-out rates, by the year 2016 there will be approximately 500 million people in the country with less than five years of schooling, and another 300 million that will not have completed high school. In other words, about two-thirds of the population will lack the minimum level of education needed to keep pace with and take advantage of the social changes occurring within the country and worldwide.

Extending the primary school system to over 500,000 villages in India has brought education to the masses. Unfortunately, this huge quantitative expansion has been accompanied by a tremendous dilution in the quality of schooling. High drop out rates in rural areas is one result of single room schools, with few teaching aids and inadequate instruction both in terms of quantity and quality. Qualitative improvement in the system can be accomplished by promoting centralised schools serving clusters of 10 or more villages, wherever distances and transportation links make that feasible. This will permit greater investment in educational infrastructure, including introduction of computers.

Achieving 100 per cent enrolment of all children in the 6 to 14 year age group is an ambitious but achievable goal for 2020. This must be coupled with efforts to increase the quality and relevance of school curriculum to equip students not only with academic knowledge but also with the values and practical knowledge needed for success in life. Table 4 depicts a business-as usual scenario for primary and secondary education in 2020, based on recent trends as well as an alternative scenario designed to radically enhance the quantity and quality of school education in the country.

A tremendous expansion of schools and classrooms will be required to support a quantitative and qualitative improvement in the country's school system. In order to achieve the best-case scenario depicted in Table 4, total school enrolment would have to increase by 75 million or 44 per cent. That will require a proportionate expansion in the number of classrooms. In addition, efforts to improve the quality of education by reducing the class size would require a further 20 per cent increase in the number of classrooms. Together, this will necessitate increasing the total number of classrooms by 65 per cent within 20 years.

An enormous increase in the number of teachers will also be required to achieve the alternative scenario, i.e., eliminating primary school drop outs and reducing the teacher-pupil ratio from the present high level of 1:42 down to around 1:20, which is the UMI reference level. Together, this will require an additional three million primary school teachers, more than twice the number currently employed. Similar increases will be required at middle and secondary school levels. The training of such large number of teachers will require the establishment of additional teacher training colleges and much larger budget allocations for teachers' salaries.

Table – 4

Education Scenarios in 2020

	1980 Actual	2000 Estimated	2020 Business-as-usual	2020 Best-case Scenario
Primary enrolment (1-5)	80%	89%	100%	100%
Elementary enrolment (1-8)	77%	79%	85%	100%
Secondary enrolment (9-12)	30%	58%	75%	100%
Drop-out rate (1-5)	54%	40%	20%	0%
Drop-out rate (1-8)	73%	54%	35%	0%

Source: Garry Jacobs "Vision 2020: Towards a Knowledge Society", paper prepared for Planning Commission.

Qualitative improvements in education should reflect a change in pedagogical methods and lay emphasis on several dimensions, including:

- A shift from methods that emphasize passive learning to those that foster the active interest and ability of children to learn on their own.
- A shift from rote memorisation to development of children's capacity for critical thinking.
- A shift from traditional academic to practically relevant curriculum.
- A shift from imparting information to imparting life values such as independent thinking, self-reliance and individual initiative that are essential for success in any field of endeavour.

An important role of education is to foster in each child the attributes and values of a responsible, capable, active and healthy member of the family and society. The rigidity of curriculum, testing and teaching methods need to be relaxed so that innovative methods and new models of education can be evolved, tested and perfected. Vocational streams have to be developed and expanded to equip larger numbers of high school students with occupation-related knowledge and skills.

Experimentation is needed with new methods for knowledge delivery. Television can be a very effective means for educating both school going and non-school going children and adults. It can deliver teaching materials in a more dynamic, entertaining, and interesting manner, utilising the nation's best teachers and multimedia teaching materials on each subject. A TV based curriculum can help slow learners to supplement classroom teaching, fast learners to learn at much faster rates than the rest of the class, drop outs to acquire knowledge they missed out in school, and adults to expand their level of education without returing to school.

New methods of delivery will be particularly necessary to augment access and improve delivery at higher levels of education. Although India's college and university network has expanded dramatically as shown in Table 5, it is able to accommodate only a tiny fraction of the college-age population. In addition, the quality of facilities, teaching and course materials leaves much to be desired. Recruitment and promotion are highly politicised; seniority rule precludes merit advancement; and the cost of delivery is beyond the means of the vast majority of young Indians.

Table – 5

Growth of Higher Educational Institutions

Years	*Colleges for General Education*	*Colleges for Professional Education*	*Universities*
1951	370	208	27
1998	7199	2075	229

Source: Department of Education, Govt. of India.

India in 2020 must be a nation in which all those who aspire for higher education have access to college and university level courses. A national network of community colleges, similar to the highly successful American system, is needed to provide knowledge and job-oriented skills to millions of young people who lack interest in or capacity for more stringent academic studies.

The advent of computer and the Internet-based educational methods offer an exciting new learning medium that can literally transform our concept of school and classroom from physical into virtual realities. Studies in the USA project a radical reshaping of higher education over the next two decades as a result of the digital revolution. Many traditional colleges will close as more course works are delivered at a distance through alternative channels. The traditional boundaries between education and other sectors will fade, as publishers, for-profit and non-profit organisations, offer accredited, multimedia-enhanced courses directly to students, by-passing the university. The traditional classroom type of education, which is most useful for students that require personal attention and assistance and for subjects that involve hands-on experimentation, will no longer be the predominant model of education. For all other purposes, it is very costly and not very efficient in the way it uses the time of both teachers and students.

Experience shows that computer-based educational methods can lead to much faster rates and higher quality of learning, which is more inter-active and motivating for students at all levels of education from pre-school to post-graduation. It is extremely effective for enhancing reading and language skills and general knowledge among the very young and even for some sophisticated professional courses such as medicine and engineering.

Given the huge number of young students that will quest for all levels of higher education in the coming decades and the severe shortage of qualified instructors, and in the light of India's outstanding expertise in the IT industry, the country needs to embark on a massive programme to convert the entire higher educational curriculum into a multi-media, web-based format and to establish accreditation standards for recognition of the distance education so imparted.

Our vision of India in 2020 is predicated on the belief that human resources are the most important determinants of overall development. As India's IT revolution has been fuelled by the availability of a very large reservoir of well-trained engineers, its future development in many different spheres will depend on commensurate development of sufficient and surplus capabilities.

Full development of India's enormous human potential will require a shift in national priorities, to commit a greater portion of the country's financial resources to the education sector. India currently invests 3.2-4.4 per cent of GNP on education. This compares unfavourably with the UMI reference level of 4.9 per cent, especially with countries such as South Africa, which invests 7.9 per cent of GNP on education. A near doubling of investments in education is the soundest policy for quadrupling the country's GDP per capita.

S&T Capabilities

Literacy and general education form the base of the knowledge pyramid that is essential for rapid and sustained development in the 21st century. The continuous advancement of science and application of improved technology form the middle rung; and social ideals and spiritual values form the apex.

Technical education, both vocational and professional, constitutes the foundation for development of science and technology. India is rightly proud of the international standing of its IITs, but a handful of world class technical institutions is not sufficient. A large number of the country's approximately 500 engineering colleges need to be upgraded to quality standards nearer to those of the IITs, and given similar autonomy. Private sector initiative and investment, whether from Indian corporates or NRIs or reputed foreign universities, need to be fully encouraged. Close links need to be fostered between technical institutions and industry.

India's enormous manpower base of scientists and engineers is often coveted. President Kalam observed that India's human resource base is one of its greatest core competencies. This is true in absolute terms, but as a percentage of the total population, we are at 1/100th of the US levels and 1/50th of the Korean level. Even China's manpower base of scientists and engineers as a percentage of its population exceeds ours by more than three times.

Absolute numbers do count, but manpower alone is not sufficient to excel in the development and application of science and technology. In terms of total investment in R&D, India's expenditure is 1/60th of that of Korea, 1/250th of that of the USA, and 1/340th of that of Japan. More significantly, atomic energy, space and defence research account for 71 per cent of all central spending on science and technology, which means that relatively little is left for investment in agriculture, energy, telecommunications and other crucial sectors within the sphere of science and technology. R&D

expenditure even in India's fast-growing IT sector has been averaging around 3 per cent of sales turnover (STO), which is much lower as compared to the 14-19 per cent expended by internationally reputed software firms.

These low figures reflect on our R&D performance. India's share of global scientific output in 1998 was only 1.58 per cent of the world's total. Out of 500,000 new patent applications filed globally each year, China accounts for 96,000 and Korea accounts for 72,000, while India accounts for only 8,000. Of greater concern has been the country's inability to capitalise on our huge pool of manpower and extensive network of scientific research organisations for transferring proven technologies from the lab to the land and to the factory. Despite possessing the world's largest cadre of agricultural scientists, we have not been able to extend the momentum of Green Revolution to other regions and crops and to update the scientific practices of our farmers to levels comparable with most other nations. Crop productivity remains far below and production costs far above world averages. A similar gap exists in the application of science and technology for food processing and many other industries. High technology exports account for only 6 per cent of total manufacturing exports for India, compared to over 20 per cent for the UMI reference level.

India has a number of premier universities for scientific and technical education which produce world class scientists and engineers, but the national research system rarely produces world class results. One reason is the missing link between scientists in universities and research institutes and practitioners in agriculture and industry. Another is that non-teaching research institutes lack the continuous inflow of young talented researchers required to challenge assumptions and infiltrate new ideas and approaches. Bureaucracy, tenure and lack of accountability minimise the pressure for practical application of scientific knowledge. Other countries have done a much better job of providing optimum incentives to their scientific community and creating close linkages between science and industry. The management of technology and the administration of government require different sets of skills and a different culture. Management of technology demands innovation, global competitiveness, and wide latitude for individual freedom characteristics that are difficult to foster under an administrative regime.

The objectives of many institutes and the mechanisms for achieving them need a radical reorientation to bring them in tune with the changing environment brought about by liberalisation of imports, technology tie-ups with foreign agencies and foreign direct investment in key sectors. If the national R&D bodies do not reorganise themselves to face globalisation and global competition, nor take into consideration the nature of the factor endowment of the country along with many existing indigenous technologies so far neglected, then they risk becoming irrelevant to the mainstream activities of industrial development. The nature of service offered by these institutions has to undergo a sea change. Grass-root consultancy and turnkey project consultancy, including project implementation and monitoring are increasingly in demand.

Another essential step is to improve the linkages between technology development and technology application by fostering close ties between basic research and business. In the USA, a large proportion of scientific research at the university level is financed by business, and most leading universities operate technology incubators designed to promote commercialisation of new products and processes. India's recent experiment with the Science and Technology Entrepreneur Parks (STEPs) has been successful in promoting application of technologies, new business start-ups, and employment. The STEPs in combination with technology incubators need to be rapidly multiplied around the country. Effective R&D management backed by suitable incentives for commercialisation are essential for bridging the gap between the lab and the land or factory.

R&D is not only essential for propelling growth in industrial fields. It can also become a growth industry on its own. Much of the work done by Indian software companies for overseas clients and parent companies rightly fall under the category of new product development. Vast potential exists for complementing India's strengths in IT with corresponding strengthening of fields such as biotechnology, pharmaceuticals, designer-made materials, and others.

India's investment in the biotechnology sector is expected to increase five-fold by the end of the current decade, from US $2 billion to $ 10 billion, largely as a result of growing collaboration between multinational corporations and indigenous research efforts. Huge opportunities also exist for R&D in the field of genomics, bioinformatics, DNA technologies, clinical studies and genetically modified crops. Rationalisation of procedure, backed by effective bio-safety regulations are needed to govern testing and approval of biotech products.

India has the potential of converting its strong R&D infrastructure into a global research, design and development platform.

Vocational Training

The knowledge and skill of our workforce will be a major determinant of India's future rate of economic growth as well as the type and number of jobs we create. The greater that knowledge and skill, the higher will be the productivity, the better the quality, and the lower the cost of the products and services we generate. Similarly, the better the quality and lower the cost, greater will be the comparative advantage and market potential. Currently only 5 per cent of the country's labour force in the 20-24 age category have undergone formal vocational training, compared with 28 per cent in Mexico, 60 to 80 per cent in most industrialised nations, and as much as 96 per cent in Korea. A strategy to achieve full employment must include as an important component, a strategy to ensure that all new entrants to the workforce are equipped with the knowledge and skill needed for high productivity and high quality.

India has over 4,200 industrial training institutes (ITI) imparting education and training in 43 engineering and 24 non-engineering trades. Of these, 1,654 are government run ITIs, while 2,620 are private. The total seating capacity in these ITIs is 6.28 lakh. Most of this training is conducted in classroom style in the form of one to two year diploma courses. In addition, about 1.65 lakh persons undergo apprenticeship vocational training every year in state-run enterprises. If a wider definition of applied courses is taken that includes agriculture, engineering and other professional subjects, the total number receiving job related training is about 17 lakh per annum, which still represents only 14 per cent of new entrants to the workforce.

The nature of vocational skills makes it impossible for vocational schools to fully address the nation's needs. The variety of skills needed by the workforce is far too great. The changes in technology and work processes are too rapid for training courses and their instructors to stay up-to-date. The cost of training is also relatively high as it often demands full time enrolment for a prolonged period. Some vocational fields do not lend themselves to classroom or laboratory study at all.

A comprehensive strategy is thus needed to enhance the nation's employable skills. It must begin by preparing a catalogue of the entire range of vocational skills needed to support the development of the country. The network of vocational training institutes and the range of vocational skills taught needs to be expanded substantially to impart those skills for which institutional training is most suitable. The private sector, which promoted the rapid proliferation of computer training institutes throughout the country, should be encouraged to recognise the commercial potential of vocational training in many other fields.

Use of Computers in Vocational Training

- Rates of learning on computer for both academic as well as vocational or skill-based subjects are four to ten times faster than they are in a classroom setting, and learning retention is likely to be much higher.
- Computers can provide multimedia, interactive, customised and individually-paced learning with instantaneous feedback and testing.
- It eliminates the need for producing and deputing a large number of highly skilled instructors. Course contents can be rapidly modified to reflect changing needs.
- For many types of vocational skills, computerised training also offers specific advantages over the live delivery of skills in a classroom.
- Training can be delivered wherever computers are available. A nationwide network of 50,000 computerised vocational centres, run as private self-employed businesses similar to the STD booths and Internet cafes, can deliver low-cost, high-quality training to 10 million workers every year — more than five times the total number covered by existing programmes.

In addition, it is essential to fashion more effective and efficient mechanisms for disseminating useful knowledge and skills, especially through the TV media and through computerised vocational training. The importance of computer has been widely recognised as a means to improve efficiency in business, government and formal education, but its application in vocational training is not fully appreciated.

Although 58 per cent of Indians are engaged in agriculture, vocational training for farmers is one of the weakest links in the Indian educational system. Agricultural universities cater to the nation's need for agricultural scientists and extension officers. An extensive network of more than 300 Krishi Vignan Kendras (KVK) offers short and medium term courses for farmers on specialised subjects. The KVK network provides training to several hundred thousand farmers each year, but it can cater to the needs of only a miniscule percentage of all farmers. Agricultural education can be moved from the campus into the village by establishing a national network of farm schools, offering practical demonstration and training on lands leased from farmers in the local community. The prime objective of the schools would be to impart knowledge and skills designed to double yields on important commercial crops. Educated farmers can be trained as self-employed instructors to operate the farm schools as private enterprises on a commercial basis.

Health for All

The health of a nation is difficult to define in terms of a single set of measures. At best, we can assess the health of the population by taking into account indicators like infant mortality and maternal mortality rates, life expectancy and nutrition, along with the incidence of communicable and non-communicable diseases.

According to these measures, the health of the Indian population has improved dramatically over the past fifty years. Life expectancy has risen from 33 years to 64 years. The infant mortality rate (IMR) has fallen from 148 to 71 per 1000. The crude birth rate (CBR) has declined from 41 to 25 and the crude death rate (CDR) has fallen from 25 to under 9. The couple protection rate (CPR) and total fertility rate (TFR) have also improved substantially.

Despite these achievements, wide disparities persist between different income groups, between rural and urban communities, and between different states and even districts within states. The infant mortality rate among the poorest quintet of the population is 2.5 times higher than that among the richest. Maternal mortality remains very high. More than one lakh women die each year due to pregnancy-related complications.

Like population growth and economic growth, the health of a nation is a product of many factors and forces that combine and interact with each other. Economic growth, per capita income, employment, levels of literacy and education — especially among females — age of marriage, birth rates, availability of information regarding health care and nutrition, access to safe drinking water, public and private health care infrastructure, access to preventive health care and medical care, health insurance, public hygiene, road safety, and environmental pollution are among the factors that contribute directly to the health of the nation.

Communicable diseases such as malaria, kalaazar, tuberculosis and HIV infection remain the major causes of illness in India. During the next five to ten years, existing programmes are likely to eliminate polio and leprosy and substantially reduce the prevalence of kalaazar and filariasis. However, TB, malaria and AIDS will continue to remain major public health problems. India has about 1.5 million identified cases of TB that are responsible for more than 3,00,000 deaths annually. Improved diagnostic services and treatment can reduce the prevalence and incidence of TB by 2020. About 2 million cases of malaria are reported in India each year. Restructuring the "malaria workforce" and strengthening health infrastructure can reduce the incidence of this disease by up to 50 per cent within a decade. Assessing the impact of HIV epidemic is more difficult; according to an estimate, there are about 4 million persons infected with HIV. The National Health Policy aims at achieving a plateau in the prevalence of HIV infection by 2007.

Childhood diarrhoea, another major cause of illness, is largely preventable through simple community action and public education, and deaths due to diarrhoea can be eliminated by 2010. Childhood under-nutrition, the other major area of concern, can be addressed by targeting children of low birth weights and employing low-cost screening procedures to detect under-nutrition at an early age. Given the projected improvement in living standards, food security, educational levels and access to health care among all levels of the general population, substantial progress can be made in reducing the prevalence of severe under-nutrition in children by 2020. China's remarkable success in combating disease over the past two decades is proof that a determined commitment to improving public health can dramatically reduce the incidence of infectious diseases within one or two decades.

With the demographic and epidemiological transition taking place in the coming years, non-communicable diseases are also likely to emerge as major public health problems. Modernisation of life styles will further aggravate health problems. The rapid proliferation of two and four wheel motor vehicles, increasing congestion on city roads and intercity highways have all contributed to an increasing number of deaths and serious injuries from traffic related accidents. Greater emphasis on education and enforcement of road safety rules by both drivers and pedestrians is an urgent need of the hour.

As already noted, there will be a massive increase in population in the 15-64 age group. Reproductive and Child Health care programmes must meet the needs of this rapidly growing clientele. The population in this age group will be more literate and have greater access to information. They will have greater awareness and expectations about access to quality services for maternal and child health, contraceptive care, management of gynaecological problems, etc. A major focus of vision 2020 must be on improving access to health services to meet the health care needs of women and children.

India's significant achievements in the field of health have been made possible by the establishment of a huge rural health infrastructure, along with the formation of a massive health care manpower consisting of over five lakh trained doctors working under plural systems of medicine, and a vast frontline of over seven lakh nurses and other health care workers; 25,000 primary and community health care centres; and 1.6 lakh sub-centres, complemented by 22,000 dispensaries and 2,800 hospitals practicing Indian systems of medicine and homeopathy. This infrastructure remains under-equipped, under-manned and under-financed to cope with the challenge of eradicating major threats to human life.

The inadequacy of the current health care system is starkly illustrated by the fact that only 35 per cent of the population have access to essential drugs, while the UMI reference level is above 82 per cent. Infant immunisation against measles and DPT for children under 12 years is only 60 per cent and 78 per cent compared to the UMI level of over 90 per cent for both diseases.

As a larger proportion of the population reaches middle class standards of living, an increasing number of people will turn to private health care providers. This development is welcome, because it will permit the public health care system to concentrate more resources on meeting the needs of the poorer sections. But at the same time, the level of public expenditure on health care needs to rise about four-fold from the current level of 0.8 per cent of GDP to reach the UMI reference level of 3.4 per cent. Rapid growth of the private health care system, however, requires the formulation of competence and quality standards to check and balance the increasing emphasis on health care as a business.

Criteria for a More Equitable and Effective Health Care System

- Universal access and access to an adequate level of health care without financial burden.
- Fair distribution of financial costs for access and fair distribution of burden in rational care and capacity.
- Ensuring that providers have the competence, empathy and accountability for delivering quality care and for effective use of relevant research.
- Special attention to vulnerable groups such as women, children, the disabled and the aged.

Development plans for India's health care systems need to place greater emphasis on public health education and prevention. The wide dissemination of health and nutrition related information through traditional channels should be supplemented by an ambitious and persistent programme of public health education through the print, television, radio and electronic media.

Health insurance can play an invaluable role in improving the overall health care system. The insurable population in India has been assessed at 250 million and this number will increase rapidly in the coming two decades. This should be supplemented by innovative insurance products and programmes by panchayats with reinsurance backup by companies and government to extend coverage to much larger sections of the population.

The life expectancy of the Indian population is expected to reach above 65 years in 2020, which compares favourably with the UMI reference level of 69 years. Mortality rates for infants is expected to decline to about 20 per 1000 in 2020, which compares favourably with the UMI reference level of 22.5.

Vulnerability

Economic growth, rising levels of education among the young, expansion of employment opportunities for the working age population, slower population growth, and declining infant mortality, however, will not eliminate and may even aggravate, inequalities between different age groups, the sexes, income groups, communities and regions, unless specific corrective steps are taken for levelling the different degrees of capacity and opportunity. The Vision 2020 must have special focus on bridging the existing gaps in the various levels of development and endeavour its best to fulfil the Constitutional commitment of raising the status of the vulnerable groups vis-a-vis the rest of the society.

During the next 20 years, the aged population in India will nearly double, placing much greater demand on the infrastructure of hospitals and nursing homes, while at the same time shifting the profile of health disorders from problems of the young to those of the aged. The population above 65 years of age will increase from 45 to 76 million persons by 2020. Reference has already been made to the very high incidence of malnutrition among this group and the growing incidence of diseases associated with aging, such as cancer and cardiovascular diseases. A disproportionate number of the aged population are illiterate and living below the poverty line. While majority of these people live in rural areas where the extended family system remains prevalent, increasing urbanisation and mobility will destabilise their situation in future. The problem of coping with a larger aged population will be partially solved by a big surge in the size of the working age labour force and a reduction in the dependency ratio, meaning that there will be a larger proportion of workers to support the aged. Specific strategies will be needed to provide targeted assistance for the most vulnerable members of this group, including research on the disabilities of the aged, greater development of geriatric medicine, training of minders for the aged, and establishment of innovative support systems such as the highly successful Japanese model.

Like the aged, the disabled persons also form another subgroup that is particularly vulnerable and unlikely to benefit directly from the general advance of society, unless specific provisions are made to address their particular needs, including a special system of schools, clinics and home-based learning programmes, combined with therapeutic and institutional care.

Increasing gender equity is an important challenge of the coming years. Literacy rates for females are 40 per cent lower than for males. Females represent only 43 per cent of all students at primary level, 37 per cent at higher secondary level, and 35 per cent of those in higher education. Drop out rates are also higher for girls. The UNDP's gender development index ranks India 108th among 174 countries in terms of gender equity. It is no coincidence therefore that countries ranking highest on this index are among the most prosperous in the world. Gender equity and social development are inseparably interlinked. Reducing the disparity in nutritional, literacy and educational levels between the sexes is essential for realisation of the country's full potentials.

Children being the supreme assets of the country, the 'Rights' based approach will continue to play an important role in ensuring their 'survival', 'protection' and 'development', with special attention to the girl child. *Our vision for 2020 in this regard is to see a nation free from all forms of child labour.* However, complete elimination of child labour through legal means is not only difficult to implement but may also prove to be counter productive in protecting the interest of these very children. While legal enforcement can contain the demand for child labour, it may leave the poor households supplying child labour more vulnerable rather than addressing the underlying socio-economic compulsions generating the supply of such labour. Indeed, poverty eradication combined with educational reforms to provide free (or affordable) access to quality education with an interesting, innovative and job-oriented curriculum for all can effectively eliminate child labour once and for all.

The other categories of the vulnerable groups include the scheduled castes (SC), scheduled tribes (ST), other backward classes (OBC) and minorities, constituting nearly three-fourths of the country's total population. They require special attention in order to narrow down the disparities between them and the more privileged section of the population. Literacy rates for SCs and STs are 25 per cent lower than for other communities. Education enrolment rates among this group, especially for females, lag significantly behind that of other communities. Low levels of education lead to lower paying employment opportunities and lower incomes. Thus, it becomes exceedingly difficult for these communities to come out of the vicious circle. Large number of people in other communities also suffer from similar disparities.

Regional disparities in rates of development are of similar concern. Regardless of the community or the region, the overall progress of the nation will depend to a large extent on its ability to provide increasing opportunities for the disadvantaged to take initiative for their self-development. Otherwise, these disadvantaged will exact an increasing toll on the stability, well-being and development of the country as a whole. It is notable that rising levels of violence and crime in society are not so much associated with overall low levels of development, as they are with wide disparities between levels of development, which create frustration and resentment. The progress of the whole will ultimately depend on the progress of its weakest links. *India's Vision of 2020 must be one in which all levels and sections of the population and all parts of the country march forward together into a more secure and prosperous future.*

4

Infrastructure

Urban Development

Disparities between the social and physical infrastructure of the urban and rural areas are common to all countries. In India they are a continuing source of concern and will become further aggravated unless innovative strategies are evolved to accelerate the development of rural infrastructure. A Vision of India 2020 must assess and try to anticipate the complexion of the future urban-rural divide.

Recent evidence confirms that the rate of growth of urban centres in the country is declining more rapidly than was previously anticipated, though the proportion of people living in urban areas continues to rise. According to the 2001 Census, 27.8 per cent of the Indian population reside in cities, compared with 25.5 per cent in 1990. The urban population is expected to rise to around 40 per cent by 2020. As India's cities continue to swell, the challenge of improving the urban infrastructure will be magnified. For instance, only 73 per cent of India's urban population has access to improved sanitation facilities, compared to the UMI reference level of 95 per cent.

The trend towards concentration of urban population in a small number of large urban centres has been taking shape over a century. While the number of urban centres doubled between 1901 and 1991, the urban population increased eight-fold, resulting in a top heavy urban hierarchy. Future demographic and economic growth is likely to concentrate in and around 60 to 70 large cities in the country having a population of a million people or more.

The demographic trends towards urbanisation are accompanied by a change in the management and financing of urban development as a result of liberalisation. Decentralisation of municipal governance has led to a substantial reduction in budgetary allocations for infrastructural development. Greater reliance is now placed on institutional financing and capital markets for resource mobilisation and on private companies for service delivery.

Disparities in infrastructure between large and small urban areas have always been prevalent, but these disparities can be expected to increase significantly in future years. The stricter fiscal disciplines imposed by government and credit rating agencies will make it increasingly difficult for all but the largest urban centres to attract finance for infrastructural development. The large cities may be expected to experience modest to high rates of growth and to absorb a large part of the incremental migration in their peripheries and neighbouring towns. Being linked to the national and global economy, these large areas are likely to attract investment from the corporate sector and experience a stable demographic growth, while small and medium towns, particularly in backward regions, attract little industrial and infrastructural investment and report low and unstable demographic growth. This almost exclusive focus on improving infrastructure and basic amenities in the large cities is misplaced. Still greater inequality may be expected in the level of basic services across urban centres of different sizes by the year 2020, unless concerted initiative is taken to reverse the trend.

The gross inadequacies of infrastructure, especially those of public transport, water supply and sanitation, demand corrective action. A strategy for developing capabilities within the urban local bodies to cope with the infrastructural deficiencies must be adopted, with genuine decentralisation of financial and administrative powers and restructuring of the entities on the basis of sound management practices.

The face of urban poverty in 2020 is unlikely to be very different from what it is today, given that the largest indicator of poverty in cities is not so much lack of income, as lack of decent housing and civic amenities. These call for a change in a number of policies, especially those relating to land regulation, zoning, and development. The activities relating to provision of health care, water supply and sanitation, education and vocational training need to be carried out with higher levels of efficiency, to help the urban poor upgrade themselves.

While improving infrastructure in existing cities/towns is not to be ignored, in the next two decades there will be need to encourage growth of new townships and take up regional urban development plans where growth corridors can be identified and public-private partnerships promoted for investment in alternative nodes of development. Such centres will have considerable impact in improving the urban profile of the country. They will, however, need to make provision for adequate supply of water and sanitation as well as other civic amenities. They will also need to chalk out more liberal policies towards education and health care in order to attract a cosmopolitan group of investors, professionals and providers of other services. While a large part of it will cater to the affluent, through imaginative planning the new centres can serve the needs of the hinterland also by offering avenues for employment, housing and other needs of a large workforce.

Urban development represents one of the great challenges for India over the next two decades. Given the socio-political reality in India, it will be difficult for the private sector to bring about changes in the pattern of investment in infrastructure without the state becoming an active partner, bringing about the required legislative and administrative changes. A satisfying outcome will depend on the formulation of effective public policy to accelerate all-round development of smaller urban centres and to refashion the role of the state as an effective facilitator to compensate for the deficiencies of market mechanisms in the delivery of public goods. Anti-poverty programmes should primarily be directed towards creation of a community-based infrastructure.

Rural Infrastructure

Along with the development of urban infrastructure, simultaneous efforts are also needed for strengthening rural infrastructure. Specific aspects of the rural infrastructure are discussed elsewhere in this report under the headings of education, health care, transport, telecom, power and water. Our vision is to create a rural infrastructure which connects every village with paved roads and telecommunication facilities, provides electricity and an assured supply of safe drinking water to all rural households, offers access to quality primary and secondary education to all children and medical services to all citizens.

The rural electrification programme, launched in 1951, has succeeded in bringing electricity to more than 5 lakh villages. However, 80,000 villages are yet to get electricity connections. Out of these, 18,000 are in remote areas where electrification through the conventional electricity grid may not be feasible. To achieve 100 per cent rural electrification, we must rely on non-conventional sources of energy, especially for the remote villages. A detailed discussion regarding the potential for such energy sources is given elsewhere in this report.

But the problem of rural infrastructure cannot be viewed or tackled in terms of a composite of separate services or in isolation from changes affecting the urban landscape. A comprehensive and integrated strategy is required. The future development of urban centres will widen the disparities in civic infrastructure that exist between urban and rural communities, thereby stimulating greater migration to the cities and rapid expansion of urban slum areas. The natural growth of urban areas will make this trend inevitable unless bold steps are taken to promote an alternative, more geographically dispersed and equitable development paradigm. Past efforts to develop satellite townships and growth centres in the vicinity of large cities have mitigated the concentration of population in central urban business districts to some extent, but in the process it has furthered the concentration of population in mega cities.

Rural livings offer several considerable advantages over their urban counterparts: However, any successful alternative approach must address the crucial issues of infrastructure and civic amenities that make urban areas so attractive.

Comparative Advantages

Urban

- Domestic services: piped water, electricity, telecommunications and sanitation.
- Primary or localised services: shops, dispensaries, and playgrounds.
- Secondary services: schools, police stations, railway, fire-fighting services, and hospitals, which need not be local but must be readily accessible when required.
- Tertiary services: airports, wholesale markets, referral hospitals, etc. which are less frequently demanded.

Rural

- Living space is much cheaper and more abundant.
- The environment is much healthier.
- Commuting times between work and home are much shorter.

One promising alternative is to link clusters of ten villages together by a high speed circular highway, thereby bringing 100,000 or more people into a circular community that can be crossed within 30 minutes travel time, and promoting a balanced and well spread out development of urban services along the periphery of the ring road. This arrangement would vastly reduce the length and cost of constructing good roads between all the villages, and enable establishment of quality services at any point around the ring to be accessible to all members of the linked community. Telecom links and sanitation systems would naturally develop around the ring at far lower cost, and better quality schools and hospitals could develop to support the larger community. Industrial parks could be established to utilise the large workforce available within the ring. These and similar models need to be tried and modified, on a priority basis, otherwise it requires little stretch of imagination to anticipate the increasing congestion and immobility of large urban areas that is bound to occur in the near future.

Telecom

Telecom acts as a stimulus for the development process. Over the past decade, India's achievement in this sector has been quite impressive. In terms of the overall size of main telephone lines in operation, the country rose from its 14th rank in the world in 1995 to 7th in 2001.

India has adopted a gradual approach towards telecom sector reforms, through selective privatisation and managed competition in different market segments. Since the early 1990s, it has introduced private competition in value-added services, and national and international long distance telephony. Two state-owned public sector incumbents with a large existing subscriber base still dominate the fixed line service, in which they own about 35 million direct exchange lines (DEL). While the number of DELs has multiplied six-fold since 1991, demand for new lines has grown nearly as fast, resulting in persistent shortfall of supply and a current waiting list of nearly 3 million lines. India has also achieved significant quality upgradation of its network in the 1990s, achieving almost 100 per cent conversion to digital lines. At the same time there has been a significant reduction in telecom rates paid by consumers.

The opening up of the cellular market has unleashed real dynamism in the marketplace. Cellular mobile telephone subscribers in India increased from 77 thousand in 1995 to 7.3 million by June 2002, rising from a 0.6 per cent of the total subscribers to 17 per cent. This level is still relatively low compared with the average level of about 25 per cent achieved by low-income countries, 42 per cent by middle-income countries, and upwards of 50 per cent by upper middle-income and high-income countries. The mobile explosion is helping in improving telecom penetration, bringing along the concomitant economic benefits of enhanced telecom accessibility, while at the same time promoting a better entrepreneurial culture, generating additional employment, and fostering a shift in the investment burden from the state to the private sector and the consumers.

In spite of a significant expansion of capacity, however, India's tele-density remains appallingly low, as shown in Table 6, and closing the digital divide in terms of tele-density remains a daunting task. In order to attain the current network size of UMI countries by 2020, India will have to increase the number of telephone lines seven-fold in 18 years.

Table - 6

Number of Main Telephone Lines per 100 Inhabitants

Country	2001
USA	66.45
Germany	63.48
Japan	59.69
UK	57.78
France	57.35
Korea, Rep.	47.60
Russia	24.33
Turkey	28.52
Brazil	21.69
China	13.81
India	3.38

Source: Manas Bhattacharya: "Telecom Sector in India: Vision 2020", Paper prepared for Planning Commission.

Targeted intervention through access promotion can be an important strategy for achieving growth with greater equity. The launching of private franchises for public call offices (PCOs) handling both domestic and long distance services has resulted in an increase in the number of PCOs from 0.2 million in 1993 to 0.9 million in 2001, including 0.4 million in villages. The presence of the private sector is widespread in PCOs and Internet Kiosks in the cities and towns, but remains insignificant in rural areas which account for only about 23 per cent of the country's fixed phone lines. The aggressive expansion of public sector telecommunications infrastructure in geographically remote parts of the country, where private industry cannot venture profitably, is essential for unleashing the latent economic energies and market forces in these regions.

Looking forward from now to 2020, the rapid expansion of India's fixed line network is likely to continue. As the fixed line market matures, more and more users will cross over to mobile communications as well, spurring a mobile revolution in India. Mobile telecommunications and the Internet are going to set the contours of further technological progress over the next two decades. The recent convergence of voice and data transmission, global satellite systems, mobile handsets and calling cards have overcome the technological barriers of distance, topography and remoteness. By 2020, third generation (3G) mobile devices with access to mobile data and voice should be within the reach of wider sections of the Indian population.

The last decade also witnessed a phenomenal growth in the use of Internet. Private Internet service providers have been allowed to set up international Internet gateways, as well as both satellite and landing stations for submarine optical fiber cables. Internet telephony is also opening up. India must strive to complete the transition into digital switching and transmission, voice over Internet protocol (VoIP), broadband and 3G by 2020.

Despite differences across countries, the global trend is towards growing privatisation and competition in telecommunications. Global experience suggests that this process is likely to undergo alternating cylces of differentiation and convergence. The convergent nature of technology may dictate mergers and acquisitions between companies in certain cases. Network operators and service providers may have to merge with content developers to add value to their services. This may create temporary conditions of oligopoly until the emergence of new firms, offering multiple services, intensifies competition. India in 2020 is likely to see competition among big firms offering innovative value-added services to capture market share. The regulatory environment should therefore forster maximum flexibility and freedom to encourage innovation and expansion, consistent with this process of evolution.

Rapid flow of information is a catalyst for social development. Vision 2020 conceives of India evolving into an information society and knowledge economy built on the edifice of information and communication technology (ICT), of which telecommunications is the springboard. Telecom is improving opportunities for people across different social strata. A whole range of information-based industries and applications have come up, creating new sources of employment and earnings with welfare enhancing consequences for both the poor and the wealthy. As a metatechnology, ICT has caused rapid innovations to occur in other areas of material sciences. It has improved access in the fields of education, healthcare, governance and business services. It has also enhanced the ability of the poor to manage risks and mitigate vulnerabilities through provision of timely information. Rapid expansion and extension of the country's fixed and mobile telecom infrastructure is essential for stimulating growth of both the ICT sector and the economy as a whole.

Transport

Development involves a continuous increase in the number of physical transactions and the speed with which they occur, both of which are highly dependent on the size and quality of the nation's transport system. India's network of roads, railways, air services and ports is one of the largest in the world, serving a land mass of 3.3 million square km and a population of over one billion. Over the last 50 years, the growth of this network and of the demand for transport services has been enormous. The volume of railway freight has increased five-fold and passenger kilometers nearly seven-fold. The length of surfaced roads has multiplied nine-fold. The number of goods vehicles has increased 40-fold, buses 20-fold and four-wheel passenger vehicles 30-fold. The tonnage of freight handled by the nation's expanding system of major and minor ports has grown more than 16-fold. Air-freight tonnage has increased about 30-fold.

Currently, about 800 billion tonne km of freight and 2,3000 billion passenger km are handled by the transport system, with the total transport demand growing at around 10 per cent a year for the past decade. The modal growth rates have varied, with road transport and air services growing at a much faster rate than the railways. The relative share of railways in total freight and passenger traffic has declined dramatically over the past five decades, from 90 to 25 per cent of inland freight and from 75 to 18 per cent of inland passenger. Meanwhile, the share of road transport has increased from 12 to 60 per cent of freight and from 32 to 80 per cent of passenger business.

Growing urbanisation is a natural phenomenon and despite all its implications has beneficial effects on economic growth. Increasing population combined with continued urbanisation are likely to raise India's urban population to around 540 million over the next two decades, resulting in the emergence of about 60 to 70 cities with population of more than a million. Lack of adequate public transport has resulted in a rapid increase in private ownership of vehicles, particularly two wheelers, with consequent adverse effects of air and noise pollution. In most cities, two wheelers comprise more than 70 per cent of total motor vehicles. Based on current growth rates, two-wheeler ownership in cities with more than 100,000 inhabitants is likely to rise from 102 to 393 per thousand population in the next 20 years, while the number of cars increases from 14 to 48 per thousand.

To contain this explosion of personal vehicle movement in cities, massive investment in mass transport services will become necessary. Public investment in transport has declined steadily over the past four decades from 23 per cent of the total plan funds in 1960 to around 12 per cent in the 1980s and 1990s. Considering the developing nature of the country and the deficiencies in its transport system, a larger proportion of resources will need to be invested in improvements to the transport infrastructure.

Among the most daunting problems faced by India's cities are the inadequate public transport infrastructure, long travel times and high transport cost for both passenger and goods traffic. The growth of cities has been haphazard, expanding around a compact central core with industrialisation and migration bringing about rapid change in peripheral land use, resulting in urban sprawl. No organised, viable and significant public transport system is available in major cities, except the four metro areas of Mumbai, Kolkata, Chennai and Delhi. Bus and rail systems are the mainstay of public transport in these cities. Transport planning must go hand-in-hand with land use planning. Specific plans will need to be formulated by each urban authority, starting with the provision of bus services, developing intermediate public transport and identifying corridors for future growth, including reserving land for such activity.

In the long run, rail-based mass transport systems appear to be the only viable solution to the problems of urban transport in India's major metropolitan areas. Where flexibility of land use is possible, electrified surface rail transport can be adopted. In the case of highly developed and congested areas, underground or flyover systems will have to be considered. On medium density corridors, electric trolley buses or CNG operated buses may be best suited.

A key component of rural development is the provision of roads for connectivity, access being essential for social and economic well-being. Families residing along side roads benefit from better health, greater educational opportunities, smaller sized families and higher ownership of assets, compared to those families living in remote villages. While almost all villages with population above 1,500 are now connected by road, more than 45 per cent of villages with less than 1,000 people still need to be connected. There are also significant regional imbalances in the connectivity of villages. Poor road maintenance is a related problem. The Government has allocated resources to achieve all-weather road access to all villages with population above 1,000 by 2003, and for villages with population between 500 and 1,000 by 2007.

While the progress made in the transport sector has been significant, it has not been able to meet the growing demand, particularly in the last decade when economic reforms triggered an unprecedented growth of GDP. Efforts to achieve even higher GDP growth rates in future years cannot be sustained without correspondingly greater efforts to strengthen the nation's transport system. The existing issues and concerns, the congestion and constraints in movement leading to higher transport costs, and other unfinished tasks will be some of the challenges that need to be met during the next two decades. A huge increase in demand for both railways and road transport will require not only massive investments but also modification in pricing policies, increasing customer focus, improved terminal management, enhanced safety, reduced transit times, and other changes required to provide adequate and efficient services for meeting the growth in demand and public expectations.

Based on projected GDP growth of 8 per cent per annum, the total freight traffic is likely to reach about 5,500 billion tonne km by the year 2020, five times the level in year 2000. If a 10 per cent growth is achieved, the traffic demand would exceed 10,000 billion tonne km. Assuming that railways retain a 20 per cent market share, rail freight traffic, measured in tonne km, will increase three to six-fold. The proportion of manufactured products to bulk cargo will also rise, with a larger proportion of liquids being carried through the pipelines. General merchandise will travel longer distances and in much smaller consignments, favouring smaller carrying units. The rising value of consignments will place a higher premium on the speed of transit in order to minimise inventories. The total logistical management of transportation, marketing and distribution will become commonplace for most general merchandise. These changes, together with the impact of other factors such as energy efficiency, environmental pollution, and technological changes in each mode, will result in changing preferences for alternative modes of transport.

Passenger traffic is expected to increase more than four-fold over the next 20 years. For long distance travel, the demand for air services will grow rapidly, as speed becomes an increasingly important consideration. Already more people travel between Delhi and Mumbai by air than by rail. Overnight sleeper class travel will continue to be the railways' strength, as long as booking, reservations, comfort and other customer services are continuously enhanced to keep pace with rising customer expections.

For medium distances up to 500 kms — with four-lane highways connecting the country, expressways coming up close to the main metro cities, and car ownership increasing rapidly — the bulk of the passenger travel may start moving towards 'own vehicle travel', a phenomenon already observed in most countries. Fast inter-city rail services will have an edge over air travel for this segment of traffic.

Road transport is best suited for short distance traffic, except where volumes increase to very high levels and rail-based mass rapid transport offers a cost-effective alternative.

Future Trends in Transport

- Improvement in the length, quality and speed of transport networks.
- Increase in productivity and economic efficiency of transport.
- Higher frequency and quality of services.
- Better control of air and noise pollution.
- Increased mobility for commuters, business and recreational travel.
- Improved urban transport systems.
- Corresponding improvements in rural transport.
- Fewer transport constraints to trade.
- Reduced transport transit times in general and at initial loading and terminal points.
- Better energy efficiency.
- Improved safety with fewer accidents.

Our vision of India 2020 is of a country with a well-developed network of roads and railways and adequate capacity to handle the growth in demand for transport. The volume of road traffic will multiply about five-fold, carried over a 70,000 km network of National Highways, including 5,000 to 10,000 km of expressways, linking the golden quadrangle of Delhi-Mumbai-Chennai-Kolkata-Delhi as well as northern, southern, eastern and western portions of the country, mostly with four or more lanes. State Highways with at least two ways lanes will link most districts. Rural roads will provide access to the furthest outlying villages. Technological progress will generate vehicles that are pollution free and fuel-efficient. An efficient public transport system will lead to a reduction in the population of two-wheelers in major urban areas.

The railways will have to be expanded to handle a three-fold increase in traffic. Improved customer service, comfort and safety, a reduction in freight costs and tariffs, elimination (or at least reduction) of the uneconomic services, non-paying projects and subsidies will be necessary for this. India will need airports of international standards for passenger and cargo handling and modern handling systems at major ports to reduce delays in berthing. Institutional arrangements will need to be in place with adequate funds for proper maintenance, especially of roads. Urban transport systems will be needed in all cities with a population of a million plus.

We envisage that connection of several distributaries of the rivers through a network of canals will give impetus to the development of inland water transport.

Investment requirements to meet these needs will increase to levels three to four times higher than the present in real terms. While the government will continue to be a major source of funds for infrastructure, internal generation of resources by the transport services will have to increase, supported by more realistic pricing of transport services and reduction in operating costs. The private sector will need to play a more central role in the development and operation of transport systems.

5

Energy and the Environment

Economic growth the world over is driven by energy, whether in the form of finite resources such as coal, oil and gas or in renewable forms such as hydroelectric, wind, solar and biomass, or its converted form, electricity. This energy generation and consumption powers the nation's industries, vehicles, homes and offices. It also has significant impact on the quality of the country's air, water, land and forest resources. For future growth to be both rapid and sustainable, it needs to be as resource-efficient and environmentally benign as possible.

Power

India's installed capacity for power generation has tripled over the last 20 years and now exceeds 101,000 MW. However, the total demand is expected to increase by another 3.5 times in the next two decades, even under a best-case scenario that envisions intensified efforts to modernise power plants, improve transmission and distribution efficiency, and adopt more efficient generation technologies. Figure 2 depicts power consumption by various sectors in 1997 compared to a business-as-usual (BAU) and an alternative scenario which we will consider as the best-case scenario (BCS) for 2020.

The soaring demand for power will necessitate a tripling of the installed generation capacity from 101,000 to 292,000 MW over the next two decades. The projected fuel mix for power generation from various sources is shown in Figure 3. At least two-thirds of this power will have to come from thermal sources — coal, oil and gas — even under the BCS. This will mean a spiralling cost for imported fuels, including coal, since even a doubling of domestic coal production would not be sufficient to meet the demand. It will also mean a surge in emission of environmental pollutants. Even under this alternative scenario, the contribution of renewable energy does not exceed 5 per cent of the total production.

FIGURE – 2

Projected Power Demand (TWh)

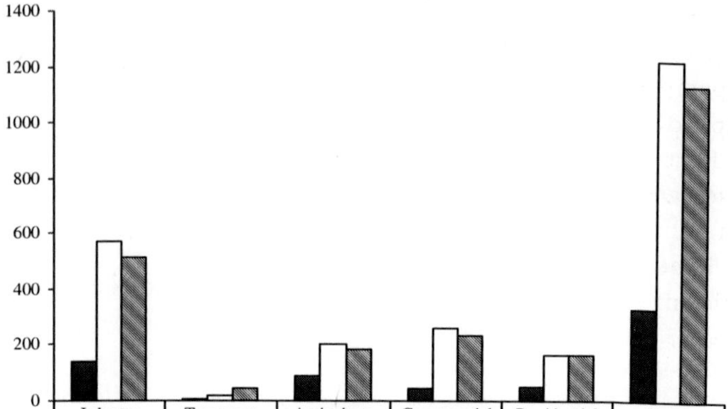

	Industry	Transport	Agriculture	Commercial	Residential	Total
■ 1997	137	7	89	47	48	329
□ BAU2020	570	22	202	262	165	1221
▨ BCS 2020	510	45	181	235	163	1134

Source: Based on R.K. Pachauri and Pooja Mehrotra, "Vision 2020: Sustainability of our Material Resources", paper prepared for Planning Commission.

FIGURE – 3

Fuel Mix for Power Generation (TWh)

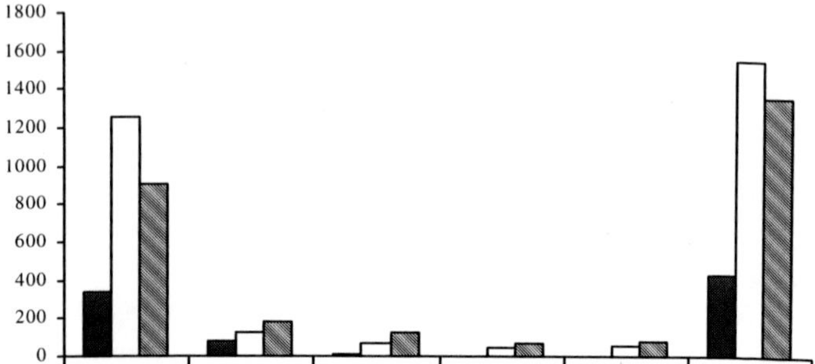

	Thermal	Hydro	Nuclear	Renewables	Hydro (Import)	Total
■ 1997	336	75	10	4	1	426
□ BAU2020	1259	119	70	49	54	1551
▨ BCS 2020	911	181	127	68	76	1363

Source: Same as Figure 2.

Fuel Demand

The overall growth in demand for all forms of fuel will mirror the growth in the power sector. Even under the alternative scenario, total coal demand will nearly double, and both oil and gas demand will triple, as shon in Table 7. Expanding domestic production capacity will require substantial investments, while increasing dependence on imported forms of energy will increase vulnerability to fluctuations in global energy prices. The surging demand will also place an increased burden on the physical and social environments. An enhanced exploration by the public and private sectors, adoption of best practices and environment-friendly technologies, more efficient use of energy, promotion of private sector investment, and greater efforts to protect the environment will be required to cope effectively with the nation's growing energy needs.

Table – 7

Projected Fuel Demand

	Coal (million tons)	*Oil (million tons)*	*Gas (billion cubic mtrs)*
1997	311	83	21.5
2020 BAU	688	245	70.8
2020 BCS	538	195	64.7

Source: Same as Figure 2.

The growth in demand for oil depicted in Figure 4 shows that the largest increases will be for transportation and industry. Domestic oil production has remained relatively constant over the past decade, while oil imports have more than doubled. If the BAU scenario depicted in Table 7 were to be realised, it would require a more than tripling of oil imports. Even under the BCS, oil imports would have to increase two-fold.

Long-term forecasts for the price of oil are at best precarious. A recent forecast by the Institute of Energy Economics of Japan shows the price fluctuating within a band from $ 17 to $ 23 per barrel over the next 20 years.

FIGURE – 4

Projected Demand for Oil

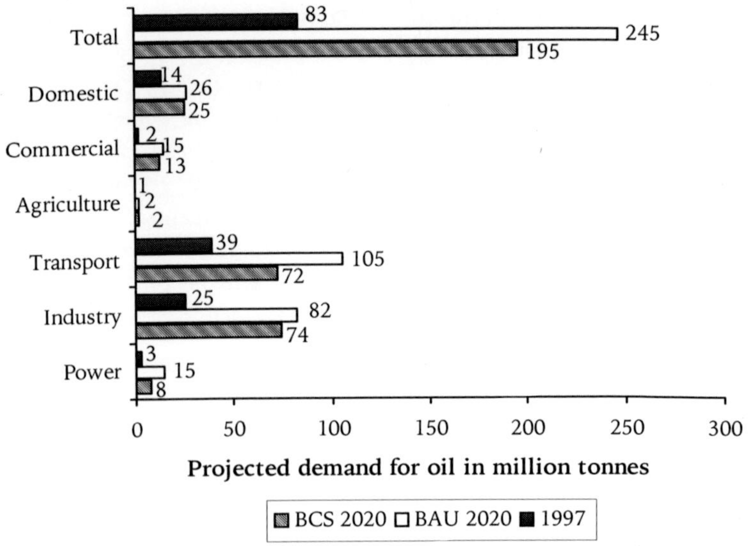

Source: Same as Figure 2.

The growth in demand for natural gas depicted in Figure 5 shows that the largest increases willl be for power and industry, especially fertilisers. Domestic gas production is expected to meet around 20 per cent of the total demand, thereby requiring massive import of gas. Plans for gas pipeline projects from Bangladesh and Iran as well as LNG terminals along India's coastlines are already being contemplated.

The alternative scenario for oil and gas presents a combination of technological developments, governance measures, and market-based instruments that will reduce resource requirements. It places greater reliance on gas for environmental considerations. The spread of cleaner technologies among transport vehicles should lead to improved air quality in the cities.

FIGURE – 5

Projected Demand for Natural Gas

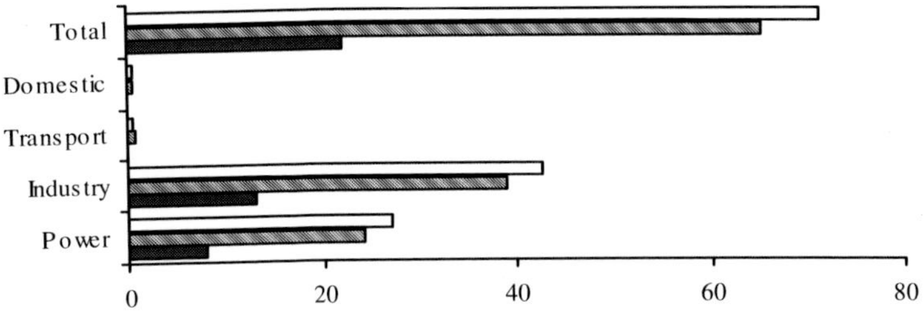

	Power	Industry	Transport	Domestic	Total
□ BAU2020	27	42.6	0.5	0.6	71
▧ BCS 2020	24.3	39	0.9	0.5	65
■ 1997	8.1	13.1	0.1	0.2	22

Projected demand for gas in billion cubic meters

Source: Same as Figure 2.

Renewable Energy

Greater reliance on renewable energy sources offers enormous economic, social and environmental benefits. India is already the world's fifth largest producer of wind power, with more than 95 per cent of the investment coming from the private sector. Other renewable energy technologies, including solar photovoltaic, solar thermal, small hydro and biomass power are also spreading. Under the BAU scenario the contribution of renewable forms of energy is expected to be quite modest, but a concerted effort to implement a more visionary plan could significantly alter this outcome. Apart from reducing India's dependence on imported fuels and the strain on the environment, some forms of renewable energy such as biomass power production and ethanol motor fuel offer the added advantage of potentially creating millions of rural employment opportunities and contributing to higher rural incomes, rather than higher outflows of foreign exchange. Tapping this potential will require conducive national policies and programmes designed to attract active participation from the private sector.

However, a far more aggressive alternative scenatio is also possible in which the country makes a massive commitment to the development of biomass power, biogas and biofuels that could act as a powerful stimulus to rural job-creation and prosperity, while radically reducing India's dependence on imported fuels. (See box)

Biomass Power & Bio-fuels for Rural Job-creation & Prosperity

India has approximately 50 million hectares of degraded wasteland that lie outside the areas demarcated as national forests, and another 34 million hectares of protected forest area, in much of which tree cover is severely degraded. A massive programme to develop energy plantations consisting of fast-growing tree crops such as Bamboo, Casuarina and Eucalyptus can serve as the raw material for a national network of small, decentralised biomass power plants. These power plants, ranging in size from 10-25 MW, can generate thousands of megawatts of power from renewable, forest-based fuel sources in a cost-effective manner. This would reduce India's dependence on imported fuel oils, stimulate private investment in the power sector, and generate massive income and employment opportunities for the rural poor. Establishment of 40 million hectares of energy plantation would be sufficient to generate 100,000 MW of power and provide year-round employment for 30 million people.

India also has the capacity to generate biofuels in massive quantities. Curcas (*jatropha curcas*) is a plant introduced from Africa, which already grows wild in India. The plant produces large quantities of seeds which contain up to 35 per cent oil that is a substitute for No. 2 diesel and kerosene and can be blended in diesel motor fuels up to 15 per cent. The cost of production is competitive with other fuel oils. Cultivation of 10 million hectares of this crop could generate 7.5 million tons of fuel annually, while generating year-round employment for 5 million people.

Ethanol, which can be produced from maize, tapioca, sugarcane, sugar beet and other crops, is another biofuel with enormous potential. It can be mixed as a pollution-free blend with petrol and diesel. Ethanol-petrol fuel blends are utilised in more than 20 countries, including Brazil, Canada, Sweden and USA. Between 1979 and 1992, this enabled Brazil to reduce reliance on imported oil by 70 per cent. Introducing 10 per cent ethanol fuel with petrol and diesel could create potential demand for more than 10 million tons of ethanol per annum.

The greatest advantage of biomass power and bio-fuels is that they can generate tens of millions of rural jobs and stimulate enormous growth of rural incomes, especially among the weaker sections. Therefore, these strategies should not be regarded from the narrow perspective of energy alone, but from the wider perspective of national development.

Air Quality

Transport, manufacturing, the power sector, commercial and residential energy use, all contribute to problems of air quality. Motor vehicles contribute to all forms of air pollution. Residential burning of unprocessed biomass fuel is the single largest source of carbon monoxide and suspended particulate matter. Power generation contributes most of the nitrogen oxides and sulphur dioxide.

The escalating demand for power, rapid proliferation of motor vehicles, expansion of industries and rising living standards will all combine to have significant impact on the quality of air, especially in urban areas, as depicted in Figure 6. Appropriate strategies and actions are required to address the various forms of pollution in each of these sectors. Stricter enforcement of environmental regulations, rapid adoption of pollution-free and more efficient technologies, and higher standards for fuel quality are needed to reduce the environmental costs of growth.

FIGURE – 6

Projected Air Emissions

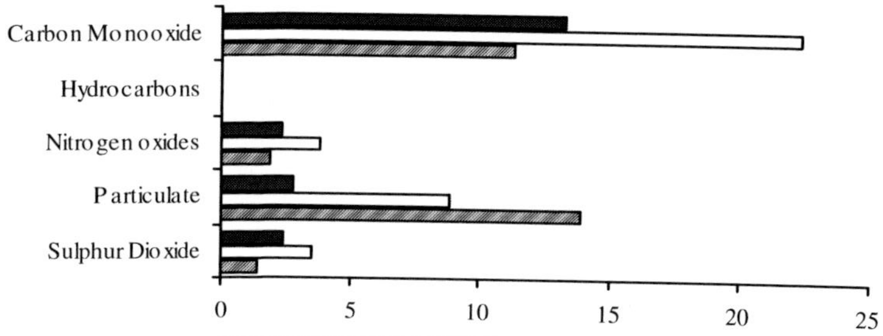

	Sulphur Dioxide	Particulate	Nitrogen oxides	Hydro carbons	Carbon Monooxide
■ 2020 BCS	2.47	2.83	2.37	0.04	13.27
□ 2020 BAU	3.57	8.82	3.84	0.07	22.32
▨ 1997	1.38	13.93	1.91	0.02	11.33

Projected Emissions in Million Tonnes

Source: Same as Figure 2.

Water Management

India possesses 16 per cent of the world's population but just 4 per cent of its water resources. Overall, at the national level, current water resources are more than sufficient to meet the demand, but future studies project that the supply situation could become difficult over the next half century. However, water shortage has already become a serious and recurring source of concern for a large number of people in different parts of the country and for a number of the major metropolitan areas. Only 70 per cent of the people in urban areas have access to basic sanitation services. A large number of rural habitations remain without any identified source of safe drinking water. Groundwater tables are receding, rivers are silting up, and leaching of chemical fertilizers is polluting drinking water supplies.

The rising consumption will further aggravate water scarcity as population, food production, industrialisation and living standards continue to rise over the next two decades. The total water consumption in India is expected to rise by 20-40 per cent over the next 20 years. Figure 7 shows the current and projected consumption of water for different categories of use.

FIGURE – 7

Projected Water Consumption

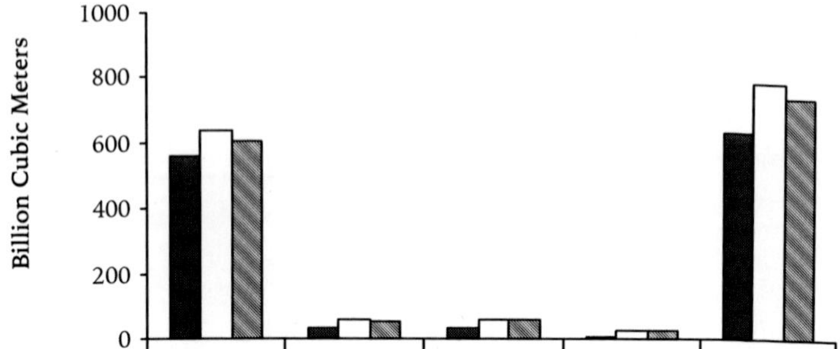

	Irrigation	Domestic	Manufac-turing	Power	Total
■ 1997-98	560	30	30	9	629
□ 2020 BAU	640	56	57	28	781
▨ 2020 BCS	602	51	57	27	737

Source: Water Resources Division, Planning Commission.

To meet the rising demand for water in 2020, it is essential to develop potential storage capacities and strengthen existing storage facilities. Agriculture accounts for 89 per cent of the total water consumption and domestic consumption accounts for 4.8 per cent. Subsidised or free supply of power and water has resulted in overexploitation and inefficient use of water in agriculture, leading to water-logging and salinity on 5.76 million hectares. Tremendous wastage occurs as a result of evapostranspiration, distribution losses, seepage through unlined channels and excess application. Canal-irrigation efficiency in India is estimated at around 35 to 40 per cent, which is below international standards. Government policies need to be revised to provide incentives for efficient use of water, including appropriate water pricing and more effective institutional mechanisms for water management.

India is not poor in water resources. What it lacks is the ability to efficiently capture and effectively utilise the available resources for the maximum benefit. Enormous potential exists for increasing the productivity of water in agriculture by raising crop productivity, combined with better water management. Deep soil chiseling prior to planting can dramatically improve water retention by the soil, while reducing run-off and flooding. Crops grown in these conditions require less irrigation and generate much higher yields.

Both urban and rural water resources can be substantially enhanced by widespread adoption of rainwater harvesting techniques. These techniques need to be applied throughout the country, in both rural and urban areas, to capture run-off water during the monsoon season and channel it into ponds, tanks and bore wells in order to recharge both surface water and underground aquifers.

A serious degradation in the quality of groundwater and river water has occurred due to excessive and indiscriminate use of pesticides and chemical fertilisers in agriculture, as well as salinity resulting from overexploitation of groundwater. The deterioration of water quaity is compounded by lack of proper effluent treatment for domestic waste water and industrial wastes. Stricter enforcement of environmental regulations is essential for stemming further degradation, and enactment of groundwater legislation is necessary to check over exploitation.

Given the enormous cost of major water projects, emphasis needs to shift from large scale projects for augmenting water supply to decentralised projects designed to manage water demand and conserve water resources. The National Water Policy 2002 advocates an integrated approach to water resources development with a river basin as a planning unit. The Policy emphasises community participation in management of water resources, appropriate pricing for water, tackling of pollution of surface and ground water bodies, and encouragement to the private sector to invest in water resources development. What is now required is to operationalise the policy by preparing state level policies and drawing up action plans to implement the various recommendations.

For the past fifty years, public imagination has been stirred by proposals to link major rivers together in a manner that would channel surpluses from flood-prone areas into drought-prone regions, create millions of hectares of additional irrigated land, provide an inexpensive system of inland water transport, and generate millions of additional employment opportunities in construction, agriculture, trade and industrial development. The high cost estimates of such a system — recent estimates place the cost at more than Rs. 500,000 crores — as well as some technical and political issues involved have been perceived as serious obstacles to implementation. However, the potential benefits to the nation of linking even some of the major rivers, subject to technical feasibility, are so vast that pragmatic proposals demand serious consideration. Given the vision and political will, India can convert the present water problem into a huge opportunity.

Land, Forest and Biodiversity

India's wide range of agro-climatic regions, vast extent of land and forest, and rich variety of biodiversity, rank it among the most naturally endowed nations of the world. But its huge and still expanding human and animal populations and its urge for industrialisation tax these resources to the limit. Competing uses of land for agriculture, forestry, pastures, human settlements and industries exert increasing pressure on the country's finite land resources, influencing land-use patterns and sometimes causing degradation of forests and soils. Changes in land use and land cover, together with land degradation have adverse impacts on forest resources and biodiversity. Increasing demand for forest resources is of particular concern.

Yet the potential exists for dramatically reversing this pattern of degradation during the next two decades. It can be done by a concerted and systematic effort to halt soil erosion, restore precious nutrients and organic material to crop lands, recharge groundwater tables, and re-establish depleted forest lands, together with a holistic approach to land management that combines technologies and policies to integrate ecological, socio-economic, and political principles.

Figure 8 shows current and projected land use pattern under the business-as-usual and alternative scenario. While the amount of land under agriculture remains constant, the quality of that land will be enormously enhanced by the policies and programmes already mentioned. The most significant improvement under the alternative scenario is the increase in land under forest and tree cover from the current level of 71 million hectares to 83 million hectares (See Table 8).

At present, 40 per cent of the commercial demand for timber and less than 20 per cent of the demand for fuel wood are being met by sustainable supply from the forests. Population growth will result in rising demand for both. Over-grazing and over-extraction of green fodder lead to forest degradation through decreased vegetative regeneration, soil compaction and erosion.

FIGURE – 8

Projected Land Use

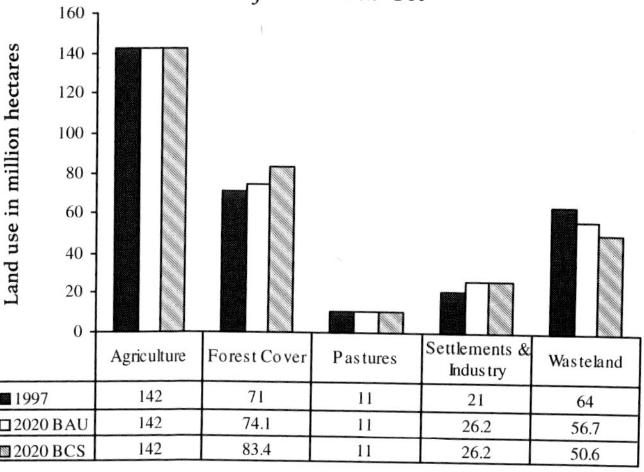

	Agriculture	Forest Cover	Pastures	Settlements & Industry	Wasteland
1997	142	71	11	21	64
2020 BAU	142	74.1	11	26.2	56.7
2020 BCS	142	83.4	11	26.2	50.6

Source: Same as Figure 2.

Table – 8

Projected Land Use - Percentage Distribution

	1997	*2020 BAU*	*2020 BCS*
Agriculture	45.9	45.8	45.3
Forest Cover	23.0	23.9	26.6
Pastures	3.5	3.5	3.5
Settlements & Industry	6.8	8.5	8.4
Wasteland	20.7	18.3	16.2

Source: Same as Figure 2.

Combating the pressure on forests requires a combination of measures. A superior genetic stock is required to correct the poor productivity of Indian forests, which is a third below world averages. Extensive areas should be brought under joint forest management and plantation forestry. Plantation forestry can be expanded through the combined efforts of local communities, NGOs, and the corporate sector, which will provide the technological, financial and organisational resources required, while generating millions of employment opportunities for rural and tribal communities. Removal of legal and technical barriers by rationalising land-ceiling laws, removing restrictions on harvest and sale of timber, and devising incentives to attract private investment are essential for achieving these goals.

The degradation of land and forest is also endangering India's rich biodiversity. Maintaining viable populations of plant and animal species which form the basis for traditional systems of medicine and also hold vast potential for modern science, requires the conservation of important ecosystems, habitats and the ecological processes of which they are a part. While the country has nearly achieved the international goal of reserving 5 per cent of its area as protected, some important biomes and species are not yet covered. This can be accomplished by an expansion of the system of national parks and sanctuaries combined with enhancing control and enforcement of wildlife trade, creation of new conservation reserves, conservation forestry, integration of rural development and biodiversity strategies, and a range of other legal, administrative and technical measures.

6

Globalisation

India's progress over the next 20 years will be intimately linked to events within the region as well as around the world. Both opportunities and challenges will arise as the result of transformations in the regional and global political and security environments. World trade under WTO will determine access to markets and international competitiveness, particularly after the ascension of China. The economic growth rates of other regions will influence demand for exports and foreign capital flows. Some other developments that will influence India's progress in the coming two decades are: pressure on energy prices as a result of global economic growth; continued spread of the information revolution; and technological innovations, such as those with regard to disease prevention and treatment.

Global Trends and Institutional Framework

Although these external factors are too many and too complex for us to reliably predict their impact, what we can do is recall some of the most significant and broad global trends that are likely to exert a powerful influence on India's progress over the coming two decades.

1. Population Growth

Global population will continue to grow from 6 billion to around 7.5 billion people, fuelling a large increase in global demand for food, goods and services. Life expectancy will rise significantly, leading to a larger proportion of the aged in all regions. At the same time a swelling of the working age population will lead to a significant increase in the global labour force.

2. Economic Expansion

The phenomenal achievements of the last half century have been the results of a fortuitous blend of forces — the absence of a world war, the spread of democracy to countries around the globe, rising levels of education everywhere, rising social aspirations and expectations, rapid technological development and diffusion, advances in the science and the practice of management, and development of a more efficient and sophisticated economic and financial organisation for global commerce. All of these driving forces should continue to exert strong positive pressure for global economic expansion in the next century. If world real GDP continues to expand at an average rate of 3.14 per cent per annum as it did over the past 12 years, real world GDP will increase by 85 per cent over the next 20 years. A substantial rise in incomes and living standards will act as an additional stimulus to global demand for food, manufactured goods, services and energy.

3. *Growth of World Trade*

World trade grew by an average of about 7 per cent per annum in the decade of 1990s. By reducing and eventually eliminating all forms of trade barriers, the emerging institutional framework under WTO is likely to accelerate the expansion of world trade in the coming years. This will open greater opportunities for domestic producers while making them more vulnerable to international competition. At the same time, with the spread of new technologies and production capabilities, economies of scale are becoming increasingly important in reducing costs and prices. Increasingly, single countries or even single producers are becoming globally dominant in specific product categories. This trend has already resulted in global surpluses in categories such as steel, basic chemicals and computer memory chips. Growing surpluses will bring even greater competition between companies and countries producing the same products, as well as cheaper products for consumers, and higher standards of living. Opportunities in business will gradually shift from volume production to special value-added categories of products and services.

4. *Growth of Services Sector*

The driving force for economic growth and employment will increasingly come from the services sector. Rising living standards will fuel the demand for commercial, social and community services. Construction, retailing, education, health, entertainment and tourism will expand more rapidly than ever before. The incorporation of services under the WTO framework has opened up enormous opportunities for hitherto non-tradable sectors to expand their horizons across borders. This will enhance the quality, range and affordability of services to the domestic economy and add a further stimulus to a service-led economic growth around the world. At the same time, the efforts will be needed to secure a level playing field and fairness in the trading system.

5. OECD Labour Shortages

Demographic trends in the OECD countries will create acute labour shortages, opening up unprecedented opportunities for countries that can provide skilled manpower and outsourcing services. A UN study released in March 2000 estimates that the 15-nation European Community would have to accept 150 million new immigrants over the next 25 years in order to maintain the present levels of working population. By 2013, labour force growth in the USA will be zero. The UN estimates that Japan would need to admit 600,000 immigrants annually for the next 50 years in order to maintain the size of its working population at the 1995 level. Significant labour shortages will develop in the OECD countries unless immigration policies are dramatically liberalised or large numbers of manufacturing and service jobs are shifted overseas. This trend will further accelerate the outsourcing of production of goods and services to locations where infrastructure, ease of doing business, quality, costs and availability of labour are most attractive, which will be beneficial for many labour surplus countries like India.

6. Capital Flows

The new institutional framework will promote freer flow of capital and foreign investment, both direct as well as portfolio. Capital rich nations will seek out investment destinations generating higher returns. This trend will be reinforced by rising income levels and the aging of the OECD population, which will swell the size of pension, insurance and mutual funds, resulting in a continued increase in international capital flows in search of secure and attractive returns. At the same time, large manufacturing companies will increasingly move from national to global production strategies, resulting in further shifting of production and direct investment in countries or regions in which markets exist or in which production costs are lowest.

7. Technology & Infrastructure

The TRIPS will promote even faster technological innovation. Application and diffusion of technologies in a wide range of fields across international borders will also accelerate. Agricultural technology, biotechnology, information & communications technology, computerised manufacturing technologies will transform the way human beings learn, communicate, produce, and care for their health. The most important technological breakthroughs of the coming decade are expected in areas such as precision farming, fuel cells, alternative energy, genetic engineering, portable information devices, robotics, mass customisation, and computerised health care. Application of computers will continue to spread rapidly, influencing all aspects of the global society, especially communication, manufacturing, finance and trade, scientific research, education, and medicine. The cost of global communications will continue to decline rapidly, reducing barriers of distance and making global production, distribution and marketing strategies more viable.

Implications and Options for India

1. Trade in goods

Liberalisation of trade will open up new opportunities for export of goods, while increasing pressures on India's domestic industry to cope with competition from imports, especially from China. The global market for textiles and clothing will expand dramatically and the phasing out of quantitative restrictions will increase trade in these categories. But India's ability to export will depend on its capacity to keep pace with the rising international standards of price, quality, productivity, and service. Global trade in agricultural products will also grow rapidly, though it is not yet clear to what extent the OECD countries will remove the barriers and subsidies that hinder exports to these markets. However, India's ability to become a major exporter of agricultural products will depend most on its ability to improve crop quality and productivity, while lowering costs to international levels. India missed out on the boom in manufactured exports that occurred from the 1970s to 1990s. Increasing overcapacity in basic manufacturing industries, coupled with mechanisation of processes, which eliminates the advantage of low cost labour, will limit future opportunities and benefits for export of manufactured commodity goods such as cars, TVs, and computers. Future opportunities for manufactured exports will be focused on the high end of the technology chain, computerised, customised manufacturing processes and sophisticated engineering and capital goods, areas in which India has not yet strongly positioned itself internationally.

2. *Trade in services*

The World Bank estimates that India will possess the fourth largest economy in the world by 2020. The emerging global scenario will open up greater opportunities for countries with a surplus of well-educated, highly skilled labour that can provide an attractive commercial environment for the outsourcing of manufacturing and service businesses from high and even middle income countries. India's recent boom in outsourcing of IT services, further facilitated by declining costs of international communication and transportation, only points to the wide range of economic opportunities existing in the manufacturing and service businesses. At the same time, the pressure for export of highly educated and highly skilled individuals will also increase, so that a significant migration of scientific, engineering and medical talent is likely to continue. Steps however need to be taken to ensure that such migration is not detrimental to the country's development.

Export of services is a field in which India can excel. Computerisation, coupled with low-cost global telecommunications are generating rapid growth of trade in service businesses, such as software and IT enabled services. This trend will further accelerate, opening up vast opportunities for countries with the capacity to deliver low-cost, high-quality services. India already commands an impressive 18.5 per cent share in the global market for customised software and the Indian software industry is the fastest growing in the world. A NASSCOM-McKinsey report estimated that by 2008, the global market for IT enabled services alone will exceed $ 1,000 billion, and that India's export of IT services will exceed $50 billion, which is double the country's total export of goods and services in 2000. In addition, India's established credentials in IT and IT enabled services can be leveraged to develop a competitive advantage in other fields, including other branches of engineering, branches of scientific research, especially biotechnology, medicine, pharmaceuticals, and agriculture, as well as education. Performance in these sectors will depend on the country's capacity to generate larger numbers of well-educated and competent scientists, engineers and professionals.

3. Capital Flows and FDI

The enlargement of the international capital market will open up increasing opportunities for India to attract foreign direct and institutional investment. Foreign direct investment (FDI) expanded globally from $159 billion in 1991 to $1,270 billion in 2000, but with an increasing proportion of these flows moving between developed nations. During this period, FDI flows to India increased six-fold to $2.3 billion, which represents less than 0.2 per cent of global FDI. The amount of capital globally available will continue to grow, but improvements in infrastructure and elimination of bureaucratic barriers will be major determinants of India's success in attracting a greater share of FDI flows. The size and prosperity of China's non-resident population has been a vital link for the channelling of technology, investment and business back to the mainland. A similar mobilisation of India's expatriate population could have momentous impact on the inflow of FDI in 2020. Likewise, multinational investments in India should be encouraged, especially in technology-intensive sectors where they can supplement and strengthen India's technological capabilities.

4. Technology

India's technology policy needs to be reformulated in the light of the emerging international economic environment, to capitalise on the accelerated global development and diffusion of technologies, and keep pace with more demanding international standards for cost, quality and productivity. India will need to be far more aggressive in acquiring and applying advanced technologies in a wide range of fields, including agriculture, information technology, energy, health and education. At the same time, India can also aspire to become an important contributor to the expansion of global frontiers of technology by building upon and leveraging its already significant achievements in fields such as pharmaceuticals, biotechnology, software, space and energy. It can also revive, simultaneously, it's traditional knowledge and technologies through formal R&D efforts.

7

Peace and Security

India is in the midst of a great experiment. It is in the process of transforming a weak agrarian economy into a modern multi-dimensional economic enterprise and a traditional stratified society into an egalitarian society, while simultaneously fashioning and transforming itself into a modern democracy through consultative politics. It is inevitable that the rapid social, economic, technological and political development of one billion people should cause turbulence. Yet it is essential that this turbulence be managed and confined within limits that preserve the social fabric and cultural values and permit the nation's transformation to continue.

Underlying all our plans and hopes for a better future, underpinning all our efforts to evolve into a harmonious and prosperous democratic nation, is the shared aspiration of all Indian people for peace. Peace is not merely the absence or avoidance of conflict. It is the essential foundation for all human and social development, the fertile ground on which we can strive to elevate our minds in knowledge, hone our productive skills, strengthen our physical infrastructure, and fashion our multitudinous communities into a strong, united and harmonious nation.

The challenges to peace are numerous and they come from all directions — from outside our border and within, as well as from within our minds. Our capacity to preserve and build lasting peace for all Indians will depend on the strength of our military to defend our borders and the potential of our economy to generate increasing employment and income opportunities for all citizens. Our education system will need to inculcate knowledge and skills in our youth. Our legal and judicial system will be required to safeguard the rights of individuals and communities. Our scientists and engineers will have to develop and harness technologies for the benefit of the people. Most of all, the wisdom and determination of our political leaders to remove injustices and to direct the collective energies of the nation for greater achievement in every field of endeavour will go a long way towards maintaining peace and harmony in the country.

Revolution of Rising Expectations

It is widely believed that poverty begets violence, but if that were true then violence both within the country and around the world would be rapidly diminishing, for both India and the world have attained unprecedented levels of development. But on closer examination it appears that violence is often associated with higher levels of development, because of the widening gap that emerges between peoples' aspirations and their accomplishments. Development leads to an awakening of human aspirations — a raising of expectations that releases people's energy and initiative for improving their lives. Yet, as it proceeds, the gap between those rising aspirations and present conditions widens. Up to a point, the widening gap acts like a voltage differential, increasing the force available for progress. But beyond that point, the widening gap leads to increasing frustration, resentment, instability and violence.

The greatest global challenge facing the international community as well as our own country is this transnational revolution of rising expectations. Recent advances in communications and information, coupled with rising levels of education, have further hastened and intensified this revolution by spreading awareness and raising aspirations. This revolution presents a challenge that must be managed by socio-economic advancement, social justice and political leadership. The peace of our nation as well as that of the world community will depend on our ability to channel the energies released by this movement into constructive initiatives for national and global prosperity.

Conventional wisdom has tended to treat national security and national defence as synonymous, but whereas defence is primarily concerned with military preparedness to combat external threats, national security covers a much broader spectrum of challenges, threats and responses. National security can be conceived of as the preservation of core values and vital interests critical to the nation-state from external and internal challenges and threats. Although we distinguish between the external and internal, in fact the two spheres are closely related. The political, economic, social and military spheres are mutually dependent.

Internal security problems in a newly emerging, independent, developing country like India essentially grow out of the laborious processes of nation-state building. At the root of the problem lies the issue of economic disparities and social inequities. Development tends to reduce the extent of these disparities in some ways while aggravating them in others. It increases the life expectancy nutritional security, health, education, social and legal protection, and economic opportunities of the masses, while at the same time enabling the more talented, enterprising, fortunate or unscrupulous to derive disproportionately greater benefits and leaving others untouched or even harmed by the general progress. Economic disparities aggravate perceptions of difference between sub-national, linguistic and communal groups, fostering ethnicity and communalism. A positive strategy for national security must reinforce the secular and democratic values of the Indian nation which derive their strength from our culture, civilization and freedom struggle.

External security depends on national power. It requires a continous enhancement of the country's capacity to use its tangible and intangible resources in such a manner as to affect the behaviour of other nations. While power is often conceived in narrow terms as military power, in the world that is emerging it must be much more broadly conceived to include political, economic, technological, social and intellectual dimensions. A vibrant economy and a leading role in international affairs may be as important as a strong military to the preservation and development of national power.

International affairs have been altered so radically by the end of the Cold War, and more recently by emergence of an international coalition against terrorism, that it is difficult to anticipate the complextion of the international environment for peace and security two decades hence. However, we can identify several of the factors that have consistently influenced our security environment in the past and which are likely to remain active for years to come.

Factors influencing Security Environment in 2020

- The twin revolutions of rising expectations and information-communications will continue.
- The fundamental ideological conflict between Pakistan and India is unlikely to be resolved without a major social-political change in Pakistan.
- Territorial disputes with neighbours that have defied resolution for fifty years may not lend themselves for easy solution.
- Religious extremism and radical politics will continue to have adverse impact on our core values.
- Rising dependence on energy imports will make us increasingly vulnerable economically, as well as diplomatically.
- Public opinion, both domestic and international, and the media will be increasingly important forces in international affairs.
- The international order is likely to evolve into a polycentric configuration with its centre of gravity shifting increasingly to Asia, which will include seven out of the ten largest economies and six out of the eight nuclear weapon states.
- The increasing economic and military strength of China may pose a serious challenge to India's security unless adequate measures are taken to fortify our own strengths.

The current global security paradigm is a competitive system founded upon the relative military power of nation states. The competitive security paradigm is a state-centered and egocentric approach in which the security of each nation is perceived in terms of its military superiority over potential adversaries. The push of each nation for unlimited security through military power is inherently de-stabilising, since it inevitably increases the level of insecurity of other sovereign states. In practice, the effort of nations to arm themselves against perceived external threats generates a sense of insecurity among other nations and compels them in turn of increase military preparedness, thus initiating a vicious spiral, as it did during the Cold War. The highly militarised approach contains an in-built mechanism for escalation that was responsible for the growth of global military expenditure to an all time peak of $1.2 trillion in 1988. The competitive security paradigm cannot provide a stable basis for global peace and security. What is needed is a quantum shift from the competitive security paradigm to a cooperative security system in which countries mutually and collectively agree to refrain from acts of aggression and to protect each other from such acts by any nation. We are now at a historic crossroads: one path leads us back to a static, unstable and exclusive competitive security paradigm; the other leads to a far more stable and dynamic cooperative security paradigm, inclusive of all nations and responsive to future needs and challenges.

Human development in all its dimensions is and will remain our highest strategic priority. Peace in search of human development must not only be durable but also seek harmony between peace and security at different levels. Internationally, we must gravitate from a state-centered, egocentric and competitive security paradigm to a co-operative security paradigm that enhances the security of each nation by reducing potential threats to all nations.

8

Governance

India's economic and technological transition is accompanied by a multifaceted political transformation which may well be slower, less clearly defined and less visible, but will nonetheless have profound impact on the functioning of the government 20 years from now. The main consequences of that transformation are likely to include:

1. Decentralisation and People's Participation

- Devolution of power to local bodies will continue at an accelerated rate. Pressure from the grassroots will increasingly supplant governance from the top down.
- Local communities will come to depend less on state and central government action and more on their own initiative and organisational capacity.
- Financial devolution will give local bodies more authority to levy taxes and greater control over the use of local natural resources. It will also make them increasingly responsible for financing local infrastructure.
- Direct democracy through gram sabhas, as opposed to representative democracy, will become more prevalent at the local level. People at the local level will be more directly involved in setting priorities for distribution of resources and managing local projects.
- A better educated and better informed electorate will be increasingly demanding of its rights and increasingly critical of non-performing governments and their individual members.

2. Efficiency, Transparency and Accountability

- Government agencies of all types at all levels will be more responsive and accountable to the public as customers.

- Mechanisms will be evolved to increase transparency and reduce corruption.
- E-government will improve responsiveness and reduce corruption in some areas. Computerisation of information systems coupled with downsizing, higher recruitment standards and stricter discipline will increase administrative efficiency.
- The educational, technical and professional qualifications of political leaders will rise.

The problems of governance 20 years from now will still include those issues which occupy our attention today — transparency, corruption, non-responsiveness, favouritism, bureaucracy, inefficiency, lack of accountability, ineffectiveness of implementation, etc. But rising expectations, increasing levels of education, greater access to information and greater prosperity will be working to mitigate these factors to a large extent.

Worldwide E-governance is such a recent development, that it is difficult to assess its potential impact 20 years hence. However, the plans and projects already being implemented by various state governments within the country suggest that it has the potential, if fully harnessed and rightly utilised, to radically improve the speed, convenience, quality and transparency of public administrative services, while enhancing the ability of individual citizens to express and exercise their democratic rights.

The essence of good governance is the capacity to envision the opportunities that lead to a better future, to build a broad consensus in support of that vision, to take the bold decisions necessary to realise the vision, and to exercise the determination and perseverance required for overcoming obstacles and resistances that arise along the way.

9

Conclusion

Best-case Scenario for India 2020

Identifying potentials and anticipating the challenges to our future progress in different sectors of the national economy does not constitute a vision of the country's future. These disparate threads need to be woven together to reflect the integrated nature of our national life. Then, there still remains the question of whether to be preoccupied by the negative possibilities or to throw our full weight behind efforts to fully realise the positive potentials revealed by this analysis. That will determine whether we regard the following statement as a promising glimpse of what India can become in 2020, or as mere fantasy and wishful thinking.

India 2020 will be bustling with energy, entrepreneurship and innovation. The country's 1.35 billion people will be better fed, dressed and housed, taller and healthier, more educated and longer living than any generation in the country's long history. Illiteracy and all major contagious diseases will have disappeared. School enrolment from age 6 to 14 will near 100 per cent and drop out rates will fall to less than one in twenty.

A second productivity revolution in Indian agriculture, coupled with diversification to commercial crops, agri-business, processing industries, agro-exports and massive efforts towards afforestation and wasteland development will generate abundant farm and non-farm employment opportunities for the rural workforce. These in turn will stimulate demand for consumer goods and services, giving a fillip to the urban economy and the informal sector as well as rapid expansion of the services sector.

India's claim to the title Silicon Valley of Asia will be followed by the diversification from IT to biotechnology, medical sciences and other emerging fields of technology, widening the field of India's international competitiveness and generating a large number of employment opportunities for the educated youth. These developments, driven by the firm commitment of the government and a quantum expansion of vocational training programmes, will ensure jobs for all by 2020.

Inequalities between different age groups, the sexes, income groups, communities and regions will come down dramatically. The old disparities between the very rich and the poor will not have disappeared, but the nature of poverty in 2020 will not be nearly as harsh and oppressive as it was at the turn of the millennium. Regional disparities will remain visible, though all regions will have advanced significantly in two decades. India's achievements have been fuelled by the realisation that the progress of the whole ultimately depends on the progress of its weakest links; India 2020 must be one in which all levels and sections of the population and all parts of the country march forward together towards a more secure and prosperous future.

The increasingly congested urban traffic will be motorised as never before. Two wheelers will be ubiquitous and cars will be considered essential for most middle class families. City roads and rural highways will improve substantially in number, capacity and quality, but a four-fold multiplication in the number of vehicle will tax the urban infrastructure to the limit. Urban congestion will accelerate the movement of business, middle class families and even government offices into new self-contained suburban centres. Cell phones, computers and the Internet will permeate every aspect of life and every corner of the country.

Computerisation of education will dramatically improve the quality of instruction and the pace of learning, so that many students will complete the first twelve years of school curriculum in as little as eight. Computerised distance education will catch on in a big way and enable tens of thousands more students to opt for affordable higher education. Computerisation in government will streamline procedures and response times to a degree unimaginable now. Perceptive observers will find that India is leapfrogging directly into a predominantly service economy.

Environmental issues will remain a serious concern. Urban air pollution will come under control by strict enforcement of motor vehicle emission standards and widespread use of ethanol-blended motor fuels, but water shortages in major metropolitan areas will continue despite a national programme to popularise water harvesting techniques in both urban and rural areas. A massive afforestation programme will reverse the depletion of forest areas, raise the nation's Green cover to 33 per cent of area, generate millions of rural employment opportunities, and provide abundant renewable energy from biomass power production.

India will be much more integrated with the global economy and will be a major player in terms of trade, technology and investment.

Rising levels of education, employment and income will help stabilise India's internal security and social environment. A united, and prosperous India will be far less vulnerable to external security threats.

A more prosperous India in 2020 will be characterised by a better-educated electorate and more transparent, accountable, efficient and decentralised government.

Some may regard this vision as an anxious attempt to imitate and catch up with the West. But there is an important distinction to be made between blind imitation and intelligent emulation that draws upon the discoveries and experiences of others to address universal needs common to all human beings and all societies. India, with its rich cultural heritage and thousands of years of history of civilisation, need not aspire to become like country A or B. For India, realising the vision for 2020 is not an end in itself, but rather an essential condition for allowing the spirit of this country to emerge and flourish.

Decision Points

There is a natural temptation to attempt to reduce two decades of future progress to a concise formula and prepare a manifesto of policies or strategies that will enable the country to realise its full potential during that period. But a list of such policies or strategies will always remain unsatisfactory unless it is made comprehensive, and a comprehensive list needs to include hundreds of necessary and desirable initiatives.

However, in addition to these policy and strategy prescriptions, or rather underlying and supporting them, there are some nodal points of action which, when touched, can release the enormous pent-up energy of the society and throw it into constructive action. It is well that we conclude our summary by identifying those nodal points which will be most powerful for propelling forward the development of Indian society over the next two decades.

These nine nodes are not independent powers. Each draws upon and contributes to the power of the other seven. They are mutually supportive and reinforcing. They are not a hierarchy of powers that can be developed sequentially, but rather eight essential forces that need to be developed simultaneously. As peace and education are essential for growth of employment and living standards, so are food security and employment opportunities essential for peace and social stability, and so forth.

But beyond these physical, social and mental powers, this country possesses something even more powerful and essential to its existence. India is a nation with a soul and a great spiritual tradition founded upon faith in the power of the spirit to create and manifest in the world. It is our spiritual values, our psychic essence, which is the core strength of Indian civilisation that has sustained it for millenniums and will elevate the quality of our national life in future. These values possess the ultimate power both for national prosperity and to propel India to be a proud member of the world community. *True spirituality will not make us less tolerant*. Though our spiritual tradition takes on an infinite variety of forms, they all share a common faith in our capacity as human beings to realise whatever we aspire for.

Our future depends not on what will happen to us, but on what we decide to become, and on the will to create it.

Nodal Points of Indian Prosperity

1. *Peace, Security and National Unity* — Physical security both from external and internal threats — strong national defence, domestic law enforcement and social harmony.
2. *Food & Nutritional Security* — A vibrant, highly productive commercial farm sector that can ensure food & nutritional security, generate employment opportunities, stimulate industrialisation, and produce renewable energy from biomass and fuel crops.
3. *Jobs for All* — A constitutional commitment to ensure the right of all citizens to a sustainable livelihood that will provide them with the purchasing power needed to freely cast their economic votes in the market place.
4. *Knowledge* — 100 per cent literacy & school education, and vocational training for all new entrants to the workforce, to equip youth with the knowledge and skills needed to thrive in an increasingly competitive world: adult education programmes to compensate working age school drop-outs for the lack of education, and continued investment in science and technology to improve productivity, quality of life and the environment.
5. *Health* — Expansion of the infrastructure for public health and medical care to ensure health for all.
6. *Technology & Infrastructure* — Continuous expansion of the physical infrastructure for rapid low-cost transportation and communication that is required for rapid economic growth and international competitiveness. Application of computers to improve access to knowledge and information, and increase in the speed, efficiency and convenience of activities in all fields of life.
7. *Globalisation* — Successful integration of India with world economy.
8. *Good Governance* — Farsighted and dynamic leadership to maximise national prosperity, individual freedom and social equity through responsive, transparent and accountable administration that removes all the bottlenecks to economic development.
9. *Work Values* — Activation of all these nodal points requires firm and determined adherence to high values, including prompt decision-making, disciplined execution, systematic implementation, finely tuned co-ordination, unceasing effort and endurance.

Annexures

Annexure 1

Rabindranath Tagore's Vision

> *Where the mind is without fear and the head is held high.*
> *Where knowledge is free.*
> *Where the world has not been broken up into fragments*
> *By narrow domestic walls.*
> *Where words come out from the depth of truth.*
> *Where tireless striving stretches its arms towards perfection.*
> *Where the clear stream of reason has not lost its way*
> *Into the dreary desert sand of dead habit.*
> *Where the mind is led forward by Thee*
> *Into ever-widening thought and action.*
> *Into that heaven of freedom, my Father, let my country awake.*
>
> *Rabindranath Tagore*

The vision articulated by Rabindranath Tagore is all encompassing in every sense. It has laid down what he considered to be the basic constituents of the "heaven of freedom". We can identify eight components of this vision reflected in the poem quoted earlier, which we can attempt to translate into operational terms for India's vision 2020.

Where the mind is without fear — Peace and security, internal as well as external, is the first and most essential foundation for the nation's future progress. Fearlessness can only be attained when this security extends to cover, over and above our physical safety, our social rights and economic well being, to eliminate all forms of vulnerability and discrimination.

Where the head is held high — Self-respect and self-esteem are the psychological foundations for the development of individuality and individual initiative, which are the means through which the nation builds its strength and fulfils its aspirations. The nation prospers through the development and flowering of all its citizens as individuals. Health, education and employment opportunities for all, and awareness of our rich spiritual and cultural heritage are the essential bases for fostering self-respect and self-esteem.

Where knowledge is free — Development takes place when people become aware of opportunities for advancement and acquire the knowledge needed to convert those opportunities into practical accomplishments. Knowledge in the form of education, technology and access to a wide range of information is a catalyst for individual and social progress. The free flow of knowledge is the basis for a free and prosperous society.

Where the world has not been broken up into fragments by narrow domestic walls — The spirit of globalisation which is rapidly reshaping the world today cannot be better expressed. The accelerated flow and exchange of trade, capital, technology, information and people will create unprecedented opportunities for the progress and prosperity of all countries that can transcend the narrow confines of national boundaries. India can however realise its full potential in the wider world only when it is internally united, surmounting all the centrifugal forces that overlook our common heritage and accentuate our differences.

Where words come out from the depth of truth — Integrity, honesty and trustworthiness are the essential foundations for a successful democracy and a prosperous society. Both good governance and commercial success demand rigorous standards of transparency, accountability and reliability in word and action.

Where tireless striving stretches its arms towards perfection — Prosperity is the result of productivity and efficiency which require the highest level of productive skills, technological excellence and human effort.

Where the clear stream of reason has not lost its way into the dreary desert sand of dead habit — Nations develop by choosing the best the future has to offer, while being willing to discard outmoded ideas and behaviours that retard future progress and even threaten to undermine the country's unity and strength.

Where the mind is led forward by Thee into ever-widening thought and action — Education, innovation and creativity are the ultimate driving forces for the continous advancement of scientific knowledge and material accomplishment.

These threads from Rabindranath's poem are the vital strands from which a fulfilling vision of India 2020 can be woven.

Annexure II

No.M-110022/1/2000-PP
Government of India
Planning Commission

Yojana Bhavan, Sansad Marg,

New Delhi, the 12th May 2000

ORDER

It has been decided to set up a Committee on Vision 2020 for India. The composition of the Committee will be as follows.

Chairman

Dr. S.P. Gupta, Member, Planning Commission, New Delhi.

Member

1. Dr. R.K. Pachauri, Director, Tata Energy Research Institute, New Delhi.
2. Dr. R. Radhakrishna, Vice Chancellor, Andhra University, Vishakhapatnam.
3. Dr. Panjab Singh, Director, Indian Agriculture Research Institute, New Delhi.
4. Prof. Ashish Bose, Former Professor, Institute of Economic Growth, Delhi.
5. Prof. Pravin Visaria, Director, Institute of Economic Growth, Delhi.
6. Shri K.L. Thapar, Director, Asian Institute of Transport Development, New Delhi.
7. Dr. Padam Singh, Additional Director General, ICMR, New Delhi.
8. Prof. C.P. Ramaswamy, Centre for Policy Research, New Delhi.
9. Shri K.C. Sivaramakrishnan, Centre for Policy Research, New Delhi.
10. Dr. V.A. Pai Panandiker, Director, Centre for Policy Research, New Delhi.

11. Shri Jasjit Singh, Director, Indian Institute of Defence Studies and Analysis, New Delhi.
12. Prof. V.R. Panchmukhi, Director-General, Research and Information System for the Non-Aligned and other Developing Countries, New Delhi.
13. Prof. P.V. Indiresan, Centre for Policy Research, New Delhi.
14. Dr. J.S. Rajput, Director, NCERT, New Delhi.
15. Dr. Prema Ramachandran, Adviser (Health), Planning Commission, New Delhi.
16. Dr. Pronab Sen, Adviser (PP), Planning Commission, New Delhi.
17. Dr. Shovan Ray, Consultant, Planning Commission, New Delhi.

2. The Committee will be serviced by the Perspective Planning Division with Shri J.N. Maggo, Joint Adviser, (IIP) acting as Secretary to the Committee.

3. The Committee may co-opt other experts as and when deemed necessary.

4. Non-officials shall be entitled to TA/DA as permissible to Grade I officers of Government of India and the expenditure will be borne by Planning Commission. The TA/DA of Government and Public Sector officials will be borne by their respective organisations.

(Arvind K. Alipura)

Director (Admn.)

Members Co-opted Subsequently

1. Dr. Amit S. Ray, Consultant, Planning Commission, New Delhi. (Member Secretary, Vision 2020 Committee)
2. Dr. Garry Jacobs, Mother Service Society, Plot No. 4, Venkata Nagar, Pondicherry-605011.
3. Dr. K. Srinivasan, Population Foundation of India, B-28, Qutab Institutional Area, Tara Crescent, New Delhi-110016.
4. Shri R. Srinivasan, B-4, Hiranya Apartments, (off Greenway Road), Mylapore, Chennai-600028.
5. Shri G.N. Kathpalia, E-190, Greater Kailash, Delhi-110048
6. Shri P. Chaturvedi, Chairman, The Instt. of Engineering, Engineer Bhavan, Bahadur Shah Zafar Marg, New Delhi-110001.
7. Prof. Amitabh Kundu, CSRD, School of Social Sciences, JNU, New Delhi.
8. Dr. Krishna Sondhi, 7, Amrita Shergill Marg, New Delhi-110003.
9. Prof. Ramaswamy R. Iyer, Centre for Policy Research, Dharma Marg, Chanakya Puri, New Delhi-110021.
10. Shri Anwar ul-Hoda, ICRIER, India Habitat Centre, Lodhi Road, New Delhi.
11. Dr. Nagesh Kumar, RIS, Zone IV B 4th Floor, India Habitat Centre, Lodhi Road, New Delhi-110003.
12. Dr. Sarala Gopalan, 138 Vasant Enclave, New Delhi-110057.
13. Dr. Hira Singh, 183, Munirka Enclave, New Delhi-110067.
14. Shri M.C. Verma, Adviser, Ministry of Labour, 1st Floor, Shram Shakti Bhavan, New Delhi-110001.
15. Shri M.C. Gupta, Director, Indian Instt. of Public Administration, Indraprastha Estate, Ring Road, New Delhi-110022.
16. Shri H.S. Saksena, Editor, Eastern Anthropologist, Lucknow.
17. Dr. Manas Bhattacharya, Dy. Director General, Dept. of Telecommunications, Ministry of Telecom & IT, Govt. of India.

18. Shri Mahesh Kapoor, New Delhi.
19. Shri H. Ramachandran, Director, IAMR, New Delhi.
20. Major Gen. S.S. Sandhu, New Delhi.
21. Shri Durganand Jha, Executive Director, Association for Social and Economic Transformation.

The Terms of Reference of this Committee are:

1. To prepare an outlook for India in 2020, especially focusing on the opportunities and challenges.
2. To envision the possibilities of India's development potential over the next two decades in a multi dimensional framework, including aspects of human development, social & physical infrastructure, knowledge resources & technology, energy & environment, economy, governance and security.
3. To seek inputs from members of the Committee and from other sources from within and outside the Planning Commission.
4. To come out with a document on "India: Vision 2020".

LIST OF CONTRIBUTORS

1. Dr. Manas Bhattacharya: Telecom
2. Mr. P. Chaturvedi: Energy
3. Dr. Sarala Gopalan: Empowerment of Women
4. Mr. M.C. Gupta: Governance (published)
5. Mr. Anwar-ul-Hoda: International Economy
6. Dr. P.V. Indiresan: Rural Development
7. Prof. Ramaswamy R. Iyer: Water (published)
8. Mr. G. Jacobs: Knowledge Society
9. Prof. Amitabh Kundu: Urbanisation
10. Mr. G.N. Kathpalia: Water
11. Mr. Mahesh Kapoor: Transport
12. Dr. Nagesh Kumar: External Sector
13. Mr. R.K. Pachauri: Energy, Environment
14. Dr. J.S. Rajput: Education
15. Dr. H. Ramachandran: Governance
16. Dr. R. Radhakrishna: Food Security, Nutrition and Poverty
17. Mr. H.S. Saksena: Vulnerable Groups
18. Maj-Gen. S.S. Sandhu: Older Persons
19. Dr. S.K. Sarkar: Energy
20. Dr. Rohit Sarkar: Financial Sector
21. Dr. Hira Singh: Social Defence
22. Air Comdr. Jasjit Singh: Peace
23. Dr. Padam Singh: Fertility, Mortality
24. Dr. Panjab Singh: Agriculture
25. Dr. K. Srinivasan: Population
26. Mr. R. Srinivasan: Health
27. Dr. Krishan Sondhi: Information Technology
28. Swami Agnivesh: Child Labour
29. Mr. M.C. Verma: Social Dimension

From Planning Commission:

30. LEM Division: Employment
31. Health Division (Dr. Prema Ramachandran): Health Nutrition, Population

Part Two

Background Papers

(by Various Authors)

Contents : See Pages 9-11

1

Indian Demographic Scenario: Vision 2020

P. N. MARI BHAT

Introduction

India's population stood at about 350 million at the time of independence in 1947. Belying Malthusian fears, it grew at an unprecedented rate to reach the one billion mark at the dawn of the new millennium. The Census of 2001 has put the population figure provisionally at 1,027 million, even though it registered a significant reduction in the growth rate of population. During the latter half of the twentieth century, India's population had grown by nearly 650 million. How much more will it grow in the first twenty years of the twenty-first century? What will be the geographical distribution of this growth? What changes are expected in the age and sex structure of the population? Any serious attempt to paint a portrait of India around the year 2020 would have to confront these questions, and make a proper assessment of the country's demographic prospectus.

With the emergence of 'the component method' of projection, the art of making population forecasts has acquired the rigour of a science. The rationale of the component method rests on the undisputable fact that the growth of population is determined by fertility, mortality and migration rates. As each of these forces have distinct age and sex profiles, it becomes possible to mathematically carry forward the base-year population by age to any future date, by making assumptions about the three components of growth. The time-honoured theory of demographic transition provides the necessary framework to make assumptions about the future course of fertility and mortality rates with a fair degree of precision. Although making assumptions about migration could prove difficult, in many a case, this is an inconsequential part of population change.

The accuracy of demographic projections can be gauged by examining how close they have come in predicting the India's population at 2001. It is to be noted that demographers generally make 'high', 'medium' and 'low' projections; but the high and low variants are often presented for pedagogical purposes only, and are not to be treated as serious forecasts. Table 1 lists ten important forecasts of India's population at 2001 that were made before 1980 using the component method. The table shows in each case, the forecasts corresponding to the medium variant, or the median of the projected population figures.

Table 1

Comparison of Provisional Population Estimate for India from the Census of 2001 with Some Selected Projections Made Before 1980 Using the Component Method

Author/Organization	*Year of projection*	*Population projected for 2001 (millions)*	*Percentage deviation from 1027 million*
Das Gupta and Majumdar	1954	667	-35.1
United Nations	1963	922	-10.2
World Bank	1972	1109	8.0
Frejka	1972	955	-7.0
United Nations	1973	1078	5.0
Operations Research Group	1974	973	-5.3
Raghavachari	1974	935	-9.0
Ambannavar	1975	1003	-2.3
Cassen and Dyson	1976	934	-9.1
United Nations	1978	1056	2.8

Source: Natarajan (1982).

Note: In some cases, the estimate for the year 2000 has been brought forward by a year using the growth rate internal to the projection. If more than one estimate was made, that based on the medium variant, or the median of the estimates, has been taken as the most likely forecast. Some projections have adjusted the base-year population for under enumeration, and some estimates are for July 1. These discrepancies have been ignored while computing the percentage deviation from the census count for March 1, 2001.

Except for the first one that was made way back in 1954, all other nine population projections have come within ten per cent of the census estimate for 2001. Only three have erred on a higher side, but two of them were so because they carried a correction for under enumeration of population in the base-year census. Among the ten forecasts, the one made by J.P. Ambannavar in 1975 had an error of only two per cent, but allowing for some under enumeration in the census count, the two projections of the United Nations made in 1973 and 1978 can also be regarded as falling within the bull's eye.

Several lessons can be learnt from this comparison. First, it appears not too hazardous to make population projections using the component method, provided the time horizon for the projection is within 25-30 years. Second, projected population totals generally have a downward bias, perhaps because assumptions regarding levels and trends in fertility tend to be too optimistic. Third, forecasting errors tend to reduce with time because of better information on the nature and tempo of demographic transition.

Recent Demographic Trends

Any serious attempt to assess future prospectus must begin with a review of past trends. Such a review would be critically important in formulating assumptions about future trends of each component of growth. With this in mind, Table 2 shows some basic demographic indicators for India since 1951. It is to be noted that fertility and mortality indicators that are shown in the table are not the ones routinely found in statistical publications of the Government of India. The official estimates, especially those for the period before the appearance of the Sample Registration System (i.e., before 1971), are grossly deficient and do not accurately depict the trends in vital rates. Although the estimates based on the SRS are more accurate, they too need to be corrected for under enumeration of vital events in the system. Even the more carefully derived estimates shown in Table 2 can show only an approximate range for the levels of fertility and mortality that prevailed before the 1970s. The major source for the uncertainty is the lack of reliable information on the levels of infant and child mortality prevailed during this period. However, it is fairly certain that their levels were higher than those shown in the official life tables of the period (for details, see Bhat 1998).

As per the estimates shown in Table 2, the crude death rate in India has declined from about 30 per 1,000 in 1941-51 to 15 in 1971-81 and 10 in 1991-2001. In the meanwhile, the expectation of life at birth has increased from about 33 years in 1941-51 to about

50 years in 1971-81 and 60 years in 1991-2001. Thus during the last 20 years, the expectation of life at birth has increased roughly by half a year per annum. There also is an indication that the life expectancy has increased somewhat faster among females than males.

The estimates presented in Table 2 show that the fertility level in India may have increased before it began to fall. The crude birth rate may have increased from about 43 per 1,000 in 1941-51 to 47 in 1951-61, and then slowly began to fall to reach 29 during 1991-2001. The total fertility rate (TFR) may have increased from a level lower than 6 births per woman to around 6.5 births between 1941-51 and 1951-61. Subsequently, it has shown a steady fall to reach 3.7 during 1991-2001. The early rise in fertility is attributable to declines in the incidence of widowhood and diseases such as malaria that held levels of natural fertility in check. The annual fall in TFR appears to be declining. Between 1961-71 and 1971-81 TFR fell by 0.14 births per year, while during the last 20 years the TFR has fallen only by half of this rate.

While making population projections, it is necessary to be as precise as possible about the current levels of fertility and mortality. Their under estimation could result in significant under assessment of future possibilities for growth and an overly optimistic date for population stabilization. Some indirectly made estimates suggest that about 10 per cent of deaths and 5-7 per cent of births are omitted in the SRS (Bhat 2000). Therefore, levels of fertility and mortality shown in Table 2 for the period 1991-2001 are somewhat higher than what is implied by the SRS estimates available up to the year 1999. They are however broadly consistent with the provisional results of the Census of 2001.

While assessing future prospects, it is also necessary to take into account the large regional differences in demographic parameters (see Bhat 1999). Several states in south India have already reached, or are about to attain, the replacement level of fertility (a TFR level of about 2.2 - 2.1) that, if maintained, would ensure a zero growth rate of population in the long run. On the other hand, TFR is over 4 births per woman in many states in north India, and it would take several decades for them to reach the replacement-level fertility. There are also similar differentials in levels of mortality, especially in infant and child mortality.

Table 2

Some Selected Demographic Indicators for India, 1951 to 2001

Census year	*Enumerated population in million*	*Rates/measures for the ten-year period before the census*					
		Percent change in	*Crude birth rate*	*Crude death rate*	*Total fertility rate*	*Expectation of life at birth*	
						Male	*Female*
1951	361.1	13.3	40-44	28-32	5.3-6.0	32-34	32-34
1961	439.2	21.6	46-48	26-28	6.3-6.6	37-39	37-39
1971	548.2	24.8	43-44	21-22	6.4-6.6	43-45	42-44
1981	683.3	24.6	37	15	5.1	50	49
1991	846.4	23.9	35	13	4.3	54	53
2001*	1027.0	21.3	29	10	3.7	59	60

Source: India, Registrar General (2001), Bhat (1998, 2000).

*: Population estimates for 2001 and demographic indicators for 1991-2001 are provisional.

It is beyond the scope of this paper to discuss the population prospectus on a state-by-state basis. But because they make telling contrasts, two broad regions - north and south - will be considered for detailed treatment. The 'north' in our discussions comprises Uttar Pradesh, Bihar, Orissa, Madhya Pradesh, Rajasthan, and newly-formed states of Uttaranchal, Jharkhand and Chhatisgarh. The 'south' comprises Kerala, Tamil Nadu, Andhra Pradesh and Karnataka. During 1991-2001, the average population growth rate was 2.22 per cent per annum in the north while it was only 1.24 per cent in the south.

Projection Assumptions

The base-year of our population projection is 2000 A.D. Based on the provisional results of the 2001 Census, India's population on March 1, 2000 is estimated to be 1,010 million. The age-sex distribution of the population on this date is estimated by projecting forward a smoothed age-sex distribution of population from the 1991 Census. This projection used slightly adjusted rates of fertility and mortality from the SRS so that the projection would give a growth rate of 1.9 per cent per annum during 1991-2001. This projection suggests that in the year 2000, TFR was 3.4 and expectation of life at birth was 60 for males and 62 for females.

At the national level, two alternate scenarios of achieving population stabilization have been considered (see Table 3). In the first scenario, it is assumed that India would able to achieve the demographic goals of the National Population Policy 2000 (Government of India 2000). The NPP has set a target of achieving a TFR of 2.1 and an infant mortality rate of 30 per 1,000 by the year 2010. The mortality target implies an expectation of life at birth of 68 for males and 71 for females (under the 'West' model life table system that has been assumed to apply at the national level). After 2010, the TFR has been assumed to remain constant at 2.1. But the life expectancy has been assumed to rise further, though at a reduced pace, to reach 71 for males and 74 for females by 2020.

Considering the pace at which fertility and mortality rates have fallen in the past, the NPP goals appear to be highly optimistic. As noted above, TFR has fallen only by 0.07 births per year during the last 20 years. As more and more states of India complete the transition to low fertility, the average pace of decline is likely to slacken further. In the case of mortality, diseases such as malaria and tuberculosis are becoming intractable and the threat of HIV/AIDS is looming large on the horizon. The pace of decline in infant and child mortality, hitherto largely driven by immunization, also seems to be slowing down.

Table 3

Mortality and Fertility Assumptions for India Under Two Scenarios, 2000-2020

Year	*Expectation of life at birth*				*Total fertility rate*	
	Males		*Females*			
	Optimistic	*Realistic*	*Optimistic*	*Realistic*	*Optimistic*	*Realistic*
2000	60.0	60.0	62.0	62.0	3.40	3.40
2005	64.0	61.0	66.5	63.7	2.75	3.10
2010	68.0	62.0	71.0	65.3	2.10	2.80
2015	69.3	63.0	72.7	67.0	2.10	2.50
2020	70.7	65.0	74.3	69.0	2.10	2.30

Therefore, under the more realistic scenario, TFR has been assumed to fall from 3.4 in 2000 to 2.8 in 2010, and to 2.3 in 2020. Under this scenario, the replacement level fertility would be reached around 2025, or approximately 15 years after the date targeted in the NPP. The life expectancy at birth has been assumed to rise by only 4 years (3 years among males and 5 years among females) during the next 15 years. By 2020, it has been assumed to reach 65 for males and 69 for females, i.e., about 6 year shorter for males and 5 year shorter for females than under the optimistic projection.

Under both the scenarios, net migration to India has been assumed to be negligible. In the past, while some regions of India were indeed affected by emigration of labourers, there were compensating inflows of illegal immigrants and refugees in other parts. In future, both internal and external demographic and economic conditions may make India a net exporter of labourers and technicians. However, immigration is unlikely to be of such proportions as to make a significant dent on India's population size.

For north and south India, only one scenario that seemed realistic has been considered (see Table 4). The provisional results of the 2001 Census suggest that in the year 2000 the northern and southern regions had a population of 450 and 220 million, respectively. As with all-India, the age-sex distribution of the population was carried forward from 1991 using slightly adjusted estimates of fertility and mortality levels from the SRS. In the case of south India, TFR has been assumed to fall progressively from 2.3 in 2000 to 1.9 in 2010 and then to remain constant at 1.8 until 2020. In north India, TFR has been assumed to decline from 4.4 in 2000 to 3.6 in 2010 and further to 3.0 by 2020. Between 2000 and 2020, the expectation of life at birth in south India has been assumed to rise from 64 to 68.5 for males and from 67 to 72.3 for females. During the same period in north India, the expectation of life at birth has been assumed to rise from 59 to 64.6 for males and 58 to 65.2 for females. As south India appears to be hit more by the AIDS epidemic, a slower rate of increase in life expectancy has been assumed there.

Table 4

Mortality and Fertility Assumptions for North and South India, 2000-2020

Year	*Expectation of life at birth*				*Total fertility rate*	
	Males		*Females*			
	North	*South*	*North*	*South*	*North*	*South*
2000	59.0	64.0	58.0	67.0	4.40	2.30
2005	60.4	65.0	59.8	68.2	4.00	2.10
2010	61.8	66.0	61.6	69.3	3.60	1.90
2015	63.2	67.0	63.4	70.5	3.30	1.80
2020	64.6	68.5	65.2	72.3	3.00	1.80

Note: Bihar, Jharkhand, Orissa, Chhatisgarh, Madhya Pradesh, Rajasthan, Uttar Pradesh and Uttaranchal are included in the North, while Andhra Pradesh, Karnataka, Tamil Nadu and Kerala are included in the South.

It is also appropriate to mention briefly here a couple of other assumptions made while projecting the population to the year 2020. For converting the assumptions on life expectancies to age-specific mortality rates, a model life table system is required. As India's mortality patterns by age appear to be getting closer to Coale and Demeny's West model system (see Bhat 1998), this model system has been assumed to be applicable to all-India during the entire projection period. The same system has also been used in the projections for south India. However, for north India the South model life table system has been preferred, as the region has relatively higher levels of under-5 mortality for its level of life expectancy at birth. With respect to age pattern of fertility, it has been assumed that child bearing would be increasingly concentrated at ages under 30, especially in the age group 20-24.

Another assumption of some consequence is about the sex ratio at birth. A sex ratio at birth of 105 males per 100 females is normally assumed. But the deteriorating juvenile sex ratios suggest that the sex ratio at birth may have gone up by couple of percentage points owing to sex-selective abortions in some parts of India. Accordingly, a sex ratio at birth of 107 has been used in the case all-India, while it is assumed to be 108 in the north and 106 in the south. It is possible that the sex ratio at birth would rise further, but it may partially be compensated by improvements in sex-differentials in mortality in childhood ages. Therefore, no further change in this ratio has been assumed during the projection period.

Projection Results for All-India

Population projections were carried out using the DEMPROJ computer programme of the Futures Group International. Tables 5 and 6 show the key results of population projections for India under the optimistic and realistic scenarios. Interestingly, both the variants imply that India's population would be slightly over 1.3 billion in the year 2020 (1305 million under the optimistic scenario and 1331 million under the realistic scenario). Indeed, though based on very different assumptions on mortality and fertility, several recent projections made for India have arrived at roughly the same population estimate for 2020:

Author/organisation	*Population in 2020 (millions)*
World Bank, 1994	1,304
Visaria and Bhat, 1999	1,328
Population Foundation, 1999	1,329
Dyson and Hanchate, 2000	1,318
United Nations, 2001	1,291

Source: Bos et al (1994), Visaria and Bhat (1999), Natarajan and Jayachandran (2001) Dyson and Hanchate (2000) and United Nations (2001).

Note: Estimates for the year 2021 were brought to 2020 using the growth rate internal to the projection.

The main reason for this remarkable agreement on the likely size of India's population in the year 2020 is that differences in the assumptions regarding mortality and fertility levels tend to cancel themselves out in their effects on the growth rate of population. The optimists assume both fertility and mortality levels to fall sharply while pessimists assume both to decline slowly. However, when projected population totals for different age segments are compared, differences would start to show up. For example, in our optimistic and pessimistic scenarios, the projected population in the school-going age of 6-14 for the year 2020 is, respectively, 190 and 224 million - a difference of 18 per cent as compared to less than 2 per cent in the total population.

As per our projection results, the sex ratio of population (females per 1000 males) would marginally increase from 932 in 2000 to 945-950 in 2020. Thus a reversal of the historical trend of falling sex ratio is expected in the twenty-first century. The projected improvement in the sex ratio is directly attributable to the assumption that by 2020, the expectation of life at birth for females would be higher than for males by at least 3.5 years. While this seems a fair assumption to make, it is not altogether clear what would happen to the sex ratio at birth. There is some fragmentary evidence to suggest that son preference is actually falling in India, but its manifestation in the sex ratios is on the rise because of the increased access to the technology of sex-selective abortion. One could expect the effect of the diffusion of this technology to be a temporary phenomenon.

We can be more certain of the changes in the age structure of the population. Under the realistic scenario, between 2000 and 2020, the percentage of population under 15 years of age is expected to fall from 36 to 28 per cent. Actually, the population under 15 years is expected to increase only marginally from 360 to 373 million in 20 years (see Figure.1). On the other hand, the adult population in the age group 15-64 is expected rise from 604 million in 2000 to 882 million in 2020. i.e., from 60 per cent to 66 per cent of the total population. The elderly population is also expected to rise sharply from 45 to 76 million, and their share in the total population would rise from 4.5 to 5.7 per cent. As a consequence of these age structural changes, the age-dependency ratio (ratio of non-working age population to working age population) is expected to fall from 67 per cent in 2000 to 51 per cent in 2020.

Figure 1

Projected Population of India Under Realistic Scenario by Broad Age Groups, 2000-2020

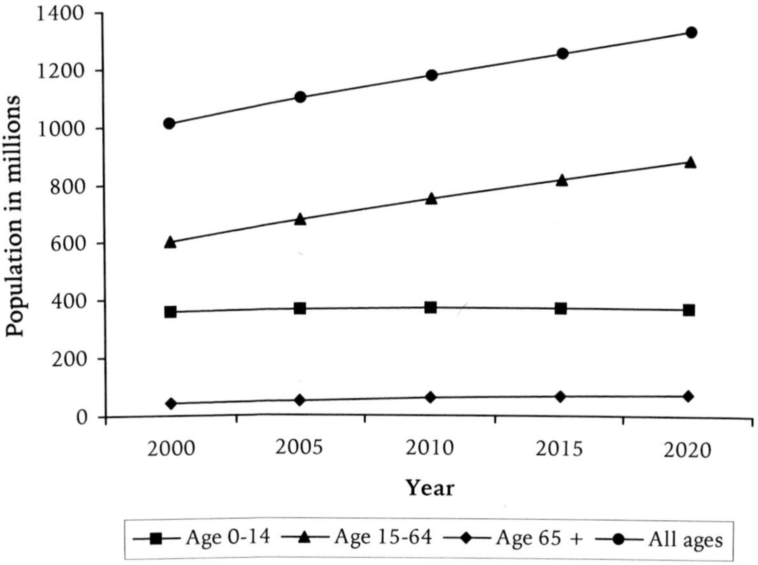

The age-structural changes are best studied through population pyramids. These are horizontal bar charts showing the male and female population at different age groups, in opposing direction. Figure 2 shows the shape of India's population pyramid in 2000. As on this date, older cohorts were invariably smaller than younger cohorts, the diagram truly has the shape of a pyramid. Figures 3 and 4 show the population pyramid in 2020 as per the two alternate scenarios. The population pyramid in 2020 is expected to assume a tower-like shape. The base of the pyramid would narrow down while the middle would be broadened. The pyramid under the optimistic scenario would show the 'scars' of the spectacular fall in fertility assumed to take place during 2000-10. The implications of these dramatic changes in the age structure of the population to the economy and society will be discussed after considering the regional differences.

Figure 2

Population Pyramid of India, Year 2000

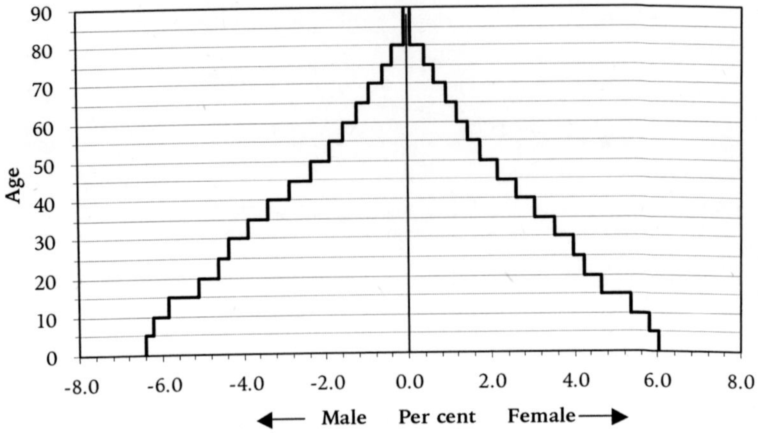

Table 5

Key Results of Population Projection for India Under the Optimistic Scenario, 2000-2020

Demographic Indicators	*2000*	*2005*	*2010*	*2015*	*2020*
Total population (millions)	1010	1089	1159	1229	1305
Population density (per sq. km)	307	331	353	374	397
Females per 1000 males	932	935	938	941	945
Growth rate for preceding 5-years (%):					
Total population	1.82	1.52	1.25	1.17	1.19
Population age 15-64 years	2.05	2.23	2.19	1.97	1.50
Per cent 0-14 years	35.7	33.3	29.9	26.7	25.0
Per cent 15-64 years	59.8	62.0	65.0	67.7	68.7
Per cent 65+ years	4.5	4.8	5.1	5.6	6.3
Median age	23	24	25	27	29
Dependency ratio (per cent):					
Child (0-14)	60	54	46	40	36
Elderly (65+)	8	8	8	8	9
Total	67	61	54	48	46
Population 6-14 years (millions)	210	220	218	201	190
Crude birth rate (per 1000)	26.5	22.1	17.9	18.5	18.4
Crude death rate (per 1000)	9.9	8.1	6.7	6.7	6.6
Crude growth rate (per 1000)	16.6	14.0	11.2	11.8	11.8
Net reproduction rate	1.42	1.21	0.96	0.97	0.98

Figure 3

Projected Population Pyramid of India Under Optimistic Scenario, Year 2020

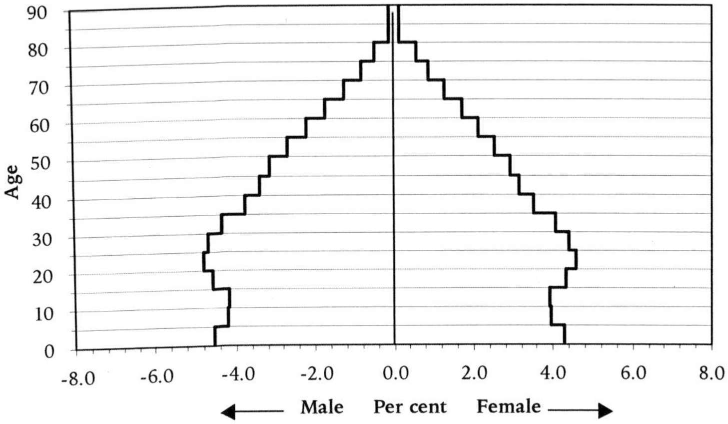

Table 6

Key Results of Population Projection for India Under the Realistic Scenario, 2000-2020

Demographic Indicators	*2000*	*2005*	*2010*	*2015*	*2020*
Total population (millions)	1010	1093	1175	1256	1331
Population density (per sq. km)	307	332	357	382	405
Females per 1000 males	932	935	940	945	950
Growth rate for preceding 5-years (%):					
Total population	1.82	1.58	1.45	1.33	1.17
Population age 15-64 years	2.05	2.17	2.07	1.82	1.51
Per cent 0-14 years	35.7	33.7	31.5	29.6	28.0
Per cent 15-64 years	59.8	61.6	63.6	65.2	66.3
Per cent 65+ years	4.5	4.7	4.9	5.2	5.7
Median age	23	23	24	26	27
Dependency ratio (per cent):					
Child (0-14)	60	55	50	45	42
Elderly (65+)	8	8	8	8	9
Total	67	62	57	53	51
Population 6-14 years (millions)	210	219	220	220	224
Crude birth rate (per 1000)	26.5	24.5	23.0	21.1	19.4
Crude death rate (per 1000)	9.8	9.4	9.1	8.8	8.3
Crude growth rate (per 1000)	16.7	15.1	13.9	12.3	11.1
Net reproduction rate	1.42	1.32	1.22	1.11	1.04

Figure 4

Projected Population Pyramid of India Under Realistic Scenario, Year 2020

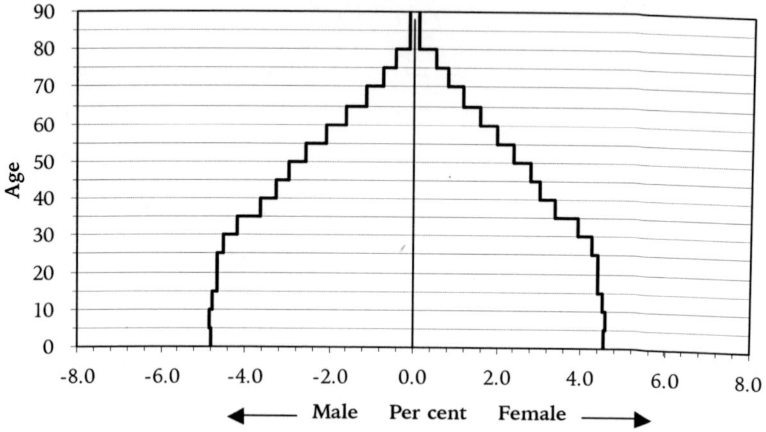

Regional Scenario

The existence of two different demographic regimes in north and south India dictates that regional differences are examined at some length. The main results of the regional projections are presented in Tables 7 and 8. According to our projections, the population of the northern region would rise from 450 million in 2000 to nearly 650 million in 2020, and its share of India's population would go up from 45 per cent to 49 per cent. On the other hand, in the southern region the population would increase only marginally from 220 million in 2000 to 258 million in 2020. In the meanwhile, its share of India's population would decline from 22 per cent to 19 per cent.

The average population density per square kilometre in the year 2000 was 319 in the north and 346 in the south. While the former is expected to increase to 461 by 2020, the latter is expected to increase only to 406 by this date. Also to be noted is that by the year 2020, population of north India would still be growing at a rate of 1.7 per cent per annum while the growth rate in south India would have fallen to 0.6 per cent. The advantages, the south would derive from its early demographic transition are thus obvious. But the regional demographic imbalances may induce large population movements from the north to the south. It remains to be seen whether this would develop into a serious regional conflict.

By the year 2020 the population of south India would have begun to 'grey'. The median age of the population would have gone up from 26 years in 2000 to 32 years in 2020, and 8 per cent of the population would be of age 65 years and over. On the other hand, the north India would have a relatively young population with a median age of 25 and only 5 per cent of the population aged 65 and over. The population pyramids shown in Figures 5 and 6 bring out the expected differences very clearly.

Table 7

Key Results of Population Projection for North India, 2000-2020

Demographic Indicators	*2000*	*2005*	*2010*	*2015*	*2020*
Total population (millions)	450	498	547	597	649
Population density (per sq. km)	319	353	388	424	461
Share of All-India population (%)	45	46	47	48	49
Females per 1000 males	924	920	918	917	918
Growth rate for preceding 5-years (%):					
Total population	2.17	2.02	1.88	1.78	1.66
Population age 15-64 years	2.23	2.45	2.39	2.24	2.04
Per cent 0-14 years	38.1	36.6	34.9	33.3	31.8
Per cent 15-64 years	57.6	58.9	60.4	61.8	63.0
Per cent 65+ years	4.3	4.5	4.7	4.9	5.2
Median age	21	22	23	24	25
Dependency ratio (per cent):					
Child (0-14)	66	62	58	54	50
Elderly (65+)	8	8	8	8	8
Total	74	70	66	62	59
Population 6-14 years (millions)	97	105	111	115	120
Crude birth rate (per 1000)	32.4	29.9	27.8	26.4	24.4
Crude death rate (per 1000)	11.3	10.5	9.7	9.2	8.6
Crude growth rate (per 1000)	21.1	19.4	18.1	17.2	15.8
Net reproduction rate	1.68	1.57	1.45	1.35	1.26

Table 8

Key Results of Population Projection for South India, 2000-2020

Demographic Indicators	*2000*	*2005*	*2010*	*2015*	*2020*
Total population (millions)	220	232	242	251	258
Population density (per sq. km)	346	365	381	394	406
Share of All-India population (%)	22	21	21	20	19
Females per 1000 males	988	987	987	988	989
Growth rate for preceding 5-years (%):					
Total population	1.26	1.05	0.86	0.70	0.61
Population age 15-64 years	1.79	1.67	1.39	1.15	0.83
Per cent 0-14 years	30.0	27.5	25.3	23.2	21.7
Per cent 15-64 years	64.4	66.4	68.2	69.8	70.5
Per cent 65+ years	5.6	6.0	6.5	7.0	7.8
Median age	26	27	29	31	32
Dependency ratio (per cent):					
Child (0-14)	47	41	37	33	31
Elderly (65+)	9	9	9	10	11
Total	55	51	47	43	42
Population 6-14 years (millions)	40	39	38	36	34
Crude birth rate (per 1000)	20.7	18.3	16.4	15.1	14.5
Crude death rate (per 1000)	8.6	8.6	8.6	8.7	8.7
Crude growth rate (per 1000)	12.1	9.7	7.8	6.4	5.8
Net reproduction rate	1.03	0.95	0.87	0.83	0.84

Figure 5

Projected Population Pyramid of North India, Year 2020

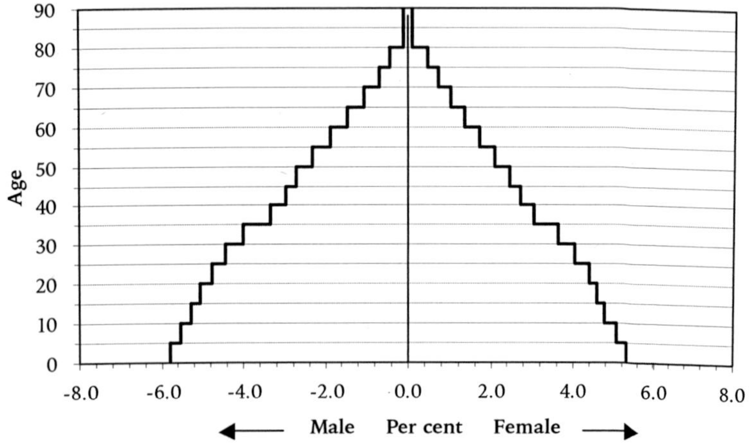

Figure 6

Projected Population Pyramid of South India, Year 2020

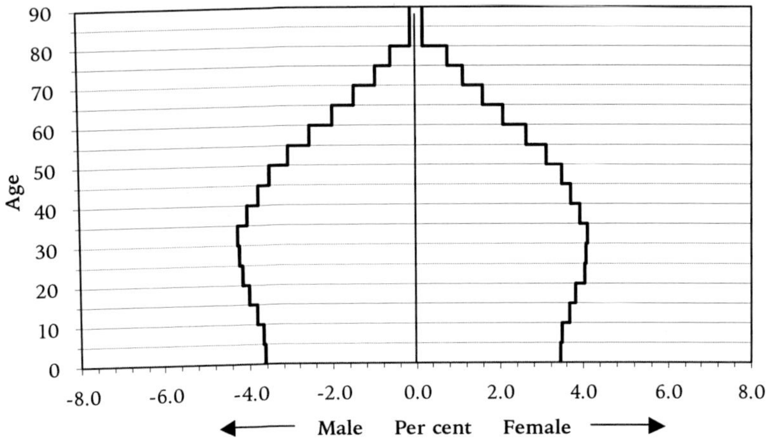

Demographic Bonus

Even though population has been estimated to increase by about 320 million between 2000 and 2020, according to the realistic scenario, as much as 87 per cent of the total growth would be in the age interval 15-64. This can have a far-reaching impact on the economy. Two Harvard economists have recently revived an earlier thesis of Coale and Hoover (1958) that demographic transition could contribute significantly to economic growth (Bloom and Williamson 1998). In the context of East Asia's economic miracle, they have noted that the working-age population there grew at a much faster rate than the dependent population during 1965-90, which provided an opportunity for raising the saving rate and expanding the productive capacity of workers. Population projection can help to pinpoint when such a demographic bonus period would occur during the transition.

Figure 7 shows the plot of the difference between the projected growth rate of the working-age population and that of the total population under the two scenarios. From the graphs, it is clear that during 2000-2020 the growth rate of working age population would exceed the growth rate of the total population. The demographic bonus would be larger in the case of the optimistic scenario, but it would be of shorter duration than that of the more realistic scenario where the pace of demographic change is slower. Figure 8 shows a similar plot for north and south India. As the figure shows, south India had already entered the demographic bonus phase by the 1990s. Perhaps the economic buoyancy being currently seen in south India is a reflection of its favourable demographic conditions. But it is expected to slip out of this phase in 15-years time. On the other hand, the north will enter this phase in the next 10 years, and remain in this phase until 2025.

Figure 7

Demographic Bonus Implied by the Difference Between the Growth Rate of Working-age Population (15-64) and Growth Rate of Total Population Under Optimistic and Realistic Scenarios, India 1995-2020

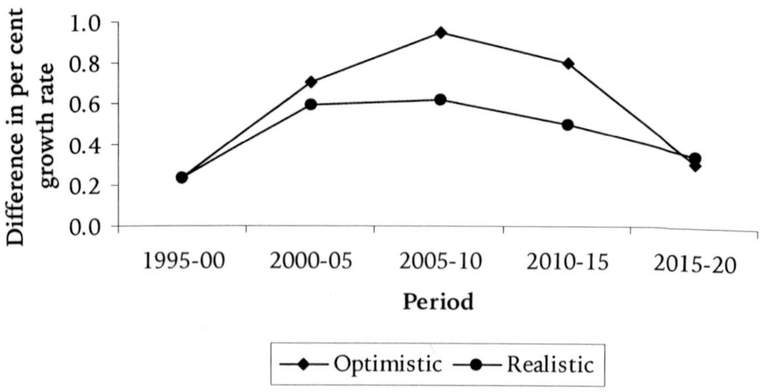

Thus, during the next 10-20 years demographic conditions would be favourable to economic growth in India. However, as Bloom and Williamson note, their effect is by no means inevitable. The one-time gift of the demographic transition would need the backing of appropriate economic, social and political institutions and policies. Otherwise, it would only lead to higher levels of unemployment.

Figure 8

Demographic Bonus Implied by the Difference Between the Growth Rate of Working-age Population (15-64) and Growth Rate of Total Population, North and South India 1995-2020

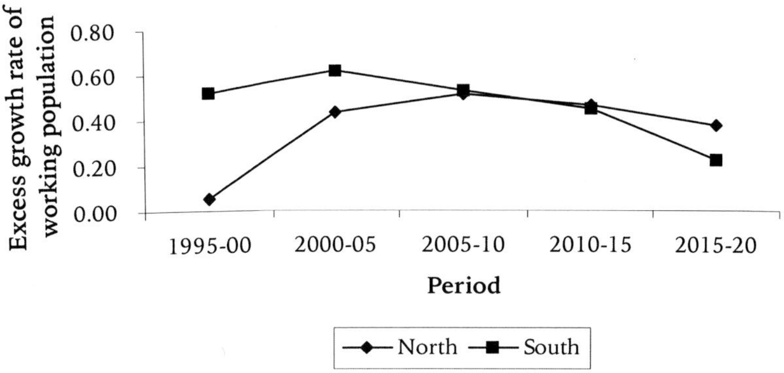

A more permanent bonus has also been quietly accruing from the demographic transition. Owing to fertility decline, the time spent by women in bearing and rearing children is falling while mortality decline is lengthening the life span remaining after the cessation of fertility. A woman's reproductive period, which used to span over 20 years and take away the better part of her working life, would be cut to half by the end of the demographic transition. Also, an average woman could expect to live for about 45 years after the termination of childbearing. It is unlikely that women would be content to spend an extended period of time in leisure. Slowly, but surely, a revolution in sex roles would begin to occur. As Kingsley Davis (1984) has put it so elegantly, it used to be that a woman would be asked what her husband does for a living; but increasingly men would now be asked what their wives do, provided they have one! However, the expected rapid expansion of the male labour force during the next quarter of century may delay the entry of women to labour market in large numbers.

Urbanization

Urban population growth is likely to be one of the major concerns of the twenty-first century. Despite rapidly increasing population pressure on arable land and planning for industrialization, according to the provisional results of the Census of 2001, only 28 per cent of India's population was living in urban areas. The census data for the period 1961 to 2001 suggest that the difference in the growth rates of urban and rural population has remained more or less constant at about 1.4 per cent. If the same difference were to continue, 33 per cent of India's population would be living in urban area by 2020. However, if the growth difference doubles in the coming years, 40 per cent of the population would be urban by 2020. As much as 50-75 per cent of the total population growth between 2000 and 2020 would be in cities and towns.

The past trends indicate a continued process of concentration of the urban population in cities with a population of 100,000 or more (65 per cent by 1991). Such a trend is likely to continue, and the pressure on urban amenities can be expected to accentuate. Owing to its demographic advantage, and rapid strides made in levels of literacy and education, south India is poised for faster rates of urbanization than north India. If this relieves the pressure on arable land in south India, it may induce migration of labourers from north India to farmlands of the south.

Conclusion

The population of India is expected to be around 1.3 billion in 2020. Interestingly, the population size is expected to reach this mark whether India attains the goals of the National Population Policy for 2010 or not. By 2020, India's population would almost be equal to that of China's. But India's population would still be growing at a rate of one per cent per annum, even though the level of fertility required for long-run population stabilization would have been achieved by then.

Even though population has been estimated to increase by 320 million between 2000 and 2020, as much as 87 per cent of the total growth would be in the age interval 15-64 years. The age interval of 65 years and over would account for another 10 per cent of the growth while the share of the interval 0-14 would be just 3 per cent of the total. This should have a far-reaching impact on the Indian economy.

Three-quarters of India's population growth during 2000-2020 would be in the northern states of Uttar Pradesh, Bihar, Madhya Pradesh, Rajasthan, Orissa, Jharkhand, Chhatisgarh and Uttaranchal. Consequently, their share in India's population is expected to rise from 45 to 49 per cent. The population in this region would still be growing at about 1.7 per cent per annum.

On the other hand, south India would have completed the demographic transition, and the growth rate of the native population would be extremely moderate, at about 0.6 per cent per annum. The population there would have also begun to 'age', as about 8 per cent of the population would be aged 65 years or more. The demographic imbalances may have begun to induce significant immigration flows from the north.

By 2020, India would be in the last few years of the 'bonus-period' of the demographic transition where the growth rate of working-age population exceeds that of total population. India is expected to go through this phase during 2000-2020. This one-time gift of the demographic transition is expected to provide a window of opportunities to raise the productivity of labour. If appropriate policies were pursued to realize the demographic gift, India would be in a comfortable position in the year 2020. Otherwise, higher levels of unemployment and its associated social evils would be on the cards.

The demographic transition also accrues a more lasting bonus in the form of women wanting to enter the labour force. The decline of fertility would reduce by half the time spent by women in raising children while mortality decline would double the life span remaining after the cessation of childbearing. Slowly, but surely, this would bring a quiet revolution in sex roles. However, the expected rapid expansion of the male labour force during the next quarter century may delay the entry of women to the labour market in significant numbers.

By 2020, about 35 per cent of India's population is expected to be urban. The urban growth would account for about 50-75 per cent of total population increase in the next twenty years. This would certainly accentuate the already existing pressure on urban amenities. But, if India finds a way of harnessing the demographic gift, urban centres would be full of buoyancy rather than despair.

References

Bhat, P. N. Mari (1998), "Demographic estimates for post-independence India: A new integration", *Demography India* 27(1), pp 23-57.

———. (1999), "Findings of National Family Health Survey: Regional analysis", *Economic and Political Weekly* 34, October 16-23.

———. (2000), "Generalized growth-balance method as an integrated procedure for evaluation of completeness of censuses and registration systems: A case study of India", 1971-1991, Delhi: Institute of Economic Growth.

Bloom, David E. and Jeffrey G. Williamson (1998), "Demographic transitions and economic miracles in emerging Asia", *The World Bank Economic Review* 12(3), pp 419-55.

Bos, Edurad, My T. Vu Ernest Massiah and Rodolfo A. Bulato (1994), *World Population Projections, 1994-95 Edition,* Baltimore and London: The Johns Hopkins University Press.

Coale, Ansley J. and Edgar Hoover (1958), *Population Growth and Economic Development in Low-Income Countries,* Princeton N.J.: Princeton University Press.

Davis, Kingsley (1984). "Wives and work: Consequences of the sex role revolution", *Population and Development Review* 10(3), pp 397-418.

Dyson, Tim and Amresh Hanchate (2000). "India's demographic and food prospects: A state-level analysis", *Economic and Political Weekly* 35, November 11.

Government of India (2000). *National Population Policy 2000,* New Delhi: Ministry of Health and Family Welfare.

India, Registrar General (2001). *Provisional Population Totals.* Census of India 2001, Series-1, India, Paper-1 of 2001, Delhi: Controller of Publications.

Natarajan, K. S. (1982). Population projection, In *Population of India.* Country Monograph Series No. 10, New York: United Nations.

Natarajan K.S. and V. Jayachandran (2001). Population growth in 21st century India, In K. Srinivasan and Michael Vlassoff (eds.), *Population-Development Nexus in India: Challenges for the New Millennium,* New Delhi: Tata McGraw-Hill.

United Nations (2001). *World Population Prospectus: The 2000 Revision,* Volume I, Comprehensive Tables, New York: United Nations.

Visaria, Pravin and Bhat, P. N. Mari (1999). Population growth in south Asia and its consequences, 1990-2051, Paper presented at the national seminar on Economy, Society and Polity in South Asia, held at Institute of Economic Growth, Delhi, November 16-17.

2

Agriculture Policy: Vision 2020

PANJAB SINGH

India has made impressive strides on the agricultural front during the last three decades. Much of the credit for this success should go to the several million small farming families that form the backbone of Indian agriculture and economy. Policy support, production strategies, public investment in infrastructure, research and extension for crop, livestock and fisheries have significantly helped to increase food production and its availability. During the last 30 years, India's foodgrain production nearly doubled from 102 million tons in the triennium ending 1973 to nearly 200 million tons (mt) in the triennium ending (TE) 1999. Virtually all of the increase in the production resulted from yield gains rather than expansion of cultivated area. Availability of foodgrains per person increased from 452 gm/capita/day to over 476 gm/capita/day, even as the country's population almost doubled, swelling from 548 million to nearly 1000 million.

Increased agricultural productivity and rapid industrial growth in the recent years have contributed to a significant reduction in poverty level, from 55 per cent in 1973 to 26 per cent in 1998. Despite the impressive growth and development, India is still home to the largest number of poor people of the world. With about 250 million below the poverty line, India accounts for about one-fifth of the world's poor. Child malnutrition extracts its highest toll in this country. About 25 per cent children suffer from serious malnutrition. More than 50 per cent of the pre-school children and pregnant women are anemic. The depth of hunger among the undernourished is also high.

India has high population pressure on land and other resources to meet its food and development needs. The natural resource base of land, water and bio-diversity is under severe pressure. The massive increase in population (despite the slowing down of the rate of growth) and substantial income growth, demand an extra about 2.5 mt of foodgrains annually, besides significant increases needed in the supply of livestock, fish and horticultural products. Under the assumption of 3.5 per cent growth in per capita GDP (low income growth scenario), demand for foodgrains (including feed, seed, wastage and export) is projected in the year 2020 at the level of 256 mt comprising 112 mt of rice, 82 mt of wheat, 39 mt of coarse grains and 22 mt of pulses. The demand for sugar, fruits, vegetables, and milk is estimated to grow to a level 33 mt, 77 mt, 136 mt and 116 mt respectively. The demand for meat is projected at 9 mt, fish 11 mt and eggs 77.5 billion (Table 1).

Table 1

Demand for Agricultural Commodities

Item	*Achieved TE 1997-99 (million tons)*			*Demand in 2020 in 2020*		*Yield target*	
	Area (Million ha)	*Production (Million tons)*	*Yield (Kg/ha)*	*LIG*	*HIG*	*LIG*	*HIG*
Rice	42.2	85.7	1903	112.4	111.9	2664	2652
Wheat	26.2	69.1	2582	82.3	79.9	3137	3045
Coarse cereal	30.7	30.4	1041	38.9	37.3	1268	1214
Cereal	99.1	185.2	1814	233.6	229.0	2357	2311
Pulses	21.7	13.8	608	22.3	23.8	1029	1095
Foodgrains	120.8	199.0	1595	255.9	252.8	2119	2092
Edible oil	28.6	6.4	269	10.8	11.4	379.7	399
Potato	1.2	21.6	17188	27.8	30.6	22279	24566
Vegetables	5.3	74.5	14204	135.6	168.0	25673	31812
Fruits	3.2	43.0	13437	77.0	93.6	24064	29259
Sugarcane Gur	3.7	26.9	7006	32.6	33.7	8788	9088
Milk	–	71.2	–	115.8	137.3	–	–
Meat	–	5.0	–	8.8	11.4	–	–
Eggs number	–	2873	–	7750	10000	–	–
Fish	–	5.3	–	10.1	12.8	–	–

Source: R.S.Paroda and Praduman Kumar (2000). Food Production and Demand in South Asia. Agril. Econ. Res. Rev. 13(1):1-24.

LIG: Low income growth 3.5 per cent per capita GDP growth.

HIG: High income growth 5.5 per cent per capita GDP growth.

Demand includes export 4.7 mt rice, 3.6 mt wheat, and vegetables 2.2 mt fruits 1.4 mt and fish 0.49 mt.

Future increases in the production of cereals and non-cereal agricultural commodities will have to be essentially achieved through increases in productivity, as the possibilities of expansion of area and livestock population are minimal. To meet the projected demand in the year 2020, country must attain a per hectare yield of 2.7 tons for rice, 3.1 tons for wheat, 2.1 tons for maize, 1.3 tons for coarse cereals, 2.4 tons for cereal, 1.3 tons for pulses, 22.3 tons for potato, 25.7 for vegetables, and 24.1 tons for fruits. The production of livestock and poultry products must be improved - 61 per cent for milk, 76 per cent for meat, 91 per cent for fish, and 169 per cent for eggs, by the year 2020 over the base year TE 1999. Average yields of most crops in India are still rather low.

Emerging Trends

The agriculture sector recorded satisfactory growth due to improved technology, irrigation, inputs and pricing policies. Livestock, poultry, fisheries and horticulture are surging ahead in production growth in recent years and will have greater demand in the future. Industrial and service sectors have expanded faster than agriculture sector resulting in declining share of agriculture in national accounts. Despite the structural change, agriculture still remains a key sector, providing both employment and livelihood opportunities to more than 70 per cent of the country's population who live in rural areas. The contribution of small farmers to the national and household food security has been steadily increasing. The water availability for agricultural uses has reached a critical level and deserves urgent attention of all concerned.

India has high population pressure on land and other resources to meet its food and development needs. The natural resource base of land, water and bio-diversity is under severe pressure. Food demand challenges ahead are formidable considering the non-availability of favourable factors of past growth, fast declining factor productivity in major cropping systems and rapidly shrinking resource base.

Vast uncommon opportunities to harness agricultural potential still remain, which can be tapped to achieve future targets. There are serious gaps both in yield potential and technology transfer as the national average yields of most of the commodities are low, which if addressed properly could be harnessed.

Concentration was on enhanced production of a few commodities like rice and wheat, which could quickly contribute to increased total food and agricultural production. This resulted in considerable depletion of natural resources and the rainfed dry areas having maximum concentration of resource poor farmers remained ignored, aggravating problems of inequity and regional imbalances. This also led to a high concentration of malnourished people in these rainfed, low productive areas. This era also witnessed rapid loss of soil nutrients, agro-biodiversity including indigenous land races and breeds.

The agriculture policy must accelerate all-round development and economic viability of agriculture in comprehensive terms. Farmers must be provided the necessary support, encouragement and incentives. It must focus both on income and greater on-farm and off-farm job and livelihood opportunities.

Main Issues

In national priority setting, the following recurring and emerging issues for sustainable agricultural development and poverty alleviation must be considered:

(i) Population pressure and demographic transition;

(ii) Resource base degradation and water scarcity;

(iii) Investment in agriculture, structural adjustment and impact on the poor;

(iv) Globalization and implication on the poor;

(v) Modern science and technology and support to research and technology development; and

(vi) Rapid urbanization and urbanization of poverty, and deceleration in rural poverty reduction.

In addressing the above issues, a policy statement on agriculture must take note of the following uncommon opportunities:

- Conservation of natural resources and protection of environment.
- Vast untapped potential of our soil and water resources, and farming systems.

- Technology revolution especially in the areas of molecular biology, biotechnology, space technology, ecology and management.
- Revolution in informatics and communication and the opportunity of linking farmers, extension workers and scientists with the national and international databases.

Vision

The Agriculture Policy document must articulate a clear vision on following few basic parameters of the agricultural sector around which a policy framework must be developed:

- Organization of agriculture: A clear long-term vision where inter-sectoral linkages are explicit.
- Sustainability and natural resource management: Prescription must lie in the domain of political economy. Otherwise, allocating funds for watershed development, agro-forestry, soil conservation, and so on will not produce desired results.
- Institutional change: Policy document must spell out new approaches and new institutions free from the shackles of bureaucratic and self-help framework.
- Investment priorities: There is a need to develop a consensus on investment themes, priorities and policies. Policy document must lend strength to the claim for greater investment in rural areas, and also re-examine its programmes in the light of complementarities.
- Incentives: Document must articulate a clear vision on the incentive framework.
- Risk management.

CHALLENGES, POLICIES AND STRATEGIES

Enhancing Yield of Major Commodities

Yield of major crops and livestock in the region is much lower than that in the rest of the world. Considering that the frontiers of expansion of cultivated area are almost closed in the region, the future increase in food production to meet the continuing high demand must come from increase in yield. There is a need to strengthen adaptive research and technology assessment, refinement and transfer capabilities of the country so that the existing wide technology transfer gaps are bridged. For this, an appropriate network of extension service needs to be created to stimulate and encourage both top-down and bottom-up flows of information between farmers, extension workers, and research scientists to promote the generation, adoption, and evaluation of location-specific farm technologies. Ample scope exists for increasing genetic yield potential of a large number of vegetables, fruits as well as other food crops and livestock and fisheries products. Besides maintenance breeding, greater effort should be made towards developing hybrid varieties as well as varieties suitable for export purposes. Agronomic and soil researches in the region need to be intensified to address location-specific problems as factor productivity growth is decelerating in major production regimes. Research on coarse grains, pulses and oilseeds must achieve a production breakthrough. Hybrid rice, single cross hybrids of maize and pigeonpea hybrids offer new opportunities. Soybean, sunflower and oil palm will help in meeting future oil demands successfully. Forest cover must be preserved to keep-off climatic disturbances and to provide enough of fuel and fodder. Milk, meat and draught capacity of our animals, needs to be improved quickly through better management practices.

Integrated Nutrient Management: Attention should be given to balanced use of nutrients. Phosphorus deficiency is now the most widespread soil fertility problem in both irrigated and unirrigated areas. Correcting the distortion in relative prices of primary fertilizers could help correct the imbalances in the use of primary plant nutrients-nitrogen, phosphorus, and potash and use of bio-fertilizers. To improve efficiency of fertilizer use, what is really needed is enhanced location-specific research on efficient fertilizer practices (such as balanced use of nutrients, correct timing and placement of fertilizers, and, wherever necessary, use of micronutrient and soil amendments), improvement in soil testing services, development of improved fertilizer supply and distribution systems, and development of physical and institutional infrastructure.

Arresting Deceleration in Total Factor Productivity: Public investment in irrigation, infrastructure development (road, electricity), research and extension and efficient use of water and plant nutrients are the dominant sources of TFP growth. The sharp deceleration in total investment and more so in public sector investment in agriculture is the main cause for the deceleration. This has resulted in the slow-down in the growth of irrigated area and a sharp deceleration in the rate of growth of fertiliser consumption. The most serious effect of deceleration in total investment has been on agricultural research and extension. This trend must be reversed as the projected increase in food and non-food production must accrue essentially through increasing yield per hectare. Recognising that there are serious yield gaps and there are already proven paths for increasing productivity, it is very important for India to maintain a steady growth rate in total factor productivity. As the TFP increases, the cost of production decreases and the prices also decrease and stabilise. Both producer and consumer share the benefits. The fall in food prices will benefit the urban and rural poor more than the upper income groups, because the former spend a much larger proportion of their income on cereals than the latter. All the efforts need to be concentrated on accelerating growth in TFP, whilst conserving natural resources and promoting ecological integrity of agricultural system. More than half of the required growth in yield to meet the target of demand must be met from research efforts by developing location specific and low input use technologies with the emphasis on the regions where the current yields are below the required national average yield.

Literacy had a positive and significant relation with crop productivity and a strong link exists between literacy and farm modernisation. A recent study (Kumar and Mittal, 2000) has shown that literacy emerged as an important source of growth in adoption of technology, use of modern inputs like machines, fertilisers, and yield. Recognising that in the liberalised economic environment, efficiency and growth orientation will attract maximum attention. Literacy will play a far more important role in the globalised world than it did in the past. Contribution of literacy, through TFP, will be substantial on yield growth and domestic supply. As future agriculture will increasingly be science-led and will require modern economic management, high return to investment on education is expected.

The investments that are good for agricultural growth-technology and its dissemination, rural infrastructure (roads), education and irrigation - amount to a 'win-win' strategy for reducing rural poverty by also increasing the non-farm economy and raising rural wages. Creating infrastructure in less developed areas, better management of infrastructure and introduction of new technologies can further enhance resource productivity and TFP. Generation and effective assessment and diffusion of packages of appropriate technologies involving system and programme based approach, participatory mechanisms, greater congruency between productivity and sustainability through integrated pest management and integrated soil-water-irrigation-nutrient management, should be aggressively promoted to bridge the yield gaps in most field crops. Besides this, efforts must be in place to defend the gains and to make new gains particularly through the congruence of gene revolution, informatics revolution, management revolution and eco-technology.

Many observers have expressed concern that technological gains have not occurred in a number of crops, notably coarse cereals, pulses and in rainfed areas. Recent analysis on TFP growth based on cost of cultivation data does not prove this perception (Table 2). In all the 18 major crops considered in the analysis, several states have recorded positive TFP growth. This is spread over major cereals, coarse grains, pulses, oilseeds, fibres, vegetables, etc. In most cases, in the major producing states, rainfed crops also showed productivity gains. There is thus strong evidence that technological change has generally pervaded the entire crop sector. There are, of course, crops and states where technological stagnation or decline is apparent and these are the priorities for present and future agricultural research. Farming system research to develop location-specific technologies and strategy to make grey areas green by adopting three-pronged approach – watershed management, hybrid technology and small farm mechanisation will accelerate growth in TFP. It is necessary to enlarge the efforts for promoting available dry land technologies. Promoting efficient fertiliser practices, improving soil-testing services, strengthening distribution channel of critical inputs especially quality seed and development of physical and institutional infrastructure will help resource-poor farmers.

Table 2

Total Factor Productivity Trends for Crops in Selected States

Crop	*TFP trend*		
	Increasing	*No change*	*Declining*
Paddy	Andhra Pradesh, Orissa, Punjab, Tamil Nadu, Uttar Pradesh, West Bengal	Assam, Haryana	Bihar, Karnataka, Madhya Pradesh
Wheat	Haryana, Punjab, Rajasthan, Uttar Pradesh	Madhya Pradesh	
Sorghum	Andhra Pradesh, Maharashtra, Karnataka	Madhya Pradesh, Rajasthan	
Pear millets	Gujarat, Haryana, Rajasthan		
Maize	Madhya Pradesh	Rajasthan, Uttar Pradesh	
Barley	Uttar Pradesh	Rajasthan	
Chickpea	Haryana	Rajasthan, Uttar Pradesh	Madhya Pradesh
Black gram	Maharashtra	Andhra Pradesh, Madhya Pradesh, Uttar Pradesh	Orissa
Moong	Madhya Pradesh	Andhra Pradesh , Rajasthan	Orissa
Pigeon pea	Madhya Pradesh	Gujarat, Uttar Pradesh	
Groundnut	Andhra Pradesh , Karnataka, Maharashtra, Orissa	Gujarat, Tamil Nadu	
Rapeseed & Mustard	Rajasthan, Uttar Pradesh	Assam, Haryana	Punjab
Soyabean		Madhya Pradesh	
Sugarcane	Bihar	Andhra Pradesh , Haryana, Karnataka, Maharashtra, Uttar Pradesh	
Cotton	Gujarat, Haryana, Tamil Nadu	Andhra Pradesh, Karnataka, Madhya Pradesh, Maharashtra, Punjab	
Jute	Assam, Bihar, West Bengal		Bihar
Onion	Maharashtra	Himachal Pradesh	
Potato	Uttar Pradesh	Himachal Pradesh	

Source: IARI-FAO/RAP study (2001) based on cost of cultivation data, DES, GoI.

Bridging Yield Gaps: Vast untapped potential in the yield exists for all crops in most of the states accounting for more than three-fourths of crop area. Emphasis must be given to the states in which current yield levels are below the national average yield. Bihar, Orissa, Assam, West Bengal and Uttar Pradesh are the priority states accounting for 66 per cent of rice area which need emphasis on bridging yield gaps to attain target demand and yield growth. For wheat we must focus mainly on Uttar Pradsh, Madhya Pradesh, Bihar and Rajasthan accounting for 68 per cent of wheat area. For coarse cereals, major emphasis must be given to Rajasthan, Maharashtra, Karnataka, Madhya Pradesh, Andhra Pradesh and Uttar Pradesh. To meet the demand for pulses, greater emphasis is needed in almost all the states with particular focus on Madhya Pradesh, Maharashtra, Rajasthan, Gujarat, Andhra Pradesh, Karnataka and Uttar Pradesh which have three-fourths of total pulse area. The target growth in pulse yield from these states annually must be six per cent; otherwise the nation will experience shortage of pulses for all times to come. The task of attaining self sufficient in pulses production looks difficult without area expansion and irrigation. In cases of oilseeds greater emphasis is needed on Andhra Pradesh, Madhya Pradesh, Rajasthan, Maharashtra, Karnataka, West Bengal and Uttar Pradesh to increase the yield by about four per cent. The possibilities of developing processing industry for extracting edible oils from non-oilseeds commodities, like rice bran etc, needs to be explored. The introduction of palm cultivation for oil production may release pressure on traditional oilseeds crops to meet future edible oil demand. In case of sugarcane, research and development efforts are to be strengthened in Uttar Pradesh and Bihar to increase the yields per hectare by about four per cent per annum. The demand for sugar can also be met by developing mini sugar mills so that substantial sugarcane production can be diverted from *Khandsari* to sugar production. This may also help release some sugarcane area to other crops. Cotton crop requires greater yield improvement emphasis on 81 per cent of the cotton area in Maharashtra, Gujarat and Andhra Pradesh.

Water for Sustainable Food Security

India will be required to produce more and more from less and less land and water resources. Alarming rates of ground water depletion and serious environmental and social problems of some of the major irrigation projects on one hand, and the multiple benefits of irrigation water in enhancing production and productivity, food security, poverty alleviation, as mentioned earlier, are well known to be further elaborated here: In India, water availability per capita was over 5000 cubic metres (m^3) per annum in 1950. It now stands at around 2000 m^3 and is projected to decline to 1500 m^3 by 2025. Further, the quality of available water is deteriorating. Also, there are gross inequalities between basins and geographic regions.

Table 3

Priority States for Increasing National Average Yield of Crops, India

Crops	*Target growth Per cent*	*Priority states*	*Percent share of priority states in total crop area*
Rice	2.35	BH, OR, AS, WB, UP	66
Wheat	2.22	UP, MP, BH, RJ	68
Sorghum	1.36	MH, KN, MP, AP	82
Pear-millets	0.43	RJ	47
Maize	2.00	BH, UP, MP, RJ	60
Chickpea	4.34	MP, RJ, UP, MH	83
Pigeon pea	4.28	MH, GJ, KN, AP, MP	72
Groundnut	2.51	AP, GJ, KN, MH	76
Rapeseed & Mustard	2.11	RJ, UP, MP, WB	74
Soybean	1.11	MP, RJ	83
Cotton	3.78	MH, GJ, KN, RJ, AP	74
Sugarcane	3.07	UP	51

Note: AP: Andhra Pradesh. AS: Assam. BH: Bihar. GJ: Gujarat. KN: Karnataka. MP: Madhya Pradesh. MH: Maharashtra. OR: Orissa RJ: Rajasthan. UP: Uttar Pradesh. WB: West Bengal.

Agriculture is the biggest user of water, accounting for about 80 per cent of the water withdrawals. There are pressures for diverting water from agriculture to other sectors. A study has warned that reallocation of water out of agriculture can have a dramatic impact on global food markets. It is projected that availability of water for agricultural use in India may be reduced by 21 per cent by 2020, resulting in drop of yields of irrigated crops, especially rice, thus price rise and withdrawal of food from poor masses. Policy reforms are needed from now to avoid the negative developments in the years to come. These reforms may include the establishment of secure water rights to users, the decentralization and privatization of water management functions to appropriate levels, pricing reforms, markets in tradable property rights, and the introduction of appropriate watersaving technologies.

The needs of other sectors for water cannot be ignored. Therefore, it is necessary that an integrated water use policy is formulated and judiciously implemented. Several international initiatives on this aspect have been taken in recent years. India should critically examine these initiatives and develop its country-specific system for judicious and integrated use and management of water. A national institution should be established to assess the various issues, regulatory concerns, water laws and legislations, research and technology development and dissemination, social mobilization and participatory and community involvement, including gender and equity concerns and economic aspects. This institution should function in a trusteeship mode and seen as the flagship of a national system for sustainable water security.

Emphasis on Rainfed Ecosystem

Resource-poor farmers in the rainfed ecosystems practice less-intensive agriculture, and since their incomes depend on local agriculture, they benefit little from increased food production in irrigated areas. To help them, efforts must be increased to disseminate available dry land technologies and to generate new ones. It will be necessary to enlarge the efforts for promoting available dry land technologies, increasing the stock of this knowledge, and removing pro-irrigation biases in public investment and expenditure, as well as credit flows, for technology-based agricultural growth, watershed development for raising yields of rainfed crops and widening of seed revolution to cover oilseeds, pulses, fruits and vegetables. Farming system research to develop location-specific technologies must be intensified in the rainfed areas. Strategy to make grey areas green will lead to second Green Revolution, which would demand three-pronged strategy - watershed management, hybrid technology and small farm mechanisation.

Accent on Diversification of Agriculture and Value Addition

In the face of shrinking natural resources and ever increasing demand for larger food and agricultural production arising due to high population and income growths, agricultural intensification is the main course for future growth of agriculture in the region. Research for product diversification should be yet another important area. Besides developing technologies for promoting intensification, the country must give greater attention to the development of technologies that will facilitate agricultural diversification particularly towards intensive production of fruits, vegetables, flowers and other high value crops that are expected to increase income growth and generate effective demand for food. The per capita availability of arable land is quite low and declining over time. Diversification towards these high value and labour intensive commodities can provide adequate income and employment to the farmers dependent on small size of farms. Due importance should be given to quality and nutritional aspects. High attention should be given to develop post-harvest handling and agro-processing and value addition technologies, not only to reduce the heavy post-harvest losses but also to improve quality through proper storage, packaging, handling and transport. The role of biotechnology in post-harvest management and value addition deserves to be enhanced.

Accent on Post-Harvest Management, Value Addition and Cost-Effectiveness

Post-harvest losses generally range from 5 to 10 per cent for non-perishables and about 30 per cent for perishables. This loss could be and must be minimized. Let us remember, a grain saved is a grain produced. Emphasis should therefore be placed to develop post-harvest handling, agro-processing and value-addition technologies not only to prevent the high losses, but also to improve quality through proper storage, packaging, handling and transport. With the thrust on globalization and increasing competitiveness, this approach will improve the agricultural export contribution of India, which is proportionately extremely low. Cost-effectiveness in production and post-harvest handling through the application of latest technologies will be a necessity. The agro-processing facilities should preferably be located close to the points of production in rural areas, which will greatly promote off-farm employment. Such centres of processing and value addition will encourage production by masses against mass production in factories located in urban areas. Agricultural cooperatives and Gram Panchayats must play a leading role in this effort. In doing so, the needs of small farmers should be kept in mind.

Increased Investment in Agriculture and Infrastructures

The public investment in agriculture has been declining and is one of the main reasons behind the declining productivity and low capital formation in the agriculture sector. With the burden on productivity-driven growth in the future, this worrisome trend must be reversed. Private investment in agriculture has also been slow and must be stimulated through appropriate policies. Considering that nearly 70 per cent of India still lives in villages, agricultural growth will continue to be the engine of broadbased economic growth and development as well as of natural resource conservation, leave alone food security and poverty alleviation. Accelerated investment are needed to facilitate agricultural and rural development through:

- Productivity increasing varieties of crops, breeds of livestock, strains of microbes and efficient packages of technologies, particularly those for land and water management, for obviating biotic, abiotic, socio-economic and environmental constraints;
- Yield increasing and environmentally-friendly production and post-harvest and value addition technologies;
- Reliable and timely availability of quality inputs at reasonable prices, institutional and credit supports, especially for small and resource-poor farmers, and support to land and water resources development;
- Effective and credible technology, procurement, assessment and transfer and extension system involving appropriate linkages and partnerships; again with an emphasis on reaching the small farmers;
- Improved institutional and credit support and increased rural employment opportunities, including those through creating agriculture-based rural agro-processing and agro-industries,

improved rural infrastructures, including access to information, and effective markets, farm to market roads and related infrastructure;

- Particular attention to the needs and participation of women farmers; and
- Primary education, health care, clean drinking water, safe sanitation, adequate nutrition, particularly for children (including through midday meal at schools) and women.

The above investments will need to be supported through appropriate policies that do not discriminate against agriculture and the rural poor. Given the increasing role of small farmers in food security and poverty alleviation, development efforts must be geared to meet the needs and potential of such farmers through their active participation in the growth process.

Government should facilitate and support community level action by private voluntary organizations, including farmers groups aimed at improving food security, reducing poverty, and assuring sustainability in the management of natural resources. In addition, governments should enhance efforts to ensure good nutrition and access to sufficient food for all through primary health care and education for all.

Modern biotechnology tools, genetic engineering, as well as conventional breeding methods are all expected to play important roles in the generation of higher yielding, pest and stress resistant varieties of rice, wheat, maize and other cereal crops. The availability of genetic innovations in developing countries will depend on continued high levels of investments in agricultural research, both at the international and the national levels. Free and unhindered access to germ plasm to breeders worldwide is absolutely crucial to the rapid dissemination and adoption of improved germ plasm. This free movement and the dissemination of modern biotechnology innovations to developing countries are hampered by increased patent protection and private sector investments. There is an urgent need to address this problem of free access to technology in the future.

Increased attention will also have to be given to development of sustainable systems that protect the natural resource base. Recent evidence of resource degradation and declining productivity in some intensively cropped areas is of particular concern. Also, population driven intensification of agriculture without the use of external inputs is leading to a serious problem of mining soil fertility.

Sustaining global food supplies will depend on continued high levels of investments in research and technology development. It is essential that research capacity has to be increased substantially. In addition to investments in research, infrastructure investments, particularly in irrigation, transport and market infrastructure development are equally important for sustaining the productivity and profitability of food crop production.

There is need to mobilize the best of science and development efforts (including traditional knowledge and modern scientific approach) through partnerships involving national and international research institutions, NGOs, farmers' organizations and private sector in order to tackle the present and future problems of food security and production.

Donors and Government must urgently increase funding for agricultural research targeted at the needs of the rural and urban poor, and every effort must be made to ensure the free flow of information, technology and germ plasm so that a proper sustainable agriculture can be achieved.

Fighting Poverty and Hunger

Nearly one-fourth of India's population, 251 million out of nearly one billion, is below the poverty line. One hundred seventy millions of the poor, 68 per cent, are rural and the remaining 32 per cent are urban (Table 4). Number at the national level in rural area has decreased after 1983; the number of poor in the cities has been increasing. This is essentially due to migration of the destitute from villages to cities. There are serious implications of this trend on feeding the cities and food security of urban people, urban poverty and environment. A question may be asked as to whether the rural settings and opportunities could be improved for securing livelihood security and consequently rationalizing the migration to the cities.

Table 4

Number and Percentage of Population Below Poverty Line in India

Year	*Rural*		*Urban*		*All India*	
	No. of persons	*% of person (million)*	*No. of persons*	*% of person (million)*	*No. of persons*	*% of person (million)*
1973	261	56	60	49	321	55
1983	254	46	74	41	328	45
1993	213	33	75	32	288	32
1998	170	24	81	30	251	26

Source: IARI-FAO/RAP study (2001) based on 50th NSS round (1993-94)

An analysis of the incidence of rural poverty and hunger by farm size revealed that more than half of the landless people are poor. Poverty got significantly reduced from 54 per cent in the landless group to 38 per cent in the submarginal group (Table 5) suggesting that even a small piece of land, less than 1/2 hectare, can greatly reduce both poverty and hunger[1]. The incidence of hunger and poverty gets reduced as one is able to meet even part of his/her dietary energy requirement through growing his/her own food (Table 6). Studies show that even a small plot of one's own helps women to escape extreme poverty and deprivation. Land is the main asset for livelihood security.

Although several factors affect the extent and depth of poverty and hunger, some of them have overwhelming impacts under the Indian setting. These include, irrigation, farming system and literacy. Generally, there is higher concentration of poor, and hungry people in rainfed areas as compared with those in irrigated zones. Even with 20 per cent of the irrigation intensity, there is a sharp fall in the proportion of hunger and poverty and it remains there irrespective of further intensification of irrigation (Table 7). Evidences suggest that extensive irrigation will prove much more effective than to

1. Energy intake below minimum energy requirement (kcal/person/day). Three-fourth of recommended calories (2400/person/day) for rural India that is 1800 kcal/person/day is used the threshold level. An average individual has an intake below this level (the threshold) is undernourished because they do not eat enough to maintain health, body weight and to under take light activity.

adding more and more water, and often wasting it along with the associated degradation of the natural resources. Such a policy will not only reduce poverty and hunger, but will also promote equity and environmental protection and natural resource conservation. An effective water policy and institutional support is needed to ensure judicious and equitable allocation, distribution and exploitation of water and water resources.

Table 5

Incidence of Hunger and Poverty by Farm Size in Rural India

Land class	*Per cent of population*	
	Hungry	*Poor*
Land less	49	54
<0.5 ha	32	38
0.5-1 ha	24	27
1.0-2 ha	17	19
2.0-4 ha	12	14
>4 ha	12	13

Source: IARI-FAO/RAP study (2001) based on 50th NSS Round(1993-94)

Table 6

Relationship between Home Produced Calories and Hunger and Poverty in Rural India

Degree of home produced calories	*Per cent of population*	
	Hungry	*Poor*
0	49	41
< 25 per cent	36	34
25-50 per cent	26	25
50-75 per cent	23	20
>75 per cent	17	29

Source: IARI-FAO/RAP study (2001) based on 50th NSS Round (1993-94)

Table 7

Impact of Irrigation on Alleviation of Hunger and Poverty in India

Irrigated area (%)	*Per cent of population*	
	Hungry	*Poor*
Rainfed	33	35
<20	20	22
20-50	22	23
50-80	18	24
>80	19	26

Source: IARI-FAO/RAP study (2001) based on 50th NSS Round (1993-94)

Livestock has the highest effect on reducing poverty and hunger. In rural India, 43 per cent of the people who do not own even a single livestock are malnourished. Addition of one cattle or one buffalo to their assets reduces the hunger prevalence by 16 and 25 percentage points, respectively (Table 8). Only 14 per cent of the people who owned one cattle and one buffalo were malnourished. In urban areas also, the addition of one cattle or one buffalo had significant impact on reduction of proportion of malnourished people. Livestock sector should also receive high priority with multiple objectives of diversifying agriculture, raising income and meeting the nutritional security of the poor farm households.

Table 8

Impact of Livestock on Alleviation of Hunger and Poverty in India

Livestock	*Per cent of population*			
	Rural		*Urban*	
	Hunger	*Poor*	*Hunger*	*Poor*
None	36	28	43	55
Cow	31	25	29	42
Buffalo	26	18	20	33
Cow & buffalo	14	8	7	4

Source: IARI-FAO/RAP study (2001) based on 50th NSS Round (1993-94)

Literacy has a very high impact on poverty alleviation as well as on hunger reduction (Table 9). The illiterate people, whether urban or rural, are the most poor and malnourished. In urban areas the impact of literacy on poverty is the highest. Education, even above primary level, is extremely effective in reducing both poverty and hunger. Graduate and technical education is, of course, the most important instrument for reducing both poverty and hunger. But its impact is most visible on poverty reduction. Therefore, the education policy of the country must be geared to remove illiteracy as soon as possible, as 50 per cent of our people are still illiterate. Free education up to 8th standard coupled with mid-day meal in the schools will go a long way in reducing both poverty and hunger and will thus help build a strong India. Further, this move will greatly reduce the violation of child labour laws and will offset some of the non-tariff restrictions imposed by developed countries on exports from developing countries on the grounds of use of child labour.

Table 9

Impact of Literacy on Alleviation of Hunger and Poverty in India

Literacy level	*Per cent of population*			
	Malnourished		*Below poverty level*	
	Rural	*Urban*	*Rural*	*Urban*
Zero	36	28	43	55
Below Primary Level	31	25	29	42
Above Primary Level	26	18	20	33
Graduate and Technical	14	8	7	4

Source: IARI-FAO/RAP study (2001)based on 50th NSS Round (1993-94)

Accent on Empowering the Small Farmers

Contributions of small holders in securing food for growing population have increased considerably even though they are most insecure and vulnerable group in the society. The off-farm and non-farm employment opportunities can play an important role. Against expectation under the liberalized scenario, the non-agricultural employment in rural areas has not improved. Greater emphasis needs to be placed on non-farm employment and appropriate budgetary allocations and rural credit through banking systems should be in place to promote appropriate rural enterprises. Specific human resource and skill development programmes to train them will make them better decision-makers and highly productive. Human resource development for increasing productivity of these small holders should get high priority. Thus, knowledge and skill development of rural people both in agriculture and non-agriculture sectors is essential for achieving economic and social goals. A careful balance will therefore need to be maintained between the agricultural and non-agricultural employment and farm and non-farm economy, as the two sectors are closely interconnected.

Raising agricultural productivity requires continuing investments in human resource development, agricultural research and development, improved information and extension, market, roads and related infrastructure development and efficient small-scale, farmer-controlled irrigation technologies, and custom hiring services. Such investments would give small farmers the options and flexibility to adjust and respond to market conditions.

For poor farm-households whose major endowment is its labour force, economic growth with equity will give increased entitlement by offering favourable markets for its products and more employment opportunities. Economic growth if not managed suitably, can lead to growing inequalities. Agrarian reforms to alleviate unequal access to land, compounded by unequal access to water, credit, knowledge and markets, have not only rectified income distribution but also resulted in sharp increases in productivity and hence need to be adopted widely. Further, targeted measures that not only address the immediate food and health care requirements of disadvantaged groups, but also provide them with developmental means, like access to inputs, infrastructure, services and most important, education should be taken.

Identification of need-based productive programs is very critical, which can be explored through characterisation of production environment. We have to develop demand-driven and location-specific programs to meet the requirements of different regions to meet the nutritional security of most vulnerable population in the rural areas. Improved agricultural technology, irrigation, livestock sector and literacy will be the most important instruments for improving the nutritional security of the farm-households. Watershed development and water saving techniques will have far reaching implications in increasing agricultural production and raising calorie intake in the rainfed areas. Livestock sector should receive high priority with multiple objectives of diversifying agriculture, raising income and meeting the nutritional security of the poor farm households. Need based and location-specific community programs, which promise to raise nutritional security, should be identified and effectively implemented. Expansion of micro credit programmes for income-generation activities, innovative approaches to promote family planning and providing primary health services to people and livestock and education should enhance labour productivity and adoption of new technologies. Development of the post-harvest sector, co-operatives, roads, education, and research and development should be an investment priority.

A congenial policy environment is needed to enable smaller holders to take the advantage of available techniques of production, which can generate more incomes and employment in villages. For this, poor farmer needs the support of necessary services in the form of backward and forward linkages. Small mechanised tools, which minimise drudgery and do not reduce employment, but only add value to the working hours are needed to enhance labour productivity. Special safety nets should be designed and implemented for them. Can agricultural co-operatives internalise and galvanize these marginal and excluded people? Off-farm employment provided through co-operatives will go a long way in pulling them out of the state where poverty breeds poverty. Therefore, investment in the empowerment of the small landholders will pay off handsomely. Let us create rural centres of production and processing by masses through co-operatives or empowerment of Gram Panchayats to promote co-operatives. This will improve efficiency of input and output marketing and give higher income. There is need to disseminate widely post-harvest handling and agro-processing and value addition technologies not only to reduce the heavy post-harvest losses but also improve quality through proper storage, packaging, handling and transport. Panchayati Raj Institutions and co-operatives can play significant role in all these directions. Giving them power over the administration, as contemplated under the 73rd and 74th Amendment of the Constitution has not been implemented seriously so far in any of the states.

Disaster Management

The frequency and intensity of disasters such as floods, droughts, cyclones and earthquakes have increased in the recent years. The devastating earthquake in Gujarat has brought untold miseries to the whole state and caused a national disaster. Special effort should be made to develop appropriate technologies for increasing preparedness to predict and to manage the disasters. Effective and reliable information and communication systems, contingency planning and national and international mobilization of technologies and resources are a must. Experiences of other countries in prevention and management of the disasters should be shared.

Keeping Pace with Globalisation

The globalization of agricultural trade will bring to the fore access to markets; new opportunities for employment and income generation; productivity gains and increased flow of investments into sustainable agriculture and rural development. I believe that if managed well, the liberalization of agricultural markets will be beneficial to developing countries in the long run. It will force the adoption of new technologies, shift production functions upwards and attract new capital into the deprived sector. However, this will only come to pass if we are mindful of the interests of billions of small and subsistence oriented farmers, fisherfolk and forest dwellers in the short and medium term. So far the magic of globalization has not been felt in India. During the past one decade of liberalization, certain trends such as deceleration of the growth rate of agricultural GDP, deceleration in yield growth rates, and low non-agricultural employment have emerged against expectations. As we globalize, however, it is imperative that we do not forget social aspirations for a more just, equitable and sustainable way of life. Trade agreements must be accompanied by operationally effective measures to ease the adjustment process for a small farmer in developing countries.

Exploiting Cyberspace

Information is power and will underpin future progress and prosperity. Efforts must be made to strengthen the informatics in agriculture by developing new databases, linking databases with international databases and adding value to information to facilitate decision-making at various levels. Development of production models for various agro-ecological regimes to forecast the production potential should assume greater importance. Using the remote sensing and GIS technologies, natural and other agricultural resource should be mapped at micro and macro levels and effectively used for land and water use planning as well as agricultural forecasting, market intelligence and e-business, contingency planning and prediction of disease and pest incidences.

3

Food Security and Nutrition: Vision 2020

R. RADHAKRISHNA & K. VENKATA REDDY

I. Introduction

The concept of food security has undergone considerable changes in recent years. Food availability and stability were considered good measures of food security till the Seventies and the achievement of self-sufficiency was accorded high priority in the food policies of developing countries. Though India was successful in achieving self-sufficiency by increasing its food production and also improved its capacity to cope with year-to-year fluctuations in food production, it could not solve the problem of chronic household food insecurity.

This necessitated a change in approach and as a result, food energy intake at household level is now given prominence in assessing food security. It has become common practice to estimate the number of food insecure households by comparing their calorie intake with required norms. However, the widely accepted norms of the level of calorie intake required for overcoming under-nutrition have been questioned. Nutritionists argue that the energy intake is a poor measure of nutritional status, which depends not only on the nutrient intake but also on non-nutrient food attributes, privately and publicly provided inputs and health status (Martorell and Ho, 1984). The non-food factors which influence biological absorption are also considered as important for food security as food factors.

It is suggested that the assessment of malnutrition should be based on outcome measures rather than input measures (ibid). The suggested outcome measures include anthropometric measures, clinical signs of malnutrition, biochemical indicators and physical activity. Outcome indicators are more closely related to health and functional capacity. Among the outcome measures, anthropometric measures are considered to have an advantage over other indicators since body measurements are sensitive to even minor levels of malnutrition whereas biochemical and clinical indicators, on the other hand, are useful only when the level of malnutrition is extreme.

In policy design, a distinction is made between transient and chronic food security. Transitory food insecurity is associated with the risks related to either access or the availability of food during the off-season, drought and inflationary years and so forth. Policies such as those relating to price stabilization, credit, crop-insurance and temporary employment creation are initiated for stabilizing the consumption of the vulnerable groups. In contrast, the problem of chronic food insecurity is primarily associated with poverty and arises due to continuously inadequate diet. The strategy to overcome this problem includes intervention (agricultural production programmes, infrastructure, human resource development, etc.) to raise the purchasing power of the poor through the endowments of land and non-land assets and by generating employment opportunities, as well as long-term growth-mediated interventions to improve food availability and incomes of the poor.

India is one of the few countries which have experimented with a broad spectrum of programmes for improving food security. It has already made substantial progress in terms of overcoming transient food insecurity by giving priority to self-sufficiency in foodgrains and through procurement and public distribution of foodgrains, employment programmes, etc. However, despite a significant reduction in the incidence of poverty, chronic food insecurity persists in a large proportion of India's population. At the national level, we have solved the problem of food security which is reflected in mounting buffer stocks. Yet, there are millions of food insecure and undernourished people in India. The limitation is not food supply, but food distribution. Careful consideration of food security requires moving beyond food availability and recognizing the low incomes of the poor. It is also important to recognize the choices that households and regions face, including exploitation of natural resources when incomes fall short. Substantial human resources are wasted due to malnutrition related diseases. Vision 2020 should aim at complete eradication of food insecurity, both chronic and transient. Productivity generated by technological innovation, particularly in less endowed areas and vibrant rural non-farm sector hold the key to eradicate food insecurity. The Asian countries which made substantial progress in the reduction of poverty, created productive off-farm opportunities. What factors are critical for facilitating this transition in the rural India? What are the required policy reforms and their companion institutional arrangements? Some of these issues are addressed in Radhakrishna (2002).

II. Trends in Food Production

Over the years, India has made rapid progress in the production of food (Table 1). The annual growth rate of food production including non-cereal food increased from 2.1 per cent during the 1960s to three per cent in the subsequent decade and further to 3.8 per cent during the 1980s. Between 1960 and 1980, food production barely kept pace with the population but in the 1980s per capita food production increased at a satisfactory rate of 1.6 per cent per annum. There seems to have been some diversification in food production in the 1980s on account of the impressive growth of output of oilseeds and livestock products. The diversification of food production more or less conforms to the growth pattern of domestic demand.

India achieved near self-sufficiency in the availability of foodgrains by the mid-Seventies. The trend rate of foodgrain production improved from 2.3 per cent during the 1960s and 1970s to 2.9 per cent in the Eighties (Bhalla and Singh 2001). It is particularly noteworthy that India could build enough buffer stocks to cope with year-to-year variations in foodgrain production. Field studies reveal that during the 1987 drought, stable foodgrain prices, PDS supplies and the availability of consumption credit enabled drought affected villages to maintain their consumption at the same level as in normal years (Acharya, 1989; Bidinger, *et al.*, 1990). The annual fluctuations in the per capita availability of foodgrains declined in the Eighties and Nineties when compared to the previous period (Rao and Radhakrishna, 1997) and there was a decline in the seasonal as well as regional variations in the prices of foodgrains (Bhalla, 1994).

Table 1

Annualised Compound Growth Rates of Food Production and Population Growth

(Per cent per annum)

Year	*Food production*		*Population Growth Rate*
	Aggregate	*Per capita*	
1961-63 – 1971-73	2.11	-0.10	2.24
1971-73 – 1981-83	3.00	0.84	2.23
1981-83 – 1991-93	3.77	1.62	2.02
1991-93 – 1997-99	2.72	0.90	1.84

Sources: FAO, *State of Food and Agriculture;*

The growth of food production slowed down to 2.72 per cent per annum in the Nineties. Ironically, even at the low growth rate of foodgrain production, the supplies outstripped the effective demand and the Nineties has seen a rapid increase in the stock of foodgrains held by the Government. Disposal of stocks has become a cause of concern. The domestic supplies are more than adequate to prevent food gaps.

The relative cereal price which showed a decline in the Seventies and Eighties, registered a rise in the Nineties. Moreover, in high inflation years, cereal prices rose even higher (Ravi, 2000). An increase in cereal price significantly reduce the calorie intake of the poor as their price elasticity of food/calorie estimates of price elasticity is numerically large. The upward trend in the real price of cereals in the Nineties had coincided with a slowdown in the decline of poverty.

Despite favourable terms of trade for agriculture and normal behaviour of the South-West monsoon, the growth of food production has been sluggish during the Nineties and agricultural product diversification in the poor rain-fed areas from coarse cereals to oilseeds and horticultural production has come to a slowdown. The sluggish growth of agricultural production could be attributed to:

(a) Decline in public investment in agriculture particularly in irrigation since the early 1980s (the annual growth rate being 4.0 per cent in 1980s and 1.9 per cent in the 1990s); as a result, expansion in irrigation input usage and technological improvement have slowed down in the last decade.

(b) The low public investment on agricultural research (0.5 per cent of GDP as against the one per cent recommended by the ICAR) adversely affecting the technological progress in agricultural production;

(c) Decline in the annual growth rate of fertilizer consumption from 7.8 per cent in the 1980s to 4.3 per cent in the 1990s;

(d) Deceleration in the annual growth rate of area under HYV from 4.9 per cent in the 1980s to 2.8 per cent in the 1990;

(e) Intensive cultivation and depletion of soil fertility due to wheat-rice rotation year after year in the North-Western region.

India needs an agricultural growth rate of 4.0 to 4.5 per cent to reduce poverty and food insecurity significantly (Rao and Radhakrishna, 1997). This is within the reach. At this growth rate, agricultural development would diversify into dairying, animal husbandry, fisheries, floriculture, horticulture and other areas. These activities are likely to be labour intensive. The best strategy would seem to be to target a growth rate of about 2.2 per cent per annum and achieve it by improving the total factor productivity. This will make available more land and water resources for the cultivation of high value-added crops. If flexibility on the supply side is facilitated, production will adjust to the market forces and generate higher incomes in the rural areas. This would also spur the growth of agro-processing industries in rural areas.

The challenge to food security comes mainly from the slow growth of purchasing power of the people in the rain-fed eco-systems. Efforts must be made to help them by developing drought resistant seeds, cost-effective dry-land farming techniques. In addition, rain water harvesting techniques, moisture conservation, inter-cropping are imperative to stabilize and improve the production in the dry-land areas. It is also essential to explore the possibilities for cost-effective expansion of irrigation. Appropriate pricing of water, electricity and fertilizer and rationalization of minimum support prices would augment resources available for investment in irrigation, rural infrastructure and prevention of soil degradation.

III. Food and Nutrient Intake

Cereal Consumption

NSS consumption data reveal that the per capita consumption of cereals has been declining since the early Seventies (Radhakrishna and Ravi, 1992, Rao, 2000). Between 1970-71 and 1997-98, the per capita cereal consumption declined by 0.72 per cent per annum in the rural areas and by 0.74 per cent per annum in urban areas. The cereal consumption in rural areas fell from 15.35 kgs per capita/month in 1970-71 to 12.5 kgs in 1997-98 while the same in urban areas fell from 11.36 kgs to 10.4 kgs during the same period. The declining trend is visible in most of the states. The decline is very prominent in Punjab and Haryana where the decline is as much as about 6 kgs per capita per month in rural areas. What is most striking is the low per capita intake of cereals in the most prosperous Punjab (9.8 kgs in rural and 9.7 kgs in the urban areas in 1997-98) and the converse in the backward state of Orissa (16 kgs in rural and 13.25 kgs in urban areas). The striking decline in serial consumption is attributed to changes in consumer tastes and preferences towards superior food items as the incomes of the household increases (Radhakrishna and Ravi 1990, 1992). This is partly due to the diversification of the food basket in Punjab and Haryana in favour of superior non-cereal foods, particularly milk and milk products, vegetables and fruits, etc. More recently, Rao (2000) has shown that the decline has been sharper in the rural areas where improvements in rural infrastructure made other food and non-food items available to the rural households. Reduction of manual work in agriculture due to farm mechanization might have also reduced the felt need for cereals. Rao further observes that a reduction in the intake of food grains on this account should not be taken as a deterioration in human welfare.

IV. Food Expenditure, Food Consumption, and Calorie Intake

Data from NSS surveys show that per capital consumer expenditure at constant (1990-91) prices steadily increased since 1970, both in rural and urban areas. It increased around 1.5 per cent per annum in both the areas during '70s and '80s; and around 1.2 per cent per annum in rural areas and 2.8 per cent per annum in urban areas during the '90s (Table 2). It appears that economic reforms benefited the urban households more than the rural ones. But the increase in consumption expenditure did not reflect in food expenditure. Per capita food expenditure at constant prices increased around 0.9 per cent per annum during the first two decades while it declined at 0.9 per cent per annum in rural areas and stagnant in urban areas during the last decade.

Table 2

Growth Rates of Total Expenditure, Food Expenditure and the Cereal Expenditure at 1990-91 Prices and Per Capita Calorie Intake

(Per cent per annum)

	Bottom 30%	*Middle 40%*	*Top 30%*	*All classess*
Rural				
Per capita cereal expenditure				
1970-89	0.09	-0.58	-1.28	-0.69
1990-98	-1.38	-2.34	-2.43	-2.14
Per capita food expenditure				
1970-89	1.34	0.87	0.74	0.89
1990-98	-0.48	-0.78	-1.12	-0.88
Per capita calorie intake				
1970-89	0.16	0.15	0.40	0.23
1990-98	-0.96	-1.63	-1.76	-1.53
Per capita total expenditure				
1970-89	1.71	1.40	1.45	1.54
1990-98	1.19	1.11	1.23	1.18
Urban				
Per capita cereal expenditure				
1970-89	0.07	-0.33	-0.18	-0.18
1990-98	-0.67	-0.55	0.30	-0.28
Per capita food expenditure				
1970-89	1.29	1.19	0.69	0.97
1990-98	0.08	0.03	-0.23	-0.08
Per capita calorie intake				
1970-89	0.31	0.05	0.32	0.21
1990-98	-0.58	-0.74	-0.05	-0.44
Per capita total expenditure				
1970-89	1.44	1.50	1.40	1.45
1990-98	1.70	2.27	3.31	2.77

Source: Ravi (2000).

Per capita cereal consumption expenditure at constant prices declined both in rural and urban areas throughout this period for all the expenditure classes, except the bottom 30 per cent during the first two decades (Table 2). The decline is more in rural areas than in urban areas. The fall in cereal consumption was more than compensated by increased consumption of non-cereal food during the first two decades and as a result, per capital calorie intake increased at 0.2 per cent during this period both in rural and urban areas. However, this did not continue during the '90s when the per capita calorie intake fell by about 0.4 per cent in urban areas and by twice as much in rural areas. It implies that the consumption of non-cereal food items could not compensate the loss of energy intake due to fall in cereal consumption during this period.

In the case of the bottom 30 per cent of the population, there has been hardly any perceptible improvement in the cereal and nutrient intake in the rural and urban areas despite a significant improvement in their real per capita expenditure. There has been a substantial diversification of the consumption basket of the poor in favour of non-cereal food items such as milk and milk products, sugar and gur and other food items. These tendencies would not be a major cause of concern if the intake levels were nutritionally adequate. The per capita intake of the bottom 30 per cent at 1600-1700 K.Cal/day, falls short of the required norm. The food gap of the bottom 30 per cent can be met by providing to them around 10 million tones of foodgrains.

Micro nutrient deficiency is equally common among the population, more so in the vulnerable groups such as women and children. These two groups are more prone to certain deficiencies than the adult male population. Iodine deficiency is common among the populations living in the sub-Himalayan region and other hill regions of the country. Vitamin-A deficiency, which leads to preventable blindness in the children is more common among the children from the rural households. Iron deficiency is widely prevalent among the pregnant women. As per the latest NFHS-2 survey, about half of the pregnant women suffer from iron deficiency and consequent anemia, 35 per cent suffer from mild anemia, 15 per cent from moderate and two per cent from severe.

Even though the question of desirable diet from nutritional perspective is still controversial, we can make certain policy options to overcome the nutritional deficiencies. The most important problem to be attended is to increase the energy intake of the bottom 30 per cent of the expenditure class. The deficiency of energy intake of the bottom 30 per cent can be rectified by increasing agricultural productivity in rain fed areas, making available food at an affordable price through the public distribution sytem (PDS), and other poverty alleviation programmes. The micro-nutrient deficiency can be cost-effectively rectified by supplementary nutritional programmes to the children and the expectant and lactating mothers.

V. Nutritional Status

The National Nutrition Monitoring Bureau (NNMB) and National Family Health Survey (NFHS) provide data on nutritional status, general as well as vulnerable groups, using Gomez classification (in case of children) and Bio-mass Index (BMI) classification in the case of others. The NNMB data show that the instance of under-nutrition among children and Chronic Energy Deficiency (CED) among other population, even though slowly declining was still alarmingly high in the late Nineties and their incidence is higher than that of income poverty.

The percentage of children suffering from severe malnutrition in rural areas of eight states covered by the NNMB declined from 15.0 in 1975-79 to 6.4 in 2000-01 (Radhakrishna 2000). If moderate and severe malnutrition is taken together, the percentage of children suffering from malnutrition declined from 62.5 to 47.7 per cent during the same period (ibid). The decline in the percentage of severely malnourished children is visible across all National Nutrition Monitory Bureau (NNMB) sample states except Orissa. The decline is very striking in Kerala and Tamil Nadu. In spite of some improvement in nutritional status, nearly half of the rural children are suffering from malnutrition.[1]

1. Children of the poor communities suffering from malnutrition not only do not achieve full genetic growth potential and end up as adults with small body size but are also exposed to a greater risk of child mortality. Pelletier et.al. (1996) identify malnutrition as a major cause of death in developing countries. Their results reveal that malnutrition, by virtue of its synergistic relationship with infectious disease has a powerful impact on child mortality in India.

There are substantial inter-state variations in the malnutrition levels of children under-five years; in 2000-01, the percentage of moderately and severely malnourished children varied between 29 in Kerala and 64 in Madhya Pradesh (Table 3). In terms of nutritional status of children, middle-income states such as Kerala, Tamil Nadu and Andhra Pradesh performed better than higher-income states like Gujarat and Maharashtra. Not surprisingly, poorer states such as Madhya Pradesh and Orissa showed worst performance. It is worth noting that with low food energy intake, Kerala and Tamil Nadu could perform better. National Family health Survey (NFHS) data also reveals similar pattern (Table 3).

NNMB data indicate that in 1996, around half of the rural adult population in the eight sample states suffered from Chronic Energy Deficiency (CED) and the extent of malnutrition among the adults was almost as much as that of children (Table 3). The regional patterns are similar to those of malnutrition among the children (NNMB). CED was found to be lower in Kerala (33 per cent) and Tamil Nadu (37 per cent) and higher in Gujarat, Maharashtra and Madhya Pradesh (above 50 per cent).

Inter-state variations reveal weak correlation between nutritional status and calorie consumption. The state-level mismatch between food intake and nutritional status could be attributed to the differences in education, health, availability of safe drinking water, environmental sanitation and personal hygiene which intervene between the food intake and nutritional status. A better environment would reduce food wastage due to infections and diseases. The better nutritional status at a comparatively lower level of food consumption in Kerala and Tamil Nadu could be due to the better health care and nutritional interventions[2].

Does all this imply that the calorie intake matters little? While empirical evidence tends to suggest a positive association between the calorie intake and nutritional status, the responsiveness is likely to be affected by the factors relating to health and environment. What is a desirable diet from a nutritional perspective thus remains unsettled in view of the controversies. It is also unclear as to how

---

2. Kerala and Tamil Nadu have better health care and educational facilities and coverage of the PDS. The per child public expenditure on nutrition as well as per capita public expenditure on social sector have been high in these two states for the past few decades.

much of the malnutrition is due to an inadequate diet and how much due to the environment[3].

Table 3

Malnutrition among Children and Adults

State	Malnutrition among children					CED among Adults
	Rural (1993) NFHS*	Urban (1993) NFHS*	Total (Rural and Urban) (1993) NFHS*	Total (Rural and Urban) 1998-99 NFHS**	Rural 2000-01 NNMB***	1996 Rural NNMB@
Andhra Pradesh	52.1	40.2	49.1	37.7	39.9	39.9
Assam	51.8	37.3	50.4	36.0	—	—
Bihar	64.1	53.8	62.6	54.4	—	—
Gujarat	45.8	40.5	44.1	45.1	48.9	53.1
Haryana	39.4	33.0	37.9	34.6	—	—
Himachal Pradesh	48.3	30.2	47.0	43.6	—	—
Jammu & Kashmir	N.A.	N.A.	44.5	34.5	—	—
Karnataka	N.A.	N.A.	N.A.	43.9	47.6	53.8
Kerala	30.6	22.9	28.5	26.9	28.8	33.2
Madhya Pradesh	59.4	50.1	57.4	55.1	63.9	53.3
Maharashtra	57.5	45.5	52.6	49.6	52.2	51.0
Orissa	N.A.	N.A.	55.3	54.4	54.4	57.3
Punjab	47.4	40.0	45.9	28.7	—	—
Rajasthan	41.1	43.9	41.6	50.6	—	—
Tamil Nadu	42.1	32.3	46.6	36.7	39.0	37.3
Uttar Pradesh	N.A.	N.A.	49.8	51.7	—	—
West Bengal	N.A.	N.A.	56.8	48.7	—	—
Arunachal	40.3	36.2	39.7	24.3	—	—
Manipur	31.6	25.9	30.1	27.5	—	—
Nagaland	30.5	19.7	28.7	24.1	—	—
Tripura	50.0	31.6	48.8	N.A.	—	—
Meghalaya	47.2	37.5	45.5	37.9	—	—
Mizoram	34.5	22.0	28.1	27.7	—	—
All-India	59.9	45.2	53.4	47.0	47.7+	48.5+

*: Children under four years, Weight for age, Percentage below two standard deviations, NFHS-1.

**: Children under three years, Weight for age, Percentage below two standard deviations, NFHS-2.

***: Children between one to five years, Weight for age, Gomez Classification, NNMB.

@: BMI < 18.5 kgs./m^2.

+: All-India estimate is an average of its eight sample states.

---

3. Sekler (1982) observes that severe malnutrition is caused by nutrient intake deficiency and the 'moderate' and 'mild' malnutrition is due to environmental factors. He argues that the former problem calls for nutritional intervention and the latter environmental intervention. There is, as yet, not much empirical basis for his position.

VI. Public Distribution System (PDS)

India has a large programme of public food distribution through fair price shops, accounting for a significant part of the government's budgetary subsidies. The PDS in its present form—a producer price-support-cum-consumer subsidy programme—has evolved in the wake of foodgrain shortages of the Sixties. It was then mainly confined to urban and food deficit areas with its emphasis primarily on price stabilisation till the late Seventies. The welfare dimension of the PDS has gained importance since the early Eighties and its coverage has been extended to rural areas in some states as well as to areas with a high incidence of poverty. The food subsidy of the Central Government, at Rs.17,612 crores, accounted for 0.89 per cent of GDP in 2001-02. In the wake of economic reforms, the PDS is perceived to be the main safety net to protect the poor from potential short-run price-induced adverse effects of economic reforms.

PDS supplies have increased rapidly since the mid-Sixties: the annual average supply increased from 6.5 million tonnes during 1961-65 to 18.4 million tonnes during 1990-92, declined to 12.86 million tonnes in 1994-95 and then increased to 18.69 million tonnes in 1998-99. A noteworthy feature of these trends is the response of government supply to fluctuations in production; it is higher in drought years than in normal ones. For instance, in 1979-80 and 1987-88—the years associated with low foodgrain production—the government supplies were substantially higher than in normal years. In both the years, the Government increased the supplies through both PDS and employment generation programmes to prevent famine, though the procurement levels were lower than in normal years. It is noteworthy in this context that there were only a few instances of deaths due to starvation.

The recent large increases in procurement prices and the consequent upward revisions in the central issue prices have had an adverse impact on the efficacy of the PDS. The price advantage to the farmers has resulted in the parastatal Food Corporation of India (FCI), buying up more wheat and rice than it can manage for the simple reason that it had no option but to buy whatever is offered to it at the minimum support price. The procurement of cereals for Central pool was 35 mt in 2000-01 and 46 mt in 2001-02 as against the off-take of cereals of 11 mt in 2000-01 and 12 mt in 2001-02.

Buffer stocks have reached uneconomic levels of 46 mt on 1st January, 2001 which further increased to 58 mt on 1st January, 2002, exceeding the norms. The carrying cost of buffer stocks accounted for 42 per cent of the Central food subsidy in 2001-02.

The substantial increases in Minimum Support Price (MSP) benefited mainly the farmers with marketable surplus from Punjab, Haryana, Western U.P. and Andhra Pradesh, which account for 80 per cent of wheat and rice procurement. In other states without food procurement, wheat and rice have been sold at less than MSP as market could not absorb all the market arrivals at high MSP.

It is important to ask whether the poor have benefited from the increased tempo of the PDS operations and what is the efficacy of the PDS in distributing food to the poor. Many empirical studies have shown severe biases in the inter-regional distributions of the PDS supplies—states with the high incidence of poverty such as Bihar, Orissa and Madhya Pradesh received a lower share. Further, with few exceptions, the PDS remained an untargeted programme (Radhakrishna, et al., 1997). In comparison with other anti-poverty programmes, PDS has been found to be the costliest (ibid). PDS has been found to deliver 100 kcal of nutrients at three times the cost under the direct nutrition programmes like Integrated Child Development Scheme (ICDS). In terms of cost of per rupee income transferred, PDS has also been found to be inferior to employment programmes.

Re-focusing of PDS should be a priority task. Welfare gains from food subsidy can be substantially enhanced by rationalizing minimum support prices scheme and improving the targeting efficiency of subsidized food distribution. If India sustains a growth rate higher than six per cent per annum and succeeds in maintaining food price stability, there may not be much need for subsidized grain distribution after 2010 other than for feeding the malnourished children, aged etc. and for food distribution in extreme scarcity situations in drought prone areas. However, fresh challenges to PDS may come from price volatility in the world market. Price stabilization will soon emerge as a major function of food management.

VII. Food Demand

The food demand will be driven by income and population growth, urbanization, food prices and income distribution. Food demand projections have been made using the piece-wise Linear Expansion System (LES) model developed at Centre for Economic and Social Studies (CESS), Hyderabad. The projections given below assume real expenditure growth of five per cent per annum between 2000 and 2020, increase of population to 1.343 billion in 2020, rate of urbanization and rural-urban disparity consistent with the historical trends and the inequality in the income distribution and relative prices same as in 1998. Under these assumptions, the demand is projected to grow at 2.2 per cent for cereals during 2000-10 and two per cent during 2010-20, three to four per cent for edible oils and pulses, and four to five per cent for milk and milk products, meat, fish, eggs, fruits, vegetables, sugar and gur.

At the current cereal intake of 143 kgs./per capital annum, cereal requirement for household consumption will be around 192 million tons in 2020. The requirement will be more if the increase in household demand due to income growth is also considered. At five per cent per annum growth in total expenditure, and population of 1.343 billion, household cereal demand works out to 221 million tons in 2020 and for foodgrains 241 million tons (Table 4). With a grossing factor of 1.14, the total (household plus non-household) demand for cereals may be around 253 million tons. The above cereal demand projections are made with the assumption of stability of tastes and preferences in food consumption. If the secular trend of food grain production, as witnessed during the last two decades is sustained, the production of additional 57 million tons of cereals and 76 million tons of total food grains in the coming two decades may not be out of reach for India. The demand projections may turn out to be on a higher side if the secular trend of change in consumer preferences away from cereal consumption persists. Demand for superior food items such as dairy and animal husbandry products, sugar, fruits and vegetables are expected to grow much faster during the coming decades. The estimated demand in 2020 for milk and milk products will be around 166 million tons, edible oils 11 million tons, meat, fish and eggs 11 million tons, sugar and gur 25 million tons and fruits and vegetables 113 million tons. However, there may be a significant growth of demand for feed grains as milk consumption is likely to increase at a high rate. The balance of 35 million tons over and above the direct household cereal consumption can absorb any reasonable increase in feed grain demand.

A major challenge to food security comes from dietary diversification of the poor. If cereal pricing is left to the market forces, government playing the facilitating role, land will be released from rice and wheat cultivation to meet the growing demand for non-cereal crops such as oilseeds, fruits and vegetables in accordance with diet diversification. This policy would facilitate agricultural diversification in tune with emerging demand patterns. Long term food security demands that research in production technology of non-cereal food as well as technology access to the poor small producers should be promoted. Improvement in the quality of food items and reduction in transaction costs associated with their market access need to be policy priorities.

Table 4

Projections of Households Food Demand-All India

(Million tons per annum)

	2010	2020
Rice	97.99	118.93
Wheat	72.07	92.37
Other Cereals	14.11	15.57
All Cereals	181.12	221.11
Pulses	14.58	19.53
Food grains	195.69	240.64
Milk & Milk Prod.	106.43	165.84
Edible Oils	7.67	10.94
Meat and Fish	7.25	10.80
Sugar & Gur	17.23	25.07
Fruits & Vegetables	75.21	113.17

VIII. WTO and Food Security

The Indian agricultural scene has witnessed changes following the economic reforms in the Nineties as well as with the establishment of World Trade Organisation (WTO) in the mid-Nineties. While the world trading environment has become more liberal, transparent and rule-bound than before, it would have become even more favourable had the developed countries adhered strictly to the Uruguay Round agreement and permitted better access to imports from developing countries.

India seems to be a victim of thirty years of agricultural policy with an exclusive focus on spreading HYV seed fertilizer technology in a few potential regions for achieving food self-sufficiency. Consequent to the adoption of this stategy, India achieved self-sufficiency in foodgrains by the mid-Seventies and is currently facing the problem of disposing off huge foodgrains stocks. It is observed that self-sufficiency in foodgrains is partly due to the weak purchasing power of the poor. As a remedial measure, it is suggested that India should diversify its agriculture and get a foothold in the world food market. The diversified and accelerated agricultural growth would enhance the food security by improving the purchasing power of the poor.

However, even after the establishment of WTO, the agricultural trade did not improve much during the transition period since agricultural prices have sharply declined in the world markets and there has been no reduction in the degree of protection by the developed countries. The protectionist measures are coming in the form of non-tariff measures and preventing the entry of agricultural commodities from developing countries by resorting to anti-dumping restrictions in one form or another. Some concessions under the Green and Blue Boxes do not favour developing countries. Some of these concerns should figure in future negotiations.

The deceleration in the agricultural growth during the Nineties is more due to internal factors such as decline in public investment in agriculture (irrigation and research), slow down in the growth in fertilizer consumption and slow rise in the expenditure on agricultural research and so on. It is argued that if India is to benefit from the emerging opportunities opened up by liberalized agricultural trade, major reforms have to be undertaken on the domestic front. It is recognized that cereal prices in the world market which have declined during the Nineties are unlikely to rise on account of reforms in the developed countries. Fresh challenges have also come from the sharp fall in the international price of some commercial crops. For instance, Kerala's agricultural economy has been severely affected by a dramatic drop in world prices which has led to greater transient poverty among its farming community. As domestic food economy gets integrated with the world market, it will experience price volatility.

India should depend on cost-reducing technology through domestic reforms, promote agricultural diversification and put pressure on the developed countries to open up their markets for value added agricultural products. While formulating an appropriate agricultural strategy some key issues of concern are[4]:

(a) How to utilise the emerging opportunities from liberalised trade for the diversification of economic activities in rural areas?

(b) What reforms are needed to improve the purchasing power of the poor?

(c) What type of safety nets are needed to protect the domestic food security from the fluctuations in international agricultural prices which are more volatile than domestic prices?

IX. Concluding Observations

While India achieved success in combating transient food insecurity caused by droughts or floods, it miserably failed to make much dent in chronic food insecurity as reflected in the low energy intake and high incidences of malnutrition. The overall improvement in nutritional status has also been very slow. There is a chronic under-nourishment in about half of the population, particularly among the vulnerable groups of children, women and elderly from the lower half of the expenditure class. Curiously, the proportion of consumption expenditure spent on food is slowly going down even in the households with chronic under-nourishment. Under nourishment in the bottom 30 per cent of the expenditure class is alarming. And even the middle 40 per cent is not free from it. The

---

4. C.H. Hanumantha Rao has suggested an agricultural strategy for accelerating agricultural growth in the changed context. See his presidential remarks in Krishna Rao (2000). See also Rao and Jeromi (2000).

mounting food stocks miserably failed to banish mass under-nourishment. While the current growth rate would significantly reduce income poverty by 2010, the chronic food insecurity is likely to persist. Moreover, with the recent shift to a more market-oriented and outward-looking macro-policies, the poor are likely to be exposed to the resultant risk of market uncertainties. As a result, several types of programmes need to be targeted exclusively to the poor aimed at: (i) eliminating transient food insecurity on account of inadequate access to food in periods of crises; (ii) reducing chronic food insecurity by enhancing their capabilities to participate in the growth process; (iii) reducing malnutrition among pre-school children and women; and (iv) improving basic services (safe drinking water, health care etc.) to the poor. The portfolio of poverty alleviation programmes (PAPs) should be contextual and suit the specific needs of the poor communities. Socially excluded groups are highly heterogeneous and, therefore, poverty reducing effects of any intervention based on a uniform package of programmes would be weak.

Improvement in food consumption is a necessary but not a sufficient condition for overcoming the problem of malnutrition in India. Apart from inadequate food consumption, the other important causes of malnutrition are high incidence of gastrointestinal and respiratory infections and behavioural factors such as faulty child feeding and weaning practices, all of which contribute to the low absorption of nutrients from the food consumed. Economic growth, left to itself, may not have a dramatic impact on nutritional status in the near future, although it provides greater opportunities for public intervention. Effective and efficient food and environmental interventions are needed, until all the citizens are adequately fed.

[This paper substantially draws on Rao and Radhakrishna (1997) and Radhakrishna (2002)]

References

Acharya, S.S. (1989), *Socio-economic Impact of 1987 Drought in Rajasthan*, Department of Agricultural Economics, Rajasthan Agricultural University, Jaipur.

Bhalla, G.S. and Gurmail Singh (2001), Indian Agriculture: Four Decades of Development, Sage Publications, N. Delhi.

Bhalla, G.S. (1994), "Policies for Food Security in India", in Bhalla, G.S. (ed.) *Economic Liberalisation and Indian Agriculture*, Institute for Studies in Industrial Development, New Delhi.

Bidinger, P.D., T.S. Walker, B. Sarkar, A. Ram Murthy and P. Babu (1990), *Economic, Health and Nutritional Consequences of the Mid-1980s Drought on a Tank Irrigated, Deccan Village in South India*, Resource Management Programme, Economics Group, Progress Report 98, ICRISAT, Hyderabad.

Gopalan, C. (1995), "Towards Food and Nutritional Security", *Economic and Political Weekly*, Vol. 30, No. 52, December 1995, pp. A-134-141.

Krishna Rao, Y.V. (ed.) (2000), *New Challenges Facing Indian Agriculture*, Visalaandhra Publishing House, Hyderabad.

Mortorell, R. and T.J. Ho (1984), "Malnutrition, Morbidity and Mortality", *Population and Development Review*, A Supplement to Vol. 10, pp. 49-68.

Meenakshi, J.V. (1996), "How Important are Changes in Taste? A State Level Analysis of Food Demand", *Economic and Political Weekly*, Vol. 31, No .50, December 14, pp. 3265-69.

Minhas, B.S. (1991), "On Estimating the Inadequacy of Energy Intakes: Revealed Food Consumption Behaviour Versus Nutritional Norms (Nutritional Status of Indian People in 1983)", *The Journal of Development Studies*, Vol. 28, No. 1, pp. 1-38.

Pelletier, D.L., E.A. Frongillo, Jr., D.G. Schroeder and J.P. Habicht (1995), "The Effects of Malnutrition on Child Mortality in Developing Countries", *Bulletin of the World Health Organisation*, Vol. 73, No. 4, pp. 443-448.

Radhakrishna, R. (1991), "Food and Nutrition: Challenges for Policy", *Journal of the Indian Society of Agricultural Statistics*, Vol. 43, No. 3, pp. 211-227.

Radhakrishna (2001), "Agricultural Growth, Employment and Poverty: A Policy Perspective", Presidential Address, 43rd Annual Conference of Indian Society of Labour Economics, December 18-21.

Radhakrishna (2002), "Food and Nutrition Security" in Kirit S. Parikh and R. Radhakrishnas (eds.) *India Development Report, 2002*, Oxford University Press.

———. and C. Ravi (1990), *Food Demand Projections for India*, Centre for Economic and Social Studies, Hyderabad.

———. (1992), "Effects of Growth, Relative Price and Preferences on Food and Nutrition", *Indian Economic Review*, Vol. 27, Special Number, pp. 303-323.

———. K. Subba Rao, Indrakant, S. and Ravi, C. (1997), *India's Public Distribution System: A National and International Perspective*, World Bank Discussion Paper No. 380.

Rao, C.H.H. and Radhakrishna, R. (1997), "National Food Security: A Policy Perspective for India", Plenary paper, 27th *International Conference of Agricultural Economists*, August 10-16, Sacramento, California and published in G.H. Peter and J.V. Braun (ed.) *Food Security, Diversification and Resource Management: Re-focussing the Role of Agriculture*, Ashgate, 1999.

Rao C.H.H. (2000), "Declining Demand for Foodgrains in Rural India: Census and Implications", *Economic and Political Weekly*, January 22.

Rao V.M. and Jeromi P.D. (2000), "Modernizing Indian Agriculture: Priority Tasks and Critical Policies" Study No.21, Department of Economic Analysis and Policy, Reserve Bank of India, Mumbai.

Ravi, C. (2000), *Complete Demand Systems, Welfare and Nutrition: An Analysis of Index Consumption Data,* Centre for Economic and Social Studies, Hyderabad.

Sekler, D. (1982), "Small but Healthy", in Sukhatme, P.V. (ed.).

Sukhatme, P.V. (1982), "Poverty and Malnutrition", in Sukhatme, P.V. (ed.), *Newer Concepts in Nutrition and Their Implications for Policy,* Maharashtra Association for the Cultivation of Science, Pune, pp. 11-64.

4

Employment in India: Vision 2020

SHAILENDRA SHARMA

A significant change in inequality in income and wealth is possible only in a longer term perspective. Employment structure of an economy is the normal instrument that can cause a change in inequality either way, i.e., an increase or a decrease in the inequality. Other economic instruments such as target group policies and programmes have a short term impact, but the redistribution through employment is sustainable. Since the governments function within the administrative and fiscal constraints, the target group programmes normally have a marginal impact on income redistribution. Income of labour enables flow of resources across income classes of people and across the social and ethnic groups. Flows of income across locations are influenced both by assets available and by other modes of creating employment opportunities. However, income generated by employment of migrant labour, facilitates flow of resources across regions for a given regional distribution of capital assets. Employment and equity of income across classes of people and across regions are, therefore, closely related to each other in the long term.

Current Employment and Unemployment Situation

As noted earlier, any vision of the future has to be rooted in the current reality and policies and processes have to be identified to bridge the gap between the current reality and the future vision. It is, therefore, essential to have an understanding of the broad employment picture as it exists today, which would also indicate the directions for improvement in future. Some aspects of the current employment scenario are listed below –

- 7.32 per cent of the labour force, in the year 1999-2000, was unemployed. In absolute terms the number of unemployed stood at 26.58 million.

- Since the above estimates are on Current Daily Status basis, the number of unemployed also includes the number of those who are underemployed in terms of underutilization of the labour time. But it excludes such underemployed who are working at very low levels of income and productivity.
- Among the employed, the proportion of poor is as high as in the population at large, suggesting a large proportion of workers engaged in subsistence employment.
- Only about eight per cent of the total employment is in organized sector. More than 90 per cent are engaged in informal sector activities, which is largely outside the reach of any social security benefits and also suffers from many handicaps in the form of limited access to institutional facilities and other support facilities.
- The educational and skill profile of the existing workforce is very poor.

Factors determining the Employment Situation in the Long Term

A. Supply of Labour

The factors which influence employment outcomes of an economy in the long term, operate both on the demand side of the labour as well as on the demand side. The supply side factors which need to be considered include the following:

A.1 Age structure of population.

A.2 The participation of population in labour force; and

A.3 Characteristics of labour force.

A.1 Age Structure of Population

The size of economically active population is determined by the age structure. Population growth will reduce from the current level (1991-2001) of 1.95 per cent per annum to about 1.25 per cent by 2020. Growth of population in the working age group (15 to 59) is at present around 2.4 per cent, substantially higher than growth of overall population. This will continue to be so for many years. Convergence between growth of population and that in the age group 15-59 years occurs around the year 2030.

Since labour force participation is not uniform across age groups, the size of labour force is influenced by age structure. Participation in labour force, i.e., the Labour Force Participation Rate (LFPR) is influenced by need to work versus other alternative uses of one's time. A unidirectional relationship between growth of population and labour force has not been observed in the past (Table 1).

Table 1

Growth of Population and Labour Force – 1972-73 to 1999-2000

(per cent per annum)

Period	*Rate of Growth of Population (UPSS)*	*Rate of Growth of Labour Force*
1972-73 to 1977-78	2.27	2.94
1977-78 to 1983	2.19	2.04
1983 to 1987-88	2.14	1.74
1987-88 to 1993-94 (1983 to 1993-94)	2.10 (2.12)	2.29 (2.05)
1993-94 to 1999-2000	1.93	1.03

The question is whether the observed deceleration in the labour force growth would continue into the future. It could be so if it has been caused by a structural change in the economy. Some decline in labour force growth could be due to a lower growth in population, which also implies a slower growth in working age population. However, the decline in labour force growth from 2.29 per cent per annum to 1.03 per cent between 1983/1993-94 and 1993-94/1999-2000 is too sharp to be explained by deceleration in population growth alone. Deceleration in population growth during this period has to be seen together with the decline in Labour Force Participation Rates (LFPRs) for a possible explanation.

A.2 Labour Force Participation

The decline in participation rates observed during 1993-94 to 1999-2000 needs to be carefully examined in terms of trends in different segments of the population and by different age groups and in a longer-term perspective. Participation rates thrown up by various rounds of National Sample Surveys during 1983 to 1993-94 are given in Annexure-1. It can be seen that the decline in participation rates across age groups, in most of the cases, either fit into a longer term trend or changes are not very significant. The decline in the LFPR in the younger age group reflects longer term trend of shift in activity status of this group towards education. This trend is likely to continue in future. Similarly, in the age group 60 and above the decline in the LFPR can be explained by increase in the share of more aged in the 60 and above population, where the LFPRs are expected to be low. In a few cases the declines are sharper and the reasons need to be looked into.

In this background, the future projections of labour force in relation to working age population have to be considered. The participation rates for younger age groups have dropped much more than other age groups (Table 2). In the 10-14 years age group, the decline will be to near zero in the next five to eight years as elementary education becomes compulsory.

Table 2

Labour Force Participation Rates for Rural Male in 1999-2000 relative to 1983.*

Age group	*LFPR 1999-2000* / *LFPR 1983*
10-14	0.389
15-19	0.809
20-24	0.972
25-29	0.999
All ages	0.985

*: UPSS Basis

A countervailing factor to prevail in the long run is the reduction in differentials between male and female labour force participation rates. In the past 17 years, female/male LFPR differential has increased. (Table 3) However, some increase of LFPR (Female) relative to LFPR (Male) was observed in the decade 1983 to 1993-94. In the States having high per capita income, the female/male LFPR ratio is higher. In the older age groups, the female to male LFPR differential is less than those in the younger (reproductive) age groups. During the next 20 years as the average age of female labour force increases, the female-male LFPR differential should reduce. It is also seen that as per capita income levels rise, the gap between male-female LFPRs reduces after touching a bottom level. That is when the excess supply of labour reduces and labour demand-supply gaps begin to emerge.

Table 3

*Ratio of Female to Male Labour Force Participation Rates**

Age Group	*Rural (R) / Urban (U)*	*1983*	*1993-94*	*1999-2000*
20 - 24	R	0.540	0.521	0.478
	U	0.267	0.280	0.253
24 - 29	R	0.556	0.539	0.511
	U	0.251	0.259	0.225
30 - 34	R	0.585	0.594	0.564
	U	0.271	0.288	0.250
40 – 44	R	0.622	0.614	0.596
	U	0.311	0.325	0.291
50 - 54	R	0.550	0.560	0.540
	U	0.286	0.304	0.281
All Age Groups	R	0.606	0.590	0.559
	U	0.289	0.303	0.271

*: Usual Status Basis

A.3 Labour Force Skills

Income of labour, i.e., its wage level is determined by productivity. Both the technology used (i.e. capital intensity) and the skill level of worker determine labour productivity.

Current State of Labour Force Skills[1]

It is not easy to quantify the level of skills in the labour force because data on skill levels are not readily available. What is available is information on the educational attainments of the labour force and the relevant data for 1999-2000 are summarized in Table 4. It is

1. This Section draws upon the Report of Task Force on Employment Opportunities, Planning Commission (2001)

evident that education levels in the labour force in India are very low. About 44.0 per cent of all workers in 1999-2000 were illiterate and another 22.7 per cent had schooling only up to the primary level. If we define the minimum level of education necessary to function in a modern economy as schooling up to the middle level, then only about 33.2 per cent of the labour force had schooling of that level and above. The percentage was higher at 57.4 per cent for the urban labour force, but it was correspondingly worse in rural areas, with only 25.4 per cent for the rural labour force meeting these standards.

Table 4

Composition of Workers of Age 15 Years and Above by Level of Education 1999-2000

(per cent)

	Not literate	Literate & schooling upto primary level	With schooling upto middle & higher level	Total	Share in Work Force
Rural Areas					
Male	39.6	27.3	33.1	100	49.74
Female	74.0	15.5	10.5	100	25.77
Person	51.3	23.3	25.4	100	75.51
Urban Areas					
Male	16.0	21.9	62.0	100	19.72
Female	43.9	17.6	38.5	100	4.76
Person	21.5	21.1	57.4	100	24.49
All Areas					
Male	32.9	25.8	41.3	100	69.46
Female	69.3	15.8	14.9	100	30.54
Person	44.0	22.7	33.2	100	100.00

Source: National Sample Survey on Employment & Unemployment, 55th Round.

A positive feature of the situation is that education levels will improve over time because the younger age groups are much better educated. Table 5 presents the educational attainment of youth (15-29) in labour force for the year 1999-2000 (and 1993-94). The percentage with middle school education or above in this age group for the country as a whole is 49.3 compared with 33.2 per cent for the total labour force. This percentage itself is increasing over time. It was 42.5 per cent in 1993-94 and has increased to 49.3 per cent in 1999-2000. There are of course sharp variations across gender and place of residence; for urban males it is as high as 72.1 (66.7 in 1993-94), whereas for rural females, it is as low as 29.0 (21.7 in 1993-94).

Table 5

Percentage of Persons in Labour Force Educated Middle and Above 1999-2000[a]

Sex	*Age Groups*	*Rural*	*Urban*	*All areas*
Male	15-29	50.9 (44.2)	72.1 (66.7)	56.4 (49.8)
	15-19	55.1 (49.5)	71.9 (67.4)	58.7 (52.1)
	20-24	53.8 (47.4)	73.8 (69.7)	59.2 (53.1)
	25-29	45.2 (36.6)	70.7 (63.5)	52.3 (44.0)
Female	15-29	29.0 (21.7)	62.5 (54.5)	33.5 (26.5)
	15-19	40.6 (30.6)	69.7 (63.6)	44.3 (34.7)
	20-24	28.9 (21.1)	64.6 (56.0)	33.9 (26.2)
	25-29	21.3 (14.2)	55.9 (47.0)	25.9 (19.6)
Persons	15-29	43.4 (36.6)	70.3 (64.1)	49.3 (42.5)
	15-19	50.2 (43.1)	71.4 (66.5)	54.2 (47.2)
	20-24	45.3 (38.0)	72.1 (66.7)	51.5 (44.3)
	25-29	36.7 (29.4)	68.0 (60.2)	44.1 (36.9)

Source : NSSO.

Note : NSS Reports on Employment/Unemployment Survey give (i) labour force participation by age groups and (ii) level of education of population by age group. However, the Reports do not give labour force participation rates by age groups cross-classified by level of education. Therefore, estimates presented in this table are based on the assumption that distribution of labour force, in an age group, by level of education, is the same as the distribution of population in that age group by level of education.

a : Figures in parenthesis are for the year 1993-94.

It should be noted however that the category "middle school and above" includes all those who have had some middle school education even though they may have dropped out before completing middle school. Provisional gross enrollment rates for the year 1998-99 in the primary and the middle school levels are 92 per cent and 58 per cent, respectively (Table 6). However, the provisional dropout rates at primary and middle levels are quite high at 42 per cent and 57 per cent, respectively, in the year 1998-99. According to a rough estimate from the 52nd round (1995-96) of National Sample Survey, around 44 per cent of the population (age group 14–16 years) was enrolled in the Class IX and X levels. However, only about 20 per cent of the population in this age group actually completes secondary school education. These figures indicates that significant deficiencies in the general education level of the labour force are likely to remain in the next ten to 15 years, though one can say from the past trends of increase in enrolment ratio and decrease in dropout ratio that the new entrants to the labour force will be significantly better educated than at present.

Table 6

Enrolment in Different Stages of Education as Per cent of Population in the Appropriate Age Groups 1961, 1981, 1990, & 1999

(per cent)

Education stage/ age group	*Enrolment as proportion of appropriate age group*			
	1961	*1981*	*1990*	*1999*
Primary classes(6-11 yrs.)	62.4	80.5	95.9	92.1
Middle classes(11-14 yrs.)	22.5	41.9	57.4	57.6
High/higher Secondary(14-17 yrs.)	10.6	17.3	24.0	N.A.

Source: Manpower profile of India, year book 2000 (IAMR); Table 2.1.2.0.

The statistics discussed above relates to general education, which is not the same thing as possession of "marketable skills". While some jobs in a modern economy, especially clerical office jobs, may not require anything more than specified levels of formal academic education, most other jobs require specific skills. The NSSO Survey on Employment and Unemployment (1993-94) sought information on the possession of 30 specific marketable skills by persons in the labour force and the results are summarized in Table 7. The skilled percentage of the work force is evidently very low. In the rural areas, only 10.1 per cent of the male workers and 6.3 per cent of female workers possessed specific marketable skills. The percentages were higher in urban areas, but they were still woefully low in absolute terms – only 19.6 per cent for male workers and 11.2 per cent for female workers.

Table 7

Percentage Distribution of Persons by possession of marketable skill: 1993-94[1]

Possessing	*Rural*		*Urban*	
	Male	*Female*	*Male*	*Female*
No Skill	89.9	93.7	80.4	88.8
Some Skill[2]	10.1	6.3	19.6	11.2
Total	100.0	100.0	100.0	100.0
Sample persons	(183464)	(172835)	(109067)	(99283)

Source: NSSO Report No. 409 on Results of 50th round (1993-94) survey on Employment and Unemployment.

Notes:

1.: Information for 1999-2000 not yet available, since the results released by NSSO for that year Employment Survey give the skill classification of Non Workers.

2.: Marketable skills that are reported by respondents are specified in Annexure 2.

The levels of vocational skills in the labour force in India compare poorly with the position in other countries. Annexure-3 shows the percentage of younger members of the labour force (age group 20-24), which have vocational training. Only 5 per cent of the Indian labour force in this age category has vocational skills whereas the percentage in industrial countries is much higher, varying between 60 per cent and 80 per cent, except for Italy, which is 44 per cent. The percentage for Korea, which has recently been categorised as an industrialised country, is exceptionally high at 96 per cent. The developing countries listed have percentages which are significantly lower than the developed countries, but they are still much higher than India e.g. Mexico at 28 per cent and Peru at 17 per cent. Differences in definition may make inter-country comparison somewhat unreliable, but the level in India is clearly far too low.[2]

2. One reason why the comparison may exaggerate the difference is because, as pointed out in the footnote to Table 6.4, it is based on those having received training in formal institution.

These figures reveal that education and skill levels of our labour force are relatively low compared with other fast growing developing countries. The system is also excessively oriented towards general academic education with little or no vocational orientation. The preference for general education is driven primarily by the perception that an academic degree is necessary to obtain a government job, which is highly valued because job security is virtually complete and pay scales are typically much above market wages. The net result is that the education system has neglected the need to provide vocational skills and to generate awareness and demand among students for acquiring marketable skills.

In the long term, a strategy to impart vocational skills will facilitate increase in income of labour. A massive expansion of training facilities is needed. As we shall see in later section, the occupational profile of workers will change at a rapid pace because the traditional avenues for work in agriculture are poised to alter substantially, as ability of this sector to absorb labour force will diminish at a fast pace. Greater emphasis on vocational training in relation to general education is required.

B. Demand for Labour

The preparation of a longer term vision for employment must take into consideration the developments taking place on the supply side of labour while planning for a strategy to absorb the annual additions to the labour force. The longer term vision, however, needs to look beyond mere absorption of the labour force in any activity irrespective of the quality of work that an activity can offer in terms of improving the living conditions of workers. The Report of the Special Group on Targeting 10 Million Employment Opportunities per year has established that with slightly altering the structure of growth in favour of labour intensive sectors, it is possible to achieve the overall balancing between the supply of labour and demand for labour even in a shorter term perspective. Also, the demand for labour thus generated will be of gainful nature in terms of ensuring availability of work on a regular basis. However, the larger question of improving the income and productivity levels of existing workers and those who are likely to enter the labour force within the perspective period can be squarely addressed only in a longer term perspective. This would call for concerted efforts on many fronts, some of which are discussed below.

B.1 Structure of Economy

Input of labour in production process depends upon technology used, and technology used varies across the industries. Traditional agriculture is more labour intensive than the modern manufacturing industries. With the modernization of economy, share of agriculture in workforce reduces due to two factors; food demand grows at a much slower pace at high levels of income, which moderates the demand for food-grains. Secondly, the technology used in agriculture, at higher yield levels is much less labour absorbing than traditional agriculture.

Agriculture absorbed 65 to 70 per cent of workforce between the years 1991 and 2001 as per demographic Census (Table 8). At all India level the proportion of workers getting work in agriculture came down by nine percentage points between 1991 and 2001. In some of the states the number of agricultural workers in 2001 is less than in 1991. These substantial shifts in ability of agriculture to absorb labour are also confirmed by the NSSO survey on Employment – 55th Round (1999-2000) (Table 9).

Table 8

Dependence on Agriculture for Work

(per cent)

	Cultivators among workers	*Agricultural Labour among workers*	*Cultivators & agricultural Labourers among workers*
	Proportion to main workers		
1971	42.9	26.9	69.8
1981	41.5	25.1	66.6
1991	38.4	26.4	64.8
	Proportion to total workers (main + marginal)		
1991	39.7	27.4	67.1
2001	31.7	26.7	58.4

Table 9

Employment growth – 1993-94–1999-2000 (UPSS & CDS basis)

Sector	% Change per annum in employment growth 1999-2000/1993-94	
	UPSS#	CDS*
Agriculture	-0.34	-0.12
Mining & Quarrying	-2.85	-2.55
Manufacturing	2.05	2.66
Electricity, Gas & Water Supply	-0.88	-3.43
Construction	7.09	5.22
Trade, Hotels and Restaurents	5.04	5.85
Transport Storage and Communication	6.04	5.61
Financing, Insurance, Real Estate and Business Services	6.20	5.62
Community, Social and Personnel Services	0.55	-2.0
All India Work Force	0.98	1.07
All India Labour force	1.07	1.31
Unemployment Rate (%) (1999-2000)	2.20	7.32

#: Based on Old Population Census and Technical Group.

*: Based on 2001 Population Census.

Source: Report of Special Group on Targeting 10 Million Employment Opportunities a Year in Tenth Plan; Planning Commission (2002).

Though, as noted above, the share of agriculture in the total employment has been declining over the years, the pace of this decline has been slower than the decline in the share of agriculture in the GDP. As a result, a clear divergence has emerged between the shares of primary, secondary and tertiary sectors in employment and output, suggesting thereby large intersectoral differences in the per worker productivity.

The secular decline in the importance of agriculture sector in the overall economic structure is a part of economic development. Work opportunities that are lost in traditional agriculture have to be replaced by work opportunities in some other sector. In the normal course it is the secondary sectors (manufacturing, electricity and construction) that grow much faster than agriculture during transition of an economy. However, in the post-reform period the growth of manufacturing industries has been constrained by competition from imports. Thus, in the medium term, the ability of manufacturing sector to replace the work opportunities lost in traditional agriculture is rather limited over the next five to ten years. However, there are immense possibilities for diversification in agricultural sector towards more value added activities such as food processing. This is an area, which has by and large remained unexploited, because reforms in agriculture sector having been very slow, resources have not yet started flowing into food processing industries. Involvement of state governments in implementing reforms in agriculture and food processing sectors is of crucial importance. Economic returns from states initiatives in transforming the rural economy from traditional agriculture to more value added activities in horticulture, etc., has been demonstrated well in some of the states, such as Maharashtra and Himachal Pradesh. Such diversification has immense potential for bridging some of the gaps in producitivity levels of workers in agriculture *vis à vis* other sectors.

Besides diversification of agriculture there is a strong need to restructure the rural economy by way of promotion of non farm activities in rural areas. Whatever non-farm activities are being carried out in the rural areas now are more out of a desperation to eke out a living rather than an informed choice of a vocation, backed by infrastructural and institutional facilities. A massive improvement in infrastructure is required to promote growth of rural industries on a sustainable basis. This will go a long way in generating good quality employment and meeting many of the consumption requirements of rural people. Many steps have been taken in regard to village connectivity, e.g., Prime Minister Gram Sarak Yojana (PMGSY) and telecommunication. But power sector reforms are urgently needed to set up modern processing facilities.

Another area requiring attention is tackling the bottlenecks in the availability of business services institutions – training, banking, insurance, storage facilities etc.

B.2 Formal and Informal Sector

In the current phase of economic reforms, a sharp deceleration in growth of organised sector has been observed. This has largely occurred because employment opportunities in public sector and Government have stagnated since 1994. (Table 10)

Table 10

Organised Sector Employment

Sector	Employment (Million)				Growth rate (% per annum)	
	1983	1988	1994	1999-00	1983-94	1994-2000
Organised Sector						
Employment	24.01	25.71	27.18	28.11	1.13	0.56
-Public Sector	16.46	18.32	19.30	19.41	1.46	0.10
-Private Sector	7.55	7.39	7.88	8.70	0.39	1.64

Note : 1. The Organised sector employment figures are as reported in the Employment Market Information System of Ministry of Labour and pertain to 1st March of 1983, 1988, 1994 and 1999.

A matter of great concern is that employment elasticity of organised sector has been very low at 0.066 during 1993-94 to 1999-2000, whereas it has been 0.213 for the unorganised sector (Annexure-4). Employment elasticity of private corporate sector at 0.133 is much less than that of the unorganised sector. On the basis of these trends, there could be hardly any replacement by the organised sector of the work opportunities that shrink in agriculture. Hence, there will be a fast growth of informal sector by influx from rural areas. These trends suggest two kinds of policy initiatives in regard to organised sector.

Firstly, we should promote use of labour intensive and capital saving technologies. And secondly, the way the "organised sector" is defined at present, needs a review. One definition of organised sector is based on its capital intensity, i.e., the technology used. Other definition of organised sector is in terms of employment – the terms of contract between the employer and employee. At present the terms of employment are seen to be rigid by the organised sector, with the result that though organised sector needs and uses a lot of labour input, it does not show up in jobs created. Similar tendencies have forced the capital intensity to increase even in the small-scale sector. One of the suggestions has been that, if employment is the social purpose of a small-scale policy or small and medium enterprise policy then the policy should be designed in terms of jobs created rather than investments made.

The growth of formal sector (i.e., organised sector) has to be based on private sector in future. In some of the states, share of private sector jobs in organised sector has increased. (Table 11)

Table 11

Share of Private Sector in Total Organised Jobs

(per cent)

Selected States	*1987*	*1999*	*Organised Jobs in Pvt. Sector 1999- '000 Nos.*
Private Sector Share Rising			
Andhra Pradesh	21.47	26.70	549.9
Gujarat	43.01	46.33	819.8
Haryana	33.57	35.36	234.2
Himachal Pradesh	7.56	14.82	44.2
Karnataka	28.32	40.94	576.9
Madhya Pradesh	14.08	14.80	239.1
Maharashtra	38.23	39.49	1504.8
Punjab	26.83	29.42	251.2
Rajasthan	18.67	20.62	263.6
Tamil Nadu	31.67	35.98	916.0
Uttar Pradesh	20.28	20.44	528.9
Private Sector Share Falling			
Assam	52.15	49.20	515.5
Bihar	16.25	15.73	254.1
Kerala	47.12	46.68	564.7
Orissa	14.02	11.59	94.8
West Bengal	36.59	34.63	810.9
All India	**29.00**	**30.94**	**8698.2**

These states have been able to attract investment for private corporate sector; whereas Bihar, Kerala, Orissa and West Bengal have had not been successful in this way.

In so far as employment is concerned, the term organised sector has at present a narrow coverage. It so happens because the labour regulations and credit policy are not designed to be sensitive to the requirements of smaller establishments. If this were possible, an increase in the share of organized sector would be a desirable objective to be pursued in a longer term perspective as steps to improve quality of employment are more feasible to be taken in a structured environment of exchange of labour services, than under purely informal conditions (conditions in this sector are better and it also offers workers in its fold the advantages of a fairly comprehensive social security).

However, there are two factors which would severely affect the prospects of organised sectoras it is presently defined, emerging as a major employer even in a 20 years perspective. Firstly, the base of the sector is very small and therefore the overall impact of even a very fast growth of employment in this sectors will be only marginal. Secondly, within the organized sector, the employment growth potential in the public sector, which accounts for approximately 70 per cent of the total organized employment, is very limited. The above two factors coupled with the declining employment elasticity in the sector preclude emergence of this sector as a major job provider in the near future.

In this scenario, the predominance of informal sector, including agriculture, is likely to continue and, therefore, the concerns of the smaller establishments (informal sector) which are crucial to its growth and also of the workers, which is today a vulnerable lot, need to be attended to. Marginal improvement in the tools used by the artisans, access to institutional credit, some amount of skill orientation and the general information about the availability of markets for different products will improve the performance of the sector as well as help the individual workers immensely.

The reach of the social security benefits are largely restricted to the workers in the formal or the organized sector barring a few attempts to reach the informal sector workers through welfare boards. A large proportion of the workers is still left out of any system of social security. There is a need to earnestly address to the welfare needs of the workers in the informal sector. This does not necessarily require bringing the sector under the purview of labour laws. Introduction of labour laws might kill the greatest advantage that this sector has in terms of flexibility in operation, through rigidities which are generally inherent in application of such laws. This also can not be done on the basis of an employer-employee relationship, as in the organized sector, because majority of the workers in informal sector are self employed. Only through a participatory approach between the governments and the workers can emerge a sustainable system of social security for informal sector workers.

B.3 Labour Laws

The existing labour laws framework does not encourage growth of labour intensive sectors as matter of design. These laws need to be reviewed in such a manner that it introduces an element of incentive for greater labour absorption.

A holisitic review of the labour laws is under consideration at various foras. The guiding principle of any such review has to be encouraging faster absorption of labour, without sacrificing the core welfare concerns of labour.

C. Patterns of Labour Migration

Depending upon the stage of demographic transition a state has achieved and also on the likely growth pattern, the experience of different states in terms of labour force growth and employment generation is likely to be varied. This would have implications for the interstate variations in the incidence of unemployment and also on the migration of labour in search of work.

A typology of states based on growth of labour force and changes in employment rate shows that in states of Andhra Pradesh, Gujarat, Haryana, Karnataka, Maharashtra, Tamil Nadu and West Bengal, the labour force growth will be falling and unemployment rate will also fall, given the employment-GDP elasticity in these states. However, in the states of Bihar, Rajasthan and Uttar Pradesh, not only the unemployment rate will be rising but growth of labour force will also be accelerating. (Table 12) These patterns suggest the states of origin and destination states of migrant labour.

Migration will increase in the long terms, as the work opportunities in traditional agriculture shrink. Normally, the migrants are at the receiving end in the destination states because they have little political voice. However, better skilled migrants have better income levels and can thereby adjust better. Migrants' jobs are hardly ever single employer ones. They frequently change the employers and alternate between the wage employed and self employed status. In this long-term perspective, a social security system for unorganised workers that is designed for such transient employment categories will have to be developed.

Table 12

Changes in Unemployment and in Labour Force in post-Ninth Plan Quinquennium (2002-07)

*Unemployment rate in post Ninth Plan period (2002-07)**	*Labour Force Growth in post Ninth Plan Period (2002-07) compared to Ninth Plan (1997-2002)*	
	Accelerating	*Decelerating*
Increasing	Bihar, Rajasthan, Uttar Pradesh	Kerala, Punjab
Decreasing	Assam, Madhya Pradesh, Orissa	Andhra Pradesh, Gujarat, Haryana, Karnataka, Maharashtra, Tamil Nadu, West Bengal

Note: * Direction of change in unemployment in States was indicated under the assumption that the growth of employment in 2002-07 is the same as in Ninth Plan.

Source: Ninth Plan, Volume I, Employment Perspective.

Summing up

It is not appropriate to project GDP growth and employment elasticities over a long period of 25 years. The scenario of employment in 2020 will develop based on certain underlying trends in regard to factors which prevail in the longer term. Though the growth of labour force will slow down, but the elasticity of employment will also fall, which means that pressure on labour market will not ease. As agricultural work opportunities continue to shrink, the informal sector will grow rapidly. To cope up with such expected trends, strategies are needed to promote labour intensive and capital saving technologies. Employment creation in small establishments will have to be promoted by incentives linked with jobs created rather than capital invested. Migrant labour will increase social pressures. A strategy to raise the wage levels of those who migrate will have to be based on a massive programme for development of vocational skills. A simple but broad based social security system will have to be developed to improve quality of employment in a scenario where migrant workers will be rapidly growing. Such a social security system coupled with better labour incomes, based on better productivity of trained manpower, will facilitate the conversion of emerging work opportunities into meaningful jobs, where chances of extreme exploitation of labour get eliminated.

ANNEXURE 1

Labour Force Participation Rates by Sex and Age, 1983 to 1999-00

Age Group	*Rural Male*				*Rural Female*			
	1983	*1987-88*	*1993-94*	*1999-00*	*1983*	*1987-88*	*1993-94*	*1999-00*
5-9	25	23	11	7	23	24	14	7
10-14	239	193	139	93	225	183	142	96
15-19	658	630	598	532	442	415	371	314
20-24	915	918	902	889	494	484	470	425
25-29	976	981	980	975	543	539	528	498
30-34	986	990	988	987	577	588	587	557
35-39	988	991	992	986	607	608	610	579
40-44	981	984	989	984	611	620	607	586
45-49	978	982	984	980	589	590	594	566
50-54	957	962	970	953	526	530	543	515
55-59	920	929	941	930	476	463	468	450
60+	660	670	699	640	227	220	241	218
All Ages	548	549	561	540	332	331	331	302
	Urban Male				*Urban Female*			
	1983	*1987-88*	*1993-94*	*1999-00*	*1983*	*1987-88*	*1993-94*	*1999-00*
5-9	7	5	4	3	7	3	4	2
10-14	114	92	71	52	65	66	47	37
15-19	472	429	404	366	164	169	142	121
20-24	816	792	772	755	218	225	230	191
25-29	965	967	958	951	242	244	248	214
30-34	985	985	983	980	267	282	283	245
35-39	987	989	990	986	292	313	304	289
40-44	982	986	984	980	305	311	320	285
45-49	977	977	976	974	284	307	317	269
50-54	943	944	945	939	270	269	287	264
55-59	843	849	856	811	230	235	225	208
60+	509	482	443	402	124	123	114	94
All Ages	536	534	542	542	155	162	164	147

Note: On Usual Status Basis

ANNEXURE 2

Profile of Persons having some Marketable Skill by type of Skill Possessed – 1993-94

Skill	*Code*	*Rural Male*	*Rural Female*	*Urban Male*	*Urban Female*
Typist/Stenographer	01	3	2	14	10
Fishermen	02	5	-	2	-
Miner, Quarryman	03	2	-	1	-
Spinner including Charkha operator	04	1	3	2	3
Weaver	05	6	10	11	8
Tailor cutter	06	6	18	15	54
Shoemaker, cobbler	07	1	-	2	-
Carpenter	08	6	-	8	-
Mason, bricklayer	09	5	-	9	-
Moulder	10	-	-	1	-
Machine man	11	2	-	8	-
Fitter die maker	12	1	-	6	-
Welder	13	1	-	4	-
Blacksmith	14	2	-	2	-
Goldsmith	15	1	-	4	-
Silversmith	16	-	-	1	-
Electrician	17	2	-	8	-
Repairer of electronic goods	18	1	-	5	-
Motor vehicle driver, tractor driver	19	11	-	27	1
Boatman	20	-	-	-	-
Potter	21	2	1	1	-
Nurse midwife	22	-	-	-	2
Basket maker, wicker product maker	23	3	4	1	1
Toy maker	24	-	-	-	-
Brick maker, tile maker	25	2	1	-	-
Bidi maker	26	3	7	-	7
Bookbinder	27	-	-	2	-
Barber	28	3	-	3	-
Mud house builder & thatcher	29	9	1	1	1
Others	30	24	15	57	21
Any skill possessed (Sub-total 01-30)		**101**	**63**	**196**	**112**
No skill possessed		**899**	**937**	**804**	**888**
Total		**1000**	**1000**	**1000**	**1000**

Source: NSSO Report No. 409 on Results of 50th round (1993-94) survey on Employment and Unemployment.

ANNEXURE 3

Proportion Vocationally Trained among the Youth in Labour Force-International Comparison[2]

Country	*Age Group*	*Vocationally trained (per cent of those in labour force).*
India	**20-24**	**5.06@**
Developing Countries		
Botswana	20-24	22.42
Colombia (1998)	20-29	28.06
Mauritius (1995)	20-24	36.08
Mexico (1998)	20-24	27.58
Developed Countries		
Australia (1998)	20-24	64.11
Canada (1998)	20-24	78.11
France (1997)	20-24	68.57
Germany (1998)	20-24	75.33
Israel (1998)	18-24	81.23
Italy (1997)	20-24	43.88
Japan (1997)	15-24	80.39
Korea Republic (1998)	20-24	95.86
New Zealand (1997)	20-24	63.03
Russian Federation (1998)	20-24	86.89
Singapore (1998)	20-24	66.24
United Kingdom (1998)	20-24	68.46

Note:

1. Vocationally trained persons are defined here as those having education level three or five as per ISCED clarifications which classifies the population across age groups & levels of education starting with level X, i.e., no education and the highest level being level 7 which post graduate level specialisation in a field. Levels 4 & 8 are not used. Level 3 of education: General education continues to be an important constituent of the programmes, but separate subject presentation and more specialisation are found at this level. Also to be classified under Level 3 are programmes consisting of subject matter mainly with a specific vocational emphasis of apprenticeship programmes, with an entrance requirement of eight full years of education, or a combination of basic education and vocational experience that demonstrates the ability to handle the subject matter of that level. Level 5 of education: Programmes of this type are usually "practical" in orientation in that they are designed to prepare students for particular vocational fields in which they can qualify as high level technicians, teachers, nurses, production supervisors etc. It may be noted however that in developing countries, economically productive skills are acquired not only in training/education institution but also through the family. Only the formal institute/school vocationally trained are shown above.
2. Only those who have received formal vocational training are shown as trained in this Table. To the extent that training and skills in India are acquired through informal methods, including training in the family, the Indian figures are understated.

@. Estimates are based on (NSSO Report No.409 on Results of 50th round (1993-94) survey on Employment and Unemployment; Table 20) distribution of persons by technical education in India adjusted by labour force participation rate by sex. The corresponding percentages by sex and residence are rural female 1.7, rural male 2.3, urban male 9.4, and urban female 17.0.

ANNEXURE 4

Output, Employment & Productivity of Organised, Unorganised and Public Sector

(Employment in million #GDP in crores at 1993-94 prices)

	Organised			*Un-Organised*	*Grand Total*	*% composition*		*Public Sector (a)*	*Private Organised (b)*
	Total	*Public*	*Private*			*Organised (a+b)*	*Un-Organised*		
Value added (GDP) (NET)									
1993-94	256849	180843	76006	441143	697992	36.80	63.20	25.9	10.89
1999-2000	418920	266519	152401	600425	1019345	41.10	58.9	26.1	15.0
Growth in per cent	8.50	6.68	12.30	5.27	6.52				
Employment									
1993-94	27.18	19.3	7.88	288.66	315.84	8.61	91.39	6.1	2.51
1999-2000	28.11	19.42	8.69	308.64	336.75	8.34	91.66	5.8	2.54
Growth in per cent	0.56	0.10	1.64	1.12	1.074				
Employment Elasticity	0.066	0.015	0.133	0.213	0.165				
Labour Productivity growth per annum (%) (1993-94 to 1999-2000)	7.88	6.67	8.38	4.10	5.38				
Relative Labour Intensity organised/unorg.(1999-2000)	0.1305								

#: Person years.

Source: Derived from Report of Special Group on Targetting Ten Million Employment Opportunities a year in the Tenth Five Year Plan; Planning Commission, (2002).

Notes:
1. For organised employment, classified by DGE&T, reported in the Economic Survey of Government of India.
2. Organised sector GDP is as classified by CSO.
3. Unorganised sector is by residual.
4. The classifications of the economy by value added and employment are not strictly comparable. But even with reasonable margin of error, the dimensional differences in the features of the two sectors – organised and unorganised – are so significantly large as to give enough confidence about the robustness of the findings of this Table.

References

Gupta, S.P. (2002), Report of Special Group on "Targeting Ten Million Employment Opportunities a Year in the Tenth Plan period", chaired by Dr. S.P. Gupta, Member; Planning Commission, Government of India.

Government of India. (1999), Ninth Five Year Plan; Planning Commission, Government of India.

———. (2001), Task Force on "Employment Opportunities", Planning Commission, Government of India.

———. (2001), Approach Paper to the Tenth Five Year Plan, Planning Commission, Government of India.

5

Education: Vision 2020

J. S. RAJPUT

SECTION 1

Vision building is a challenging exercise as it aims to construct future scenarios and link the present with the future. It is true that without vision, cultures, communities and civilisations perish. The exercise of vision building can neither be done by only re-structuring the present realities nor by sheer dreaming. Vision, dreams and future expectations must merge into contemporary realities. Visions can be realised and transformed into realities by understanding, initiative, commitment and hard work and dreams can be transformed into realities if full trust is put in self, society and the nature. Envisioning is a part of an individual's planning activities as also that of a nation. Nations, big or small, developed or developing, all conceive and construct future visions and prepare strategies to achieve them.

Vision is not to be seen either as a long term planning exercise or as a road map. In both these cases there is something given, something existing which forms the base. On the other hand, future

---

Prompted by the Prime Minister's vision for India's development as Knowledge Society, the Planning Commission constituted a Vision 2020 Group to look into the various parameters of knowledge society which relate to knowledge as a base to create values to be shared through global networking. NCERT was assigned the task to develop the educational aspect of Vision 2020.

The paper defines Knowledge Society as a society where caring, sharing and using knowledge are key factors promoting prosperity and well being of the people.

The paper has three sections, the first relates to Knowledge Society and its various parameters, the second looks at knowledge *per se* from Indian point of view and the third section presents Vision Statement, specific themes and strategies to achieve educational vision.

The author is greatly obliged to various insights he received from members of the group specially Shri K.C. Pant, Vice Chairperson, Planning Commission and Bharat Ratna Dr. Abdul Kalaam.

aspiration generates vision and that stirs us to action. Through the eye of creative imagination, the vision builder develops a constructive picture about the present. Unlike activities involved in annual planning, wherein the present shapes the future, the activities in vision building are guided by the future to shape the present. Thus, the construction of vision is a type of dreaming rooted in the contemporary contextual social realities. With respect to education, this exercise is being attempted here under three sections, the first relates to knowledge society which for, our purpose means a society where caring, sharing and using of knowledge are key factors promoting prosperity and well being of the people, the second section relates to knowledge as seen from the institution perspective and the third presents vision statement themes and strategies to achieve them.

In the last decade India has seen a revolution in knowledge and information sectors. It has gained a special position in the comity of information communication technology oriented nations. It would thus be advisable to give some space here to the term "knowledge society".

The term 'Knowledge Society', 'Information Society' and 'Learning Society' have now become familiar expressions in the educational parlance, communicating emerging global trends with far-reaching implications for growth and development of any society. These are not to be seen as mere cliché or fads but words that are pregnant with unimaginable potentialities. Information revolution, information technologies and knowledge industries, constitute important dimensions of an information society and contribute effectively to the growth of a knowledge society.

The term "Knowledge Industry" was coined by Princeton Economist Friz Machlup in his book, 'Production and distribution of Knowledge' in 1962. The term 'knowledge society' has been used by Peter F. Drucker (1971) in his book 'The Age of Discontinuity'. The term 'Learning Society' was used by Torsten Husen in 1974 and Hutchins (1970), the genesis of which lies in the concept of life long or continuous learning, which was later on stressed in UNESCO reports of 1972 and 1996. The concept of global village has its genesis in the concept information society, "information revolution" and communication technologies. The world has shrunk into a small village due to the emergence of information and communication technologies. Alvin Toffler (1980) has advanced the idea that power at the dawn of civilization resided in the 'muscle'. Power then got associated with money and in 20th century it shifted its focus to 'mind'. Thus the shift from physical power to wealth power to mind power is an evolution in the shifting foundations of economy. This shift supports the observation of Francis Bacon who said 'knowledge itself is power'; stressing the same point and upholding the supremacy of mind power, in his characteristic expression, Winston Churchill said, "the Empires of the future shall be empires of the mind". Thus, he corroborated Bacon and professed the emergence of the knowledge society.

Information and Knowledge Revolution

In the last fifty years, information and knowledge revolution has become a reality. With the advent of satellites, televisions and computers, there is a great flow of information and knowledge. Boundaries between many disciplines are blurring. New disciplines have emerged. There are institutions which evaluate and undertake research on various aspects of knowledge and information. Knowledge and information are imported and exported. There is a constant sharing of knowledge going among institutions and individuals. Institutions have become information and knowledge-oriented institutions. Even daily newspapers have become knowledge papers.

With the advent of knowledge industry, the epistemology of knowledge has also undergone change. Theory of chaos, fuzzy logic and theories of probability have become important. New sciences like Neuro-biology are emphasizing on mind-body symbiosis.

Knowledge workers play a crucial part in the knowledge industry where knowledge is produced, transmitted and consumed. There is also networking of knowledge workers and of knowledge institutions.

The management system of knowledge industry has to be closely re-looked into. Effective and efficient ways to manage knowledge workers are to be evolved. Obviously, the traditional, administrative and bureaucratic approach will not be adequate with respect to management of knowledge workers. Universities, colleges, schools, institutions of professional learning are all crying for a new management system that would be dynamic and responsive.

There are places where knowledge is produced. Sufficient resources have to be made available to these centres. The processes and procedures which govern knowledge institutions, are to be made more innovative, creative, flexible and responsive. Faculty members of world-class competence have to be nurtured and recruited, retrained and retained to ensure maintenance of levels, standards and dynamism. A constant research and review activity has to go into the various aspects of knowledge projects.

Responsive and effective distribution systems are an essential pre-requisite in a knowledge industry. These often are weak. Within the knowledge distribution systems there are leakages. There are information rich and information poor societies and there is a skewed distribution of knowledge. Yet an average person today has more knowledge than his counterpart had a hundred years ago. An average patient today has more medical knowledge, an average individual has more legal knowledge and an employee has more managerial knowledge than his counterpart had say 50 years ago. Thus in the knowledge revolution, knowledge has not remained the monopoly of a few. And yet the distribution system has gaps and leaks and presents a skewed picture.

Knowledge or information revolutions have become a reality because of some outstanding breakthroughs in the human history. Some of them occurred when:

- Alphabets were created
- Paper was invented
- Zero was discovered
- Decimal system was invented
- Printing press was invented
- Telegraph and radio were invented
- Telephone, television, fax machines and Xerox were invented
- Computers and internet were invented and
- Satellites were put into orbit and telecommunication became a common experience.

These breakthroughs have resulted in the present information and knowledge revolution. Fruits of knowledge revolution are available but there is mal-distribution. This has contributed to development of islands of prosperity and continents of ignorance, poverty, illiteracy, over-population, backwardness and poor health. If knowledge industry and knowledge society is to develop properly then information has to be structured in such a way that it fulfils some basic conditions of inter-activity, mobility, convertibility, connectivity, ubiquity and globalization, as given by Toffler (1990).

Distances have shrunk in time and inter-activity is instantaneous. Inter-activity results when the sender and the receiver both interact and when electronic messages of one medium interact with messages of another medium. Video conferencing is one such example.

Another feature of the knowledge society is mobility in the information technologies. Mobile phones and lap top computers are examples which have made mobility a positive attribute of communication revolution. Another feature of information revolution is convertibility. With appropriate machines, messages of one medium can be transferred on to another, for example, films can be transferred on to video. Connectivity is another important feature of information revolution where different devices are connected with one another. Multimedia is an example of connectivity where audio, video, text and graphics are combined to produce information. Now the computers can be connected with audio and video by attaching audio CD or video CD players to them. Presentation of computers can be displayed on screen, thus connecting it with the functions of OHP. Ubiquity means the way in which various messages are made available everywhere to different economical layers of the society. During the Iraq war the messages were available in metropolitan cities, state capitals, district headquarters and even in small villages where antenna discs were available. The future of economy, stability and development of any country would depend upon how wisely it masters information and knowledge technologies.

The first important fact is to ensure that knowledge does not remain a prerogative of a few but is accessed by a large number of persons. The second important thing is to create facilities for accessing knowledge. The third important thing is to set up national and international knowledge corporations which will use knowledge, both as raw material as well as the product. Knowledge networks also need to be built between the main land and Indian diaspora. With knowledge industry, internal threats and external intervention will increase. The main question is how rationale, intellectual, emotional, aesthetic and spiritual knowledge can increase our happiness, harmony, peace, justice and a sense of proportion.

In a knowledge society, one has to guard against cultural colonization. Globalization will have a direct impact on culture. One has to make distinction between knowledge society and consuming society. Consuming society will have different keynote and ideological images and may lead to cut throat competition.

A system's approach should be followed in a knowledge society with respect to hardware, software, maintenance and management. Each situation should be examined on the basis of its inherent Strength, Weakness, Opportunities and Threat (SWOT). The critical points that need attention is the management of knowledge workers and knowledge institutions.

The economic, social, cultural and technological changes in the national and international scene contribute to the knowledge society. The present rate of economic growth can be substantially increased if India becomes super power in knowledge sector and if information and technology revolutions are properly understood and exploited. India can substantially eliminate poverty, generate wealth and can play a meaningful role in the international world order. Thus, keeping in view the emergence of knowledge society we briefly present below, the existing educational scenario.

Education as an Engine of Development

Education is an important input both for the growth of the society as well as for the individual. Properly planned educational input can contribute to increase in the Gross National Products, cultural richness, build positive attitude towards technology and increase efficiency and effectiveness of the governance. Education opens new horizons for an individual, provides new aspirations and develops new values. It strengthens competencies and develops commitment. Education generates in an individual a critical outlook on social and political realities and sharpens the ability to self-examination, self-monitoring and self-criticism.

During the last five decades we have gained valuable experiences in all spheres and stages of education in the country. The expectations from education perceived by learners, communities and people are being understood better. The potentialities for future growth are also before us. The expectations and the chance of their being achieved are separated by a wide gap of resource crunch, credibility of institutions, levels of commitment, efficacy of functioning and several others. Any vision of education 2020 would have to take these into consideration. The success of the 'vision' would depend upon the extent to which it would be realised in actual practice. Essentially, one could visualise dreams which would be converted into reality through diligence, commitment and comprehensive action oriented strategies.

Contrary to the expectations from education at the time of independence, gaps in education in the context of have and have-nots are increasing. The thin line separating privatisation and commercialisation is getting blurred. Merit alone no longer remains the criteria for moving upwards in education. There is a visible loss of credibility of existing systems of imparting education in schools and also in institutions of higher learning. On one hand we are short of basic infrastructures and on the other, optimum utilisation of existing infrastructures has not been ensured.

Mere appreciation of creating a knowledge society and knowledgeable people is not sufficient. The message must reach each individual that these are times when every nation needs to move towards a learning society and knowledge society. People in India are better equipped to understand and appreciate it. They are familiar with traditional systems of creating, generating, transferring knowledge and the in-built respect in the society for the learned and the knowledgeable. These could become the cornerstones in moving ahead in building a Vision 2020.

Specific approach should be necessary to ensure extended outreach of scientific and technological literacy to every category of people. It would become an essential component of school education on one hand and that of the adult education initiatives on the other. The curricula have to be regularly reviewed and revised. Obsolescent must be discarded and new areas introduced without delay. Lack of attention to this aspect has resulted in avoidable curriculum load on young learners.

Education system of the country is already being influenced by international trends and scenarios. During the last couple of years, provision for admission to NRIs in various professional and academic courses have been made. A large number of foreign universities are opening avenues to young persons in India to get their degrees without leaving the country. There are trends to liberalise university systems which would permit more and more private universities. However, the impact on university education could become more evident in a couple of years. The nature of programmes to be offered by universities and institutions will continuously undergo drastic changes and transformation. Acquisition of mastery level skills and competencies would be the demand. Degrees may not retain their importance in relation to jobs.

Greater attention would be paid to understand and analyze learner interests, learning needs and learning choices. Specific learning needs shall have to be responded at each stage of education at secondary and university levels. Cafeteria approach in the choice and selection of areas to be studied will become a common practice. Evaluation systems of the present will be discarded. Focus would shift more to accreditation and certification. These will have to be made available at the choice and convenience of the learner. Towards this, an active interface of the formal education system with open learning and distance education shall have to be concretised. The Constitutional amendments leading to Panchayat Raj Act is one of the critical decisions which will have impact on the entire educational process in terms of its system, management, content, utility and credibility. It would ensure community accountability and responsibility coupled with necessary power and authority.

Education of the children will have to be examined in their specific contexts. The learning needs of the children in slums, in rural areas and in urban area would have to be met with strategies that would be appropriate to the situation and as such would differ vastly and widely. Issues of equity and equality would become very prominent. In a learning society none would tolerate being ignored or deprived of their right to a fair chance and equality of opportunities. The competition shall have to be transparent and honest. Favourtism, nepotism, corruption and other such practices, having reached their nadir, shall be resisted vehemently and violently.

The content of education shall no longer be determined centrally. There would be greater pressures from various sectors to develop content, learning and materials that would meet their requirements and needs. Issues which are emerging fast as areas of concern like energy, environment, pollution, land degradation, drinking water, health and sanitation, drugs and drinking, HIV/AIDS, malnutrition, mental and physical stresses emerging out of life styles and others would have to find appropriate response in the process of learning and skill development.

Regeneration of Indian economy shall continue to be highly dependent on re-generation of rural economy. This in turn would depend on achievement of universal elementary education and simultaneously on the quality of elementary education being imparted. The acquisition of skills during the first eight years in school shall become very important and relevant when this aspect is considered suitably. While focus on vocational education at secondary stage would gain strength, skill development in the earlier years would no longer remain neglected.

At present India has achieved a literacy rate of 64 per cent but still the gross number of illiterates is the largest in the world. India has the third largest scientific and technological manpower of the world but it has also a high drop-out rate, only two out of 10 students reach the 9th standards. India has institutions like Indian Institute of Technology, Indian Institute of Management and several schools that can be compared with the best of the institutions in the world. It also has institutions where required infrastructure facilities are awefully lacking. There is a great disparity of educational achievements between good public schools and government-run institutions in rural and slum metropolitan areas.

There is a great pressure on educational system and it seems the existing system as such cannot bear the burden of pupils' pressure. There are examples of excellent dedicated teachers but there are many teachers who would rate poorly on competency, commitment and performance. Although Panchayat Raj Amendment Act provides decentralisation and flexibility, there are also entrenched trends of bureaucratization and centralization.

Changes in the society are coming thick and fast. The changes are explicit in the sectors of economy and technology. They call for new shape of schools, new learner profile, teacher profile, and administrator's profile. More attention has to be given now to excellence, quality and efficiency so that peace and harmony in the society can be maintained. Acceptance and appreciation for diversity and pluralism is inevitable.

The future agenda for education will be to empower individuals, assure high quality of life and pave way to learning society. The new system of education has to be rooted to culture and committed to progress.

For taking India in the midst of knowledge society and for ensuring India becoming knowledge super power we propose an Education Vision for 2020 but before that we will like to see how knowledge has been perceived in the Indian context.

SECTION 2

Knowledge: The Indian Perspective

The term "knowledge Society" cannot be accurately translated into Indian language with its nuance intact and at the same time, one cannot conceive of a society without knowledge. The emergence of any society has always been through knowledge. In the context of the term as used now a days, knowledge society (Venkatasubramanian, 2000) means "creating, sharing and using knowledge as the key factor in bringing about prosperity and well being of people."

The Sanskrit word for knowledge is *'gyan'*. In day-to-day language we also use words like 'education' or *'taleem'* or *'elm'*. Though these words differ with one another, there is a lot which is common amongst them. If one looks at the word *'gyan'* one sees it has semantic relationship with *'shiksha'* and *'vidya'*. *'Shiksha'*, as defined in *Upanishads,* is basically related to language, its use, articulation, its pronunciation, stress intonation, modulation etc.

The acquisition of knowledge is explained on the basis of two theories, one presumes that knowledge exists outside the learner and the teacher has to teach and provide that knowledge. The other explanation is that, knowledge resides within the learner and the teacher has to remove the learner's ignorance so that the learner can see his own knowledge and acquire it by self efforts. Indian perspective, supports and stresses the latter concept which represents constructivistic aspect of knowledge.

Various metaphors have been used in education to convey its essence. Education has been equated to activities undertaken by a gardener, i.e., looking after and developing young saplings. It has also been equated with banking, i.e., depositing knowledge in the mind of the learner. These metaphors communicate two different approaches of education. In the first case the potentiality of education resides within the learner and the teacher is seen only providing supportive help, whereas, in the second metaphor the student is seen as a blank slate and the teacher deposits knowledge. Now-a-days, industry-oriented terms are used in the context of education. The terms like "knowledge workers", "knowledge producers", "knowledge brokers", etc. are in fashion. Other words that one hears are productivity, utility, profitability, salability, marketability, etc.

In ancient India there were other metaphors and similes used for knowledge. They put education at the transcendental level. Knowledge (*Gyan*) was considered as *Amrit*. In *Isa Upanishad* it has been said that through *Vidya* one attains immortality. As Sri Aurobindo (1994) says 'Reality has Unity'. "Consciousness about multiplicity is due to *Avidya*. The realization that "Unity" is the ultimate truth brings immortality.

The *Mundak Upnishad* (1.1.4) talks about two types of knowledge *Para* and *Apara*:

तस्मै स होवाच। द्वे विद्ये वेदितव्ये परा चैवापरा च ।।

Apara Vidya, includes the study of all the four Vedas, Shiksha, Grammar, Vedic rituals, Etymology, Prosody and Astronomy:

तत्रपरा, ऋग्वेदो यजुर्वेदः
सामवेदोउथवर्वेदः शिक्षा कल्पो
व्याकरणं निरुक्तं ज्योतिषमिति।
अथ परा यया तदक्षरमधिगम्यते।

मुण्डक उपनिषद्
मन्त्र 4 व 5

Para Vidya included spiritual knowledge relating to their cosmic reality which is inexpressible, infinite, indestructible, beyond the life and death. In this context *Avidya* does not mean lack of knowledge *Avidya* is not ignorance, it means knowledge which relates to doing activities related to worldly subjects which does not lead to life immortal.

Knowledge has been considered as bliss that removes doubts, confusion and ignorance. The Gita (Chapter IV) uses three similes with reference to 'gyan', as a rapier (sword) which cuts asunder doubts and suspicions ज्ञानासिना (4.42), second as boat, which helps one to cross the sea of ignorance ज्ञानप्लवेनैव (4.36), and third as fire, that burns out results of one's deeds ज्ञानाग्निदग्धकर्माणं (4.19). It is also mentioned there that those who are in doubt cannot achieve tranquility and peace of mind संशयात्मा विनश्यति (4.41).

The world needs peace, progress, social cohesion and spirit to live together. These are the basic requirements which Delors Commission (UNESCO 1996) identified as the pillars of education. If we shape education on the principles of ancient Indian school of thought, we will be in a position to prepare our youth for learning to live together. The need for international understanding was never so imperative as it is today. As Dr. Karan Singh (1996) in his thoughtful article observes, "knowledge is expanding but the wisdom languishing". There is a need to expose our young generation to ideas of universal love, tolerance and peace. "We have to work to remove orthodoxy and obsolescence orientations. There is a need to offer holistic education with multiple dimensions of human personality. There is a need that education should provide experiences which would reduce hatred, bigotry, fundamentalism fanaticism, greed and jealousy."

The Gita in a subtle way gives prominence to self-directed, self generated, self-initiated learning. It says one should raise oneself with own efforts उद्धरेदात्मनात्मानं नात्मानमवसादयेत् आत्मैव ह्यात्मनो बन्धुरात्मैव रिपुरात्मनः (6.5), One should realize one's goals and aims through one's own efforts. Metaphysically speaking, it means realisation and actualisation of self is through self only. Educationally, this means that the process of education has to be self-directed and self-generated. The sense of fulfilment by self efforts was the core of ancient education. The "Learning To Be" (UNESCO 1972) mentions that man is an unfinished being and can only fulfill himself through constant learning. If this is so then education takes place at all ages of life, in all situations and in all circumstances of existence. Education must transcend its limits of institutions, programmes and methods. And this concept was presented in all ancient literature on education.

The concept "life long education" has been emphasised in the Delors Report (UNESCO 1996). It bases its faith in the concept of continuing education. It makes distinction between initial education and continuing education and finds the later in harmony with the needs of the learning society. The commission observes that in 21st century, learning throughout life will be essential for evolving requirements of labour market, for mastery of the changing time frames and gaining rhythm of individual existence. Delors report interprets continuing education and life long learning as key concepts and finds it most relevant in the era of rapid globalization. Major transformation in the nature of employment and advances in science and technology make life long learning and continuing education a core component of the educational process. At this stage we must be very clear that illiteracy of the developing countries is as big an obstacle as functional illiteracy of the developed world. Both hamper the genuine growth of a learning society. In Indian tradition, there is an injunction that activities relating to teaching and learning should never be abandoned or postponed. In *Traitriya Upanishad* it has been repeatedly said that self learning should never be abandoned, स्वाध्यायान् मा प्रमदितव्यम्।

Open learning and continuing education are two important concepts which have come in educational vocabulary in the last 30 years. This does not mean that the ancient Indian thinkers were unaware of these developments. Open learning continuing education which emphasise on life long learning has been a corner stone of Indian thinking.

Ancient Indian thinking has never given hundred per cent credit to formal institutionalized learning. In one of the *slokas,* four sources of education have been identified through which learning takes place: It says "one fourth of the learning is done when the student is with the teacher, one fourth of learning by the learner's self-study and self-reflection. One fourth of the learning results by peer interaction and the last one fourth comes out of time context.

आचार्यात पादम् आदत्ते, पादं शिष्यः स्वमेधया

पादं सब्रह्मचारिभिः, पादं कालक्रमेण तु।

There are also other powerful expressions which appear in Vedas, Upanishad and Puranas. One of the significant utterances of Atharva Veda is that the aim and goal of every man's life is self-growth and self-enrichment and the mechanism for this is continuing life long learning: उद्यातं ते पुरुषनावयानम्।

अथर्ववेद (8,16)

In Indian thinking education and learning is not an inert activity. It is dynamic and interactive. It depends upon thoughtful listening, quick grasp and wise application and thoughtful reflection:

सुश्रूषा श्रवणं चैव ग्रहणं धारणं तथा
उहापोहार्थविज्ञानं, तत्त्ज्ञाचं धीगुणाः।

Formation of character development of values, inculcation of commitment is at the root of Indian thinking. Accumulation of knowledge and development of skills is only the first preliminary step. The flowering of education must be seen in modification of one's behaviour, in developing an open mindset, and in cultivating the finer sense of discrimination. *Achar Pratham Dharma* means behaviour is the first requirement.

In the Indian context, *gyan* (knowledge) is a spiritual activity. It is the aim and objective of all individuals, to equip themselves with knowledge and attain *Vivek* and *Vinay*. *Vivek* is the discriminating wisdom: नित्यानित्य वस्तुविवेक,

Arrogance and pride have been considered as negative human dispositions. It will be appropriate to recall, A.N Whitehead who said "I plead for a little humility. The self confidence of the learned people is the cosmic tragedy of civilisation".*

As opposed to narrowness, self-centredness, greed, anger, worldly infatuation, true knowledge as explained in the Gita, inculcates truthfulness, fearlessness and an abiding faith in non-violence.

अभयं सत्वसंशुद्धिर्ज्ञानयोगव्यवस्थितिः
दानं दमश्च यज्ञश्च स्वाध्यायस्तप आर्जवम्। (16.1)

---

*: Quoted in Radhakrishnan, The Present Crisis of Faith, New Delhi, Orient Paper Book.

The word *Vidya* as explained by Prof. Misra (1998) is made up of the root word '*Vid*' which has four meanings and comes very close to the four pillars of learning Delors Commission (UNESCO 1996):

Vid	=	To know (Cognitive aspect)
Vid	=	To acquire (psychomotor aspect)
Vid	=	To perceive (perceptual aspect)
Vid	=	To internationalise.

Similarly, the other word *Shiksha* comes from the root *Sak* that denotes "potentiality". In that sense, *Shiksha* means empowerment. *Shiksha* was considered as one of the six branches of Vedanga which stressed on pronunciation intonation, modulation, etc. The advantages of knowledge and the *gyan* have been elaborately discussed by Bhrataari:

साहित्यसंगीतकलाविहीनः
साक्षात् पशु पुच्छविषाणहीनः।

It has also been observed that without diligence and practice, one will never attain *Vidya*. Further, *Vidya* gets destroyed or diluted if it is not practised or revised from time to time what Bruner calls as "revisitations". The process of attaining *Vidya* through analysis, synthesis and reflection is based on sound pedagogical principles. Importance of questions and cross questions have been greatly recommended.

Self actualisation, a term used in modern psychology comes closer to *Aatma Darshan*. This point has been stressed by Goldstein (1940) and Maslow (1954, 1962).

In Indian perspective, a school is an abode of *Vidya* (abode where one knows, thinks and becomes someone) it was called 'Ashram', the term that stresses the need of hardwork, labour both physical and intellectual.

The aim of education is not to know things superficially. Sri Aurobindo (1994 p.248) says "Simply to know the eternal and to remain in pain, the struggle and inferiority of our present way of being, would be a poor and lame advantage". Thus, knowledge brings us the fullness of being 'brahmavid', "Being" is an existence in its fullness. Being itself is power, consciousness and delight. Thus, the emphasis was on "Being" (*Vid)* rather than on empowerment which is the trend today.

SECTION 3

Educational Vision

Two of the finest statements of educational vision in India must be recalled while attempting to perceive Vision 2020 for education in the country. The first of these was made by Gandhiji in 1931 in London in the context of universalising education in India:

> *'India lives in its villages. It is there that our producers live, voters live, the poor and illiterate live. It is the villages that hold the key to the country's problems. So vision of future India can be greater than to rebuild its half a million villages. The irony is that in terms of the teaming millions inhabiting these villages our developments, our democracy, and our education have all become irrelevant. But once we decide to approach them in the right spirit they are bound to respond, and rise to end their suffering. It may be that in the first phase selected homogenous SC/ST and other backward villages may have to be taken up. In case whole villages do not come forward in the beginning, then mutual-aid teams may have to be formed. Naturally in the whole process of rebuilding villages education will have the most vital part to play, because it alone can prepare people's mind to receive new ideas, and accept new tools, new relationships, and new forms of organization'.*

The second vision statement is contained in Article 45 of the Constitution of India: The state shall endeavour to provide within a period of ten years from the commencement of this Constitution, for free and compulsory education for all children until they complete the age of fourteen years.

The framers of the Constitution, knowing fully well that literacy rates were only 17 per cent at that stage, had the courage and conviction coupled with confidence and self-assurance that it would be possible to universalise education within the next ten years. In fact, the mandate given in the Constitution is pregnant with 'dream' potentialities like equality of opportunity to all children in terms and participation and success. It also unfolds the possibilities for better quality of life, freedom from ignorance and obscurantism.

India after 1947 has most assuredly marched ahead as a free, democratic, secular republic. During these years education has always been considered as the engine of personal, social and economic growth. Over the years, at regular intervals, the nation has taken stock of growth and developments in education and planned activities for its future development accordingly. In 1947, 1953 and 1966 it has looked, respectively at university education, at secondary education and education in its totality. The nation has made concrete formulations on educational policy in 1968, 1986 and 1992.

Elementary Education

Universalisation of Elementary Education has been given the highest priority since Independence of the country. In an attempt to fulfill this mandate, several interventions and initiatives were undertaken in the past, such as enrolment drives, community awareness campaigns and incentive schemes. They brought remarkable progress as is evident from the enclosed Table 1 giving state-wise number of schools and enrolment in primary and upper primary schools. The goal still remained to be fulfilled because in 1998-99 approximately 407 lakh children of the age-group six to below 11 years and 306 lakh children belonging to the age-group 11 to below 14 year were out of school (refer Table 2). The Ninth Five-Year Plan (Planning Commission, 1999) document envisaged additional enrolment of lower primary stage during Ninth and Tenth Five Year Plans as 250 lakh and 300 lakh, respectively. The progress achieved so far is much below than the envisaged targets by the end of 2001-2002, i.e. end of Ninth Five-Year Plan (Table 2) approximately 487 lakh and 386 lakh children of the age group six to below 11 and 11 to below 14 years, respectively will likely to remain out of school. The progress of individual states is at variance. Especially the educationally backward states like Andhra Pradesh, Assam, Bihar, J&K, Madhya Pradesh, Orissa, Rajasthan, Uttar Pradesh and West Bengal have to put more efforts. The new thrust under Sarva Shiksha Abhiyan and empowering the Panchayati Raj Institutions for development of education at the grass root level are the vehicle to fulfill the goal of UEE. To fulfill the target by the end of 2007, special attention is to be paid to enroll the poor children, slum dwellers and working children. As per 1991 Census, the working children were 112.8 lakh and their number must have increased substantially during the last nine years. Besides, the most important activity during this period is required to be effectively monitoring of the aforesaid interventions.

Secondary Education

Demand for secondary education depends upon the performance of upper primary stage, which in turn depends upon the performance of lower primary. During the Eight and Ninth plan period, focussed attention has been paid to improve lower primary, followed by improving upper primary sub sectors under UEE commitment of the nation. The Tenth Five-Year plan will be facing the issue of increased demand for places in secondary schools. The state-wise position as on 1998-99 for number of schools and enrolment are given in Table 3. Estimation of demand for secondary stage of education is given in the annexure. Based on the above estimation, around 5000 to 6000 schools having secondary sections having IX and X classes are to be opened and around 50 to 60 thousand additional teachers are to be appointed annually during the Tenth Five-Year Plan. Apart from the quantitative dimension, the secondary education has to face the demand for quality of education in the rapidly changing economic and social contexts in different parts of the country.

Vocationalisation of Secondary Education

The Ninth Five-Year Plan laid down the criterion of diversion of 25 per cent students of 10+2 stage to vocational stream so that they become self-employed or wage-earner in the field of their choice. The scheme is to be properly strengthened by establishing various linkages, as envisaged in the Ninth Plan document.

Need for Higher Priority to Improve Quality and Relevance

Optimum utilisation of resources made available for secondary education depends upon the priority to quality as compared expansion. The post-independence scenario of secondary education indicates that the policies followed have not focused on the quality. There is an excessive dependence on the examination based outcome indicators. Examinations for certification do not indicate the changes in the quality of secondary education. The nation has no database on the school outcomes beyond lower primary stage. Even at the lower primary stage, only at one point of time (1989) we have achievement indicators comparable across states. Even to get feedback for curriculum revision, one needs indicators of processes and outcomes at given points of time. During the remaining term of the Ninth Plan, serious efforts should be made to generate such data to obtain the perspective of the Tenth Plan. The Tenth Five-Year Plan should provide for quality audit of schools in different states. Quality audit should focus on functional input factors, the education process itself and obtaining achievement levels based on standardised achievement tests. At present, the All India Educational surveys carried out by NCERT contain some parameters related to quality. This has to be supplemented by National Level Studies on the utilisation of inputs and school outcomes. NPE (1986) and POA (1992) suggest establishment of National Testing Organization. This needs implementation. Further, special attention needs to be given for quality improvement of teaching in the mathematics, science and computer education, as stressed in the Ninth Five Year Plan document to bring improvement in quality. There has been a widespread decline in demand for higher education in basic sciences. In the long run this may adversely affect scientific advancement in the country. Partly low demand is due to the curriculum and teaching-learning processes carried out in secondary schools and partly it is due to the attraction towards professional courses. In order to attract and retain bright minds in the fields of basic sciences, identification of talents and its nurturing, attracting them to the careers in basic sciences and improvement of science teaching in schools should find place in the strategy.

Vision Statement

Keeping in view the achievements and gaps of education and keeping in view the present mood of the country and the economic and technological upswing, we would like to construct a vision statement based on the faith that India will become a developed country by 2020 and all activities be taken up in a mission mode.

By 2010, India will have 100 per cent elementary education for the age group 6-14. School curriculum will be so planned that it will promote peace, harmony, social cohesion and composite culture. Education will empower learners for self growth and higher quality of living. Distance and open learning will become an integral part of instruction at all levels. Virtual classroom and self learning (using networks and websites) will get strengthened. Education will protect and promote ancient wisdom and will be indigenous in nature. School and university education will have an open window to international achievements. Educational management systems will become more sensitive, open, transparent and learner friendly and will focus on to provide academic support to students. The overall vision of Education-2020 is to create a learning and knowledge society.

Thrust Areas

- With elementary education becoming universal, more efforts will be put to provide quality secondary education, parent education, vocational education and teacher education.
- Intensive efforts will be made to provide educational opportunities through distance education using information and communication technologies. Students evaluation will become more formative and flexible. Curriculum will have a provision to offer cafeteria approach.
- School curriculum will not unnecessarily load students. At the same time, it will have comparative international standard and promote critical and independent thinking.
- Pre-primary education and early childhood education will become an important element of school education supported through public funds. At present it is offered by non-governmental agencies only at few places. Government's efforts in this direction will also continue through Anganwadis and Integrated Child Development Scheme (ICDS). By 2020 it will become a regular feature, available to all children.
- Adult education will be of comprehensive nature encompassing, functional, literary, post literacy programmes and life long continuing education.
- Universities will take greater interest in college education and support Staff Development Programmes through extension activities and Academic Staff Colleges. By 2020 each university will have Academic Staff Colleges which will undertake in-service education of college and university teachers on a regular and continuous basis.

- All educational resource institutions like National Council of Educational Research and Training, State Council of Educational Research and Training, National Institute of Educational Planning & Administration and District Institute of Education and Training will get electronically connected and so will the UGC with its Regional Offices.
- Teacher education programmes, both Pre and In-service, will undergo drastic changes to make them relevant and rigorous. In-service programmes will become more communication technology oriented and will use virtual classroom teaching practices and will utilize internet facilities.
- Educational management will become efficient, effective, sensitive, responsive and performance oriented.
- Income generation projects will become a regular feature of all institutions.
- Preservation, protection and modification of indigenous knowledge and composite culture will become an important objective of education.

Strategies

To achieve the above areas, the same strategies are suggested as illustration. When elementary education becomes universal and adult illiteracy gets liquidated, the education thrust will shift to the remaining two important educational issues, strengthening of secondary education and vocationalising education. These priorities were identified decades earlier but steps taken in achieving these aspirations have been partly inadequate and partly *ad-hoc*. These need to be reiterated and reinforced here. In such ventures, potential of communication technologies should be fully and optimally utilised.

Networking School-level Resource Institutions

This strategy is based on the assumptions that resources are always inadequate, and widely distributed, it is by their proper mobilisation that they can be put together and make a critical mass. At present, there are resource institutions at national, state and district levels. National Council of Educational Research and Training, National Institute of Educational Planning and

Administration and National Open School are resource institutions at the national level. State Council of Educational Research and Training, State Institute of Education and Central Institute of Educational Technology are institutions at the state level and District Institute of Education and Training at the district level. The first requirement is to build a network of these institutions and establish links amongst them. To take up a concrete example, electronic links between National Council of Educational Research and Training and all the State Council of Educational Research and Training should be established preferably by 2001. This will make National Council of Educational Research and Training and State Council of Educational Research and Training interact closely on various issues related to school curriculum, teacher training, research projects. In case the technological facilities are made available in National Council of Educational Research and Training to undertake 'one-way-video' and 'two-way-audio', many programmes can be speeded-up and streamlined. Similarly, even on experimental scale, one or two educationally backward states may be identified where State Council of Educational Research and Training could be electronically connected with all its District Institute of Education and Training. As an illustration, if State Council of Educational Research and Training Rajasthan located at Udaipur gets connected with all the 23 District Institute of Education and Training of the state, then it would be very easy to deliberate on programmes, prioritise the programmes, monitor them and provide timely feedback. If this is done, District Institute of Education and Training can get continuous and instant feedback from the State Council of Educational Research and Training. We propose that some of district level resource institutions be electronically linked to state level once and the state level resource institutions with national level institutions. This could be a concrete activity for the next two or three years.

Building Strong Educational Information Management System

This action area is based on the assumption that in the existing situation most of the actions are taken on the basis of personal liking and disliking, personal preferences and on hunches. If decisions are made on the basis of information available, they would be more objective. Thus developing a management information system is the first pre-requisite.

At present there are no Educational Management Information Systems (EMIS) in many institutions. The Educational Survey and Data Processing Unit of National Council of Educational Research and Training makes available school surveys in CD ROM hard copy. Survey of educational research that National Council of Educational Research undertakes in areas like teacher education, educational philosophy, distant education, education psychology, teaching methodology is another input for Educational Management Information Systems (EMIS). It is now proposed that a mechanism should be designed whereby institutional resources are made available on Internet and anyone who wants access to it, is free to do so. The EMIS could be thought of in various fields, for example they may be EMIS on teacher training institutions, schools qualification of teaching etc. In the first step, teacher training institutions of the secondary level may be enlisted with specific details related to location, address, telephone number, etc. In the second step, various courses offered by these institutions could be made available. In the third step, institutions which have facilities for M.Phil. and Ph.D work should also be enlisted. The point is that the strong EMIS should be built in areas like educational research, education publications, etc.

Making Available Parent Education Programmes Round the Clock

This action area is based on the assumption that parents want to increase their awareness about various educational matters. If appropriate educational awareness programmes are telecast and made available to the general public especially parents, it will help them to become better productive members of the society.

A society cannot be considered a knowledge society unless the members of the society have facilities and opportunities for life long learning. With the coming up of educational channel, the nation should be in a position to offer educational programmes of various types through satellite and computer networks. This means there would be programmes for adults, parents, etc. These programmes should be telecast round the clock.

Change to digital economy will call for new steps, such as need for high speed and large band width networks so as to ensure last mile connectivity. A lot of content centres will have to be set up to accumulate, collect and preserve ancient knowledge. Efforts to preserve folk stories, folk proverbs, folk sayings, etc., will also be made. Attempts will also be made to put some items of curriculum on the Website. Thus, by 2005 e-books and e-magazines may be available in schools and universities. The role of teachers as facilitators would expand when facilities of Internet are made available in schools.

Offering Special Programmes for Gifted and Talented Students

It is known to everyone that the real treasure of a country is its youth and specially youth who are gifted and talented. Any country which does not nurture the giftedness and the talent of its youth can never dream of becoming a progressive and forward-looking society.

There are programmes which are in place that are geared to search and nurture national talent research but they are sketchy and inadequate. Central Government and the state governments have some plans to identify young talents, both in science and social science streams. There are also certain incentives for those who have been identified as talented but these are too inadequate and do not cover a great mass of students. It is, therefore, proposed that to celebrate "knowledge society", the nation must develop a comprehensive programme to identify, nurture and support the talent at block and district level. It should be the duty of the panchayats as well as of the state governments to identify the talent and create special facilities for their growth and nurturance.

In every district there will be a strong provision for education of gifted students. To begin with, each district will have schools for the gifted in the area of academic subjects, music, dance and painting and sports. Curricular activities will be so structured that they promote student mobility.

Special Programmes for Girls Education

Providing girls education and ensuring their full enrolment should be the educational objective to be attained by 2020. At present, the drop out rate in class VIII is as high as 82 per cent in Bihar, 83 per cent in Meghalaya and nearly 80 per cent in Rajasthan. One must remember that if we educate a boy we educate a human being and if we educate a girl we educate several generations. Article 45 of the Constitution provides free and compulsory education both for boys and girls up to 14 years of age. Education for All (UNESCO 1990) highlights education for women claiming that it is impossible to have the educated people if there are no educated women. Amendment 73 and 74 of the Indian Constitution which gives special power to Panchayati Raj envisages that a third of the seats in local governments, rural Panchayats and urban environments be reserved for women. However, present position is alarming. The percentage of girls in classes VI-VIII is approximately 25 per cent in Rajasthan, 29 per cent in Bihar, 34 per cent in Madhya Pradesh and 31 per cent in Uttar Pradesh*.

Education of Scheduled Castes, Scheduled Tribes and other Disadvantaged Groups

For achieving cohesive and productive society, special programmes have to be launched for the Scheduled Castes, Scheduled Tribes and other disadvantaged groups. This can be done by providing positive protective discrimination and also by integrating socio-cultural and linguistic specificities into pedagogical and curricular requirements. Contextualization of curriculum will be very important if drop-out rate of scheduled castes, scheduled tribes students is to be arrested. Facilities like mid-day meals incentive schemes and of residential schools will have to be augmented.

Inclusive Education for Special Needs Students

By 2020 attempts will be made to offer integration education on comprehensive basis for physically and mentally handicapped children. In 1974, Government of India started Centrally sponsored scheme for Integrated Education of the Disabled Children (IEDC) in the Department of Social Welfare, which was later on transferred to Department of Education in 1981. On the international scene the World Conference on "Education for All" (UNESCO 1990) advocated that steps need be taken for education of every category of disabled person as an integral part of education system. Another UN initiative was equalization of opportunities for persons with disabilities (1993), wherein it was proposed that members States will provide education for persons with disabilities as integral part of the education system.

Source: *. NCERT (1999) School Education in India as on 30.09.1993.

The Salamanca Statement and Framework for action on Special Needs Education (1994) provides for education of disabled children in nearby neighbourhood schools and recommends that children with special needs must have access to regular schools. Inclusive education for special needs students has a wider connotation than merely providing education. It includes combating discriminatory attitudes of students and teachers and creating a community that welcomes inclusive education. One of the important features of inclusive education would be to set up resource rooms for supporting special needs children in schools.

Special Programmes for Countries which have Indian-origin Population

Countries like USA, Canada, South Africa, U.K, Australia, Caribbean Islands have large population of Indian origin. These people still keep up the Indian traditions and want to maintain their cultural roots. The younger generation in these countries is keen to know about the culture of India and also their provincial language like Gujarati, Marathi, Tamil, Telugu, etc. It would be most appropriate if suitable programmes are launched for teaching these languages to the willing people as well as exposing them to common features of Indian culture. This is a Herculean task, difficult and complicated but will be greatly appreciated by the Indian people abroad.

Income generation should be one of the objectives of knowledge society. International markets may be explored where Indian textbooks or other materials like computer programmes can find access. There are about 20 million Indian diaspora. Educational links through University Grants Commission, National Council of Educational Research and Training, Indira Gandhi National Open University and Central Board of Secondary Education will be developed and programmes will be designed to keep Indian origin persons in close touch with Indian culture and Indian Languages.

Providing and Promoting Indigenous Knowledge

In the knowledge society communities will assess education in quality and utility as per their own norms. During the first two decades in the post Independence period, the process of expansion of education created awareness and consciousness amongst the people on the need for sending children to school. A certificate at the matriculation level or a graduate degree was a great achievement in Fifties and Sixties. The situation at the beginning of 21st century is different. Mere education does not convey much meaning to the parents and communities. Children rarely learn anything substantial of their own environment, flora and fauna, social and cultural context, local resources, skills, traditions, festivals and economic scenario. Had we realised the significance of acquainting children with the indigenous techniques of water resource management, traditional method of preparing fertilisers, preserving foodgrains, utilising herbs and ensuring cleanliness and developing a sense of attachment and responsibility towards people and the community, the scenario would have been very different in every sphere of human development. We would not have landed up in such a crisis as the water famine, wastage of foodgrains and non-availability of health support to the majority of the people in the country.

The Report of UNESCO Commission on Education for 21st Century entitled: 'Learning – The Treasure Within' pleads for an education which is 'rooted to culture and committed to progress', Gandhiji wanted education to be so rooted that there would be a continuity in the social, cultural and economic environment of life. A sound education, according to him, would prepare the present generation to take up activities which relate to the previous generation and ensure a continuity for the next generation. A sense of pride in the achievements of the predecessors and in the culture of the country is a pre-requisite for a dynamic and forward-looking society. He always pleaded for preservation of the culture, heritage and its enlargement for the posterity. To him, these were most important functions of education. Development of a harmonious and integrated personality would just not be possible if the system does not believe in this philosophy.

Curriculum: Review, Revision and Development

School level resource institutions like National Council of Educational Research and Training, State Council of Educational Research and Training, Central Institute of Educational Technology etc., as well as universities, will have to develop a mechanism for curriculum review, revision and development, both at schools and university level, which should expose students to latest global developments as well as to indigenous knowledge. Curriculum will pay attention to indigenous tradition and enormous amount of wisdom and experience that has been drawn from various regions and sections of the Indian society in knowledge relating to Ayurveda, herbal treatment, massage therapy, achievements in psychology, mental health, logic, epistemology, jurisprudence, pedagogy, etc. Curriculum will also offer fast track and front line curriculum in areas such as information technology, bio-technology etc. Curriculum will emphasise value education, meditation and importance of silence. It will gradually build in students higher levels of awareness from animality to humanity to rationality to civility to divinity. Curriculum should make students aware of positive and critical thinking and the harms of negativity and negative thinking.

Curriculum will be so designed that it will not load students; neither with the physical load, nor with the load of non-comprehension, and irrelevance. Curriculum will stress on joyful learning, functional science and functional mathematics. It will not unmindfully reject memorisation. A mechanism will be evolved to ensure that school college and university curriculum as well as the curriculum of teacher education gets reviewed, revised and updated every five years. It may also be stressed that Curriculum in school education provides enough stress and importance to computer education, information and communication technologies and other frontline curriculum. It should also be stressed that distance education and open learning systems are optimally used.

Computer education will be introduced in a phased manner:

- Computer literacy in all schools.
- Computer assisted learning in a large number of schools (10,000).
- Computer-aided learning in some schools (1,000).
- Intensive computer education in some selected schools (100 called as smart schools).

Teaching-learning material which is largely in the form of textbooks and workbooks, now will accordingly change when facilities of Internet and website are made available in schools. Multimedia packages, CD ROMs and hyper texts need to be developed and made available in the library and students.

Adult Education

It is heartening to note that India has attained literacy rate of 64 per cent. We hope by 2020 illiteracy will be totally eradicated. In the subsequent decades, comprehensive adult education programmes including parent education will be launched. One set of adult education programmes will relate to post literacy education, another set of programmes will be vocational and technical in nature. The third type of programmes will be related to life enrichment activities, culture, etc. These new initiatives will call for setting up community colleges in each district.

Adult education as literacy activity should continue till we achieve 100 per cent literacy. Simultaneously, we should plan programmes for neo-literates and post literacy programme to consolidate the gains achieved in the literacy phase. The post literacy phase should enhance adults reading, writing capabilities, as well as give them an adequate orientation about social and cultural environment. The third phase of functional literacy will be to provide specific inputs to specific target groups. For example, functional programmes may be designed in music, media appreciation, computers, literacy, agriculture, horticulture, banking, hotel management, etc. The important thing while designing these programmes is to ensure that under these programmes, the learners are offered specific content which meet their vocational, professional and interest needs. In a way, functional programmes become the beginning point for life enrichment. The types of life enrichment programmes fall in the category of social, political, moral, philosophical literacy programmes as well as may encompass areas relating to aesthetics, painting, interior decoration and language courses. Community colleges are conspicuous by their absence in India. One can see these colleges in Canada, Australia and USA. India should not copy the western model but should launch community colleges of a new type which will educate learners to senior secondary level as well as provide life enrichment courses. They would become adult education centers with links with school education.

Teacher Education

Teacher education programmes by 2020 will be drastically revised. At present, in most of the teachers colleges, the teacher education programme (B.Ed.) is of one year duration after graduation. This trend will change and teacher education after graduation will become of two year duration. This is because in one year the knowledge base relating to pedagogy cannot be developed fully. Further, pre-service education should also provide enough exposure to teacher so that they can fully utilise information and communication technologies.

Initial teacher education programme (B.Ed.) by 2020 all over the country will be of longer duration, four years after +2 and two years after graduation. The focus of teacher training will become more school based. Teacher education programmes will offer inputs, so that the teachers become more commitment oriented. All teacher education programmes – pre-service as well as in-service – will have substantial input of information and communication technology.

In-service education at the moment is *ad-hoc*. Enough resources will have to be provided to District Institute of Education and Training so that they become think tanks of education in the district. The linkages between National Council of Educational and Training, and State Council of Educational Research and Training should be electronically built with the objective that its connectivity will facilitate decision making and programme formulation.

The thrust of teacher education programmes go to developing thinking capabilities in student teachers. In that case, present programmes which emphasize memory will be appropriately modified. This does not mean that memory and fact learning has no place in school education. As a matter of fact, in the initial years, there is a need of memorization and this point has been fully endorsed by UNESCO Report 1996.

Teacher education programmes will develop in teachers a new insight about plurality of perspectives. This means each individual is unique and different from the other.

There is another aspect which relates to developing collaborative programmes of teacher education jointly by the National Council of Educational and Training, National Institute of Educational Planning and Administration, State Council of Educational Research and Training and District Institute of Education and Training. At the moment, these different institutions, which are research and resource organizations work more or less in isolation (Trist 1983). Complexity and the flux of environment give rise to meta problems which are different from discreet problems. Meta problems require inter-organization collaborations which provide poly dimensional and multi-facet solutions. Thus, it is necessary that institutions like National Council of Educational and Training, National Institute of Educational Planning and Administration, National Council of Teacher Education, University Grants Commission and others have more collaborative projects.

Educational Management

Education management, or for that matter any management system, whether in education or defence or industry or health or social sector, has to abandon its *babu* culture. It should optimide resource utilisation rather than saving resources; it should meet objectives and criteria rather than show internal efficiency; it should satisfy needs rather than reduce costs. Management should see a problem in the holistic manner rather than offer solutions for bits and peaces and it should create alternatives rather than follow holy procedures. Education management must become more effective doing the right things rather than being more efficient.

Educational management will need a paradigm shift. It must have and create a culture of performance. (Volcker Commission, 1990) and must show a bias for action (Peters & Waterman,1982). It has to be efficient, effective, transparent and sensitive to future needs. It must provide single window service facility. The present administrative style would undergo a change. The future administrative configurations will be such that they can be restructured, relocated or co-located. Management will give greater emphasis on appointment of project and contract based staff.

All administrative units will be electronically connected and will have strong component of Educational Information Management Systems (EIMS). It should have more decentralization, less bureaucracy and more converging governance. In each State, there will be a State Educational Council which would look into the total gamut of activities relating to school from pre-primary to university level. There will also be District Education Councils with appropriate authority and responsibilities. The planning unit will become District and then subsequently Block. There will be more convergence of funding.

Higher Education

Universities will give more attention to under graduate teaching. By 2020 at least 50 per cent of university age learners will receive higher education. Each university will have some special programmes suited to the genius of that locality. University Education Departments will undertake more programmes relating to extension and research in school education. Links will be developed between school education and higher education.

In many universities teaching at under graduate level is not given full attention. This trend harms university education and must be checked. Most of the teaching in universities and colleges do not keep the potentialities of the learner in view. University teachers often keep only the prescribed content in focus and are unmindful of the learner's abilities to assimilate. University teachers will have to be oriented towards this through Academic Staff Colleges.

References

Drucker, P. F. (1971), *"The Age of Discontinuity"*, London, Pan Paper Books Ltd.

Goldstein, Kurt. (1940), *"Human Nature in the Light of Psychopathology"*, Cambridge Mass. Harvard University, Press (1940).

Husen, Torsten. (1974), *"The Learning Society"*, London, Methuen & Co.

Hutchins, R.M. (1970), *"The Learning Society"*, Penguine Books.

Singh, Karan (1996), *"Education for the Global Society"*, the UNESCO (1996) *Learning: The Treasure Within*, Paris.

Maslow, A.H. (1954), *"Motivation and Personality"*, New York, Harper & Row 1954.

Maslow, A.H. (1962), *"Towards a Psychology of Being"*, New York, D. Van Nostand 1962.

Misra, Vidyanivas. (1998), *"Teaching: Indian Perspective"*, New Delhi, NCTE.

Peters, T. and Waterman, R. (1982), *"In Search of Escellence: Lessons from America's best run companies"*.

Radhakrishan, *"The Present Crisis of Faith"*, New Delhi, Orient Paper Book.

Sri Aurobindo, *"The Upanishadas"*, Sri Aurobindo Asharam Pondicherry (5th impression of work done in 1900-1910) p 61, 1994.

Toffler, Alvin. (1980), *"The Third Wave"*, New York Morrow.

Toffler, Alvin. (1990), *"The Power Shift"*, New York Bantam Books.

Trist. E., "Referent Organization and the Developemnt of inter-organizational domains", *"Human Relations"*, 36(3) March 1983, pp 269-84.

UNESCO (1972), *"Learning To Be"*, UNESCO, Paris Harrap.

UNESCO (1990), World Conference on Education for All: Meeting Basic Learnng Needs, Jomtion.

UNESCO (1994), *Final Report:* World Conference on Special Needs Education: Access and Quality, Salamanca, June 7-10, Paris, UNESCO.

UNESCO (1995), Review of the Present Situation in Special Needs Education. p 30.

UNESCO (1996), *"Learning: The Treasure Within"*, Paris.

UNESCO (1996), Legislation Pertaining to Special Needs Education.

Venkatasubramanian, K. (2000), *"India's Development as Knowledge society"*, *The Hindu*. September 5, 2000.

Volcker Commission Report (1990), *"Learnership for America; Rebuilding the Public Service"*.

ANNEXURE

Estimation of Future Enrolment in Class IX and X Using Trends during 1993-98 Period

Projected enrolments are rough estimates. The procedure is as follows:

(i) Based on the aggregation of actual enrolment for each state using the grade-wise enrolment, figures for India for 1993 and 1998 was obtained.

(ii) Annual average growth rate during 1993-1998 of Upper Primary stage was obtained. It was found to be 3.8 per cent per year between 1993 and 1998.

(iii) Using the average annual growth, total enrolment at Upper primary stage was estimated annually for 2001 to 2007.

(iv) The actual enrolment in the terminal grade (VII/VIII) for each state was aggregated to get the all India figures for 1993 and 1998.

(v) The proportion of terminal grade enrolment in the total upper primary enrolment was obtained for 1993 and 1998. These were 28.8 and 30.16, respectively.

(vi) Based on the proportion of terminal year enrolment for 1998 taken as 30 per cent and the projected total enrolment in upper primary stage, the number of students in terminal year from 2001 to 2007 were obtained.

(vii) Proportion of enrolment in the beginning year of secondary stage out of enrolment in terminal year of upper primary stage for 1993 and 1998 was obtained separately. This was 86 per cent in 1993 and 83 per cent in 1998. These were used as a proxy to the transition rate. Using the transition rate of 83 per cent observed in 1998, enrolment was estimated for the period from 2001 to 2007.

(viii) The observed proportion of beginning year of the secondary stage in the total enrolment of secondary stage was 55 per cent in 1993 and 45 per cent in 1998. Having estimated the enrolment in beginning year of secondary stage for each year, the total enrolment of the secondary stage for respective years were obtained by doubling the beginning year enrolment (i.e., 50 per cent as beginning year and 50 per cent in the remaining classes of secondary stage). The Table 1 provides the result of the exercise.

Table 1

Estimated Demand for Secondary Places during X Plan Period

Source	*Year*	*Total enrolment in upper primary*	*Enrolment of terminal class of upper*	*Enrolment in Beginning class of secondary*	*Total Enrolment in secondary*
VI AIES	1993	34071058	9841148	8428490	15219392
MHRD	1995	41014136	11814891	8987834	16779905
MHRD	1998	41926086	12644079	10469101	22861119
Estimated	2001	46705660	14011698	11629709	23259418
	2002	48480475	14544142	12071637	24143274
	2003	50322733	15096820	12530360	25060720
	2004	52234997	15670499	13006531	26013028
	2005	54219927	16265978	13500761	27001522
	2006	56280284	16884085	14013790	28027580
	2007	58418935	17525680	14546314	29092628

Estimation of Additional Schools and Teachers

According to the Sixth All India Education Survey (1993), the average size of secondary stage (including all types of schools having secondary stage) was 174. Similarly teacher pupil-ratio for secondary stage was 1:17. Extrapolating these values, the number of schools and additional teachers have been arrived as given below.

Year	*Enrolment*	*No. of schools*	*No. of teachers*	*Additional schools*	*Additional teachers*
1993	15219392	87238	895431	—	—
2001	23259418	133674	1368201	46436	472770
2202	24143274	138754	1420192	5080	51991
2003	25060720	144027	1474160	5273	53968
2004	26013028	149500	1530178	5473	56018
2005	27001522	155181	1588234	5681	58066
2006	28027580	161078	1648681	5897	60447
2007	29092628	167199	1711331	6121	62650

6

Towards a Knowledge Society: Vision 2020

GARRY JACOBS & N. ASOKAN

INTRODUCTION

India: Vision 2020

Imagine an India in which elementary school enrolment (I-VIII) and adult literacy are approaching 100 per cent, school drop out rates are nearly zero, all children who are not going on for higher academic studies receive vocational training, and computer literacy is almost up to the standard of Western nations. Imagine a country in which nearly all citizens have access to all forms of print and electronic communication media — television, telephone, the internet.

Compare that with India as it is today, with only 64 per cent of its people meeting even the most minimum standard of literacy, where 59 per cent of students never complete 5th standard, where secondary enrolment is 58 per cent but of those that enrol 54 per cent (68 per cent of the total age group) never complete 8th standard, where only a small percentage of youth receive vocational training before entering the workforce, and where probably less than 1 per cent of the working age population is computer literate.

Now try to conceive of how much more productive, prosperous, dynamic and expansive would be the India that you have imagined. Think about the potential benefits of new educational methods that would make it possible for school children to complete the entire secondary school curriculum within the first five or six years of education, with greater comprehension and retention and greater capacity for thinking, problem solving and creativity. How much more knowledgeable, skilled, and competent would be the nation's workforce? Imagine the impact on social productivity and living standards of corporations, universities, and government administrations staffed by such a workforce. How much more efficient and innovative they would be? How much better informed would be the decisions taken by individuals regarding education, occupation, politics, business investment, health, child-rearing and life-style? How much more effective will be the institutions operating for the development of society? Imagine a workforce able to meet the entire world's shortage of technical and professional graduates. Imagine companies and universities from around the world gravitating to India as the premier scientific and technological research and development environment. Imagine an India in which cities are far cleaner and more modern, citizens more enlightened and responsible, entrepreneurs more dynamic and sophisticated, institutions far more effective and responsive. Surely as a minimum, this India would enjoy a per capita income three to four times higher, perhaps ten times higher, than the country does today.

This India of your imagination is merely a dream today, but it can become a reality within the next two decades, provided the nation's intellectual, political and business leaders have the vision to perceive the country's enormous untapped human potentials and make a full and determined commitment to fully develop those potentials. Knowledge is the key to realizing this vision of India in 2020.

Knowledge Society

Knowledge has always been an essential and distinguishing characteristic of human society, for human beings are unique among all species in their extended capacity to formulate, systematize, preserve and consciously transmit organized bodies of knowledge from one individual, community, generation and location to another. That is the essence of all that is known as education.

The term 'knowledge society' has gained prevalence in recent years due to the revolutionary strides in technology and the rapid evolution of new systems for the gathering, transmission and application of information. A confluence of technologies—television, computers, networking, satellite communications and the internet—constitute the technological basis for the knowledge revolution. Their rapid proliferation over the past decade has made possible movement of information around the world at lightning speed. This dramatic acceleration in the development of information technologies; in the speed and extent of global knowledge accumulation, dissemination and exchange; in the blurring and transcendence of traditional boundaries between fields of knowledge; and in the emergence of new knowledge-based industries are defining characteristics of the knowledge revolution.

The knowledge revolution marks a fundamental shift in human development beyond the limitations imposed by material processes towards the unlimited, indeed, infinite creative potential, of human processes. In fact, this shift is really not as unusual as we may have thought. All resources, even land and minerals, are products of the human mind. Anything becomes a resource only when the human mind recognizes a valuable use for it. Development has always been based on the creative and imaginative capacity of the human mind. In this sense, the Knowledge Society is not really something that has just suddenly emerged out of nowhere.

The concept of Knowledge Society includes also that of the learning society. The pace of knowledge generation and adoption is so rapid in the world of today that learning can no longer be confined to formative years of youth. All members of the population must continue to acquire knowledge throughout their adult lives in order to avail of the economic opportunities that rapid development makes possible. This requires the development of innovative delivery systems for dissemination of practically useful information on a continuous basis.

A guiding and inspiring vision of what India has the opportunity to become by 2020 must take into account the enormous productive potential of knowledge to accelerate the development and transformation of the country. The knowledge revolution is not a fashion or a fad. However, in striving to adapt and respond to the opportunities generated by the knowledge revolution, two guiding principles should be kept in mind. First, efforts to spread the Knowledge Society should avoid as far as possible the empty hype and fads currently sweeping the world and concentrate rather on the real role of knowledge as a catalyst for development. Second, rather than blind imitation of other countries, India should seek to innovate new strategies and new applications of the knowledge revolution adapted to local needs, conditions and culture. To do so it is necessary that we appreciate the true role of knowledge in development.

The Question of Resources

All efforts to project India's future progress get blinded sooner or later by the question of resources, by which is meant the financial resources needed for investment in infrastructure, industry and institutions. Annual budgets, Five-Year Plans, company reports place primary emphasis on the importance of capital investment. But money is not the most important contributor to a nation's growth. A study by Denison of the factors contributing to growth of the US economy from 1929 to 1982 attributes 94 per cent of the total to factors relating to knowledge generation and dissemination: 64 per cent of that growth is linked to advances in knowledge generation (i.e. R&D) and another 30 per cent to advances in education. Better resource management, which is an application of knowledge, is also identified as a more important factor than capital. This fact bodes well for countries whose economic planners are able to escape from their faith in the pre-eminent importance of capital and fully tap the enormous productive potential of non-material, knowledge resources.

The knowledge revolution is not just a short term blip on the radar screen which peaked in 2000 with the boom in dot.com companies. It is a real and profound opportunity for countries around the world to increase the speed and spread the benefits of development. What is termed the knowledge revolution marks a significant shift in the relative importance of different resources or factors of production in the development process. As futurist Alvin Tofler has documented, the shift from physical power to wealth power to mind power is an evolution in the foundations of the global economy. It marks a fundamental shift in the character of social evolution.

In earlier stages of development, land and minerals constituted the principal resources for development. Technology was rudimentary. Human beings were valued mainly for their physical labour. Today, technology, organization and information—three basic components of the knowledge revolution—have become critically important resources for development. All economic activities are becoming more knowledge-intensive. By one recent estimate, 50 to 60 per cent of all industrial output is based on information. Modern manufacturing industries depend as much for their success on the management of information relating to quality, cost and scheduling as they do on the management of materials and production processes. The service sector, which is the greatest source of new jobs and economic growth in the world economy, is essentially knowledge-based. The phenomenal growth of employment opportunities in this century has been mostly driven by the rapid expansion of services. The four most important service sectors in the US economy today—financial services, insurance, health and education—are especially knowledge-intensive. This shift from material to knowledge-based resources opens up vast opportunities for developing countries to accelerate the pace of development. India's rate of economic growth can be substantially increased if the country becomes a superpower in knowledge and if the potentials of information and information technology are fully understood and exploited.

These knowledge-based resources differ significantly in character from the scarce natural resources on which traditional economic assumptions have been made. Natural resources are subject to inherent limits of availability. The knowledge-based resources are not. Natural resources are consumed when they are utilized. The knowledge-based resources are not. Knowledge expands as it is shared rather than being consumed. Knowledge is not lost when it is freely given away. Knowledge is readily transportable at rapid speed and very low cost. Development today depends to a much larger extent than ever before on resources that can be freely multiplied, distributed and utilized by the entire population, provided people have the educational background to receive and utilize it effectively. This makes possible a vast acceleration in rates of development.

Historically, development has occurred under conditions in which access to critical resources was restricted to a relatively small portion of the population. The distinguishing characteristics of knowledge as a resource make it possible for the first time to spread and share a resource among the entire population. The pace of India's progress towards a Knowledge Society will depend to a large extent on its ability to make available the latest and most useful knowledge to vast sections of the population.

Role of Knowledge in Development

We now understand that the pace and extent of development is determined to a very large extent by a host of non-material, intangible factors: access to information; knowledge and skill; generation and application of technology; the quality and efficiency of social systems and public institutions; expertise in building and managing organizations of all descriptions; and ultimately on the aspirations and attitudes of the people.

In its essence, development is a human process that is determined by the response of people to their external environment. Development is the process by which human beings become aware of opportunities and challenges, formulate responses, make decisions, and initiate organized actions. This process follows the sequence from knowledge to inspiration to action. When human beings acquire knowledge, they become aware of opportunities and challenges. When that knowledge matures, they acquire the motivation or urge to translate that knowledge into action. No matter how great the opportunity or how dire the necessity, without that knowledge no adaptive response occurs. Knowledge is fundamental to each step in the development process. It is essential for creating awareness of opportunities and challenges, evaluating alternatives, formulating responses, effective planning, organizing initiatives, and implementing those initiatives.

Development depends on a very broad range of knowledge—technical knowledge of productive processes, commercial knowledge of markets and business practices, personal knowledge of human health and nutrition, knowledge of laws and legal processes, knowledge of political and administrative processes and public policies, knowledge of organization and management, knowledge of emerging fields of science, and a conceptual knowledge of the nature of the development process itself, by which we may acquire the wisdom to unleash and harness the energy, resourcefulness and creativity of the people.

Knowledge contributes to development in several different ways: as a productive resource; as an essential input for education; scientific research and industrial technology; as a catalyst for social change and economic development; and as a basis for civilization and cultural values that promote social integrity and harmony, which is the essential foundation for all development.

Knowledge is only one input to the development process, but it is an absolutely essential one. Without adequate knowledge all the other essential inputs—land, infrastructure, factories, capital, technology, administrative and social organization—cannot yield full results. Enhancing knowledge generation, dissemination and application is the fastest, most cost-effective means of increasing the productivity of all these other resources and accelerating national development.

Development depends on four knowledge processes:

- Knowledge generation and acquisition through scientific discovery, R&D and transfer of technology.
- Knowledge adaptation through innovation to particular fields, needs and operating environments.
- Knowledge dissemination through formal and informal channels from knowledge developers and adapters to those responsible for applying the knowledge in society.
- Knowledge application through skilled action in fields, factories, classrooms, hospitals and every other field of activity to achieve practical results.

INDIA'S KNOWLEDGE GAP

The task of harnessing available knowledge for development is complicated by the fact that the rate of global knowledge generation is growing exponentially and old knowledge is quickly superseded or nullified by new knowledge which generates more and better results, faster and at lower cost. Humanity's knowledge base, which has been accumulating slowly over centuries, is now doubling every three to five years.

Not only is knowledge much more available, it is also much more essential for survival in an increasingly complex and competitive world. Factory workers, urban citizens and even housewives today require a much broader range of knowledge and practical skills to perform even routine functions such as operating sophisticated machinery and appliances, complying with laws, interacting with government departments, benefiting from modern medical technology, etc. The minimum knowledge required of every Indian citizen is increasing. At the same time, the maximum opportunities for those that acquire the most knowledge in any field are boundless, as the recent surge in the IT industry dramatically illustrates.

The pace of knowledge dissemination in India has also been growing rapidly. The expansion of media coverage through cable TV has multiplied the range of programming. Rising levels of education have fueled a proliferation of specialized journals on a wide range of topics. The spread of information technology, telecommunication facilities and the Internet have created far wider access to a much greater range of knowledge. But, in spite of these significant achievements, there is a growing gap between the rate of knowledge generation and knowledge dissemination in the country as illustrated in Figure 1.

Figure 1

India's Knowledge Gap

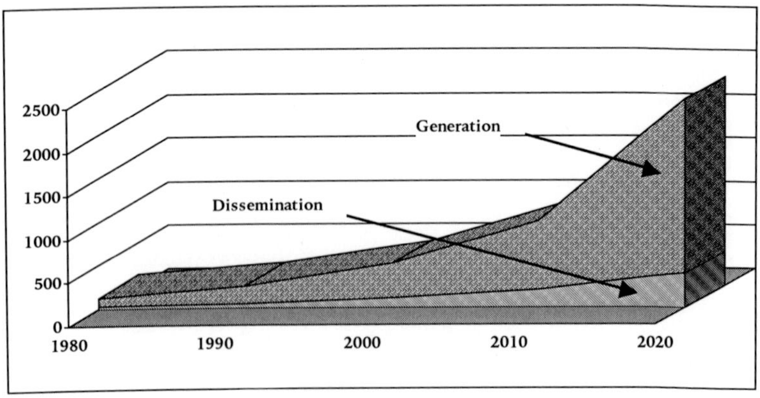

India's knowledge gap is not easily quantified, but we can roughly measure it by examining the country's progress on literacy, education, application of technology, R&D and growth of the media.

Literacy

Literacy rates in India have doubled over the past four decades. This impressive progress is diminished by the fact that the starting rates were extremely low. This still leaves approximately 300 million illiterate adults in the country, 30 per cent of the entire population. For these people, the traditional avenues of knowledge dissemination through education and printed information are ruled out. It is precisely the people in this group that are most vulnerable to the challenges posed by the knowledge revolution because they are least equipped to rapidly expand their knowledge base. Since many of them are relatively young adults who will still be active in 2020, the country cannot afford to ignore them or leave them behind. Innovative approaches will be needed to increase knowledge dissemination to this group.

Figure 2

Growth of Literacy in India

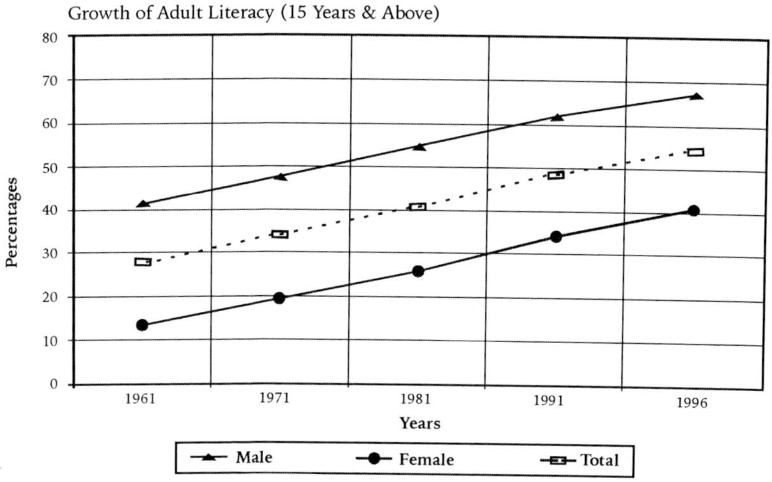

Education

A second way of estimating India's knowledge gap is to look at the number of people who do not acquire even a minimum of formal education. Education is the primary and most effective means so far evolved for transmitting practically useful knowledge from one generation to another. Education is the process of passing on to future generations in a concentrated and abridged form the essence of knowledge accumulated by past generations.

India's educational system has expanded exponentially over the past five decades. But drop-out rates from primary and secondary school remain so high that a very large proportion of children do not acquire even high school education, which must be considered the minimum education required to adapt and succeed economically in modern society.

Figure 3

Drop-out Rates at Elementary Stage: 1960-1997

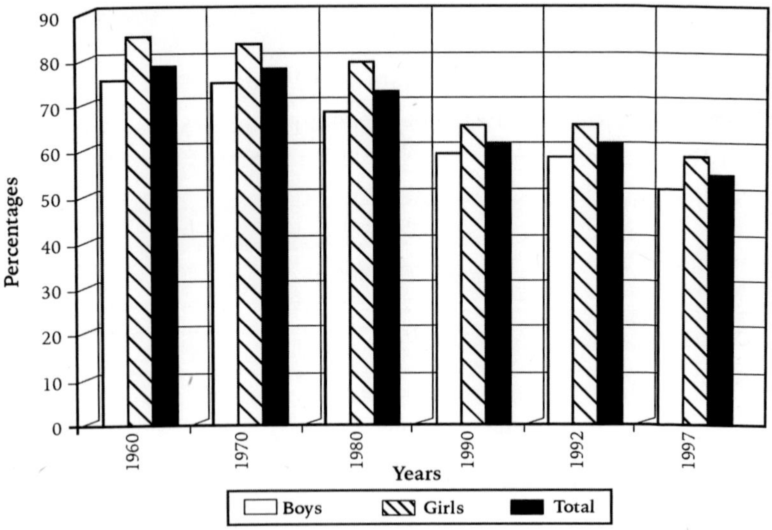

In spite of significant progress in reducing school drop-outs, 40 per cent of children still drop out before completing the 5th grade and 70 per cent drop out before completing high school. Therefore, apart from addressing the needs of a large illiterate population, India's knowledge strategy must also develop innovative approaches to enhance knowledge acquisition among the large community of school drop-outs. Unless something is done to drastically reduce drop-out rates, by the year 2016 there will be approximately 500 million people in the country with less than five years of schooling and another 300 million that will have not completed high school. In other words, about two-thirds of the population will lack the minimum level of education needed to keep pace with and take advantage of the social changes occurring within the country and worldwide.

R&D

The rate of knowledge generation in the country is another aspect of the knowledge gap. At the global level, science and technology are expanding at unprecedented rates. There are many ways in which this global knowledge permeates into the domestic economy, but the capacity of any country to adapt and fully harness these advances depends to a significant extent on domestic R&D activity.

Estimates of R&D activity can only be taken as crude indices of the knowledge gap, but the figures do suggest that knowledge generation in the country is not keeping pace, even proportionately, with the global knowledge revolution.

Table 1

R&D Expenditure

Country	*Exp. in US $*	*Exp. as % GNP*
Japan	825	3.0%
USA	568	2.9%
Korea	146	2.1%
India	**2.4**	**0.8%**

Two points are important to note about India's performance. First, atomic energy, space and defense research account for 71 per cent of all Central Government spending on science and technology, which means that relatively little is left for investment in agriculture, energy, telecommunications, health, education and other crucial sectors. Second, R&D expenditure in India's fast growing IT sector is currently 3.1 per cent, suggesting a strong correlation between investment in R&D and economic growth.

There are other indicators that also suggest an increasing knowledge gap resulting from inadequate knowledge generation.

- India's share of global scientific output in 1998 was only 1.58 per cent of the world's total.

- India's annual output of science papers declined from 13,000 in 1981 to 12,000, while world output has risen from 4 lakh to 7.6 lakhs per year.
- India's share of global scientific citations in 1997 was only 0.7 per cent of the world's total.
- India's rank on the Science Citation Index has fallen from 8 to 13 since the early 1980s.

Knowledge generation directly impacts national development when it results in new and improved, patentable industrial processes. Every year more than 500,000 new patent applications are filed globally. Of these, China accounts for 96,000 and Korea accounts for 72,000, while India accounts for only 8000. Korea produces nine times as many patents as India with only twice India's total investment in R&D, suggesting that not only the quantum of investment but the management of R&D activities is a critical determinant of knowledge generation.

Application of Technology

A fourth way to estimate the country's knowledge gap is to examine the extent to which commercially viable technology is being applied in the country. Since agriculture is still the largest source of employment in India, the application of technical knowledge in this field can be a useful index of knowledge dissemination through agricultural education, agricultural extension services and other delivery systems.

The table below compares agricultural productivity in the USA and India. There are many reasons for these differences in productivity, including size of land holdings, level of investment and quality of inputs. But in addition to these, there are vast differences in the extent to which available scientific knowledge is applied by farmers in their fields. According to the empirical studies and field research conducted in India by California Agricultural Consulting Services, knowledge accounts for more than 50 per cent of the difference in productivity on American and Indian farms.

Table 2

Agricultural Productivity in USA & India (kg/hectare)[1]

Crop	*USA*	*India*	*USA/India*
Rice	6622	2928	2.3
Maize	8397	1666	5.0
Wheat[2]	4400	2583	1.7
Groundnut	3038	912	3.3
Soya beans	2452	1007	2.4
Potato	40,238	17,307	2.3
Lint Cotton	700	333	2.1
Tomato	59,295	15,138	3.9

Note: 1. Data in this table is from the FAO web database for 1999.
2. The figure for USA wheat yield is for irrigated wheat which is the best comparison since almost all Indian wheat is irrigated. The overall average yield for irrigated and rainfed wheat in the USA is 2872 kg/ha.

To test this conclusion, numerous experiments have been conducted in which the knowledge available to California farmers has been provided to Indian farmers. Without any change in the size of the land holdings or quality of inputs, productivity on the Indian farms rose by 100 to 300 per cent as shown below.

Table 3

Crop Productivity Improvement by Knowledge Application

	Crop	*Yield (kg/ha)*		*Increase*
Location		*Local*	*Test*	
Tamil Nadu	Tomatoes	31,250	1,05,000	236%
Tamil Nadu	Lint Cotton	335	978	192%
Kerala	Black Pepper	426	1716	303%
Bihar	Maize	1125	2568	128%
Karnataka	Lint Cotton	347	1045	202%

Note: These results illustrate the enormous potential for accelerating India's development by closing the knowledge gap and point to the great importance of improving the quality and relevance of the rural educational system.

Knowledge Dissemination through the Media

Knowledge dissemination occurs through the system of formal education and through a variety of informal channels, of which the media is the most prominent. Therefore, the development of the media can be taken as another rough index of knowledge dissemination in the country.

The number of publications and growth of readership in India is expanding rapidly, as shown below:

Table 4

Indian Newspapers & Journals

Year	*Publications*	*Circulation*	*Circulation/1000*
1987	24629	57 million	71
1997	41705	89 million	91

The Indian newspaper industry has expanded enormously as the population has expanded and literacy rates have risen. India currently publishes 4719 daily newspapers with a total circulation of 40 million. Still, the percentage of the Indian population reading newspapers remains relatively low.

Table 5

Daily Newspaper Circulation per 1000 Population (1992)

Country	*Circulation*
Korea	412
Singapore	336
USA	236
France	205
India	**31**
Pakistan	6

The number of publishers and books published is another index of the capacity for knowledge dissemination. Currently India has about 3000 active publishing firms publishing at least 20,000 books annually.[1] This figure compares favourably with 49,000 books published annually in the USA, the world's largest publisher, however, there is still a huge difference in the number of copies of each title printed and circulated.

Cable television coverage has expanded very rapidly in India over the past two decades and currently reaches 37 million people. While little current programming is directed at knowledge dissemination, this medium has enormous potential for closing the knowledge gap.

The Internet is currently the fastest growing media channel in India and around the globe. The table below compares India's current position with that of some other countries.

Table 6

Internet Penetration (1999)

Country	*Netizens*	*% of Households*
India	**2 million**	**2.5%**
China	10 million	1.7%
Japan	20 million	30.0%
Taiwan	4 million	35.0%
USA	80 million	50.0%

The following table projects the growth of India's IT infrastructure over the next eight years. Cable TV is included in this list because it will become a important means of delivering internet access to households.

NASSCOM projects that the number of television sets will triple from 75 million to 225 million by 2008 and that cable television coverage will expand from the current level of 37 million households to 70 million. While little current programming is directed at knowledge dissemination, this medium has enormous potential for closing the knowledge gap.

1. Some sources indicate the number may be as high as 56,000 books, taking into account multiple language editions, but the authors preferred to cite the more conservative figure.

Table 7

India's IT Infrastructure

	2000	*2008*
PCs	4.3 million	20 million
Internet subscribers	1.0 million	35 million
Internet users	3.7 million	100 million
Cable TV subscribers	37.0 million	70 million

The Internet is the fastest growing media channel in India and around the globe. Currently 2.5 per cent of Indian households are connected to the web compared with 30 per cent in Japan and over 50 per cent in USA. According to a recent study by Pricewaterhouse Coopers, the number of Internet current users will rise to more than 25 million by 2005, representing a 50 per cent annual growth rate. Other studies project that by the end of 2008, 100 million Indian will have access to the Internet, of which 25 per cent will be serious users. India is also investing in IT infrastructure to support rapid growth in this field. Over 200 Indian cities and towns have Internet access. Seven private international gateways were operational by the end of 2000 and at least 12 are expected to be operational during 2001. It is projected that between 2000 and 2008 the number of PCs in the country will increase five-fold from the current base of five million.

These various measures indicate that the Knowledge Gap in India is indeed very great and very great will be the benefits of implementing strategies to close that gap. The measures also reveal that India has a substantial media infrastructure that is not being effectively utilized for knowledge dissemination.

Knowledge is only one input to the development process, but it is an absolutely essential one. Without adequate knowledge all the other essential inputs—land, infrastructure, factories, capital, technology, administrative and social organization—cannot yield full results. Enhancing knowledge generation and dissemination is the fastest, most cost-effective means of increasing the productivity of all these other resources and accelerating national development.

In formulating a realistic, achievable vision of India in 2020, we need to take into account both the magnitude of the challenges the country faces and the magnitude of the opportunities afforded by the still nascent revolution in knowledge. As the evidence indicates, the nation's knowledge gap is widening and this trend will not be arrested by incremental changes in strategy or implementation. It will require bold innovative initiatives to formulate and experiment with new models suited to the new context. The primary incentive for bold initiatives is not the pressure of physical circumstances, since India today is more prosperous and comfortable than at any time since Independence. It is rather the recognition, that it is possible within a short period of time, to bridge the great developmental distance that presently separates this country from other nations that were not more advanced than India was just a few decades ago and now stand out among the most developed nations of the world.

Essential Role of Education

It is now evident that capital is a result and product of the development process rather than its source. The true source and driving force for development is human capital—the values, attitudes, knowledge, skills, organization and motivation of the people. The current knowledge gap points to the vast underdevelopment and underutilization of that most precious of all resources, a resource which India possesses in greater abundance than all but one other nation. Accelerating the development of the country's human resource base by imparting greater knowledge and greater access to information should be the mainspring of our efforts to leap forward into a more prosperous future.

Education is the process of passing on to future generations in a concentrated and abridged form the essence of knowledge accumulated by past generations. It is arguably the single most important input both for the growth of the society as well as for the individual. Properly planned, educational input can contribute to increase the Gross National Product, enhance cultural richness, build greater receptivity to technology, and improve the quality and effectiveness of Government. Education opens new horizons for the individual, releases new aspirations and develops new values. It strengthens competencies and develops commitment. Education generates in an individual a critical outlook on social and political realities and sharpens the ability for self-examination, self-monitoring and self-criticism.

During the last five decades India has gained valuable experience in all spheres and stages of education. The expectations of the people regarding education and the potentialities for future growth are better understood. But the present reality and future potential are separated by a wide gap in the level of social commitment, institutional credibility, quality of human and institutional resources, and efficiency of functioning. Contrary to expectations at the time of Independence, disparities in levels of education within the society are increasing. There is a visible loss of credibility of existing systems of imparting education in schools and institutions of higher learning. In addition, educational infrastructure is inadequate and even the effective utilization of existing infrastructure has not been ensured.

Table 8 estimates the probable state of education in India 2020 based on current policies and trends and compare it with a best-case scenario in which maximum attention, resources and effort are directed to raise the educational status of the population.

Table 8

Education Scenarios in 2020

	1980 Actual	*2000 Estimated*	*2020 Business -as-usual*	*2020 Best-case Scenario*
Primary enrolment (1-5)	80%	89%	100%	100%
Elementary enrolment (1-8)	77%	79%	85%	100%
Secondary enrolment (9-12)	30%	58%	75%	100%
Drop-out rate (1-5)	54%	40%	20%	0%
Drop-out rate (1-8)	73%	54%	35%	0%

This is the time when the nation should commit to a whole-hearted effort to move toward a learning society and a knowledge society. That effort must begin by ensuring 100 per cent literacy by 2020, including all those who have already passed into adulthood without acquiring this minimum capacity for knowledge acquisition. It should also commit to fulfil the objective of Article 45 of the Constitution of India to provide a minimum of 10 years of free and compulsory education to all children up to 14 years of age. Universal primary education should be considered one of the most essential objectives and highest priorities of the coming decade. Extending the reach of scientific and technological literacy to all sections of the population should become an essential aim of all child and adult educational programmes. These achievements are essential for providing all citizens with more equitable access to knowledge and more rapid economic advancement.

Beyond this minimum level, greater efforts need to be made to enhance the quality and increase the breadth of educational options at all levels. India has a few institutions such as the Indian Institute of Technology and Indian Institute of Management that compare with the best in the world, but it also has a vast multitude of institutions that lack even the minimum infrastructure required to function effectively. The minimum standard of these institutions needs to be elevated in order to serve the vast majority of the population.

Other qualitative changes are needed as well. Present evaluation systems need to be discarded and replaced by a shift to accreditation and certification. There is need to create an active interface between the formal educational system and systems of open learning and distance education that are now emerging via television and the Internet. A concerted effort is also needed to improve the management and administration of educational processes and institutions in terms of their systems, content, utility and credibility.

Our vision of India in 2020 is to create a learning and a knowledge society. By 2020, India must achieve nearly 100 per cent adult literacy and elementary education for the age group 5-14 years. School curriculum need to be enhanced to promote creative thinking, initiative, self-respect, social responsibility, peace, harmony, social cohesion and a composite culture. Education should empower learners for self-employment, self-growth and higher quality of living. Distance and open learning need to become an integral part of education at all levels. Virtual classrooms and self-learning *via* the Internet and television need to be strengthened. Educational management systems need to become more sensitive, open, transparent and learner friendly.

Elementary Education

In spite of increased efforts to impart literacy, reduce the drop out rates and expand the educational system to accommodate more children, the quantitative expansion of the educational system is still too slow to meet the country's needs, depriving tens of millions of young people of the minimum education required for their development. India rightly prides itself on its adherence to democratic principles, but the effective exercise of those principles depends directly on the education of the electorate. Nothing can have greater impact on the preferences of the nation's voting public, the quality of elected government officials, and the productivity of the workforce.

Upgrading rural primary and secondary education is possibly the single most important initiative that the country can take to secure a better future for its people. The very low productivity of Indian agriculture, which is the main source of income for the majority of people, is one reflection of the inadequacy of the rural educational system. India has followed a policy of opening a school in every village on the principle that no child should be far away from a primary school. As a result, the rural primary school system consists predominantly of single teacher schools that lack the minimum infrastructure and teaching staff to provide a relevant quality education. The task of upgrading the rural primary school system can be facilitated by adopting a strategy presented by Professor P. V. Indiresan. The present system of 500,000 village primary schools can be consolidated into around 60,000 centralized schools established in each cluster of eight or nine villages and located at the epicentre of the clusters. This would provide each school with at least nine teachers. Such consolidation offers substantial economies of scale in terms of cost of management and cost of delivery of quality.

Improving the Quality of Education

A quantitative expansion of the educational system will provide access to more young people, but it will not ensure that the education provided is of adequate quality to keep them enrolled or dramatically improve their capacity for social adaptation and achievement. Many of the methods commonly adopted in the nation's schools are based on practices developed in the distant past that have outlived their value and utility. Simultaneous with the quantitative expansion of the educational system, there needs to be a concerted effort to experiment with new approaches to education that will increase the quality and speed of knowledge transmission. The qualitative change needed should include:

Shift from Teaching to Learning

The traditional emphasis on the teacher as the active source of knowledge and the student as the passive recipient who simply receives what is taught needs to be replaced by a pedagogical system in which the student is taught to actively seek knowledge through a variety of means from a variety of sources and the role of the teacher is as facilitator and guide for that process.

Shift from Traditional Academic to Life-based Curriculum

The current curriculum is a product of many different influences. Most of it was developed in countries with very different values and social conditions, some of it in earlier centuries when life was altogether different than it is today. The high dropout rates in India reflect the fact that the school curriculum is only distantly related to the knowledge and skills needed by most Indians for adaptation and achievement in life, especially in rural areas. The dawn of a new millennium is an appropriate time to begin formulation of an entirely new educational curriculum, one which will relate to the cultural, social, political and economic life of the country and the skills, attitudes and values needed for individual initiative, personal achievement and nation-building.

Computer Education

Computer literacy is an increasingly important qualification for both for individual employment and growth of the national economy. It requires a minimum of 10 to 20 computers for the operation and maintenance of a computer laboratory to be economical. The consolidation of primary schools into clusters would facilitate investment in adequate centralized facilities to provide at least minimum access to computer training for all students. But teaching students how to operate computers represents only a tiny part of the benefits of computerization. The greater potential of computerization is as a medium and aid for teaching any subject. Experience shows that computer-based general education can be at least twice as fast and effective as normal classroom methods now employed in India.

Value-based Education

The word 'values' is normally employed with reference to ethical and moral concepts. But it can also be used in a much wider sense to connote principles that are essential for national development. Values are those attitudes which are based on long experience society has come to recognize as most essential for individual and collective achievement. Values represent the quintessence of life wisdom about what is necessary for continued social progress. It is possible to identify a list of 20 or 30 work values that will be critical for the future growth and development of Indian society and its greater participation in the emerging global economy, values such as cleanliness, punctuality, self-reliance, self-respect, honesty in trade, entrepreneurship, systematic functioning, etc. As practical skills can be trained, values can be trained too. Rather than merely imitating the West, a study of India's most successful individuals, organizations and communities will reveal the core values that form the inner foundation for their outer accomplishments. Efforts should be initiated to identify those values that are most critical to India's future development and to evolve a curriculum to effectively impart them to students of all ages.

Model Schools

Even while the effort is still underway to expand the school system to cover the entire population, a simultaneous effort is needed to introduce and experiment with new philosophies and methods of education more in tune with the needs and possibilities of the 21st Century. As a modest beginning, experimental schools can be established in every district to test and demonstrate new methods and serve as models for other schools to emulate.

Promoting Indigenous Knowledge

For learning to be relevant it must be tailored to local needs and encompass indigenous knowledge systems. Knowledge about indigenous techniques for water resource management, preparation of fertilizers, preservation of foods, utilization of herbal medicines for better health and nutrition, personal and community hygiene are essential elements of a complete education that should be incorporated in the school curriculum. The curriculum needs to be expanded to include traditional knowledge systems such as Ayurveda, Siddha and other forms of herbal medicine.

English Language Education

In this era of globalization, command over the English language is a precious asset. It significantly improves access to information and employment. There is enormous popular interest in learning English, but most existing teachers are not qualified to teach it and fear for their careers if it is given importance. As a consequence, the rich-poor divide only widens. Rich children learn English and monopolise high paid jobs and the poor are condemned to low paid ones. Without antagonising existing teachers, the Government can encourage private initiative to provide supplementary courses in English and support it to the extent that it will be affordable by all families.

New Methods and Delivery Systems for Adult Education

A mere expansion of the educational system will do little to help the hundreds of millions of people who have already missed or dropped out of the formal educational system. Innovative alterative methods are needed to extend basic education to these people as well.

Utilize Flash Card Method for Early Childhood Learning, Adult Literacy and School Dropouts

Applied research in India based on methods developed in the USA has demonstrated that flash cards can be very effective for both early childhood and adult learning. These methods, which can be applied at home, in school, on television or over the Internet, involve very rapid flashing of words or general information on large cards at the rate of one card per second with simultaneous oral pronunciation of the words or explanation of related facts. Research indicates that the rate of learning achieved by these methods can be at least double those achieved through conventional classroom techniques. Delivered over the television, these method can rapidly improve reading capabilities at a far lower cost than alternative methods.

Develop Video Versions of the Entire School Curriculum for Delivery over Cable TV

Television can be a very effective means for educating both school going and non-school children and adults. It can deliver teaching material in a more dynamic, entertaining, and interesting manner, utilizing the nation's best teachers and multimedia teaching materials on each subject. A TV based curriculum can be utilized by slow learners to supplement classroom teaching, by fast learners to learn at much faster rates than the rest of the class, by dropouts to acquire knowledge they missed in school and by adults to expand their level of education without returning to school.

Farm Schools for Applied Agricultural Science

Knowledge leads to development when it is expressed in skilled action. That action requires practical skills for knowledge application. A primary reason for the phenomenal success of India's IT industry is the fact that India operates the world's largest system of computer training institutions. Over the past decade thousands of training institutions have sprung up around the country to provide knowledge and practical skills relating to every aspect and level of the IT industry.

Earlier we stated that the gap in India's agricultural productivity is primarily the result of a knowledge gap, rather than to the small size of land holdings or a shortage of sunlight and water essential for plant growth. In spite of the fact that agriculture is the primary occupation for two-thirds of the population, the agricultural education system primarily caters to those who seek employment in Government or research rather than application of agricultural knowledge on the farm.

The highest priority should be given to establishing a national system of farm-based training institutions to impart advanced knowledge and farming skills to the nation's farmers. Farm schools should be established in every block of the country. Each farm school should consist of 10 to 20 acres of irrigated farm lands equipped with a sophisticated computer program for analyzing soil types and recommending best practices to achieve maximum yield and profitability and supported by access to a high quality, soil testing lab capable of accurately analyzing the complete spectrum of plant nutrients. Cultivation on the farm schools can be carried out on lands leased from local farmers by student farmers enrolled at the school and drawn from the local population, so that the demonstrations will have maximum impact. The farm schools should be self-sustaining, profit-making educational organizations. Each farm school should demonstrate multiple cropping patterns that generate a minimum of Rs. 25,000 to 50,000 per acre annual income. In this way, each farm school can achieve a minimum annual revenue of Rs. 5 to 10 lakhs and minimum annual profit of Rs. 2.5 to 5 lakhs from ten acres. Farm school instructors should be offered profit-sharing incentives to achieve maximum yields. After demonstrating high yields for three consecutive years, they should become eligible for special loan programs to enable them to establish their own private farm schools.

Vocational Training for All Productive Skills

In most countries the ratio between engineers and technicians is 1:3, but in India their numbers are nearly equal. That forces many engineers to perform tasks that can be done better by technicians. The problem lies in the poor state of vocational training in the country. Vocational education is one of the weakest links in the educational system. Little social recognition is accorded to vocational skills or certification because of relatively poor career prospects and emoluments paid for vocational skills. Responsibility is divided between the Ministries of Education and Labour. Industries are lukewarm to the idea of supporting this type of education, except in fields such as computerization where the commercial rewards can be enormous. Academic institutions are not geared to provide quality vocational training in all its myriad forms.

Currently only five per cent of the country's labour force in the 20-24 age category have undergone formal vocational training, compared with 28 per cent in Mexico, 60 to 80 per cent in most industrialized nations, and as much as 96 per cent in Korea. This is an important reason why our share in global trade is very low. A strategy to achieve full employment must include as an important component a strategy to ensure that all new entrants to the work force are equipped with the knowledge and skill needed for high productivity and high quality.

The Government has created a national infrastructure of industrial training institutes that has been taken down to the block level. India has over 4200 Industrial Training Institutes imparting education and training in 43 engineering and 24 non-engineering trades. Of these, 1654 are government run ITIs, while 2620 are private. The total seating capacity in these ITIs is 6.28 lakh. Most of this training is conducted in classroom style in the form of one to two year diploma courses. In addition, about 1.65 lakh persons undergo apprenticeship vocational training every year in state-run enterprises. If a wider definition of applied courses is taken that includes agricultural, engineering and other professional subjects, the total number receiving job related training is about 17 lakh per annum, which still represents only 14 per cent of new entrants to the workforce.

But it is now clear that national development involves upgrading the skills of the workforce on a much wider range of activities relating to every occupation. In addition to carpenters, metal workers, machinists and computer programmers, the country needs to produce large numbers of qualified journalists and illustrators to meet the needs of newspapers, television stations, and internet companies. It needs trained entrepreneurs, managers and supervisors to start and operate new and existing businesses. It needs more qualified lawyers', clerks, inventors, mechanics, marketers, trainers, physiotherapists, dental and medical technicians, teaching assistants and hundreds of other skilled workers for which there is no training or insufficient training presently available.

The existing institutions for imparting basic technical and vocational skills are limited in number, enrolment and the variety of skills they offer. There is already a shortage of basic skills in the country, which is why carpenters, masons and electricians are scarce and command such high wages. Craftsmen and vocational training institutes can be established in every block to impart a wide variety of basic technical skills including vehicle and pump repair, house and building construction, furniture making, printing and book binding, lathe operation, etc.

Vocational education can be split into two parts and offered as a sandwich consisting of academic courses after the elementary school stage and hands-on apprenticeship training under master craftsmen.

Employers can be asked to offer at least one apprenticeship for every ten employees with a stipend equal to, say, half the minimum wage or pay the equivalent of a cess.

The tremendous success of private computer training institutions in India, frowned on by some as an instance of commercialization, has enabled the nation to respond to the rapid surge in demand for trained software professionals which the public education system could not have accomplished on its own. Investment and active involvement of business in the development and delivery of vocational training programmes is vital for creation of a viable system. Rather than frown on profit making, incentives should be offered to businesses that evolve quality certification training programmes.

A comprehensive strategy is needed to enhance the nation's employable skills. It must begin by preparing a catalogue of the entire range of vocational skills needed to support development of the country. The network of vocational training institutes and the range of vocational skills taught needs to be expanded substantially to impart those skills for which institutional training is most suitable. The private sector, which promoted the rapid proliferation of computer training institutes throughout the country, should be encouraged to recognize the commercial potential of vocational training in many other fields.

A comparison of India with countries at higher levels of development will reveal that the workforce in these countries have acquired a greater range and higher level of skills in every field of activity. A comprehensive list should be prepared of those skills needed to support development of the country over the next two decades and a plan prepared to expand both public and private training institutions to offer these skills to the population. The farm school model can be adapted and applied to many other fields of activity such as school management, hospital management and small enterprise management.

Computer-based & TV-based Vocational Training

The nature of vocational skills makes it impossible for vocational schools to fully address the nation's need. The variety of skills needed by the workforce is far too great. The changes in technology and work processes too rapid for training courses and their instructors to stay up-to-date. The cost of training is also relatively high and often demands full time study for a prolonged period. Some vocational fields do not lend themselves to classroom or laboratory study.

In addition, it is essential to fashion more effective and efficient mechanisms for disseminating useful knowledge and skills, especially through the TV media and through computerized vocational training. The importance of computer has been widely recognized as a means to improve efficiency in business, government and formal education, but its application in vocational training is not fully appreciated. Rates of learning on computer are four to ten times faster than they are in classroom setting and learning retention is likely to be much higher. This is true for both academic as well as vocational or skill-based subjects. Computers can provide multimedia, interactive, customized and individually-paced learning with instantaneous feedback and testing. It eliminates the need for producing and deputing large numbers of highly skilled instructors. Course content can be rapidly modified to reflect changing needs. For many types of vocational skills, computerized training also offers specific advantages over the live delivery of skills in a classroom. Training can be delivered wherever computers are available.

Private software companies can be commissioned to develop education and training CD-ROMs and videotapes to disseminate useful knowledge and skill in many different fields. In the USA such material already exists for acquiring knowledge and skills in such diverse fields as CNC machining, mining and excavation, foundry maintenance, aluminium smelting, engine repair, aviation training, law, psychiatry, fire-fighting, furniture and upholstery making, door panelling, industrial safety, driving and police training. Programmes can be developed in crucial areas such as methods to improve crop productivity, recharging aquifers, machinery maintenance, machining and tool making, medical testing, etc.

A nationwide network of 50,000 computerized vocational centres, run as private self-employed businesses similar to the STD booths and Internet cafes, can deliver low cost, high quality training to 10 million workers every year—more than five times the total number covered by existing programmes. Incentives can be introduced to encourage private sector investment to establish computerised vocational training centres to offer knowledge and skills for a wide range of vocations.

Higher Education

Since Independence, India has built up a substantial infrastructure for higher education, yet the system suffers from a variety of inadequacies. In most cases, education does not match job requirements. A large percentage of graduates remain unemployed. The content of the curriculum does not keep pace with rapid advances in knowledge. Most teachers are under-qualified or of poor calibre. Most talented students migrate abroad. Infrastructure facilities are insufficient. Recruitment and promotion are politicized and caste-based. Seniority rules preclude recognition of merit. University bureaucracy and policy-making are too slow to keep pace with rapid advancements of knowledge. There is no system for discontinuing outdated courses. Research positions are not sufficiently attractive to the brightest students. These deficiencies are not easily eradicated from the system without changes in the basic strategy for delivery of higher educational content. A new approach is needed that shifts the emphasis from classroom based teaching to full utilization of all available technologies to delivery content in the most cost- and quality-effective manner.

Develop Multimedia Forms of the School and College Curriculum for Delivery over the Internet

The advent of the Internet offers an exciting new learning medium that can literally transform our concept of school and classroom from physical into virtual realities. Future studies in the USA project a radical reshaping of higher education over the next two decades as a result of the digital revolution. Many traditional colleges will close as more course work is delivered at a distance through alternative channels. The traditional boundaries between education and other sectors will fade as publishers, for-profit and non-profit organizations offer accredited, multimedia-enhanced courses directly to students by-passing the university. The traditional classroom type of education, which is most useful for students that require personal attention and assistance and for subjects that involve hands-on experimentation, will no longer be the predominant model. For all other purposes, it is very costly and not very efficient in the way it uses the time of both teachers and students. Given the huge numbers of young Indians that will quest for higher education in the coming decades and given India's outstanding expertise in the IT industry, the country should embark on a massive program to convert the entire higher educational curriculum into a multi-media, web-based format and to establish accrediting standards for recognition of distance education courseware.

Community Colleges

Education begins with literacy but should not end there. Adult literacy programmes should be augmented by post-literacy and vocational programmes to transmit knowledge related to the individual's social and cultural environment. Drawing lessons from the phenomenal success of community college systems in Australia, Canada and USA in providing wider access to higher education to both students and adults, India should develop its own system adapted to the specialized needs of the country. India's model should include courses designed to meet vocational, professional and personal interest needs including subjects such as music, media, computer, agriculture, horticulture, banking, hotel management.

Social Systems for Knowledge Dissemination

In addition to the educational system, India can adapt from other countries and originally innovate a wide variety of other organizations to facilitate the generation and dissemination of Knowledge to the population.

Build a National Rural Information Delivery System

Knowledge is a catalyst for the development process. The gaps in practical knowledge that retard development can be identified and filled by creating new systems and institutions to transmit information that is not being adequately conveyed by traditional means.

Several efforts are already underway in the country to utilize the Internet as a medium for delivering practically useful information to the rural population. Within five years, every revenue village in the country should be equipped with a web-based computer system providing timely information, including prices for agricultural commodities in local and regional markets, technical advice on issues such as pest alerts for local crops, advice on health and nutrition, announcements of government programs, credit schemes, school and college scholarship applications, and self-employment opportunities. Such a system can form the backbone of a national development information system that caters to a wide range of practical needs.

Awards for Social Innovation

Awards can be a highly effective means to stimulate innovation, dissemination and application of knowledge in new ways. Three different levels of award can be established: for imitation from other countries or fields, for imitation adapted to local conditions, and for pure original innovation. Literally hundreds of awards can be introduced at the national, state and local level to promote research, innovation and application of better methods.

- Awards for improving utilization of any resource such as water conservation methods or reduced electricity consumption: In the 1980s, the State of California instituted a prize leading to the development of refrigerators consuming 50 per cent less electricity. The resulting savings eliminating the need for constructing thousands of megawatts of additional power generation capacity.
- Awards for innovation of practical technologies: When Napoleon was seeking a means to conserve food so that his army could move more quickly and further from base, he instituted an award that led to the development of canned foods.
- Awards for application of technology to achieve higher productivity or better quality: One pioneering farmer has recently demonstrated maize yields four times higher than the average in India. Another has achieved levels of productivity for vegetables equivalent to those reached by California farmers.
- Awards for improved government administration to provide faster, more convenient or quality public service.

- Awards for high performing public and private sector companies that demonstrate highest productivity, efficiency, quality and profitability.
- Awards for management excellence in fields such as banking, medicine, hotels, retail, transportation, telecom and industry.
- Awards for innovation in education, including development of new vocational courses and more effective teaching methods.
- Awards for public education: Television stations that develop outstanding educational or vocational training programmes, computer companies that produce innovative educational software, and newspapers that publish the best educational columns can be recognized.

Establish a National Knowledge Foundation

In earlier centuries, development has been an unconscious process of the society that occurred gradually over decades by trial and error exploration and experimentation. Only in the 20th century did Government take upon itself primary responsibility for directing and achieving the development of society in order to accelerate and abridge the process. But experience has proven time and again that Government cannot develop a nation. Development is a process that involves awakening and releasing the energies of the whole population and propelling them into action. At most, Government or any institution can only guide, support and facilitate that process.

A new possibility exists today, drawing upon the experience of this country and other nations, to convert the *unconscious process* of development into a *conscious social movement*. Indian development is taking place as an unconscious process. What now occurs in 10 or 25 years can be abridged to three or five years by making the process fully conscious. Making it conscious means that the society as a whole becomes aware of the process of development taking place in the country and endeavours to support it. Objective, factual information and rejection of superstitions—both traditional and modern—are essential conditions for making it conscious.

The leader of this movement can be any institution that understands the process, identifies the stage of society's current development and recognizes what is needed to propel it to the next stage. An institution of this type can accomplish in many fields what until now Government has sought to accomplish through huge investments and comprehensive programs. The creation of a National Knowledge Foundation can accelerate the gradual process of social development in the country and convert it into a National Prosperity Movement. A National Knowledge Foundation can play a central and unique role in the development of the country and evolve a new type of social institution as a model for India and for other nations to emulate.

In India today there are many areas where considerable progress has been made and many in which neither the goals or right methods and steps are very clear. The creation of a National Knowledge Foundation can help make Indian society conscious of its direction and goals and offer it the intellectual clarity and practical guidance needed to achieve those goals. This can speed up the process, avoid lapses and pitfalls, inspire the elite with hope and give the masses material support to progress.

The role of the Foundation could be to:

- Disseminate information about opportunities, technologies, programs, accomplishments, and achievements.
- Conduct and commission studies and surveys to obtain quantifiable statistical data in support of important issues and then publicize the data to educate policy and decision-makers.
- Prepare documentaries presenting effective strategies to achieve the results; compile directories of best practices in each field.
- Publish reports on the suitability and profitability of more productive technologies.
- Study and publicize successful systems and organizational innovations in every field.
- Publish newspapers, journals and syndicated columns in other journals to disseminate information on success stories and best practices, publicize research findings, challenge superstitions and out-moded beliefs, and report on successful initiatives that should be imitated.
- Establish models and demonstrations of new development potentials and solutions to problems.

- Provide assistance to pioneers who agree to take up a new activity as an example to others; establish programs to support those who want to imitate the pioneer, and
- Institute national and local awards to encourage and recognize innovation; and commission short stories and novels portraying the development potentials and achievements in dramatic and interesting fashion.

The Foundation would have the option of supporting constructive programs in a wide variety of fields without being guided by any overall master plan or strategy to accomplish any specific development goals. This is, in fact, the normal mode of functioning for institutions of this type. However, it would also have the option of trying to become an institution of a new type, which assumes for itself certain overall national objectives and develops an agenda of programs designed to achieve them.

It is in this sense that the Foundation can play a role in promoting Indian prosperity akin to that which the Indian National Congress played in Indian freedom. As the Congress awakened the nation to its political potentials and generated a mass movement in support of specific political goals, the Foundation can awaken the nation to its vast economic and social potentials and unleash a mass movement of the popu-lation for national prosperity.

Rightly conceived and properly executed, the Foundation's programs can highlight literally hundreds of "next steps" which Indian society can take to further its development. By studying the process of development in more advanced nations and more advanced parts of the country or sections of the population, these steps can be readily identified, appropriately modified to suit present conditions, and then presented to the population in a form that the people will readily understand and act upon.

The Foundation can generate a 'national register' of possibilities and potentialities of the country covering all fields of the national life and make it available to the public so that it can be made more comprehensive by their further contributions. When the initiative for development is taken up by the people, then development ceases to be a program of the Government and becomes a movement of the whole society. Once created, the Foundation can achieve in a brief period and with token investment developmental results comparable to those achieved by the five year plans.

A comprehensive strategy covering major sectors such as agriculture, industry, commerce, education, environment, health, management and public administration can be developed and executed over a five year period. The strategy could be implemented with an investment ranging from Rs. 100 to 500 crores, much of which could be funded on a project basis rather than from the Foundation's endowment.

The programs could include—

- 100-500 studies of development potentials and problems to get at the facts
- 100-500 information publicity campaigns to project the opportunities
- 100-500 documentaries to educate and motivate people for action
- 100-500 syndicated columns to disseminate new perspectives and findings
- 100-500 articles to dispel out-dated superstitions and beliefs
- 100-500 short stories to dramatize development potentials
- 100-500 demonstrations of how to tap the potentials
- 100-500 success stories to publicize achievements
- 100-500 seed projects to support pioneers
- 100-500 programs to encourage imitation of the pioneers
- 100-500 awards to recognize pioneers, innovators and high achievers

The Foundation can educate the elite of the country, the framers of public opinion, which means the national mind, and create a Blue Book on Indian Prosperity spelling out actions that are needed for achieving rapid development in all fields. The Foundation can become a model for a new type of institution, not only for India, but for other developing and developed nations and for the international community.

Promote Professional Associations

Government, business, educational institutions and the media can play crucial roles in national development. But, in addition, there are many types of non-governmental, non-commercial organizations that can make vital contributions to the country's progress. Among these, professional associations are a category whose importance is often overlooked. There are over 16,000 professional associations in the USA covering the entire gamut of human activities from broad general categories such as law, medicine, engineering, agriculture and computer science to highly specialized fields such as tool & die manufacturing, plastic injection mould-making, custom home electronics installation, hybrid seed production, irrigation engineering, mining technology, internet banking and web marketing. Associations of this type can serve as powerful instruments for the generation, adaptation, dissemination and application of knowledge. They can sponsor research, conduct conferences, encourage pooling of information and exchange of experiences, publish new research findings and best practices, propagate management practices appropriate to each specialized field. India can benefit enormously by a proliferation of professional associations. Creation of new professional associations can be supported by the formulation of criteria and standards for professional associations; establishment of a national, non-governmental agency for accreditation of new associations; and creation of a venture capital fund to provide seed money for the promotion of new associations.

Establish National Network of Centres for Research and Public Debate on Development Issues

Public debate is a well-developed institution in India, but too often it focuses on emotionally charged political issues backed by little supporting information, rather than on objective analysis of the nation's development opportunities and challenges—a role which public television very effectively plays in the USA and other Western countries. When properly conceived and executed, public debate can be an effective mechanism for creating awareness, disseminating information and sensitizing the population to development issues.

As the national scientific laboratories were established in the 1950s to create the essential infrastructure for research, we propose the establishment of a national network of centres for research and public debate on development issues. Each centre could conduct research on pressing regional and national development issues, host public debates open to specialists and the general public, and arrange coverage of these topics by regional newspapers, radio and television. These debates should focus on issues that can strongly influence the general public and spur people to constructive action. Debate topics could include —

- *Solutions to national and international disputes:* such as political, social and economic solutions to the Kashmir problem and to water disputes between states.
- *Educational standards and curriculum:* Comparison of educational standards in different types of schools, regions of India and different countries to assess the scope for improving standards and making the school curriculum more relevant to the needs of individual students and the development of the country.
- *Self-employment vs. Salaried jobs:* The opportunities and benefits of self-employment for achieving higher income and greater economic security.
- *Management practices:* The tremendous importance of management practices in determining the success or failure of business enterprises of any type and size, indices of good practices and ways to acquire greater knowledge and skill.
- *Labor productivity:* Differences in labor policies, attitudes and practices in different regions and countries and their impact on the development of business and the prosperity of the working class.
- *New forms of democracy:* Examination of practices in different parts of the world designed to make democracy more representative and effective in fulfilling people's needs and national goals.
- *Savings vs. investment:* Discussion of strategies to tap India's huge reserve of private gold savings (estimated value is upwards of $200 billion) for investment in national development.

Compile an Internet-based Development Encyclopaedia

Over the past five decades, the pace of development has accelerated around the world. Changes that used to occur over centuries or decades are now occurring within a few years. Humanity's knowledge of development is accumulating so rapidly that it is difficult to keep track of all that has been learned or to access information on relevant experiences in specific fields.

The advent of the World Wide Web now makes it possible to create a compendium of development knowledge, information and experience, a well documented and continuously updated source of knowledge and practical experience on all fields of national development. This Development Encyclopedia could view every subject from the perspective of social development. It could catalog proven technologies, successful strategies and best practices in different fields, so that the information is readily accessible to people all over the country.

Compilation of the encyclopedia would need to be managed by a central editorial team, but the actual generation of material could be contributed by thousands of experts located around the country. All contributions could be screened and edited, placed in a central repository on the web and updated regularly for a fraction of the cost of printed sources of information. Since publication of new material would be progressive and continuous, the encyclopedia could be launched and operative very quickly and continue to grow in value as additional material was added.

The Encyclopedia could contain both theoretical knowledge and practical information. On the theoretical side, it could examine topics such as the role of agriculture as an engine for employment and industrialization, the global growth of the service sector as the major source of new jobs, the impact of information technology on productivity and economic growth, the role of social and cultural values in development, the relationship between peace and development, the impact of rising levels of education on democracy and economic development, the relationship between education, prosperity and corruption, and the relationship between inflation and development. It could contain articles examining the factors responsible for the development achievements of different countries. It could formulate a series of scales and indices to compare the effectiveness of social organizations in different countries.

On the practical side, the encyclopedia could document both in text and multimedia format methods to improve agricultural productivity, preserve foodgrains, conserve water, recharge aquifers, improve nutrition and health care, create low-cost housing, introduce complementary local currencies, stimulate entrepreneurship and job creation. It could catalog and evaluate alternative technologies for power generation, agriculture and aquaculture, various industries and environmental protection. It could compare the effectiveness of public policies and administrative systems in different countries and regions.

The Encyclopedia could also become a virtual forum for national and international debate on policies, priorities and strategies for national and international development.

Formulate a Comprehensive Theory of Development

Theoretical knowledge is the highest level in the hierarchy of knowledge that rises from data to information to ideas. Good theory represents the essential knowledge contained in vast quantities of data, information and practical experience. While it is relatively easy to compile a large quantity of data and information about development, when it comes to drawing theoretical conclusions that will be valid over time and space, all the knowledge we have acquired over decades and centuries gets distilled into a few principles.

Looking back on the impressive accomplishments of the 20th century, a vast multitude of technological inventions, economic activities, political and social organizations, and material riches have emerged from the relatively less complex and accomplished centuries that preceded it. A whole new range of problems and challenges has accompanied these achievements. Looking forward on the century now commencing, we may well wonder what further accomplishments await humanity, what new challenges they will pose, and what ultimate limits there may be to the creative process that drives these changes.

Regardless of whether we look backward or forward, the same questions arise: what is the essential nature of human development? By what process does it occur? What force accomplishes it? What factors propel and retard it? What conditions are essential or detrimental to it? Through what stages or phases does it pass? What is the role of the individual in this process? What is the relative importance of subjective factors such as ideas, attitudes, values and choices, compared with objective factors such as material resources, political systems and technology? What is the source of the problems and failures that it generates? And, most importantly, what is the role of the human being in this process?

The formulation of valid theory possesses enormous power to elevate and accelerate the expansion and development of human capabilities in any field, leading to fresh discoveries, improvement of existing activities and capacity for greater results. Science is replete with examples of theoretical formulations that have led to important breakthroughs, such as the discoveries of Neptune and Pluto, electromagnetic waves, subatomic particles, and new elements on the periodic table. A broad range of technological achievements in this century has been made possible by the emergence of sound theoretical knowledge in fields such as physics, chemistry and biology. As management expert Peter Drucker put it, "There is nothing more practical than a good theory." Valid theory can tell us not only what should be done, but also what can be done and the process by which it can be achieved.

Social development can be summarily described as the process of organizing human energies and activities at higher levels to achieve greater results. Development increases the utilization of human potential. In the absence of valid theory, social development remains largely a process of trial and error experimentation, with a high failure rate and very uneven progress. The dismal consequences of transition strategies in most Eastern Europe countries, the very halting progress of many African and Asian countries, the increasing income gap between the most and least developed societies, and the distressing linkage between rising incomes, environmental depletion, crime and violence reflect the fact that humanity is vigorously pursuing a process without the full knowledge needed to guide and govern it effectively.

Advances in development theory can enhance our social success rate by the same order of magnitude that advances in theoretical physics have multiplied technological achievements in this century. The emergence of a sound theoretical framework for social development would provide the knowledge needed to address these inadequacies. It would also eventually lead us to the most profound and practical discovery of all – the infinite creative potentials of the human being.

Now is an appropriate time to launch a new inquiry into the theoretical basis for human development, drawing upon five decades of rich experience, both within India and internationally, in order to fashion a fresh conceptual framework for the development process that will give us a greater theoretical understanding of its essential nature and a greater practical knowledge of how it can best be fostered and accelerated.

Knowledge-based Industries

No discussion of India's emergence as a Knowledge Society would be complete without reference to the central role played by knowledge-based industries in this transformation. This term is often used with reference to industries directly involved in the creation and application of computer hardware and software and the information and communication technologies that have spurred the growth of the global IT industry over the passed two decades. Numerous studies have been undertaken by NASSCOM identifying specific strategies that will support and accelerate the development of the IT industry in India. These strategies call for increased public and private investment in telecommunications infrastructure, liberal policies regarding investment, trade and taxation, and increasing investment in technical education.

Enhancing educational capabilities in software services is one of the essential thrust areas for upgrading technical education. Currently, India trains some 68,000 software professionals a year and has around 280,000 people working in the software service sector. To maintain and enhance its capabilities, India needs to develop over 2.2 million additional knowledge workers by 2008 and it needs to ensure that this workforce is equipped with the right mix of technical, business and functional skills to meet the needs of different business segments and customer markets. This will require a significant development of IT related education both in quantitative and qualitative terms.

But the term 'Knowledge-based industries' includes a much wider range of commercial opportunities. The recent growth of IT enabled service businesses in India—call centres, medical transcription, technical support and back office processing—are powerful evidence that the potential of IT technology and knowledge based industries extends far beyond the development of software and hardware. As the application of Information Technology spreads and saturates traditional industries, it can generate new employment opportunities ten times greater in number than those directly involved in core IT industries.

The concept of knowledge-based industries can be extended still further to encompass all those in which the application of mental judgment and skill rather than the application of mechanized production technology is the core resource. Education, health services, insurance and financial services are among the leading industries in this category. They are also among the fastest growing industries in the world. Added to these there is enormous scope for other knowledge intensive activities such as clinical drug trials and many types of scientific research.

The management of all types of information is emerging as a major growth industry worldwide and India is well poised to become a global leader in these fields. Increasing demand for education within the country and worldwide will create tremendous demand for qualified teachers with adequate language skills. Increasing demand for health services will create even greater demand around the globe. Already nurses and medical technicians are in short supply. The USA has a doctor-nurse ratio at least twice that of India. Yet the US currently faces a shortfall of 117,000 nurses, which is more than three times India's total annual production of new nurses. Physicians, nurses, medical technicians and other scientific occupations will become growth industries to rival the IT sector within the next decade.

PUBLIC POLICIES

What can India do to avail these emerging opportunities? Foremost priority must be given to education of all types and at all levels. It should now be abundantly clear that India's vast population can be converted into a tremendous development asset by equipping all its people with the requisite knowledge and skills. Whatever the country may be lacking, intellectual capacity is not among those deficiencies. But development of that native capacity to its full potential will require an enormous commitment and effort by the entire society. India's leaders need the clarity and far sight of vision to see that knowledge in all its forms offers a key to the country's emergence as an economic superpower.

Among the most critical, policy issues will be those relating to formal education and the development of the electronic media as instruments of education.

Investment in Education

Our vision of India in 2020 is predicated on the belief that human resources are the most important determinant of overall development. But full development of India's enormous human potential will require a shift in national priorities to commit a greater portion of the country's financial resources to the educational sector. India currently invests 3.4 per cent of GNP and 12 per cent of total government spending on education. This compares unfavourably to countries such as Mexico which invests 5.5 per cent of GNP and 23 per cent of total government spending on education. A doubling of investments in education is the soundest policy for doubling the country's GDP.

Expanding the Nation's Corps of School Teachers

A tremendous expansion in the number of teachers will be required to support a quantitative and qualitative improvement in the country's school system. Eliminating primary school dropouts and reducing the teacher-pupil ratio from the present high level of 1:42 down to around 1:20 will together require an additional three million primary school teachers, tripling of the number currently employed. Similar increases will be required at upper primary and secondary school levels. The training of such large numbers will require the establishment of additional teachers training colleges and much larger budget allocations for teachers' salaries.[2]

Expansion of Schools and Classrooms

A tremendous expansion in the number of schools and classrooms will be required to support a quantitative and qualitative improvement in the country's school system. In order to achieve the best case scenario depicted in Table 8, total school enrolment would have to increase by 75 million students or 44 per cent. That would require a proportionate expansion in the number of classrooms. In addition, efforts to improve the quality of education by reducing class size would require further 20 per cent increase in the number of classrooms. Together, this would require increasing the total number of classrooms by 65 per cent within 20 years.

Role of Private Sector

Such a dramatic improvement in the quantity and quality of the nation's educational institutions cannot be achieved without enlisting and unleashing the full and active participation of the private sector in the expansion and upgradation of educational facilities and operations. Introduction of more modern curricula, upgrading teaching skills and standards, more efficient management of schools and financial resources, and innovation in teaching methods will all require strong involvement by private corporations. This can be achieved by policies to encourage investment in education and incentives for delivering quality educational content to poor sections of the population.

---

2. Current TPR is 1:42 for primary, 1:37 for upper primary and 1:31 for secondary level. An additional 9 lakh primary teachers will be required to support 100 per cent net primary enrolment in 2016 (an increase from 79 million to 116 million students). To reduce TPR from 1:42 to 1:30, an additional 11 lakh teachers will be required, bringing the total to 39 lakh teachers, which is double the present number. An additional 5 lakh upper primary teachers will be required to support 100 per cent net upper primary enrolment in 2016 (a net increase from 46 million to 66 million students). To reduce TPR from 1:37 to 1:30, an additional 4.5 lakh teachers will be required, bringing the total to 22 lakh teachers, compared to the present level of 12.5 lakh. Higher enrolment and lower drop out levels in secondary school could require a doubling of the high school teaching corps which presently consists of 15 lakh teachers.

Computerizing General Education and Vocational Education

Mere quantitative expansion in classrooms and teaching staff is an efficient way of tackling the nation's educational deficit in the age of computer. Recent experience has proven that computerizing education, i.e. utilizing computer and computerized teaching materials as instruments for general education, can dramatically increase the quality of education and the speed of knowledge acquisition, while dramatically decreasing dependence on the knowledge and skill of teaching staff.

A fundamental policy decision should be made to fully utilize the capacities of computer for general education, not just for computer training, and to launch a major initiative to convert the entire school curriculum to computer-based, CD-Rom teaching materials.

The effort at computerization can be extended to include not only general school curriculum but vocational training on a very wide range of occupational skills, which can then be made accessible through private and public vocational training outlets throughout the country.

At the same time, a national campaign should be launched to develop low-cost teaching computers that can introduced into existing schools on a very large scale. A tie-up may be possible with major international computer manufacturers to provide long term credit for this investment as it will serve as model for other countries and expand the entire world market for educational computers.

7

Health Care in India: Vision 2020

R. SRINIVASAN

Introduction

Key Linkages in Health

Health and health care need to be distinguished from each other for no better reason than that the former is often incorrectly seen as a direct function of the latter. Heath is clearly not the mere absence of disease. Good health confers on a person or groups freedom from illness and the ability to realize one's potential. Health is therefore best understood as the indispensable basis for defining a person's sense of well being. The health of populations is a distinct key issue in public policy discourse in every mature society often determining the deployment of huge economic and social resources. Final decisions in this regard will be influenced as much by the cultural understanding of health, illness and well being in that society, as by the other relevant determinants namely, extent of social disparities, reach of health services, quality and costs of care and current bio-medical understanding about health and illness.

Health care covers not merely medical care but also all aspects of pro preventive care too. Nor can it be limited to care rendered by or financed out of public expenditure within the government sector alone but must include incentives and disincentives for self care and care paid for by private citizens to get over ill health. Where as in India, private out-of-pocket expenditure dominates the cost financing health care, the effects are bound to be regressive. Heath care at its essential core is widely recognized to be a public good. Its demand and supply cannot, therefore, be left to be regulated solely by the invisible hand of the market. Nor can it be established on the considerations of utility-maximizing conduct alone.

What then could form the basis for a just health care system even as an ideal? Four criteria could be suggested- *first,* universal access, access to an adequate level, and access without excessive burden; *second,* fair distribution of financial costs for access and fair distribution of burden in rationing care and capacity and a constant search for improvement to a more just system; *third,* training providers for competence, empathy and accountability, and in the pursuit of quality care and cost-effective use of the results of relevant research. Last, special attention must be vigilantly provided to vulnerable groups such as children, women, disabled and the aged.

Forecasting in Health Sector

In general, predictions about future health of individuals and populations can be notoriously uncertain. Moreover, all projections of health care in India must in the end rest on the overall changes in its political economy and the progress made in poverty mitigation (health care to the poor) in reduction of inequalities (health inequalities affecting access/quality), in generation of employment/income streams (to facilitate capacity to pay and to accept individual responsibility for one's health), in public information and development communication (to promote preventive self care and risk reduction by conducive life styles) and in personal life style changes (often directly resulting from social changes and global influences). Of course, it will also depend on progress in reducing mortality and the likely disease load, efficient and fair delivery and financing systems in private and public sectors, attention to vulnerable sections, family planning and nutritional services, women's empowerment and the confirmed interest of the state to ensure just health care to the largest extent possible. To list them is to recall that Indian planning had at its best attempted to implement such a comprehensive synergistic approach within a democratic structure. It is another matter that it is now remembered only for its mixed success in tackling this gigantic problem.

Available Health Forecasts

Some forecasts are available on the new health challenges likely to emerge in India over the next few decades. Murry and Lopez (World Bank 2000) have provided a possible scenario of the Burden Of Disease (BOD) for India in the year 2020, based on a statistical model calculating the change in Disability-Adjusted Life Years

(DALYs) as applied to the population projections for 2020. The key conclusions must be understood keeping in the mind the fact that the concept of DALYs incorporates not only mortality but also disability, viewed in terms of healthy years of life lost. In this forecast, DALYs are expected to dramatically decrease in respect of diarrhoeal diseases and respiratory infections and less dramatically for maternal conditions. TB is expected to plateau by 2000, and HIV infections are expected to rise significantly up to 2010. Injuries may increase less significantly, the proportion of people above 65 will increase and as a result the burden of non-communicable disease will rise. Finally, cardio-vascular diseases, resulting from any of the risk associated with smoking, urban stress and improper diet, are expected to increase dramatically.

Under the same BOD methodology, another view is available from a four-state analysis done in 1996 (World Bank 2000). These four-states - AP, Karnataka, W. Bengal and Punjab represent different stages in the Indian health transition. The analysis reveals that the poorer and more populated states like West Bengal will still face a large incidence, of communicable diseases. More prosperous states, such as Punjab, further along the health transition profile, will witness sharply increasing incidence of non-communicable diseases especially in urban areas. The projections highlight the fact that we are still operating on unreliable or incomplete base data on mortality and causes of death, in the absence of vital registration statistics and know, as yet, little about how they differ between social classes and regions or about the dynamic patterns of change at work.

It also highlights the policy dilemma of how to balance between the articulate middle-upper class demand for more access to technologically advanced and subsidized clinical services and the more pressing needs of the poor for coverage of basic disease control interventions. This conflict over deployment of public resources will only get exacerbated in future. What matters further in such estimates are not societal averages with respect to health but sound data illumining specifically the health conditions of the disadvantaged among social groups in local areas. There has been a long tradition of health sector analysis carefully looking at unequal access, income poverty and unjustly distributed resources as the trigger that deny health needs of the poor. That tradition has been totally replaced by the currently dominant school of international thought about health which is concerned primarily with efficiency of systems measured by cost-effectiveness criteria and massive use of technology [Gwatkin 2000].

Future of State Provided Health Care

Historically, the Indian commitment to health development has been guided by two principles, leading to three consequences. The first principle was State responsibility for health care and the second (after independence) was free medical care for all (and not merely to those unable to pay).

The first set of consequences was inadequate priority to public health, poor investment in safe water and sanitation and to the neglect of the key role of personal hygiene in good health, culminating in the persistence of diseases like Cholera.

The second set of consequences pertains to substantially unrealized goals of National Health Policy (NHP) 1983 due to funding difficulties from compression of public expenditures and from organizational inadequacies. The ambitious and far reaching National Population Policy (NPP) 2000 goals and strategies have however been formulated on that edifice in the hope that the gaps and the inadequate would be removed by purposeful action. Without being too defensive or critical about its past failures, the rural health structure would have to be strengthened, funded and managed efficiently in all states by 2005. This can trigger many dramatic changes over the next twenty years in neglected aspects or rural health and of vulnerable segments.

The third set of consequences appears to be the inability to develop and integrate plural systems of medicine leading to the further failure to assign practical roles to the private sector and to assign public duties for private professionals.

To set right these gaps demanded patient redefinition of the State's role keeping the focus on equity. But during the last decade there has been an abrupt switch to market-based governance styles and much influential advocacy to reduce the State role in health in order to enforce overall compression of public expenditure and reduce fiscal deficits. People have therefore been forced to switch between weak and efficient public services and expensive private provision or, at the limit, forego care entirely except in life threatening situations, in many cases sliding into indebtedness. Health status of any population is not only the record of mortality and its morbidity profile but also a record of its resilience based on mutual solidarity and indigenous traditions of self-care assets normally invisible to the planner and the professional. Such resilience can be enriched only with the State retaining a strategic directional role for the good health of all its citizens in accordance with the constitutional mandate. Within such a framework the heterogenous private sector can be engaged as an additional instrument or a partner for achieving shared public health outcomes. Similarly there is some scope for getting basic skills regarding key community health issues developed and upgraded among the less than qualified medical force already serving in rural areas. Public programs in rural and poor urban areas engaging indigenous practitioners and community volunteers can prevent much seasonal and communicable disease using low cost traditional knowledge and based on the balance between food, exercise, medicine and moderate living. Such an overall vision of the public role of the heterogenous private sector must inform the course of future of State-led health care in the country.

Key Achievements in Health

Our overall achievement in regard to longevity and other key health indicators are impressive but in many respects uneven across states, The two Data Annexure at the end indicate selected health, demographic and economic indicators and highlight the changes between 1951 and 2001. In the past five decades, life expectancy has increased from 50 years to over 64 in 2000. Infant Mortality Rate (IMR) has come down from 147 to 75. Crude birth rates have dropped to 26.1 and death rates to 8.7.

At this stage, a process understanding of longevity and child health may be useful for assessing future progress. Longevity, always a key national goal, is not merely the reduction of deaths as a result of better medical and rehabilitative care at old age. In fact, without reasonable quality of life in the extended years marked by self-confidence and absence of undue dependency longevity make men only a display of technical skills. So quality of life requires as much external bio-medical interventions as culture-based acceptance of inevitable decline in faculties starting at sixty but run across life lived at all ages in reduction of mortality among infants through immunization and nutrition interventions and reduction of mortality among young and middle aged adults, including balanced information to adolescents about sexuality, reproduction and safe motherhood. At the same time, some segments will remain always more vulnerable - such as women due to patriarchy and traditions of infra-family denial, aged (whose survival but not always quality of life will increase with immunization) and the disabled (constituting a tenth of the population).

Reduction in child mortality involves as much attention to protecting children from infection as in ensuring nutrition and hence calls for a holistic view of mother and child health services. The cluster of services consisting of antenatal services, delivery care and post mortem attention and low birth weight, childhood diarrhoea and ARI management are linked priorities. Programme of immunization and childhood nutrition seen in better performing states indicate sustained attention to routine and complex investments into growing children as a group to make them grow into persons capable of living long and well. Often interest fades in pursuing the unglamorous routine of supervised immunization and is substituted by pulse campaigns etc. which in the long run turn out counter-productive. Indeed, persistence with improved routines and care for quality in immunization would also be a pathway to reduce the world's highest rate of maternal mortality.

In this context we may refer to the large ratio-based rural health infrastructure consisting of over five lakh trained doctors working under plural systems of medicine and a vast frontline force of over seven lakh Auxiliary Nurse Mid wives (ANMs), Multi Purpose Workers (MPWs) and Anganwadi workers besides community volunteers. The creation of such public work force should be seen as a major achievement in a country short of resources and struggling with great disparities in health status. As part of rural primary health care network lone, a total of 1.6 lakh subcenters, (with 1.27 lakh ANMs in position) and 22,975 PHCs and 2,935 CHCs (with over 24,000 doctors and over 3,500 specialists to serve in them) have been set up. To promote Indian systems of medicine and homeopathy, there are over

22,000 dispensaries 2,800 hospitals. Besides six lakh angawadis serve nutrition needs of nearly 20 million children and four million mothers. The total effort has cost the bulk of the health development outlay, which stood at over Rs. 62,500 crores or 3.64 per cent of total plan spending during the last fifty years.

On any count these are extraordinary infrastructural capacities created with resources committed against odds to strengthen grass roots. There have of course been facility gaps, supply gaps and staffing gaps, which can be filled up only by allocating about 20 per cent more funds and showing determined will to ensure good administration and synergy from greater congruence of services, but given the sheer size of the endeavour, there will always be some failure of commitment and in routine functioning. These get exacerbated by periodic campaign mode efforts and vertical programmes, which have only increased compartmentalized vision and over-medicalization of health problems. The initial key mistake arose from the needless bifurcation of health and family welfare and nutrition functions at all levels instead of promoting more holism. As a result of all this the structure has been precluded from reaching its optimal potential. It has got more firmly established at the periphery/subcenter level and dedicated to Reproductive and Child Health (RCH) services only. At Primary Health Centre (PHC) and Community Health Centre (CHC) levels this has further been compounded by a weak referral system. There has not been enough convergence in "escorting" children through immunization coverage and nutrition education of mothers and ensuring better food to children, including cooked midday meals and health checks al schools. There has also been no constructive engagement between allopathic and indigenous systems to build synergies, which could have improved people's perceptions of benefits from the infrastructure in ways that made sense to them.

One key task in the coming decades is therefore to utilize fully this vast created potential by attending to well known organizational motivational and financial gaps. The gaps have arisen partly from the source and scale of funds and partly due to lack of persistence, both of which can be set right. PHCs and CHCs are funded by states several of whom are unable to match Central assistance offered and hence these centers remain inadequate and operate on minimum efficiency. On the other hand, over two-thirds cost of three-fourths of subcenters are fully met by the Center due to their key role in family welfare services. But in equal part these gaps are due to many other non-monetary factors such as undue centralization and uniformity, fluctuating commitment to key routines at ground level, insufficient experimentation with alternatives such as getting public duties discharged through private professionals and ensuring greater local accountability to users.

Health Status Issues

The difference between rural and urban indicators of health status and the wide interstate disparity in health status are well known. Clearly the urban rural differentials are substantial and range from childhood and go on increasing the gap as one grows up to five years. Sheer survival apart, there is also the well-known under provision in rural areas in practically all social sector services. For the children growing up in rural areas the disparities naturally tend to get even worse when compounded by the widely practiced discrimination against women, starting with foeticide of daughters, often in prosperous States.

In spite of overall achievement, therefore, it is a mixed record of social development specially failing in involving people in imaginative ways. Even the averaged out good performance hides variations by social class or gender or region or state, many who have had to suffer the most due to lack of access or denial of access or social exclusion or all of them. This is clear from the fact that compared to the richest quintile, the poorest had 2.5 times more IMR and child mortality, TFR at double the rates and nearly 75 per cent malnutrition - particularly during the Nineties.

Not only are the gaps between the better performing and other states wide but in some cases have been increasing during the Nineties. Large differences also exist between districts within the same better performing state and the picture in urban areas which appear to have better health outcomes than rural areas although the figures may not fully reflect the situation in urban and peri-urban slums with large in migration with conditions comparable to rural pockets. It is estimated that urban slum population will grow at double the rate of urban population growth in the next few decades. India may have by

2020 a total urban population of close to 600 million living in urban areas with an estimated 145 million living in slums in 2001. What should be a fair measure for assessing success in enhancing health status of population in any forecast on health care?

Disease Load in India and China

We also need a basis for comparative scenario building. Among populous the nations of the world, China alone ranks in size and scale and in complexity comparable to India. Differences between an open and free society and a semi-controlled polity do matter. But the remarkable success in China in combating disease is due to sustained attention on the health of the young in China, and of public policy backed by resources and social mobilization. While comparing China and India in selected aspects of disease load, demography and public expenditures on health, the record of India must seem mixed compared to the more all round progress made by China. But this should also be seen in the perspective of the larger burden of disease in India compared to China and of the transactional costs of an open and free democracy.

Though India and China recorded the same rate of growth till '70s, China initiated reforms a full decade earlier. This gave it a head start for a higher growth rate and has resulted in an economic gap with India which has become wider over time. This is because domestic savings in China are 36 per cent of GDP whereas in India it hovers at 23 per cent, mostly in house-hold savings. Again, China attracted $40 billion in Foreign Direct Investment against $2 billion in India. Special Economic Zones and relaxed labour laws have helped. Public expenditure on health in China has been consistently higher, underlining the regressive nature of financing of health care in India. Nevertheless, it is not too unrealistic to expect that India should be able to reach by 2010 at least three-fourth the current level of performance of China in all key health indices.

India's current population is now a bit more than 75 per cent that of China and India will of course be catching up even more with China into the 21st century. This would be offset by the handicap that Indian progress will have to be steering through an open, free and democratic society. A practical rule-of-thumb measure for an optimistic forecast of future progress in India could be that between

2000 and 2010 India should do three fourth as well as China did in 1990-2000 and, after 2010, India should try to catch up with the rate of performance of China and do just as well thereafter. This will translate into, for instance, a growth rate of about 8 per cent for India till 2010 and as close to 10 per cent as possible thereafter thus enabling doubling first in ten years and doubling twice over every seven years thereafter prior to 2025. Keeping this perspective in mind, we may now examine the profile of major disease control effort, the effectiveness of available instruments for delivery and financing public health action and assess factors relevant to the size of our vulnerable segments within our emerging social pyramid over next two or three decades.

Major Disease Control Efforts

A careful analysis of the Global Burden of Disease (GBD) study focusing on age-specific morbidity during 2000 in ten most common diseases (excluding injuries) shows that 60 per cent of morbidity is due to infectious diseases and common tropical diseases, a quarter due to life-style disorders and 13 per cent due to potentially preventable perinatal conditions. Further, domestic R&D has so far been muted in its efforts against an estimated annual aggregate health expenditure in India of Rs. 80,000 crores. R&D expenditure in India for public and private sector combined was Rs. 1,150 crores only. India must play a larger part in its own efforts at indigenous R&D as very little world-wide expenditure on R&D is likely to be devoted to infectious diseases. For instance, out of the 1233 new drugs that came into the market between 1975 and 1997 only 11 were indicated specifically for tropical country diseases.

We already have the distinction of elimination or control acceptable to public health standards of smallpox and guinea worm diseases. In the draft National Health Policy-21 it has now been proposed to eliminate or control the following diseases within limits acceptable to public health practice. A good deal of the effort would be feasible.

- *Polio Yaws and leprosy by 2005* which seems distinctly feasible though the removal of social stigma and reconstructive surgery and other rehabilitation arrangements in regard to leprosy would remain inadequate for a decade or more.

- *Kalaazar by 2010 and Filalriasis by 2010* which also seems feasible due to its localized prevalence and the possibility of greater community-based work involving PR institutions in the simple but time-limited tasks or public health programs.
- *Blindness prevalence to 0.5 per cent by 2010* sees appears feasible due to a graying population. At present the programme is massively supported by foreign aid, as there are many other legitimate demands on domestic health budgets.
- *AIDS reaching zero growth by 2007* appears to be problematic as there are disputes even about base data on infected population. On most reckonings, affordable vaccines are not likely to be available soon nor anti-retro viral drugs appear likely at affordable prices in the near future. Further, the prevalence curve of Aids in India is yet to show its shape. There is also larger unresolved question of where HIV/AIDS should be fitted in our priorities of public health, especially in this massively foreign aided programme what will happen if aid does not become available at some point.

Unfinished Burden of Communicable Diseases

Apart from the above, there remains a vast unfinished burden in preventing, controlling or eliminating other major communicable diseases and in bringing down the risk of deaths in maternal and perinatal conditions. Endemic diseases arising from infection or lack of nutrition continue to account for almost two-thirds of mortality and morbidity in India. Indeed, eleven out of thirteen diseases recommended by the Bhore Committee were infectious diseases and at least three of them may well continue to be with us for the next two decades. Barring Leprosy which is almost on the path to total control by 2005, the other key communicable diseases will be TB Malaria and AIDS- to which diarrhoea in children and complicated and high risk maternity should be added in view of their pervasive incidence and avoidable mortality among the poorer and underserved sectors.

Tuberculosis

Tuberculosis has had a world wide resurgence including in India. It is estimated that about 14 million persons are infected, i.e., 1.55 per cent of total population suffer from radiologically active

Tuberculosis. About 1.5 million cases are identified and more than 3,00,000 deaths occur every year. Between NFHS 1 and NFHS 2 the prevalence has increased from 467 per lakh population to 544. Unfortunately, prevalence among working age adults (15-59) is even higher at 675. All these may well be underestimates in so far as patients are traced only through hospital visit. Only about half reach the hospital. Often wrong diagnosis by insufficiently trained doctors or misunderstood protocols is another key problem in both public and private sectors. TB is a wide spread disease of poverty among women living and working in ill ventilated places and in other undernourished persons in urban slums it is increasingly affecting the younger adults also in the economically productive segments. No universal screening is possible. Sputum positive test does not precede diagnosis but drugs are prescribed on the basis of fever and shadows, as a result, incomplete cure becomes common and delayed tests only prove the wrong diagnosis too late. Improved diagnosis through better training and clear protocols and elimination of drug resistance through incomplete cure should be a priority. Treatment costs in case of drug resistance can soar close to ten times the normal level of Rs. 3,000 to 4,000 per person treated. Similarly, even though the resistant strain may cover only 8 per cent at present, it could suddenly rise and as it approaches 20 per cent or so, there is a danger that TB may get out of control. The DOTS programme trying for full compliance after proper diagnosis is settling down but has already some claims of success. More than 3000 laboratories have been set up for diagnosis and about 1.5 lakh workers trained and with total population coverage by 2007, cure rates (already claimed to have doubled) may rise substantially. There is reason to hope that DOTS programs would prove a greater success over time with increased community awareness generation. The key issue is how soon and how well can it be integrated into the PHC system and made subject to routines of local accountability, without which no low cost regime of total compliance is feasible in a country as large as India.

An optimistic assessment could be that with commitment and with full use of infrastructure it will be possible to arrest further growth in absolute numbers of TB cases keeping it at below 1.5 million till 2010 even though the population will be growing. Once that is done TB can be brought down to less than a million, lie within internationally accepted limits and disappears as a major communicable disease in India by 2020.

Malaria

As regards malaria, we have had a long record of success and failure and each intervention has been thwarted by new problems and plagued by recrudescence. At present, India has a large manpower fully aware of all aspects of malaria but often low in motivation. It can be transformed into a large-scale work force for awareness generation, tests and distribution of medicine. In spite of past successes, there is evidence of reemergence with focal attacks of malaria with the virulent falciparum variety especially in tribal areas. Priority tribal area malaria stands fully funded by the Center. About two million cases of malaria are recorded all over India every year with seasonal high incidence local failures of control. Drug resistance in humans and insecticide resistant strains of mosquitoes present a significant problem. But there is a window of opportunity I respect of DDT sensitive areas in eastern India where even now malaria incidence can be brought down by about 50 per cent within a decade and be beneficial for control of kalazaar and Japanese ehcephalities (JE). There is growing interest and community awareness of biological methods of control of mosquito growth. Unfortunately, diligent ground level public health work is in grave disarray in these areas but can be improved by better supervision, greater use of Panchayat Raj Institutions and buildings on modest demonstrated successes. As regards a vaccine, there seems to be no sufficient incentive for international R&D to focus on a relatively lower priority or research. Roll back malaria programmes of the WHO are more likely to concentrate on Africa whose profile of malaria is not similar to ours. The search for a vaccine continues but has little likelihood of immediate success.

In spite of various difficulties, if the restructuring of the malaria work force and the strengthening of health infrastructure takes place, one can expect that the incidence can be reduced by a third or even upto half in the next decade or so. For this it is necessary that routine tasks like timely spraying and logistics for taking blood slides testing and their analysis and organic methods of reducing mosquito spread etc. are down staged to community level and performed under supervision through Panchayat with community participation, public education and local monitoring. Malaria can certainly be reduced by a third even upto a half in ten years, and there is a prospect of near freedom from malaria for most of the country by 2020.

The Case of AIDS

There is finally the case of HIV/AIDS. The magnitude in the numbers of HIV infected and of AIDS patients by 2025 can be known only as trends emerge over a decade from now when better epidemiological estimates are available but at present these figures are hotly contested. 'We can not start with the number infected with HIV as per NACO sentinel surveillance in 2000 at a cumulative total of 3.86 million, a figure disputed in recent public health debate. We can then assume that about 10 per cent will turn into full-blow cases of severe and intractable stage of AIDS. There is as yet no basis to know how many of those infected will become AIDS patients, preventive efforts focused on behaviour change will show up firmly only after a decade or so. During this period one can assume an additional 10 per cent growth to account for new cases every year. The NHP 2001 seeks to stop further infection by educating and counseling and condom supplies to level it off around 2007, which seems somewhat ambitious. We have yet to make a decisive dent into the problem of awareness with the broader population and so far we have been at work only on high risk groups. NFHS 2 shows that only a third of woman reported that they even knew about the HIV/AIDS. Further, such awareness efforts must be followed by multi-pronged and culturally compatible techniques of public education that go beyond segments easier to be convinced or behaviour changed. There are voices already raised about the appropriateness of IEC mass media content and of the under emphasis of face to face counseling, calling for innovative mobilization strategies rooted in indigenous belief systems.

What it implies is that we may be carrying by 2015 close to 5 million infected and upto a tenth of them could turn into full blown cases. We may not be able to level off infection by 2007. Further, the base magnitudes may turn out in actual fact to be wildly off the mark. On any account it is clear that AIDS can lead to high mortality among the productive groups in society affecting economic functioning as also public health. Even if 10 per cent of them, say 50 to 60000 cases, becomes full blown cases, the state has the onerous and grim choice to look at competing equities and decide on a policy for free treatment of AIDS patients with expensive anti-retro viral drugs. And if it decides not to, the issue remains as to how to evolve humane balanced and affordable policies that do not lead to a social breakdown. In about a decade vaccine development may possibly be successful and drugs may by more effective but they may not always be affordable nor can be given free.

There would hopefully be wider consultation with persons with caring sensibilities including AIDS patients on how to counsel in different eventualities and to get the balance right between hospital and home care and how to develop a humane affordable policy for anti retroviral drugs for AIDS patients. Is there a case for providing them with drug free of cost merely to extend their lives for few years? The matter involves a true dilemma, for public health priorities themselves certainly argue for more funds should address diseases constituting bigger population based hazards. Investments made in such expensive interventions can instead be made in supporting hospice efforts in the voluntary and private sectors.

Whatever position may emerge in research or spread of infection of case fatalities, a multipronged attempt for awareness must continue and tough choices must get discussed openly without articulate special, often urban middle class interests denying other views and especially public health priorities of the poor. The promotion of barrier protection must increase but has to be related to a system of values, which would be acceptable to the people's beliefs. We need to strengthen sentinel surveillance systems and awareness effort. We also need sensitive feed back on the effects they leave on younger minds for a balanced culturally acceptable strategy. All this is feasible and can be accomplished if we are not swept away by the power of funding and advocacy and fear of being accused to be out of line with dominant world opinion.

In any case, many of the ill cannot afford the high prices or have access to it from public agencies. The strict patent regime under TRIPS is bound to prevail, notwithstanding the ambivalently worded Doha decision of WTO, that public health emergencies provide sufficient cause of countries to use the flexibility available from various provisions of TRIPS. A recent analysis reveals that the three drug regime recommended will cost $10,000 per person per year from Western companies and the treatment will be lifelong. Three Indian companies are offering to Central Government anti retro viral drugs at $600/Rs. 30,000/per person per year and to an international charity at an even lower price $350/Rs. 13,000/per year provided it was distributed for humanitarian relief free in South Africa. It has been a public policy in Brazil that the drug is supplied free to all AIDS patients should be no exception. If drugs are supplied acting on a public health emergency basis and prices can stabilize at Rs. 1,000 or so per year the public health budget should be able to accommodate the cost weighed against true public criteria. But the aim of leveling off infection of 2007 still seems unlikely.

Maternal and Perinatal Deaths

Maternal and perinatal deaths are sizeable but the advantage here is that they can be prevented merely by more intensive utilization of existing rural health infrastructure. Policy and implementation must keep steady focus on key items such as improved institutional deliveries, better trained birth attendants and timely antenatal screening to eliminate anaemia and at the same time isolate cases needing referral or other targeted attention. After all, Tamil Nadu has by such methods ensured closed to 90 per cent institutional deliveries backed by a functional referral. Firm administrative will and concurrent supervision of specified screening tasks included in MCH services can give us a window of opportunity to dramatically bring down within a few years alarming maternal mortality, currently one of the highest in the world. From NFHS I data, it was estimated at 424 per lakh births. It has risen to 540 per lakh births in NFHS 2, but the WHO estimate puts it higher at 570.

There can be a systematic campaign over five years to increase institutional deliveries as near as possible to the Tamil Nadu level, also taking into account assisted home deliveries by trained staff with doctors at call. For the interim TBAs should be relied on through a mass awareness campaign involving Gram Panchayats too. Over a period of time there is no reason why ANMs entitled benefits of children to help in their growth and not remain as welfare measure. Using the infrastructures fully and with community participation and extensive social mobilization many tasks in nutrition are feasible and can be in position to make impact by 2010.

Child Health and Nutrition

Associated with this is the issue of infant and child mortality, (70 out of 1000 dying in the first year and 98 before vide years) and low birth weight (22 per cent underweight at birth and 47 per cent age adjusted weight at below three years) most mortality occurs from diarrhoea and the stagnation in IMR in the last few year is bound to have a negative effect on population stabilization goals. A recent review of the Ninth Plan indicated that even with accelerated efforts we may reach at best IMR/50 by 2003, but more likely IMR/56. Since the easier part of the problem is taking child mortality is over, every point gain hereafter will deal with districts at greater risk and needing better organizational efficiencies in immunization. At the same time, more streamlined RCH services are getting established as part of public systems and through private partnerships. Therefore, there is every reason to hope that the NPP 2000 target of 30 per thousand live births by 2010 will be met barring a few pockets of inaccessible and resource lean areas with stubborn persistence of poverty and dominantly composed of weaker sections (e.g., in part of Orissa as seen from NFHS 2).

As regards childhood diarrhoea, deaths are totally preventable by simple community action and public education by targeting children of low birth weights and detecting early those children at risk from malnutrition through proper low cost screening procedure, the present arrangement has got too burdened with attempting total population coverage getting all children weighed even once in three months and making ANMs depots for ORS and for simple drugs for fever and motivating the community to take pride in healthy children are the lessons of the success of the Tamil Nadu Nutrition Project. If this is done there is a reasonable chance of two-third decline in moderate malnutrition and abolition of serious grades completely by 2015. The success can be built upon till 2025 for reaching levels comparable to China.

Concentration on preventive measures of maternal and child health and in particular improved nutrition services will be particularly useful because it will help that generation to have a head start in good health who are going to be a part of the demographic bonus. The bonus is a young adult bulge of about 340 million (with not less than 250 million from rural population and about 100 million born in this century). The bonus will appear in a sequence with South Indian states completing the transition before North Indian states spreading it over the next three decades. To ensure best results at this stage the present nutritional services must be converted into targeted (and entitled) benefits of children to help in their growth and not remain as welfare measure. Using the infrastructures fully and with community participation and extensive social mobilization many tasks in nutrition are feasible and can be in a position to make impact by 2010.

Mild and moderate malnutrition still prevalent in over half of our young population can be halved if food as the supplemental pathway to better nutrition becomes a priority both for self reliance and lower costs. There has been a tendency for micro nutrient supplementation to overwhelm food derived nourishment. This trend is assisted by foreign aid but over a long run may prove unsustainable. By engaging the adolescents into proper nutrition, education and reproductive health awareness we can seamlessly weave into the nutritional security system of our country and a corps of informed, interconnected and imaginative ideas can be tried out. Such social mobilization at low cost can be the best preventive strategy as has been advocated for long by the Nutrition Foundation of India (Gopalan 2001) and can be a priority in this decade over the next two plan periods.

Unfinished Agenda - Non-communicable Diseases and Injuries

Three major such diseases, *viz.*, cancer, cardiovascular diseases and renal conditions - and neglect in regard to mental health conditions, have of late shown worrisome trends. Cures for cancer are still elusive in spite of palliatives and expensive and long drawn chemoor radiotherapy which often inflict catastrophic costs. In the case of CVD and renal conditions known and tried procedures are available for relief. There is evidence of greater prevalence of cancer even among young adults due to the stress of modern living. In India cancer is a leading cause of death with about 1.5 to two million cases at anytime to which seven lakh new cases are added every year with three lakh deaths. Over 15 lakh patients require facilities for diagnosis and treatment. Studies by WHO show that by 2026 with the expected increase in life expectancy, cancer burden in India will increase to about 14 lakh cases. CVD cases and diabetes cases are also increasing with an eight to 11 per cent prevalence of the latter due to fast life styles and lack of exercise.

Traumas and accidents leading to injuries are offshoots of the same competitive living conditions and urban traffic conditions. Data show one death every minute due to accidents or more than 1800 deaths every day. In Delhi alone about 150 cases are reported every day from accidents on the road and for every death eight living patients are added to hospitals due to injuries. There is finally the emerging aftermath of insurgencies and militant violence leading to mental illnesses of various types. It is estimated that 10 to 20 persons out of 1000 population suffer from severe mental illness and three to five times more have emotional disorder. While there are some facilities for diagnosis and treatment exist in major cities there is no access whatever in rural areas. It is acknowledged that the only way of handling mental health problems is through including it into the primary health care arrangements implying trained screening and counseling at primary levels for early detection.

All these are eminently feasible preventive steps and can be put into practice bv 2005 and we should be doing as well or better than China by 2020 considering the greater load of non-communicable diseases they bear now. The burden of non-communicable diseases will be met more and more by private sector specialized hospitals which spring up in urban centers. Facilities in prestigious public centers will also be under strain and they should be redesigned to take advantage of community-based approach of awareness, early detection and referral system as in the mode developed successfully in the Regional Cancer Center Kerala. Public sector institutions are also needed to provide a comparative basis for costs and evaluating technology benefits. For the less affluent sections, prolonged high tech cure will be unaffordable. Therefore, public funds should go to promote a routine of proper screening health education and self care and timely investigations to see that interventions are started in stages I and II.

Health Infrastructure in the Public Sector

Issues in regard to public and private health infrastructure are different and both of them need attention but in different ways. Rural public infrastructure must remain the mainstay for wider access to health care for all without imposing undue burden on them. Side by side the existing set of public hospitals at district and subdistrict levels must be supported by good management and with adequate funding and user fees and out contracting services, all as part of a functioning referral network. This demands better routines more accountable staff and attention to promote quality. Many reputed public hospitals have suffered from lack of autonomy, inadequate budgets for non-wage O&M leading to faltering and poorly motivated care.

All these being tackled in several States as part health sector reform, and will reduce the waste involved in simpler cases needlessly reaching tertiary hospitals directly. These attempts must persist without any wavering or policy changes or periodic denigration of their past working. More autonomy to large hospitals and district public health authorities will enable them to plan and implement decentralized, flexible and locally controlled services and remove the dichotomy between hospital and primary care services. Further, most preventive services can be delivered by down staging to a public health nurse much of what a doctor alone does now. Such long-term commitment for demystification of medicine and down staging of professional help has been lost among the politicians bureaucracy and technocracy after the decline of the PHC movement. One consequence is the huge regional disparities between states which are getting stagnated in the transition at different stages and sometimes, polarized in the transition. Some feasible steps in revitalizing existing infrastructure are examined below drawn from successful experiences and therefore feasible elsewhere.

Feasible Steps for Better Performance

The adoption of a ratio based approach to creating facilities and other inputs has led to shortfalls estimated upto 20 per cent. It functions well whereever there is diligent attention to supervised administrative routines such as orderly drugs procurement, adequate O&M budgets and supplies and credible procedures for redressal of complaints. Current PHC, CHC budgets may have to be increased by 10 per cent per year for five years to draw level. The proposal in the NHP 2001 is timely that state health expenditures be raised to 7 per cent by 2015 and to 8 per cent of state budgets thereafter. Indeed, the target could be stepped up progressively to 10 per cent by 2025. It also suggests that Central funding should constitute 25 per cent of total public expenditure in health against the present 15 per cent. The peripheral level at the subcenter has not been (and may not now ever be) integrated with the rest of the health system having become dedicated solely to reproduction goals.

The immediate task would be to look into deepening the range of work done at all levels of existing centers and in particular strengthen the referral links and fuller and flexible utilization of PHC/CHCs. Tamil Nadu is an instance where a review showed that out of 1400 PHCs 94 per cent functioned in their own buildings and had electricity, 98 per cent of ANMs and 95 per cent of pharmacists were in position. On an average every PHC treated about 100 patients, 224 out of the 250 open 24 hour PHCs had ambulances. What this illustrates is that every state must look for imaginative uses to which existing structures can be put to fuller use such as making 24 hours services open or trauma facilities in PHCs on highway locations etc.

The persistent under funding of recurring costs had led to the collapse of primary care in many states, some spectacular failures occurring in malaria and kalazar control. This has to do with adequacy of devolution of resources and with lack of administrative will, probity and competence in ensuring that determined priorities in public health tasks and routines are carried out timely and in full. Only genuine devolution or simpler tasks and resources to panchayats, especially when there will be a third women members - can be the answer as seen in Kerala or MP where panchayats are made into fully competent local governments with assigned resources and control over institutions in health care. Many innovative cost containment initiatives are also possible through focused management – as for instance in the streamlining of drug purchase stocking distribution arrangements in Tamil Nadu leading to 30 per cent more value with same budgets.

The PHC approach as implemented seems to have strayed away from its key thrust in preventive and public health action. No system exists for purposeful community focused public information or seasonal alerts or advisories on community health information to be circulated among doctors in both private practice and in public sector. PHCs were meant to be local epidemiological information centers which could develop simple community information sheets based on reporting from a network associating private doctors also as has been done successfully at CMC Vellore in their rural health projects or by the Khoj projects of the Voluntary Health Association of India. It is only through such community based approach that revitalization of indigenous medicines can be done and people trained in self care and accept responsibility for their own health.

PHC approach was also intended to test the extent to which non-doctor based healthcare was feasible through effective down staging of the delivery of simpler aspects of a care as is done in several countries through nurse practitioners and physician assistants, ANMs; etc. can each get trained and recognized to work in allotted areas under referral/supervision of doctors. This may indeed be more acceptable to the medical profession than the NHP proposal to restart licentiates in medicine as in the Thirties and give them shorter periods of training to serve rural areas. Such a licentiate system cannot now be recalled against the profession's opposition nor would people accept two level services.

Finally it is important to note some dangers inherent in arrangements that promote delivery systems substantially outside government channel either through NGOs or through registered societies at state and district levels. Clearly this may be a better approach than leaving it to the market and welcome as path breaking innovative efforts as a precursor to launching a public program. But as a long run delivery mechanism it is neither practical nor sustainable, as such arrangements tend to bypass government under our constitutional scheme of parliamentary responsibility and would also cut into the potential of Panchayat Raj Institutions. Each major disease control program has now got a separate society at state and district levels often as part of access to foreign aid. What is lost is the principle of parliamentary accountability over the flow of funds that arise out of voted budgets and international agreements to which Government is a party and answerable to Parliament. Like campaign modes and vertical interventions, the registered society approach may weaken the long-term commitment and integrity of public health care systems.

Shape of the Private Sector in Medicine

The key features of the private sector in medical practice and health care are well known. Two questions are relevant. What role should be assigned to it? How far and how closely should it be regulated? Over the last several decades, independent private medical practice has become widespread but has remained stubbornly urban with polyclinics, nursing homes and hospitals proliferating often through doctor entrepreneurs. At our level tertiary hospitals in major cities are in many cases run by business houses and use corporate business strategies and hi-tech specialization to create demand and attract those with effective demand or the critically vulnerable at increasing costs. Standards in some of them are truly world class and some who work there are outstanding leaders in their areas. But given the commodification of medical care as part of business plans it has not been possible to regulate the quality, accountability and fairness in care through criteria for accreditation, transparency in fees, medical audit, accountable record keeping, credible grievance procedures etc. Such accreditation, standard setting and licensure systems are best done under self regulation, but self regulation systems in Indian medical practice have been deficient in many respects creating problem in credibility. Acute care has become the key priority and continues to attract manpower and investment into related specialty education and facilities for technological improvement. Common treatments, inexpensive diagnostic procedures and family medicine are replaced and priced out of the reach of most citizens in urban areas.

Tertiary hospitals had been given concessional land, customs exemption and liberal tax breaks against a commitment to reserve beds for poor patients for free treatments. No procedures exist to monitor this and the disclosure systems are far from transparent, redressal of patient grievances is poor and allegations of cuts and commissions to promote needless procedure are common.

The bulk of non-corporate private entities such as nursing homes are run by doctors and doctors-entrepreneurs and remain *unregulated either in terms of facility competence standards or quality and accountability* of practice and sometimes operate without any systematic medical records and audits. Medical education has become more expensive and with rapid technological advances in medicine, specialization *has more attractive rewards*. Indeed, the reward expectations of private practice formerly spread out over career long earnings are squeezed into a few years, which becomes possible only by working *in hi tech hospital some times run as businesses.* The responsibilities of the private sector in regard to clinical and preventive tasks were not specified in the NHP 1983. Nor is there any coherent and practical strategy developed by government to engage the private sector in major public health tasks. The last decade of reforms in the health sector has tried to decrease the state's role in health permitting the possibility of its substitution by market forces. However, the details of a sound public-private partnership in health care has not yet emerged as a working proposition because there is still no clear commitment to shared public health outcomes in respect of national health goals. It is doubtful if such sharing is likely to be easy or reliable in the current context of the retreat of the state from its welfare functions which are expected to be performed through market forces. Hence there is likely to be little effective monitoring or regulation of private health care in the near future to minimize its escalating costs to patients. In fact, it has required the Supreme Court to lay down the professional obligations of private doctors in accidents and injuries who used to be refused treatment in case of potential becoming part of a criminal offence.

In doing so, there is a clear danger of exclusion of access for those not in a position to pay. For them it is sometime argued that risk pooling arrangements should act as a cushion to lighten the burden on those facing priced services essential to them but out of their normal reach. While conceding the fact that it is difficult for government to bear the entire clinical and public health tasks within limited resources, it is important to devise risk pooling arrangements that are not only innovative but also strongly in favour of fairness.

To a large extent the course of health sector reform in India confirms this trend. The distribution of the burden between the two sectors at state level would depend on the shape and size of the social pyramid in that state & its vulnerablity profile. There is no objection to introduce user fees, contractual arrangements, risk pooling, etc. for mobilization of resources for health care. But, the line should be drawn not so much between public and private roles, but between institutions and health care run as businesses and those run within a wider public perspective as a social enterprise with economic dimensions. Much experimentation in community services for basic health needs would be needed. In a market economy, health care will always be subject to three links, none of which should become out of balance with the other — the link between state and citizens' entitlement for health, the link between the consumer and provider of health services and the link between the physician and patient.

Health Financing Issues

Public Expenditure Levels

Fair financing of the costs of health care is an issue in equity and it has two aspects: how much is spent by Government on publicly funded health care and on what aspects? And secondly how heavily does the burden of treatment fall on the poor seeking health care? Health spending in India at 6 per cent of GDP is among the highest levels estimated for developing countries. In per capita terms it is higher than in China, Indonesia and most African countries but lower than in Thailand. Even on PPP $ terms India has been a relatively high spender.

Public health spending accounts for 25 per cent of aggregate expenditure the balance being out of pocket expenditure incurred by patients to private practitioners of various hues. Public spending on health in India has itself declined after liberalization from 1.3 per cent of GDP in 1990 to 0.9 per cent in 1999. Central budget allocations for health have stagnated at 1.3 per cent to total Central budget. In the states it has declined from 7.0 per cent to 5.5 per cent of State health budget. Considering the contrast with the Bhore Committee recommendation of 15 per cent committed to health from the revenue expenditure budget, Indeed WHO had recommended 5 per cent of GDP for health. The current annual per capita public health expenditure is no more than Rs. 160 and a recent World Bank review showed that over all primary health services account for 58 per cent of public expenditure mostly on salaries, and the secondary/tertiary sector for about 38 per cent, perhaps the greater part going to tertiary sector, including government funded medical education. Out of the total primary care spending, as much as 85 per cent was spent on curative services and only 15 per cent for preventive service (World Bank 1995). About 47 per cent of total Central and state budget is spent on curative care and health facilities. This may seem excessive at first sight but in face the figure is over 60 per cent in comparable countries, with the bulk of the expenditure devoted to publicly funded care or on mandated or voluntary risk pooling methods. In India close to 75 per cent of all household expenditure on health is spent from private funds and the consequent regressive effects on the poor is not surprising. In this connection, the proposals in the latest NHP are welcome seeking to restore the key balance towards primary care, and bring it to internationally accepted proportions in the course of this decade.

Private Expenditure Trends

Many surveys confirm that when services are provided by private sector it is largely for ambulatory care and less for inpatient care. There are variations in levels of cost, pricing, transactional conveniences and quality of services. There is evidence to suggest that disparities in income as such do not make a difference in meeting health care costs, except for catastrophic or life threatening situations. Finally, it has been established that between two-third to three-forth of all medical expenditure is spent on privately provided care. Every household on an average spends up to 10 per cent of annual household consumption in meeting health care needs. This regressive burden shows up vividly in the cycle of incomplete cure followed by recurrence of illness and drug resistance that the poor face in diseases like TB or Kalazar or Malaria especially for daily wage earners who cannot afford to be out of work.

Privatization has to be distinguished from private medical practice which has always been substantial within our mixed economy. What is critical however is the rapid commercialization of private medical practice in particular its uneven quality of care. There are complex reasons for this trend. First is the high scarcity cost of good medical education, and second the reward differential between public and corporate tertiary hospitals leading to the reluctance of the young professional to be lured away from the market to public service in rural areas and finally there is the compulsion of returns on investment whenever expensive equipment in installed as part of practice. Increasingly, this has shifted the balance from individual practice to institutionalized practice in hospitals, polyclinics, etc. This conjunction explodes into unbearable cost escalation when backed by a third party payer system. This in turn induces increases in insurance premiums making such cover beyond the capacity to pay. There is a distinct possibility of such cycles of cost escalation periodically occurring in the future, will be promoted further by global transfer of knowledge and software, tele-medicine etc., especially after the advent of predictive medicine and gene manipulation.

Doctors practicing in the private sector are sometimes accused of prescribing excessive, expensive and risky medicines and with using rampant and less than justified use of technology for diagnosis and treatment. Some method of accreditation of hospitals and facilities and better licensure systems of doctors is however likely within a decade. This will enables some moderation in levels of charges in using new technology. High cost of care is sometimes sought to be justified as necessary due to defensive medicine practiced in order to meet risks under the Consumer Protection Act. There is little evidence from decisions of Consumer Courts to justify such fears. While the line between mistaken diagnosis and negligent behaviour will always remain thin, case law has already begun to settle around the requirement of the doctor's ability to apply reasonable skills and not the highest degree of skill. What has been established is the right of the patient to question the treatment and procedures if there is failure to treat according to standard medical practice or if less than adequate care was taken.

As health insurance gets established it may be necessary to impose more stringent criteria and restrictions on physician performance which may tempt them into defensive medicine. There may also be attempt at collusive capture and (indirect ownership) of insurance companies by corporate hospitals as in other countries. Advances in medical technology are rapid and dominant and easily travel world wide and are often seen as good investment and brand equity in the private sector. Private independent practices - and to a smaller extent hospitals, dispensaries, nursing homes tele- are seen as markets for medical services with each segment seeking to maximize gains and build mutually supporting links with other segments. More than one study on the quality of care indicates that sometimes more services are performed to maximize revenue, and services/medicines are prescribed which are always not necessary.

Allegations are also widely made of collusive deals between doctors and hospitals with commissions and cuts exchanged to promote needless referral, drugs or procedures (World Bank 1995). Appropriate regulation is likely in the next decade for minimum standards and accountability and that should consist of a balanced mix of self-regulation external regulation by standard setting and accreditation agencies including private voluntary health insurance.

How far can Health Insurance Help?

What constitutes a fair distribution of the costs of care among different social groups will always be a normative decision emerging out of political debate. It includes risk pooling initiatives for sharing costs among the healthy and the sick leading to insurance schemes as a substitute for, or as supplementary to, State provision for minimum uniform services. It also covers risk sharing initiatives across wealth and income involving public policy decisions on progressive taxation, merit subsidy and cross subsidization by dual pricing. Both will continue to be necessary in our conditions with more emphasis on risk sharing as growth picks up. Risk pooling within private voluntary and mandated insurance schemes has become inevitable in all countries because of the double burden of sickness and in order to ensure that financial costs of treatment do not become an excessive burden relative to incomes. It is difficult but necessary to embed these notions of fair financing into legislation, regulations and schemes and programs equity is aimed at in health care.

With the recent opening up of the general Insurance sector to foreign companies, there is the prospect of two trends. There is likely to be a highly competitive new health insurance market in the future. Business will expand easier by deepening existing risk areas covered rathar than by widening ambit of coverage. The second trend would be to concentrate on urban middle and upper classes and settled jobholders with capacity to pay and with a perceived interest in good health of the family. Both trends make sound business sense in a vast growth market and would increase extensive hospital use and protection against huge hospitalization expenses, and will get promoted by urban private hospitals since their clientele will increase.

Insurance is a welcome necessary step and must doubtless expand to help in facilitating equitable health care to shift to sections for which Government is responsible. Indeed, for those not able to access insurance it is the Government that will have to continue to provide the minimum services, and intervene against market failures including denial through adverse selection or moral hazard. In the long run the degree of inequity in health care after insurance systems are set up will depend ironically on the strength and delivery of the public system itself as a counterpoise in holding costs and relevance in technology.

The insurable population in India has been assessed at 250 million and at an average of Rs. 1,000 per person the premium amount per year would be Rs. 25,000 crores and is expected to treble in ten years. While the insurance product will dutifully reflect the demands of this colossal market and related technological developments in medicine, it should be required to extend beyond hospitalization and cover domiciliary treatment too in a big way; for instance, extending cover to ambulatory maternal and selected chronic conditions like Asthma more prevalent among the poor.

The insurance regulatory authority has announced priority in licensing to companies setting up health insurance as key business and has emphasized the need for developing new products on fair terms to those at risk among the poor and in rural areas. Much will turn on what progress takes place through sound regulation covering some aspects indicated below. In order to be socially relevant and commercially viable the scheme must aim at a proper mix of health hazards and cover many broad social classes and income groups. This is possible in poor locations or communities only if a group view is taken and on that basis a population- based risk is assessed and community rated premiums determined covering families for all common illnesses and based on epidemiologically determined risk.

In order that exclusions, co-payments, deductibles etc. remain minimum and relevant to our social situation, some well judged government merit subsidy can be incorporated into anti poverty family welfare or primary education or welfare pension schemes meant for old age. Innovative community based new products can be developed by using the scattered experience of such products for instance in SEWA, so that a minimum core cover can be developed as a model for innovative insurance by panchayats with reinsurance backup by companies and government bearing part of promotional costs. The bulk of the formal sector may be covered by an expanded mandatory insurance with affordable cover and convenient modes of premium payment. Outside the formal manufacturing sector innovative schemes can be designed around specific occupation groups in the informal sector which are steadily becoming a base for old age pension entitlements, as in Kerala and Tamil Nadu - and these can be brought under common risk rating. Finally, as in the West, health insurance should develop influence and capacity as a bulk purchaser of medical and hospital services so as to impact on quality and cost and provide greater understanding about Indian health and illness behaviours, patterns of utilization of care and intra family priorities for accessing medical care. Health insurance should be welcomed as a force for a fairer healthcare system. But its success should be judged on how well new products are developed with a cover beyond hospitalization, how fairly and inclusively the cover is offered and how far community rated premiums are established. The IRDA has an immense responsibility and with its leadership one can optimistically expect about 30 per cent coverage by 2015 relieving the burden on the public systems.

Health Perceptions and Plural Systems

Health perceptions play an important part in ensuring sound health outcomes. To a large extent they are culturally determined but also subject to change occurring with economic growth and social development. People intuitively develop capacity to make choices for being treated under the western of indigenous systems of medicines, keep a balance between good habits traditionally developed for healthy living and modem lifestyles, decide on where to go for chronic and acute care and how to apportion intra-family utilization of health care resources. The professional is generally bound by his discipline and its inherent logic of causation and effect and tends to discount even what work as successful practice, but does not fall within the accepted understanding of his profession.

Some movement is occurring among eminent allopathic doctors trying, for instance, to rework Ayurveda theory in a modem idiom starting from respectful reverse analysis for actual successful contemporary practice of Ayurveda and provide a theoretical frame linking it to contemporary needs. There is evidence from public health campaigns in Tamil Nadu where every seventh person spontaneously expressed a preference for Sidda Medicine. Homeopathy for chronic ailment is widely accepted. The herbal base for Ayurveda medicine widely practiced in the Himalayan belt has drawn world attention. A huge export market remains to be tapped according to the knowledgeable trade sources but the danger of bio-privacy remains and legal enablements should be put in place. Soon that would fully expand on our rights under the WTO agreements. The national policy on ISM&H has attempted to place these plural systems in a modem service delivery and research and education context, it has covered its natural resource base, traditional knowledge base and development of institutions to carry a national heritage forward.

There is hope for the survival and growth of the sector only if it becomes an example of convergence between people's and planner's perceptions and ensure its relevance, accountability and affordability to contemporary illnesses and conditions. At the same time it is undeniable that there is much cross practice by ISM practitioners which usually include prescriptions under western medicine but as part of indigenous treatment. Appropriate regulation is needed to protect people from fraud and other dangers but the larger question is how to make the perceptions of the professionals and planners regarding indigenous system of medicine less ambivalent. The separate department for ISM&H should be able to bring about some functional integration of ISM and western medicine in service delivery for common illnesses at PHC levels by 2005 whereby it will usher in an uniquely Indian system of care.

Emerging Scenario

What then can we conclude about the prospects of health care in India in 2020? An optimistic scenario will be premised on an average 8 per cent rate of economic growth during this decade and 10 per cent per annum thereafter. If so, what would be the major fall out in terms of results on the health scene? In the first place, longevity estimates can be considered. China in 2000 had a life-expectancy at birth of 69 years (M) and 73(F) whereas India had respectively 60(M) and 63(F). More importantly, healthy life expectancy at birth in China was estimated in the World Health Report 2001 at 61(M) and 63.3(F) whereas in

Indian figures were 53(M) and 51.7(F). If we look at the percentage of life expectancy, i.e. years lost as a result of the disease burden and effectiveness of health care systems, Chinese men would have lost 11.6 years against Indian men losing 12.7 years. The corresponding figures are 13.2 for Chinese women and 17.5 for Indian women. Clearly, an integrated approach is necessary to deal with avoidable mortality and morbidity and preventive steps in public health are needed to bridge the gaps, especially in regard to the Indian women. Taking all the factors into consideration, longevity estimates around 20-25 could be around 70 years, perhaps, without any significant distinction between men and women.

This leads us to the second question of the remaining disease burden in communicable and non-communicable diseases, the effectiveness of interventions, such as, immunization and maternal care and the extent of vulnerability among some groups. These issues have been dealt with in detail earlier. Clearly, an optimistic forecast would envisage success in polio, yaws, leprosy, kalazar filaria and blindness. As regards TB it is possible to arrest further growth in absolute numbers by 2010 and thereafter to bring it to less than an million within internationally accepted limits by 2020. With regard to Malaria, the incidence can be reduced by a third or even upto half within a decade. In that case, one can expect near freedom from Malaria from most of the countries by 2020. As regards AIDS, it looks unlikely that infection can be leveled of by 2007. The prognosis in regard to the future shape of HIV/AIDS is uncertain. However, it can be a feasible aim to reduce maternal mortality from the present 400 to 100 per lakh population by 2010 and achieve world standards by 2020.

As regards child health and nutrition, it is possible to reach IMR/30 per thousand live births by 2010 in most parts of the country though in some areas, it may take a few years more. What is important is the chance of achieving two-third decline in moderate malnutrition, and abolition of serious malnutrition completely by 2015. In the case of cancer, it is feasible to set up an integrated system for proper screening, early detection, self care and timely investigation and referral. In the matter of disease burden as a whole, it is feasible to attempt to reach standards comparable to China from 2010 onwards.

Taking the third aspect, *viz.*, fairness in financing of health care and reformed structure of health services, an optimistic forecast would be based on the fact that the full potential of the vast public health infrastructure would be fully realized by 2010. Its extension to urban areas would be moderated to the extent substantial private provision of health care is available in urban areas, concentrating on its sensible and effective regulation. A reasonably wide network of private voluntary health insurance cover would be available for the bulk of the employed population and there would be models of replicable community-based health insurance available for the unorganized sector. As regards the private sector in medicine, it should be possible in the course of this decade to settle on the fair basis the public role of private medical practice - independent or institutional. For this purpose, more experiments are to be done for promoting public-private partnerships, focusing on the issue of how to erect them on the basis of shared public health outcome as the key basis for the partnership. A sensible mixture of external regulation and professional self-regulation can be devised in consultation with the profession to ensure competence, quality and accountability. The future of plural systems in medical understanding and evaluation of comparative levels of competence and reliability in different systems - a task in which, the separate department for Indian systems of medicine and homeopathy will play a leading role in inducting quality into the indigenous medical practices.

The next issue relates to the desirable level of public expenditure towards health services. China devotes 4.5 per cent to its GDP as against India devoting 5.1 per cent. But this hides the fact that in China, public expenditure constitutes 38 per cent whereas in India, it is only 18 per cent of total health expenditure. An optimistic forecast would be that the level of public expenditure will be raised progressively such that about 30 per cent of total health expenditure would be met out of public funds by progressively increasing the health budget in states and the centre and charging user fees and improve local facilities in appropriate cases. The figure mentioned would perhaps correspond to the proportion of the population which may still need assistance is social development by 2020.

Finally, it is proper to remember that health is not a mere technical or management issue but at bottom an issue in justice. It is in this context that we should ask the question as to how far and in what way would politics get engaged in health care? The record is disappointing. Most health sector issues figuring in political debate are those that affect interest groups and narrow but dramatised issue seldom central to choices in health care policy. For instance, conditions of service and reward systems for government doctors have drawn much attention often based on interservice comparison of no wider interest. Intersystem problems of our plural medical care have drawn more attention from courts than from politics. Hospital management and strikes, poor working of the MCI and corruption in recognition of colleges, dramatic cases of spurious drug supply etc. have been debated but there has been no sustained attention on such issues as to why malaria recrudescence is so common in some parts of India or why complaints about absence of informed consent or frequent in testing on women, or on the variations in prices and availability of essential drugs or for combating epidemic attacks in deprived areas seldom draw attention. The far reaching recommendations made by the Hathi Committee report and the Lentin Commission report, have been implemented patchily. The role to be assigned to private sector in medicine, the need for a good referral system or the irrationality in drug prescriptions and sue have seldom been the point of political debate. Indeed, the lack luster progress of MNP over the Plans shows political disinterest and the only way for politics to become more salient to the health of the poor and the reduction of health inequalities is for a much greater transfer of public resources for provision and financing - as has happened in the West, not only in UK or Canada but in the US itself with a sizable outlay on Medicaid and Medicare.

8

Health, Nutrition, Population: Vision 2020

PREMA RAMACHANDRAN

Health

Improvement in the health status of the population has been one of the major thrust areas for the social development programmes of the country. This was to be achieved through improving the access to and utilization of health services with special focus on underserved and underprivileged segments of the population. Over the last five decades, India has built up a vast health infrastructure and manpower at primary, secondary and tertiary care in Government, voluntary and private sectors. Professionals and paraprofessionals trained in the medical colleges in modern medicine and ISM&H and paraprofessional training institutions man these institutions. The population has become aware of the benefits of health-related technologies for prevention, early diagnosis and effective treatment for a wide variety of illnesses and accessed available services. Technological advances and improvement in access to health care technologies, which were relatively inexpensive and easy to implement, had resulted in substantial improvement in health indices of the population and a steep decline in mortality (Table 1). The extent of access to and utilization of health care varied substantially between states, districts and different segments of society; this to a large extent, is responsible for substantial differences between states in health indices of the population.

During the 1990s, the mortality rates reached a plateau and the country entered an era of dual disease burden. Communicable diseases have become more difficult to combat because of development of insecticide resistant strains of vectors, antibiotics resistant strains of bacteria and emergence of HIV infection for which there is no therapy.

Longevity and changing life style have resulted in the increasing prevalence of non-communicable diseases. Under nutrition, micro nutrient deficiencies and associated health problems coexist with obesity and non-communicable diseases. The existing health system suffers from inequitable distribution of institutions and manpower. Even though the country produces over 17,000 doctors in modern system of medicine and similar number of ISM&H practitioners and paraprofessionals, there are huge gaps in critical manpower in institutions providing primary healthcare, especially in the remote rural and tribal areas where health care needs are the greatest.

Table 1

Time Trends (1951-2000) in Health Care

	1951	*1981*	*2000*
SC/PHC/CHC	725	57,363	1,63,181 (99-RHS)
Dispensaries & Hospitals (all)	9209	23,555	43,322 (95-96-CBHI)
Beds (Pvt. & Public)	117,198	569,495	8,70,161 (95-96-CBHI)
Doctors (Modern System)	18,054	1,43,887	7,37,000 (98-99- MCI)
Nursing Personnel	61,800	2,68,700	5,03,900 (99-INC)
Malaria (cases in million)	75	2.7	2.2
Leprosy (cases/ 10,000 population)	38.1	57.3	3.74
Small Pox (no. of cases)	>44,887	Eradicated	
Guineaworm (no. of cases)		>39,792	Eradicated
Polio (no. of cases)		29709	265
Life Expectancy (Years)	36.7	54	64.6 (RGI)
Crude Birth Rate	40.8	33.9 (SRS)	26.1 (99 SRS)
Crude Death Rate	25	12.5 (SRS)	8.7 (99 SRS)
IMR	146	110	70 (99 SRS)

Source: National Health Policy - 2002

As the country undergoes demographic and epidemiological transition, it is likely that larger investments in health will be needed even to maintain the current health status because tackling resistant infections and non-communicable diseases will inevitably lead to escalating health care costs. Last two decades have witnessed explosive expansion in expensive health care related technologies and broadening diagnostic and therapeutic avenues. Increasing awareness and rising expectations to access these have widened the gap between what is possible and what is affordable for the individual or the country. Policy makers and programme managers realise that in order to address the increasingly complex situation regarding access to good quality care at affordable costs, it is essential to build up an integrated health system with appropriate screening, regulating access at different levels and efficient referral linkages. However, both health care providers and health care seekers still feel more comfortable with the one-to-one relationship with each other than with the health system approach.

Another problem is the popular perception that curative and preventive care compete for available resources, with the former getting preference in funding. Efforts to convince the public that preventive and curative care are both part of the entire spectrum of health care ranging from health promotion, specific protection, early diagnosis and prompt treatment, disability limitation and rehabilitation and that to improve the health status of the population both are equally essential have not been very successful. Traditionally, health service (both government and private) was perceived as a social responsibility albeit a paid one. Growing commercialisation of health care and medical education over the last two decades has eroded this commitment, adversely affecting the quality of care, trust and the rapport between health care seekers and providers.

Faced with the problems of sub-optimally functioning health care system and providing adequate investment for improving health, Ninth Plan emphasized the need for:

- Reviewing the changing health scenario and assess response of the public, voluntary and private sector health care providers as well as the population themselves to the changing situation.
- Reorganizing health systems so that they become efficient and effective.
- Introducing health system reforms which ensure access to public health programmes free of cost to all and enable the population to obtain essntial health care at affordable cost.

The ongoing health system reforms broadly fall into three categories: structural and functional, aimed at improving efficiency, financial, aimed at improving resource available and governance related, aimed at improving transparency and accountability. It was envisaged that the public sector will play the lead role in health systems reform.

The Health Care System

The Health care system consists of:

- Primary, secondary and tertiary care institutions, manned by medical and paramedical personnel;
- Medical colleges and para-professional training institutions to train the needed manpower and give the required academic input;
- Programme managers managing ongoing programmes at central, state and district levels; and
- Health management information system consisting of a two-way system of data collection, collation, analysis and response.

So far the interaction between these components of the system had been sub-optimal. In spite of the plethora of primary, secondary and tertiary care institutions and medical college hospitals there are no well organised referral linkages between the primary, secondary and tertiary care institutions in the same locality. The programme managers and teachers in medical colleges do not link with institutions in any of the three tiers; essential linkages between structure and function are not in place. The health sector is currently undertaking structural and functional reforms aimed at correcting these problems and improving efficiency. Major efforts include:

- Reorganisation and restructuring the existing government health care system including the ISM&H infrastructure at the primary, secondary and tertiary care levels with appropriate referral linkages. These institutions will have the responsibility of taking care of all the health problems (communicable, non-communicable diseases) and deliver Reproductive and Child Health (RCH) services for people residing in a well-defined geographic urban and rural area;
- Development of appropriate two-way referral systems utilising Information Technology (IT) tools to improve communication, consultation and referral right from primary care to tertiary care level;

- Building up an efficient and effective logistics system for the supply of drugs, vaccines and consumables based on need and utilisation;
- Horizontal integration of all aspects of the current vertical programmes including supplies, monitoring, information education communication and motivation (IECM), training, administrative arrangements and implementation so that they are integral components of health care; there will be progressive convergence of funding, implementation and monitoring of all health and family welfare programmes under a single field of administration beginning at and below district level;
- Building up efficient and effective logistic system for supply of drug, vaccines and, consumables based on the need and utilisation;
- Mainstreaming ISM&H practitioners, so that in addition to practising their system of care, they can help in improving the coverage of the National Disease Control Programmes and Family Welfare Programme;
- Increasing the involvement of voluntary and private organisations, self-help groups and social marketing organisation in improving access to health care;
- Improving the efficiency of the existing health care system in the government, private and voluntary sectors and building up appropriate linkages between them;
- Building up tele linkages between villages, Subcentre, PHC, FRU, district and tertiary care centers; linking tertiary care institutions especially in the remote areas (eg north-eastern states) with major super-speciality institutions for other regions so that patients could benefit from tele-consultations;
- Increasing use of Information Technology for health management. All subsectors dealing with the generation, transmission and utilisation of demographic and epidemiological data such as bio-informatics, bio-statistics, HMIS and the Decision Support Systems (DSS) will be used in health planning and management building up a fully functional, accurate Health Management Information System

(HMIS) utilising currently available IT tools; this real time communication link will send data on births, deaths, diseases, request for drugs, diagnostics and equipment and status of ongoing programmes through service channels within existing infrastructure and manpower and funding; it will also facilitate decentralized district based planning, implementation and monitoring;

- Building up an effective system of disease surveillance and response at the district, state and national level as a part of existing health services; and
- Improving inter sectoral coordination.

Human Resource Development for Health

During new century, medical education faces newer opportunities and challenges. The country has to train an adequate number of health professionals with appropriate knowledge, skill and attitude to meet the health care needs of the growing population and dual disease burden. Priority areas for Human Resources Development for Health were:

- Creation of a district data base on requirement, demand and availability for health manpower in the government, private and voluntary sectors;
- Periodic updating of information on
    - Requirement availability and of different categories of health manpower;
    - Health manpower production based on the needs;
    - Improvement in quality of undergraduate/postgraduate education;
- Promotion of equitable and appropriate distribution of health manpower;
- Continuing medical education for knowledge (using distance education technology and IT linkages) and skill upgradation and appropriate people and programme orientation; and
- Continuing multiprofessional education for promoting team work and intersectoral co-ordination.

In this era of globalization, India with its excellent teachers and abundant clinical material can become a key player in medical education. The health care institutions can transform India into a major medical tourism destination. Appropriate investment in research and development and quality control can result in a massive expansion of the pharmaceutical sector. The next two decades will show whether the country has successfully used these opportunities to:

- train and provide gainful employment to the highly skilled medical manpower;
- improving community awareness, participation and effective utilisation of available services; and
- use of PRIs in improving community participation and monitoring implementation of programmes.

Indian Systems of Medicine and Homoeopathy

The Indian Systems of Medicine and Homoeopathy consist of Ayurveda, Siddha, Unani and Homoeopathy, and therapies such as Yoga and Naturopathy. Some of these systems are indigenous and others such as Homeopathy have over the years become a part of Indian tradition. Prior to the advent of modern medicine these systems had, for centuries, catered to the health care needs of the people; these systems are widely used even today because their practitioners are acceptable both geographically and culturally, are accessible and their services and drugs are affordable.

During the next two decades a major thrust will be given to mainstream ISM&H system and utilise ISM&H practitioners by,

- Ensuring that ISM&H clinics are located in the primary, secondary and tertiary care institutions providing complimentary system of care in these institutions and ISM& H care is funded as a part and parcel of funds provided for these institutions;
- Specially focusing on use of ISM&H therapeutic modalities for diseases for which effective drugs free of serious side effects are not available in the modern system of medicine and for prevention and management of lifestyle-related chronic diseases;
- Increasing utilisation of ISM&H practitioners working in Government, voluntary and private sector to improve IEC,

counselling so that utilisation and completion of treatment in National disease control and Family Welfare programmes improve;

- Explore opportunities in public and private sector for health tourism and set up regulations in this regard.

Prevention and Management of Communicable and Non-communicable Diseases

Appropriate strategies for combating the dual disease burden for prevention, detection and management of communicable and non-communicable disease through existing health care infrastructure will be evolved, implemented and evaluated. Modalities to improve delivery of services pertaining to these programmes through the existing health services should be worked out. Efforts will be made to improve states ownership of the programmes, participation of the community, private sector and NGOs. Local accountability and intersectoral co-ordination should be improved through the involvement of PRIs. Evaluation and operational research to rectify problems in implementation and improving efficiency will receive attention.

Appropriate modification will be required in the health care delivery as the country undergoes demographic and epidemiological transition and non communicable disease emerge as major public health problems. In view of this there is a need to obtain data on not only mortality but also morbidity due to chronic illnesses and disabilities and take them into account while formulating public health programmes. There are wide inter-state in differences health indices, morbidity rates and rate of demographic and epidemiological transition. Under these conditions, it is important to:

- ascertain and document morbidity and mortality due to major health problems in different states/districts;
- evolve appropriate interventions programmes;
- invest adequately in well targeted interventions;
- implement intervention effectively by modifying the health care system; and
- monitor the impact on the morbidity and mortality.

Such an effort would require a reliable sustainable database for mortality and morbidity. While mortality data can be obtained through strengthening of CRS/SRS and ascertainment of the cause of death, the data base for morbidity can come only through a strengthened HMIS supplemented by the data from disease surveillance. When sustained, these three systems should, over the next two decades, provide valuable insights regarding time trends in morbidity and mortality in different states/districts. Development of this data base is critical for evolving appropriate health policies and strategies, identifying priority areas for investment of available funds and bring about modifications in the existing health system to ensure equitable, efficient and effective implementation of the programmes to tackle dual disease burden.

In addition to these the health system is getting geared up to tackle some of the emerging problems through:

- Strengthening programmes for the prevention, detection and management of health consequences of the continuing deterioration of the ecosystems; improving the linkage between data from ongoing environmental monitoring and that on health status of the people residing in the area; making health impact assessment a part of environmental impact assessment in developmental projects;
- Improving the safety of the work environment in organized and unorganised industrial and agricultural sectors especially among vulnerable groups of the population;
- Developing capabilities at all levels, for emergency and disaster prevention and management; evolving appropriate management systems for emergency, disaster, accident and trauma care at all levels of health care;
- Effective implementation of the provisions for food and drug safety; strengthening the food and drug administration both at the centre and in the states;
- Screening for common nutritional deficiencies especially in vulnerable groups and initiating appropriate remedial measures; evolving and effectively implementing programmes for improving nutritional status, including micronutrient nutritional status of the population.

Medical Research

Medical research can play a major role in improving access to health care. In India, most of the morbidity and mortality is due to illnesses for which simple, inexpensive and effective preventive measures and time-tested cost-effective curative interventions are available. Therefore, priority has been given to health systems research for improving service delivery and coverage as well as operational research aimed at improving access to technological advances. Basic and clinical research leading to development of products, drugs, vaccines for prevention, diagnosis and management of illnesses especially major health problems for which currently there is no effective cure are encouraged. Health policy research and health system research at the national level is essential and a reliable information base is a pre-condition for effective investment in health care and performance assessment of the health system.

Currently, Indian industry is investing about five per cent of turnover on research and development. These investments may have to be augmented so that the Indian pharmaceutical industry achieves its full potential. Parallel efforts to improve public sector-funded research are also essential for the development of drugs for the treatment of public health problems such as emerging drug resistance development of newer contraceptives and vaccines. The private sector may not be willing to make requisite investments in these areas because of very low profit margins.

Quality Assurance and Redressal Mechanisms

Quality assurance and redressal mechanism is another major area that will require increasing attention during the next two decades. A transparent procedure for defining the norms of quality and cost in various settings and then review is an essential step in improving quality of care. There will be efforts to,

- introduce a range of comprehensive regulations prescribing minimum requirements of qualified staff, conditions for carrying out specialized interventions and a set of established procedures for quality assurance.
- evolve standard protocols for care for various illnesses; at primary, secondary and tertiary care settings public sector hospitals, medical colleges, professional associations to play

a major role in this exercise; improvement in the quality of care at all levels and settings by evolving and implementing a whole range of comprehensive norms for service delivery; prescribing minimum requirements of qualified staff, conditions for carrying out specialised interventions and a set of established procedures for quality assurance.

- evolve treatment protocols for the management of common illnesses and diseases; promotion of the rational use of diagnostics and drugs.
- evolve, implement and monitor transparent norms for quality and cost of care in different health care settings.
- improve quality assurance and redressal mechanism such as Consumer Protection Act and Citizens' Charter for hospitals.
- ensure appropriate delegation of powers to Panchayati Raj Institutions (PRIs) so that the problems of absenteeism and poor performance can be sorted out locally and primary health care personnel function as an effective team.
- increase Involvement of the Panchayati Raj Institutions in the planning and monitoring of ongoing programmes and taking timely corrections for optimal utilisation of services.
- devolution of responsibilities and funds to Panchayati Raj Institutions (PRIs); besides participating in area-specific planning and monitoring, PRIs can help in improving the accountability of the public health care providers, improve inter-sectoral co-ordination and convergence of services.

Financing Health Care

As a part of economic reforms, health sector reforms are perhaps inevitable; however, due care will be taken to ensure that poorer segments of population are able to access services they need. In view of the importance of health as a critical input for human development, there will be continued commitment to provide essential primary health care, emergency life saving services, services under the National disease control programmes and the National Family Welfare programme totally free of cost to individuals based on their needs and not on their ability to pay. Data from NSSO indicate that escalating health care costs is one of the reasons for indebtedness not only among the poor but also in the middle income group. It is therefore essential that appropriate mechanisms by which cost of severe illness and hospitalisation can be borne by individual/organisation/State are explored and affordable appropriate choice made. Global and Indian experience with health insurance/health maintenance organisations have to be reviewed and appropriate steps initiated. In order to encourage healthy life styles yearly 'no claim bonus'/adjustment of the premium could be made on the basis of previous year's hospitalisation cost reimbursed by the insurance scheme. The Centre and the states will :

- Evolve, test and implement suitable strategies for levying user charges for health care services from people above poverty line while providing free service to people below poverty line; utilise the collected funds locally to improve quality of care.
- Evolve and implement a mechanism to ensure sustainability of ongoing government funded health and family welfare programme especially those with substantial external assistance.
- Work out cost of diagnosis and therapeutic procedures for major and minor ailment in different levels of care and setting cost of care norms.
- Explore alternative systems of health care financing including health insurance so that essential, need-based and affordable health care is available to all.
- Initiate appropriate interventions to ease the existing funding constraints at all levels of health system and to promote the complete and timely utilization of allocated funds.

Different models of health care financing at the individual, family, institution and state level will be evolved, implemented and evaluated. Models found most suitable for providing essential health care to all will be replicated.

The issue of how much the government sector, private individuals and the country as a whole is spending on health care and which segments of the population are benefiting, has been debated widely during the last decade. As there is no National Health Accounting system, there is no information on total government expenditure on health and categories of people who benefit from this expenditure. It is imperative that a system of National Health Accounting, reflecting total government expenditure on health is established. This will enable periodic review and appropriate policy decisions regarding modalities for ensuring optimal utilisation of the current government investment in the health sector and also future investments to meet public health needs.

The Ninth Plan Recommended a Review of the National Health Policy in View of:

- Ongoing demographic transition;
- Ongoing epidemiological transition;
- Expansion of health care infrastructure;
- Changes in health care seeking behaviour;
- Availability of newer technologies for management;
- Rising expectations of the population, escalating cost of health care.

National Health Policy 2002

The NHP (1983) provided a comprehensive framework for planning, implementation, monitoring of health services and goals to be achieved by 2000. The Department of Health has reviewed the performance since 1983 and formulated the NHP 2002 which emphasises that any significant improvement in the quality of health services and health status of the citizens would depend on increased financial and material inputs, service providers treating their responsibility not as a commercial activity but as a service (albeit a paid one), the citizens demanding improvement in the quality of services, a responsive health delivery system, particularly in the public sector and improved governance. Recognising that the health needs of the country are enormous and dynamic and acknowledging the human and financial resource constraints, the NHP 2002, attempts to make choices between various priorities and has set the goals for the next two decades. It is expected that with effective implementation of the policies and strategies indicated in the Tenth Plan and NHP 2002, the country will achieve goals set and complete the health and demographic transition within the set time frame.

NHP 2002 - Goals to be achieved	
Eradicate Polio and Yaws	2005
Eliminate Leprosy	2005
Eliminate Kala Azar	2010
Eliminate Lymphatic Filariasis	2015
Achieve zero level growth of HIV/AIDS	2007
Reduce Mortality on account of TB, malaria and other vector and water-borne diseases by 50 per cent	2010
Reduce prevalence of blindness to 0.5 per cent	2010
Reduce IMR to 30/1000 and MMR to 100/100,000 live births	2010
Increase utilisation of public health facilities from the current level of <20 per cent to >75 per cent	2010
Establish an integrated system of surveillance, national health accounts and health statistics.	2005

Family Welfare

India, the second most populous country in the world having a meagre 2.4 per cent of the world's surface area sustains 16.7 per cent of the world's population. Realising the inevitable high population growth during the initial phases of demographic transition and the need to accelerate the pace of the transition, India became the first country in the world to formulate a National Family Planning Programme in 1952, with the objective of "reducing birth rate to the extent necessary to stabilise the population at a level consistent with requirement of national economy". The First Five-Year Plan stated, "The main appeal for family planning is based on considerations of health and welfare of the family. Family limitation or spacing of children is necessary and desirable in order to secure better health for the mother and better care and upbringing of children. Measures directed to this end should, therefore, form part of the public health programme". Thus the key elements of health care to women and children and provision of contraceptive services have been the focus of India's health services right from the time of India's independence. Successive Five-Year Plans have been providing the policy framework and funding for planned development of nationwide health care infrastructure and manpower to deliver these services. The centrally sponsored and 100 per cent Centrally Funded Family Welfare Programme provides the states additional infrastructure, manpower and consumables needed for improving health status of women and children and to meet all the felt needs for fertility regulation.

The technological advances and improved quality and coverage of health care resulted in a rapid fall in Crude Death Rate (CDR) from 25.1 in 1951 to 9.8 in 1991. In contrast, the decline in Crude Birth Rate (CBR) has been less steep, from 40.8 in 1951 to 29.5 in 1991. As a result, the annual exponential population growth rate has been over 2 per cent in the period between 1971-1991. The pace of demographic transition in India has been relatively slow but steady. Census 1991 showed that after three decades the population growth rate declined below 2 per cent. In order to give a new thrust and dynamism to the Family Welfare Programme and achieve a more rapid decline in birthrate, death rate and population growth rate in the last decade of the century, the National Development Council (NDC) set up a Sub Committee on Population and endorsed its recommendations in 1993.

Census 2001

Census 2001 recorded that the population of the country was 1027 million – 15 million more than the population projected for 2001 by the Technical Group on Population Projections. The decadal growth during 1991-2001 was 21.34 per cent (decadal growth in 1981-91 was 23.86 per cent). Analysis of growth rates of the states from the decade 1951-1961 indicates that it took four decades for Kerala to reach a decadal growth rate of less than 10 per cent from a high growth rate of 26.29 per cent during 1961-71. Tamil Nadu also took 40 years to reduce its growth rate from a high of 23.2per cent during 1961-71 to 11.2 per cent during 1991-2001. Andhra Pradesh has shown an impressive fall in growth rate by over 10 percentage points within a short span of a decade during nineties. The growth rate in Bihar has shown an upward swing during 1991-2001; the growth rates in Rajasthan, UP and MP are now at a level where Kerala and Tamil Nadu were 40 years ago.

Population Projections and their Implications to the Family Welfare Programme

The Technical group projected the total population, population growth rates (Fig) and the year by which the replacement level of TFR of 2.1 will be achieved by different states in India if the pace of decline in Total Fertility Rate observed during 1981-93 continues in the future years. The projections regarding some of these indicators are given in the box.

Population Projections 1996-2016

The population will increase from 934 million in 1996 to 1264 million in 2016. Between the periods 1996-2001 and 2011-2016 there will be a decline of:

• CBR	from 24.10 to 21.41
• CDR	from 8.99 to 7.48
• NGR	from 1.51 per cent to 1.39 per cent
• IMR	
Male	from 63 to 38
Female	from 64 to 39

Inter State Differences

The projected values for the total population in different regions are shown in the Figure. There are marked differences between states in size of the population projected, population growth rates and the time by which TFR of 2.1 is likely to be achieved. If the present trend continues, most of the southern and the western states are

Population Projections
(Region Wise)

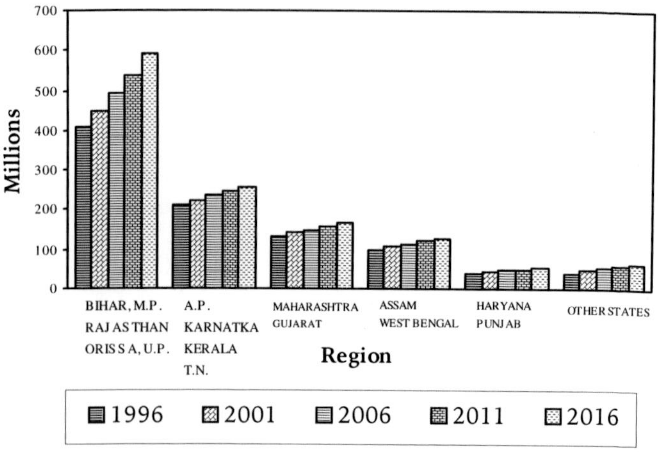

Source: Registrar General India.

likely to achieve TFR of 2.1 by 2010. Urgent energetic steps to assess and fully meet the unmet needs for Maternal and Child Health (MCH) care and contraception through improvement in availability and access to service are needed in Rajasthan, Orissa, Uttar Pradesh, Madhya Pradesh and Bihar (before division) in order to achieve a faster decline in their mortality and fertility rates. The performance of these states would determine the year and size of the population at which the country achieves replacement level of fertility. It is imperative that special efforts are made during the next two decades to break the vicious self-perpetuating cycle of poor performance, poor per capita income, poverty, low literacy and high birth rate in the populous states so that further widening of disparities between states in terms of per capita income and quality of life is prevented. An Empowered Action Group has been set up to provide special assistance to these states. The benefits accrued from such assistance will depend to a large extent on the states' ability to utilize the available funds and improve services and facilities.

Changes in Age Profile of the Population

The projected population of India in the three major age groups (less than 15, 15-59, 60 years or above) between 1996 and 2016 are shown in Figure. In the country as a whole, there will be a marginal decline in less than 15 years of age population (352.7 million to 350.4 million), even though in poorly performing states there will be continued increase in the number of children requiring care. The health care infrastructure will, therefore, not be under pressure to provide care to an ever increasing number of children. They will be able to concentrate on:

Projected Population - India

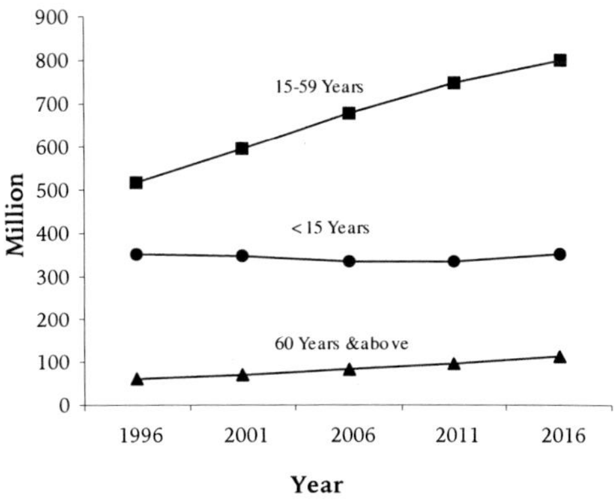

Source: Registrar General India

- Improving quality of care.
- Focus on antenatal, intra natal and neonatal care aimed at reducing neonatal morbidity and mortality.
- Improve coverage for immunisation against vaccine preventable diseases.
- Promote inter sectoral coordination especially with the ICDS programme so that there is an improvement in health and nutritional status, and
- Improve coverage and quality of health care to vulnerable and underserved adolescents.

Age group < 15 years

There will be no increase in numbers. Focus will be to improve:

- Quality and coverage of health and nutrition services and achieve improvement in health and nutritional status.
- Improve access to education & skill development.

The economic challenge is to provide needed funds so that these children have access to nutrition, education and skill development. The challenge faced by the health sector is to achieve reduction in morbidity and mortality rates in infancy and childhood, to improve nutritional status and eliminate ill effects of the gender bias.

Age group 15-59 years

The challenge is the massive increase in the number of people in this age group. They will:

- Need wider spectrum of services :
    - maternal and child health services
    - contraceptive care
    - gynaecological problems
    - RTI/STD management
- Expect better quality of services
- Expect fulfillment of their felt needs for MCH/family planning care.

If their felt needs are met through effective implementation of RCH programme, it is possible to accelerate demographic transition and achieve rapid population stabilisation.

There will be a massive increase of population in the 15-59 age group (from 519 million to 800 million). The RCH care has to provide the needed services for this rapidly growing clientele. The population in this age group is more literate and has greater access to information. These people will, therefore, have greater awareness and expectation regarding both access to a wide spectrum of health care related services and the quality of these services. The Family Welfare Programme has to cater to a wider spectrum of health care needs of this population – including Maternal and Child Health (MCH) care, contraceptive care, management of gynaecological problems, the quality of services also needs to be improved.There will be a substantial increase in the population more than 60 years (62.3 million to 112.9 million) in the next two decades. Increasing numbers of the population beyond 60 years would necessitate provisions for the management of some of the major health problems in this age group, including early detection and management of cancers.

Progress in Implementation of the Family Welfare Programme during the Ninth Plan

Review of the FW programme have shown that Governmental network provides most of the MCH and contraceptive care (NFHS 1998-99). During the Ninth Plan period the Department of Family Welfare has implemented the recommendations of the NDC Subcommittee on Population. The centrally defined methods specific targets for family planning were abolished; emphasis shifted to decentralised planning at district level based on community needs assessment and implementation of programmes aimed at fulfilment of these needs. RCH programme aimed at providing integrated good quality maternal, child health and contraceptive care. A massive pulse polio campaign was taken up to eliminate polio from the country. The Department of Family Welfare set up a Consultative Committee to suggest appropriate restructuring and revision of norms for infrastructure funded by the states and the Centre and has initiated implementation of the recommendations. Monitoring and evaluation have become part and parcel of the Family Welfare Programmes and the data is used for midcourse corrections.

It was expected that these initiatives would lead to substantial improvement in the coverage and quality of services. The health systems in the states required longer time to adapt to decentralised planning and RCH programme implementation. In an attempt to improve coverage under specific components of the RCH programme, some states embarked on campaign mode operations which took their toll on routine services. Efforts to eliminate polio by the winter of 2000 through massive pulse polio campaign also had some adverse effect on routine delivery services. As a result of all these it is unlikely that Ninth Plan goals for CBR, Couple Protection Rate, Maternal Mortality Ratio and Infant Mortality Rate will be achieved. However, the country is likely to achieve elimination of polio by 2004.

Independent surveys have shown that several states have achieved goals set for some aspect of the RCH programme during the Ninth Plan, demonstrating that these can be achieved within the existing infrastructure, manpower and inputs. For instance,

- Andhra Pradesh, Punjab, West Bengal and Maharashtra have shown substantial decline in birth rates; the latter three states are likely to achieve replacement level of fertility, ahead of the projection made.
- Punjab has achieved couple protection rate and use of spacing methods far ahead of all other states.
- Tamil Nadu and Andhra Pradesh have achieved increase in institutional deliveries.
- Kerala, Maharashtra, Punjab and Tamil Nadu improved immunization coverage.
- Tamil Nadu and Andhra Pradesh had achieved improvement in coverage and quality of Antenatal care.

Major Areas of Concern

Some of the major areas of current concern include:

- The massive interstate differences in the fertility and mortality - the rates are high in the states where nearly 50 per cent of the country's population lives;
- Gaps in infrastructure/manpower/equipment and mismatch between infrastructure and manpower in PHC/CHC; lack of referral services;

- Decline in mortality during the Nineties was slow; the goals set for mortality and fertility in the Ninth plan will not to be achieved;
- There has been no decline in the Maternal Mortality Ratios over the Nineties; neonatal and Infant Mortality Rates have remained essentially unaltered in the Nineties;
- The routine service coverage has declined perhaps because of the emphasis on campaign mode operations for individual components of the programme;
- In spite of the emphasis on skill upgradation training for delivery of integrated reproductive and child health services, the progress in in-service training has been very slow; the anticipated improvement in the content and quality of care has not taken place;
- Evaluation studies have shown that the coverage under immunization is not universal even in the best performing states; coverage rates are very low in states like Bihar; elimination of polio is yet to be achieved;
- Logistics of drug supply has improved in some states but remains poor in populous states;
- Decentralised district based planning, monitoring and midcourse correction utilising the locally generated service data and CRS has not yet been operationalised fully.

Approach during the Next Two Decades

The current high population growth rate continues to be due to:

- The large size of the population in the reproductive age-group (estimated contribution 60 per cent);
- Higher fertility due to unmet need for contraception (estimated contribution 20 per cent);
- And high wanted fertility due to prevailing high IMR and other socio-economic reasons (estimated contribution about 20 per cent).

During the next two decades paradigm shift (will be fully operationalised), which began in the Ninth plan from:

- Demographic targets to *focus on enabling the couples to achieve their reproductive goals;*
- Method specific contraceptive targets *to meeting all the unmet needs for contraception to reduce unwanted pregnancies;*
- Numerous vertical programmes for family planning and maternal and child health to *integrated health care for women and children;*
- Centrally defined targets to *community need assessment and decentralised area specific microplanning* and *implementation of health care for women and children to reduce infant mortality and reduce high desired fertility;*
- Quantitative coverage *to emphasis on quality and content of care;*
- Predominantly women centred programmes *to meeting the health care needs of the family with emphasis on involvement of men in Planned Parenthood;*
- Supply driven service delivery *to need and demand driven service; improved logistics for ensuring adequate and timely supplies to met the needs;*
- Service provision based on providers perception *to addressing choices and conveniences of the couples.*

The focus will have to be on improving access to services to meet the health care needs of women and children by:

- Decentralised area specific approach to planning, implementation and monitoring of the performance and effecting mid course corrections;
- Differential strategy to achieve incremental improvement in performance in all states/districts;
- Special efforts to improve access to and utilisation of the services in states/districts with high mortality and /or fertility rates;
- Filling the critical gaps (especially CHCs) in existing infrastructure through appropriate reorganisation and restructuring primary health care infrastructure;

- Ensuring that post of specialists in CHC/FRU do not remain vacant; skill upgradation and redeployment existing manpower to fill other critical gaps;
- Streamlining the functioning of the primary health care system in urban and rural areas; providing good quality integrated reproductive and child health services at primary, secondary and tertiary care and improving the referral services;
- Providing adequate supply of essential drugs, diagnostics and vaccines; improving the logistics of supply;
- Well co-ordinated activities for delivery of services by public, private and voluntary sectors to improve coverage;
- Involvement of the PRI in planning, monitoring and midcourse correction of the programme at local level;
- Involvement of the industries, organised and unorganised sectors, agriculture workers and labour representatives in improving access to RCH services;
- Effective use of social marketing to improve access to simple OTC products such as ORT and condoms;
- Effective Information, Education, Communication and Motivation;
- Effective intersectoral co-ordination between concerned sectors.

National Population Policy

The National Population Policy was drawn up by the Department of Family Welfare and was approved by the cabinet in 2000. As envisaged in NPP, National Commission on Population was constituted on 11th May, 2000 under the Chairmanship of the Prime Minister of India. Deputy Chairman, Planning Commission, is the Vice Chairman.

During the next two decades efforts will be directed to:

- Assess and meet the unmet needs for contraception;
- Achieve reduction in the high desired level of fertility through programmes for reduction in IMR and Maternal Mortality Ratio (MMR); and

- Enable families to achieve their reproductive goals.

If the reproductive goals of families are fully met the country will be able to achieve the National Population Policy goal of replacement level of fertility by 2010. The medium and long term goals will be to continue this process to accelerate the pace of demographic transition and achieve population stabilisation by 2045. Reductions in fertility, mortality and population growth rate will be major objectives during the Tenth Plan. Three of the 11 monitorable targets for the Tenth Plan and beyond are:

- Reduction in IMR to 45 per 1,000 live births by 2007 and 28 per 1,000 live births by 2012;
- Reduction in maternal mortality ratio to 2 per 1,000 live births by 2007 and 1 per 1,000 live births by 2012; and
- Reduction in decadal growth rate of the population between 2001-2011 to 16.2.

In view of the massive differences in the availability and utilsation of health services and health indices of the population, a differential strategy is envisaged so that there is incremental improvement in all districts. This, in turn, is expected to result in substantial improvement in state and national indices and enable the country to achieve the goals set for the Tenth Plan. The steep reduction in mortality and fertility envisaged are technically feasible within the existing infrastructure and manpower as has been demonstrated in several states/districts. It is imperative that the goals set are achieved within the time frame as these goals are essential prerequisites for improving the quality of life and human development.

Nutrition

Importance of optimal nutrition for health and human development is well recognised. At the time of Independence the country faced two major nutritional problems - one was the threat of famine and acute starvation due to low agricultural production and lack of appropriate food distribution system. The other was chronic energy deficiency due to:

- Low dietary intake because of poverty and low purchasing power.

- High prevalence of infection because of poor access to safe-drinking water, sanitation and health care.
- Poor utilisation of available facilities due to low literacy and lack of awareness.

Chronic Energy Deficiency (CED), kwashiorkor, marasmus, goitre, beriberi, blindness due to Vitamin-A deficiency and anaemia were major public health problems. The country adopted multi-sectoral, multi-pronged strategy to combat these and to improve nutritional status of the population. Constitution of India (Article 47) states that "the State shall regard raising the level of nutrition and standard of living of its people and improvement in public health among its primary duties". Successive Five Year Plans laid down the policies and strategies for achieving these goals.

During the last 50 years considerable progress has been achieved. Country has achieved self sufficiency in food grain production; famines no longer stalk the country. There has been substantial reduction in moderate and severe undernutrition in children and some improvement in nutritional status of all segments of population. Kwashiorkor, marasmus, pellagra, lathyrism, beriberi and blindness due to severe Vitamin-A deficiency have become rare. However:

- While mortality has come down by 50 per cent and fertility by 40 per cent, reduction in under nutrition is only 20 per cent.
- Under nutrition in pregnant women and low birth weight rate has not shown any decline India with less than 20 per cent global children accounts for over 40 per cent under nourished children.
- Even though there has been 50 per cent decline in severe under-nutrition reduction in mild under-nutrition is marginal under nutrition associated with HIV/AIDS is emerging as newer public health problems.
- There had been major alterations in the life styles and dietary intake and consequently the prevalence of obesity and non-communicable diseases are increasing.

Distribution of Children (1-5) years according to Gomez Classification

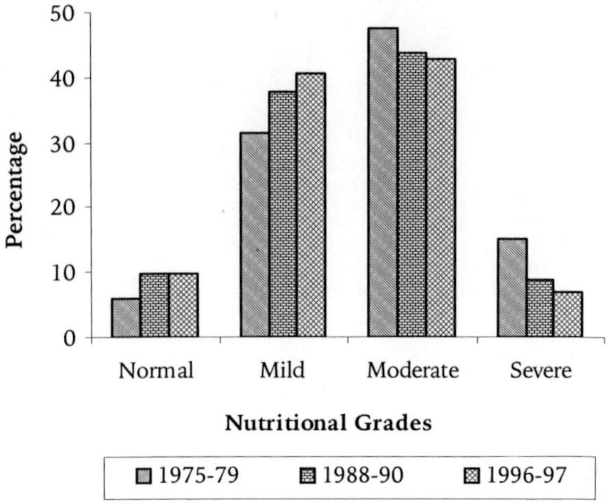

Source: NNMB

Currently, the major nutrition related public health problems are:

- Chronic energy deficiency and under-nutrition
- Micro-nutrient deficiencies
    - Anaemia due to iron and folate deficiency
    - Vitamin A deficiency
    - Iodine Deficiency Disorders
- Chronic energy excess and obesity

Initiatives in the Next Two Decades

During the next two decades they will have to implement focused and comprehensive interventions aimed at improving the nutritional status of the individuals; this in turn will enable the country to achieve rapid reduction in severe forms of under-nutrition and ill health and lead to improvement in nutritional and health status of the population to achieve this objective, coordinated multisectoral interventions for increasing food production, effective processing and distribution, improvement in purchasing power, generating awareness, ensuring optimum utilisation of well targeted interventions for prevention, detection and management of macro and micronutrient deficiencies are needed. As the country enters the era of dual nutritional burden of under and over nutrition and associated health hazards, efforts to define the nutritional requirements of Indian population, nutritive values of common and unconventional Indian foods and norms for anthropometric indices of Indian population will receive adequate support. It is important to embark on a paradigm shift from:

- Household food security and freedom from hunger to nutrition security for the family and the individual.
- Untargeted supplementation to screening of all the persons from vulnerable groups, identification of those with various grades of under-nutrition and their appropriate management.
- Lack of focused interventions on over-nutrition to promotion of appropriate lifestyles and dietary intakes for prevention and management of over nutrition and obesity.

Path Ahead and Goals Set

Prime Minister in his Independence Day Speech on 15th August, 2001 announced the,

- Setting up of the National Nutrition Mission;
- Providing Foodgrains at subsidized rates to adolescents girls and expectant and nursing mothers belonging to Below Poverty Line (BPL) families;

The National Nutrition Mission has the following objectives:

- Reduction in under nutrition;
- Reduction/elimination of micronutrient deficiencies - iron, iodine and Vitamin A;
- Reduction in chronic energy deficiency.

In addition the Mission would co-ordinate and monitor,

- Implementation of National Nutrition Policy;
- Strengthening of existing programme;
- R&D
- Nutrition education and IEC;
- Strengthening of ICDS and Mid-Day Meal Programme;

- Relief in Natural Calamities.

National Nutrition Mission will be supervised by the National Nutrition Council headed by the PM as envisaged in the National Nutrition Policy.

Interventions will have to be initiated to,

Achieve adequate household/individual nutrition security by

- Ensuring production and availability of cereals, pulses and vegetables to meet the nutritional needs.
- Making them available at affordable cost throughout the year to urban and rural population through reduction in post harvest losses and appropriate processing.
- More cost-effective and efficient targeting of the PDS to address macro and micronutrient deficiencies (such as providing coarse grains, pulses and iodised salt to BPL families through TPDS).
- Improve purchasing power by appropriate programmes including food for work programmes.

Prevent under-nutrition through nutrition education aimed at

- Ensuring appropriate infant feeding practices (universal colostrums feeding, exclusive breast feeding upto six months, introduction of semisolids at six months).
- Promoting appropriate intra-family distribution of food based on requirements.
- Dietary diversification to meet the nutritional needs of the family.

Operationalize universal screening of

- All pregnant women for under-nutrition.
- All infants and preschool and school children for under-nutrition.

Initiate appropriate nutrition interventions for management of under-nutrition through

- Targeted food supplementation and health care for those with under-nutrition.
- Effective monitoring of these individuals and their families.

- Utilisation of the PRI for effective intersectoral coordination and convergence of services, improving community participation in planning, monitoring of the ongoing interventions for prevention and management of under-nutrition.

Focus on prevention, early detection and appropriate management of micronutrient deficiencies and associated health hazards through

- Nutrition education to achieve dietary diversification and balanced intake of all micronutrients;
- Universal access to double fortified salt;
- Screening of
  - all children with severe under-nutrition for micronutrient deficiencies
  - all pregnant women for micronutrient deficiencies
  - all school children for micronutrient deficiencies
- Appropriate intervention for treatment of micronutrient deficiencies;

Promotion of appropriate dietary intake and life style for prevention and management of obesity and prevention and management of diet-related chronic diseases

Nutrition monitoring and surveillance will be given high priority to enable the country to closely monitor the impact of on going demographic, developmental, economic transition and ecological and life style changes on nutritional and health status of the population to ensure that the existing beneficial strategies are fully exploited and emerging problems are identified early and corrected expeditiously.

Goals Set

The following goals have been set for the Tenth Plan period:

- Enhance early initiation of breast-feeding (colostrum feeding) from the current level of 15.8 per cent (as per NFHS 2) to 50 per cent.
- Enhance exclusive breast-feeding rate for children upto the age of 6 months from the current rate of 55.2 per cent (as per NFHS 2) to 80 per cent.

- Enhance Complementary Feeding rate at six months from the current level of 33.5 per cent (as per NFHS 2) to 75 per cent.
- Bring down the prevalence of under-weight in children under 3 years from the current level of 47 per cent as per NFHS-2 to 40 per cent.
- Reduce prevalence of severe undernutrition in 0-6 year children by 50 per cent.
- Universal screening of pregnant women for anaemia and appropriate treatment.
- Reduce prevalence of moderate/severe anaemia by 50 per cent.
- Reduce prevalence of night blindness to below 1.0 per cent and that of Bitot Spots to below 0.5 per cent in children between 6 months to six years of age.
- Eliminate Vitamin A deficiency as a public health problem.
- Achieve universal access to iodised salt.
- Generate district-wise data on iodised salt consumption.

Tenth Plan has set specific nutrition goals to be achieved by 2007. In view of the massive interstate/interdistrict differences in availability and access to the nutrition-related services and in nutritional status of the population, the state specific goals to be achieved by 2007 have been evolved based on the current level of these indices and the Tenth Plan goals for the country has been derived from the state specific gaols. The progress achieved in terms of the process and impact indicators will be reviewed yearly and if necessary goals may be reset at the time of mid-term appraisal. Intensification of the efforts during the next two decades can result in elimination of severe forms of macro and micro nutrient under nutrition and prevent any increase in prevalence of over nutrition and associated health hazard.

9

The Profile of the Empowered Woman: Vision 2020

SARALA GOPALAN

People all over the world want peace, security and development. In a world of violence and bloodshed, they seek a new world order, which is just, and humane. Women, who form nearly half of the people of the world, have been advocating peace between nations, races, religions and every other divide, as mothers and citizens. Women have intensely realized the need to be at the top – at decision making levels to steer the course of decisions at all levels to shape this new world, beyond international borders, within the country, within the community and within the households. There is greater understanding of human rights today than ever before and women are much aware of their deprivations in this regard more intensely. Illiterate, poor and socially backward women living in less developed parts of the world; as well as the educated, accomplished women in economically advanced regions of the world recognize 'inequity' and 'in-equality' wherever and whenever it occurs. Women have come forward to become change agents to alter this situation of deprivations, discrimination and decadence. This effort is getting further strengthened through their global networking. They want for themselves and their families "better lives" in a "decent society". Governments and civil society world-over have to play the catalytic role that is necessary to create the environment conducive for removing barriers for the realization of good living.

India with its vision of a new economic regime has an urgency to guarantee the spirit of equality and social justice envisioned in the Constitution. The greater awareness of human rights and the need to realize such rights without any barriers has also been accepted as a goal in all the sectors of development. In the coming twenty years, the social environment conducive for realizing human rights, equality and justice, therefore, assumes great importance. The National Policy for Empowerment of Women, 2001, sets the pace for creating a gender-just society for human resource development and the elimination of all discrimination to make place for capacity building, access and empowerment. It is naturally presumed that the priority of planning will be the creation of this social environment, conducive for exercise of human rights accompanied with the required social infrastructure for women and men to have better lives.

My Vision for 2020 will depend on who I Am Today.

If I have just been conceived,

- I am doubtful if my mother will go through her pregnancy, when the tests reveal who I am – a baby girl!
- I believe the 2001 census has clearly brought out that there is less space for baby girls.[1]
- I understand states are getting strict on families having only two children, therefore, my chances of being born are getting lesser and lesser as the second girl child in the family.
- If I am that unfortunate one – 'bye' to all of you, I am not going to be around in 2020!
- Otherwise.............

If I am a millennium baby girl born in this century, then, in 2020,

- I would expect to live a very purposeful healthy life till I am eighty-plus with assured access to nutrition, clean water and unpolluted air, assured of quality shelter.
- Attend school and learn skills for my livelihood.
- Choose my career in any avenue according to my skills and capabilities and contribute to the best of my ability to the well being of my family, community and nation.

1. Juvenile Sex Ratios, Census 2001, see Table 1 on page 11.

- Marry according to my desire after I am 21 years of age and have a small family when I think it is appropriate, and be able to give a good healthy environment for my child or a maximum of two children.
- My life would be a shared, one with my brother/sister and later my husband – all of us being conscious of our rights and responsibilities to each other.
- Get good support from the society to pursue my career and vocations.
- Be a well-accomplished young woman in good health and capable of taking all my decisions and participating in all decisions in the family, community and administration at all levels.

If I have turned 16 at the beginning of this millennium,

- I expect fewer struggles to live and make both ends meet in the next 20 years of this millennium than my mother did.
- I will use all opportunities to build up my capacity – education, skill development and other facilities.
- I will wait to be 18-plus to be married. My marriage will be with no dowry.
- My husband and I will wait till I am 21 to have a child, and another, may be three years later.
- I will fully avail the health services, antenatal care, attendance of trained persons at the time of delivery, post-natal care and avoid morbidity of any kind.
- I will avail of a child-care support network in my neighbourhood, I expect to be in place soon.
- I expect things to improve on all scores, with access improving for me to information, services and a better quality of economic and social life.
- I will be an active member of my community taking part in all activities for the advancement of my community and accept any positions in bodies of governance to ensure good governance, gender justice, security and peace.

If I am a senior citizen,

- I expect good geriatric care.
- Food security, nutrition and shelter.
- Healthy environment, clean water and unpolluted air.
- Security for my life.
- A responsive family and community that respects senior citizens and makes provisions for their care.

The vision of 2020 for the empowered woman is:

- To be a human being with dignity and respect as an individual first and as a citizen next.
- To be a capable human resource that can make the family, society, economy and country, proud and strong.
- Equal status in all spheres – social, economic and political.
- A pervading environment of equity and gender justice without any kind of discrimination.

This would call for,

- Optimum development of infrastructure for quality of life with easy access to water, fuel, food and fodder; eliminating all kinds of deprivations and eradicating poverty.
- A network of childcare and healthcare services.
- A strong system of education and skill development with unrestricted access.
- A high-level of technology development including information, bio-technology and other production technologies accompanied with the necessary skill development and technocracy to use new technologies.
- Complete access to information, education and awareness.
- A full appreciation of gender roles with male and female responsibilities and sharing of reproductive and family responsibilities.
- The establishment of equal status in decision-making in the family and outside the family at all levels; and

- Special care for the aged, and women in various vulnerable situations.

The situation, as it exists today, is one of low status of woman that is powerless, endangered by development and further suppressed by poverty and oppressed by patriarchy.

The status of the Indian woman today depends very much on where she is in the country at this time (June, 2001). Let us look at the difference.

If I am a girl child in Kerala[@],

- I am sure to be born.
- I will survive.
- I will attend school and at least reach 10th class.
- I will struggle to get employed, and may spend long years looking for a job. I have little chance of getting into a primary school as a teacher in Kerala, as schools there are closing down for want of children, surplus teachers themselves being treated as "protected teachers", and as new jobs are rare to come by. If I do well and get some technical qualifications, I may venture outside the state to be a lab technician in the Middle-east, or a nurse any where in the world, or sometimes land up in one of the dormitories of shrimp peeling units in some coastal area of any of the nine maritime states of the country.
- I will be quite mature when I get married, may be past 25 years.

@: Data compiled from following sources for all the States:

Sex ratios and literacy – Census 2001.

Life expectation from Women in India: A Statistical Profile, 1997.

Age at marriage for all major States relates to 1994 quoted from - Dr. Sarala Gopalan and Dr. Mira Shiva, "National Profile on Women, Health and Development", April 2000; for other States the data relates to 1993 - from "Women in India: A Statistical Profile -1997".

Antenatal check-up, deliveries, vaccination, aneamia, TFR from NFHS-2.

Victims of rape and rank on the basis of crime committed against women from Crime in India, 1998.

- I will not have more than two children. I may even stop with one. I would have regular antenatal check-ups, institutional delivery attended by a trained professional, my child will have all the immunization.
- My child will be in nursery and then go to school and will get qualified, of course in the hope that at least the labour market of the future would hold out opportunities for reasonable employment.
- I hope to see my 80th birthday.
- I still have to struggle to gain a position in decision making and etch a place for women in the social and political platforms.

If I am a girl child in Uttar Pradesh,

- I would be lucky to survive at birth, nine out of ten chances of reaching age one, and a slightly lesser chance of reaching age five.
- I am not certain I will reach school. I might most probably be helping my mother with the care of

Kerala	
Sex Ratio (Per 1000 Males)	1,058
Juvenile Sex Ratio	963
Female Literacy	87.86 %
Life Expectancy for Females	74.7
Infant Mortality	16.3 %
Under 5 Mortality Rate	18.8 %
Mothers Receiving Antenatal Checkup	98.8 %
Deliveries Assisted by a Health Professional	94.0 %
Per cent of Children, Age 12-23 Who Received All Vaccination	79.7 %
Per cent of Women, Age 15-49 with any Anemia	22.7 %
Mean Age at Marriage	22.3
Total Fertility Rate	1.96 %
Victims of Rape 1998 (cases)	589
Rank on the basis of percentage share of crime committed against women in States/UTs.	11

Uttar Pradesh	
Sex Ratio	898
Juvenile Sex Ratio	916
Female Literacy	42.98 %
Life Expectancy for Females	55.1
Infant Mortality	86.7 %
Under 5 Mortality Rate	122.5 %
Mothers Receiving Antenatal Checkup	34.6 %
Deliveries Assisted by a Health Professional	22.4 %
Per cent of Children, Age 12-23 Who Received All Vaccination	21.2 %
Per cent of Women, Age 15-49 with any Anemia	48.7 %
Mean age at Marriage	19.5
Total Fertility Rate	3.99 %
Victims of Rape 1998 (cases)	1605
Rank on the basis of percentage share of crime committed against women in States/UTs.	1

siblings and other household chores.

- I will be married early, much before my 18th birthday.
- I may conceive before I am 18 years old and go through several pregnancies.
- I am not sure all my children will survive.
- There may not be enough to eat in the house all the year round.
- I may not live beyond 50 years.

If I am a girl child in Rajasthan,

- I would be lucky to survive at birth, nine out of ten chances of reaching age one, and a slightly lesser chance of reaching age five if I am not neglected or starved.
- I am hopeful of becoming literate, with opportunities opening up for informal learning.
- I have to help my family in their struggle for drinking water and fuel for their meagre cooking.
- My marriage will be very early and child births too.
- I have no hope of any medical care with no roads to take me anywhere.
- I will struggle through life and put in hard work to keep my body and soul together.
- I may not see my 16th birthday.

Rajasthan	
Sex Ratio	922
Juvenile Sex Ratio	909
Female Literacy	44.34 %
Life Expectancy for Females	58.5
Infant Mortality	80.4 %
Under 5 Mortality Rate	114.9 %
Mothers Receiving Antenatal Checkup	47.5 %
Deliveries Assisted by a Health Professional	35.8 %
Per cent of Children, Age 12-23 who Received All Vaccination	17.3 %
Pe rcent of Women, Age 15-49 with any Anemia	48.5 %
Age at Marriage	18.4
Total Fertility Rate	3.79 %
Victims of Rape 1998 (cases)	1266
Rank on the basis of percentage share of crime committed against women in States/UTs.	4

If I am a girl child in Bihar,

- My chances of survival on birth, is uncertain, in a Rajput family; while I may be born in a SC/ST or other community.

- I have nine out of ten chances of reaching age one, and a slightly lesser chance of reaching age five if I am not neglected or starved.
- I have little chance of becoming literate, with no opportunities opening up for informal learning and not many schools within reach.
- I have to help my family in their struggle for drinking water and fuel for their meagre cooking.
- My marriage will be very early and child births too.
- I have no hope of any medical care with the health infrastructure in a dire state.
- I am scared of violence and molestations.
- I will struggle through life and put in hard work to keep my body and soul together.
- I may not see my 16th birthday.

If I am a girl child in Mizoram,

- I am sure to be born.
- I will survive.
- I will attend school and at least reach 10th class.

Bihar	
Sex Ratio	921
Juvenile Sex Ratio	938
Female Literacy	33.57 %
Life Expectancy for Females	57.2
Infant Mortality	72.9
Under 5 Mortality Rate	105.1
Mothers Receiving Antenatal Checkup	36.3 %
Deliveries Assisted by a Health Professional	23.4 %
Per cent of Children, Age 12-23 who Received All Vaccination	11.0 %
Per cent of Women, Age 15-49 with any Anemia	62.4 %
Mean age at Marriage	18.6
Total Fertility Rate	3.49
Victims of Rape 1998 (cases)	1421
Rank on the basis of percentage share of crime committed against women in States/UTs.	7

Mizoram	
Sex Ratio	938
Juvenile Sex Ratio	971
Female Literacy	86.13 %
Life Expectancy for Females	
Infant Mortality	37.0 %
Under 5 Mortality Rate	54.7 %
Mothers Receiving Antenatal Checkup	91.8 %
Deliveries Assisted by a Health Professional	67.5 %
Per cent of Children, Age 12-23 who Received All Vaccination	59.6 %
Per cent of Women, Age 15-49 with any Anemia	48.0 %
Mean age at Marriage	NA
Total Fertility Rate	2.89 %
Victims of Rape 1998 (cases)	84
Rank on the basis of percentage share of crime committed against women in States/UTs.	20

- I will have to try hard for employment.
- I will marry not very early.
- Have a small family.
- I expect reasonable access to health care and delivery.
- I am worried of internal security due to the socio-political situation.
- Molestations too are due to the failing law and order situation.

If I am a girl child in Haryana,

- My family does not want me.
- It will be quite a chance that I appear on earth.
- I am not sure of being given all the nice things my brothers get to eat.
- If I succeed crossing my fifth year, I am not certain of going to school.
- I will do a lot of work at home and help my parents.
- I will get married early, even when I would have liked to play like my brothers do.
- I will have children and may go through several abortions till my family is satisfied that I have a son or two.
- Each time I go for an abortion, it is going to be a risk for my life, because I may not get a professionally trained person to handle my case, may even die in the process.
- I have to be careful for my personal honour and dignity.

Haryana	
Sex Ratio	861
Juvenile Sex Ratio	820
Female Literacy	56.31 %
Life Expectancy for Females	63.7 %
Infant Mortality	56.8 %
Under 5 Mortality Rate	76.8 %
Mothers Receiving Antenatal Checkup	58.1 %
Deliveries Assisted by a Health Professional	42.0 %
Per cent of Children, Age 12-23 who Received All Vaccination	62.7 %
Per cent of Women, Age 15-49 with any Anemia	47.0 %
Mean age at Marriage	19.2
Total Fertility Rate	2.88 %
Victims of rape in 1998 (cases)	364
Rank on the basis of percentage share of crime committed against women in States/UTs.	14

If I am a girl child in Delhi,

- I may not be conceived, except by accident.
- I will be checked in the womb for my sex, and aborted for being the wrong one – female.

- If I get through these stages and come alive I have reasonable chances of survival and access to some development.
- I will do a lot of work at home and help my parents.
- I have to struggle for my safety and security all through.
- I will get married and may experience the wrath of my in-laws if they are not satisfied with the dowry; they may even burn me alive.
- As in Haryana, I will have children, but may go through several abortions till my family is satisfied that I have a son or two.

Delhi	
Sex Ratio	821
Juvenile Sex Ratio	865
Female Literacy	75 %
Life Expectancy for Females	
Infant Mortality	46.8
Under 5 Mortality Rate	55.4
Mothers Receiving Antenatal Checkup	83.5 %
Deliveries Assisted by a Health Professional	65.9 %
Per cent of Children, Age 12-23 who Received All Vaccination	69.8 %
Per cent of Women, Age 15-49 with any Anemia	40.5 %
Mean age at Marriage	19.8
Total Fertility Rate	2.40 %
Victims of rape in 1998 (cases)	438
Rank on the basis of percentage share of crime committed against women in States/UTs.	15

INFLUENCE OF PATRIARCHY

In the patriarchal setting in India today, the girl grows up in the natal family as 'paraya dhan' with least investment in her capacity development. In her marital home, she suffers for not bearing sons and is tortured mentally and sometimes physically by the family. She is compelled to abort if she is carrying a female foetus in her womb. She may die too in the process.

She suffers all deprivations; she is unwanted by families as evidenced through son preference, female foeticide and infanticide, she is victim to great deal of violence both inside the home and outside in the society.

Policy implementors consider her more as a demographic tool to curb population growth and sterilize her.

Why Do Baby Girls Die?

Improvements in medial technology have made it possible to determine the sex of the unborn child, so that families can decide whether or not to let a girl be born. Sex selection (carrying out a sex detection test and getting rid of unwanted female children before birth) is a phenomenon about which much is known but little is discussed. There is very little formal data on sex-selective abortions, although several micro-level studies indicate very disturbing trends. There is a visible proliferation of ultrasound clinics in rural areas of Uttar Pradesh, Rajasthan, Bihar and Haryana. The clientele of these clinics includes women from educated and well-off backgrounds, who are trying to "balance" their families.

Even worse, there is now enough evidence that female infanticide – killing of girl infants – is still prevalent in parts of India.

Female foeticide and female infanticide signal the grossest form of discrimination against women in India. However, these practices by themselves do not account for the fact that there are as many as 20-25 million missing girls and women in India's population.

Girls in India are discriminated against in several ways – fewer months of breast-feeding, less of nurturing and play, less care or medical treatment if they fall ill, less of "special" food, less of parental attention. As a result, girls are far more susceptible than boys to disease and infections, leading to poor health and a shorter life span. It is this life-long discrimination in nurturing and care that is the real killer of girls – less visible and dramatic, but as unequivocally lethal as female foeticide and infanticide.

Source: "Women in India – How Free? How Equal?", Kalyani Menon Sen, A.K. Shiva Kumar.

She is the caregiver in the family, often the beast of burden, attending to all the domestic chores and working from dawn to dusk – with no reward, no asset and no count in the System of National Accounts.[2]

She works for the family too in its economic enterprise, but her work is neither counted nor paid.[3]

When she does bring some income, she gives it all to the family and tries to work more to battle against poverty. She even has to finance the husband for his 'leisure activities' – that is alcohol, only to be beaten and raped by him in his drunkenness.

2. See Table 1 and 2 in Appendix I based on the Report of the Time Use Survey, CSO, Government of India, 2000.

3. See Table 2 in Appendix I based on the Report of the Time Use Survey, CSO, Government of India, 2000.

Practices for getting rid of Unwanted Baby Girls

Women's groups and grassroots NGOs in many parts of India are reporting that the supposedly "primitive" practice of female infanticide is still flourishing.

There are many ways to kill a baby girl. Commonly reported methods include lacing their feed with pesticides, forcing down a few grains of poppy seed or rice husk to slit their tender gullets, or stuffing their mouths with black salt or urea. In some regions, babies are fed the juice or paste of poisonous oleander berries. Yet others are suffocated with a wet towel or a bag of sand, or exposed to the strong current of pedestal fans to make them asphyxiate. Others are simply starved to death.

The worst betrayal is when poison is rubbed on the mother's breast, so that the baby girl is poisoned as she suckles.

Millions of Indian women simply lack the freedom to go out of the house in search of the health services they need. According to the National Family Health Survey-2, 1998-99, only 52 per cent of women in India are even consulted on decisions about their own health care. In Madhya Pradesh, the figure is as low as 37 per cent.

Source: "Women in India – How Free? How Equal?", Kalyani Menon Sen, A.K. Shiva Kumar.

Otherwise, she is the symbol of pleasure and entertainment for the dominant male. She is looked at as a piece of advertisement to lend more lust to the machine or any product that has to sell. The girl child and women are trafficked for prostitution and suffer infection of HIV/AIDS and get isolated for the rest of their lives.

There is no better evidence than the data emerging from the Census about the treatment meted out to the females in this part of the world. Data is presented in Table 1. In 2001 there are only 933 females in India for every 1000 males. When it comes to the juvenile sex ratio, it has become even lower at 927 females per 1000 males, despite evidence of more than 1000 baby girls being born for every 1000 boys.

Table 1

Census 2001- Sex Ratio Variations

India/States/UTs	*Sex ratio 2001*	*Rank*	*Sex ratio for 0-6 only*	*Ratio of males per 1000 females at birth 1981-90**
Kerala	1,058	1	962	1055
Pondicherry	1001	2	958	
Chattisgarh	990	3	975	
Tamil Nadu	986	4	939	1049
Manipur	978	5	961	
Andhra Pradesh	978	6	964	1047
Meghalaya	975	7	975	
Orissa	972	8	950	1062
Himachal Pradesh	970	9	897	
Uttaranchal	964	10	906	
Karnataka	964	11	949	1073
Goa	960	12	933	
Tripura	950	13	975	
Lakshadweep	947	14	974	
Jharkhand	941	15	966	
Mizoram	938	16	971	
West Bengal	934	17	963	1056
India	933		927	1095
Assam	932	18	964	1064
Maharashtra	922	19	917	1085
Rajasthan	922	20	909	1141
Gujarat	921	21	878	1113
Bihar	921	22	938	1117
Madhya Pradesh	920	23	929	1082
Nagaland	909	24	975	
Arunachal Pradesh	901	25	961	
Jammu and Kashmir	900	26	937	
Uttar Pradesh	898	27	916	1116
Sikkim	875	28	986	
Punjab	874	29	793	1132
Haryana	861	30	820	1150
Andaman and Nicobar Island	846	31	965	
Delhi	821	32	865	
Dadra and Nagar Haveli	811	33	973	
Chandigarh	773	34	845	
Daman and Diu	709	35	925	

Source: RGI, India.

*: Estimated male live births per 1000 female live births based on SRS.

Table 2

Female/Male Ratios in Under-Five Mortality, 1992-93

States & UTs	*Female/Male Ratios*		
	Neonatal	*Post neonatal*	*Child*
Haryana	0.80	1.59	2.35
Punjab	0.82	0.97	1.81
Uttar Pradesh	0.96	1.24	1.70
Jammu and Kashmir	0.99	1.47	1.69
West Bengal	0.95	0.84	1.63
Rajasthan	0.99	1.20	1.59
Delhi	0.84	1.41	1.56
Bihar	0.78	1.14	1.55
Orissa	0.82	0.96	1.45
Himachal Pradesh	0.83	1.11	1.44
Gujarat	0.93	1.24	1.42
Karnataka	0.83	1.06	1.30
Andhra Pradesh	0.75	1.21	1.28
Maharashtra	0.62	1.21	1.24
Madhya Pradesh	0.78	1.18	1.22
Assam	0.76	0.96	1.13
Goa	0.65	1.11	1.11
Kerala	0.88	0.68	0.94
Tamil Nadu	0.73	0.87	0.80

Source: IIPS, various volumes.

This has been further analysed on the basis of data available on female/male ratios of mortality for the under five age group as shown in Table 2. The ratio which is less than unity at the neonatal stage rises to more than unity for several states in the post-neonatal stage, and in almost all states in the child stage, with the exception of Kerala and Tamil Nadu. This is an indication of the wastage of baby girls more than baby boys. This is a significant reason for the sex ratio (females to 1000 males) being lower than 950 in 143 districts in six major states in 2001 as well as in 1991 as shown in Table 3. The silver lining is the slight improvement in sex ratios by a reduction of 27 districts below 850, 12 crossing the 850 barrier and 15 crossing 899 to get into 900-950 range of sex ratio. The differences in the female infant mortality rates in major states, which could be one of the reasons for the low female sex ratios, is presented in Chart 1. There is a close relationship between the levels of health and nutrition awareness of the mother and infant mortality. Level of literacy/education significantly influences awareness.

The absence of awareness or ignorance of women on several matters impacting quality of life is a contributory factor to the high levels of infant mortality in those states. Lack of awareness restricts access to facilities and services in turn.

Chart 1

Female Infant Mortality Rate in India: 1998

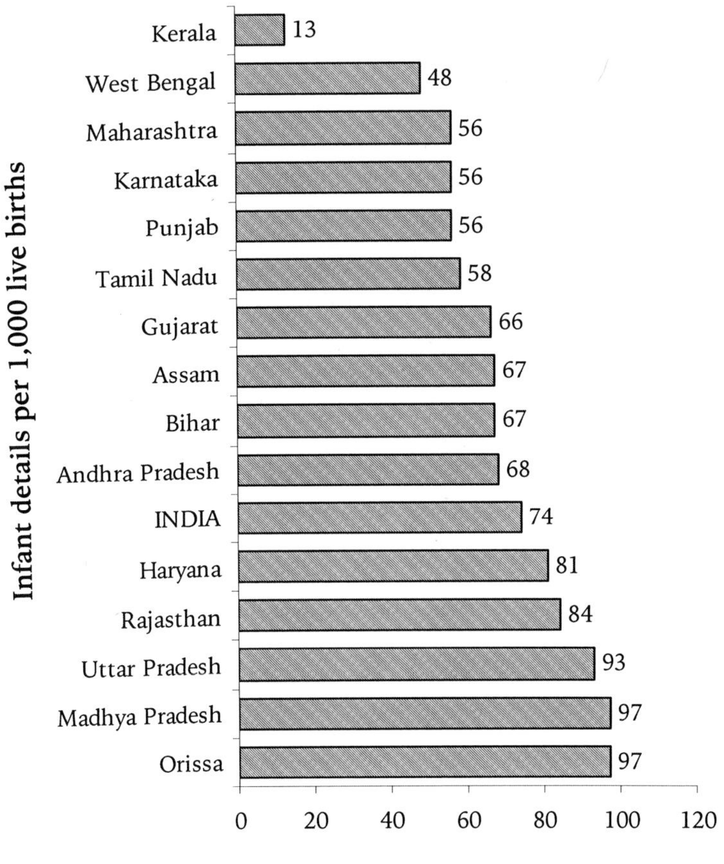

Table 3

Low Sex Ratio: Important States

State	1991 Less than 850	1991 850-899	1991 900-950	2001 Less than 850	2001 850-899	2001 900-950
Uttar Pradesh	28	20	1	7	39	3
Madhya Pradesh	5	7	0	3	7	2
Haryana	4	10	1	5	10	0
Bihar	1	14	2	0	8	9
Rajasthan	4	11	0	2	11	2
Punjab	1	13	1	1	13	1
INDIA	**58**	**80**	**5**	**31**	**92**	**20**

Being unaware, ill-informed and uneducated about living more comfortably with less drudgery, morbidity and the threat of mortality often coupled with absence of access, women are not able to get the benefit of the superior biological strength endowed to them by nature. The social, economic and political environment around women is suffocating and stifles their existence. At every age, more numbers of the species (female) die than is warranted, which keeps the sex ratio adverse to females in many parts of the country at almost all ages, as shown in Chart 2.

Trends in Vital Statistics

Trends in vital statistics in India for the past fifty years is presented below in Table 4. While the life expectation for women has increased to over 63 years, they still have early marriage, high total fertility rate, high incidence of maternal mortality, high levels of infant and child mortality, low couple protection rate etc. which impacts on their quality of life. Their morbidity is high. The decline in Infant Mortality Rate (IMR) is substantially due to improvement in immunization, which is yet to reach 100 per cent – we are just around 65 per cent.

Chart 2

Sex Ratio (Males per 100 Female) of Population by Age Groups 1988-92

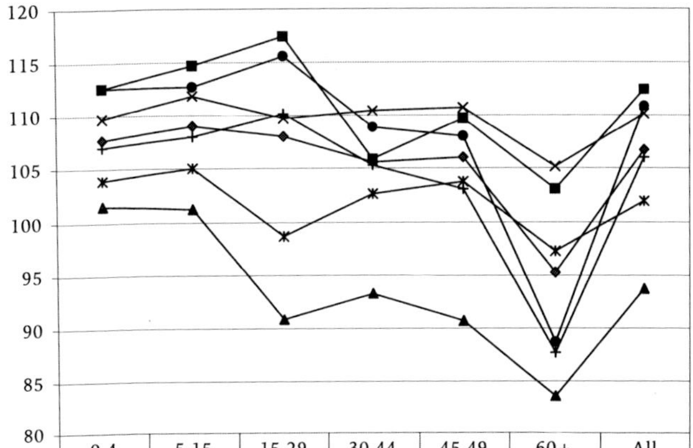

	0-4	5-15	15-29	30-44	45-49	60+	All
All India	107.8	109	108.1	105.6	106	95.3	106.8
UP	112.6	114.8	117.5	105.9	109.8	103.1	112.4
Kerala	101.5	101.2	90.8	93.3	90.7	83.6	93.7
Punjab	109.7	111.9	109.8	110.5	110.7	105.2	110.2
Tamil Nadu	103.9	105.1	98.7	102.6	103.8	97.2	101.9
Rajasthan	112.6	112.8	115.6	108.9	108.1	88.7	110.9
MP	107	108	110.2	105.4	103	87.7	106.1

The national health goals and achievements are given in Appendix II. While we should have reached an IMR of 56-50 for All India by the end of the Ninth Plan, we are just around the Eighth Plan goal of 70, having achieved 72 in 1998. We need to concentrate more intensively on neonatal and perinatal mortality, if we are to get nearer the goal for IMR. As it is, against National Health Policy (NHP) goal of 30-35 for perinatal mortality, we have reached 44.3 in 1993. The NFHS-2 records post-neonatal (1-12 months) mortality at 25.3 which is encouraging.

We are still far off the mark with regard to decreasing LBW babies to 10 per cent. It remains above 30 per cent and even higher at 47 per cent according to NHFS-2. The absence of nutrition for the mother and poor health care is writ large in this data. Significant proportion of girls in the 15-19 age group get married as shown in Table 4 and become teen age mothers with LBW babies.

Table 4

Trends in Vital Statistics

Year	*1951*	*1981*	*1991*	*Current level*
Birth rate (per 1000 population)	39.9	33.9 (SRS)	29.5 (SRS)	26.1 (SRS, 99)
TFR	6.0	4.5 (")	3.6 (")	3.3 (SRS, 97)
IMR (Per 1000 live birth)	146	110 (")	80 (")	70 (SRS, 99)
Child mortality rate (0-4 year per 1000 children)	57.3 (1972)	39.1 (1982)	26.5 (")	23.9 (SRS, 96)
*Age at marriage				
Males	22.6 (1971)	23.5	24.0	24.9 (NFHS-2)
Females	17.2 (1971)	18.4	19.3	19.7 (NFHS-2)
+Proportion of female married in the age group15-19 years	R 61.03('71) U 35.91('71)	R 48.92 U 27.89	R 40.68 U 21.32	R34.4(NFHS-2) U16.4(NFHS-2)
Couple protection rate (%)	10.4 (1971)	22.8	44.1	46.2 (31.3.2000)
Expectation life at birth				
Male	37.2	54.1	60.6	62.36 (1996-01)
Female	36.2	54.7 (1991-96)	61.7	63.99 (Projects)

Source: Page 204, Economic Survey, Government of India, 2000-2001.

* : Page 21, IIPS (1998-99).

+ : Census 1991, RGI Quoted in Women in India, Statistical Profile, 1997.

This goal can be reached only if there is greater quality of health service including antenatal and post-natal care in the high IMR states. It may be pertinent to point out that the higher rate of female mortality at the post-neonatal stage is a serious matter reflecting the poor social status of the girl child in the family that should cause great social concern. The female juvenile sex ratio surfacing in the 2001 census is a pointer to this.

"Goals fixed for women's health have only been related to Family Planning and later for MCH (such as the number of beneficiaries, and the number of deliveries Ante and Post-Natal Care and the number of women and children being immunised). However, there have been no targets for women's health in the context of Revised National Tuberculosis Control Programme (RNTCP) and National Leprosy Eradication Programme (NLEP). This situation needs to be changed by fixing special targets for covering women patients under all diseases." (National Profile on Women, Health and Development, 2000).

The National Population Policy, 2000, was announced in 2000. The immediate objective of the National Population Policy 2000 is to address the unmet needs for contraception, provision of health care infrastructure and health personnel and ensure integrated service delivery for basic reproductive and child health care. The medium term objective is to bring the TFR to replacement levels by 2010, through vigorous implementation of intersectoral operational strategies. The long-term objective is to achieve a stable population by 2045, at a level consistent with the requirements of sustainable economic growth, social development and environmental protection.

The national demographic goals for 2010 to achieve NRR 1 according to the National Population Policy 2000 is also presented in Appendix II. The CBR, CPR and NRR (NRR has to come down to 1.0) are still far off the mark. The National Population Policy has sought to achieve these goals by 2010 only. The TFR that was aimed at 2.3 by 2000 has not been realized. These need multi-pronged action from various social development sectors.

Achievement of many of these goals would benefit women immensely. Tardy implementation and poor delivery of services and inadequate access to them has left the woman in India a much deprived person compared to her sisters in the developed countries of the world. The comparison is brought out in Table 5.

The situation of women in South Asia is much poorer than the rest of the developed world with regard to health and nutrition. Sri Lanka is the only country in the group which has made more significant advancement. The situation in South Asia with regard to health and nutrition of women is presented in Table 6.

Table 5

Sex Ratio, Maternal Mortality Rate, Life Expectancy by Sex of Selected Countries

Country	Life Expectancy		Females as % of Males Sex Ratio (1992)	Maternal Mortality Rate (1990)
	Male	Female		
Japan	76.8	82.9	103.0	18.0
France	74.2	82.0	105.0	15.0
USA	73.4	80.1	105.0	12.0
UK	74.5	79.8	108.0	9.0
Republic of Korea	68.8	76.0	100.0	130.0
Sri Lanka	70.9	75.4	99.0	140.0
China	67.9	72.0	94.0	95.0
Brazil	63.1	71.0	101.0	220.0
South Africa	61.2	67.2	101.0	230.0
Pakistan	62.9	65.1	92.0	340.0
India	**61.4**	**61.8**	**93.0**	**570.0**
Bangladesh	58.1	58.2	94.0	850.0
Uganda	38.9	40.4	102.0	1200.0

Sources: UNDP, Human Development Reports – 1994, 1997 and 1999.

Education and Skill Development

Female adult literacy in India has just crossed 50 per cent and reached 54.2 per cent in 2001. Yet, 46 per cent of the females in the country are illiterate and also unaware of various factors of life to improve its quality. The school enrolment rates at all stages of education are much below the levels for males in India and also remain low in comparison to other countries of the world as brought out in Table 7.

The state of literacy at the district level is an important indicator of the development at the decentralised level. The picture we have now is of districts with a high level of literacy for females at 96.06 per cent at one hand and less than 20 per cent at the other as given below. The distribution of districts at different ranges of

Table 6

Health and Nutrition

	India	*Pakistan*	*Bangladesh*	*Nepal*	*Sri Lanka*	*Bhutan*	*Maldives*	*South Asia (weighted average)*
Life expectancy at birth (years)								
1960	44	43	40	38	62	37	44	44
1998	63	64	58	58	73	61	65	63
Infant mortality rate (per live 1000 births)								
1960	144	139	151	212	90	175	158	144
1998	69	95	79	72	17	84	62	72
Daily calorie supply (as a % of requirement)								
1966	89	76	91	87	100	n/a	n/a	n/a
1997	114	107	97	108	99	n/a	82	111
Under-weight children under age 5 (%)								
1975	71	47	84	63	58	n/a	n/a	69
1997	53	38	56	47	34	38	43	51

Source: HDSA 2000 Background Tables; MHHDCA 1999a; UNDP 1999c and UNDP 1990 quoted in "Human Development in South Asia 2000 – The Gender Question, Mahbub ul Haq Human Development Centre, Oxford".

Table 7

Gender Gaps in Education

Name of the Country	Female Adult Literacy		Female primary net enrolment ratio		Female secondary enrolment ratio		Female Tertiary Students		Female Tertiary science enrolment
	Rate % 1997	As % of male rate 1997	As % of relevant age group	As % of male rate 1997	As % of relevant age group	As % of male rate 1997	Per 10,000 women 1996	As % of male 1996	As % of female Teriary Students 1995
Bangladesh	27.4	55.0	69.6	87.0	15.6	58.0	...	...	...
Bhutan	30.3	52.0	12.3	88.0	...	...	...	...	...
India	**54.2***	**71.4***	**71.0**	**91.0**	**48.0**	**68.0**	**481**	**61**	
Pakistan	25.4	46.0	...	...	...	...	...	...	...
Sri Lanka	87.6	93.0	99.9	100.0	79.3	109.0	388	69	...
Indonesia	79.5	88.0	98.6	99.0	53.4	91.0	812	53	23
Malaysia	81.0	90.0	99.9	100.0	68.5	115.0	...	...	...
Philippines	94.3	99.0	99.9	100.0	78.5	102.0	3404	133	27
Singapore	87.0	91.0	89.5	98.0	74.8	98.0	2250	81	...
Thailand	92.8	96.0	89.2	103.0	36.9	97.0	..	...	23
Vietnam	89.0	94.0	99.9	100.0	54.2	97.0	..	...	...
Korea, Republic of	95.5	97.0	99.9	100.0	99.9	100.0	4182	60	16
China	74.5	82.0	99.9	100.0	65.1	88.0	327	54	...

Source: UNDP, Human Development Report, 1999 quoted in ESCAP's "Overall Review of Regional Implementation of the Beijing Platform for Action.

*: Figures as per Census 2001.

literacy is given in Table 8. There has been quite significant shift of districts from a lower range of literacy to a higher range between 1991 and 2001. Yet there are 232 districts with less than 50 per cent female literacy. This is a rather high proportion of districts lagging behind.

- Aizawl district in Mizoram recorded highest female literacy rate (96.06 per cent).
- Kishanganj district in Bihar recorded lowest female literacy rate (18.49 per cent).
- 143 districts in 1991 had female literacy rate of over 50 per cent. The corresponding number has significantly gone up to 335 in 2001.

Table 8

Distribution of Districts by Range of Female Literacy Rates: 1991, 2001

Ranges	*No. of Districts*	
	1991	*2001*
Less than 10	3	–
10-20	100	2
20-30	125	40
30-40	122	76
40-50	84	124
50-60	74	136
60-70	36	117
70-80	17	59
80-90	11	16
90+	5	7
Total	**577**	**577**

Note: Excludes Jammu & Kashmir, Kinnaur District of Himachal Pradesh and Kachchh District of Gujarat.

This deprivation of education not only affects the advancement of women in life but also influences nutrition, health and disease burdens. The relationship between female literacy and infant mortality is brought out in Chart 3. Lower literacy and education level of the mother has an impact on the infant mortality and child mortality rates. States with lower female literacy generally have higher infant mortality. This relationship has been emphasised in the National Family Health Surveys.

Chart 3

Infant Mortality by Level of Mother's Education

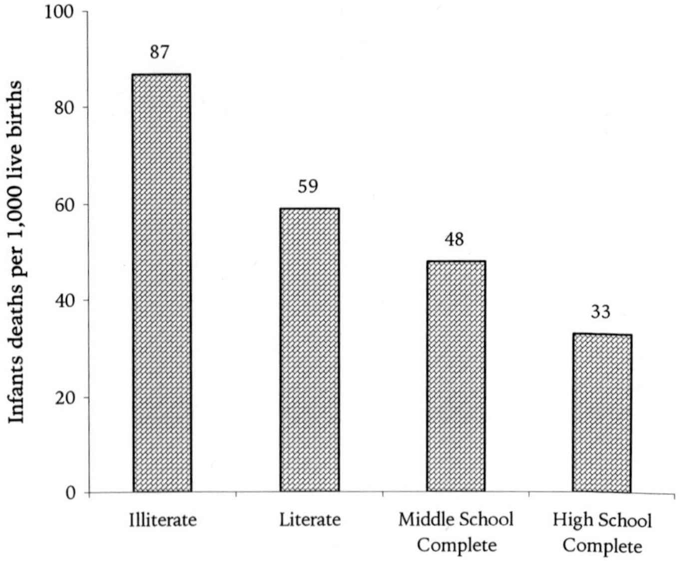

There is great disparity between states in India in the provision of social infrastructure for health and education. This is reflected in the various ranges of achievements by the different states. Consequently, women living in different parts of India have different levels of satisfaction and access. The richer states are able to provide comparatively better facilities for education and health than the poorer states where the needs are even greater. The variation in the provision of expenditure for social services is brought out in Table 9. Compared to levels of public expenditure in 1990-91 on health and education, there has generally been a decline in the poor states as well as middle-income States. Only rich states have done slightly better in education and all social services in the subsequent years. The analysis of the Central Budget for 2000-01 and 2001-02 highlights that the allocations of women specific schemes form 0.76 to 0.87 per cent of the total expenditure of Rs. 336000 – 375000 crores and about 0.12 – 0.17 per cent of the GDP. The situation of backwardness of women cannot be dramatically altered with these kinds of meagre allocations and low public expenditure. There is urgency for dedicating much larger amounts of expenditure for women specific programmes and women components in other general programmes.

Table 9

Index of Per Capita Public Expenditure on Social Services (at 1981/82 prices)

	1990-91	1991-92	1992-93	1993-94	1994-95
	Health				
Poor states	100	96	95	102	97
Middle income states	100	94	93	99	98
Rich states	100	96	97	97	96
All states	100	95	94	100	97
	Education				
Poor states	100	90	92	87	91
Middle income states	100	95	94	99	99
Rich states	100	101	100	104	104
All states	100	95	95	95	97
	All social services*				
Poor states	100	94	93	92	93
Middle income states	100	96	93	97	97
Rich states	100	99	98	100	101
All states	100	96	95	96	97

Note: Poor states include Bihar, Madhya Pradesh, Orissa, Rajasthan, and Uttar Pradesh. Middle income states include Andhra Pradesh, Assam, Karnataka, Kerala, Tamil Nadu, and West Bengal. Rich states include Gujarat, Haryana, Maharashtra and Punjab.

#: includes medical and public health, and family welfare.

*: includes, inter alia, education, health, housing & urban development, and social welfare.

Source: RBI Bulletin, various issues cited in Tulasidhar (1997).

Women in Economic Activity

The profile of women workers relative to men in India is significantly lower by all parameters – in terms of proportion to total workers, work participation, work share in urban areas, as well as number of workdays in a year. Women have a work participation rate of 23 per cent as main workers. A profile of the working population of the country as per 1991 census is presented in Table 10.

Table 10

Profile of Working Population as per 1991 Census

Working Population	*Persons*	*Males*	*Females*
Total population (million)	838.6	435.2	403.4
Workers (million)	314.1	224.4	89.7
% of workers to population (Work Participation Rate)	37.5	51.6	22.3
% of male and female workers to total workers	100.0	71.4	29.6
Workers in rural areas (million)	249.0	168.6	80.4
% of workers in rural areas to total workers	79.2	75.0	89.6
Workers in urban areas (million)	65.1	55.8	9.3
% of workers in urban areas to total workers	20.8	25.0	10.4
Main workers (million)*	285.9	221.6	64.3
% of Main workers to total workers	91.0	98.7	71.7
% of male and female workers to total main workers	100.0	77.5	22.5
Marginal workers (million)**	28.2	2.7	25.5
% of Marginal workers to total workers	9.0	1.3	28.3
% of male and female workers to total marginal workers	100.0	9.6	90.4

Source: Census 1991.
*: Workers getting work for 183 or more days in a year.
**: Workers getting work for less than 183 in a year.

As regards the quality of their employment, the National Sample Survey brings out their lower status in employment as largely casual workers and a lesser proportion of self-employed or regular salary employees.

Quality of employment for females as well as males has generally been deteriorating. Table 11 brings out the details for 1999-2000. Increasing casualisation of employment is seen in both males and females in rural areas and for males in urban areas.

Table 11

Quality of Employment

Details	*1999-2000*		
	Male	*Female*	*Total*
Population (in million)			
Rural	367.24	344.64	711.88
Urban	147.44	135.01	282.44
Total	514.68 (531.3)	479.65 (495.7)	994.33 (1027.0)
Estimated employment (in million)			
Rural	*193.8	*88.7	*282.5
Urban	*71.6	*14.6	*86.2
Workforce participation rate			
Rural	53.1	29.9	41.7
Urban	51.8	13.9	33.7
Self employment (%)			
Rural	55.0	57.3	
Urban	41.5	45.3	—
Total			
Regular salaried Employment (%)			
Rural	8.8	3.1	
Urban	41.7	33.3	
Total			
Casual wage employment (%)			
Rural	36.2	39.6	
Urban	16.8	21.4	
Total			
Unemployment rate			
Rural	1.7	1.0	
Urban	4.5	5.7	
Unemployment rate of the Educated			
- *Secondary and above**			
Rural	6.9	20.4	
Urban	6.6	16.3	
- *Graduate and above*			
Rural	10.7	35.1	
Urban	6.6	16.3	

Source: Population figures given in parentheses relate to census figures. Other data are based on the figures of the National Sample Survey Organization during 1972-73 and 1999-2000.

*: Figures relate to 1998 – NSS 54th round.

Women's share of the labour force averages 40 per cent or more in all of the developed regions, the Caribbean, Eastern and Southeastern Asia. The participation rates for South Asia, West Asia are comparatively low as shown in Table 12. There are cultural factors associated with work participation in these regions.

Table 12

Economic Activity Rates of Persons Aged 15 and over, each Sex, 1970-1990

(percentage)

	1990[a]	
	Women	Men
Developed regions		
Eastern Europe[b]	58	74
Western Europe[b]	51	72
Other developed	54	75
Africa		
Northern Africa	21	75
Sub-Saharan Africa	53	83
Latin America and Caribbean		
Latin America	82	82
Caribbean	77	72
Asia and Pacific		
Eastern Asia	56	80
South-eastern Asia	54	81
Southern Asia	44	78
Central Asia[b]	58	79
Western Asia[b]	30	77
Oceania	48	76

Sources: Prepared by the Statistical Division from ILO, *Year Book of Labour Statistics*, various years up to 1993 (Geneva) and national census and survey reports.

a: Based on national population census and survey data as reported by countries and not adjusted for comparability to internationally recommended definitions. Covers fewer countries than the ILO estimates.

b: Figures for 1970 and 1980 include ILO estimates for States succeeding the former USSR.

Living Conditions

Living conditions are far from satisfactory for majority of the households in India. In the existing pattern of gender roles and division of labour in the households, collection of water, fuel and fodder, cooking, cleaning and caring are the responsibilities of females; they have to spend several hours each day on these domestic chores. In several cases, these have a great impact on their health and also take away a lot of their time from using it for productive purposes and schooling in the case of girls.

The urban population has the problem of inadequate infrastructure owing to a great deal of over crowding. The rural population, on the other hand, does not have many basic necessities for good living. The rural population is scattered in a very large number of small villages. 67 per cent of the population lives in 3,90,093 villages. It is uneconomical to provide various services for households in very small villages and therefore, they have to travel long distances to access services. The degradation of the environment has made life difficult with receding forests and depleting fuel resources.

Women, confined to domestic chores, spend long hours trudging in inhospitable climes, to fetch water, fuel, and fodder and remain poor and sick without care, nor count and reward for the hours they slog. The time spent on activities not included in the System of National Accounts (SNA) have been mapped out in the Time Use Survey, in Table 1 and the unpaid work which is SNA activity in Table 2 of Appendix I. The proportion of time spent by men and women in rural and urban areas on SNA, extended SNA and non-SNA activities are given in Charts 4 and 5.

The details of living conditions are presented in Table 13.

Safe drinking water is a serious problem even for those households that have tap connections with the water sources being enormously polluted even in urban areas. Over 80 per cent of households in rural areas have to rely on wells, tube well/hand pump, tank, river, spring etc. for their supply of water against 30 per cent of households in urban areas. Wells and tubewells are drying up with the groundwater depletion and also deterioration of quality. Water borne diseases are also becoming more serious in many habitations.

Chart 4

Average Time (hours) Spent per week on Various Type of Activities by Sex (Rural)

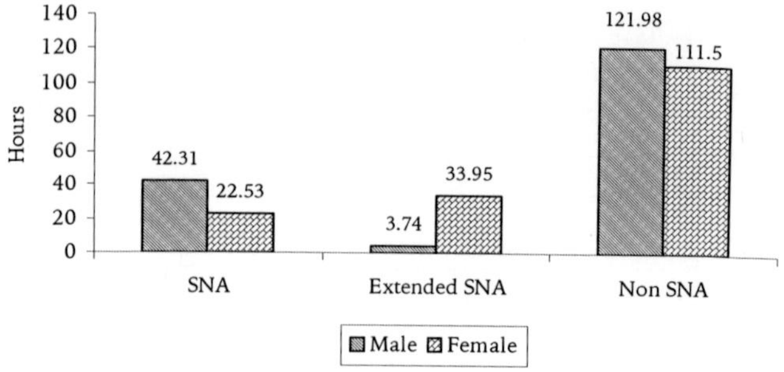

Chart 5

Average Time (hours) Spent per week on Various Types of Activities by Sex (Urban)

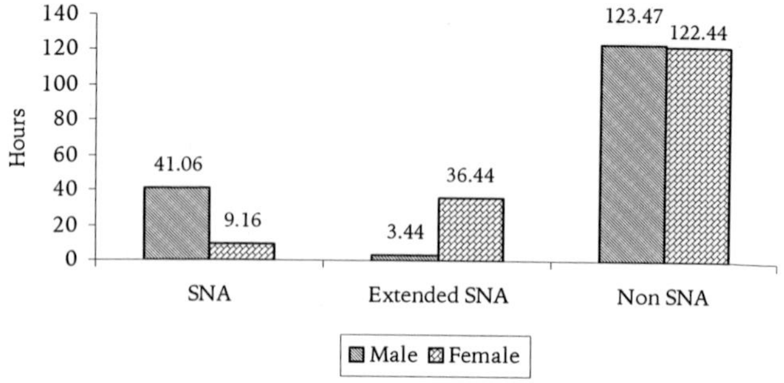

The enormous time a woman (women and girls) spends on these chores as some of her sisters in other parts of the world is illustrated in Table 14. The data in Table 14 also informs about the exposure to air pollution in cooking in different parts of the world where biomass is being used for cooking and the number of hours of exposure. These are severe health hazards for women.

The type of housing is poor for the majority as 58 per cent live in *kuccha* and *semi pucca* houses. 62.10 per cent of households in rural areas are not electrified against 17.20 per cent of urban households. Even those electrified often do not get regular supply of power.

82.5 per cent of rural households do not have any kind of latrine, while 25.5 per cent of urban households still do not have latrines.

Table 13

Details of Living Conditions

(This Table is further subdivided in 7 parts: 13A, 13B, 13C, 13D, 13E, 13F and 13G)

13(A)

Distribution of Villages according to Population 1991

Size of population	No. of villages	% of villages
< 1000	390,093	67.17
1000 to 1999	114,395	19.70
2000 to 4999	62,915	10.83
5000 to 9999	10,597	1.82
10000 and over	2,779	0.48
Total	580,781	100.00

13 (B)

Percentage of Total Population in Urban Areas by Size of Town

Class	Size of town	1991
Class I	1,00,000 & above	16.55
Class II	50,000 – 99,999	2.76
Class III	20,000 – 49,999	3.31
Class IV	10,000 – 19,999	1.96
Class V	5,000 – 9,999	0.65
Class VI	Less than 5000	0.07

Source: Manpower Profile India Yearbook 2000.

13 (C)

Type of House 1991

Details	Rural & Urban Combined
Pucca	42%
Semi Pucca	31%
Kuccha	27%

Source: Statistical Abstract, India 1999.

13 (D)

Type of Dwelling Units (%)

Details	*Rural*	*Urban*
Independent house	87	58
Flat	2	14
Chawl/Basti	5	15
Others	6	13
Total	**100**	**100**

Source: Statistical Abstract, India 1999.

13 (E)

Percentage of Households having Electricity
(NSS 51st Round: July 1994 to June 1995)

Details	*Rural*	*Urban*
Electrified	37.90	82.80

Source: Statistical Abstract, India 1999.

13 (F)

Percentage of Households by Type of Latrine
(NSS 54th Round: January – June 1998)

Type of Latrine	*Rural*	*Urban*
No Latrine	82.50	25.50
Service Latrine	2.70	5.90
Septic Tank	7.50	35.20
Flush System	2.90	8.40
Sewerage System	0.80	22.50
Other	3.50	2.50
Total	100.00	100.00
Toilet facility available (1991 census)	9.48%	63.85%

Source: Statistical Abstract, India 1999.

13 (G)

Distribution of Household by Source of Drinking Water

Details	*Rural*	*Urban*
Tap	(10.29)18.70	(63.24)70.10
Well	(61.63)25.80	(20.40)6.70
Tube Well/Hand pump	(16.21)50.10	(11.82)21.30
Tank/Pond	1.90	0.30
River, Canal and Lake	1.30	0.20
Spring	1.70	0.10
Others	0.40	1.10
Total	100.00	100.00

Source : NSSO, NSS 54th Round January – June 1998. NSS Report No. 449. Figures in parenthesis relate to 1981.

Table 14

Women's Exposure to Indoor Air Pollution from Biomass Fuel Combustion in Selected Countries and Time Spent for Collection of Water and Fuel

(This table is further subdivided in 3 Parts: Table 14A, 14B and 14C)

14 (A)

*Women's Exposure to Indoor Air Pollution from Bio-mass Fuel Combustion. Kitchen Area Concentration Levels**

Countries	*Measurement conditions*	*Particulate concentration (micrograms of pollutant per cubic metre of air)*	*Suspended particulate micrograms as multiple of WHO peak guideline*
India, 1998	Cooking	4000-21000	17-91
	Individual exposure (2-5 hrs. per day) in five villages, 1988	4700	20
China, 1997	All day in wood-burning kitchen	2600	11

14 (B)

*Time Women Spent Collecting Water***

Region	*Time spent to collect water (hrs. per week)*
India	
Baroda region	7.0
Rajasthan	2.9
West Bengal	2.5
Punjab (Ludhiana)	0.5
Karnataka (Gulbarga)	2.6
Nepal villages	4.9
Pakistan villages	3.5
Africa	
Egypt	4.9
Kenya	4.2
Nigeria	3.5-10.5
Latin America	
Ecuador, Northeast Amazon region	0.7-1.3

14 (C)

*Time Women Spent Gathering Fuel Wood****

Region, Village and Forest Status	*Time collecting fuel wood (hours per day)*
Uttar Pradesh, Chamoli Hills (1982)	4.0-5.0
Gujarat (1980)	4.0-5.0
Assam (1983-84)	1.0
Maharashtra (1983-84)	4.0-5.0
Madhya Pradesh (1983-84)	2.2
Indonesia – Java (1983-84)	0.1-2.0
Nepal (1982-83)	1.1-2.5
Latin America – Ecuador (1990)	1.2

Source: The World's Women 1995, Trends and Statistics, UNITED NATIONS;

*: adopted from Chart 2.12, page 49.

**: adopted from Chart 2.13, page 50.

***: adopted from Chart 2.15, page 55.

Human Development and Gender Development Indicators for India

UNDP has been analysing the status of the UN members countries with reference to various parameters of development. They rank countries according to the social and economic development parameters. India has only recently graduated to the middle income group of countries. According to the UNDP analysis in their Human Development Report of 2000, India is 128 out of 170 countries on the Human Development Index (HDI). The details of various groups of countries is given in Table 1 of Appendix III with reference to HDI. The HDI index value for India stands at 0.563 against 0.935 for Canada which ranks first, 0.924 for Japan which stands 9th, 0.733 for Sri Lanka which stands 84th.

The Gender Development Index (GDI) takes India to the 108th rank amongst 174 countries as shown in Table 2 of Appendix III against Sri Lanka which climbs up to the 68th rank. India has a very long way to go to catch up with other countries even in Asia and South Asia.

A ranking has been worked out for different states using the same methodology of Human Development Index and Gender Development Index. The analysis is presented in Table 15. Amongst major States superceding Punjab (which has high per capita income). Kerala ranks first and Uttar Pradesh ranks last.

Action Ahead

The scenario as it exists today is rather dismal as captured in Chart 2 which emphasises the subservient position of women owing to a variety of social, cultural, economic and political factors. If things are to improve for them to achieve empowerment, quality of life and capacity building to be a competent person, as envisaged in Chart 1, it is critical to understand what goals should be aimed at for 2020 in various sectors and the action required to achieve them. A brief sketch of the goals to be achieved for 2020 to satisfy this vision is attempted in Table 16.

Table 15

HDI and GDI for Major States

States	Life Expectancy at birth (years)[a] (1989-93)	Literacy Rate (7+)[b] (%) (1991)	State Domestic Product per capita (Rupees)[c] (At Current Prices) (1992-93)	Human Development Index (HDI)[d] (1991-92)	Gender Development Index (GDI)[e] (1991-92)
1. Kerala	72.0	90	5,768	0.603	0.565
2. Punjab	66.4	59	11,217	0.529	0.424
3. Maharashtra	64.2	65	9,795	0.523	0.492
4. Haryana	62.9	56	9,037	0.489	0.370
5. Gujarat	60.1	61	8,045	0.467	0.437
6. West Bengal	61.5	58	5,633	0.459	0./399
7. Himachal Pradesh	63.6	64	6,390	0.454	0.432
8. Karnataka	61.9	56	6,331	0.448	0.417
9. Tamil Nadu	62.4	63	6,809	0.438	0.402
10. Andhra Pradesh	60.6	44	5,718	0.400	0.371
11. Assam	54.9	53	4,973	0.379	0.347
12. Orissa	55.5	49	4,114	0.373	0.329
13. Rajasthan	58.0	39	5,086	0.356	0.309
14. Bihar	58.5	38	3,053	0.354	0.306
15. Madhya Pradesh	54.0	44	4,558	0.349	0.312
16. Uttar Pradesh	55.9	42	4,345	0.348	0.293
India	*59.4	*52		0.423	0.388

States have been ranked in descending order of HDI.

(*): Excludes Jammu and Kashmir.

a: Sample Registration System, cited in: Government of India (1997 a);

b: Census of India 1991, cited in Government of India (1997 b);

c: Government of India (1997c);

d&e: Shiva Kumar A.K. (1996).

Table 16

Projection of Goals for 2020 to Achieve the Vision of 2020 for Women

Details	*Latest*	*2010*	*2020*
IMR	70 (1999)	30	20
Prenatal Mortality	44.3 (1993)	20	10
Crude Death Rate (CDR)	8.9 (1996)	8	7
Maternal Mortality Rate (MMR)	407 (1997) 540(1998-99)	100	50
Life Expectancy (years)			
Male	63 (1996-2000)	70	74
Female	63.4 (1996-2000)	72	77
Babies with birth weight not below 2.5 kg.	47% (1998-99)	20%	15%
Crude Birth Rate (CBR)	26.1 (SRS 99)	18.0	10.0
Couple Protection Rate (CPR)	46% (2000)	80%	90%
Net Replacement Rate (NRR)	—	2.1	1.6
Total Fertility Rate (TFR)	3.3 (SRS 97)	2.1	1.6
Annual Growth Rate	1.6	1.1	0.9
Immunization	—	100%	100%
Age at marriage for girls		20+	20+
Antenatal care	65% (1998-99)	90%	95%
Deliveries Institutional	35%	80%	90%
Trained Attendant	76.7%	100%	100%
Projected Age Composition (%)			
Below five years	10.70	10.10	9.7
0-15 years	34.33	28.48	27.73
>15-59 years	58.70	63.38	63.33
+ 60 years	6.97	8.14	8.94

Source: Compiled from data from NFHS-2, National Profile on Women, Health and Development, 2000 and National Population Policy. The projections for 2020 are based on assumption of best practices.

In very simple terms, the entire priority of planning has to shift to providing basic infrastructure for life with amenities of food security, nutrition security, safe drinking water, sanitation, sustainable environment for basic needs and good health, security of life with law and order and recognition of human rights to a decent life. Ordinarily, all these are the basic functions of good governance.

People have to learn to insist on accountability of their elected representatives to deliver good governance and assure the basic needs of life.

This calls for great awareness of deprivations and human rights to demand them. This has to become a process of awareness generation and education–both within the curriculum and outside the curriculum. The effort has to be a partnership between people, the civil society and the Government at all levels. Even advanced countries are recognising the need to fulfil these basic needs of people as the responsibility of democracy and elected governments.

Certain specific action that would be required are detailed below:

1. Reverse the Low Sex Ratio

The analysis of the sex ratio in 593 districts shows that it is above 1000 only in 76 districts in 2001, a slight improvement over the 54 districts in 1991. It continues to be less than 800 in eight districts. The range of sex ratios in the districts are given in Table 17.

Table 17

Distribution of Districts by Range of Sex Ratio: 1991, 2001

Ranges	*No. of Districts*	
	1991	*2001*
Less than 800	8	8
800-849	59	74
850-899	130	78
900-949	181	194
950-999	161	163
1000-1049	38	56
1050+	16	20
Total	**593**	**593**

There is urgency to look at the districts with low sex ratios. The cause for the low sex ratio needs to be studied deeply to find out whether it is due to:

- Technology of sex selection.

- Female Foeticide.
- Female Infanticide.
- Maternal mortality.
- Higher female mortality in all age groups due to negligence in nutrition and overall health care for females.
- Migration.

The Central and state governments have initiated programmes to change mindsets with incentives to allow the girl child to survive and develop through specific schemes. The religious groups and courts have also become aware of this critical need to change attitudes in families and bring about a shift from son preference. More active action would be necessary in this direction, and may be campaigns would have to be supported in a big way to remove gender biases.

2. The Integrated Child Development Services (ICDS)

The package of services envisaged in the ICDS is very critical for the community at this juncture with high levels of malnutrition, under development, morbidity and mortality. The quality of service, no doubt needs great improvement with more investment in training the service delivery agents and due compensation for the work they do. Unfortunately, in many parts of the country, the essence of this programme has not been understood and it has been treated as *"daliya centres"* and closed when the state government runs out of resources to provide supplementary food for the beneficiaries. In fact, it is ironic that with abundance of food in the granary, the poor should remain hungry. The ICDS should be used effectively to reach food and nutrition to the needy persons, particularly, children, lactating and pregnant women and the old people who are in destitution. States like Kerala and Tamil Nadu who have used the ICDS channel effectively and mid-day meal programmes have reached high levels of human resource development in the last two decades in India. This should be a good example for other states to design their programmes.

The integration of health services in a more coordinated manner with the ICDS is very urgent to achieve several health goals for women and children. The elimination of anemia, antenatal checkups, immunization depend very heavily on a good ICDS support programme. Currently, the coordination is not effective. This needs attention and improvement. The functionaries at the grassroots level have to be brought together to work on common goals with coordinated activities.

3. Traditional Dais

The institution of the traditional *dai* needs to be strengthened with training on technically correct methods and information on techniques. Their services can be harnessed very effectively for delivery of a variety of basic health services. Other areas relating to reproductive and child health need urgent attention and care for the survival of mothers and children. The health infrastructure needs to be given priority for filling up all the gaps in terms of manpower and infrastructure so as to fulfil the needs of the population in the rural and urban areas. The National Population Policy 2000 has already identified the gaps. Their can be nothing more urgent than putting the supply of services in order.

The reproductive rights of women needs to be recognised as their human right to choose their priorities. They must have choice of timing and the choice of number of children and choice of methods of contraception. They have to be educated about their rights. Their partners should be educated to respect women's reproductive rights.

4. Care of the Aged

The age composition of the population is already changing. By 2010, those above 60 would have exceeded eight per cent of the population and would be near nine per cent in 2020. This would increase the dependency ratios and call for special services including specialised geriatric care. The proportion of females in the higher age group will be higher and this calls for additional responsibility. Old age homes to look after them and other social security benefits for the aged become more urgent.

5. Working Women

Women in the labour force will increase rapidly in the years to come with increase in the proportion of people in the 15-59 age group. It is possible that the work participation rates will touch 40 per cent as in most other parts of the world. A very serious handicap today for working women is the absence of a secure child care support service. The services so far attempted in India have just been pilot programmes. It is now necessary to scale up these services with proper system of registration, standardisation of services, norms for fees and standards of quality and training. The potential for employment generation in this service sector is enormous, but it needs very careful regulation. It would be impossible for Government to undertake the running of creches directly. Models that are available of child care services even in other smaller countries like Mauritius are worth emulation. This involves zoning of areas and running child care services with a charge on every employer and employee and a share by the Government/local body. In fact, a proper system of child care service will release a lot of women into productive labour and may be a very strong instrument for elimination of poverty.

6. *Education*

Our progress towards universal elementary education has been rather slow. The target date for achievement has been staggered every time we have come close to the year (see Table 7). It is now expected to be reached by 2005. It must be reached. Literacy for women has to be made a priority as it holds the key to all other development, both of themselves and the community. May be, all the resources that are warranted should be allocated for the purpose on a priority basis to achieve 90 per cent literacy in all the districts by 2020. More than half the districts are currently lagging behind with less than 50 per cent literacy for women as mentioned in Table 8.

7. *Skill Development*

Efforts undertaken so far for skill development for women have been far too inadequate. In the new economic regime of competition, survival would be difficult without the right skills to avail of new employment opportunities. Intensive studies to track the need for various skills to suit economic development is urgent to design the right programmes for training women. The existing training institutions and programmes need to be strengthened, effectively based on field studies.

8. Credit and Organisation

A big stride has been taken in India with formation of self-help groups for micro-credit. This needs to be scaled up as an access point or "means towards advancement" and not as an end in itself. Credit availability through regular lending institutions has to be expanded to help women achieve economic advancement beyond subsistence levels. The mode of self-help groups should be treated as a way of organisation for achieving several common goals including infrastructure, skill and other entitlements for empowerment. The form of organisation could be societies, cooperatives or any form that is conducive for democratic government.

9. Participation in Decision-Making

Elected women members in the local bodies (Panchayats and Municipalities) need to be intensively trained to perform their roles effectively. It is important to use strategies for gender sensitisation of the male members on the Panchayats and Municipalities, including the bureaucracy, to accept the elected women members and allow them to play their roles.

10. Male Responsibilities

Vision 2020 for women cannot be realised without women and men understanding and appreciating male responsibilities at the family and social levels if a thorough shift from patriarchy is to take place. May be, this is the most difficult part of the strategy to bring gender justice and a society of equity and equality. This has to come through a very systematic approach of gender sensitisation of all organisations, systems and practices. Right from achieving demographic goals to sharing power from the Panchayats to the Parliament, gender sensitisation is necessary. This calls for serious gender analysis and gender budgeting in all allocations, performance evaluations and measurement of achievements. A beginning should be made with the 10th Five-Year Plan to lay down a strong course of action in this direction.

APPENDIX I

Accounting for Women's Work in India

Women's work is underestimated. A lot of work they do is unremunerated. The System of National Accounts (SNA) includes only productive work which has market value and is included in exchange for value. A great deal of work women do for the household which is in the nature of care of the household is not included in the System of National Accounts. Some part of the work women do for value addition in the household also do not get paid as it is merged in the household economic activity. Consequently, women become invisible in these activities. The Time Use Survey measures the time devoted for SNA activities and Extended SNA activities and evaluates the contribution of men and women to the household. "The full visibility of the type, extent and distribution of this unremunerated work will also contribute to a better sharing of responsibilities."[4]

Time Use Survey by the Central Statistical Organisation, 2000

Time use data consists of information on-

Time spent on activities within and outside households;

Nature of work undertaken, paid, unpaid etc;

Time spent on, and intensity of, drudgerous work like collecting fuel, fodder and water;

Pattern of use of child labour;

Sharing of work between women and men within households etc;

These data help in understanding the various socio-economic and cultural aspects of life of the people in terms of burden of work and leisure, community activities, mobility outside the households, survival strategies and livelihood patterns. They are of considerable use in planning for skill training and employment.

Time Use Survey was conducted in India from July 1998 to June 1999 over six selected states namely, Haryana, Madhya Pradesh, Gujarat, Orissa, Tamil Nadu and Meghalaya by the Central Statistical Organisation with the objective of collecting data for

4. Platform for Action and the Beijing Declaration, Fourth World Conference on Women, Beijing, 1995.

properly quantifying the economic contribution of women in national economy and to study gender discrimination in household activities. The survey found that out of 168 hours in a week, on the average, males spent about 41.96 hours in 'System of National Accounts' (SNA) activities as compared to only about 18.72 hours by females. While females spent 34.63 hours on extended SNA activities, males spent only 3.65 hours. Taking SNA and extended SNA activities together, males spent 45.61 hours against 53.35 hours spent by females; rural males spent only 46.05 hours as compared to 56.48 hours spent by rural females on SNA and extended SNA activities. In the case of urban males, this figure works out to 44.50 hours as compared to 45.60 hours spent by urban females. Females, thus, work for longer hours than males. In other words, women's contribution worked out to 55 per cent of the total work done as compared to 45 per cent by men. Therefore, if extended SNA activities are included in the economic activities, the contribution of women will be higher as compared to men. Women spent another 25.56 hours per week on cooking, cleaning and childcare. Men spent only 0.32 hours per week on childcare. Including household work, women worked 82.04 hours out of 168 hours in a week.

The total time spent on SNA, extended SNA and non-SNA activities by males and females in the six states surveyed is presented in Table 1.

The survey notes "in India no payment is made for a number of economic activities". Such activities are performed either by family labour or through exchange labour. For the states combined, payment was not made for about 38 per cent of the time spent in SNA activities. The amount of unpaid activities was more (51 per cent) for females as compared to only 33 per cent for males. The predominance of females in unpaid activities was visible in all the states. The percentage of time spent by females in unpaid activities was highest in Haryana (86 per cent followed by Meghalaya, 76 per cent and Orissa, 69 per cent). The percentage was lowest for Tamil Nadu (32 per cent). Table 2 brings out the differences in regard to unpaid work between the states for men and women.

Table 1

Time Spent on Various Activities: State-wise Weekly Average Time (In Hours Spent on SNA, Extended SNA and Non-SNA Activities by Sex and Place of Residence)

States	*Activities*	*Rural*			*Urban*			*Total*		
		Male	*Female*	*Total*	*Male*	*Female*	*Total*	*Male*	*Female*	*Total*
Haryana	SNA	37.98	23.49	31.36	36.54	11.21	24.97	37.72	21.26	30.19
	Extended SNA	1.74	30.67	14.91	3.11	32.74	16.68	1.99	31.06	15.24
	Non-SNA	128.22	113.81	121.69	128.31	124.08	126.36	128.23	115.67	122.52
	Total	**167.94**	**167.97**	**167.96**	**167.96**	**168.03**	**168.01**	**167.94**	**167.99**	**167.95**
Madhya Pradesh	SNA	43.55	22.62	33.64	36.35	8.50	23.37	42.07	19.85	31.54
	Extended SNA	4.22	35.47	19.12	4.43	36.99	19.60	4.43	35.79	19.22
	Non-SNA	119.98	109.85	115.20	127.19	122.53	125.03	121.47	112.38	117.19
	Total	**167.95**	**167.94**	**167.96**	**167.97**	**168.02**	**168.00**	**167.97**	**168.02**	**167.95**
Gujarat	SNA	44.83	23.90	34.74	41.81	7.02	25.45	43.63	17.60	31.24
	Extended SNA	3.25	37.55	19.73	3.09	41.57	21.18	3.19	39.08	20.27
	Non-SNA	119.93	106.52	113.49	123.09	119.47	121.99	121.12	111.36	116.44
	Total	**168.01**	**167.97**	**167.96**	**167.99**	**168.06**	**168.62**	**167.94**	**168.04**	**167.95**
Orissa	SNA	39.54	19.03	29.26	42.19	8.37	26.46	40.12	17.07	28.69
	Extended SNA	4.34	35.28	19.83	5.00	37.61	20.18	4.47	35.70	19.91
	Non-SNA	124.10	113.67	118.92	120.81	122.06	121.41	123.45	115.20	119.36
	Total	**167.98**	**167.98**	**168.01**	**168.00**	**168.04**	**168.05**	**168.04**	**167.97**	**167.96**

(Contd...)

(...Contd...)

States	*Activities*	*Rural*			*Urban*			*Total*		
		Male	*Female*	*Total*	*Male*	*Female*	*Total*	*Male*	*Female*	*Total*
Tamil Nadu	SNA	42.02	23.46	32.77	43.28	11.02	27.09	42.54	18.97	30.68
	Extended SNA	3.51	29.52	16.53	2.70	32.08	17.44	3.19	30.46	16.87
	Non-SNA	122.43	114.99	118.71	121.94	124.89	123.47	122.27	118.61	120.45
	Total	**167.96**	**167.97**	**168.01**	**167.92**	**167.99**	**168.00**	**168.00**	**168.04**	**168.00**
Meghalaya	SNA	48.28	29.12	38.45	35.42	14.42	24.23	45.94	26.34	35.88
	Extended SNA	7.02	34.55	21.13	7.96	34.39	21.99	7.16	34.52	21.28
	Non-SNA	112.70	104.31	108.38	124.60	119.24	121.77	114.78	107.15	110.84
	Total	**168.00**	**167.98**	**167.96**	**167.98**	**168.05**	**167.99**	**167.88**	**168.01**	**168.00**
Combined States	SNA	42.31	22.53	32.72	41.06	9.16	25.77	41.96	18.72	30.75
	Extended SNA	3.74	33.95	18.40	3.44	36.44	19.26	3.65	34.63	18.69
	Non-SNA	121.98	111.50	116.89	123.47	122.44	123.03	122.42	114.58	118.62
	Total	**168.03**	**167.98**	**168.01**	**167.97**	**168.04**	**168.06**	**168.03**	**167.93**	**168.06**

Note: The figure of total time for each may not be exactly equal to 168 due to effect of rounding.

Source: Table 5.3, Report of the Time Use Survey, Central Statistical Organisation, Ministry of Statistics and Programme Implementation, Government of India, New Delhi, April 2000.

Table 2

Time Spent on Paid and Unpaid Activities

States	*Male*			*Female*			*Total*		
	Paid	*Unpaid*	*% time on unpaid activities*	*Paid*	*Unpaid*	*% time on unpaid activities*	*Paid*	*Unpaid*	*% time on unpaid activities*
Haryana	33.09	18.12	35.38	4.13	25.34	85.99	20.06	21.37	51.58
Madhya Pradesh	29.41	23.34	44.25	14.31	15.75	52.40	22.99	20.12	46.67
Gujarat	44.37	15.17	24.27	17.18	13.87	44.67	33.26	14.05	29.70
Orissa	31.25	22.42	41.77	8.00	18.18	69.44	20.55	20.47	49.90
Tamil Nadu	41.42	13.36	24.39	21.48	10.32	32.45	32.74	12.04	26.89
Meghalaya	17.34	35.39	67.12	7.83	25.34	76.39	12.65	30.44	70.64
Combined States	36.54	18.12	33.15	14.87	15.18	50.52	27.16	16.85	38.29

Source: Report of the Time Use Survey, Central Statistical Organisation, Government of India, April 2000.

APPENDIX II

Table 1

National Health Policy: Goals and Achievements

Indicator	Prior to NHP	EIGHTH PLAN		NHP Goal for 2000	9th Plan Goal	Most recent estimate
		Goal	Achievement (1996)			
IMR	125 (1978)	70	72	60	56-50	72 (1998)
Perinatal mortality rate				30-35		44.3 (1993)
CDR	12.5 (1981)		9	9	9	8.9 (1996)
MMR	4-5 (1976)		4.7 (1993)	Below 2	3	4.07 (1997)
Life Expectancy						
a) Male	52.6(1976-81)		59.0 (1989-93)	64	62 (1996-2001)	63.0 (96-01)
b) Female	51.6		59.7 (1989-93)	64	63 (1996-2001)	63.4 (-DO-)
Babies with weight below 2.5 Kg.(%)	30##		30##	10##		30 (1993) 47 (98-99)@
CBR/1000	35	26	27.5	21	24/23	26.5 (1998)
CPR %	23.6 (1982)	56	45.4	60	51-60	46.2 (2000)&
NRR	1.48 (1981)					
Growth Rate % (Annual)	2.24 (1971-81)		1.8	1.2	1.6/1.5	
TFR	4.4 (1975)		3.5	2.3	2.9/2.6	2.85 (96-98)

(Contd...)

(...Contd...)

Indicator	Prior to NHP	EIGHTH PLAN		NHP Goal for 2000	9th Plan Goal	Most recent estimate
		Goal	Achievement (1996)			
Immunisation						
BCG (Infants)		100	97 (1996-97)	100	65[$]	
Polio (Infants)		100	90 (1996-97)	100	65[$]	
DPT (children < 1 year)		100	89 (1996-97)	100	65[$]	
Measles		100		100	65[$]	
DT (new school entrants) (5-6 years)		100	48 (1995-96)	100		
T.T. (for school children)						
a) 10 years		100	47 (1995-96)	100		
b) 16 years		100	41 (1995-96)	100		
Immunisation by TT (%) (for Pregnant Women)	20	100	79	100	95	66.8 (98-99)[@]
Pregnant mothers receiving antenatal care(%)	40-50	100	76	100	90	65.1 (98-99)[@]
Deliveries by trained personnel (%)	30-35		13	100	45	76.7 (98-99)[%]
Institutional Deliveries %	-	-	-	-	35	
Leprosy (% arrested cases among detected cases)	20			80		
Prevalence per thousand TB (% of arrested cases among detected)	57.3 (1981)**		5.8 (1995) 30 (1995)	90	1/10,000 85[#]	

Source: GOI, Planning Commission, Ninth Five Year Plan 1997-2002.
*: National Health Policy ** : Ministry of Health and FW $: Fully immunized against 6 VPD by 1 year

#: 85% cure rate in RNTCP districts @ : IIPS – NFHS-2 1998-99 &: Economic Survey 2000-2001
##: "Women in India – How free? How equal?", Kalyani Menon & A.K. Shivakumar

APPENDIX II

National Population Policy 2000

National Socio-Demographic Goals for 2010

1. Address the unmet needs for basic reproductive and child health services, supplies and infrastructure.
2. Make school education up to the age 14 free and compulsory, and reduce drop outs at primary and secondary school levels to below 20 per cent for both boys and girls.
3. Reduce infant mortality rate to below 30 per 1000 live births.
4. Reduce maternal mortality ratio to below 100 per 100,000 births.
5. Achieve universal immunization of children against all vaccine preventable diseases.
6. Promote delayed marriage for girls, not earlier than age 18 and preferably after 20 years of age.
7. Achieve 80 per cent institutional deliveries and 100 per cent deliveries by trained persons.
8. Achieve universal access to information/counseling, and services for fertility regulation and contraception with a wide basket of choices.
9. Achieve 100 per cent registration of births, deaths, marriage and pregnancy.
10. Contain the spread of Acquired Immune Deficiency Syndrome (AIDS), and promote greater integration between the management of Reproductive Tract Infections (RTI) and Sexually Transmitted Infections (STI) and the National AIDS Control Organisation.
11. Prevent and control communicable diseases.
12. Integrate Indian Systems of Medicine (ISM) in the provision of reproductive and child health services, and in reaching out to households.
13. Promote vigorously the small family norm to achieve replacement levels of TFR.
14. Bring about convergence in implementation of related social sector programs, so that family welfare becomes a people centered programme.

NFHS-2 FACT SHEET – STATES

State	Population, 1 July, 2000 (in millions)[1]	Per cent of females literate (age 6+)	Per cent of females age 6-14 attending school	Per cent of ever-married women age 15-49 who are: Urban	Not regularly exposed to any media	Per cent of households: With electricity	With drinking water piped or from hand pump	With no toilet/ latrine facility	Using adequately iodized salt[2]	Per cent of women involved in decisions about own health care	Per cent of women age 20-24 married by exact age 18
India[#]	**1002.1**	**48.6**	**73.7**	**26.2**	**40.3**	**60.1**	**77.9**	**64.0**	**49.3**	**51.6**	**50.0**
North											
Delhi	14.1	21.7	90.8	92.1	7.3	97.7	98.7	5.6	89.2	68.7	19.8
Haryana	19.9	42.7	85.5	28.8	33.1	89.1	88.0	60.9	71.0	67.2	41.5
Himachal Pradesh	6.7	31.3	97.3	9.1	16.3	97.2	77.4	73.0	90.5	80.8	10.7
Punjab	23.6	35.1	90.0	30.8	18.0	95.5	98.9	48.6	75.3	78.5	11.6
Rajasthan	53.9	62.9	63.2	24.2	63.1	64.4	69.8	71.8	46.3	40.6	68.3
Central											
Madhya Pradesh	80.2	55.5	70.8	25.3	45.2	68.1	63.5	77.8	56.7	36.6	64.7
Uttar Pradesh	171.5	57.3	69.4	20.0	54.7	36.6	85.6	73.3	48.8	44.8	62.4
East											
Bihar	100.6	65.2	54.1	10.2	72.7	18.2	75.4	83.2	46.9	47.6	71.0
Orissa	36.0	48.7	75.1	11.0	55.7	33.8	65.3	86.5	35.0	38.6	37.6
West Bengal	79.3	42.6	76.7	23.8	38.6	36.7	89.3	54.9	61.7	45.1	45.9

(Contd...)

(...Contd...)

State	Population, 1 July, 2000 (in millions)[1]	Per cent of females literate (age 6+)	Per cent of females age 6-14 attending school	Per cent of ever-married women age 15-49 who are:		Per cent of households					
				Urban	Not regularly exposed to any media	With electricity	With drinking water piped or from hand pump	With no toilet/ latrine facility	Using adequately iodized salt[2]	Per cent of women involved in decisions about own health care	Per cent of women age 20-24 married by exact age 18
Northeast											
Arunachal Pradesh	1.2	43.0	77.3	15.9	36.7	68.9	80.7	26.1	84.1	70.0	27.6
Assam	26.3	40.9	75.0	8.5	47.4	26.4	60.1	36.8	79.6	65.1	40.7
Manipur	2.5	41.3	87.8	33.7	16.2	75.3	48.9	8.0	87.9	43.3	9.9
Meghalaya	2.5	33.2	85.2	20.0	37.3	41.2	42.1	48.0	63.0	78.9	25.5
Mizoram	1.0	10.6	90.8	52.9	16.9	84.1	63.2	2.3	91.3	73.2	11.6
Nagaland	1.7	31.7	83.5	20.3	35.7	56.3	40.5	25.6	67.2	69.4	22.9
Sikkim	0.6	35.6	88.5	14.2	21.5	80.7	84.6	27.3	79.1	60.2	22.3
West											
Goa	1.6	25.2	93.2	41.6	11.6	93.5	61.8	41.1	41.9	61.6	10.1
Gujarat	48.5	46.4	72.8	42.5	33.8	84.3	84.5	54.9	56.1	71.4	40.7
Maharashtra	91.4	38.6	86.9	41.3	29.6	82.1	81.9	54.0	60.1	49.9	47.7
South											
Andhra Pradesh	75.9	54.0	70.5	24.9	23.7	74.4	78.5	72.7	27.4	56.1	64.3
Karnataka	52.3	44.5	77.6	34.8	21.4	80.9	87.0	61.4	43.4	49.3	46.3
Kerala	32.4	14.9	97.4	23.1	11.5	71.8	19.9	14.8	39.3	72.6	17.0
Tamil Nadu	61.9	41.7	88.5	34.6	20.3	78.8	85.0	65.9	21.2	61.1	24.9

1 : Registrar General of India.

2: Cooking salt that has an iodine content of at least 15 parts per million (ppm).

: Excludes Tripura.

NFHS-2 FACT SHEET – STATES

State	Total fertility rate[3]	Wanted total fertility rate[4]	Per cent of currently married women[5] using: Any contraceptive method	Sterilization[6]	Unmet need for family planning[5]: For spacing	For limiting	Total
(1)	(2)	(3)	(4)	(5)	(6)	(7)	(8)
India	**2.85**	**2.13**	**48.2**	**36.0**	**8.3**	**7.5**	**15.8**
North							
Delhi	2.40	1.72	63.8	28.6	5.9	7.5	13.4
Haryana	2.88	2.10	62.4	40.8	2.9	4.7	7.6
Himachal Pradesh	2.14	1.50	67.7	52.4	3.6	4.9	8.6
Jammu & Kashmir	2.71	1.74	49.1	30.7	7.4	12.6	20.0
Punjab	2.21	1.55	66.7	30.8	2.8	4.5	7.3
Rajasthan	3.78	2.57	40.3	32.3	8.7	8.9	17.6
Central							
Madhya Pradesh	3.31	2.40	44.3	38.0	8.9	7.3	16.2
Uttar Pradesh	3.99	2.83	28.1	15.6	11.8	13.4	25.1
East							
Bihar	3.49	2.58	24.5	20.2	12.6	11.9	24.5
Orissa	2.46	1.90	46.8	35.6	8.7	6.8	15.5
West Bengal	2.29	1.78	66.6	33.8	6.3	5.5	11.8
Northeast							
Arunachal Pradesh	2.52	1.74	35.4	20.7	17.2	9.3	26.5
Assam	2.31	1.75	43.3	16.6	7.0	10.0	17.0
Manipur	3.04	2.50	38.7	15.5	13.6	10.0	23.6
Meghalaya	4.57	3.83	20.2	6.5	23.4	12.1	35.5
Mizoram	2.89	2.66	57.7	45.4	11.7	3.7	15.5
Nagaland	3.77	2.98	30.3	12.2	18.3	11.9	30.2
Sikkim	2.75	1.65	53.8	24.8	9.9	13.2	23.1
West							
Goa	1.77	1.47	47.5	28.2	7.3	9.8	17.1
Gujarat	2.72	29.08	59.0	45.2	4.8	3.7	8.5
Maharashtra	2.52	1.87	60.9	52.2	8.1	4.9	13.0
South							
Andhra Pradesh	2.25	1.88	59.6	57.0	5.2	2.5	7.7
Karnataka	2.13	1.56	58.3	52.1	8.3	3.2	11.5
Kerala	1.96	1.81	63.7	51.0	6.9	4.9	11.7
Tamil Nadu	2.19	1.71	52.1	46.0	6.6	6.4	13.0

(Contd...)

(...Contd...)

State	Per cent of users of modern contraceptive methods who were told about side effects or other problems with method[7]		Per cent of currently married women who received follow-up[8] for:	
	Sterilization	Other modern method	Sterilization	Other modern method
(1)	(9)	(10)	(11)	(12)
India	**21.9**	**20.6**	**24.6**	**39.9**
North				
Delhi	27.8	26.7	67.9	54.8
Haryana	61.9	40.0	99.8	33.7
Himachal Pradesh	35.8	23.0	97.8	25.2
Jammu & Kashmir	7.8	12.7	88.4	54.5
Punjab	55.6	30.9	99.4	29.6
Rajasthan	13.1	14.2	73.6	49.2
Central				
Madhya Pradesh	11.3	18.8	82.0	44.7
Uttar Pradesh	15.5	11.3	54.3	41.4
East				
Bihar	15.8	16.0	78.3	65.5
Orissa	35.7	28.9	62.9	34.3
West Bengal	10.1	9.9	38.8	12.6
Northeast				
Arunachal Pradesh	31.0	34.2	79.9	84.2
Assam	10.6	17.1	91.1	74.3
Manipur	41.0	47.4	63.8	36.5
Meghalaya	16.4	25.3	94.3	86.1
Mizoram	47.6	49.8	73.8	61.1
Nagaland	18.5	15.9	58.0	45.6
Sikkim	23.8	29.5	95.2	55.4
West				
Goa	16.3	16.5	83.0	26.5
Gujarat	9.5	9.9	78.5	27.7
Maharashtra	20.6	27.8	74.6	50.7
South				
Andhra Pradesh	13.2	16.7	80.7	55.9
Karnataka	35.9	47.3	83.8	62.3
Kerala	9.2	14.9	91.1	26.2
Tamil Nadu	54.8	43.7	73.3	50.4

3 : Based on births to women age 15-49 during the three years preceding the survey.

4 : Calculated in the same way as the TFR, except that unwanted births are excluded from the numerators of the age-specific fertility rates on which the TFR is based.

5 : Among currently married women age 15-49.

6 : Female or male sterilization.

7 : By a health or family planning worker at the time of accepting the method.

8 : After accepting the current method.

(Contd...)

NFHS-2 FACT SHEET – STATES (...Contd...)

State	*Infant mortality rate*[9]	*Under five mortality rate*[9]	*For births in the three years preceidng the survey*[10]*, per cent of:* *Mothers receiving at least one antenatal check-up*	*Mothers receiving two or more tetanus toxoid Injections*	*Mothers receiving iron and folic acid tablets or syrup*	*Deliveries in medical institutions*	*Deliveries assisted by a health professional*
(1)	*(13)*	*(14)*	*(15)*	*(16)*	*(17)*	*(18)*	*(19)*
India	**67.6**	**94.9**	**65.4**	**66.8**	**57.6**	**33.6**	**42.3**
North							
Delhi	46.8	55.4	83.5	84.9	77.8	59.1	65.9
Haryana	56.8	76.8	58.1	79.7	67.0	22.4	42.0
Himachal Pradesh	34.4	42.4	86.8	66.2	85.6	28.9	40.2
Jammu & Kashmir	65.0	80.1	83.2	77.7	70.8	35.6	42.4
Punjab	57.1	72.1	74.0	89.9	79.6	37.5	62.6
Rajasthan	80.4	114.9	47.5	52.1	39.3	21.5	35.8
Central							
Madhya Pradesh	86.1	137.6	61.0	55.0	48.9	20.1	29.7
Uttar Pradesh	86.7	122.5	34.6	51.4	32.4	15.5	22.4
East							
Bihar	72.9	105.1	36.3	57.8	24.1	14.6	23.4
Orissa	81.0	104.4	79.5	74.3	67.6	22.6	33.4
West Bengal	48.7	67.6	90.0	82.4	71.6	40.1	44.2
Northeast							
Arunachal Pradesh	63.1	98.1	61.6	45.6	56.3	31.2	31.9
Assam	69.5	89.5	60.1	51.7	55.0	17.6	21.4
Manipur	37.0	56.1	80.2	64.2	50.0	34.5	53.9
Meghalaya	89.0	122.0	53.6	30.8	49.5	17.3	20.6
Mizoram	37.0	54.7	91.8	37.8	72.7	57.7	67.5
Nagaland	42.1	63.8	60.4	50.9	42.5	12.1	32.8
Sikkim	43.9	71.0	69.9	52.7	62.4	31.5	35.1
West							
Goa	36.7	46.8	99.0	86.1	94.7	90.8	90.8
Gujarat	62.6	85.1	86.4	72.7	78.0	46.3	53.5
Maharashtra	43.7	58.1	90.4	74.9	84.8	52.6	59.4
South							
Andhra Pradesh	65.8	85.5	92.7	81.5	81.2	49.8	65.2
Karnataka	51.5	69.8	86.3	74.9	78.0	51.1	59.1
Kerala	16.3	18.8	98.8	86.4	95.2	93.0	94.0
Tamil Nadu	48.2	63.3	98.5	95.4	93.2	79.3	83.8

(Contd...)

(...Contd...)

State	Per cent of children: Age 12-23 months who have received all vaccinations[11]	Age 12-35 months who have received at least one dose of Vitamin A	Age 0-3 months exclusively breastfed
(1)	(20)	(21)	(22)
India	**42.0**	**29.7**	**55.2**
North			
Delhi	69.8	32.7	13.2
Haryana	62.7	45.2	47.2
Himachal Pradesh	83.4	71.1	17.5
Jammu & Kashmir	56.7	36.0	41.5
Punjab	72.1	56.5	36.3
Rajasthan	17.3	17.6	53.7
Central			
Madhya Pradesh	22.4	24.4	64.2
Uttar Pradesh	21.2	13.9	56.9
East			
Bihar	11.0	10.2	55.2
Orissa	43.7	42.0	58.0
West Bengal	43.8	43.4	48.8
Northeast			
Arunachal Pradesh	20.5	20.9	(33.9)
Assam	17.0	15.4	42.5
Manipur	42.3	38.4	69.7
Meghalaya	14.3	24.7	16.1
Mizoram	59.6	70.6	40.7
Nagaland	14.1	6.8	43.9
Sikkim	47.4	45.8	16.3
West			
Goa	82.6	78.0	*
Gujarat	53.0	51.9	65.2
Maharashtra	78.4	64.7	38.5
South			
Andhra Pradesh	58.7	24.8	74.6
Karnataka	60.0	48.4	66.5
Kerala	79.7	43.6	68.5
Tamil Nadu	88.8	16.2	48.3

( ) : Based on 25-49 unweighted cases.
* : Percentage not shown; based on fewer than 25 unweighted cases.
9 : Per 1,000 live births for the five years preceding the survey (1994-98).
10 : Includes only the two most recent births.
11 : BCG, measles, and three doses each of DPT and polio vaccines.

(Contd...)

NFHS-2 FACT SHEET – STATES (...Contd...)

State	Per cent of children			Per cent of children under age three years[13]		
	Age 6-9 months receiving breast milk and solid/ mushy food	Age 1-35 months with diarrhoea who received ORS[12]	Age 6-35 months with any anaemia	Underweight	Stunted	Wasted
(1)	(22)	(24)	(25)	(26)	(27)	(28)
India	**33.5**	**26.8**	**74.3**	**47.0**	**45.5**	**15.5**
North						
Delhi	37.0	39.1	69.0	34.7	36.8	12.5
Haryana	41.8	25.7	83.9	34.6	50.0	5.3
Himachal Pradesh	61.3	45.6	69.9	43.6	41.3	16.9
Jammu & Kashmir	38.9	47.5	71.1	34.5	38.8	11.8
Punjab	38.7	42.3	80.0	28.7	39.2	7.1
Rajasthan	17.5	20.3	82.3	50.6	52.0	11.7
Central						
Madhya Pradesh	27.3	29.8	75.0	55.1	51.0	19.8
Uttar Pradesh	17.3	15.8	73.9	51.7	55.5	11.1
East						
Bihar	15.0	15.4	81.3	54.4	53.7	21.0
Orissa	30.1	35.1	72.3	54.4	44.0	24.3
West Bengal	46.3	40.5	78.3	48.7	41.5	13.6
Northeast						
Arunachal Pradesh	(60.2)	40.2	54.5	24.3	26.5	7.9
Assam	58.5	37.1	63.2	36.0	50.2	13.3
Manipur	86.8	50.7	45.2	27.5	31.3	8.2
Meghalaya	77.1	22.4	67.6	37.9	44.9	13.3
Mizoram	(74.2)	44.7	57.2	27.7	34.6	10.2
Nagaland	81.3	29.7	43.7	24.1	33.0	10.4
Sikkim	87.3	27.0	76.5	20.6	31.7	4.8
West						
Goa	(65.4)	55.6	53.4	28.6	18.1	13.1
Gujarat	46.5	28.9	74.5	45.1	43.6	16.2
Maharashtra	30.8	33.2	76.0	49.6	39.9	21.2
South						
Andhra Pradesh	59.4	39.6	72.3	37.7	38.6	9.1
Karnataka	38.4	34.3	70.6	43.9	36.6	20.0
Kerala	72.9	47.9	43.9	26.9	21.9	11.1
Tamil Nadu	55.4	27.9	69.0	36.7	29.4	19.9

(Contd...)

(...Contd...)

State	Per cent of women with BMI[14] below 18.5 kg/m²	Per cent of women age 15-49 with any anaemia	Per cent of women reporting a reproductive health problem[15]	Per cent of women age 15-49 who have heard of AIDS
(1)	(29)	(30)	(31)	(32)
India	**35.8**	**51.8**	**39.2**	**40.3**
North				
Delhi	12.0	40.5	36.5	79.2
Haryana	25.9	47.0	38.2	44.3
Himachal Pradesh	29.7	40.5	33.7	60.9
Jammu & Kashmir	26.4	58.7	60.5	31.9
Punjab	16.9	41.4	28.3	54.6
Rajasthan	36.1	48.5	43.2	20.8
Central				
Madhya Pradesh	38.2	54.3	44.9	22.7
Uttar Pradesh	35.8	48.7	38.1	20.2
East				
Bihar	39.3	63.4	44.2	11.7
Orissa	48.0	63.0	27.5	39.0
West Bengal	43.7	62.7	45.3	26.4
Northeast				
Arunachal Pradesh	10.7	62.5	42.1	60.4
Assam	27.1	69.7	50.6	33.7
Manipur	18.8	28.9	56.0	92.9
Meghalaya	25.8	63.3	66.9	44.2
Mizoram	22.6	48.0	52.5	93.2
Nagaland	18.4	38.4	45.6	72.4
Sikkim	11.2	61.1	48.6	53.6
West				
Goa	27.1	36.4	40.2	76.3
Gujarat	37.0	46.3	28.6	29.8
Maharashtra	39.7	48.5	40.0	61.1
South				
Andhra Pradesh	37.4	49.8	48.5	55.3
Karnataka	38.8	42.4	18.8	58.1
Kerala	18.7	22.7	42.4	86.9
Tamil Nadu	29.0	56.5	27.8	87.3

( ): Based on 25-49 unweighted cases.

12: Oral re-hydration salts.

13: Underweight assessed by weight-for-age, stunting assessed by height-for-age, wasting assessed by weight-for-height; undernourished children are those more than two standard deviations below the median of the International Reference Population, recommended by the World Health Organization.

14: Body mass index.

15: Currently married women with abnormal vaginal discharge, symptoms of a urinary tract infection, painful intercourse, or bleeding after intercourse.

APPENDIX III

Table 1

Human Development Index

Regions/Countries	*HDI Rank*	*Life expectancy at birth (years) 1998*	*Adult literacy rate (% age 15 and above) 1998*	*Combined primary secondary and tertiary gross enrolment ratio (%) 1998*[a]	*GDP per capita (PPP US$) 1998*
(1)	(2)	(3)	(4)	(5)	(6)
All developing countries		64.7	72.3	60	3,270
Least developed countries		51.9	50.7	37	1,064
Arab States		66.0	59.7	60	4,140
East Asia		70.2	83.4	73	3,564
East Asia (excluding China)		73.1	96.3	85	13,635
Latin America and the Caribbean		69.7	87.7	74	6,510
South Asia		63.0	54.3	52	2,112
South Asia (excluding India)		63.4	50.5	47	2,207
South-East Asia and the Pacific		66.3	88.2	66	3,234
Sub-Saharan Africa		48.9	58.5	42	1,607
Eastern Europe and the CIS		68.9	98.6	76	6,200
OECD		76.4	97.4	86	20,357
High Human Development		77.0	98.5	90	21,799
Medium Human Development		66.9	76.9	65	3,458
Low Human Development		50.9	48.8	37	994
High Income		77.8	98.6	92	23,928
Medium Income		68.8	87.8	73	6,241
Low Income		63.4	68.9	56	2,244
World		66.9	78.8	64	6,526
Canada	1	79.1	99.0[c]	100	23,582
Japan	9	80.0	99.0[c]	85	23,257
India	**128**	**62.9**	**55.7**	**54**	**2,077**
China	99	70.1	82.8	72	3,105
Malaysia	61	72.2	86.4	65	8,137
Brazil	74	67.0	84.5	84	6,625
Sri Lanka	84	73.3	91.1	66	2,979

(Contd...)

(...Contd...)

Regions/Countries	*Life expectancy index*	*Education index*	*GDP index*	*Human Development Index (HDI) value 1998*	*GDP per capita (PPP US$) rank minus HDI rank*[b]
(1)	(7)	(8)	(9)	(10)	(11)
All developing countries	0.66	0.68	0.58	0.642	-
Least developed countries	0.45	0.45	0.39	0.435	-
Arab States	0.68	0.60	0.62	0.635	-
East Asia	0.75	0.80	0.60	0.716	-
East Asia (excluding China)	0.80	0.93	0.82	0.849	-
Latin America and the Caribbean	0.74	0.83	0.70	0.758	-
South Asia	0.63	0.54	0.51	0.560	-
South Asia (excluding India)	0.64	0.49	0.52	0.550	-
South-East Asia and the Pacific	0.69	0.81	0.58	0.691	-
Sub-Saharan Africa	0.40	0.53	0.46	0.464	-
Eastern Europe and the CIS	0.73	0.91	0.69	0.777	-
OECD	0.86	0.94	0.89	0.893	-
High human development	0.87	0.96	0.90	0.908	-
Medium human development	0.70	0.73	0.59	0.673	-
Low human development	0.43	0.45	0.38	0.421	-
high income	0.88	0.96	0.91	0.920	-
Medium income	0.73	0.83	0.69	0.750	-
Low income	0.64	0.65	0.52	0.602	-
World	0.70	0.74	0.70	0.712	-
Canada	0.90	0.99	0.91	0.935	8
Japan	0.92	0.94	0.91	0.924	1
India	**0.63**	**0.55**	**0.51**	**0.563**	**-7**
China	0.75	0.79	0.57	0.706	7
Malaysia	0.79	0.79	0.73	0.772	-10
Brazil	0.70	0.84	0.70	0.747	-16
Sri Lanka	0.81	0.83	0.57	0.733	25

Note: The Human Development Index has been calculated for UN member countries with reliable data in each of its components, as well as for two non-members, Switzerland and Hong Kong, China (SAR). For data on the remaining 16 UN member countries see table 32.

a. Preliminary UNESCO estimates, subject to further revision.

b. A positive figure indicates that the HDI rank is higher than the GDP per capita (PPP US$) rank, a negative indicates the opposite.

c. Human Development Report Office estimate.

d. For purposes of calculating the HDI, a value of 100.0 per cent was applied.

e. The ratio is an underestimate, as many secondary and tertiary students pursue their studies in nearby countries.

f. Not including Turkish students or population.

Table 2
Gender-Related Development Index

Regions/Countries	*Gender-related development index (GDI) 1998*		*Life Expectancy at birth (Years) 1998*		*Adult literacy rate (% age 15 and above) 1998*	
	Rank	*Value*	*Female*	*Male*	*Female*	*Male*
(1)	(2)	(3)	(4)	(5)	(6)	(7)
All developing countries	-	0.634	66.4	63.2	64.5	80.3
Least developed countries	-	0.427	52.9	51.2	41.0	61.4
Arab States	-	0.612	67.5	64.6	47.3	71.5
East Asia	-	0.710	72.5	68.2	75.5	91.1
East Asia (excluding China)	-	0.846	76.4	69.7	95.1	98.6
Latin America and the Caribbean	-	0.748	73.2	66.7	86.7	88.7
South Asia	-	0.542	63.6	62.6	42.3	65.7
South Asia (excluding India)	-	0.533	64.2	62.7	38.8	61.7
South-East Asia and the Pacific	-	0.688	68.3	64.2	85.0	92.4
Sub-Saharan Africa	-	0.459	50.3	47.6	51.6	68.0
Eastern Europe and the CIS	-	0.774	73.8	64.1	98.2	99.1
OECD	-	0.889	79.6	73.2	96.7	98.2
High human development	-	0.903	80.3	73.8	98.3	98.7
Medium human development	-	0.665	68.9	65.0	69.7	83.7
Low human development	-	0.411	51.9	50.1	38.9	59.9
High income	-	0.916	81.0	74.6	98.4	98.7
Medium income	-	0.743	72.2	65.8	85.0	90.4
Low income	-	0.594	64.7	62.2	59.6	78.1
World	-	0.706	69.1	64.9	73.1	84.6
Canada	1	0.932	81.9	76.2	99.0[c]	99.0[c]
Japan	9	0.916	83.0	76.9	99.0[c]	99.0[c]
India	**108**	**0.545**	**63.3**	**62.5**	**43.5**	**67.1**
China	79	0.700	72.3	68.1	74.6	90.7
Malaysia	57	0.762	74.5	70.1	82.0	90.7
Brazil	66	0.736	71.2	63.3	84.5	84.5
Sri Lanka	68	0.727	75.6	71.1	88.3	94.1

(Contd...)

(...Contd...)

Regions/Countries	*Combined primary, secondary and tertiary gross enrolment ratio(%) 1997*		*GDP per capita (PPP US$) 1998*[a]		*HDI rank minus GDI rank*[b]
	Female	*Male*	*Female*	*Male*	
(1)	*(8)*	*(9)*	*(10)*	*(11)*	*(12)*
All developing countries	55	63	2,169	4,334	-
Least developed countries	32	42	771	1,356	-
Arab States	54	65	1,837	6,341	-
East Asia	67	71	2,788	4,297	-
East Asia (excluding China)	81	88	9,414	17,744	-
Latin America and the Caribbean	73	72	3,640	9,428	-
South Asia	44	59	1,147	3,021	-
South Asia (excluding India)	38	55	1,263	3,108	-
South-East Asia and the Pacific	63	66	2,316	4,154	-
Sub-Saharan Africa	37	46	1,142	2,079	-
Eastern Europe and the CIS	78	74	4,807	7,726	-
OECD	86	86	14,165	26,743	-
High human development	91	88	15,361	28,448	-
Medium human development	60	67	2,319	4,566	-
Low human development	31	42	693	1,294	-
High income	93	90	16,987	31,100	-
Medium income	72	73	3,948	8,580	-
Low income	50	60	1,549	2,912	-
World	60	67	4,435	8,587	-
Canada	101[d]	98	17,980[e]	29,294[e]	0
Japan	83	86	14,091	32,794	0
India	**46**	**61**	**1,105**[e]	**2,987**[e]	**-2**
China	67	71	2,440[e]	3,732[e]	3
Malaysia	66	64	4,501[f]	11,674[f]	-3
Brazil	82	78	3,830	9,483	-3
Sri Lanka	67	65	1,927	4,050	4

a.: Data refer to the latest available year.
b.: The HDI ranks used in this column are those recalculated for the universe of 143 countries. A positive figure indicates that the GDI rank is higher than the HDI rank, a negative the opposite.
c.: Human Development Report Office estimate.
d.: For purposes of calculating the GDI, a value of 100.0% was applied.
e.: No wage data available. An estimate of 75% was used for the ratio of the female non-agricultural wage to the male non-agricultural wage.
f.: The manufacturing wage was used.

Source: *Columns 1 and 2*: Human Development Report Office calculations; see the technical note for details, *columns 3 and 4*: interpolated on the basis of life expectancy data from UN 1998c; *Columns 5 and 6:* UNESCO 2000a; *columns 7 and 8:* UNESCO 2000c; *columns 9 and 10*: unless otherwise noted, calculated on the basis of the following: for GDP per capita (PPP US$), World Bank 2000a; for wages, wage data from ILO 1999c; for economic activity rate, data on economically active population from ILO 1996; for population shares, population data from UN 1998c; for details on the calculation of GDP per capita (PPP US$) by gender see the technical note; *column 11*: Human Development Report Office calculations.

10

Social Defence: Vision 2020

HIRA SINGH

Social defence is generally understood as the protection of society against crime through a systematically organized and coherent action by both the State and civil society. Though this term has long been in use in the criminological and penological literature, the modes and modalities of achieving its inherent objective have been shifting with the advancement in social sciences and behavioural disciplines. Even today, because of the complexity of issues involved, it has not been possible to evolve a wholly satisfactory theoretical framework for policy formulation and programme development in this field. It is true that crime is essentially an offshoot of the disorganizational process of society itself and, as such, it is difficult of visualize a system that could completely neutralize an 'aggression' which originates from within. Then, in the absence of any fool-proof theory of crime causation, it is beyond human capacity to create a society entirely free from crime. Moreover, the definition of crime itself may vary from country to country and within the same country from time to time, in keeping with the changes in social structure, cultural values and normative expectations and no single system can hold good for different situations. Despite this position, there is a candid awareness that the objective behind social defence cannot be realized merely by focussing on individuals who are recognized as offenders; it inevitably requires, also reaching out to those who are vulnerable to crime. Thus, the social defence approach aims not only at perfecting the system that deals with offenders but also at forestalling conditions that generate criminality. In this process, it closely interacts with various sectors of socio-economic development in creating an environment conducive to the prevention of crime and in mobilizing resources appropriate for the treatment and rehabilitation of offenders in the totality of their life situations.

Crime Trends

The phenomenon of crime has baffled humankind down the ages. It is usually explained as a by-product of the interaction that takes place between the individual and his environment. But both these aspects being dynamic in character, the prognosis of any socially deviant behaviour becomes highly problematic. In fact, the perception of crime is dependent on several variables, such as the fabric of a society, the extent of which a particular behaviour is deemed anti-social and the manner in which it is sought to be tackled. For instance, in India, as in other developing countries, much of crime has hitherto been largely pulled back or absorbed by the traditionally operative informal controls of the family, the community and religion. Now, with changes in socio-economic milieu, and an increasing centralization of authority in the hands of the State, crime situation is in a state of flux. Further, in order to maintain an orderly functioning of the society in transition, there is an exaggerated need for an effective enforcement of the existing laws, and even the enactment of new laws, to adequately cope with the emerging forms and trends of crime. In any case, the reported crime would always remain a small part of crime as it permeates society, because of the intricate relationship between the growing individual and his fluid environment and the limitations of the formal system in plugging the malady at its genesis. Such a reality only makes it imperative that the crime prevention and control strategies must extend beyond the criminal justice system and integrate into sectors in which individuals are born and they live and grow. From this viewpoint, social defence as a comprehensive approach towards ameliorating conditions responsible for social maladjustment, deviance and crime gains significance.

Nevertheless, crime as detected and reported by the concerned official agencies is the safest way to analyzing the problem and determining its trends. According to the statistics published by the National Crime Record Bureau, while the incidence of crime has been steadily rising, crime rate (incidence of crime per lakh of population) is maintaining pace with the increase in the general population over the last five decades. Though the crime rate is still much lower than that in many other countries, the pattern of crime surely signifies certain alarming features. For instance, the share of violent crimes, including murder, attempt to commit murder, culpable homicide not amounting to murder, dowry deaths, kidnapping and abduction, dacoity, preparation and assembly for dacoity and robbery, riots and arson, and rape, has increased substantially over the last four decades. These crimes not only endanger life, property and safety of the people but also pose a serious threat to public peace. Similarly, economic offences including smuggling, money laundering, tax evasion, export and import offences, drug trafficking, trafficking in cultural property, bribery and corruption, etc., are also manifesting a challenging trend in terms of sophistication, precision and *modus operandi* on the part of organized syndicates. There are enough indications that, in the years to come, with the development of information technology and telecommunications and the acceleration of economic activities within and across national borders, organized crime is bound to acquire a much more volitional and disruptive form. The emergence of terrorism, environmental crime, cyber crime, etc., are most ominous for a developing country like India.

Crime and Development

The nexus between crime and development, especially in the wake of globalization, liberalization of trade and commerce and free market economy, has been clearly recognized at various international fora. The world community is gravely concerned about the baneful effect of crime on the peace, progress and prosperity of nations. Many countries have seen as to how crime thwarts the development process, undermines human dignity and disrupts the well-being and welfare of people. It is invariably found that the development process, if not property monitored, tends to become criminogenic. While economic development is essential to satisfy human needs and to raise living standards, it could also unleash forces of social disintegration, disharmony and disorganization, unless prompt steps are taken to counteract its negative fall-out. Failure to balance both the social and economic aspects of development has led many a nation to face a chaotic situation, rampant with crime and human misery. There is an ample evidence to surmise that unbridled economic growth is liable to push the poor, the weaker and the disadvantaged into further marginalization and vulnerability to abuse and exploitation and to their eventual induction into crime, both as offenders and victims. Being in the throes of an unprecedented development process, India has an opportunity to learn from the mistakes of others and to vigorously pursue its declared policy of economic growth with a 'human face'.

From the standpoint of social defence, the development process must be geared towards ensuring social justice, protecting human rights and providing for an equitable sharing of socio-cultural and economic opportunities by one and all. Any development process which destroys the self-generating and self-sustaining capacity of the people, alienates certain sections from the mainstream of social and economic life, widens the gap between the rich and the poor, intensifies ethnic and caste conflicts, and erodes public confidence in the rule of law, is socially destructive and, thus, breeds crime. History shows how an imbalanced development can stir social strife, racial discriminations, religious bigotry and fragmentation of society, and how authoritarian governance deprives people of a life compatible with human dignity. In a democratic structure like that of India, the development process has to aim at economic prosperity with social justice in which people have to be the first and the last and the poorest of the poor will have to be in the centre-stage. Such a course would certainly call for a concerted action, on the part of both the State and civil society, towards restoring human rights of the poor, nurturing their creative potentials, building their capacity to assert for legitimate needs, enhancing their knowledge, skills and competence, and reinforcing their intellectual and material resources so as to enable them to stand on their own and to bargain for a better quality of life. While the government tends to rely mainly on a trickle-down approach, civil society has to work from bottom upward in helping the poor to shape their destiny and to secure their place in society with dignity.

Poverty Factor

Irrespective of the debate that continues in academic circles on whether a human being is a rational-economic or emotional-social animal, the importance of poverty factor in crime could hardly be overlooked. While poverty *per se* cannot be taken as a direct cause of crime, it does make individuals in stark deprivations more prone than the others to social maladjustment and to their coming in conflict with law. The situation is further compounded when, in the wake of industrialization and consequential urbanization, the poor migrants in search of livelihood, are found to cluster around slums and squatter dwellings and to live in a state of social marginality and economic neglect. It is, therefore, encouraging that the Government of India has provided a major thrust to poverty alleviation in the national development plans. A three-pronged strategy adopted to reduce poverty includes: (i) accelerated economic growth with a focus on sectors which are employment intensive; (ii) human and social development through basic minimum services; and (iii) targeted anti-poverty programmes. A priority is placed on agriculture and rural development, food and nutrition, security for vulnerable sections of society, participation of the poor in the development process, and empowerment of women, scheduled castes and scheduled tribes and other disadvantaged groups. As a result of various measures, the poverty ratio is reported to have considerably declined in the recent years. The present trend augurs well for the creation of just society committed to the rule of law.

For this purpose, the policies for poverty alleviation will have to be vigorously pursued in the light of various civil, political, economic, social and cultural rights that all people are equally entitled to under the Constitution of India. There is a national consensus that comprehensive strategies need to be devised so that the pattern of economic growth helps the poor and the down-trodden in improving their lot. This would require not only a much larger investment on social services but also more effective measures to establish that the delivery mechanisms are non-discriminatory and the facilities created are accessible to the people at the grass-root level. In order to ascertain that the development benefits percolate down and are shared by all on an equitable basis, irrespective of their socio-cultural and economic status, local bodies and people's organizations will also have to be actively involved in the implementation of various plan schemes. People themselves will have to be sufficiently empowered to overcome poverty through self-help endeavors, collective initiatives and participation in decisions that affect their lives. While the government would be legitimately responsible for policy formulation and programme development; representatives of civil society will have to be closely associated in making the process more transparent and accountable to people.

With the globalization of national economy, the obligation of multinationals, business houses and financial institutions towards protecting the rights and interests of the poor has to be clearly spelt out. Of course, in a free society, the media has to serve as a powerful agent in promoting a social climate conducive to a solidarity with the poor in their fight against poverty.

It is well accepted that the strategies for poverty alleviation have to evolve within the framework of social justice for which the rule of law is a pre-requisite. Though law by self cannot eradicate poverty, it can definitely contribute to the national efforts towards this end by intervening specifically in three broad areas: (i) combating such crimes as are responsible for the disruption of economy, social cohesiveness and security of people; (ii) curbing conditions which perpetuate abuse and exploitation of the socially marginalized or economically backward groups in society; and (iii) protecting human rights and interests of the poor in the administration of justice. In this process, the criminal justice system as a whole may have to undergo radical reforms by way of the rationalization of the relevant laws and, if necessary, the enactment of new laws, modernization and strengthening of enforcement machinery and of its methods and apparatuses, and a purposeful use of various social support systems in enhancing its operational coverage, institutional capacity and organizational efficiency. In responding to crimes which adversely affect the well-being of people, the legal system must constantly sharpen its teeth and plug loopholes as they come to fore. In the background of a fast changing socio-economic scenario, the courts may soon have to discard its 'hands off' doctrine towards the issues of survival and sustainability of people, in favour of a judicial security and even intervention when the human rights and interests of the poor are found in jeopardy.

Vulnerable Groups

Among various groups subjected to social inequalities, cultural discrimination and economic handicaps, the condition of women below poverty line is much more precarious than that of their male counter-parts. Though a variety of schemes have been introduced for their emancipation, women in India continue to be largely dependent on and subordinated to men in different walks of life, and thus, to be devalued and socially marginalized, particularly in the lower strata. When a family is faced with any crisis, its female members suffer most and are rendered an easy prey to various kinds of abuse and exploitation. Even when recognized as offenders, they are more of a victim of situational compulsions than a perpetrator of crime. Therefore, in the planning of programmes for social defence, a vigorous drive has to be launched towards women's empowerment and gender justice and the criminal justice system has to act relentlessly against unscrupulous elements degrading their status. Already, in pursuance of its Constitutional mandate, India has enacted a number of laws to secure for women equal rights, to counter offences and atrocities against them, and to provide support services for their special care and protection. Along with various legal safeguards made available to them, a stringent action is contemplated to check crimes directed against them, which broadly fall under two categories: (i) crimes under the Indian Penal Code, such as, rape, kidnapping and abduction, homicide for dowry or dowry death or their attempts, torture, molestation, sexual harassment and importation of girls, and, (ii) crimes under special laws, such as, abrogation of their rights in the family, marriage and work place, immoral traffic, dowry, child marriage, indecent representation and commission of 'Sati'. It is, however, being strongly felt that, as law alone cannot by itself change age-old traditions and attitudes that subjugate women, the whole society has to be mobilized in preventing crimes against them.

Doubtlessly, the economic and social marginalization of the poor deprives a vast population of children in the country of their right to grow normally in body and mind. Increasing population with limited resources intensifies the problem of survival and security of the poor, creating an environment of destitution, desperation and despair for their children. As children constitute the supreme national asset for the making of tomorrow, the failure of society to bring them up as socially healthy individuals not only multiplies poverty but also leaves them extremely fragile to withstand the onslaught of anti-social elements. Apart from a widespread violence against such children within and outside the family, the problems of child labour, child prostitution and child begging are some of the most sordid forms of child abuse. In several cities, a large number of poor children are found to be living or working on the street in search of livelihood through odd jobs in extremely subhuman and hazardous conditions. A rising trend of the abuse of children for unconscionable gain and their instrumental use in crime, and of their transportation beyond national borders for nefarious purposes under the garb of adoption, marriage or employment, is also a matter of grave concern. Though definite provisions exist in the substantive and special laws against all such eventualities, there is wide gap between rhetoric and reality. Now that India is signatory to the United Nations Convention on the Rights of the Child, it is obligatory that the role of criminal justice system in protecting children against victimization is redefined and translated into concrete action. Obviously, there is a dire need for a thorough review of all the central and state laws concerning children so as to bring these in tune with our cherished goals.

It is well accepted that the criminal justice system can function as an enabling tool in the alleviation of extreme poverty by legally safeguarding the rights and interests of the weaker sections of society. India has a first-hand experience of setting in motion a host of democratic processes to resolve the problems of social inequality and class divide, including the formulation of special laws to provide a protective umbrella to all such social groups as are oppressed for centuries. The overall strategy is to secure distributive justice and allocation of resources to support programmes for the social, economic and educational advancement of the weaker sections in general and Scheduled Castes and Scheduled Tribes, Backward Classes and Minorities in particular. The protection of Civil Rights Act, 1955 has totally abolished untouchability in any form. The Scheduled Castes and Scheduled Tribes (Prevention of Atrocities) Act, 1989, aims at protecting them against any injustice and any form of abuse or exploitation. By enacting these laws, the concept of positive discrimination in favour of the weaker has been extended to the field of criminal law. The penalties prescribed in the special legislation are more stringent than those for corresponding offences in other laws. A speedy trial of cases coming within the purview of these laws has been assured by the constitution of special courts in major cities. While the legislation is seen to have a salutary impact on the process of the desired social change, there is a strong public opinion that the problems of the weaker sections of society need to be addressed in all their facets. It is also being increasingly realized that poverty is a complex problem, both a cause and an effect of disorganization at the individual, familial and societal levels, and, as such, has to be tackled through mutually reinforcing coordinated efforts on the part of various law enforcement, social welfare and development agencies. Indeed, the criminal justice system which is founded on the principles of fairness and equity has to prove its credibility of being equally fair and equitable to the poor as to the rich, in actual operation.

Correctional Strategy

In the backdrop of a rapidly changing crime situation, any action to interpret principles underlying social defence into actual practices has to start with the rationalization of sentencing policy. The penal policy should not only strive at balancing the interest of society with that of the individual involved in crime but also at addressing the plight of the victim. The range of dispositional alternatives has to be so widened as to enable the court to place a person found guilty in a setting which is most conducive to his mainstreaming. The procedure to be adopted by the court has to be so streamlined as to make it sure that a decision is arrived at not only in relation to the crime committed but also on the basis of a thorough study of the personality and background of the offender, and the circumstance in which the crime took place. Institutional treatment has to be resorted to as the last measure, only when an offender poses a real threat to public safety and peace and tranquility in the community. A community-based option for treatment has also to be based on scientifically tested and verifiable criteria. It needs to be fully appreciated that an offender placed on community correction will have a much greater stake in social conformity than the one being treated in a closed institution as a 'social misfit'. Even a non-institutional placement has to be carefully selected so as to retain, to the maximum extent possible, the usefulness of the offender to himself, his family and society. In order to ensure that the sentence is delivered in a fair, just and equitable manner, irrespective of the socio-economic status of the person involved, the State has to stand for one who cannot by himself protect his substantive and procedural rights. More importantly, the right of an accused to a speedy trail which, in the case of the poor, seems to have been severely trampled has to be restored by reinforcing the judicial system.

In India, as in many other countries, where most of the persons coming within the purview of the criminal justice system are involved in crime under various kinds of situational compulsions, correctional approach to crime control has to be pursued as an integral part of the social development process. An analysis of crime statistics would show that a large segment of offenders consists of the poor, the illiterate and the unskilled. Such offenders are seen to be victimized twice: once, when they are denied of their basic human needs in open society and forced to live in a subculture of social marginality, and, again, when they are grinded in the mill of criminal justice for having infringed the law. An increased investment on the provision of correctional services in relation to these persons would be most productive not only in reducing crime but also in improving the quality of life among the strata they come from and are ultimately to return to. In this regard, a priority attention needs to be given to raising the standards of diagnostic, educational and developmental programmes with all the necessary technical inputs, in close conjunction with community based welfare agencies. There is no dearth of success stories in this regard, but most of these have so far been confined to a few bold experiments or to some individual initiatives. It is high time that correctional measures are directed towards developing the capacity, caliber and competence of persons in conflict with law in such a manner as to assure that, after their passage through the criminal justice system, they would be able to stand on their own as dignified and law-abiding citizens. Of course, the approach towards those who indulge in crime as a way of life and refuse to understand the language of correction will have to be differentiated.

Prison Reform

Doubtlessly, prisons constitute the oldest and most widely used mode of dealing with offenders. In the recent years, it has also been a subject of unprecedented criticism, scrutiny and debate from the viewpoint of its social defence role. It is well recognized that as long as certain types of offenders are to be segregated from society in the interest of public safety, and are expected to return as better human beings than what they were when incarcerated, the institution of prison will have to play an important role in the dispensation of justice. However, there are several problems that prison administration is presently confronted with in discharging its public safety and reformative functions. In India, as in many parts of the world, imprisonment continues to be applied indiscriminately and excessively, either as a convenient way of dealing with all sorts of crime or because of the non-availability or limited range of effective alternatives. In the face of competing priorities, it is hard to mobilize adequate resources to bring in the desired systemic reforms in terms of the necessary infrastructure, scientific classification of inmates, diversification of prisons for various categories of offenders, provision of correctional services and duly qualified and professionally trained personnel to handle custodial and correctional tasks. The problem of overcrowding and a swelling proportion of undertrials among prison inmates has thrown the system haywire. As the judicial process further speeds up and the pendency of cases in courts decreases, prison population will correspondingly multiply, because a much larger number of accused persons are on bail and awaiting trail. There is also a real need to establish appropriate linkages between institutional programmes and community-based welfare resources to ensure that the processes of recovery, re-education and rehabilitation initiated in prisons are systematically followed up till the discharged prisoners are able to reintegrate themselves into society. What is most urgently called for is the formulation of a national policy and bringing in a basic uniformity in laws governing prisons, so that imprisonment as defined in the Indian Penal Code has the same meaning, when actually executed, in every part of the country.

Apart from the imperativeness of bridging the gap that exists between societal expectations and operational realities, the prisons administration has to run on the premise that its rehabilitative function can be accomplished only in an atmosphere that fosters human rights of persons in custody and generates among them a will to improve their quality of life. In this respect, the Supreme Court of India, discarding its erstwhile 'hands off' doctrine in favour of a judicial intervention when the rights of prisoners are found in jeopardy, has already enunciated three basic principles: (i) a person in custody does not become a 'non-person'; (ii) a prisoner is entitled to all human rights within the limitations of imprisonment, and, (iii) there is no justification for aggravating the suffering which is already inherent in the process of incarceration. Accordingly, the apex court has issued a number of directives for prison authorities to afford to prisoners all such facilities for self-improvement and correctional therapy as are consistent with their conditions of imprisonment. Besides a detailed interpretation of the relevant Constitutional provisions, the principles embodied in various United Nations instruments, to which India is a party, have also been invoked in guiding this process. The framework laid down by the Supreme Court of India to protect the rights and interests of prisoners has far-reaching implications for prison reform in a futuristic perspective. It not only entails a thorough overhauling of the prison administration but also an enlightened participation on the part of civil society.

The current emphasis on the humanization of prisons as an essential condition for invigorating their reformative and rehabilitative role brings into focus the issue of torture. Despite a high level of denial among the concerned authorities, torture does exist in prisons broadly in three different ways. First, there is a form of torture which may be intentional in nature and resorted to against all canons of rules and regulations to 'discipline' a prisoner or to 'set him right'. It may happen sporadically but does take place when the custodian under pressure loses his balance and the prisoner is totally at his mercy. No civilized society would ever condone such an intentional torture. Secondly, there is torture incidental to the sub-human conditions prevailing in prisons, especially in developing countries. Such incidental torture has to be prevented by adhering to certain minimum standards of institutional care in terms of living conditions, basic needs and the necessary amenities and privileges to treat prisoners as human beings. And, thirdly, there is an element of torture inherent in incarceration itself, when the individual involved is deprived of his freedom and isolated from his family and the community he belongs to. This form of torture can also be considerably reduced, if not eliminated altogether, by using prisons more selectively only for offenders who endanger public safety, by enlarging the range of alternatives to imprisonment, and, even when a offender is justifiably imprisoned, by providing him with ample avenues to maintain ties with outside world, and a possibility for an early release as an incentive for good behaviour and responsiveness to correctional treatment. Abolition of torture other than what is consequential to lawful sanctions is fast emerging as a vital issue of prison reform to be addressed squarely.

Juvenile Justice

It has long been accepted that children coming in confrontation with law, because of their physical, emotional and mental immaturity, cannot be equated with adults in terms of their culpability and accountability to crime. It is widely held that delinquency is not merely an act of social deviance on the part of a child but also a symptom of the failure of society to bring him up as wholesome individual. At the same time, no society takes crime, even if it is committed by a juvenile, as entirely value-free and expects it to be dealt with as such. There is, however, a unanimous view that the problem must be dealt with on its growth continuum by responding to all the situations before and after the onset of delinquency. While India has chosen to achieve this objective through a single law in the form of Juvenile Justice (Care and Protection of Children) Act, 2000, many countries have formulated a separate law for delinquents *vis-à-vis* those vulnerable. (The United Nations Standard Minimum Rules for the Administration of Juvenile Justice also concentrate only on children in conflict with law, while other categories of vulnerable children are envisaged to be catered to within their families and communities under a welfare regime.) While much would depend on the manner in which the newly enacted law is implemented on the ground, with children in the higher age group of 16 to 18 years now increasingly emulating adult role models in criminal behaviour, the juvenile justice approach will have to undergo a progressive refinement in the years to follow.

Significantly, the United Nations rules for juvenile justice incorporate some salutary provisions for an active involvement of civil society at various stages of the handling of juvenile offenders through the system. At the very initial stage, the police, the prosecution and other concerned agencies are proposed to be empowered with a wide discretion to divert cases from the formal system to the family and the community on a selective basis. A variety of disposition measures are contemplated, such as care, guidance and supervision, probation, community service, financial penalties, compensation and restitution, intermediate treatment, participation in group counselling and similar activities, foster care, living in communities or other educational settings, etc. While institutionalization is thought to be a disposition of last resort, non-institutional treatment has to provide juveniles with necessary assistance, including education and vocational training in order to facilitate the reformative process, and to mobilize volunteers and other community welfare resources for rehabilitation. When a juvenile undergoes institutional treatment, early recourse to conditional release under proper supervision and community support has been suggested. A provision for semi-institutional arrangements such as half-way houses, educational homes, day-time centres, etc., has also been made to assist juvenile to reintegrate into society. Though the new Indian Law on Juvenile Justice also includes some of such features, like association of volunteers and non-government organizations in the screening, treatment and rehabilitation of children, the provision for foster care, sponsorship and adoption among the modes of disposition, and linkages with community-based welfare agencies for rehabilitative purposes, the success would naturally require a massive effort towards the mobilisation of various social support systems.

Non-Custodial Measures

Whereas the rationale behind the segregation from society of certain types of offenders in the public interest and their treatment in closed institutions is firmly established, the correctional potential of non-custodial measures has yet to be fully utilized in the administration of justice. Though probation as a form of non-institutional treatment of offenders under conditions of good behaviour, with or without supervision, has been in practice since the British period, the country has yet to provide a sound basis for its application on an extensive scale. Probation is still generally perceived as a lenient approach rather than a selective device for the treatment of offenders who are no threat to public safety. In fact, for want of scientifically evolved criteria to be safely relied upon in the placement of offenders in a non-institutional setting, the range of community corrections remains limited and imprisonment continues to be followed as the most convenient course, even for offenders whose institutionalization for short periods has no therapeutic value. It is true that when non-custodial correctional measures are used arbitrarily, without being resorted to on objective grounds, there is real danger of men of means taking undue advantage and abusing the system as against those who would really deserve but have no advocacy or support, and of the whole approach becoming counter-productive and coming into public disrepute. It is, therefore, necessary that a ground is prepared for community correction to prove its credentials to function, if not more, as effectively as custodial correction in reforming and rehabilitating offenders.

For this purpose, the United Nations Standard Minimum Rules for Non-Custodial Measures which seek to strike a proper balance between the interests of the individuals involved in crime and those of society at various stages of the criminal justice process, offer a blue-print for action and strategy. In keeping with the principles of the observance of human rights, the requirements of social justice, and the rehabilitation needs of offenders, the rules spell out a wide range of disposition modalities at the pre-trial, sentencing and post-sentencing stages. Apart from empowering the police and prosecution agencies to discharge offenders under specified conditions, the suggested sentencing alternatives include: verbal sanctions, such as admonition, reprimand and warning; conditional discharge; status penalties, economic sanctions and monetary penalties; confiscation or an expropriation order; restitution to the victim or a compensation order; suspended or deferred sentence; probation and judicial supervision; community service order; referral to an attendance centre; house arrest; and any other mode of non-institutional treatment or combination of various measures. With a view to avoiding institutionalization and to secure early reintegration of offenders into society, the post-sentencing dispositions to be tried out are: furlough and half-way houses; work or education release; parole; remission and pardon. Obviously, the implementation of such non-custodial measures would call for the development of a scientific basis for the selection, placement and supervision of cases, treatment processes, staffing resources, community participation, etc. However, all these approaches are worth experimenting with so as to assess their suitability to indigenous socio-cultural and economic conditions.

Public Participation

As crime is a social phenomenon, no system for its prevention and control could ever be conceived without an active participation of the public. In fact, public participation is an inseparable ingredient of the process that defines a behaviour as crime and strives to tackle it. Whereas the critical attitude of the public that abhors crime and cries for the offender to be so punished as to become a deterrent for the others, is clearly discernible, the positive role of the public in preventing conditions which precipitate crime and in facilitating the offender to mend his behaviour and to reintegrate into society has yet to be fully recognized. Of course, the public opinion towards crime manifests in an ambivalent manner: while on one side, demanding for a stringent action against those who offend, on the other hand, pleading for the powers of those who administer punishment to be restrained and curbed. It is, therefore, logical that civil society is encouraged to take a balanced view and to guide the public in subscribing to a system that protects society against crime without impinging on the human rights of all those involved, whether as offenders or victims. For this purpose, civil society must be closely associated with the planning and execution of crime prevention and criminal justice strategies, so that it sets a direction for a momentum to public participation in this field, at the individual, group and community levels. Civil society has to serve as the primary tool for the desired transparency and accountability in the functioning of various penal institutions established by the State to control crime. The edifice of social defence can stand only on an enlightened participation of the public as the harbinger, the means and the end of the process.

In the prevention of crime, voluntary organisations that spring from within society have a definite advantage over official agencies in making a dent on the problems that culminate into crime. A variety of situation-, problem- and individual-oriented approaches to crime prevention can be devised and implemented through the self-help endeavours and collective initiatives of the people themselves. A situation-oriented strategy would be based on an optimum use of all such voluntary agencies as are engaged in protecting the vulnerable, like children, women and other economically weaker or socially disadvantaged sections in society against any form of abuse or exploitation which is likely to induce a social reaction. A problem-oriented strategy would bring within its ambit all such activities and programmes as are initiated through voluntary action to tackle social problems which have a nexus with crime. An individual-oriented strategy would obviously require working with those who, under situational compulsions, have fallen to a socially deviant behaviour and still have a chance to redeem. In all these areas, voluntary organizations have to function in conjunction with families, communities and other social institutions which have a bearing on the process of resocialization. Apart from a direct intervention in situations and problems responsible for crime, voluntary organizations can be greatly instrumental in moulding public opinion and in mobilizing social support for an effective implementation of social legislation enacted to eradicate social evils such as dowry, child marriage, 'Sati', beggary, prostitution, etc. Most of these laws contain specific provisions for public participation in different forms. Experience has abundantly shown that despite severe penalties prescribed in the law against the perpetrators, such social evils continue to persist, mainly because of the lack of public awareness about their ill-effects and the absence of an enabling social environment for the measures to succeed. It is distressing to note that, while a large number of voluntary organizations in social welfare are being financially supported by the government, very few are really coming forth to work for the mainstreaming of social deviants.

The need for public participation in the treatment and rehabilitation of offenders is equally well established. The future of various non-custodial measures is tied with not only the offender's responsiveness to community correction but also the extent to which the public is prepared to extend its helping hand in the correctional process and to accept the offender within its fold. Besides adopting a positive attitude towards the rationale and efficacy of community-based treatment, the public can substantially contribute to the reformative process by providing social and material inputs. In the sphere of institutional treatment, the public can play a significant role in two broad ways: first, by supplementing correctional programmes in custodial institutions, and, secondly, by serving as a bridge for the offender's transition from custody to free society. From this angle, the question of even privatizing prisons is being hotly debated in many countries. While a 'handing over' of prisons to private agencies may not be feasible, there is a wide scope for a constructive involvement of non-governmental organizations in strengthening the welfare content of prison programmes, especially in the areas of education, vocational training and socio-cultural and spiritual development of inmates. Further, appropriate linkages with the private sector are inescapable in the specialized treatment of terminal illnesses, including chronic drug addiction and HIV infection. The role of voluntary institutions in the aftercare and follow-up of discharged prisoners so as to facilitate their reintegration into society is quite obvious. There is, however, a strong view that public participation in institutional treatment has to be highly selective so as not to take any risk with security and safe custody. It, therefore, needs to be emphasized that whereas any transfer or dilution of the responsibility that legitimately comes within the purview of the State would be rather hazardous, civil society has every right to know as to what transpires behind walls.

In conclusion, it may be reiterated that as no formal system has a complete answer to the problem of crime, integrated efforts are needed to tackle the problem at its very source. The social defence approach is based on the premise that the criminal justice system by itself cannot undo such aberration of the wider socio-economic system as are associated with crime. However, war against crime has to be waged, if not to win, atleast to ensure that it is not being lost. Even the reduction in crime as a more realistic goal can be achieved only by extending crime prevention and control measures beyond the criminal justice system and by building these into a broader social action to curb conditions which produce crime. Such a perspective requires focussing on two major areas: (i) prevention of crime by protecting various vulnerable groups within the framework of social justice; and, (ii) treatment of offenders in a just, fair and equitable manner, with due regard to their human rights, and on the basis of a differential handling of individuals who violate law under various kinds of situational compulsion *vis-à-vis* those who perpetrate crime in an organized manner. While the prevention of crime would necessitate forging of constructive linkages between the formal system and various sectors of socio-economic development, the treatment of offenders would inevitably entail a progressive refinement of the criminal justice processes. With newly emerging forms and trends of criminality, some of which are much more volitional and disruptive in nature, a holistic strategy has to be worked out jointly by various criminal justice, social welfare and development agencies. Such a concept of social defence warrants not only a thorough reorganization of the traditionally operative crime control mechanisms but also innovation of, and experimentation with new approaches in coping more effectively with the changing crime scenario.

11

Issues Concerning Vulnerable Groups: Vision 2020

H. S. SAKSENA

This paper which is a part of the Vision 2020 exercise deals with four sections of the people of India. Unlike other such exercises which deal with sectoral development, here we have to visualise how these people, collectively, are likely to fare two decades hence, which can hardly be mechanically calculated and determined as the dynamics of change – social, economic, educational and other aspects – will not be the same for all the sub-sections, communities, castes and tribes.

The groups which can be treated as vulnerable find a mention in the Constitution itself and its frame also contains special provisions which the State is to follow for their progress and development to the level of others, particularly ensuring their special rights and implementation of certain directives for State policy. These groups are:

1. Scheduled Castes (SC) (Art. 341)
2. Scheduled Tribes (ST) (Art. 342)
3. Socially and Educationally Backward Classes, also called 'Other Backward Classes' – (Art. 340)
4. Minorities (Religious) – (Art. 30)

As first two groups have been the weakest among the vulnerables, the constitutional safeguards for them are far more elaborate and the nation's efforts to reduce their vulnerability through protection, development and a process of empowerment was initiated in the year 1950. As regards OBC a full-fledged programme sponsored by the

---

H.S. Saksena is a retired Director, National Commission for Scheduled Castes Tribes, and presently editor of The Eastern Anthropologist, the premier journal of anthropology published from Lucknow.

Table 1

Population Projections

(*In crores*)

Year	Total Population	Growth Rate	SC			ST		
			Population	% to Total Population	Decadal Growth (%)	Population	% to Total Population	Decadal Growth (%)
(1)	(2)	(3)	(4)	(5)	(6)	(7)	(8)	(9)
1971	54.82	24.80	8.00	14.59		3.80	6.93	26.2
1981	68.33	24.66	10.42	15.28	30.3	5.16	7.53	35.8
1991	84.64	23.86	13.82	16.48	32.6	6.78	8.08	31.4
2001	102.70*	21.34*	16.77			8.23		
2011	117.89**		20.35	Assumed at 21.34		9.99	Assumed at 21.34	
2020	133.47***		24.69			12.12		

* Actual.

** Ninth Five Year Plan Vol. II p.88.

*** Calculated on the basis of population in 2016.

Centre was initiated only in the early 1990s. Similarly a programme for the (Religious) minorities came on the scene around the late 1980s.

II. DEMOGRAPHIC TRENDS AMONG SC AND ST

Table 1 gives the decadal growth of only SC and ST populations *vis-à-vis* the general population, as detailed census data relating to OBC and Minorities are not being collected. It may be mentioned that a substantive part of the population growth of the SC and ST is attributable to revisions in their lists/removing area restrictions in scheduling, apart from demographic factors.

Projections in 2020 for different age groups among them are projected in Table 2. These projections are based on the likely age structure of the total population of the country in 2020. However, in the case of both SC and ST the percentage of population in the younger age group may actually turn out to be more as TFR and growth rates among them have so far been higher than the country's as a whole. Furthermore, TFR in the states like U.P., Bihar, M.P., Rajasthan which account for substantial SC/ST populations continue to remain higher. Therefore, the dependency rate among SC and ST in 2020 may come up to be more than the projections rate among SC and ST in 2020 and so will be their need for social and economic services in the future.

Table 2

Age Group Projections of SC and ST: 2020*

(In Crores)

Age groups	*India – total*	*SC*	*ST*
(1)	(2)	(3)	(4)
	133.47	24.69	12.12
0-4 (9.7%)	12.95	2.39	1.18
5-9 (9.3%)	12.41	2.30	1.13
10-14 (8.7%)	11.62	2.15	1.05
15-59 (63.3%)	84.45	15.63	7.67
60+ (9.0%)	12.0	2.22	1.19

* Based on Ninth Five Year Plan Vol.II P.87 -%.

III. DEVELOPMENT PROCESS AT WORK AMONG SC AND ST

Presently more than 750 castes including their sub-castes, synonyms, etc. are listed as SC. In 1991 their population was 13.82 crores (16.48 per cent), of whom 81 per cent lived in rural areas. There has been an increase in the percentage of SC population to the total population from 15.28 in 1981 to 16.48 in 1991, with a decadal growth rate of 32.0 per cent during 1981-91. They are dispersed all over the country, except in one state and two UTs, *viz*. Nagaland, Andaman and Nicobar Islands and Lakshadweep. In a few states, the SC constitutes more than 20 per cent of the total of the state populations. These include Punjab (28.3 per cent) Himachal Pradesh (25.34 per cent), West Bengal (23.62 per cent) and Uttar Pradesh (21.05 per cent).

The main problems of the Scheduled Castes were their marginalisation due to a low statues in the *Varna* and *Jati* system of the mainstream Hindu structure. Their exploitation, subordinated access to economic resources and lack of power, all had their nexus in this situation of theirs which was institutionalized through the wide-spread practice of untouchability in all its myriad forms. In fact, their deprivation was so pervasive that all the channels which could have even remotely led to their emancipation and development were closed to them.

The process of gaining education, economic diversification, development in levels of economy, empowerment through participation in political processes and government jobs has inevitably led to the formation of an elite class among the Scheduled Castes. Not only that, this elite class belongs not to a wide-base of castes but to a limited number of castes. Thus, there has been an increasing dualistic trend of the elite cornering the benefits for themselves and at best for their caste, and also for certain dominant and vocal castes to ensure more and more benefits for themselves alone, at the cost of a few other castes. Moreover, these comparatively advanced scheduled castes practice discriminations against the backward of 'low' scheduled castes. These trends are reflected in some of the findings of the 'People of India Project' of the Anthropological Survey of India (since 1993; 1994) completed in 1990s. The relevant observations (751 castes as universe) are:

i) Public servants came from 250 scheduled castes, teacher from 364, administrators from 155, and entrepreneurs and businessmen from 286.

ii) The benefits of political leadership were still more restricted at village level to only 39 per cent Scheduled Castes, at regional level to 18.5 per cent and at national level to just 4.5 per cent of the castes.

Mendelsohn and Vicziany (1994) report that one of the reasons for the collapse of the Dalit Panther movement in Maharashtra was its exclusivity only for the Mahar. The rise of the BSP in the north too has to be seen in this light with its predominantly Chamber base.

Among the vulnerable sections, the ST are patently the most disadvantaged. There are many facets of their existence – isolation, resources-loss, poverty exploitation at the hands of outsiders, to name a few. The Constitution, therefore, contains more elaborate set of safeguards for them which were followed up with protective legal measures particularly relating to land and indebtness and developmental programmes. The results, however, leave much to be desired after 54 years of implementation. Due to the unmatched plurality of the situation, the impact, both positive as well as negative has spread out rather unevenly. Tribal studies indicate the following broad trends of change:

1. Transformation from a marginalised and peripheral existence to an acute awareness of their civic rights.
2. Deficiencies in the formulation and implementation of the programme specially when these are handled by personnel lacking empathy and insight into the tribal culture, have led to intense neglect of certain sections, a process of elite formation; and their being pushed into a macrocapitalist market economy unprepared.
3. An elite class has emerged through the present democratic institutions and they have concerned developmental benefits.
4. The investment in tribal areas specially through the tribal subplan strategy have been going up but analysts find that investment on infrastructure which may be more beneficial to non-tribals in the area has consumed most of these resources.

5. Some of the impoverishment, deprivation and powerlessness of the common tribal is traceable to national policies like forest policy, construction of large projects, heavy mining and industrialization in their areas and the direction of agricultural policies. The situation has even been labeled as 'internal colonisation'.

The 'People of India Project' studied 635 scheduled tribal communities – tribes, their groups and segments including territorial units. It has come out with some quantitative data regarding tribal participation in the mainstream and their responses to developmental effort. The following changes are largely traceable to the development efforts:

1. An elite stratum of entrepreneurs, businessmen (156 tribes), teachers (380), administrators (156), engineers/doctors (150) and defence personnel (178) has been created.
2. There has been a rise in the political leadership with the number of tribes playing leadership role at various levels being – village panchayat (362), regional (185) and national (45).
3. Reaction to education has been favourable in case of both boys and girls. Educational levels have increased steadily.
4. The tribes avail of modern health and medical facilities and 531 tribes (83.5 per cent) expressed favourable attitudes towards these facilities. There has been a decline in death and rise in birth rate.
5. Many tribal communities are aware of and participate in self-employment schemes initiated by the government. The number being agriculture (438); animal husbandry (302); piggery (160); basketry (151); poultry (164); fishery (98); small scale industry (67); etc. The electronic media cover the tribal areas well – radio (91 per cent) and T.V. (27 per cent).
6. There has been an erosion of their traditional institutional and patterns of social and economic relations. For instance, status of tribal women which was comparatively much better has been undermined due to factors connected with development intervention.

An examination of some macro-level parameters of economic changes such as reduction in poverty, sectoral and occupational shift in livelihood patterns and the educational profile of SC and ST can further enable to assess how these disadvantaged groups have fared in development process during the past few decades. The data at Annexures 1, 2 and 3 throws up the following picture:

a) Between 1977-78 and 1993-94 the pace of poverty reduction among SC has been at a level similar to the total population – a reduction of about 14 per cent.

b) The SC workers continue to be basing their economy on the primary sector – agriculture and agricultural labour – almost to the same extent with a reduction of mere 2 per cent in the decade 1981-91 which was almost similar to the general population. There was no shift to secondary sector and the entire swing was to the tertiary sector.

c) The percentage of persons living below poverty levels among ST went down significantly between 1977-78 and 1993-94, by more than 13 per cent which was higher than the total rate of reduction in poverty.

d) The dependence of ST on primary sector remained at almost the same level in the decade 1981-91 with a reduction of just 0.8 per cent, with a shift of 1.4 per cent to the tertiary sector.

e) The occupational classification of main workers during 1971-91 indicates that among ST there has been a reduction among cultivators as well as those engaged in household industry. Correspondingly, there has been a sizeable increase in 'other workers'.

In the context of another economic parameter, *viz.* the distribution of operational holdings by size groups, during 1980-81 to 1985-86 (the latest data available), the number of holding of all social groups including SC and ST has increased in the marginal and small holding categories (except in case of SC where small holders decreased from 1.43 per cent to 1.40 per cent). The largest number of total operational holdings of each of these groups being in the category of marginal holdings, followed by small holdings.

Some vital aspects of educational development among the SC and ST have been examined now.

i) Literacy rate : Though literacy rates among the SC and ST have shown improvement, the growth is very slow as compared to the literacy rate of the general population as shown in Table 3. The gaps between literacy rates of ST and non-SC/ST population has been increasing since the 1961 census. While the gap of literacy between ST literacy and non-SC/ST population was 19.33 per cent in 1961 it has increased to 28.09 per cent in 1991.

Table 3

Literacy Rates : 1961-1991

Year	Non-SC/ST	SC	Difference	ST	Difference
1	2	3	4	5	6
1961	27.86	8.53	17.59	8.53	19.33
1971	31.80	14.67	14.78	11.30	20.50
1981	41.22	21.38	14.85	16.35	24.87
1991	57.69	37.41	14.80	29.60	28.09

ii) Drop-out-rates : The drop-out-rates (%) amongst SC and ST and non-SC/ST population for the period 1980-81 and 1988-90: (Table 4) at the primary, middle and secondary levels show that drop-out in case of SC/ST, specially among ST pupils has been rather high as compared to figures for all communities.

Table 4

Drop-out Rates (%) SC/ST and All Communities

Year	Drop-out rates for SC			Drop-out rates for ST			Drop-out rates for all communities		
	Primary	Middle	Secondary	Primary	Middle	Secondary	Primary	Middle	Secondary
(1)	(2)	(3)	(4)	(5)	(6)	(7)	(8)	(9)	(10)
1980-81	60.16	76.84	86.91	75.66	86.71	91.18	58.70	72.70	82.46
1989-90	49.03	67.62	79.42	63.81	79.35	86.28	48.08	64.09	74.45

iii) Female literacy : The low levels of female literacy among SC and ST (Table 5) is a cause for grave concern as female education contributes to vital aspects of children development, lowering of TFR and economic empowerment.

Table 5

Female Literacy Levels

Year	*All communities*	*SC*	*ST*
1	2	3	4
1961	12.9	3.3	3.2
1971	18.7	6.4	4.8
1981	29.8	10.9	8.1
1991	39.3	23.8	18.2

It is apparent from the educational profile of SC/ST that they have yet to go a long way to reach the general level. Further, educational development in India is not uniform in all states. Imbalances exist not only amongst the backward or advanced SC and ST in each state but also between males and females and one region and another within the states. A much greater thrust is, therefore, essential to achieve universalisation of elementary education and well-focussed targets for other stages. Special measures to reduce drop-out, increase enrolments and to make the content of education more attractive and functional for the SC and ST, specially the latter will be urgently needed during the current decade.

It is obvious that development has left out quite a number of castes in a comparative state of neglect. Generally, these castes are either small caste groups on the periphery of scheduled castes conglomerates, often in small pockets or nomadic groups sometimes with a stigma of criminality or the groups still following their most polluting traditional occupations. Illustratively, some such scheduled castes are the group of scavanger castes, particularly in north India and among them those living in rural areas, Dhor, Dom, Musahar, Nat (Kabutar, Kalbelia, Sapera, etc.) Sansi, Karwal, Bedia and many others. Some of them are still nomadic or semic-nomadic and were also stigmatized formerly as criminal tribes. Saksena (1997) has analysed the extremely low literacy and deprivation levels among some of the nineteen earlier notified as criminal tribes and now listed as scheduled castes in Uttar Pradesh. Even the setting apart of some funds under the Special Component Plan has not produced the desired results for them. Moreover, in Uttar Pradesh we have thirteen scheduled castes who should have been in the list of scheduled tribes. They have suffered through loss of their lands due to deficient land records and heavy industrialization in their areas, and almost no rehabilitation benefits (Saksena and Sen 1993). Their levels of illiteracy, deprivation and absence of development benefits in spite of the Special Component Plan have to be seen to be believed.

The problem faced by the groups of Scheduled Castes engaged in scavenging has led to the formulation of special programmes. The aim of this policy is to liberate them from their traditional unclean and extremely unhygienic occupation and surroundings and to rehabilitate them in alternative occupations. The scheme was started in 1991-92. So far 8.26 lakh such scavengers have been identified and 29.7 per cent of them rehabilitated in alternative occupations/employment, after imparting some training in other skills or without any training. Such trainings have been provided to nearly 1.08 per cent lakh persons (13 per cent). A commission has been set up to deal with this policy and its implementation.

Reduction in the economic deprivation of the Scheduled Castes is also targeted through a number of laws. Foremost among them have been land reforms, which aim at a more equitable re-distribution of land. But the impact of these measures has not been much. While the estimates of available surplus lands show large areas, the progress of redistribution has been tardy. The percentage of cultivators (land owners) has been going down for all, but more among the Scheduled Castes (27.9 per cent in 1971 and 23.6 per cent in 1991). Moreover, the operational holdings of the Scheduled Castes are overwhelming in the marginal (68.9 per cent in 1980-81 and 71.8 per cent in 1990-91), and small (16.4 per cent in 1980-81 and 16.0 per cent in 1990-91) categories. Though large-scale distribution of land has been attempted in some states, often these entail difficulties in ensuring physical possession to the Scheduled Castes and land has emerged as the most important cause of atrocities. The other relevant laws relate to minimum wages, and the abolition of bonded labour – widely noticed among same Scheduled Castes like the Kol and the Musahar, etc. followed up with the rehabilitation of the persons released from bondage. However, comments on the working of these laws by the former Central Labour Commissioner (Mishra 1994) place their implementation in a poor light, particularly in the context of states like Bihar which have a large Scheduled Caste population. Mishra (ibid) has advocated a comprehensive strategy for this situation: promote an in-depth understanding amongst the rural poor as to who are the oppressors, their strength and weaknesses; impart them tools, techniques and strength; and familiarize them with the craft of putting up organized resistance. Cases like that of the Nadar in Tamil Nadu and Jatava in western Uttar Pradesh show how communities can improve their status and economy and achieve empowerment through education, well-knit community organization and concerted efforts even to give up traditional occupations, if these are demeaning and bring inadequate returns due to *jajmani* and some other such systems of feudal exploitation. The signs that such moves and organizations are building up in the north are also patent and these must be extended all support by the state (Singha Roy 2001). The tendency of the local bureaucracy to either deliberately ignore such measures to avoid any conflict or treat such socio-economic movements as merely 'law and order' matters in their areas should be positively discouraged and pro-poor activism inculcated. The approach should speedily expand among the SC the 'process of broadcasting' whereby "more and more social groups that were formerly deprived or marginalized enter the mainstream of social, political and economic life to derive the same advantages as the groups already in the mainstream" (Nadkarni 1997-2160).

A comparative profiling of a dominant scheduled caste (Chamar and its sub-castes) and a small or minor scheduled caste (Musahar of Uttar Pradesh) over a span of 30 years (1961 census data and 1991 census data) can be further indicative of the trends delineated above. It is seen that:

i) Educational progress : The Chamar advanced three times (7.4 per cent literacy level to 22.1 per cent) while the Musahar could achieve a mere 4.8 per cent compared to 2.2 per cent in 1961. Moreover, the latter suffered further disadvantages in achieving matriculate and higher levels of education.

ii) Economic progress : Though both the castes registered a fall in the percentages of workers and female workers, the

> Musahar continued to have, in 1991, a much larger percentage of workers among whom female workers accounted for nearly a third of female population compared to less than one-sixth among the Chamar. Occupationally, the Musahar registered a much higher rise in the agricultural labour category in 1991. Diversions to secondary and tertiary sectors as well were seen at a much lower level among the Musahar, as compared to the Chamar.

Thus, a situation has been emerging where the more backward are not able to muster adequate developmental support and continue to remain stagnant at the lowest level. Therefore, such castes and also tribes create a dynamics of 'drag' for both the categories – SC and ST. Unless this drag is effectively arrested before 2020 the targeted levels of development for the two categories of under-privileged sections will not materialise. On the other hand, the mechanism of Special Component Plan and substantive financing through institutional process, unless fine tuned, will contribute to further aggravate the situation.

Apart from the laws referred to above, the state has decisively moved to empower the SC and also ST socially and economically, in the context of prevalent disabilities and the tendency to harass the SC, generally to reinforce traditional exploitation and achieve economic gains. The Protection of Civil Rights (PCR) Act of 1995 and the Scheduled Castes and Scheduled Tribes (Prevention of Atrocities) Act, 1989 are the two major legal instruments therefore. As many as 434 Special Courts/Mobile Courts were set up in seven states. In addition, Special Cells/Squads/Officers have also been appointed in nineteen states to ensure effective implementation of the Act. In accordance with the PCR Act of 1955, special legal aid was also extended to the victims of untouchability and other crimes through Special Officers who ensured effective implementation of the Act, besides extending support for social and economic rehabilitation of the SC/ST victims. Comparative data regarding crime is committed against the SC and ST is at Table 6.

In the year 1996 a study on the implementation of the PAA was conducted by Saksena (1996) in five districts of U.P. The study, *inter alia,* highlights that the two laws, specially the Anti-atrocity law which could be very significant instrument in the process of empowerment has not fully achieved its objectives mainly due to inadequacies of investigating and prosecuting agencies, delays in the judicial process and poor implementation of the rehabilitative and preventive measures as set down in the law and its rules – all the factors are connected with the State's enforcement machinery. This study also brings out a major trend in caste situation/relations – that more than 55 per cent atrocities/crimes were perpetrated by the middle level peasant castes (mostly listed as OBC) and not the two upper castes, viz. Thakurs and Brahmins; and land and terms of agricultural labour were the motivating factors for more than 54 per cent cases. Krishnan (2002), while analysing the PCR Act, 1955 points out that convictions under and it were low and compared to earlier years the proportion has flagged and fallen in subsequent years. He identifies wages, bondage, land and access to civic facilities as matrix of atrocities and the new phenomena of Dalit assertion of self-respect.

Table 6

Cases/Crimes under the PCR and POA Acts

Year	Under PCR	Under POA	
		SC	ST
1995	1528	32997	5498
1996	1417	31440	4973
1997	1157	26488	NA
1998	724	25638	NA

As has been pointed out earlier, the canvas relating to ST presents far more varied issues connected with their economic, educational, health, nutritional and cultural contexts for the next two decades which may now be factualised and analysed.

Economic issues : A systematised elucidation of the multiple economic involvements of tribals can help in understanding the interactive roles of cultural, ecological and technological parameters of tribal living in order to evolve better strategies and introduce innovations. Moreover, such an approach would also bring out the dynamics of institutionalisation in economic structure, adoption of technology, and march of modernisation, at a varied pace, among the different levels of tribal communities. Danda (1991) has examined the frequency distribution of economic pursuits of tribes by the levels of their involvement in each pursuit. He has pointed out that today the tribals are following a wide range of economic activities ranging from the most primitive form of collection of forest products to the latest forms of post-industrial specialized economy. Danda's analysis brings out that most of the tribals who may primarily depend on the economic pursuit, have to supplement it with upto five other activities. The data relating to 410 tribal communities collected by him as given in Table 7.

Table 7

Frequency Distribution of Economic Pursuits of Tribes

Bases of subsistence	*Frequency (number) of tribes pursing*	
	As Primary means	*As per all priorities I to VI*
A. Food gathering		
(i) Collection of forest products	39	144
(ii) Hunting	19	130
(iii) Fishing	7	69
B. Animal husbandry	**15**	**70**
C. Food producing		
(i) Shifting cultivation	84	111
(ii) Terrace cultivation	11	18
(iii) Settled agriculture	139	186
D. Institutional		
(i) Craft and professional	49	123
(ii) Trade and Commercial	7	47
(iii) Wage labour	40	171
Total :	**410**	**1069**

* The number of scheduled tribal communities comes to around 461 if synonyms, sub-communities, etc. are excluded.

It is seen that all the tribes communities excepting those depending primarily on 'institutional' pursuits have a land-based strategy of livelihood and a large number of tribal communities having settled or shifting agriculture are drawing their secondary, tertiary or even lower level of economic support from 'food gathering'. Even wage-earners may have an important secondary pursuit and craftsmen and artisans too may depend on a land base for their raw materials and secondary/tertiary support. In this situation some aspects of tribal land base and forests assume a centrality.

Land Holdings, land alienation and agriculture : In 1985-86, 41.3 per cent of STs cultivators were marginal farmers and 24.1 per cent were small farmers. Only 2.8 per cent had larger operations holdings. There has been a decrease in the average size of operations holdings in the marginal category indicating a trend of marginalisation in agriculture. Due to tardy land reforms and lack of detailed survey/settlement operations in the tribal areas, specially the scheduled areas of several states there is erosion in the titles of the tribal of their lands. Then, alienation of tribal lands remains a spiralling problem in spite of the law of ban alienation and restore illegally transferred lands. Information for eleven states till November 1996 indicates that more than 20 per cent area of total tribal holdings illegally transferred by the tribals was involved in legal proceedings for restoration. But even in cases where restoration was ordered, the tribal owners could not be put in possession. Alienation has also been going up through rising acquisitions for public purposes, a backlash of development. It is estimated that nearly 25 per cent of alienations taking place in recent decades have been through acquisitions. Low productivity of lands and chronic indebtedness among them and their failure to properly utilize and repay productive institutional loans also contribute to land alienation.

Irrigation : Lack of irrigation facilities in these areas in a major contributor to low agricultural production. According to the agricultural census of 1990-91, of the total net sown area of 143.84 lakh hectares, in the tribal areas, 13.2 per cent of the cultivated land was being irrigated through canals, tanks, wells/tubewells, etc. VIII Plan Working Group have pointed out to a drop in productivity in many tribal areas in spite of large TSP investments. Impoverishments of agriculture is reflected also in the NSS Survey (1988-89) finding that in the central belt where a majority of tribals live only, 42 per cent of tribal families were engaged in agriculture while 49 per cent were wage earners and only 2.1 per cent were in non-agricultural activities, as compared to 10.6 per cent for non-tribals.

Shifting Cultivations : Shifting cultivation is still being practiced on higher slopes of hilly areas by an estimated more than six lakh tribal families in the states of North-East, Orissa, Andhra Pradesh, Jharkhand, Madhya Pradesh, Chattisgarh and Himachal Pradesh. Shifting cultivation is integrally linked to the tribal economy in the areas where it is practiced and their social, economic and ritual activities also center around this practice. The problem of shifting cultivation is complex and needs careful micro-level agro-horticulture packages for rehabilitation.

Indebtedness : Indebtedness among the tribals is on the increase (14 per cent to 34 per cent during 1975-83) according to a survey quoted by the VIII Plan WG. They are heavily indebted to both institutional and private sources (72 per cent). Debt bondage is the worst facet of indebtedness. The Bonded Labour System (Abolition) Act, 1976, along with the rehabilitation scheme for released bonded labour was implemented vigorously earlier. But now laxity has crept in ensuring continuous vigilance and use of law. It is feared that the system is under revival. Therefore, there is a need now to make fresh surveys and search for bonded labour, specifically in the mining and construction industry in rural areas.

Migrant Labour : Low agricultural productivity and lack of employment opportunities and restrictions on rights over forest produce have forced the tribal labourers to seasonally migrate to other areas in search of wage employment. This outflow will increase heavily in the ensuring decades. The migrant labourers are subjected to a variety of exploitative practices and the law relating to migrant labour is proving inadequate in eliminating exploitation.

Displacement : The tribal areas are rich in mineral, water and other resources. A study conducted by the Ford Foundation indicated that 85 per cent of the mineral wealth of India comes from the south-east resource triangle comprising the hilly parts of Chattisgarh, Orissa, Bihar (Jharkhand) and West Bengal. It points out that the quantum of tribal land that passed on to individual non-tribals in these areas is dwarfed by the extent of the land government and industrial organizations have taken over for big projects.

Government policies and approach have been so apathetic to the problem of displacements that they have not even cared to collect proper statistics thereof. Walter Fernandes (1997) estimates that during 1951-1990, 21.3 million persons were displaced out of whom nearly nine million were tribals. The rehabilitation of these people, the quality of which is questionable, has covered only 5.38 million including only 2.12 million tribals. Because of liberalization and globalization, displacement is going to assume much larger proportions. Yet, the government has failed to come up either with a resettlement policy and a people-friendly law to replace the archaic land acquisition laws or an organization to ensure rehabilitation. In future more and more projects will be set up, particularly by private industries. The Supreme Court judgement in the Samata Case (Samata 2000) is a trend-setter, but unless the state assumes a more positive role in successful rehabilitation, movements and prolonged litigation will continue to block both the progress of projects and the future of vulnerable outsees in future.

Primitive Tribal Groups : Based on a four point criteria – i) smallness in size and diminishing numbers; ii) backwardness and isolation; iii) pre-agricultural technology; and iv) very low literacy, the Government of India have identified 75 tribal communities as Primitive Tribal Groups (PTG) with a total estimated population of 1.36 millions in 1991, spread over fifteen states/UTs. The approach was to prepare detailed tailor-made projects for their development. However, the VIII Plan WG (1996) and subsequent documents indicate that adequate information on the demographic, educational, health and economic aspects of individual primitive tribes is yet to be collected. By 2020 that population is likely to be around 2.10 million with a need to cater effectively to their development needs, particularly health and nutrition. Urgent steps have to be taken for building up a comprehensive information/data base and prepared detailed status reports which should eventually form the bases for need-based projects to improve their condition.

Forest rights : It is estimated that almost one-third of the tribal household economy is built around the forest resources and, therefore, access to these resources has been a matter of great concern. No development of forestry can be planned in isolation and it has to be an integral part of plans for tribal development. The

Forest Policy Resolution of 1988 makes a welcome change with some significant features which concretise the recommendations made by the Roy Burman Committee on Forests and Tribals in India (1982) and the Bhatia Committee on Forestry Programme for Alleviation of Poverty (1984). The Policy emphasises close association of tribals in protection, regeneration, optimal collection of MFP, arrangements for MFP marketing and development of forest-based means of livelihood. Unless these measures are sincerely taken up, ecological degradation and loss of forest cover cannot be eliminated. Protection of rights of the tribals in forests has assumed further relevance in this context. The extension of Panchayati Raj to the scheduled areas through the Panchayati Raj (Extension to Scheduled Areas) Act, 1996, if it proceeds properly, can resolve conflicts and pave the way for economic improvement. But its implementation thus far has been uneven. The Joint Forest Management approach too has been taken up in most of the States. Its impact, however, has so far been assessed to be less than equitable and needs-responsive in many tribal areas. Hence, its policy and procedures have to be recast wherever necessary by the forest, revenue and tribal development departments in the areas inhabitedly by the tribes.

Bio-diversity, Tribals' Traditional Knowledge Systems and Intellectual Property Rights : Art. 8(j) of Bio-diversity Convention adopted by the U.N. envisages IPR of indigenous peoples to be respected through special arrangements. To operationalise this process, an international conference had taken place in May 1998. However, in India it appears that due to delay in positioning adequate mechanism to protect the interests of bio-diversity and tribals' traditional knowledge systems, gene plundering of medicinal herbs and illegal taking away of tribals' traditional knowledge has been going on.

Education : The Gains and the Gaps (1971-91) in Literacy levels reflect that although there has been substantial gains during the last three decades, the gaps between the ST and the general population is not only persisting but it is also seen to be widening. Under the circumstances, apart from ensuring schools for the children, better programmes and continuous efforts in adult education are needed. This requires target oriented interventions relating to the following vital issues:

(a) Scholarships and other facilities make education attractive to the SC and ST. However, the total allotments in this field and the implementation of the schemes has not been upto the mark. The quantum of scholarships fail to meet their needs, and even these reach them late in the academic session. The hostel facilities are inadequate and also ill-equipped.

(b) The type of education and the curriculae for the tribals particularly PTG and nomadic communities should be planned keeping in view their milieu, genius and special needs.

(c) Employment oriented education and training vocational education has to be pursued.

(d) Further, in view the low literacy rates, low enrolment and high drop-out special incentives like mid-day meals, uniform, books, etc. are needed.

(e) Smaller tribes, particularly PTG and some others having exceptionally low literacy levels has to be identified and specific plans prepared for such groups and areas.

(f) Well conceived schemes focusing on the areas and tribes most backward in girls education have to be extensively undertaken.

The projections of 5-9 age group give a clear indication that the educational infrastructure for the ST at the primary level as reflected by an enrolment figure of about 86 lakh in 1993-94 will have to be increased substantially to cater to 1.23 crore ST students. The corresponding figures for SC are 1.76 crore in 1993-94 which have to be developed to have 2.51 crore students. At the middle level, the facilities will need very substantial expansion and consolidation to eliminate heavy drop-out, the 1993-94 enrolment being at 22 lakhs only for ST and 56 lakhs for SC while the projected 10-14 years population is likely to be 1.15 and 2.34 crore for ST and SC respectively.

Health : The comparative information on health indicators contained in Human Development Profile for Rural India (NCAER 1996) was :

Table 8

Health Indicators

Indicators	*Tribal*	*Rural*
(1)	(2)	(3)
1. Crude Birth Rate (CBR)	35	32 (per 1000)
2. IMR	98	77
3. ANC received by pregnant Women (%)	42.2	57.5
4. Immunization of children aged 12-23 months (%)	39.5	48.5
5. Percentage of people who fell ill during 1995-96 (PEO Survey)	21.9	24.7 (non tribals in tribal area)

High CBR and IMR reflect the weakness of rural public health care services. The tribals are worse off in terms of access to health services (Annexure 4). Further, TFR among the ST is also high and a large number of tribal districts featured among 'the demographically weak districts' in 1998-99. The tribal population, being heterogeneous there are wide variations in their health status, access and also utilization of health services. The tribals of North Eastern states show better utilization of the available health facilities. Some tribes and tribal areas have high incidence of certain diseases like leprosy, yaws, water-borne diseases, TB, anaemia, etc. Obviously health services need much better attention in the interior areas but the trends of privatization of services and reluctance of doctors and para-medical staff work in the tribal area have been severely affecting the services. A study of ITDPs by PEO (1997) clearly points out this. In the coming years this process is not likely to be arrested.

Nutrition : Malnutrition amongst the tribal especially tribal children and women is fairly common, debilitating their physical condition, lowering resistance to disease, and leading in the post-weaning period at times, even to permanent brain impairment. Maternal malnutrition common among tribal women is also serious health problem, particularly for those having closely spaced frequent pregnancies. PIG need urgent attention as some of them are demographically in danger due to starvation and diseases. Research and surveys are expeditiously needed to understand their specific diseases, genetic disorders and other health issues for remedial action. Indigenous systems of medicine should also get adequate encouragement to cater to the needs of the tribal population as the ingredients of these systems are easily available at a lower cost and investment within the tribal areas. One of the basic necessities of life, viz. safe drinking water, is yet to be provided adequately in the interior tribal.

Drinking Water: By 1995-96 nearly 85 per cent tribal population has been covered through rural water supply programme. However, clear information about the tribal habitations specially in the hilly and drought affected areas has to be clearly monitored before it can be said that potable water supply has been ensured all through the year. It is likely that these goals may not be fully met by 2020.

Culture and Heritage: As pronounced in Nehru's Tribal Panchasheel and reiterated in our Five Year Plans, the welfare programmes for Scheduled Tribes have to be based on a proper understanding of their culture and traditions and an appreciation of the social, psychological and economic problems which they face. Along with various developmental policies and programmes initiated to improve the socio-economic conditions of tribal peoples, there has also arisen an urgent and widely felt need to preserve and promote various aspects of tribal culture and heritage, including their dialects and language, values of co-operation and community feeling, music, dance, literature, language, festivals/religions, knowledge and indigenous technology, skills, arts and handicrafts, etc. The tribal communities themselves are voicing their concern in this regard through their ethnic movements. Under the circumstances, the state has to go beyond just reiterating such a policy and announce a national tribal policy encompassing the entire gamut of tribal issues.

IV. NEW ECONOMIC POLICY AND SC AND ST

Privatisation and globalisation of economy will have and are already creating a contradiction of employment in the public sector, both governmental and PSU. In this context three vital questions have arisen:

1. Will the privatization of economy and all the attendant policies create enough jobs to compensate for the loss of jobs?
2. Assuming that the private sector does so, what is likely to be the nature of these prospective jobs; and
3. What chances SC/ST persons stand for getting a fair share of these jobs so as to compensate the consequences of fall in the availability of governments and PSU jobs and the erosion of reservation policy?

The present scenario has been analysed by a number of researchers and the emerging position is likely to be as below:

1. During the last fifteen years the overall growth of economy has not been accompanied by a proportionate increase in the level of employment. This has been attributed to the decline in the elasticity of employment with respect to the growth of economy (Gupta 1994 and others). Agriculture too has ceased to be 'last resort' of employment due to mechanization and other similar devices by the better off farmers. In fact the capacity of agriculture to employ is declining and more and more people are moving to wage-earning elsewhere and service sector. Organised sector was a great failure in employment generation. During 1991-94 jobs rose by 0.64 million only in both the organized public/private sectors. Then, manufacturing sector (both public/private) is worse – an increase of just 0.08 million jobs during 1991-95. Small scale industries capacity to employ is essence but it is eroding due to multi-nationals which use capital intensive modern techniques of production. Even trade as an engine of growth may lead to 'de-industrialization' resulting in fall in both industrial and employment growth. The kind of jobs that economy reforms are likely to create will not be proportionate to either the prospective economic growth or work force increase.
2. Regarding the nature and quality of jobs – the jobs to be created may demand relatively more technical

skills and professional competence. Here the position is that the SC/ST lag far behind in possessing this capability.

3. The chances of SC/ST sharing these jobs in good measure are indeed bleak – specially when the job interests of the vulnerable groups are less than adequately protected as is the case of private sector. Even under the present reservation policy, their interests are not being fully served.

The resulting trend may be that SC/ST will crowd themselves still more in unorganized and informal sectors of economy which will lead to further economic-marginalisation. This process resulting from NEP will be further strengthened by 'commodification of social services' (Mungekar 1999) like education, medical facilities, etc.

Private sector services are unaffordable for the poor and therefore the state must continue to provide these, however, our welfare expenditure is far below – around 15 per cent - compared to Italy (56 per cent), UK (45 per cent). In India it has been going down or increasing only marginally to 19.4 per cent (1995-96). But, on the other hand, efforts are also being made to reduce benefits by cutting down subsidies, and increasing service charges (education/health for example) by the government and revising criteria to reduce beneficiaries.

The trend vision is that even when NEP may secure the country's economic growth, the highly inequitious social system creating and sustaining an unequal opportunity structure will deprive these groups of much opportunity in sharing the benefits – essentially due to the erosion of reservation policy and a growing process of commodification of social services. Therefore, the approach should be for the continuance and not dismantling of welfare state by the ruling classes.

V. OTHER BACKWARD CLASSES (OBC)

The term OBC for some sections of people was used for the first time in the Objective Resolution of the Constituent Assembly.

However, even though Article 15(4) in the constitution makes an exception in order to provide for reservations of appointments/posts in favour 'of any backward class of citizens' in the fundamental right guaranteeing equality in matters of public employment' and Articles 16(4) allows the state to make special provisions for the 'advancement of any socially and educationally backward classes of citizens', the founding fathers had left it for a Commission (Art. 340) to investigate the conditions of 'socially and educationally backward classes' and to recommend : i) steps to remove their difficulties and to improve their conditions; and ii) as to the grants that should be made for the purpose by the Union or any states and the conditions subject to which such grants should be made.

The report of the Commission appointed under this Article (Kaka Kalelkar Commission submitted in 1955) was not accepted by the Government of India. It was left to the states to continue having their own lists of OBCs or draw a fresh list and make financial provisions for their advancement. The Centre also continued with a few schemes for their educational advancement. The Kalelkar Commission had identified 2,399 castes (estimated population 11.35 crores in 1951) constituting 32 per cent of country's population to be falling in this category. The second Commission (Mandal Commission) on the bases of several social, educational and economic criteria prepared a list of such castes and classes and, further, included among them some groups of primitive tribes, exterior castes, criminal tribes, nomadics, etc. as they were more or less alike the SC and ST and, therefore, backward. The castes listed by the Commission in their report of December 1980 came to 3,743 and their calculated 'derived population' as 52 per cent of the country's population. It may be mentioned that the 'People of India Survey' (1994) had identified a total of 4,693 castes/communities in the country including 1046 OBCs.

The Government of India acting on the Mandal Report have already taken the following measures:

i) Notified lists of OBC common with States/U.T. for the purpose of reservation in Central services/posts fixed at 27 per cent along with relaxation in age and standards.

ii) Set up a National Commission for OBC through an Act in 1993 for entertaining, examining and recommending upon requests for inclusion and complaints relating to over-inclusion and under-inclusion in the OBC lists.

iii) Set up a National Backward Classes Finance and Development Corporation, upgrade the technological and entrepreneurial skills of OBC individually and a special scheme for OBC women.

iv) Taken up educational schemes – pre-matric and post-matric scholarships, hostels for boys and girls, pre-examination coaching for competitive and entrance examinations and assisting voluntary organisations for OBC welfare.

The Ninth Plan document states clearly that since these measures were introduced recently, their impact could not be assessed at this stage.

Although little specific information is available on the status on OBCs, it is apparent that a substantial section among them lives below the poverty line, possess few assets and are engaged in low-income traditional occupations. Unless the harsh conditions under which the OBCs live and work are altered it would not be possible for them to secure economic self reliance either in their traditional activities or in other diverse occupations. In this context the Mid Term Appraisal holds out a sanguine promise that our economy has reached a stage where a much larger skilled manpower would be needed and where OBCs have an edge over others. And, therefore, on-going schemes of employment-cum-income generation are being expanded to reach the unreached in the most backward rural areas.

Now, we may turn to have a closer and analytical look at the composition of the OBC with a view to commenting upon the adequacy and comprehensiveness of the approach adopted on the basis of the Mandal report. Broadly speaking, the Backward Classes still represent to a varied extend the inequalities of Indian society in different forms. In the economy, they substantially include a large number of castes and communities who were required to produce a variety of goods and provide a variety of services on terms unfair to them, thus constituting different forms and degrees of exploitation. On this basis they can be grouped under the following categories:

a. Communities without resources or skills	A good number of castes/communities are indigent and their traditional occupation has been and still is begging, sometimes with religious overtones. Many of them are nomadic or semi-nomadic.
b. Artisan castes/communities with traditional skills engaged in various crafts providing a variety of good on cottage scale like weavers, potters, black-smiths, carpenters, etc. who have been engaged in secondary production for centuries.	Their traditional occupations have been and under different forms and degrees of threat while entry into modern sectors and facilities for upward mobility are generally denied.
c. Castes/communities of artisanal producers like fisher folk, toddy tappers, stone cutters, earth workers, etc.	
d. Castes/communities providing traditional services like hair-cutting and grooming, washing of clothes, scavenging (by Muslim low castes).	
e. Castes/communities of poor peasantry including tenant peasantry of the former Zamindari and other intermediary tenures.	
f. Castes/communities engaged in activities under attack and fast shrinking demand, such as bird catchers, snake charmers, hunters, acrobats, folk art performers, musicians, Bhand (entertainers) Bahurupiyas, etc.	

The target universe i.e. the entire mass of OBC which may have to be catered to in the coming decades is difficult to quantify and analyse diagonostically due to three factors:

1. The lists of OBC are constantly undergoing revisions generally by way of expansion and this crucial act of scheduling has not remained entirely free of politics and some cases are before the apex court.
2. Exclusion of individual beneficiaries from the mass of beneficiaries will also be under regular alteration through the 'creamy layer' criteria. Generally the trend has been to raise the criteria, thereby reducing the excluded quantum.

3. Census data regarding the size and other details regarding individual castes/classes/communities are not available.

The 'derived population' formula of the Mandal Commission puts it at 52 per cent of the country's population. However, due to various reasons this estimate does not appear to be realistic. Hence, the likely target population (OBC) in the year 2020 is difficult to estimate. Undoubtedly, it is likely to be substantial. It could even be more if weightage is provided to the higher TFR among them. But it may be set off partly due to the southern states with substantial OBC populations achieving a lower TFR much earlier.

The developmental intervention in the case of OBC has so far been of a low order, specially in view of their vast numbers and difficult reach. Moreover, a considerable number of castes/classes among them have traditional skills which cannot provide them with adequate livelihood due to changing ways of life, habits, means of entertainment, etc. – for example *Bajigar, Bharbhuja, Mirasi, Rangrej, Nilgar, Nalband, Sikligar, Bairagi, Teli, Jogi.* Therefore, they have to be provided with alternative skills after a careful appraisal of their situation. Some occupational skills like those of Kumhar, Lohar, Banjaraa have to be provided with opportunities for upgradation, modern tools and designs and guided through newly created channels of marketing and sale. Studies among them have also pointed out that communities themselves have been taking to alternative and supplementary livelihood strategies quite successfully. Misra (1992) has documented this trend as seen among the *Gadiya-Lohar* and some other nomadic OBC group.

As the 'People of India Survey' has brought out, there has been a sharp decline in some traditional occupations – such as trapping of birds/animals (33 per cent), pastoral activity (10 per cent), gathering and selling of natural products (44 per cent) – while some economic activities have increased particularly wage labour (69 per cent), sericulture (80 per cent), business (70 per cent) industry (82 per cent), horticulture (40 per cent), trade (53 per cent) and government and other services (95 per cent).

Another significant emerging situation is that a number of large influential OBC communities have been progressing fast. As Lieten and Srivastava (1999) observe in the context of U.P. :

"the abolition of the Zamindari system after independence also widened the base of land-ownership to include better-off tenants who were largely from the backward and intermediate castes .... land legislation measures and the dynamism which followed the introduction of the Green Revolution, initially in the western districts but gradually spreading to other parts, have reduced the stark monopoly of the traditional proprietary groups ....the rich and upper middle farmers, often OBCs and intermediate castes, have shown more dynamism and have consolidated substantial gains in the last few decades. On the flip side, there has been some diversification in the employment structure away from agriculture, and real wages have shown an increase, even in the more backward regions............ And the OBCs, however, have been growing in importance, economically and educationally, and some of the representatives of the lower castes are well placed and provide leadership politically, to the varied groups of lower castes and Muslims."

A study on the working of the SC and ST (Prevention of Atrocities) Act 1989 in U.P. by Saksena (1996) revealed that among the perpetrators of atrocities on the SC, the Yadav came second, after the Brahmin. The overall position was that the OBC as a group were responsible for over 33 per cent crimes against the SC.

It came to be forecast that this trend will intensify in the areas and states where land reforms will proceed with some seriousness U.P. and A.P. for instance and here a core of OBC communities with agricultural traditions will further move the center-stage. A patent outcome would be that these communities will proceed to appropriate for themselves most of the benefits of 'positive discrimination' policies. This brings into sharp focus a constant and accentuated need for:

i) correcting eligibility norms and delivery mechanism for the programmes which cannot but remain limited in number and coverage due to financial constraints;

ii) avoiding further inclusions in the lists unless richly deserved and a watch over the creamy layer criteria;

iii) focussing and honing of programmes to suit and, more importantly, to reach the most backward groups, and splitting the lists into priority categories on the bases of ground realities;

iv) concurrent evaluation of programmes with a view to correcting their frame and identifying the neglected section;

v) creating an effective institutional frame, quasi-judicial in nature, to tackle the problem of bonded labour and child labour with complementary provisions for stable rehabilitation;

vi) empowerment through education, initiative for voluntary organizations of their own and well-informed participation in the process of democratic decentralisaiton;

vii) reorienting educational programmes to suit the semi-nomadic groups and communities engaged in artistic and performing activities which are losing their clientele;

viii) legal restraint on hazardous traditional occupations and health care for the affected peoples;

ix) strengthening development instrumalities like the national and state corporations, skill upgrading, training, etc. specially in the northern states – U.P., Bihar while ensuring that political mobilization does not corner the benefits which is visualized as the most dangerous trend for the development future of the OBC as a whole.

VI. MINORITIES (RELIGIOUS)

The religious minorities, as presently notified include Muslims, Christians, Sikhs, Buddhists and Zorastrians. As per the 1991 Census their population was nearly 17.4 per cent and in the state their percentage ranged from 4.01 per cent in Orissa to 94.27 per cent in Mizoram and 95.47 per cent - all Scheduled Tribe Muslims – in Lakshadweep. In all 142 districts have been listed as having 20 per cent population of the Minorities. It is however noticed that the list does not include any district from Jammu and Kashmir where several districts are having more than 20 per cent minority population. As per the 2001 census the number of such districts must have gone up and by 2020 this list will surely be considerably larger. The areas within the districts where there are pockets of thick minority populations and minority concentration districts need to be carefully demarcated so that these can be focused for their development through selected programmes and institutional arrangements can be put in position for the purpose.

The fundamental constitutional rights guaranteed to the minorities related to their language, script and culture and to establish and administer educational institutions of their choice whether based on religion or language:

Article 29. Protection of interests of minorities

(1) Any section of the citizens residing in the territory of India or any part thereof having a distinct language, script or culture of its own shall have the right to conserve the same.

(2) No citizen shall be denied admission into any educational institution maintained by the State or receiving aid out of State funds on grounds only of religion, race, caste, language or any of them.

Article 30. Right of Minorities to establish and administer educational institutions

(1) All minorities, whether based on religion or language, shall have the right to establish and administer educational institutions of their choice.

(1A) In making any law providing for the compulsory of any property of an institution established and administered by a minority, referred to in clause (1), the State shall ensure that the amount fixed by or determined under such law for the acquisition or such property is such as would not restrict or abrogate the right guaranteed under that clause.

(2) The State shall not, in granting aid to educational institutions, discriminate against any educational institution on the ground that it is under the management of a minority, whether based on religion or language.

And more importantly Article 51A relating to Fundamental Duties enjoins the citizens, *inter alia*, "to promote harmony and the spirit of common brotherhood amongst all the people of India transcending religion, linguistic and regional or sectional diversities; .... and to value and preserve the rich heritage of composite culture."

During the last about two decades some over-riding issues concerning the minorities have come to the fore and it can be clearly envisaged that in the coming two decades some of the following aspects are likely to assume a focal position in any dispensation for them:

i) Minorities must have a feeling that they are acknowledged and accepted as an intrinsic and inalienable part of Indian culture, ethos and society.

ii) Their values and perceptions, in so far as the national identity and national good are concerned, are perceived to be no different from the values and perceptions of the majority.

iii) That they are not being discriminated against on the ground of religion.

iv) The majority too has to develop a mindset which does not erroneously believe that any special dispensation is being accorded in respect of Minorities or that they are in any way being "pampered"; and all that is intended is to enable them to be, and to remain, an integral part of India, with fair access to equal rights and opportunities.

Direct development intervention in the case of the religious minorities, specially the Muslims, has come only after the Prime Minister's 15 Point Programme (1983) for them. This charter included special consideration to minorities in recruitment to State and Central police forces, railways and public sector undertakings, coaching facilities for competitive examinations and encouraging their admissions to technical courses. It is also promised that care would be taken to ensure benefits of various ongoing development programme, solve their local problems and expeditiously attend to their grievances and special problems. The Progamme also envisage measures to prevent communal riots and ensure confidence building measures.

The following special programmes have been introduced for them since the Eighth Plan:

(i) Area intensive programme for educationally backward minorities.

(ii) Financial assistance for modernizing the Madarsa education among the Muslims.

(iii) Community polytechnics in minority concentration area.

(iv) Setting up of a National Minorities Finance and Development Corporation to encourage their self employment and industries.

(v) Coaching classes for competitive examinations set up in the universities and elsewhere.

(vi) Setting up of the Maulana Azad Educational Foundation with a corpus fund of Rs. 70.01 crores.

The Ninth Plan document has observed that "........ the impact of various developmental measures in respect of the Minorities also could not be assessed in view of the short span they have been in operation. However, the general conditions reveal that the Minorities, especially the Muslims, their women and girl children, remain educationally very backward and their traditional institutions like *Madarsas* are yet to adopt the modern syllabus to get integrated into the mainstream education. A large number ...... continue to depend upon the low income traditional artisanship or similar occupations." The Ninth Plan Working Group had gone into the details of implementation of the special programmes and also several other related aspects, viz. the role of employment exchanges in placement of minority candidates, actual recruitment to police, railways, all India services, etc. and the performance of banks in providing priority sector lending. They felt that the areas where positive thinking and action in the IX Plan are called for are: general education; girl's education, technical education, recruitment to public services (including banks, railways and PSU) with particular reference to the police; health; housing; special attention to artisans and handloom weavers (who constitute a substantial segment of Minorities) and their families, bank credit in the priority sector for the setting up of micro and small enterprises; and, finally, confidence building.

A vision for the Minorities for the next 20 years should encompass the following dimensions of the scenario in order to adequately cater to their developmental needs and social dynamics:

i) A projection would indicate that in 2020 the population of India will be around 133.5 crore and the Minority population about 24 crore. (18 per cent). Some weightage has been provided in this projection to the higher TFR.

ii) The age-group composition of the minority population is estimated to be

0-4	9.7%	2.33 crores
-14	18.6%	4.32 crores
15-59	63.3%	15.20 crores
60+	9.0%	2.16 crores

iii) In the process the number of districts with 20 per cent + minority population will go up from the 142 (excluding J&K) to may be around 175).

iv) The component of minority population will rise at a higher rate in at least 42 districts (plus the valley area of J&K) as these feature in the list of 135 districts with births of order third and higher – in other words in the higher TFR category – and in the 1998-99 religion-wise TFR that of the Muslims was the highest at 3.59.

The thrust areas should, therefore, be identified with a view to promoting socio-economic development, integrative attitudes, syncretic cultural life and values and modernization of the minorities. Broadly these can be:

i) Educational policies/programmes to achieve total literacy, particularly aiming at the girl child, blending it with technical and vocational training, science and technical courses in the Madarsas to promote integration and make that pattern of education useful by way of employability/self employment.

ii) Identification of areas and sections of populations where intensive programmes can be undertaken for skill upgradation, introduction of appropriate technology, better production, marketing, etc. for traditional crafts. Also taking into account the effects ongoing liberalization and concommitant processes.

iii) Advancing suitable projects to promote confidence building and emotive environment in cultural fields, particularly language, religious traditions, art, etc.

iv) Health and family welfare programmes have to be focussed in their areas in the context of specific morbidity patterns, higher TFR and environmental factors leading to specific diseases particularly among women and children.

v) The reach of Basic Minimum Services and poverty alleviation programmes and Public Distribution System will have to take special care of the slums with minority concentration in the urban areas and similar conglomerates in the rural area.

vi) Confidence building measures would also lead to the empowerment of minorities particularly Muslims and neo-Buddhists. Empowerment of women also has to be achieved through suitable civil laws and other reformatory measures.

vii) In the field of public employment it is visualized that opportunities are likely to shrink after about five years. Nonetheless, coaching and educational improvement programmes can yield results in the fields of private employment as well e.g. in Information Technology. The minority institutions and NGOs can play a significant role in this direction.

viii) During the last two decades people from all the five minority groups have been taking good advantage of employment opportunities abroad, particularly in dominant. Minority's prosperity has achieved an unprecedented boom through it in some states. Therefore, educational and skill upgradation has to be suitably and continuously honed to the demands of the diaspora. The Government of India must also continue to intervene to ensure fair terms of employment in order to enable the minorities to fully avail of all the openings.

Annexure 1

Percentage of SC/ST and all India Populations below Poverty Line during 1977-78 to 1993-94 as per previous Estimates of the Planning Commission

Year	*Scheduled Caste*		*Scheduled Tribes*		*All India*	
	Rural	*Urban*	*Rural*	*Urban*	*Rural*	*Urban*
1	2	3	4	5	6	7
1977-78	64.6	54.3	72.4	52.6	51.2	38.2
1983-84	53.1	40.4	58.4	39.9	40.4	28.1
1987-88	43.6	31.7	51.4	30.2	33.4	20.1
1993-94	48.1	49.4	51.9	41.1	37.3	32.4

Source: National Commission for SC/ST IV Report (1996-98).

Annexure 2

Sectroal Distribution of 'Main Workers' amongst SC and ST in 1981 and 1991

Category	*Primary Sector*		*Secondary Sector*		*Tertiary Sector*	
	1981	*1991*	*1981*	*1991*	*1981*	*1991*
1	2	3	4	5	6	7
SC	79.1	77.1	9.9	9.8	10.8	13.1
ST	90.7	90.0	4.4	3.8	4.7	6.1
General	69.4	67.5	13.0	12.0	17.6	20.5

Source: Registrar General and Census Commissioner, India, Series - 1, Paper - 1 of 1993 Union Primary Census Abstract for Scheduled Castes and Scheduled Traibes.

Annexure 3

Occupational Classification of Main Workers from 1961 to 1991 Census among SC/ST and General Population

Year	*General*	*Sch. Castes*	*Sch. Tribes*
1961	52.18	37.76	68.18
1971	43.38	27.87	57.56
1981	41.53	28.17	54.43
1991	39.74	25.44	54.50
Agriculture Labour			
1961	16.71	34.48	19.71
1971	26.32	51.74	33.04
1981	26.16	48.22	32.67
1991	19.66	49.06	32.69
Household Industries			
1961	6.38	6.56	2.47
1971	3.55	3.33	1.03
1981	3.99	3.31	1.42
1991	2.56	2.41	1.04
Other Workers			
1961	24.13	21.20	9.64
1971	26.32	17.06	8.64
1981	29.32	20.30	11.84
1991	38.04	23.08	11.67

Annexure 4

Health – The Position of Sub-centres, PHCs and CHCs in Tribal Areas

S. No.	*State/UT*	*Population in tribal sub-plan areas and in tribal pockets (in Lakhs) according to 1981 Census*		*CHCs*		*PHCs*		*Sub-Centres*		*Period upto which information relates to*
		Total	*Tribal*	*Required*	*In position*	*Required*	*In position*	*Required*	*In position*	
1	2	3	4	5	6	7	8	9	10	11
1.	Andhra Pradesh	27.40	23.00	NA	12	315	115	1400	824	31.3.94
2.	Assam	24.10	13.10	NA	10	121	74	804	445	
3.	Bihar	84.75	40.78	NA	19	489	208	3522	1824	
4.	Gujarat	61.30	58.78	64.00	37	319	227	2126	1929	31.12.95
5.	Himachal Pradesh	1.99	1.33	NA	7	11	17	77	97	31.12.94
6.	Karnataka	63.46	11.23	NA	42	286	291	1850	1850	31.3.94
7.	Kerala	1.60	1.20	NA		55	58	380	131	31.12.94
8.	Madhya Pradesh	150.58	105.30	207.00	95	836	596	5562	4959	31.3.95
9.	Maharashtra	45.23	25.70	68.00	53	272	285	1815	1872	30.6.95
10.	Manipur	4.90	3.90	6.00	6	37	34	236	221	30.6.95
11.	Orissa	63.50	45.30	NA	25	354	349	2300	1485	
12.	Rajasthan	42.58	26.78	37.00	26	167	171	1116	934	31.3.94
13.	Sikkim	0.52	0.35	NA		2	3	10	19	31.3.9

(Contd...)

(...Contd...)

1	2	3	4	5	6	7	8	9	10	11
14.	Tamil Nadu	2.50	2.10	NA	2	12	15	70	111	
15.	Tripura	6.65	4.50	NA	6	30	28	275	250	30.6.94
16.	Uttar Pradesh	43.80	2.30	NA	1	219	189	1381	1376	
17.	West Bengal	117.28	21.35	NA	88	NA	435	946	738	30.9.94
18.	Daman & Diu	0.50	0.10	NA	NIL	NIL	NIL	11	9	31.12.94
19.	A&N Islands	0.40	0.30	2.00	1	4	3	34	29	31.12.94
20.	Meghalaya	13.40	10.80	NA	3	67	45	447	235	
21.	Nagaland	7.80	6.50	NA	3	63	65	418	213	
22.	Arunchal Predesh	6.30	4.40	NA	1	2	2	190	236	
23.	Mizoram	4.90	4.60	NA	6	60	38	314	261	30.9.95
24.	D&N Haveli	1.00	0.80	NA	1	5	5	34	34	
25.	Lakshadweep	0.40	0.40	3.00	3	4	4	18	14	30.9.95

Note: For predominatly tribal States/UTs having no Tribal Sub-Plan separately.
Figures are provisional

Source: Tribal Development Planning Cell, DGHS Ministry of Health & F.W.

References

Commissioner for Scheduled Castes and Scheduled Tribes Report for 1986-87 (Twenty eight Report), Reports for 1987-89 (Twenty Ninth Report)

Danda, Ajit K. (1991), Tribal Economy in India, New Delhi : Inter-India Publications.

Fernandes, W. & V. Paranjpye (1997), 'Hundred Years of Displacement in India' In W. Fernandes and V. Paranjpye (eds.) Rehabilitation Policy & Law in India: A Right to Livelihood. New Delhi: Indian Social Institute.

Government of India (1971), A Statistical Compendium on Scheduled Castes and Scheduled Tribes of Central Zone : Madhya Pradesh & Uttar Pradesh. Bhopal: Ministry of Welfare. 1989 Report of the Working Group on Development and Welfare of Scheduled Tribes during Eighth Five Year Plan. New Delhi: Ministry of Welfare. 2002 Mid-Term Appraisal of Ninth Five Year Plan (1997-2002) New Delhi: Planning Commission. N.D. C.D. Containing Census Data 1992. New Delhi : Registrar General of India.

Gupta, S.P. (1994), Recent economic reforms and their impact on the poor and vulnerable (Mines). New Delhi: National Council of Applied Economic Research.

Krishnan, P.S. (2002), 'Untouchability and atrocities'. In Ghanshyam Shah (ed.) Dalits and the State. New Delhi: Concept Publishing Co. for L.B.S. National Academy for Administration, Mussoorie.

Lieten, G.K. & Ravi, Srivastava (1999), Unequal Partners: Power Relations, Devolution and Development in Uttar Pradesh. New Delhi : Sage

Mungekar, B.L. (1999), 'State, Market and the Dalits: Analytics of the New Economic Policy'. in Modern India-Vision and Values. New Delhi: Vistaar Publications

Mendelsohn, O. and Marick, a Vicziany (1994), The 'Untouchables'. In Mandelsohn O. and Upendra Baxi (eds.) The Rights of Subordinated People. Delhi: Oxford University Press.

Mishra, L. (1994), The Anguish of the Deprived. New Delhi: Har Anand Publications.

Nadkarni, M.V. 1997 'Broad-basing Process in India and Dalits; *Economic and Political Weekly* Aug. 16-23.

Misra, P.K. (1992), 'Oral strategies among the nomadic peoples' The Eastern Anthropologist, 45, No. 3; pp. 215-226.

Saksena, H.S. (1997), 'Uttar Pradesh Mein Vimukta Jatiyon ka Swaroop' Manav (Hindi) Jan-June. 1996 The Scheduled Castes and Scheduled Tribes (Prevention of Atrocities) Act 1989: Implementation in Uttar Pradesh. Report submitted to the Ministry of Welfare Lucknow: Ethnographic & Folk Culture Society.

Saksena, H.S. and Chandra, Sen (1999), Putting People Last – Tribal Displacement and Rehabilitation, New Delhi: Inter India Publications.

Samata (2000), Survivinga Mine field – An Adivasi Triumph. Hyderabad: Samata.

Singh, K.S. (ed.) (1993), The Scheduled Castes: Vol.II People of India: National Series Anthropological Survey of India and Oxford University Press. 1994 The Scheduled Tribes: Vol.III *People of India: National Series*, Anthropological Survey of India Oxford University Press.

Singha-Roy, Debal, K. (Ed.) (2001), Social Development and the Empowerment of Marginalised Groups - Perspectives and Strategies, New Delhi: Sage Publications.

12

Social Dimensions of Long Term Growth: Vision 2020

M. C. VERMA

Economic growth in itself can not be considered the be – all and end – all of development. By its very nature however, it may lead to improvement in social conditions, social justice, reduction of inequality, gender equity, and inclusion of all sections of society in the process of development. That is why the UNDP in 1990 started releasing the Human Development Report to give comparative picture of different UN members countries on various aspects of human development. The social dimensions of structural adjustment have been studied in various institutions like World Bank and UNDP for at least 10-15 years. The appearance of shorter and shorter spans for reaching a certain level of economic prosperity in the countries during the second half of the 20th century gives the impression that more rapid economic development is feasible within a generation itself. Therefore, several visions of a relatively better society have been prepared in various countries within a short span of only twenty years. This paper focuses on the possibilities of social development in India over the next twenty years under various facets and what should be the Vision for different components. Therefore, this will cover multiple variables with gainful employment on the one side and social defence as well as protection of vulnerable groups on the other.

It is important to understand that every society has not one but a series of goals which it wants to achieve within a certain time span. Some of the goals within social development need not be fully supportive of each other and in fact, there could be some contradiction in the series of targets or goals which the society may lay down for itself. However, revolutionary strides in technology and rapid development of the Information Communication Technologies

(ICTs) has necessarily changed the perspectives of societies and the participants living there. Since information on what other societies have been able to achieve is now readily available by a click of a button, the goals or targets which each society may like to give for itself have tended to converge. For example, Universal Elementary Education could have a target laid down to be achieved within the next 50 years say, of the promulgation of the Constitution of India. It would be difficult to convince the public at large and the civil society to wait for 50 years now at the end of 2001. Similar hurry can be noticed in the demand for achievement of targets for replacement level of population, health for all, rehabilitation facilities for the disabled, empowerment of women, total elimination of child labour and protection of all types of minorities. While in the past centuries even the enlightened persons would have been willing to wait for a long time for achievement of such targets, this is no more so. The dangers of environmental degradation, the horrors of terrorism and those of the first and second world war including the nuclear holocausts, more or less make it imperative for national governments and policy makers to try to evolve a path of vary rapid social development.

One of the most serious problems of the 20th century was rapid population growth all over the world but even more so in already populous countries like India. The availability of various technologies to regulate human reproduction is rather recent and so is the situation about many other social components of development. Fortunately, India has been aware of major developments in each of these areas and all the developments of the newer technologies for the service of humanity. It has also tried through its Five Year Plans, at least half-heartedly, to utilize all such technologies, methodologies and ways of organizations of human society during the last 50 years. But it has become clear for some time now that the existing modes of operation and utilization of technologies are not good enough and would not be able to satisfy the urges of ordinary persons and of course, the enlightened sections of Indian society. Therefore, it has become necessary to not only look at what was attempted during the process of planned development but also critically examine what was not achieved despite promises. This makes it even more important that targets of development of different components of social justice are not only revisited but also cross checked with the reality of non-performance under various social heads. Simultaneously, it has become necessary to integrate such goals, targets or larger visions in the process of planned economic development. This paper critically examines each of these components of social development with reference to what has been achieved so far against what was expected and what should be the minimum goals to be achieved over the next 20 years to make sure that citizens of this country at least reach a minimum decent level of social development, social justice or whatever other phrases might be used for judging the performance of a society in the long term.

Demographic Factors – Their Impact on Social Development

One of the basic paradiagms of development in Indian context is the vision of small families for a healthy and wealthy society and achievement of replacement level of fertility as early as possible, in pursuit of population stabilization thereafter. The data from the 2001 census, though not yet available in sufficiently disaggregated forms can be considered both positive and negative for Indian social development – positive in the sense that the rate of growth of population has certainly declined more or less in line with expectation generated by the earlier surveys about fertility and other basic demographic variables. Though the 2001 census data has not been fully digested in the sense of throwing up definitive future projections, say for the year 2021, it does give the impression that the TFR has declined significantly. In the negative sense, the 2001 census figures do not validate all the assumptions and expectations enshrined in the National Population Policy 2000 (NPP 2000). The population figures for 2001 are certainly more than what would have been considered decent by the population policy makers or the national population commission. It was always difficult to believe that all the demographic goals set in the population policy would be achieved without major interventions from the government, the civil society or furies of nature or the three together.

Unlike many other countries, however, the Indian public is not unaware of the environmental degradation, which have already taken place and the difficulties of eking out a living in environmentally difficult tracts of the country. Since in quantitative and percentage terms the levels of migration in India from state to state are not very high for our larger size, the individual families are becoming more and more aware of difficulties generated due to shortages of various environmental resources and other factors which have also suddenly come up on the surface e.g., the awareness of likely HIV/AIDS disaster which has now been accepted as a strong possibility by the enlightened public and the civil society. Therefore, the 2001 census figures should be considered in balance, to be more on the positive side than on the negative and it can be expected that the demographic goals set out for the country as a whole and shown as achievable in a couple of states can be considered as feasible within the other states as well. In other words the demographic transition in the BIMARU States is not an impossibility in the medium to long term.

Trends in fertility, mortality, nutrition and health indicators have been studied in India for a long time. Indian demographers have been valued abroad for their expertise in the art and science of population projections. The same is true about Indian Population Census, which has shown remarkable continuity in the census operation for almost a century. However, the processing of census data, especially at the State and lower levels, takes a long time and adjustments to the census raw figure have to be made, in any case, for under enumeration etc., like everywhere else. Therefore, the Government also undertakes sample surveys to understand family health and other characteristics. These are the nature of sample registration system, RCH rapid household survey, ICMR surveys and of course, National Family Health Surveys, (two rounds already). From this wealth of data it appears that based on 2001 Census provisional results and assuming the same trends in fertility in the future, the population of the country could grow up to 1409 million by the year 2026 and 1345 million in 2021, also utilizing Tim Dyson's projection on life expectancy etc. on account of HIV/AIDS etc. Under this assumption, the four BIMARU States of UP, Bihar, MP & Rajasthan alone would continue to increase their population until 2051, out of the 15 larger states examined in detail by the Population Foundation of India. All other major states would show decline and the group which would start earliest by 2031 will be that of three best performing southern states of Kerala, Karnataka and

Tamil Nadu. There could be other assumptions for making alternative projections of the population, including one based on the NPP 2000 and State Government policies announced by several of them but we do not propose to give all such alternative projections here.

One of the immediate consequences of continuing growth of population linked with reduced fertility rates is increased proportion of older persons 65 plus who constituted just 4.5 per cent in 2001 in the country as a whole. This proportion could rise to as much as 7.8 per cent in 2026 (6.7 per cent in 2021) as per the assumption utilizing NPP 2000 but it could remain as low as 7.4 per cent in 2026 under the first assumption of same trends infertility rate etc. (6.4 per cent in 2021). In this respect, use of alternative assumptions for making projections of population does not make too much of difference to the total population of the older persons in the country as a whole but the situation would differ from state to state and on the basis of different assumptions. This is one category of people who need to be looked after by the society and if their proportion increases too fast, there would be excessive pressure on the working population to share their income with the very old and look after them in respect of health, disability, nutrition and other parameters of good living. On the other hand, if the fertility declines faster as per the assumption under NPP 2000, there would be decline in school going population with the consequent necessity of closing some primary/middle school and reduction in employment of teachers at the school stage as has already happened in Kerala and Tamilnadu.

The 2001 Census results and other data from other surveys, mentioned earlier, throw light on the demographic behaviour of population in greater depth. The last NFHS survey indicated in details the demographically weak districts, mostly located in the BIMARU States plus Orissa, though there are some weak districts in other States as well. If the government intervention in this rather private behaviour pattern could be effective, as it is assumed to be so far, there is every reason for major government interventions in such demographically weak districts i.e., utilizing the base district unit for intervention rather than the state as a whole. With the break up of Bihar into two states, Jharkhand also has sufficiently large number of such weak districts to attend to along with J & K and the North-Eastern States. On the assumption that continued relatively good growth itself would partly reduce fertility levels in association with growth of literacy, our vision of 2020 should include a rapid decline in fertility in these states associated with reduction in illiteracy and increases in the proportion of older persons. To what extent the Central Government could enforce this change of demographic behaviour and to what extent the State Government and civil society and the already educated persons could do so is a matter of details. The additional and new factors arising out of HIV/AIDS pandemic is also a matter of operational details to be worked out between the Central Government, on the one side and the other change agents, on the other. However, rising levels of literacy do not have that direct a correlation with reduction in HIV/AIDS as they have with levels of fertility. Therefore, much more efforts would be required to control the HIV/AIDS pandemic and rising rates of mortality associated with the same. The vision for 2020 would include control over further HIV/AIDS infections and utilization of national and international medical knowledge to provide treatment to those already infected, through use of not only existing three-drug therapy but also utilisation of traditional knowledge on the one side and foreign technical inventions, on the other.

Employment Perspective

Unemployment has been a cause of worry in India for a very long time. However, unemployment is a derivative from the variables Labour Force and Employment. The Planning Commission has had the objective of removing unemployment and severe under-employment right from 1977-78, spread over a period of ten years. This has not happened so far, though the National Development Council in its September 1992 meeting approved the strategy for removal of unemployment and severe under-employment over the next ten years. Recent evidence from NSS surveys indicate that this was not achieved. On the other hand, the 55th round data from the NSS indicates slight increases in the rate of unemployment both for the urban and rural area over the previous survey conducted in 1993-94. The rate of unemployment on the basis of Usual Principal and Subsidiary Status used by the Planning Commission has varied over the years and was perhaps at the highest in the year 1987-88, a drought year. The growth of labour force, on which basis rate of unemployment is calculated, has also varied from survey to survey and was the highest in the initial survey years of 1972-73 to 1977-78. The distribution of employment by industry however, shows considerable evolution over the last 27-28 year, from 1972-73 onwards to 1999-2000. At this stage, the most important indicator of change in the industry distribution is decline of agricultural employment from 74 per cent to around 62 per cent in the latest survey year.

The distribution of employment over different economic activities is generally based on growth of different sectors of economy which is never the same from year to year or from survey to survey. Thus, it is largely but wholly dependant on intra sectoral growth of different sectors. Alternatively or in contradictory terms, employment in national as well as international economies is affected by distribution of labour force by its age-sex-education-training levels. For example, if India did not have a reasonable surplus of educated and trained persons in the IT area, the IT component of the services sector would not have gone up rapidly as seen recently. It could not have also spared lakhs of personnel for employment abroad in the same field. Furthermore, if certain sectors of the economy are not perceived to be doing well the labour force likely to go to those sectors could possible change their educational/skill composition or improve upon the previous base. The inter-play of growth in the various components of labour force is best demonstrated from the experience of urban females' entry into various types of employment in the new economy and thereby raise the labour force participation rate of the urban females as a whole. In this dynamic situation the past rate of unemployment of different sub-categories can at best be considered an approximation to the likely future behaviour of individual components of labour force, broken up by age, sex, residence, education/skill levels.

Since it is expected that much larger proportion of labour force would be residing in the urban area by 2020 and since a large majority of them would have attained educational levels of primary and above, the dynamic behaviour of different components of labour force, mentioned above, would be even more difficult to project over the 20 years, in advance. Already the proportion of educated (matric and above) job seekers through the employment exchanges has gone well beyond 50 per cent and could go even up to 80 per cent, if the experience of metropolitan cities like Delhi can be considered pointer to the future. The recent decline in the observed rate of labour force between 1993-94 and 1999-2000 to as low as 1.03 per cent p.a. may not be terribly accurate but is definitely a pointer to a clear decline in the growth rate. It appears that the Planning Commission is not very sure of this low growth rate and is likely to utilize growth rate of 1.8 per cent p.a. for the purposes of projections of labour force in the Tenth Plan. At this stage, there are no known definite reasons for such a major drop in the growth of labour force in the recent five year survey period and till these factors are fully analyzed and understood, it could only be said that increase in the number of years spent in the educational institutions is a very likely causative factor. Considering that India still has a very low average number of years of education per capita as per the latest HDR, the effect of higher and greater use of educational/skill opportunities is likely to remain with us all through the period up to 2020.

The growth of labour force in the age group 15-29 has to be watched very carefully since the members of this age group display and have displayed in the past rather high rate of unemployment. There is a hypothesis with international experts that unemployment rate continue to grow from the level of illiterates to the level of education below university and it decline thereafter i.e., there is an inverted U-curve to display the pattern of unemployment rate. There is a parallel with the labour force participation for the same educational levels but this is better represented by the U-curve. Recent evidence of unemployment of the educated above secondary level, i.e., degree holder, technical diploma holders and above is quite disconcerting. The technical diploma holders and above are displaying almost the highest rates of unemployment, which are potentially unsustainable. There could be various factors to explain this strange behaviour but non-collection of cost and other expenditure from the beneficiaries of such education from public institutions could certainly be one of them. The other factor of relatively low quality of degree level/technical personnel from most of the institutions is also at work but both the parents and students suffer from what is called 'diploma disease', otherwise explained as 'paper qualification syndrome'. The holders of 'paper qualifications' compete for a limited number of jobs in the market organized labour since the government sector is already showing a decline, this leads to competition for displaying a bigger/higher ability by individual job seeker to the potential employers. There are already a large number of personnel with degree/diploma and the employers are utilizing the certificate basically as a screening mechanism. Therefore, if everyone in the labour market raises his educational profile one notch, the employers remain as uninformed of the potential ability of the candidates as before. The only solution to this syndrome would be to raise the private cost of higher education to the beneficiaries so that every one does not want to accumulate more certificates as a tool of competition for limited jobs in the formal labour market. Most countries, including some developing countries, are moving in that direction and there is no reason to doubt that India will also move in the same direction though with a time lag.

Another factor in a liberalized and pre-dominantly service economy is the share of female employment in the total work force. With continuous decline of employment in agricultural/farming, there is evidence of increase in non-farm sector even in the rural areas/labour force. This tendency of the non-farm sector to grow has been studied for some time and there is no doubt that like in other countries, non-farm sector both in terms of output and employment is growing in our rural areas. An important issue therefore, is quality of work likely to be available in rural areas when the increased availability of education and skills is going to raise the expectations of individual females for better quality work not merely tending of animals, forestry and other traditional occupations other than agricultural. If the economy continues to grow at 6-7-8 per cent p.a. it is likely that the diversification of rural economy would generate a lot of employment opportunities, especially in the service sectors. Since creation of social infrastructure is an accepted goal, both for urban and rural areas, females, especially educated females are likely to get the benefit of the maintenance of social infrastructure, be it health, education or social work, care of aged and disabled and so on. Therefore, there are reasons to believe that the gap between the rate of participation of labour force between sexes would decline overall and more so in the younger age group. The males on the other hand, would have to compete with educated females especially in the service sector and within the sub-sector of 'Community, social and personal' services. This is also because females are likely to accept part-time jobs while males prefer and need full time jobs of a more regular type to be able to support dependents on a sustained basis. The worldwide experience, however, points to significant reduction in manual jobs, a typical preserve of males. The trends are also pointing against any further increase in blue collar jobs of manufacture/transport & related sectors. The livelihood is therefore that of more and more under-employment for the male who would complain and demand a better job whereas the female might not do so aggressively. Many of these hypotheses are based on experiences of economic growth of difference types of economies/countries. Since India is practically open to all new technologies and has voted for ICT's, the direction of growth in India cannot be very different from the emerging market economies like Korea, Malaysia and the industrialized parts of Greater China.

Another macro factor to be taken into consideration is whether the recent reversal of growth of labour force below that of the population would continue all through to 2020 or would it revert to the previous pattern of the labour force growing faster than population. Based on the latest available growth rate of 1.03 per cent, it would be difficult to assume that in the future also there would be much lower growth rate of labour force than population. In fact, the two growth rates might converge closer by the year 2020, as has happened in many developed countries. The other macro factors relate to need for 'Decent work' on the one hand and remunerative work for older people (older than 60 as a general rule), on the other. The ILO has recently examined the issue of quality of work at the international level and has recommended to all ILO members the need to emphasize on better quality work than available so far to the masses. India is expected to fall in line with this emphasis and try its best to provide better quality work to the majority of population over the next 20 years. This would obviously imply better occupational safety and health and less accidents in all the work places. This would naturally include the major occupation of agriculture and related activities where the current Indian work force does not seem to be bothered.

Child Labour

The ILO studies in many places have indicated that replacement of child labour by the adult labour could possibly increase the final cost of product by about 2 per cent but up to a maximum of 5 per cent. Given the fact that the cost of labour as a proportion of total cost of a physical product has continuously fallen while the share of other intermediaries has arisen, on pure economic grounds there is not much justification for continuance of child labour. The country has already passed a law for making elementary education a Fundamental Right for all children in the age group 6-14 years, as already laid down in the Indian Constitution. As the law starts getting implemented, more and more children would be withdrawn systematically from the labour force and brought into school education. Our Vision of the next 20 years could obviously include total elimination of child labour and their participation in elementary education fully. In terms of employment planning, such total elimination would not change the total volume of labour force since by definition the labour force has already eliminated child labour in official calculation. However, once a child reaches Grade 8 or so, the curiosity generated by the educational programmes could possibly push him to go to higher grades and to that extent also reduce the participation rate in the labour force in the higher age group 15-29 years. The Vision 2020 should accommodate such changes in the behaviour of adolescent aged 15 and above.

Older Persons

The question of older persons' participation in work is far more complicated since the life expectancy now is around 64 years and the number of persons above 60 years has already reached 75 millions. It has to be analysed whether all of them are resting or a large proportion is engaged in economic activities. The worldwide projection of persons above 60 years is around 600 millions which could rise to 1100 million by 2025. In India the proportion of older persons i.e. above 65 years is shown to be between 6.4 and 6.7 per cent. In many countries people continue to work till the age 65 and in the Indian rural areas and even in the urban informal sector, there is no retirement age as such. Therefore, a significant proportion of persons above 60 years is already working and, over the next 20 years, this is likely to rise further, implying the need for focusing all the efforts more on the older group of 65+, rather than 60+. The current estimates made by several knowledgeable persons/ organizations indicate that the situation of even the 60+ is rather hopeless, with 40% living below the poverty line, 73 per cent illiterate and 12 million i.e. 16 per cent are blind for want of cataract operation. Over and above the bland figures, is the change in the social system with extended family breaking up into nuclear families. However, the positive picture lies in the fact that almost 80 per cent of the current 60+ are in rural area where the extended family is breaking up more slowly. The problem could however, become acute over the next 20 years even in rural areas if current trends persist and no major interventions take place.

By the year 2020, even if we take the lower figure of 6.4 per cent as the proportion of 65+, the total number is going to be rather significant i.e. over 80 million as against the current year estimate of 75 million of 60+. With continuous degradation of environment and shortages of clean air and water and other environmental resources, it is obvious that this group of over 80 million persons would need special attention, both from the government and the civil society/ younger members of the family. Given the fact that there are no private retirement pension plans and the existing efforts to start them are developing rather slowly, major interventions from the society are required for the benefit of 65+ by 2020. Some points made by the experts are the following:

- Research into the capabilities/disabilities of all such persons.
- Holistic health including development of new disciplines like geriatrics.
- Training of carers, setting up of old age homes and half-way homes etc.
- Organisation of older persons to enable them to demand better facilities.
- New avenues of engaging older persons, whether on payment or as voluntary workers with minimum support and pre-retirement training to assist this programme.
- Effective awareness campaigns to prepare the society to up-keep the older persons and reduction of direct government hand-outs etc.

Some of the recommendations made above are based on experience of Western countries where old age home is the accepted model of delivery of government-funded health care and other facilities. The cost calculations made by other experts however, indicate that the western style of old age home is beyond the means of Indian economy even by the year 2020 and that the community-based approach is likely to be the cost-effective alternative. Even in some developed countries like Japan, the older persons are linked up with very young children which is likely to be more satisfactory than plain dependence on the income earning of the young people through the mechanism of old age homes etc. Since the Indian traditions of *Vanaprashta* and *Sanyas* are not really functional any more in the sense they were visualized, the Government can not possibly withdraw from the care of older persons, but our vision of 2020 should tilt the balance of care to the community and NGO's with whatever tax benefits feasible, and less on direct dependance on the Government itself. However, not enough research and hard data is available to indicate the shares of costs to be borne between the Government and the civil society.

Gender Equity

Another issue relating to employment as well as human development is that of gender equity. It is well known that women suffer from discrimination in the work place whether in the organized or the unorganized sector. It is also well known that within the various occupations and economic activities available, women tend to concentrate on the traditional occupations or those which require less/new technologies and less manual work. The rates of participation of women in the labour force are already much lower in practically all age groups, especially if we focus on main workers. However, in terms of marginal workers, women out-number men significantly but even more than this is the fact that a lot of work done by women is invisible to the accountants of GDP. While many efforts have been made to bring on the surface different types of work which is of economic nature even in the household, the overall GDP figures still do not reflect the true contribution of women to the output of goods and services. However, this is so not only for India but also in most countries, even more in the developing world. At one time, some studies were organized to identify what was called women-prone occupations which showed that in a large number of manual occupations women constituted the dominant proportion, especially coal mining and construction work. Therefore, the picture of developed world about women-related occupations is not true of India now and might not be true even by the year 2020. Unless there is major shift of work force from farming/agriculture to non-farm occupations the continuing discrimination against women in the work place is detrimental to their health needs, apart from educational and personal care needs. It is difficult to visualise to what extent the quality of life for an average woman, leaving aside the matric and higher educated, would improve by the year 2020. It is however very clear that without massive doses of education and skills and improvement in their ability to control reproduction, these improvements would be only minor.

It is already known that intra-family nutrition distribution is against women and children or women and girl children, as against males. The earning male member obviously and naturally gets higher food intake and better care and so also the male child. This discrimination can perhaps be removed without much economic cost in view of the fact that total nutrition availability in the country has surely improved. It is expected that by 2020 the nutritional availability would further improve and therefore, without much economic costs the intra-family distribution of nutrition should also improve. Logically this should lead to lower proportion of low birth babies, lower birth related problems for women, less anaemia and possibly better ability to master new skills, so far kept by the males for themselves. Better regulation of environmental factors and higher availability of better fuel in the rural/poor family, should also lead to less pollution related difficulties for the women working in the kitchens. Better fuel availability should in fact, also reduce the number of hours spent on fuel collection and combustion and therefore, leave more time for personal care/health care. Further, availability of birth attendants for every single birth, registration of births and deaths and child care through the ICDS route should also help in reducing the drudgery and quantity of physical work for women and thereby allow them to participate in better quality work within and outside the household.

While considering the questions of gender equity, one cannot forget the stark differences, which has already come up between states. The Dender Development Index (GDI) prepared by the UNDP places India at the 108th rank amongst 174 countries. However, using the same methodology if similar indexes are prepared for different states, one finds Kerala to be similar to medium-developed countries while the BIMARU states are similar to LDCs in the UN ranking. This means that no simple strategy of development will work for all the states together. One of the important components of the Vision 2020 has therefore to be, reduction of the disparities in the HDI/GDI of different states, which in itself would go someway to reduce discrimination against women in the country as a whole. It has been repeatedly mentioned by experts that priority of planning should be on providing basic infrastructures for life including food/ nutrition security, drinking water, sanitation, other basic needs like health and education and of course, security of life/respect for human rights. The process of awareness generation and education are essential for any efforts towards gender equality. This would for example, include campaign to reverse the low sex ratio in most of the country which is based on gender discrimination at birth or even before birth. Integration of health services in a more coordinated manner would also help in this process towards reduction of anaemia, better nutrition and provision of good health care and feeding practices. In fact, one of the factors working against good nutritional status is the fact of poor food preparation practices which lose a lot of nutrition in the very process of food preparation. Literacy for women is a very important component of all these efforts and it is encouraging to know that there is a good chance that very soon there would be no district with less than 50 per cent female literacy, which appears to be a very important mile stone.

Vulnerable Groups, Including the Disabled and Crime Prone

Every democratic society has to cope up with the care of those who cannot care for themselves un-aided. These include a whole range of people, for example, the handicapped persons either due to visual or hearing or speech or orthopaedic problems and those who are mentally challenged. Another way of looking at the vulnerable sections of society is to examine the whole group of Scheduled Castes, (SCs) Schedule Tribes (STs), socially and educationally backward classes and minorities (OBCs). The last group is that of the crime prone persons or sections of society including groups of families in some parts of the country. While some data is available on the SC and ST groups of population as a result of considerable work over the last century, not much data is available on the persons handicapped due to other factors. Similarly, not much data on the motivation of the crime prone individuals, family or groups is readily available. This shortage of data or poor quality data makes it difficult to develop dependable projections up to 2020. But the Government of India already has a number of institutions and departments whose job it is to analyse the situation of each such group or section of individuals.

The Ministry of Social Justice along with the Rehabilitation Council of India and several other organizations is the most important single ministry to assist in the process of main-streaming the disabled of various kinds, into normal life and participate in all types of activities of a normal society. Over the 1990s the Government of India have enacted new laws and strengthened the legislative framework for assistance to persons with disability, along with specific rehabilitation mechanisms. It is too early to say whether these mechanisms and law/regulation are sufficient for the purpose of main-streaming persons with disability into normal life. But it is already well known that only a few buildings and some transport/ public facilities are actually accessible to the disabled persons. It is obvious that creation of non-handicapping physical environment is an absolutely basic requirement for assisting such persons. Even more, the central initiatives do not get translated well into the state governments' actions and even less at the operational level of districts. For example, rehabilitation services as per the relevant Act should have been able to reach each district through 'district rehabilitation centre' which must work as a single-window facilitation center for all requirement of persons with disabilities. The percentage of persons with obvious disability has been estimated at about 5 per cent by the NSSO/Central ministry but at the junior school level, in most of the European countries, children with this disability are known to be around 8 per cent of total students. It must also be mentioned that though 'integrated education' has been the favourite theme at the school level for a couple of decades, the actual number of students who are able to take advantage of integrated education is much less. There are cultural factors at work against persons with obvious disabilities in a tradition-ridden society like India which might explain the relatively lower number of persons picked up in the NSS survey in 1991. Even worse, many parents would not like to admit that their wards are disabled. There are now newer afflictions at work also, including HIV/AIDS, drug abuse and road accidents, which are likely to increase continuously. Finally, mental illness is hardly diagnosed in a traditional society whether rural and urban, and mental disorders tend to be ignored even by the educated persons for a long time.

The Vision for 2020 for the disabled is obviously that of creation of an environment where preventable diseases and disability are prevented while those which are not preventable, are handled with sensitivity, sympathy and best available medical knowledge. From this angle it is clear that India has a very long way to go since we have serious problems due to various diseases, lack of sanitation, poor drinking water, poor care of expectant mothers including poor nutrition and bias against those born with a disability and against the girl child. As regards attention to persons already suffering from disability including self-made disability arising out of drug abuse, the institutional care available is very minor and does not really reach the remote parts of even normal districts. Over and above the cultural factors and in-appropriate traditions, there is a problem of finding sufficient funds for looking after the disabled persons, despite a variety of organizations and ministries/departments in various governments. It has been suggested that at least 5 per cent Plan outlay should be earmarked for expenditure on such disabled persons, national or state level. It has also been visualized that there would be a single window delivery system up to '*Gram Panchayat*' level and convergence of various ministries/department looking after the disabled persons, one way or the other. The system of special school, clinic, home based learning, institutional care for the drug-dependents, and so on, is obviously too costly for a country with our per capita income and therefore, alternative modes of delivery of care have to be developed through the community NGOs and even Gram Panchayats but under the overall scientific and technical guidance of the state level apparatus.

Other Vulnerable Groups

As for the groups of SC, ST and OBCs, considerable work has been done by various government organizations and various Commissions have been set up under the Constitution to supervise all such government funded actions. However, it has to be admitted that most of the benefits of development out of government funds have not spread widely across the entire spectrum of SCs or STs and of course, OBCs (action in their regard has been relatively recent). It has also been recognized by now, right up to the level of Supreme Court that a lot of benefit of reservation of jobs and facilities or school places has been appropriated by the creamy layers of such groups. The development of SCs, STs and OBCs has therefore to be seen in this larger context of a huge variety of situations under which individual castes or tribes might be labouring. However, it is difficult to work out separate caste or tribe-specific operational strategies since this could be struck down in the Courts. A number of studies have been made on what type of castes or tribes have been left out from availing the major benefits flowing from central government funds and it is possible that some non-justiciable interventions could be made in their favour, in comparison to other castes/tribes also covered under the heading SC-ST. As regards the OBCs, the experience available is not good enough to demand any major change of government approach to their development but it must be noticed that the demands to be categorised as an OBC in the hope of government employment is now self defeating in a liberal or liberalizing Indian economy. This is because most of the wealth formation is now expected to take place outside the Government and in fact, at the national level the number of government jobs is now on a declining trend. Even if some of states are not yet on this trend, they are most likely to be so by 2020 and therefore, such states have also to find other means of assisting the individual SCs, STs and OBCs.

Minorities

The government also has the responsibility of assistance to the minorities including Muslims, Christians, Sikhs, Buddhists and Zoroastrians. They together account for 17 or more per cent of national population and there are 142 districts in the country which have in their population more than 20 per cent minorities. In a liberalizing economy the government has not too many intervention mechanisms to assist them economically but they can still be assisted through various programmes like:

- Area intensive programme for educationally backward minorities.
- Financial assistance for modernising the Madarsa education.
- Community polytechnics in minority concentration area.
- Setting up of a corporation – NMDFC.
- Coaching classes for competitive exams.
- Setting up the Maulana Azad Educational Foundation with a corpus.

The current government thinking is to assist the minorities through education including technical education, special attention to their health and housing needs and priority sector lending in their favour etc. especially to artisan and handloom weaver etc. where the minorities have concentration in many parts of the country. The vision for 2020 in respect of minorities, therefore, has to be almost total equality of opportunities in education, technical/vocational training, coaching for employment, health and family welfare, PDS, other components of minimum needs/poverty alleviation programme and finally, confidence building to make them equal members of a multi-cultural, multi-religion country. Since government intervention mechanisms are limited in a liberal economy, it is obvious that Vision 2020 would assign greater responsibility to the civil society, NGOs and to the already existing public institutions in the field of human development.

Social Defence

Though India is not a high crime society and respect for law in the general public is still high, there is a rising trend in various type of crimes practically all over the country. However, the reported crime numbers or crime rates always remain much lower than the reality and over and above this is the failure of the criminal justice system to track down crimes firstly and then to give them proper punishment in good time so as to act as a deterrent to other criminals. It is feared that with the spread/availability of ICTs and rapid economic growth, organized crime could acquire a more volitional and disruptive form, along side emergence of terrorism, environment crimes and now cyber crimes. It is also feared that rapid economic growth in many parts of the country could create imbalances and disparities between the rich and the poor. The growth of slum and unauthorized colonies in practically all the cities and un-regulated urbanization itself tends to encourage a smart persons with criminal tendencies to develop crime in an organized way, be it drug trafficking, prostitution or trafficking in women and children. Therefore, the potential of growth of crime and criminals in India by the 2020 is truly high. Given the fact that India is considered to be a poorly governed or at least a soft state, organization of crime or crime syndicates appears to be easier than before.

The existence of stark poverty in many groups of society, the patent discrimination against SCs and STs and other lower castes is itself a factor for growth of crime. While we have a whole range of civil society group, NGOs and human rights activities, the basic component of social justice are still not fully in place. The feeling of discrimination is further aggravated by ability of the relatively rich to avoid taxes and commit other economic offences without commensurate punishment. The economic and social marginal of poor also adds to the growth of diseffective children, adolescence and young adults who are frustrated with their lot. There are however, a number of new laws to protect against the atrocious on the vulnerable sections of society and children and happily, the upper judiciary is proactive in enforcing the provision of such laws and regulations.

In the back drop of a rapidly changing crime situation experts feels that a correlation strategy, widespread reform in the prison system and that of juvenile justice are not only required urgently but could be even useful in improving modification for good economic growth. It is noticed that public participation in prevention of crime as well as in treatment and rehabilitation of offender is highly desirable. In the light of low per capita income, this is perhaps more effective than the Western style and reforms of the prison system and similar other facilities. The United Nations has given a lot of thought and made recommendation toward utilizing the non-custodial system for the purpose where the civil society, relevant NGOs, community policing and voluntary efforts would play a much higher role than before. It is however, distraught to note that very few organization are active in the work of main-streaming of social deviants/criminal. The vision for 2020 has therefore, to include large scale involvement of the civil society through tax incentive on the one side and technical/judicial support from the other. This would be in addition to raising the number of judges and speeding criminal judicious system by provision of additional funds, utilization of IT and of course, widespread reform of the existing system prison/correctional home etc.

Concluding remarks

The examination of various social dimensions in the light of expected rapid growth of the economy must be seen the large context of a relatively secure society and peace at the national border. India with its vast land and maritime borders, is already committed to additional resource for national defence. This has become urgent in the light of terrorist attacks of September 11, which has bought turbulence and instability close to our hilly borders and perhaps, to the entire country. The government is already redefining its approach in the light of these developments but it is difficult to cover in this short paper the likely scenario for national defence in the year 2020 to ensure peace and all over borders. It is, however, necessary to point out that human development in all its dimension should continue to remain highest strategic priority in the forceable future.

This paper utilize the materials and analyses contained in the following papers presented in the various meeting of the Group on Vision 2020.

1. Population projections of India and the larger states based on 2001 census results by K. Srinivasan.
2. Child Labour by Swami Agnivesh.
3. Vision 2020 Older persons.
4. Issues concerning vulnerable groups by H. S. Saksena.
5. Social defence by Dr. Hira Singh.
6. The profile of the empowered woman by Dr. Sarala Gopalan.
7. Vision of Peace for 2020 by Air Commodore Jasjit Singh.
8. Employment Perspective by LEM Division, Planning Commission.
9. Population Growth in 21st century by K. S. Natarajan.
10. Disabled persons by Gauri Chatterjee.
11. Trends in Fertility, mortality, nutrition and Health indicator by Dr. Padam Singh.

13

Infrastructure Financing and Emerging Pattern of Urbanisation: Vision 2020

AMITABH KUNDU

1. Introduction

Large sections of planners and policy makers in the country have argued that there exists no serious problem of infrastructural deficiency that can not be tackled through management solutions. All that is needed is to restructure the system of governance, legal and administrative framework in a manner that the standard reform measures can be implemented. Reduction of public sector intervention, ensuring appropriate prices for infrastructure and civic amenities through elimination or reduction of subsidies, development of capital market for resource mobilisation, facilitating private and joint sector projects, simplification of legislative system to bring about appropriate land use changes and location of economic activities etc. are being advocated as the remedial package (World Bank 1995, Expert Group on Commercialisation of Infrastructure 1996, World Bank 1998).

The public sector and other para-statal agencies that had been assigned the responsibility of producing and distributing infrastructural facilities have come in for sharp criticism on grounds of inefficiency, lack of cost effectiveness, resulting in continued dependence on grants for sustenance. Some kind of "financial discipline" has already been imposed by the government and Reserve Bank of India, forcing these agencies to generate resources internally and borrow from development cum banking institutions, and, in a few cases, from capital market at a fairly high interest rate. This has restricted their areas of functioning and, what is more important, changed the thrust of activities.

Solutions are being found also in terms of their efficient, transparent and decentralised management of the facilities. With the passing of the 74th Amendment to Indian Constitution (Ministry of Urban Development 1992) and corresponding legislations, amendments, ordinances etc. at the state level, decentralisation has become the keyword in governance. The vacuum created by the limited withdrawal of the state in the provision of infrastructure is sought to be filled up also through non-governmental organisations (NGOs) and community based organisations (CBOs), besides the local authorities.

The enthusiasm for the above package of "management solutions", both among the international as also national organisations, is responsible for the issues concerning their impact on settlement structure and access of the poor to the infrastructural amenities not receiving adequate attention among researchers. However, given the disparity in economic strength of the towns and cities and their unequal access to capital market and public institutions, this perspective would enable the larger cities to corner much of the advantage from the system. Also, large sections of urban poor are likely to be priced out of the formal systems of service delivery. A few researchers have pointed out that the indifference on the part of policy makers on these issues would institutionalise inequality in infrastructural facilities and accentuate disparity in the levels of economic development.

In the light of the dominant perspective and criticisms thereof, as discussed above, the present paper overviews the recent initiatives for resource mobilisation for infrastructural investment and analyses their impact on the structure of settlements, access of poor to infrastructural facilities and process of segmentation within the cities. The analysis has been done by taking into consideration the recent changes in labour and capital market and land management development practices.

The second section in the paper analyses the shift from budgetary support to institutional finance for infrastructure development and discusses the new arrangements for mobilising resources, in the wake of the strategy of economic liberalisation and the changes in urban governance as a consequence of the 74th Constitutional Amendment. Assigning contracts to private agencies for providing infrastructural services has also been examined critically. Furthermore, infrastructure development/improvement projects being implemented by NGOs and local communities within a participatory framework have also been evaluated. The third section overviews the scenario of infrastructure financing likely to emerge in the next couple of decades and its impact on the deficiency of amenities across states and size classes. In the last section, an attempt has been made to put forward a perspective for infrastructural development that can bring about a balanced regional development in the country and fulfill other socio-economic objectives to which the country stands committed through the Constitution and Directive Principles of State Policy. It also outlines a strategy for intervention that can help in attaining the objectives.

2. Financing Infrastructure Development: Recent Trends and Institutional Initiatives

Budgetary Support and Institutional Borrowings

The system of managing and financing infrastructural facilities has been changing significantly since the mid-Eighties. The Eighth Plan (1992-97) envisaged cost recovery to be built into the financing system. This has further been reinforced during the Ninth Plan period (1997-2002) with a substantial reduction in budgetary allocations for infrastructure development. A strong case has been made for making the public agencies accountable and financially viable. Most of the infrastructure projects are to be undertaken through institutional finance rather than budgetary support. The state level organisations responsible for providing infrastructural services, metropolitan and other urban development agencies are expected to make capital investments on their own, besides covering the operational costs for their infrastructural services. The costs of borrowing have gone up significantly for all these agencies over the years. This has come in their way of taking up schemes that are socially desirable but are financially unremunerative. Projects for the provision of water, sewerage and sanitation facilities etc., that generally have a long gestation period and require a substantial component of subsidy, have, thus, received a low priority in this changed policy perspective.

Housing and Urban Development Corporation (HUDCO), set up in the Sixties by the Government of India to support urban development schemes, had tried to give an impetus to infrastructural projects by opening a special window in the late Eighties. Availability of loans from this window, generally at less than the market rate, was expected to make state and city level agencies, including the municipalities, borrow from HUDCO. This was more so for projects in cities and towns with less than a million population since their capacity to draw upon internal resources was limited.

HUDCO finances even now up to 70 per cent of the costs in case of public utility projects and social infrastructure. For economic and commercial infrastructure, the share ranges from 50 per cent for the private agencies to 80 per cent for public agencies. The loan is to be repaid in quarterly installments within a period of 10 to 15 years, except for the private agencies for whom the repayment period is shorter. The interest rates for the borrowings from HUDCO vary from 15 per cent for utility infrastructure of the public agencies to 19.5 per cent for commercial infrastructure of the private sector. The range is much less than what used to be at the time of opening the infrastructure window by HUDCO. This increase in the average rate of interest and reduction in the range is because its average cost of borrowing has gone up from about seven per cent to 14 per cent during the last two and a half decade.

Importantly, HUDCO loans were available for upgrading and improving the basic services in slums at a rate lower than the normal schemes in the early Nineties. These were much cheaper than under similar schemes of the World Bank. However, such loans are no longer available. Also, earlier the Corporation was charging differential interest rates from local bodies in towns and cities depending upon their population size. For urban centres with less than half a million population, the rate was 14.5 per cent; for cities with population between half to one million, it was 17 per cent; and for million plus cities, it was 18 per cent. No special concessional rate was, however, charged for the towns with less than a hundred or fifty thousand population that are in dire need of infrastructural improvement, as discussed above. It is unfortunate, however, that even this small bias in favour of smaller cities has now been given up. Further, HUDCO was financing up to 90 per cent of the project cost in case of infrastructural schemes for "economically weaker sections" which, too, has been discontinued in recent years.

HUDCO was and continues to be the premiere financial institution for disbursing loans under the Integrated Low Cost Sanitation Scheme of the government. The loans as well as the subsidy components for different beneficiary categories under the scheme are released through the Corporation. The amount of funds available through this channel has gone down drastically in the Nineties.

Given the stoppage of equity support from the government, increased cost of resource mobilisation, and pressure from international agencies to make infrastructural financing commercially viable, HUDCO has responded by increasing the average rate of interest and bringing down the amounts advanced to the social sectors. Most significantly, there has been a reduction in the interest rate differentiation, designed for achieving social equity.

An analysis of infrastructural finances disbursed through HUDCO shows that the development authorities and municipal corporations that exist only in larger urban centres have received more than half of the total amount. The agencies like Water Supply and Sewerage Boards and Housing Boards, that have the entire state within their jurisdiction, on the other hand, have received altogether less than one third of the total loans. Municipalities with less than a hundred thousand population or local agencies with weak economic base often find it difficult to approach HUDCO for loans. This is so even under the Central government schemes like the Integrated Development of Small and Medium Towns, routed through HUDCO, that carry a subsidy component. These towns are generally not in a position to obtain state government's guarantee due to their uncertain financial position. The Central government and the Reserve Bank of India have proposed restrictions on many of the states for giving guarantees to local bodies and para-statal agencies, in an attempt to ensure fiscal discipline. Also, the states are being persuaded to register a fixed percentage of the amount guaranteed by them as a liability in their accounting system. More importantly, in most of the states, only the para-statal agencies and municipal corporations have been given state guarantee with the total exclusion of smaller municipal bodies. Understandably, getting bank guarantee is even more difficult, specially, for the urban centres in less developed states and all small and medium towns.

The Infrastructure Leasing and Financial Services (ILFS), established in 1989, is coming up as an important financial institution in recent years. It is a private sector financial intermediary wherein the Government of India owns a small equity share. Its activities have more or less remained confined to development of industrial-townships, roads and highways where risks are comparatively less. It basically undertakes project feasibility studies and provides a variety of financial as well as engineering services. Its role, therefore, is that of a merchant banker rather than of a mere loan provider so far as infrastructure financing is considered and its share in the total infrastructural finance in the country remains limited.

ILFS has helped local bodies, para-statal agencies and private organisations in preparing feasibility reports of commercially viable projects, detailing out the pricing and cost recovery mechanisms and establishing joint venture companies called Special Purpose Vehicles (SPV). Further, it has become equity holders in these companies along with other public and private agencies, including the operator of the BOT project (Mathur 1999). The role of ILFS may, thus, be seen as a promoter of a new perspective of development and a participatory arrangement for project financing. It is trying to acquire the dominant position for the purpose of influencing the composition of infrastructural projects and the system of their financing in the country.

Mention must be made here of the Financial Institutions Reform and Expansion (FIRE) programme, launched under the auspices of the USAID. Its basic objective is to enhance resource availability for commercially viable infrastructure projects through the development of domestic debt market. Fifty per cent of the project cost is financed from the funds raised in US capital market under Housing Guaranty Fund. This has been made available for a long period of thirty years at an interest rate of six per cent, thanks to the guarantee from the US-Congress. The risk involved in the exchange rate fluctuation due to the long period of capital borrowing is being mitigated by a swapping arrangement through the Grigsby Bradford and Company and Government Finance Officers' Association for which they would charge an interest rate of six to seven per cent. The interest rate for the funds from US market, thus, does not work out as much cheaper than that raised internally.

The funds under the programme are being channelled through ILFS and HUDCO who are expected to raise a matching contribution for the project from the domestic debt market. A long list of agenda for policy reform pertaining to urban governance, land management, pricing of services etc. have been proposed for the two participating institutions. For providing loans under the programme, the two agencies are supposed to examine the financial viability or bankability of the projects. This, it is hoped, would ensure financial discipline on the part of the borrowing agencies like private and public companies, municipal bodies, para-statal agencies etc. as also the state governments that have to stand guarantee to the projects. The major question, here, however is whether funds from these agencies would be available for social sectors schemes that have a long gestation period and low commercial viability.

Institutional funds are available also under Employees State Insurance Scheme and Employer's Provident Fund. These have a longer maturity period and are, thus, more suited for infrastructure financing. There are, however, regulations requiring the investment to be channeled in government securities and other debt instruments in a "socially desirable" manner. Government, however, is seriously considering proposals to relax these stipulations so that the funds can be made available for earning higher returns, as per the principle of commercial profitability.

There are several international actors that are active in the infrastructure sector like the Governments of United Kingdom (through Department for International Development), Australia and Netherlands. These have taken up projects pertaining to provision of infrastructure and basic amenities under their bilateral co-operation programmes. Their financial support, although very small in comparison with that coming from other agencies discussed below, has generally gone into projects that are unlikely to be picked up by private sector and may have problems of cost recovery. World Bank, Asian Development Bank, OECF (Japan), on the other hand, are the agencies that have financed infrastructure projects that are commercially viable and have the potential of being replicated on a large scale. The share of these agencies in the total funds into infrastructure sector is substantial. The problem, here, however, is that the funds have generally been made available when the borrowing agencies are able to involve private entrepreneurs in the project or mobilise certain stipulated amount from the capital market. This has proved to be a major bottleneck in the launching of a large number of projects. Several social sector projects have failed at different stages of formulation or implementation due to their long pay back period and uncertain profit potential. These projects also face serious difficulties in meeting the conditionalities laid down by the international agencies.

Borrowings by State Government and Public Undertakings from Capital Market

A strong plea has been made for mobilising resources from the capital market for infrastructural investment. Unfortunately, there are not many projects in the country that have been perceived as commercially viable, for which funds can easily be lifted from the market. The weak financial position and revenue sources of the state undertakings in this sector make this even more difficult. As a consequence, innovative credit instruments have been designed to enable the local bodies tap the capital market.

Bonds, for example, are being issued through institutional arrangements in such a manner that the borrowing agency is required to pledge or escrow certain buoyant sources of revenue for debt servicing. This is a mechanism by which the debt repayment obligations are given utmost priority and kept independent of the overall financial position of the borrowing agency. It ensures that a trustee would monitor the debt servicing and that the borrowing agency would not have access to the pledged resources until the loan is repaid.

The most important development in the context of investment in infrastructure and amenities is the emergence of credit rating institutions in the country. With the financial markets becoming global and competitive and the borrowers' base increasingly diversified, investors and regulators prefer to rely on the opinion of these institutions for their decisions. The rating of the debt instruments of the corporate bodies, financial agencies and banks are currently being done by the institutions like Information and Credit Rating Agency of India (ICRA), Credit Analysis and Research (CARE) and Credit Rating Information Services of India Limited (CRISIL) etc. The rating of the urban local bodies has, however, been done so far by only CRISIL, that too only since 1995-96.

Given the controls of the state government on the borrowing agencies, it is not easy for any institution to assess the "functioning and managerial capabilities" of these agencies in any meaningful manner so as to give a precise rating. Furthermore, the "present financial position" of an agency in no way reflects its strength or managerial efficiency. There could be several reasons for the revenue income, expenditure and budgetary surplus to be high other than its administrative efficiency. Large sums being received as grants or as remuneration for providing certain services could explain that. The surplus in the current or capital account can not be a basis for cross-sectional or temporal comparison since the user charges permitted by the state governments may vary.

More important than obtaining the relevant information, there is the problem of choosing a development perspective. The rating institutions would have difficulties in deciding whether to go by measures of financial performance like total revenue including grants or build appropriate indicators to reflect managerial efficiency. One can possibly justify the former on the ground that for debt servicing, what one needs is high income, irrespective of its source or managerial efficiency. This would, however, imply taking a very short-term view of the situation. Instead, if the rating agency considers level of managerial efficiency, structure of governance or economic strength in long-term context, it would be able to support the projects that may have debt repayment problems in the short run but would succeed in the long run. The indicators that it may then consider would pertain to the provisions in state legislation regarding decentralisation, stability of the government in the city and the state, per capita income of the population, level of industrial and commercial activity etc. All these have a direct bearing on the prospect of increasing user charges in the long run. The body, for example, would be able to generate higher revenues through periodic revision of user-charges, if per capita income levels of its residents are high.

The rating agencies have, indeed, taken a medium or long-term view, as may be noted from the Rating Reports of various public undertakings in the recent past. These have generally based their rating on a host of quantitative and qualitative factors, including those pertaining to the policy perspective at the state or local level and not simply a few measurable indicators[1]. The only problem is that it has neither detailed out all these factors nor specified the procedures by which the qualitative dimensions have been brought within the credit rating framework, without much ambiguity.

Political Decentralisation and Investment in Infrastructure and Basic Services by Local Bodies

The resource scarcity being faced by the central and state governments and the consequent reduction of current and capital expenditures on infrastructure and social sectors in recent years have created serious uncertainty with regard to provision of basic amenities, particularly to the poor. Earlier, the role of central and state governments in local affairs was not clearly defined. It consisted of ad hoc and fragmented efforts at programmatic level. Since mid Eighties, however, a process of shifting the responsibility to the local level has manifested clearly. Political decentralisation through Constitutional Amendment Act has been hailed as a panacea for the problems of infrastructural deficiency in urban centres. It is argued that the Act enables the local bodies to undertake planning and development responsibility as also mobilise resources for infrastructural investment.

Transferring of responsibilities to local bodies, without examining their economic base and resource raising capacity or making provision of adequate transfer of funds, may, however, have serious consequences. Several studies suggest that there exists significant disparity in the income levels of local bodies and its

---

1. It has been argued that the outlook for the finances of the Corporation, in the medium term, is positive as it "has been able to upgrade the tax administration framework. In the long run, the Corporation's ability to implement the proposed property tax reforms would further strengthen the tax base of the Corporation. In addition, the Corporation has initiated efforts to diversify its revenue base by undertaking activities like commercial property development. These efforts are expected to be supported by the political and administrative wing at the state level ———The prevailing policy framework would have to be sustained to achieve the desired results" (Credit Rating Information Services of India Limited 1996).

various components across size class of urban centres. A study by the National Institute of Public Finance and Policy (NIPFP 1995) reveals that the per capita (own) revenue for D Class cities, having population above five hundred thousand, was more than three and a half times that of A class towns, having population below one hundred thousand, in the early Nineties. The tax and non-tax revenue together constituted 90 per cent of the total revenue in case of the former while the figure for the latter was 70 per cent only. Correspondingly, the percentage share of grants in total revenue for the D class cities was only five per cent while that for the lower class towns was as high as 18 per cent. The high dependence on external grants for the smaller towns would be a major handicap in their undertaking the development responsibility on their own[2]. One may, thus, argue that the larger cities are financially stronger and can take up public works and social infrastructure projects on their own which is not so for smaller towns.

The NIPFP study unfortunately does not give further break-ups for the towns falling in A class by considering the size classification followed by the Population Census. Also, the sample does not include many towns with less than 50,000 population and none with less than 10,000. When these towns are included in the sample, the disparity in revenue earnings across size class of urban centres would work out as much sharper (National Institute of Urban Affairs 1983). A large majority of these towns have come to depend increasingly on grants-in-aid, primarily due to their poor economic base and incapacity to mobilise adequate tax and non-tax revenues. With the decline in central or state assistance in recent years, it is not surprising that most of these towns do not make any investment for improving infrastructure and basic services. This has compounded their problems of inadequacy of basic amenities.

People in small and medium towns in the country, particularly those with less than 50,000 population, have low per capita income due to lack of employment opportunities in the organised sector, low incidence of other secondary activities, poverty induced growth of

2. The capacity of these smaller towns becomes further restricted since about twenty per cent of their total expenditure is on general administration as compared to a figure of 12 per cent for D class cities.

tertiary employment etc. Instability in their economy is reflected in high fluctuation/variation in their demographic growth over time as also across regions, as noted above. Understandably, many among the small and medium towns are not in a position to invest funds for development of civic amenities. The Constitutional Amendment, making the civic bodies increasingly dependent on their own tax and non-tax resources, would further increase the disparity in the level of services and economic infrastructure across size class of urban centres. This would adversely affect the level of basic services in these towns and their capacity to absorb future growth of population or attract new economic activities.

In an era, wherein obtaining funds for investment from private sector or capital market has become the critical factor, it is not surprising that the exercises of preparing Master Plans have been thoroughly discredited. Indeed, the city level Master Plans in recent years have been referred to more for violation than for compliance since no fund is available for their implementation. Given this emerging scenario, the option of going for project preparation in formal or informal consultation with the stake-holders through the intermediation of the financial institutions, seems to be an easy way out. This, the local governments in large cities would find hard to resist. It must, however, be pointed out that preparing a Master Plan to answer the needs and aspirations of local people (in different social and income brackets) and then breaking it down to a set of meaningful projects is a different exercise from that of identifying projects with high credit rating that would attract corporate investment. Assigning the responsibility of development planning to local bodies, thus, does not automatically enable them to design projects, based on a macro perspective for the town or region. The data available at the micro level are not adequate to support the optimism that the Amendment would indeed enhance the resources, particularly of the local bodies and enhance their capacity to invest in infrastructure.

Obtaining a hefty loan from capital market or even an international organisation may lead to disempowerment of local bodies. Sanctioning of the loan has been subject to the latter maintaining budgets of the sectors receiving the funds separate from the general budget. Bombay Municipal Corporation, for example, was obliged to maintain water supply and sewerage budget on accrual basis while the other budgets of the corporation are maintained on cash basis. This was the pre-condition for getting the World Bank loan under the International Development Assistance credit scheme. Similarly, a study on Pune Municipal Corporation under the FIRE project, proposes a budgeting discipline for the local bodies such that they maintain separate accounts for not merely capital and current expenditures but also for different set of sectors (Mehta and Satyanarayana 1996). Proposals have been put forward for revising the user charges along with the norms for sectoral transfers such that a group of sectors can become independent of the general municipal budget. This is considered necessary for attracting capital investments in future years.

Land as a Source of Infrastructure Financing

Many of the state governments are trying to create a few "global centres of the future" while the city governments are engaged in competition with their counterparts, within the state or country, to grow up to that stature by attracting private corporate investment. The prospective global cities, however, face a major problem in attracting local or international investment in infrastructural facilities. The problem is that of scarcity of land within the central city and other prime locations wherein such facilities are in high demand. An ingenious method has been worked out to solve the problem. The agencies like World Bank, USAID etc. have recommended that the Floor Space Index (FSI) in the central areas of the city should be increased so that multi-storied structures can come up, providing space for business houses, commercial activities and high income residential units. The policy of giving permission for vertical growth at a high price or selling of extra FSI in central and business districts has been welcomed by many local bodies also as an easy way of generating resources for infrastructural development. There is further incentive to this since sanctioning of loans by the international agencies is often contingent on the acceptance of a higher FSI in the central city. This has led to creation of a few high-density business and high-income residential districts and pushing out of the households that can not afford the costs.

Land is provided for infrastructural facilities and upcoming industrial and commercial houses through government intervention as also by activating the land market. Steps are taken to facilitate changes in land-use pattern through simplification of legal and administrative procedures and enabling the market to push "low valued" activities out of the city core. The low income and slum colonies are the obvious candidates for relocation in city peripheries. The shift is carried out by the state or local governments, often directly through eviction of slum dwellers, hawkers, pavement dwellers etc. Sometimes, it is done indirectly and discreetly through slum improvement schemes, "rehabilitating" them outside the city limits. Unfortunately, that has been done mostly without making any provision for alternate employment opportunities for the displaced workers[3]. This has led to high disparity in population density, quality of life and segmentation of the cities into rich and poor colonies.

Management Contracts for Provision of Services by Private Agencies

Widening gaps between demand and supply of infrastructural services have necessitated involvement of private sector and designing of alternate institutional arrangements. Different forms of participation have been worked out for investment and management of the services, with varying levels of responsibility and cost sharing between private and public agencies[4]. The most commonly used form is contracting out the tasks of capacity creation, production, distribution and management of one or a set of services to private companies for certain period. It has been argued that this would result in substantial cost saving and, at the same time, make it possible for the companies to conduct their business with profit.

In order to ensure that the contractual agreements with private or joint sector companies are executed, supervised or monitored under strict regulatory control, new regulatory/supervisory arrangements are being proposed. Under the old system of state control, the public

3. Some of the government schemes do have a provision for giving the evicted slum dwellers plots or flats, in the building being constructed at the original site. It is, nonetheless, erroneous to believe that such allottees would be able to hold on to them for a long time, given their acute need for finance, growing land values and relaxation in legal and administrative environment.

4. The arrangements are described as Build Operate Own and Transfer (BOOT), Build Operate and Transfer (BOT), Build and Transfer (BT) etc. depending on the nature of agreement with the private companies.

agencies had failed in meeting the social objectives and catering to the needs of the poor. Designing and implementing the regulatory controls in a liberalised regime is, therefore, far more challenging, in case we are serious about these objectives. Importantly, UNCHS has launched an Urban Management Programme (UMP), with offices in many developing countries including India, for creating an enabling environment for such participatory management practices and assist the local bodies in drawing up terms and conditions of the contracts, involving community participation in management. Besides, it facilitates the local bodies in establishing contacts with possible participating companies and often conducts negotiations on their behalf.

These moves in urban areas have had some success as a number of cities have come forward to institutionalise such contractual arrangements. It may, however, be pointed out that a number of companies being engaged in the provision of the services and their making profits or local bodies reducing their financial burden through privatisation of services are by themselves no indication of success of the arrangement. Such a judgement is possible only after the issues concerning quality of the services and, more importantly, the coverage of the urban poor have been analysed in a rigorous manner.

It is difficult to empirically determine the benefits and costs of this privatisation move, as it is a recent phenomenon. Reliable data on revenue and expenditure of local bodies before and after the sub-contracting arrangement or the profitability of the private agencies are yet not available. The critical information in this context would, however, be with regard to the quality of the services and the coverage of the vulnerable sections of the city population, as noted above. Unfortunately, there exists no database covering these aspects at national, state or local level. These would have to be obtained through field survey at the micro level. It is nonetheless very surprising that none of the studies conducted in connection with privatisation of services or subcontracting arrangements has attempted to focus on these aspects seriously.

An overview of studies on the contractual agreements through their progress reports and other official documents reveals that there have been problems even in operationalising the working arrangements and norms for day to day functioning even at the stage of capital investment. This is largely because India does not have much experience of partnership arrangements in the field of urban infrastructure. Many have got trapped in serious difficulties after the formal launching of the projects. In Vadodara, for example, the Municipal Corporation had worked out an arrangement with a private company to make pellets from waste, to be used as fuel. Unfortunately, the company faced serious difficulties in establishing working arrangements with the local bodies and had to finally close down its unit. Similar difficulties have been encountered in a number of other projects.

Solid waste management is one service where the local bodies have shown interest in involving the private sector. The method of collection often involves participation of citizens' groups and non-governmental organisations (NGOs). Many groups have shown willingness to spare time or money for an improved system of garbage disposal, which is behind the success stories coming from a number of cities. There is, however, no reason to believe that the coverage of the poor areas or households through basic amenities would increase after a private company takes over the responsibility. There have been demands from the companies to hike the user charges commensurate with inflation and even more. But the low income and slum colonies have resisted such moves, resulting in their exclusion from the private sector based delivery system. In such a situation, the people in these localities have not been able to raise their voices or complain against the municipal body as the latter would take the plea of passing on the responsibility to an outside agency. This has led to fragmentation of responsibility of service delivery, with marginalised areas/people remaining under serviced or unserviced, as noted above. As a consequence, there has been serious health risk for the entire urban community that may result in breaking of epidemics from time to time.

Involving Community in Infrastructure Development

Community participation in urban development projects has a history dating back to the early seventies when Urban Basic Service Programme was launched by the central government with assistance from UNICEF. The projects covered only a few slums in select number of cities. There was no perspective for building a network to cover all the slums even within the selected cities and, consequently, the solutions pursued were local in nature. Attempts were made to do social mobilisation by creating community groups and involving these in implementation of the project at the grassroots level. Community was, thus, viewed merely as an agent, providing support to state sponsored development activities to ensure better implementation, in the initial experiments of community participation.

In subsequent years it was realised that community involvement not only results in effective implementation of the projects but also leads to better designing and substantial reduction in operational costs. Following this, community was often involved not just for project implementation and supervision of work but also in designing the project. All these initiatives notwithstanding, community participation remained a state sponsored activity until the late seventies.

Community participation as a component of development strategy gained currency in the eighties as a consequence of failure of public agencies and growing deficiency in the level of basic amenities. It was argued that the community can help not only in social mobilisation but also in raising financial resources[5] that the local authorities need very badly. In many cases, it became possible to have substantial reduction in project cost as the prospective beneficiaries provided their labour free or at a wage rate much below that in the market. Further, the pressure of peer group under participatory arrangement resulted in better monitoring, more productive engagement of the beneficiaries in the project and better recovery of development loans sanctioned to individuals. The community was mobilised not merely for making contributions in terms of ideas and labour but also for sharing a part of the capital and current expenditure. Only, there was demand for making credit available outside the formal institutional structure, which was beyond the access of the slum communities. In several cases, attempts were made to build mechanisms at community level to ensure timely repayment of loans.

5. "It has been demonstrated in India that, firstly, large scale renewal can be undertaken using slums as opportunities (Indore) and secondly, huge resources can be generated from the communities and supplemented by local authorities, industries and NGOs (pilot projects in Baroda and Ahmedabad)" Verma, K., Slum Networking Project (mimeo), Office of the Municipal Commissioner, Ahmedabad.

The most innovative form of community participation in infrastructural projects, which has been hailed as an major achievement in the nineties, is the neighbourhood and slum networking schemes, launched with substantial financial support from the state or central government. The people in the project area have been associated with all stages in the development of the project and are given the overall responsibility of monitoring it as also maintaining the services.

The most celebrated case of community involvement in the nineties is the Slum Networking Project (SNP), Indore. The second case - still in the process of implementation - is SNP, Ahmedabad project. Similar projects are being tried out in a number of cities in Maharashtra by involving the local community and the NGOs. These projects often involve provision of roads, pavements, water supply, sewerage, drainage and waste disposal facilities, street lighting, water taps and toilets connected to a network provided on individual or community basis. Sometimes projects are designed to take up not the entire agenda of slum improvement but provision of one or a few of the infrastructural facilities. It is argued that "the slums typically cover only about five per cent of the land area of cities... it is thus possible to have a massive impact on the entire city and its infrastructure by working in these very small areas. Concentrating resources in these neediest areas would, thus, work out as highly cost effective"[6]. This approach, understandably, helps in mainstreaming the issue by underlining the fact that investment in slum infrastructure is a critical component of urban development, which can yield a high rate of economic and social return.

The advocates of the projects have argued that private industries can be motivated to join these projects as they have an interest in the overall hygiene and health of the city because that determines their business prospects in the long run. They can, therefore, be persuaded to share the cost of slum development. This perspective has allowed the advocates of the participatory approach to place the slum-linked activities within the mainstream of urban development strategy.

---

6. *op. cit.*

3. The Emerging System for Financing Infrastructure Development and Its Impact: A Vision for 2020

It would be interesting to speculate on the nature of the system of financing for infrastructural sector in about a couple of decades from now and what would be its impact on the availability of infrastructural facilities across states and size class of settlements. More importantly, it would be worthwhile to assess the possible impact of this new system on the urban structure in the country.

Understandably, the budgetary support for infrastructural projects, coming from central or state governments would be very low in two decades from now. As a consequence, the investment in small and medium towns, particularly in the less developed states, would be very small. The projects for the provision of basic amenities in slums or low income areas, even in large cities not having clear stipulations for total cost recovery within a reasonable period - unlikely to be fancied by public agencies.

Unfortunately, investment in infrastructure in small towns in backward states undertaken with finances from organisations like HUDCO, ILFS will be very low. This would not find favour even under the institutional arrangements of USAID FIRE project nor of private or joint sector company because of uncertainties with regard to their commercial viability.

On the face of the difficulties in obtaining loans from financial institutions, efforts are on to develop the capital market so that the public utilities and other para-statal agencies can mobilise resources directly by issuing bonds and other credit instruments. This strategy, being operationalised with support from financial intermediaries, including credit rating institutions, has serious spatial implications. Given the need to keep user charges for the basic facilities within certain limits, many of the public agencies may not be able to raise funds from the market and launch major expansion in activities in the next few decades. Further, the cities issuing bonds, SDOs etc. for undertaking investment in infrastructure, have been forced to escrow or pledge their regular earnings from octroi, property tax, grants from the state etc. as a guarantee for debt servicing. An analysis of the arrangements, worked out by financial intermediaries, including the credit rating institutions, for tapping the capital market reveals that these are already restricting the functioning of the para-statal agencies as also local bodies.

In several cases, the pubic bodies have been forced to pledge their regular earnings (from grants from the state, octroi etc.) as a guarantee for debt servicing. Alternately, the guarantee has come from the central or state governments to make up the loss or even ensure certain minimum rate of return to the private agency. Importantly, the projects that are likely to be financed through such arrangements happen to be commercially viable, catering to the demands of the upper or middle class, so as to ensure profitability to the investors and other stakeholders. The arrangements would, thus, lead to a situation wherein the finances generated from the common people would get diverted for financially profitable projects, or get pledged as a security for these that are likely to benefit better off sections of population.

In case of an eventuality of the projects failing to generate the desired rate of profit, the public bodies would have to depend on the bail out by the government. It, thus, appears that the policy of liberating the public utilities and para-statal agencies from the regulatory and legislative controls of the state would bring the former firmly under the direct control of financial institutions by 2020. The state, however, would hardly be in a position to shake off its responsibility in case of failure of a project, despite the avowed desire of the lending institutions to treat the public bodies or local governments as corporate entities. Understandably, the funds from the capital market would be used in taking up infrastructural projects that cater to the needs of upper income groups or are located in rich colonies. This would result in a dilution of their social commitments including that of reducing regional imbalances and providing infrastructural amenities to the poor.

Despite all these, the new instruments like bonds, SDO (structured Debt Obligation) are likely to emerge as the dominant method of resource mobilisation by the year 2020. These would be more acceptable to the investors than general borrowings by the local body as it insulates the former from the general risk of financial uncertainty, faced by the issuer. Its basic strength would stem from the fact that every city would have certain areas or sectors wherein it is possible to identify commercially profitable projects. Also, they would always be able to identify a few revenue sources that are lucrative and buoyant. Escrowing the earnings from the lucrative sources can, thus, support the credit instruments floated for mobilising funds for the commercially viable projects[7]. The instruments, issued through the state level financing institutions or Special Purpose Vehicles (SPVs), would possibly be made further attractive for the investors by providing certain tax benefits.

It is evident that the new institutional arrangements and the credit instruments would open up an opportunity for the large cities to tap new resources. These, nonetheless, would seriously constrain "the local fiscal flexibility" (Mathur 1999) by curbing the autonomy of the agency to utilise its own resources for carrying out its normal functions as also meeting some exigencies, as noted above.

The requirements of the capital market for issuing bonds, furthermore, would facilitate launching of projects that have short gestation period and high financial return. Understandably, those catering to the demands of the upper and middle class consumers would attract investment funds, both from within as well as outside the country. It would be extremely difficult to get funds for social sector projects or those targetted to the poor due to their low rate of return and high risk factor. The financial intermediaries including credit rating agencies would, thus, ensure that infrastructural investment takes place in projects with assured cost recovery. They would also create pressures for bringing about an appropriate legal and administrative restructuring, at the state and city level, so that the commercial viability of such projects is guaranteed. These would seriously restrict the choice of the projects, rendering launching of schemes for say, provision of water and sanitation facilities for the poor, slum improvement etc., virtually impossible in 2020. (Kundu *et. al.* 1999).

---

7. The three corporations of Ahmedabad, Bangalore and Vijaywada have successfully floated SDOs that are secured by the cash flows from certain specific assets and/ or sources of revenue. While Ahmedabad Municipal Corporation has escrowed the octroi revenues from specified entry points, Vijaywada Municipal Corporation has been obliged to escrow the property tax and revenues from its commercial property. These two sources of revenues, i.e., octroi and the property tax, account for a substantial proportion of the revenue of the two corporations. The non-availability of these revenue sources for meeting routine expenditures can, at a future date, accentuate the financial problems faced by the corporations. Far stringent are the conditions on the Bangalore City Corporation which had to escrow a part of the proceeds from property tax and State Finance Commission grants. In addition, it had to obtain guarantee from the state government.

Until recently, ULBs had no mandate to take up infrastructure development or launch capital projects for sewerage and garbage disposal. Now that the states are downloading these responsibilities to local bodies, these bodies would have passed these over to private companies through contractual arrangements by 2020. These bodies are very keen to subcontract solid waste disposal to private companies. Most of the ULBs are in a dire financial state and the very motive behind contracting out is to save on capital as well as current expenses. It would, however, be difficult by 2020 for them to ensure that the private companies meet the social obligations like covering the slum population, without their paying a substantial compensation. Many among the ULBs have already negotiated with the private agencies and agreed to compensate them not in cash but in kind. In most cases, the Corporations have leased out land to the companies on a long-term basis. The companies find this arrangement remunerative because they can thereby use the precious urban land for other purposes, earning often undeclared profits. We may find a number of companies taking up the job of waste disposal solely for the purpose of getting a hold on urban land for alternate uses, without going through the complex land acquisition procedures or paying their market price.

Unfortunately, it may not be possible to augment the technical competence of the city authorities to assess the cost implications of such arrangements for the people or urban economy in the long term. Given the financial situation, the state governments are unlikely to make serious efforts to create information base or provide technical assistance to ULBs for assessing the long-term implications of land deals and helping the latter in enforcing appropriate administrative safeguards. There would be no institutional network to which an ULB can look up for seeking guidance on technical matters like, the proposal to set up a garbage disposal plant by a private company. In fact, voices are likely to be raised against any such institutional "interventions". Given the enthusiasm for decentalisation, any such effort would be criticised as an attempt to undermine or impinge on the authority of the local bodies.

Despite formal pronouncements by the Central and state governments from time to time and some financial support given to ULBs for these purposes, it is unlikely that the latter would succeed in reaching the poor and vulnerable in any satisfactory manner. Often the Municipal Corporations, Development Authorities and the State Level Boards have admitted to providing (directly or through private arrangements) differential levels of services to different areas or failing to cover marginal areas in the cities. Understandably, the better off localities with higher tax collections are demanding high quality facilities and even pressing for creation of separate local bodies. All these have made cross subsidisation in the provision of amenities within the cities extremely difficult in another two decades.

One is, thus, not very certain that the recent moves for liberalisation, decentralisation and invigoration of the capital market would help local bodies in undertaking infrastructural investment in the new century. These developments would, while liberating the local agencies from the control of central and state governments, place the former under some trustees or commercial banks, controlled by pure market logic. Alternately, the financial powers might also go in the hands of international "donors" and credit rating agencies who, through various innovative and complicated arrangements, can influence the expenditure pattern of municipal bodies. They would also be in a position to determine the type of projects to be undertaken, and in certain cases their management system. It would be extremely important to keep a watch on the problems faced by the cities in handling their budgetary earnings and expenditures after accepting the terms and conditions for raising resources.

The adverse impact of the Constitutional Amendment on intra-urban disparity is likely to become very pronounced by 2020. Only a handful of large cities with reasonably strong economic base would have benefited from the "opportunity", opening up owing to the Constitutional Amendment. A few of these cities would possibly be able to introduce certain new taxes, increase the rates of the old ones and, at the same time, liberate themselves from the legislative and administrative controls of the state government. They might also be able to raise resources by issuing debt instruments or borrowings from international organisations, as discussed in the preceding section. It is, however, unlikely that small and medium towns would be able to benefit in a similar fashion. Consequently, the mobilisation of funds from the capital market and institutional sources would accentuate the disparity in terms of per capita expenditure and the level of amenities across the size class of urban centres during the next two decades.

Within a couple of decades from now we would face serious problems due to socio-economic segmentation in large cities. The Amendment stipulates that the ward level committees are to be constituted in all cities having more than 0.3 million people and that the former will have the powers to take decisions regarding the nature of infrastructural facilities and civic amenities, based on the capability and willingness of the residents to pay. Also, these committees will statutorily be assigned certain part of the municipal budget. The slum populations in the heart of the large cities or their peripheries, with low affordability or willingness to pay, would understandably accept a low level of civic amenities. The elite colonies, on the other hand, would be able to attract private entrepreneurs and even the subsidised government programmes for improving the quality of services, based on their capacity to pay higher user charges and political connections. This would further accentuate the disparity in the availability of basic amenities across the wards and between the city and the periphery.

A large number of the industrial units would get located in the villages and small towns around the big cities in the next few decades. The reasons for their moving out of the large cities are easy availability of land, access to unorganised labour market and lesser awareness or less stringent implementation of environmental regulations. The poor would find shelter in the "degenerated periphery", get jobs in the industries located therein or commute to the central city for work (Kundu 1989). The entrepreneurs, engineers, executives etc., associated with modern industries and business, however, would reside within the central city and travel to the periphery through rapid transport corridors. The process of segmentation, manifested in different variants in different cities, would push the incoming migrants from rural areas largely into the peripheral zones.

A number of projects would be launched with the participation of community groups and non-governmental organisations in a number of cities and towns in many of the states. This new approach, while involving the community in infrastructure development, may lead to withdrawal of the state or minimal budgetary support. In the absence of the states designing an institutional network for providing technical support, the poor may be left to themselves for designing and implementing the project or simply involving them in credit access and loan recovery mechanism.

Despite much noise being made regarding participatory projects, these are unlikely to become an alternative to the formal slum improvement programmes launched by public agencies as there is not adequate evidence that the success cases are replicable on a large scale. Although the government is placing high weightage to provision of credit and training for the participatory projects, it may not be possible to do so through institutional sources due to bureaucratic hurdles. The major handicap in large-scale multiplication of the projects would be the slum households not possessing legal title to "their land".

Changing Structure of Urbanisation and Access to Infrastructure and Basic Amenities

The changes being introduced in the system of financing infrastructural financing have serious implications for the trend and pattern of urban growth in future years. During fifties and sixties, some kind of ceiling on the absorptive capacity of large cities was sought to be imposed through physical planning and controls on location of economic activities and urban land-use, imposed through Master Plans etc. These, however, could not restrict RU migration as there was large-scale violations in the Master Plan norms and land use restrictions. The growth urban population thus worked our as high or medium during the first four decades since Independence.

The annual exponential growth rate was very high - 3.5 per cent per annum - during forties. This had prompted several scholars propound the thesis of urban explosion, dysfunctional urbanisation, urban accretion etc, basically stipulating that urban centres are growing beyond their capacity, determined by the level of infastructural facilities. The rate came down substantially during fifties and sixties but that was attributed to the adoption of a rigorous definition of urban centres in the Census of 1961. In seventies, however, the country recorded an all time high growth of

3.8 per cent. This was due not only to the existing urban centres experiencing an acceleration in their growth rates but emergence of a large number of new towns.

There has been a striking change in the urban scenario in the country since the eighties reflected in deceleration in urban growth. The annual growth rate of population recorded for urban India was as low as 3.1 per cent during 1981-91. This has gone down further to 2.7 per cent during 1991-2001. It is indeed true that the numbers of new towns identified in the last two Censuses are not as high as reported in Census 1981. The main reason for the deceleration is however, slower demographic growth recorded in existing urban centres.

The declining demographic growth goes against not only the popular perception of "urban explosion" but also questions the projections made by Expert Groups set up by various government departments during eighties and nineties, besides that of the India Infrastructure Report and the Tenth Five Year Plan. Even the United Nations had projected urban growth during nineties to be close to that of the eighties. All these can now be dismissed as overestimates. The data from Population Census 2001, thus, provides an occasion to have a fresh look at the infrastructure development policy in the country and the perspective on urbanisation.

Measures of structural reform in urban sector launched informally during eighties but formalised since 1991 were expected to accelerate rural urban migration and give boost to the pace of urbanisation. The proponents of the reform often argued that linking of India with global economy would lead to a massive inflow of capital from outside the country as also rise in indigenous investment. This, in turn, would give impetus to the process of urbanisation, since much of the investment and consequent increase in employment would be either within or around the existing urban centres. Even when the industrial units get located in rural settlements, in a few years the latter would acquire urban status, resulting in emergence of a number of new urban centres by the year 2020.

Critics of globalisation had, however, pointed out that employment generation in the formal urban economy might not be high due to capital intensive nature of industrialisation. Also, the reduction in the rate of public sector investment in infrastructure would continue for the next couple of decades, for keeping budgetary deficits low. A cut in infrastructural investment in rural areas, coupled with open trade policy, would, in turn, slow down agricultural growth, causing high unemployment and exodus from rural areas. This would lead to rapid growth in urban population. Thus, the protagonists as also the critics of economic reform converged on the proposition that urban growth in the post liberalisation phase would be high. The data from the Population Census 2020, however, is likely to prove them both wrong as there will be significant decline in urban growth not merely due to slowing down of natural growth of population but also RU migration.

More important than the decline in the growth rate of urban population is the change in the pattern of urban growth. During 1951-91, urban growth was generally high in relatively backward states, the states of Bihar, Uttar Pradesh, Rajasthan and Orissa and Madhya Pradesh topping the list. This is because the pace of RU migration and urbanisation were high in most of the backward states and regions that were stuck in the vicious circle of poverty. The relationship between urban growth and economic development was negative but not very strong as a few among the developed states such as, Maharashtra, Gujarat and Haryana, too, recorded high or medium growth. The other developed states like West Bengal, Tamil Nadu and Punjab experienced low urban growth.

The scenario of urban growth during this period was characterised by dualism. The developed states attracted population in urban areas due to industrialisation and infrastrctural investment. However, the backward states – particularly their backward districts and small and medium towns – also experienced rapid urban growth. This can party be attributed to government investment in the district and *taluka* headquarters, programmes of urban industrial dispersal, and transfer of funds from the states to local bodies through a need based approach. A part of RU migration in backward states could also be attributed to push factors, owing to lack of diversification in agrarian economy.

Nineties, however, made a significant departure from the earlier decades. The developed states like Tamil Nadu, Punjab, Haryana, Maharashtra and Gujarat have registered urban growth above the national average. West Bengal is the only exception whose growth rate is not particularly impressive. The backward states, on the other hand, have experienced growth either below that of the country or at the most, equal to that. It may, therefore, be argued that the dynamics of urban growth would become weak and tend to get concentrated more and more in developed regions, with the exclusion of the backward states, during 2001-2021.

The decline in the rate of urbanisation and the increasing concentration pattern of growth in the next couple of decades must be examined in relation to the new systems of urban governance and methods of financing infrastructural investment. Indeed, launching of the measures of privatisation, strengthening of legal system relating to pollution and land-use etc., would adversely affect the "informal and illegal" market for land and provision of civic services. It may be noted that the functioning of these informal markets had helped the poor to find a foothold in urban centres during the first few decades since Independence. The stricter implementation of planning norms and frequent invocation of legal system for eviction etc. during the incoming decades would further slow down inmigration of rural poor. Lack of their access to basic amenities, due to a reduction in public investment on urban development and social sectors, would be yet another factor, adversely affecting the pace of urbanisation.

It is possible to predict an increase in inequality in the urban structure, along with regional imbalance in the incoming decades, as discussed above. The distribution of population in different size class of settlements, as defined by the Census[8], is likely to become more and more skewed. The share of Class I towns or cities, with population size of 100,000 or more, has gone up significantly from 26 per cent in 1901 to 65 per cent in 1991. The percentage share of class IV, V and VI towns, having less than 20,000 people, on the

---

8. Population Census in India classifies urban settlement into six size classes as per the limits indicated below.

Population Size	Category
100,000 and more	Class I
50,000 to 100,000	Class II
20,000 to 50,000	Class III
10,000 to 20,000	Class IV
5,000 to 10,000	Class V
Less than 5,000	Class VI

other hand, has gone down drastically from 47 to 10 only. This is largely due to the fact that the towns in lower categories have grown in size and entered the next higher category. Unfortunately, however, there has not been a corresponding increase in the number of urban centres, especially at the lower levels, through transformation of rural settlements during the period from 1901 to 1991[9].

The slow process of graduation of large sized villages into towns, through growth of industrial and tertiary activities, would be a major problem in India's urbanisation in the next few decades. The number of additional urban centres identified by the Census of 2001 is 630 which is less than that of 1991 and much below that of 1981. The process of sectoral diversification in rural economy is so week that one would not expect more than 800 additional urban centres during the next two decades. Also, given the spatial concentration of the growth process, these new towns are likely to remain concentrated around a few large cities or regions.

The second and more important reason for the urban hierarchy to become skewed and top heavy in the year 2021 is that the larger urban centres would experience faster demographic growth as compared to smaller order settlements. The class I cities, for example, have registered an average annual growth rate[10] of 3.0 per cent during 1981-91, which is higher than that of lower order towns[11]. The same pattern is noted during 1991-2001 as well. More importantly, the class I cities exhibit a lower disparity in their growth rates, measured through coefficient of variation, compared to those in other size classes. One would expect the former to experience relatively higher and stable demographic growth in future years as these would get more and more linked to the national and even global market (Nagaraj 1987, Kundu 1983 and Bhalla and Kundu 1982). In the smaller towns that are mostly rooted in their regional economy, however, population growth would tend to be low and

---

9. The number of urban centres has doubled while urban population has become eight-fold.
10. The growth rates have been computed by considering the population of only those towns (for both initial as well as terminal year) that belonged to this size category in the base year.
11. The class VI towns, however, are exceptions to this as many of these are special purpose urban centres, established or managed by public sector agencies, military establishments or private industries.

fluctuating over time and space. This would further reinforce the dual urban structure in the country wherein the larger cities would get integrated with higher order system and would thus share the growth dynamics at national or global economy. This would, by and large, be absent in case of smaller towns.

The higher demographic growth in large cities, compared to the smaller towns, could, at least partly, be attributed to the measures of decetralisation whereby the responsibilities of resource mobilisation and launching infrastructural projects have been given to the local bodies, as noted above. The large municipal bodies, particularly those located in developed states, tend to have a strong economic base, and this would result in their high economic and demographic growth during the next couple of decades.

It has been noted that a strong lobby is emerging, particularly in these cities, pleading for disbanding all zoning restrictions, building laws and bye-laws and making them relatively independent of state and central level controls. As a consequence, decisions regarding location of industries, change in land-use etc. would be taken expeditiously at the local level. The decentralisation of responsibilities for development planning, sought to be ushered in through the 74th Constitutional Amendment, would help this lobby. The large cities that have relatively stronger economic base would be able to benefit from this opportunity of empowerment of local governments. As a consequence, a few of these cities would be able to attract infrastructural investment and record a high population growth. The small and medium towns, on the other hand, are unlikely to benefit from this changed policy regime. All these would explain the urban structure becoming more and more top-heavy by 2020, as mentioned above.

It was pointed out earlier that planning controls, bye-laws etc. have had little impact in restricting demographic growth of large cities in the past. Interestingly, the advantages of relaxation in these controls as also systems of infrastuctural financing in the next two decades would also be taken up mostly by these cities. Due to their strong economic base and consequently high tax and non-tax revenue generating capacity, these would be in a position to put in more resources in creating basic physical conditions, necessary for attracting private investment. This would make the urban structure further top heavy as these large cities and their immediate hinterland would absorb most of the migrants.

Access to Infrastructure and Basic Services

The NSS reports an interesting pattern of improvement in the level of infrastuctural facilities over time. The percentage of households having no latrine has declined significantly from 36.8 to 31.1 during the period from 1983 to 1988-89. The figure has, however, gone down only marginally to 30.6 per cent in 1993. Correspondingly, the percentage of households with flush system has moved up from 20.1 to 26.9 during the first period. The increase during the second period, however, is very modest, going up to only 28.5 in 1993. This pattern is observed also for the households having access to septic tank (toilets)[12]. Furthermore, as opposed to the increase in the coverage through safe drinking water by 6.3 percentage points during 1981-91 as per the Census, NSS reports that the figure has remained static at 88 per cent during the period from 1986-87 to 1993. One would, therefore, argue that the progress in providing basic amenities, which was reasonably high in early and mid–eighties, has slowed down in the post-liberalisation phase. Based on the trend, one would predict that the rate of coverage of household by infrastructural facilities would continue to be low in the first two decades of the present century.

Most of the indicators of basic amenities show positive correlations with those of economic development across the states in the nineties. The percentage of households having flush toilets, for example, exhibits a very strong relationship with per capita income. Those for other amenities, like drinking water, toilets and electricity, too, the correlations are positive but not always statistically significant. One would argue that economically developed states are doing fairly well in providing their people access to basic amenities (Kundu *et. al.* 1999). This trend is likely to continue in future years implying that the improvements in the availability of these amenities would be higher in the relatively developed states.

---

12. Interestingly, the trend in the percentage of households residing in pucca houses is similar - going up by 20 percentage point from 51.21 during 1983-88 (38th and 44th round) but registering a nominal increase of 2.8 points only during 1988-93 (44th and 49th round). Furthermore, the percentage figures reported in the 49th and 50th rounds are about the same.

The coverage of households through basic amenities across size class of urban centres shows regularity and a distinct pattern. The percentage of households having all the three amenities goes down systematically as we move from higher to lower size class of urban centres[13]. It is indeed very disturbing that in class V towns (having population between 5,000 and 10,000), the percentage of households not covered by toilet, electricity and drinking water are as high as 61, 41 and 28 respectively in 1991. The corresponding figures for the cities with more than half a million population are 22, 17 and 14 per cent only (Kundu *et. al.* 1999). Going by the present trend, one would expect still higher inequality in the level of basic services across urban centres in different size classes by the year 2020.

Higher rates of infrastructure investment in larger cities during 2001-21 can be explained in terms of the present development policy. Indeed, one can perceive a clear bias in favour of large cities in the current policy debate, media discussion etc. Despite the large cities having lower percentage of people below poverty line, it is mostly these cities that get covered under slum improvement and poverty alleviation programmes of international and national agencies due to reasons of greater visibility. The anomaly of giving greater attention to larger cities in all programmes for poverty alleviation and provision of infrastructure can be attributed to strong vested interests in their favour. Further, it becomes easier to cover a larger number of poor households in absolute terms because of the size factor, if larger cities are selected under a programme.

Given the present dynamics of urban industrial development in the country, the small and medium towns, located away from the "emerging global centres of growth", particularly those in backward regions, are unlikely to receive much private investment. They would find it difficult to finance any development project through internal resources or borrowings from capital market. The fiscal discipline, imposed by the government, HUDCO, credit rating agencies and other financial intermediaries, would make it impossible for them to undertake infrastructural investment of any kind. The deficiency in basic amenities would be a serious hurdle in

---

13. The exception occurs in case of the lowest class of towns (class VI) because many among these enjoy a special status, as mentioned above, and consequently have higher level of amenities.

their attracting private investment from within or outside the country. It is only a few large cities with strong economic base that would be able to secure high credit rating and raise resources through bonds and other innovative credit instruments. With governmental investment in infrastructure and basic amenities becoming less and less over the years, the disparity within the urban economy is bound to increase, as mentioned above.

4. A Perspective for Balanced Infrastructural Development and a Strategy for Intervention

It has been pointed out that launching of the programme of structural adjustment has led to a decline in public investment in infrastructure, without any compensatory gain in the contribution from the private sector. Public undertakings and para-statal agencies have become increasingly dependent on their internal resources and institutional/private finance that have constrained their capacity to take up social sector projects. With the objective of "bringing in efficiency and accountability in their functioning", the component of subsidy has also been brought down while the cost of borrowing has gone up significantly. Furthermore, there has been increasing reliance on partnership arrangements, privatisation and community participation for launching infrastructure development projects.

It has been demonstrated in the preceding section that this changed perspective and new development strategy would accentuate disparity in the levels of infrastructural facilities across the states and size class of urban settlements by the year 2020. Understandably, the poor would get priced out of the system, organised through private or joint sector initiatives. Unfortunately, the same would be true with the delivery system under the government and semi-government undertakings as well, since these have increasingly been made to depend on institutional borrowings and capital market. All these would accentuate interurban inequality in the availability of infrastructural facilities. Furthermore, this would lead to spatial segmentation, particularly in the large cities of the country.

One may ask the question whether intervention by state in India can change the process and pattern of infrastructural development, as discussed above. The analysis of the emerging policy perspectives makes it clear that posing the issue as state versus market does not give much analytical mileage. One must ask what are the tools of intervention available to the Indian state and with what objectives these are likely to be used in the next two decades.

The changes in the system of governance and financing of infrastructural investment, brought about through structural adjustment, as recommended by several international agencies and broadly accepted by the Indian planners, envisage state's role as a facilitator. If indeed the public agencies intervene as a facilitator in the market – removing its deficiencies and saving the actors from market failures – the above scenario of growing regional imbalance would emerge, possibly with a greater ease.

Given the socio-political reality in India, it is difficult for private sector to bring about the changes in the pattern of investment in infrastructure without state becoming an active partner and bringing about the required legislative and administrative changes. Indian state has indeed responded quite favourably in the past few years by ushering in the necessary changes, although the democratic structure and bureaucratic inertia have made the process slow. The government has removed impediments in the functioning of the urban land market and facilitated the necessary changes in landuse, etc. The message has come loud and clear from the Plan documents that such changes are possible and are forthcoming.

In order to make a dent on the process of infrastructural development and their impact on urban structure, it would be important to make a significant departure from the present policy of financing the investment. Based on the above overview of the trend at macro level and its negative implications, a strong case can be made for providing special assistance to the less developed states that are not in a position to allocate requisite funds for infrastructural projects. Particularly, small and medium towns in these states need to be supported, as their economic bases are not strong to mobilise resources for the purpose. This would imply increasing the resources allocated in the public sector for development of infrastructure. There must, however, be explicit stipulations in the schemes to ensure that most of the funds go to small and medium towns.

The capacity of the state or local government to generate employment directly through anti-poverty programmes would remain limited. The past experiences suggest that there has been considerable leakage in the self-employment programmes. Banks and other financial institutions have been unwilling to give loans to the poor, as the risk of non-recovery is very high. Also, the assets created through wage employment programmes have not contributed significantly to the development potential or long-term income generating capacity of the poor. It is, therefore, recommended that the anti-poverty programmes should primarily be directed to creation of community based infrastructure.

The state governments should take the overall responsibility of ensuring certain minimum level of the amenities to all sections of population, in different size class of urban centres, irrespective of their income levels or affordability. For this purpose, it would be important to set up the "standards" for the infrastructural facilities in realistic terms, based on what the country can afford. The government may, however, fulfil this responsibility by engaging/ supporting private organisations, NGOs and CBOs or strengthening the local bodies.

Constitutional amendment for decentralisation of financial powers is not adequate for augmenting resources of the local bodies for this purpose. Further, it would be erroneous to depend on the capital market or the banking sector for fulfilling the social obligations or implementing a strategy of balanced regional development. All these must be backed up by actual devolution of powers and responsibilities by state governments and their use by municipal bodies. The management capacities of these bodies need to be strengthened by giving more technical personnel and training the existing staff. Manufacturing activities at the town level are noted to exhibit a strong relationship with the availability of infrastructure and civic services. One may, therefore, argue that the provision of these services in small urban settlements, besides being a goal in itself, would help in generating non-agricultural employment and diversifying their economic base.

Much of the subsidised amenities provided through the governmental programmes during the seventies and eighties have in the past gone to a few developed regions and large cities and benefited generally the high and middle-income colonies. There is no way that this can continue in a more liberalised regime during 2001-21. However, withdrawing government support and relegating the provision of the services to the market would have adverse consequences for regional inequality as also the micro environment/ health conditions within large cities. Institutional borrowings by public agencies (involved in the provision of the amenities) at high rates of interest, reduction in their grants from government etc. are likely to erode their capacity to invest in backward states, smaller order towns, slums and low income areas.

The relationship of urban industrial growth with that of infrastructural facilities has been positive. The government and para-statal institutions providing the facilities have unfortunately not exhibited sensitivity in favour of backward states in recent years. The pattern is likely to become more unfavorable to the developed states that have little capacity to attract corporate capital in future years. Similarly, the large cities would succeed in cornering much of the investment that would come to infrastructure sector. The small and medium towns, on the other hand would attract private investment neither from within nor outside the country.

To counter the above trends, new programmes must be designed that can cover the entire urban hierarchy and all vulnerable sections of population. Importantly, the capacity of the people in small and medium towns in less developed states as also the urban poor to pay for basic services would remain low during the years of structural adjustment as the prospect of an increase in their real income does not seem very bright. The programmes must, therefore, be specifically targetted and the subsidies must be made more explicit and transparent. Above all, these programmes must emerge from a long term development plan for the regional economy that gives due weightage to the infrastructural needs of all sections of population in the city as also its rural hinterland.

References

Bhalla, G. S. and Kundu, A., (1982): "Role of small and Medium Towns in India's Regional Development", *Small Cities I National Development*, United Nations Centre for Regional Development, Nagoya.

Credit Rating Information Services of India Limited (1996): *Credit Rating of Municipal Bonds: Rating Report on Ahmedabad Municipal Corporation*, New Delhi.

Dubey A. and Gangopadhyay, S., (1999): "Poverty and Occupational Structure in Size Class of towns in India", *Regional Development Dialogue*, Nagoya, (forthcoming)

Dutta, A., (1999): "Institutional Aspects of Urban Governance", in Mathur, O. P. (ed.) *India: the Challenge of Urban Governance*, National Institute of Public Finance and Policy, New Delhi.

Expert Group on the Commercialisation of Infrastructure Projects (1996): *The India Infrastructure Report: Policy Imperatives for Growth and Welfare*, Ministry of Finance, Government of India, New Delhi.

International Institute of Population Sciences (1994): *India: Introductory Report, National Family Health Survey 1992-93*, International Institute of Population Sciences, Mumbai.

Kingsley Davis, (1962): "Urbanisation in India – Past and Future", in Turner, R. (ed.) (1962).

Kundu, A., (1983): "Theories of City Size Distribution and Indian Urban Structure – A Reappraisal", *Economic and Political Weekly*, 18(3).

———. (1989): "The Dynamic of City Hinterland Relationship: The Indian Case" in Vennetier, P., *La Peri-Urbanisation Dans Les Pays Tropicaux*, CEGET-CNRS, Talence.

———.(1994): "Pattern of Urbanisation with Special Reference to Small and Medium Towns in India" in Chadha, G. K., *Sectoral Issues in the Indian Economy*, Har-Anand Publications, New Delhi.

———.(1997): "Trends and Structure of Employment in the Nineties: Implications for Urban Growth", *Economic and Political Weekly*, 32(24).

———. and Basu, S. (1998): "Informal Manufacturing Sector in Urban Areas – An Analysis of Recent Trends", Manpower Journal, 34(1), April-June 1998.

———. and Gupta, S. (1996): "Migration Urbanisation and Regional Inequality", *Economic and Political Weekly*, 31(52), December 26.

Kundu, A., Bagchi, S. and Kundu, D. (1999): "Regional Distribution of Infrastructure and Basic Amenities in Urban India – Issues Concerning Empowerment of Local Bodies", *Economic and Political Weekly*, 34(28), July 10.

Mathur, O. P., (1999): "Fiscal Innovations and Urban Governance" in Mathur, O. P. (ed.) *India: the Challenge of Urban Governance*, National Institute of Public Finance and Policy, New Delhi.

Mehta, M. and Satyanarayana, V., (1996): *Pricing and Cost Recovery for Urban Services*, Community Consulting International, New Delhi.

Ministry of Urban Development (1992): *The Constitution Seventy-fourth Amendment Act 1992 on Municipalities*, Government of India, New Delhi.

Nagraj, K., (1987): "Urbanisation in Tamil Nadu, Karnataka and Andhra Pradesh" in Alam, S. Manzoor and Alikhan, F. (eds.) *Perspectives in Urbanisation and Migration – India and USSR*, Allied Publishers, New Delhi.

National Institute of Public Finance and Policy (1995): *Redefining State-Municipal Fiscal Relations*, vol. I (mimeo), NIPFP, New Delhi.

National Institute of Urban Affairs (1983): *A study of Resources of Urban Local Bodies in India and the Level of Services Provided*, National Institute of Urban Affairs, New Delhi.

———. (1998): *Compendium of Major Legislation in Conformity with Constitution Seventy-fourth Amendment Act*, Study Series no. 70, NIUA, New Delhi.

Planning Commission (1992): *Eighth Five Year Plan 1992-1997*, Government of India, New Delhi.

———. (1997): *Ninth Five Year Plan 1997-2002*, Government of India, New Delhi.

Premi, M. K., (1991): "India's Urban Scene and Its Future Implications", *Demography India*, 20 (1).

Nayak, P. R., (1962): "The Challenge of Urban Growth to Indian Local Government" in Turner (ed.) (1962).

Sen, A. and Ghosh, J., (1993): *Trends in Rural Employment and Poverty Employment Linkage*, ILO-ARTEP Working Paper, New Delhi.

Sovani, N. V., (1966): *Urbanisation and Urban India*, Asia Publishing House, Bombay.

Turner, R., (ed.) (1962): *India's Urban Future*, University of California Press, Berkley.

World Bank, (1995): *India Transport Sector: Long Term Issues*, Report No 13192-IN, Washington, D.C.

———. (1998): *Reducing Poverty in India: Options for More Effective Public Services*, World Bank, Washington, D.C.

United Nations, (1995): *World Urbanisation Prospects*, Population Division, New York.

14

Rural Development and Technology Management: Vision 2020

P. V. INDIRESAN

Synopsis

It is usual to plan for growth, as rapid a growth as possible. That is incremental thinking. Visionary thinking is different. It starts not from what is but from what should be, at any rate, can be. It works backwards from the end and not from now on to the end.

India is likely to attain a stationary population of 1.7-1.8 billion. It may never reach the current prosperity of the United States; may be it should not with all its attendant extravagance. Can it reach at least the average level of world's prosperity with per capita incomes of about US $ 5000-6000 per year? That much is indeed necessary. That is the minimum needed to avoid being looked down in the comity of nations. More than that runs the risk of evoking jealousy and inviting unwanted migration too.

The Planning Commission has targeted eight per cent growth rate, but agriculture (the mainstay of rural areas) cannot grow much faster than two per cent. So, either rural areas recede six per cent a year relative to cities, or there is six per cent rural-urban migration or rural areas are empowered to grow at eight per cent with non-agricultural development making rural-urban migration unnecessary. The last option is best and feasible. Then, the objective should be to enrich rural areas by employing around 80 per cent of 1.3 to 1.5 billion rural residents (out of ultimate population of 1.7-1.8 billion) in non-agricultural occupations.

Two aspects of Vision 2020 have been addressed in this presentation – ensuring the fulfilment of Maslow Needs socially and empowering the economy to face global competition. The approach to the Vision is best done by working backwards as shown in the diagram. For instance, fulfilling Maslow Needs socially requires infrastructure and that is best done by a process called Rurbanisation that combines rural ambience with the capability of cities to supply a full range of services. Like wise, empowering the economy to face global competition requires technology development and that may be generated in Science and Technology Parks (STEP) and technology incubators. Connectivity is the primary input to Rurbanisation and education the one for STEPs and incubators. Both connectivity and education require capital and optimum utilisation of capital which depends on (a) the choice made or allocation efficiency and the level chosen or optimum economy of scale. Or, primary level driving forces are infrastructure and technology, and at the secondary level, they are connectivity and education level, respectively. Capital is only tertiary and it has been shown that its importance to growth and development is relatively minor.

Figure S.1

Deriving Driving Forces of Development
By Working Backward from Vision

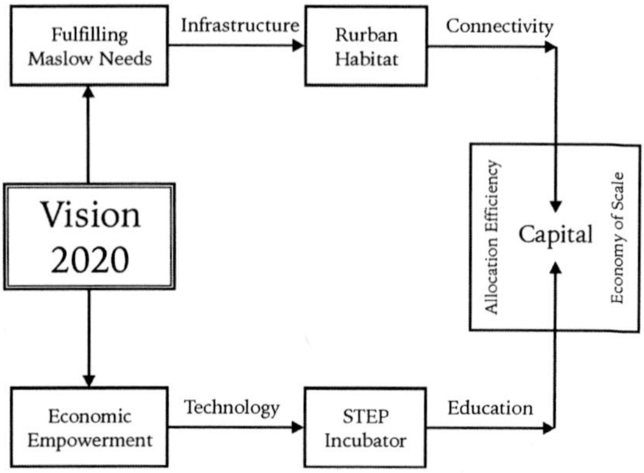

Rural areas can be empowered to compete with cities. They can be reorganised to support 80 per cent of their population in non-agricultural occupations. Rural-urban migration can be halted. All that is not only possible, that is also more economical than expanding cities without limit.

The ultimate Vision is a nation dominated by Rurban habitats, several thousand of them, virtually one for every rural development block and supporting 70-80 per cent of the total population and offering a full range of urban amenities in a rural ambience; a nation neither too rich nor too poor but one that follows the Middle Path, deploys technology extensively but wisely, where talented people are respected and ordinary people are secure.

1. TARGETS OF VISION: FULFILMENT OF MASLOW NEEDS

1.1. Maslow Needs

Thanks to Amartya Sen, UNDP has shifted emphasis from outputs to entitlements, from quantity to quality, from money to what money actually buys. As a result, UNDP has introduced this year a new measure called Human Poverty Index (HPI) to highlight more forcefully shortcomings in any economy. HPI does not replace the more orthodox Human Development Index but supplements the same. HPI is a composite of three variables:

a. Percentage of people not expected to live beyond 40 years of age;

b. Illiteracy rate and

c. Lack of access to safe drinking water, health services and sanitation.

Defined in this manner, it is possible for communities that have high per capita incomes and even a high HDI, to have relatively poor HPI. Both HDI and HPI indicate what should be done, or what the priorities should be, but not how to achieve such goals. Further, both HDI and HPI are limited to essentially economic factors whereas, ideally, a vision should take into account social, cultural, political factors too.

Maslow's postulate of hierarchy of "basic needs" offers a systematic and analytic basis for defining a Vision[1]. VISION 2020 may be interpreted as the Vision for the year 2020, or better still, as

---

1. A Maslow, Motivation and Personality, 1952.

a formulation of perfect vision. Maslow postulated that people have a hierarchy of five needs, namely, physical, security, status, autonomy and self-actualisation needs (to which ecology needs may also be added and placed between autonomy and self-actualisation). One may then define the ideal Vision 2020 as transforming the present disgruntled society into a happy one in which one and all are empowered to enjoy all six Maslow Needs.

Food, water and energy constitute the first level of physical needs. Food can be further sub-divided into its components like proteins, vitamins and the like. We could branch off still more, say, into types of vitamins. Quality too needs to be specified.

Similarly, appropriate inputs can be identified for other levels of Maslow Needs. Table 1.1 suggests a possible set of inputs to match each level of Maslow Need.

Table 1.1

Maslow Needs and Matching Inputs

Need	*Type of Input*	*Typical Examples*
Physical	Income	Food, water, clothing, energy, employment
Security	Wealth	Health care, house, vocational skill, secure employment
Status	Perquisite	Quality habitat, career, education
Autonomy	Freedom to act	Authority, connectivity
Ecology	Freedom from squalor	Waste disposal, non-congestion
Self-actualization	Culture	Higher education, leisure

1.2. The Iron Law of Economic Justice

Just as it is not obvious that the earth does go round the sun, it is not directly obvious that luxury consumption helps the poor. Strange as it may appear *the one and only way the poor can get their basic needs is to let others enjoy luxuries! Unless and until the rich enjoy luxuries, the poor cannot get their basic needs.* These are necessary (but not sufficient) conditions, yet so strict are they that this stipulation may be described as the Iron Law of Economic Justice.

For decades, the policy has been to target the poor and to target them directly. As a practical observation, *everybody cannot have identical incomes; some will always be richer than others.* So, disparities are a fact of life. In such a practical but non-ideal situation where income disparities cannot be reduced to zero, the question arises: "How small can those disparities be made?" To make an estimate of minimum practicable income disparity, let us start with Scandinavian countries that are reputed to be the most egalitarian ones in the world. Those countries are also among the richest. Hence, there is no doubt about their ability to get results. So, we will not be far wrong if we assume that they have reached the practicable limits in minimising disparity. In their case, the bottom ten per cent of the population gets three per cent of national income while the top ten per cent command 21 per cent, a ratio of 1:7. For most other countries, the variation is between 2.5 per cent and 25 per cent. Others, like Brazil, are far worse. Then, we may reasonably assume that, in practice, the ratio of incomes between the bottom and top deciles cannot be made significantly lower than 1:7, and will generally be about 1:10. By the same token, we may assume that the bottom decile will usually get no more than 25 per cent of the national average.

Let us consider the significance of this practical reality. For the sake of argument, let us assume that the average income of a country is 100 units with the bottom decile getting 25 units. Further, let us suppose that, even with an income of only 25 units, the poor are able to command all basic needs. That will happen only when the price of all basic needs is not more than 25 units. However, the average income is 100 units. Then, where can the remaining 75 units go? That can be spent only on non-basic needs, on luxuries! In other words, if the poor get all their needs, 75 per cent of national income and expenditure must be spent on luxuries! On the other hand, if luxuries amount to less than 75 units, the cost of basic needs will be more than 25 units – more than what the poor can afford. That will make the poor destitute! In this example, we have assumed that the bottom decile of the population gets 25 per cent of the national average. If it gets less, say, only 20 per cent, luxury consumption should rise to 80 per cent to avoid deprivation.

In India, we have treated only food items as necessities. Many non-food items also are essential needs, not luxuries. If entitlement to those needs too are included, the proportion of the poor will be much more than the official figure of 30 per cent. India can remedy the situation in two ways: Increase luxury consumption to 75-80 per cent of the total or *raise the income share of the poorest to 50-60 per cent of the average.* No country in the world has ever achieved that degree of equality. So, the only practical way of eliminating poverty is to raise the share of luxury consumption to 75-80 per cent of the total.

Unfortunately, this Iron Law of Economic Justice describes only a necessary condition but not a sufficient one. Hence, substantial luxury consumption is necessary for the poor to enjoy the basic amenities of life but there is no guarantee that, in that case, the poor will actually enjoy all basic needs.

1.3. Issues in Implementation

1.3.1. The Problem of Inverted Precedence

Physical needs, like food and water, are the most basic. Consider the case where a person ensures that the family gets enough to eat by becoming a bonded laborer. That may solve the problem of physical needs but, at the same time, it precludes any hope of satisfying any higher need. Or, one may get a well paid job in a city and lose all hope of enjoying an unpolluted environment. Thus, faulty processing of a lower need can block, at least impede the fulfillment of higher ones. That is a precaution that is often overlooked in designing schemes to help the poor.

Problems arise also when higher needs are allocated out of turn. For instance, lower staff in government establishments often rent out their staff quarters and remain in the slum where they came from. Here is a case where the allocation of a higher order need becomes infructuous because it preceded the full satisfaction of a lower need – in this case, income. Likewise, sophisticated instruments gifted to universities often remain idle because they were offered before establishing a culture of research. Such instances may be multiplied. Evidently, there is no point in fulfilling a higher order need until the beneficiaries are ready for the same and also till they are in a position to utilise it effectively. Many government schemes do not make allowance for this feature.

These two kinds of problems result from the hierarchical nature of Maslow Needs. These needs are not only felt in a hierarchical sequence, they cannot even be fulfilled effectively out of sequence. Neglecting that characteristic leads to waste of national resources.

1.3.2. Public Goods and Geographic Socialism

A poor servant maid in Delhi (some "middle class" families too) has no other option but live in a slum. Even then, she will almost definitely have electricity in her house if not a gas stove, refrigerator, TV or even a telephone. Her child may attend an English medium school. In several respects, she and her family will command a Quality of Life, and enjoy future prospects that are better than what "rich" landlords and their children command in India's villages. This contrast demonstrates the oft-ignored fact that poor people in a rich economy can be better off than rich people in a poor economy do. The maid and her family enjoy all they do because Delhi has a wealthy economy where electricity is readily available, telephones can be had for the asking, gas supply is well laid out, English medium schools are plenty and public transport too is extensive. In villages, practically none of these can be had, however wealthy one may be.

Typically, the state determines the allocation of 20 to 30 per cent of the national product, the single largest component in any economy. The importance of the geographical distribution of government goods is often underestimated. For instance, good schools are located only in cities like Delhi, therefore, the son of a menial employee in Delhi has better chances of education and better prospects of the future than the son of a wealthy landlord in a village. Thus, because of government's policy in the distribution of its goods – in this case that of high quality schools – every person's future is determined by where he or she resides and is quite independent of personal income or wealth. Here it is not a question of affordability, but of entitlement. The village landlord could have afforded the same kind of education as the maid if English medium schools had been nearby.

Some goods like water, kindergarten schools are of little value unless available close by. They may be called tele-ineffective goods, the kind that have little value when moved some distance away. Such goods, in particular, should be made available in the immediate vicinity of everybody. The equitable geographical distribution of all such goods is a major component of distributive justice and might be described as "Geographical Socialism"[2]. That form of justice is conspicuous by its absence in India. For example, over Rs. 1000 has been spent per capita to augment the water supply of Chennai. In Mumbai, it has cost Rs. 800 per capita merely to cart garbage. No rural area can dream of attracting that kind of allocation for such basic needs. Far less would have been adequate but even that little is denied by the state. Denial of minimum degree of Geographical Socialism is a major act of social injustice.

The government has a variety of job creation schemes for the village poor but few jobs of any kind to be had, let alone well-paid ones. On the other hand, there are next to no employment generation schemes for cities; yet, there are plenty of jobs and high-paying ones too. This anomaly is the result of government's policy of investing in the macroeconomy of cities and tackling rural poverty at the microeconomic level. Villagers cannot get rich so long as villages remain poor, too poor to attract modern industry and commerce. Conversely, if villages are enriched, there will be little need to target individual villagers.

1.3.3. Risks of Rapid Economic Development

The Planning Commission has targeted eight per cent growth for the Tenth Five-Year Plan. However, agriculture, the mainstay of villages, cannot grow faster than two per cent on an average. So, it is inevitable that either, (a) villages get relatively impoverished, or (b) massive rural-urban migration results. The probability is that both will happen. Hence, if no corrective steps are taken, over the next five years, (a) a third of the rural population will have to either migrate to cities, or (b) suffer a similar relative decline in incomes. Alternately, rural areas may be so developed that, over the next five years, a third of the population will be diverted to non-agricultural occupations. If this issue is not faced squarely and if rural development is not diverted away from agriculture (and handicrafts), rural incomes will be reduced to one-eighth of urban ones by year 2020, or urban slum populations will go up by an order of magnitude.

---

2. P. V. Indiresan, Managing Development: Geographical Socialism, Decentralisation and Urban Replication, New Delhi, Sage, 1990.

1.3.4. The Problem of Spatial Development

As matters stand, in our crowded cities, there is not enough space to provide basic amenities such as water, electricity, shelter and a healthy environment. Their congestion is such that it is physically impossible for most cities to offer these amenities. In rural areas, there is no such physical constraint (as there is in cities) but absence of investment prevents people to enjoy basic amenities there too. So, the problem in cities is physical and insurmountable; in villages, the impedance is economical but curable – provided sufficient investment is diverted to rural areas.

The Iron Law of Economic Justice is nowhere more dominant than in the field of housing – unless the wealthy enjoy spacious houses, the poor cannot hope to get a basic minimum of shelter. Consider, for instance, the designs adopted by the Delhi Development Authority (DDA). The DDA builds flats for the well to do under, what is known as, the Self-Financing Scheme. These flats are built on modules of 100 sq.m. of land area, which is shared by four flats on four floors. That is, effectively, each flat gets only 25 sqm. of space as its share. Even then, the DDA constructs so few of these flats and thereby has made them so scarce, that their market price is over Rs. 50 lakhs – so expensive that even those who occupy the highest positions in the government find it difficult to acquire them. If even such rich people can afford (with much difficulty) barely 25 sq.m. of space, what can the poor hope for? At current market prices, they cannot afford even one sq.m. of land. In effect, the government treats the poor the way *Kauravas* treated *Pandavas* – deny them land the size of a cow's foot even. The *Kauravas* triggered the Mahabharata war. Our urban planners are fuelling an even greater disaster. Bereft of all hope, slum dwellers steal other people's land. Injustice has made criminals out of basically decent people.

The model of urban development adopted by India involves (a) non-allocation of living space to the poor, (b) expansion without planning, (c) sub-standard allocation of services of each and every type, (d) concentration of capital investment, (e) adoption of expensive technology that offers no economic return.

The existing paradigm of urban development based on unbridled expansion of slums is deadly. Also, rural development that depends solely on agriculture/cottage industries will breed only poverty and not wealth. In any case, the government should tackle the poverty of villages rather than the poverty of villagers. In Germany, 80 per cent of the rural population is engaged in non-agricultural occupations. That is a useful model for India too to emulate.

1.3.5. Supplying Public Goods

The components of Human Poverty Index (life expectation, literacy and access to safe drinking water, health services and sanitation) are all largely a function of public goods. Governments in poor countries are unable to provide these services either in quantity or in quality. In contrast, the supply of public goods in "company towns" is usually of a high order. Here, these goods are paid for, not by taxes, but by the employer and provided as perquisites to the employees. Essentially, in this case, the employee remuneration is in two parts; a wage component w for private goods and a perquisite component p for the public goods allotted making a total of $w+p$ in all. When the cost of public goods is met directly by the employer, there will be constant pressure from the employees to maximise p, that is, to maximise the allocation of public goods. On the other hand, when the entire remuneration $w+p$ is paid in cash, the same employees will balk at spending the original share p on public goods. They will all try to be "free riders". In effect, the people are willing to pay a higher local tax when the remuneration is split partly in cash and the rest is given away as a perquisite in the form of public goods.

Suppose, as an alternative to providing perquisites, the employer is asked to pay the same amount p as tax to the government. Then, the employer will now turn into a free rider and the tax collected will be much less than p. Out of that reduced collection, the cost of collection will have to be deducted. For both reasons, the net amount available for public goods becomes significantly less. Further, municipal bodies are not known to be very efficient. That is a third reason why the actual delivery of public goods will be worse than in private campuses.

Thus, there are three options, with the cost of public goods met by (a) the consumer as a tax, (b) by the state as a subsidised service, and (c) by the employer providing the same as a perquisite. As we know, the consumer will not pay enough, and the employer too will evade paying the full amount of tax. Neither can the government make up the shortfall fully nor spend it efficiently.

In the past, the state has "primed the pump" by raising the supply of public goods and stimulated demand. Perquisites too work in an identical fashion and stimulate growth with the added advantage that when employers provide public goods as perquisites, they will utilise resources more efficiently than municipal bodies do. For three reasons, giving away public goods as perquisites is better than raising wages and leaving it to the discretion of individual citizens how much they will contribute for public goods: (a) they may not spend all that money and hence, curtail demand; (b) they may spend it on imported luxuries, which may not be ideal and (c) the time lag between accretion of income and actual expenditure will create inflationary pressures.

Before employers can supply public goods as perquisites, they will have to house their employees in campuses of their own. Few employers can do so. There is also the objection that few employers would be altruistic enough to accept the responsibility of supplying public goods. Instances of such altruism are not unknown; in many cities of India, open spaces at the intersections of major roads are maintained by individual firms and very well too – much better than what the local government could have done. As a reward, the company is allowed to place a small board indicating that it is maintaining the flowerbeds. Evidently, this small recognition materially changes the attitude of the employer. As Schumpeter (1961) has explained, entrepreneurs have two strong desires: (a) social recognition and (b) getting things done. Encouraging employers to supply public goods will cater to both these psychological needs of entrepreneurs.

1.4. Factors in Visionary Development

Targets do not make a vision but are derived from it. Vision is qualitative, but targets are quantitative. "Freedom from Hunger" is one expression of Vision. Providing 3000 calories a day to farm labour is a target, a target that can change to barely 2000 calories a day for sedentary office workers. Thus, targets vary from one situation to another but Visions like "Freedom from Hunger" are invariant. Targets are convenient and necessary too for implementing a Vision. Unfortunately, the tendency is to treat the target and not the Vision as the final objective. For that reason, some of the boundary conditions of development, such as the following, tend to be overlooked:

a. *The Iron Law of Economic Justice*: Unless the rich have their luxuries, the poor cannot have their needs. Unfortunately, this is only a necessary condition, not a sufficient one. Offering luxuries to the rich does not guarantee welfare of the poor.

b. *Hierarchial Nature of Maslow Needs*: In fulfilling the hierarchy of Maslow needs two precautions should be observed: One, no lower order need should be so provided that it impedes the supply of a higher one. Two, higher ones should be offered only when lower levels are reasonably well satisfied and there is no risk of the facility being diverted.

c. *Limits to Agricultural Expansion*: Agriculture cannot keep pace with industry or services. Hence, rural areas should be empowered to shift from an agrarian economy to an industry and service oriented economy. Or else, large-scale rural-urban migration and consequent social dislocation will be unavoidable.

d. *Equitable Distribution of Public Goods between Cities and Villages*: Both inefficiency and injustice are rooted in the policy of not allocating public good investment equitably (on a per capita basis) in rural areas. Geographical socialism is still valid even if other forms of socialism are not.

e. *Public Goods and The Free Rider Syndrome*: Encouraging employers to provide municipal goods, as perquisites to their employees, is an efficient way of getting round this pernicious human frailty.

1.5. Formulating A Vision

The Prime Minister's aspiration of nine per cent GDP growth is the closest to a vision that we have heard in a long time from our political leadership. The actual rate, whether it should be nine per cent or eight per cent or any other is not the issue; it could be anything provided it is the fastest growth that is possible under the prevailing conditions. Hence, the economic Vision for the Indian economy may be defined to be *"the fastest possible GDP growth"*, or better still *"the fastest growth in per capita incomes"*.

Growth cannot go on forever. So, there is a school of thought that aims at *sustainable growth* along with its counterpart *sustainable consumption*. Up to what level growth can be sustained is a matter of guesswork. In the past there have been extreme pessimists like Malthus who predicted that however prosperous an economy may be in the short run, ultimately, the wages will dwindle to subsistence levels. That is still true for economies that practice subsistence agriculture and have no population control, e.g., several areas in BIMARU states.

With modern technology and population stabilisation, per capita incomes can, and do rise above subsistence levels. Theoretically, there seems to be no limit to technological advance, and hence, no limit to per capita incomes. However, where there is free migration of people, rich countries cannot avoid in-migration from poorer ones. So, if immigration were free, the entire world would stabilise at a common per capita income. In the real world, due to economic, social and political costs of migration, that equalisation will not be exact but few countries can remain much richer than the average. That is why, compared to the world average, even the US is only about five times richer but poor countries are 30 times poorer. Then, for a poor country like India, one realistic definition of sustainable Vision can be:

> *The fastest feasible growth that will push per capita income, the Quality of Life Index and the Human Poverty Index too reasonably beyond the world average.*

In that case, the country will not invite contempt as being too poor nor invoke much jealousy for being "sinfully rich". On that basis, India may plan to raise per capita income five times on a Purchasing Power Parity basis. However, that is not enough. Disparities between the rich and the poor too should be taken into account. According to World Bank estimates, the bottom twenty per cent of India's population get a fifth of what the top 20 per cent get. That ratio of 5:1 between the top and bottom quintiles is comparable with most egalitarian countries. Then, assuming that (a) this ratio of 5:1 between the top and bottom quintiles is acceptable, (b) that India should grow five times richer to reach the world average, the socially conscious Vision 2020 may be set as:

The living standards of the bottom quintile of India's population should be raised to the level of the top quintile today by year 2020.

There is now a willingness to admit errors committed in the past. That is truly a Cultural Revolution. However, realisation of past mistakes is only half the battle. The task of finding better solutions remains. Better solutions can be discovered only through experimentation. For that reason, experiments will have to be conducted on alternative processes of development. Every such experiment involves risks. So, risk-taking will have to be encouraged and safety nets erected for unavoidable failures. Before we can reach the goal of building an economy where the poor will command all basic needs, we should induce everyone (particularly administrators and entrepreneurs) to experiment with change. That is the best way to make the country develop not only rapidly but wisely too.

2. DRIVING FORCES OF DEVELOPMENT

2.1. The Importance of Technology

There is a widespread belief that it is capital that drives the economy. Annual budgets, Five-year Plans, company reports make a great play about capital investment. While money is critical, it is not the most important contributor to a nation's growth. Denison has calculated (Table 2.1) the factors that contributed to the growth of the United States between 1929 and 1982. He found that as much as 64 per cent of that growth was attributable to advances in knowledge (that is, to R&D). Education came next with 30 per cent whereas the direct contribution of finance and capital was barely ten per cent. Management and economies of scale too contributed more than capital did. Similar conclusions were arrived at by Solow too.

In the 1920s, the situation of United States was not much different from that of India today. For instance, she was a late entrant with other countries like Britain and Germany already well entrenched each in their own market niche. Further, she too had relatively a large population. So, the 1929-1982 experiences of United States offer a useful lesson for India today. Hence, India would be wise to lay stress on R&D and education and make them the driving forces of future economic development.

Table 2.1

Components of GNP Growth in United States: 1929-82

Type	*Share*
Labour input except education	- 23
Education per worker	30
Capital	10
Advances in knowledge (R&D)	64
Better resource allocation (management)	19
Economies of scale	20
Land	- 4
Other determinants	- 20

Businessmen too would be well advised to take the same cue and concentrate more on educating workers (or recruiting educated workers) than in buying machinery, and invest more on R&D than on buying know-how. Unfortunately, Indian businessmen, and planners too, have an ineradicable conviction that money is all. They and the labour leadership too have a morbid fear of technology change. For instance, as late as 1985, the Government of Kerala banned outright the use of computers in any of its establishments.

Indian businessmen feel that they are too poor to support education and R&D. It is more than likely that they are poor only because they do NOT support education and R&D. Incidentally, according to Denison, economies of scale accounted for 20 per cent of American growth. It appears possible that India's ideological support to small-scale industries and the government's aversion to economies of scale have impeded the country's development substantially.

At the rate India is progressing, it will take 100 years to attain the per capita GNP South Korea reached by 1995. Evidently there is something wrong with our economic policies. The mistake is our policy makers worship *Lakshmi* instead of *Saraswati*. Both deities do contribute to economic growth but with a difference.

As Fig. 2.1 indicates, the money pumped in by capital increases demand and shifts the demand curve upwards, but the position of the supply curve will not change, only the limit at which the supply will saturate will be extended from S(N) to S(C). So, pumping more capital increases output but at the cost of higher prices and consequent inflation. In contrast, when technology is adopted as the growth engine, improvements in technology reduces costs all round – it reduces consumption of labour, of material and quite often even that of capital. So, it pushes the supply curve downward, generates growth and actually reduces prices too. That is why technology is a better Driving Force than money.

Figure 2.1

How Technology Promotes Growth and Lower Prices and Capital Stimulates Demand but Increases Prices

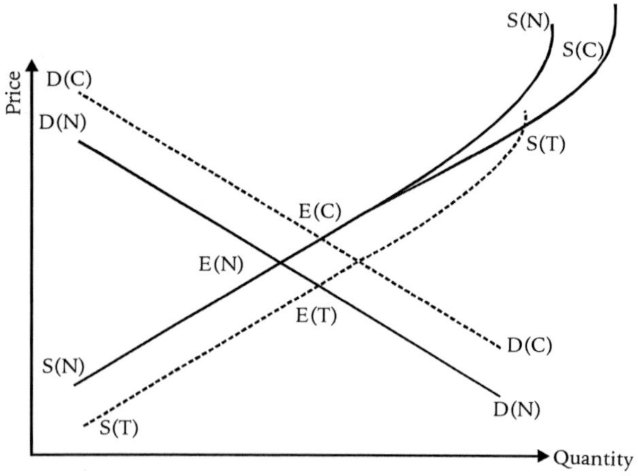

E(N) - Normal Market Equilibrium.
E(C) - Capital infusion increases output and prices too.
E(T) - Improved technology too increases output but with reduced prices.

2.2. The East Asian Model

East Asian countries are by far the most successful practitioners of capital-led growth. Paul Krugman has explained that the East Asian Model depends on increasing the inputs of labour and capital; the Western one on increasing the efficiency of utilisation of those two inputs – through technology innovation. According to Krugman (Box 2.1), the East Asian Model is liable to get saturated on the labour front once the entire population is put to work. Similarly, on the capital side, saturation will be the result when savings and foreign investment reach their peak. Further, as foreign investment is notoriously fickle, the risk is not merely saturation but instability – as demonstrated already by East Asian countries. In contrast, innovation-led development is relatively autonomous, and hence, more stable. In particular, so long as there is worthwhile innovation, there is little risk of recession. So long as a nation is building better and better mousetraps, there is little risk of shortage of customers! (However, it must be said to the credit of East Asian countries that after a foundation of capital-led growth, they are now investing heavily in R&D and in higher education too.)

Box. 2.1

Limitations of the East Asian Model

Long before the East Asian meltdown, Paul Krugman correctly predicted that the East Asians were merely paper tigers. Writing in 1994 in the journal *Foreign Affairs,* he said:

Consider in particular the case of Singapore. Between 1966 and 1980, the Singaporean economy grew a remarkable 8.5 per cent per annum, three times as fast as the United States; per capita income grew at a 6.6 per cent, roughly doubling every decade. This achievement appears to be a kind of economic miracle. But the miracle turns out to have been based on perspiration than inspiration: Singapore grew through a mobilisation of resources that would have done Stalin proud. The employed share of the population grew from 27 per cent to 51 per cent. The educational standards of that workforce were dramatically upgraded: while in 1966, half the workers had no formal education at all, by 1990, two-thirds had completed secondary education. Above all, the country had made an awesome investment in physical capital: investment as a share of output rose from 11 to more than 40 per cent.

. . . these numbers should make it obvious that Singapore's growth has been based largely on one-time changes in behaviour that cannot be repeated. Over the past generation, the percentage of people employed has almost doubled; it cannot double again. A half-educated workforce has been replaced by one in which the bulk of workers has high school diplomas; it is unlikely that a generation from now most Singaporeans will have Ph.D.s. And an investment share of 40 per cent is high by any standard; a share of 70 per cent will be ridiculous. So, one can immediately conclude that Singapore is unlikely to achieve future growth rates comparable to those of the past.

But it is only when one actually does the quantitative accounting that the astonishing result emerges: all of Singapore's growth can be explained by increases in measured inputs. There is no sign at all of increased efficiency. ... once one allows for their rapid growth of inputs, the productivity performance of the "Tigers" falls from "the heights of Olympus to the plains of Thessaly"

There is a critical reason why India may not succeed in adopting the East Asian model. Small countries — Singapore, or at the most Malaysia — can prosper through capital-driven growth. For a large population like India's, similar level of per capita Foreign Direct Investment is next to impossible. Even if such massive foreign investment materialises, that capital may be used only for the kind of goods that have been discarded by developed countries, and hence have low profit margins — television sets, for instance. Further, whatever niche there was for a large country, appears to have been captured already by China.

Imported technology is like a banana peel, the fruit from which all value has been extracted, and which can yield only a marginal profit. Small countries can prosper by selling a million TV sets at comparatively low profit margins. Taking that route, India will have to export hundreds of million sets for which a market is just not available. So, being a large country, India can prosper only by exporting products with large profit margins – that means, innovative products that will emerge only from high quality education and innovative R&D.

There is an incorrect view that India has a large manpower base in science and technology. As Table 2.2 shows, how poor India really is in this respect.

Table 2.2

A Comparison of S&T Manpower in India and Other Countries

Country	*Scientists and Technicians per 1000 of population*	*R&D Scientists per 10,000 of population*
China	4	
Germany	86	47
Israel	76	59
Japan	110	60
Korea	61	22
USA	55	
India	**1.2**	**2.5**

2.3. The Swadeshi Issue

Though the Indian government's economic policy has been strongly in favour of self-reliance, its technology policy has been equally strongly in favour of importing technology. Currently, in several ministries, it is the official policy not to accept any technology unless it has been in use for two years. That rules out indigenous innovation altogether and actually kills it because why should a foreigner accept any Indian technology if that is not acceptable in India itself? Thus, technology infanticide is the practice in India though the country won Independence on the basis of swadeshi.

In two articles entitled "Who Is Us?" and "Who Is Them?"[3] Robert B. Reich, the former US Labour Secretary argues that the labour force is always "Us" but the owners may or, may not be - even if they are citizens. According to Reich, the Corporation is "profoundly less relevant to . . . economic future than the skills, the training and knowledge commanded by . . . workers". He adds that control and ownership of corporations is NOT important. "What is crucial is how many corporations invest in the future capability of the workers, and how far they employ local scientists, engineers and technicians in R&D. A corporation which invests in the training and upgrading of human capital is "ours" even if it is owned by foreigners; a corporation which does not invest in human capital is not "ours" even if owned by our own citizens."

According to Reich, financial capital is fluid; international capital movements are far simpler and easier than international movements of human capital. So, human capital is reliable; financial capital is ephemeral and untrustworthy. Further, as a rule, financial capital chases human capital - that is why so many software firms are coming to India. Or, if we have human capital, we need not worry about financial capital. The converse is not true. That makes skilled work force a more reliable asset than financial capital. Development based on human capital is dependable; that based on financial capital is undependable. As he says:

3. Robert Reich, Harvard Business Review, 1991.

"well-trained workers attract global corporations, which invest and give the workers good jobs; the good jobs, in turn, generate additional training and experience. As skills move upward and skill accumulates, a nation's citizens add more and more value to the world — and command greater and greater compensation from the world, improving the country's standard of living."

Then, an Indian-owned firm, even if it is a Public Sector Undertaking is NOT one of "ours" if it is wedded to imported technology. In contrast, any foreign firm that brings in new technology, new management, new skills and invests in R&D employing Indian scientists, engineers and technicians, is truly one of "ours"!

Culture Receptive to Technology: All these are cultural factors, the fact emphasised by Olson. Mokyr[4] (pp. 11-12) has analysed this particular aspect, and explains that the following three conditions should be satisfied before any national culture will support innovation and development:

a. A cadre of ingenious and resourceful innovators who are both willing and able to challenge their physical environment should be available.

b. Economic and social institutions have to encourage potential innovators by presenting them with the right incentive structure.

c. Diversity and tolerance should prevail in the society to enable technological creativity overcome entrenched vested interests that might incur losses if innovations are introduced.

In other words, innovation and technological progress are unlikely in a society in which people are intellectually malnourished, are superstitious, or are extremely traditional. In brief, what any country needs most is scientific spirit. Thus, quality education is the prerequisite without which technology innovation and development will not flourish.

2.4. Education as a Driving Force

According to Denison, education contributed a massive 30 per cent to the growth of United States. Education can be classified under

4. Joel Mokyr, The Lever of Riches: Technology, Creativity and Economic Progress, New York, Oxford University Press, 1990.

three categories: school, vocational and university. Contrary to popular opinion, Indian education must be quite good – or else, India would not have been able to export skilled manpower as much as it does. At any rate, many Indian schools are apparently not so bad as to destroy the native intelligence of students. At the same time, by absolute standards, however, India's performance is admittedly unsatisfactory both in quantity and in quality.

2.4.1. School Education

The government has the policy of opening a school in every village, even hamlet, on the principle that no child should be far away from a primary school. That may be good quantitatively but not qualitatively. It is more important that every child has access to good education rather than physical proximity to a school. Single teacher schools that predominate in the rural areas do not offer, cannot offer, quality teaching, not even regular teaching.

In this era of globalisation, command over the English language is a precious asset. So, is computer literacy. Unfortunately, most state governments are lukewarm towards the teaching of English and indifferent to computer literacy. Some are actually hostile. So, only rich children who can afford private schools get the advantage depriving poor children the capability to compete on an equal footing.

It is now recognised that intelligence has many dimensions, of which eight are prominent: factual, numerate, analytic, linguistic, spatial, intuitive, athletic and emotional. Most Indian schools concentrate on rote learning that stimulates factual intelligence and little else. It would be useful if students are given individual attention and encouraged to develop whichever type of intelligence they excel most.

Strictly speaking, school education is not a preparation for the job market. It takes 10-12 years of schooling for the economic benefits of education to be realised. Few poor families have the economic strength to educate their children for that many years. So, dropouts are common, particularly in poor families. Therefore, before school education to play its due role in national development, the following issues must be addressed:

a. Providing universal access to good quality schools and at affordable cost by even the poorest families.
b. All children must have the entitlement to acquire proficiency in English and in computer skills.
c. School education should address the individual strength of each student – and the society should respect and honour all skills equitably so that every kind of talent is encouraged.
d. Suitable employment opportunities should be created for those children who have no ability or inclination to study for long years.

2.4.2. Vocational Education

On the whole, unlike in Germany, vocational education has not succeeded in India. That is because it does not address several basic features of this system of education – which would be better described as training rather than education. Some critical features of vocational training are:

a. Innumerable variety.
b. Needs years of practice.
c. Requires costly materials to practice on.
d. Skills required can change rapidly.

No school system can address these issues. A school can, at the most, have instructors in two or three specialisations, whereas the variety required in the market is enormous. Schools cannot afford to provide long years of practice and even if they try to, they will never afford the amount of materials that may be needed – except may be in computer skills. Nor can instructors in schools keep pace with rapid changes in technology. For all these reasons, vocational training is best given in the work place and under the supervision of master technicians. Bookish learning in a school need not be excluded entirely. Conceptual aspects can still be taught there. It is like a musician learning the theory of music in a school, but practising music under a guru.

2.4.3. University Education

Sir C. V. Raman, India's only Nobel Laureate in science was strongly opposed to the concept of dedicated research laboratories like the CSIR. His argument was that the money should have gone to universities. It is no accident that virtually all Nobel Prizes have gone to universities and few to far better endowed non-academic research laboratories. The reason is simple: good research needs young research students. Hence, diverting talented researchers from academic institutions to full time research hurts both ways: full-time researchers lose the stimulation that only young research students can give. Students too lose because the best minds are drawn away from teaching. In particular, applied research is liable to be siphoned away completely from universities. At the same time, without the discipline of teaching, researchers are liable to lose touch with basic principles and the quality of their research is liable to suffer. So, isolation of teaching from research will hurt both research and teaching.

Some of these fears have borne fruit. Universities are starved of funds and research laboratories too are starved of talented youth. There are over 800 engineering colleges in the country and another ten thousand arts and science colleges. Yet, there are not enough well educated students to man the laboratories. Some pertinent issues to be considered are:

a. Education provided does not match job requirements in most cases.

b. Almost invariably, graduates are under-employed.

c. Education does not keep pace with rapid advances in knowledge.

d. Most teachers are of poor intellectual calibre and are yet paid very highly compared to the ability of the economy to bear.

e. The most talented migrate abroad or opt for non-technical occupations.

f. Financial and infrastructure support is meagre.

Table 2.3 compares the finances of IITs with that of the Massachusetts Institute of Technology. The revealing factor is how much more expensive IIT Education is and how much better their faculty is paid compared to MIT – in terms of per capita income of the two countries. University education will not become universal, and poor students will be lost to higher education, until Indian education becomes as cheap as American education is in terms of ability to pay.

Table 2.3

University Financing - A Comparison

Item	*MIT, Cambridge, USA*	*IITs*
Salaries	5000 perchis	30,000 perchis
R&D Income	60%	10%
Fees Income	13%	20%
Endowments	23%	2%
Fees Rate	600 perchis	3000 perchis

Perchi = National per capita average hourly income

Though the US has several thousand colleges, the country picks on barely a score of them for substantial support. The same kind of elitism is to be found in every advanced country without exception. Apparently, higher education is not democratic and requires extra privileges to the most talented.

The issues to be borne in mind relating to higher education are:

a. Making Indian universities globally competitive.

b. Matching education to the economic needs of the country.

c. Attracting talented students to S&T occupations.

d. Financing elite institutions at international levels.

e. Making it socially acceptable to give preference to talented students and faculty.

2.5. Urbanisation as Driving Force

It is a common observation that cities generate employment in higher numbers, and of higher value too, than the same population distributed over a number of villages. It is also a fact that rich countries are, as a rule, highly urbanised and poor ones are rural. So, urbanisation appears to be a necessity for a modern economy and hence, should be treated as a driving force of development.

At the same time, not all city dwellers are rich. Many cities are infested with appalling slums. In general, the world's largest cities are in the poor nations of the Third World while some of the richest cities, like Frankfurt, Edinburgh, Amsterdam, San Francisco, have all a population of a few hundred thousand only. So villages and very large cities wallow in poverty, while rich habitats are often of a modest size. So, there must be an optimum size for cities, at any rate there is a range of population size where cities prosper best.

The Central Business District (CBD) determines the economic strength of a city. If expensive metros are ruled out, access to the CBD will be mainly by bus transport whose capacity is typically 6000 persons per hour. If the CBD is located at the convergence of four arterial roads, around 25,000 people can enter or exit it during the busy hour. As a thumb rule, the CBD employs five - ten per cent of a city's population. So, one CBD accessed by buses can support a population of about 300,000-500,000 population. If the city grows bigger, either more expensive rail or metro systems should be used or multiple CBDs installed. Either way, costs escalate. These are congestion costs that raise real estate prices beyond control, make it necessary to employ costly techniques like high rise buildings and fly overs, increase pollution, even crime. Hence, both theoretically and from practical experience, city size is best limited to a few hundred thousand.

Fig. 2.2 expresses these concerns graphically. When population size is too small, the capital cost of amenities (a railway station or a college for instance) will be spread over too few people. So, per capita costs are high. When the size becomes large, the city tends to get congested. So, congestion costs mount up raising per capita costs once again. In between, there is a broad range of population sizes where the per capita costs are low.

Population density is another critical factor in habitat design. Cities are, by definition, more crowded than villages. Yet, many Indian villages are so densely packed together that their density could be higher than that of large cities of the West. While sparsely populated villages cannot offer most services of a modern economy, crowded cities are liable to be infested by slums. So, they too deny many amenities. Hence, in this case also, there must be some in-between figure where modern services are economical and at the same time, congestion is not excessive and tolerable.

Indian cities and villages are often tightly packed. Kolkata has the dubious distinction of being the most densely populated city in the world with a density of 89,000 per sq. km. Other cities are not far behind. In contrast, New York, one of the most densely populated cities of the world has a population density of 8900. In London, the density is half as much, in Berlin a third. So, large cities need not be as crowded as Indian cities are. The fact that not one city in India is able to provide such a basic necessity as water in sufficient quantity is an indication that our urban design exceeds the carrying capacity of the soil.

Figure 2.2

Why Cities Have an Optimum Size

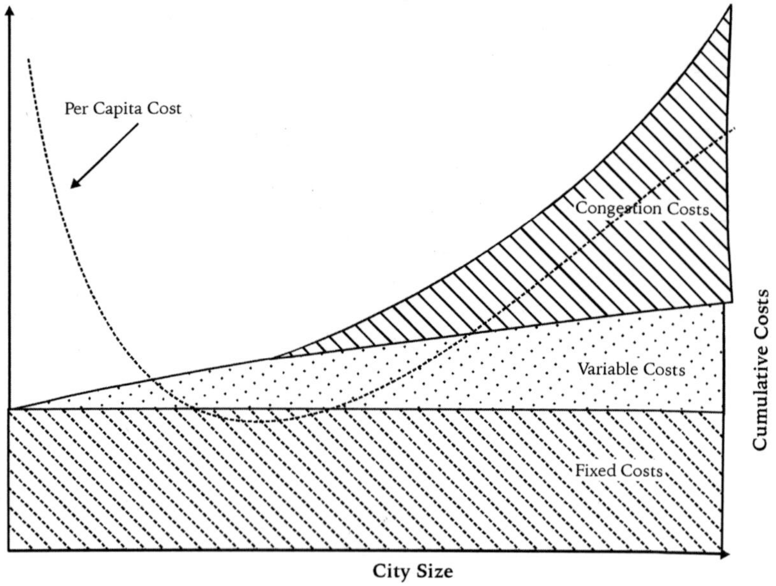

In most parts of the country, average rainfall is around 70 cm per year or 2 mm per day on an average. Assuming that half of that can be harvested, local water availability can be assumed to be one mm of rainwater per day. If a modest 100 litres of water per day is allowed per head, 500 square metres of space should be available for a family of five. (That includes non-residential space too. So, average space per house will be 200-250 square metres). Then, the upper limit will be 2000 families, or 10,000 persons per sq.km. – about the same density as New York. Similar conclusions emerge from considerations of traffic flow also.

Considering how expensive land is in Indian cities, an average allocation of 250 sq.m. space would appear a pipe dream. Actually, only 25 thousand sq.km – no more than 0.8 per cent of the land area of the country will be needed to allocate space at this rate to the entire urban population of 250 million people. So, it cannot be anyone's case that enough land is not available to entitle people to this order of space. However, though there is enough and more of land in the country to prevent slums, they are not available within existing cities – precisely where people want to reside. That too is not an insoluble problem.

2.6. Constrained Vision, Unconstrained Vision

The problem lies with our vision, rather the lack of it. There are two kinds of vision – the Constrained Vision and the Unconstrained one. We in India have been bogged down by Constrained Vision in many ways. Constrained Vision leads to dead ends, to a state of utter helplessness and hopelessness. We have got caught in that state of mind because we have been asking the wrong kind of questions. For instance, it is usual for us to ask: "How can we accommodate the growing rural-urban migration in our already congested cities?" That pre-supposes that rural migration can take place only to congested cities and nowhere else. That is Constrained Vision. When the question is posed in that manner, the inevitable conclusion is slums are unavoidable. Suppose we pose the issue in a different manner and ask: "Our Vision 2020 includes civilised habitat. Hence, how can jobs be created for surplus rural labour in places where it is possible to guarantee a minimum quantum of dwelling space?" That is the way of Unconstrained Vision. It opens up opportunities that do not exist now. It shifts emphasis from congested cities (a case of closed option) to employment generation in rural areas where land is available in plenty for housing needs. That is an unbounded option, the approach of Unconstrained Vision.

Urbanisation is always a driving force for an economy but not always a good one. Only when it is implemented within a range of suitable sizes and with appropriate population densities that it becomes a desirable driving force. Most services, including referral hospitals and universities can be supported once a population reaches three to four hundred thousand. A collection of such cities located within an hour or two of travel time, can support a large airport too. That is how Frankfurt, Dusseldorf, Cologne and Bonn operate. Cities with size larger than a few hundred thousand spawn multiple business districts and inevitably get congested. So, the optimum urban habitat will be composed of several mutually connected cities each of a few hundred thousand population and all with densities not more than 10,000 per square kilometre. Urbanisation on these lines will not only be a driving force, it will also be a good driving force.

Slums are not inevitable. Top officials need not be confined in tiny flats. Even the poor can have enough space to relax provided the rich have much larger accommodation. Many developmental problems have remained unresolved only because the vision stops at the conventional. Once the vision stretches beyond the obvious, effective solutions become apparent.

Unfortunately, these days, most people in India forsake the country at the first whiff of inconvenience and at times for self interest. Some leave the country to use their talents for the benefit of others. Others stay here but siphon away profits to deposit them elsewhere, in Swiss banks and the like. The perception that India is not the best place to exploit either talent or capital is a major hurdle and a significant impedance to the country's progress. Restoring people's confidence, particularly those of the talented, should have priority in the mind of any planner or policy maker in India.

3. IMPEDANCES TO DEVELOPMENT

According to Denison, nearly two-thirds of American growth during the mid-twentieth century was attributable to technology development. Hence, any impedance to technology innovation will be a great impediment in the path of economic progress. In India, there are plenty of such impediments, based on a variety of fears, such as:

a. Unemployment.

b. Displacement of population.

c. Environmental pollution.

Other impedances to technology-based development include:

a. Rigidity in the labour market.

b. Poor education system.

c. Industry's apathy to R&D.

d. Government bias in favour of technology imports.

e. Reservation of many products for production by small scale industries.

Behind all these impedances lies one factor – fear of change and consequent cultural suspicion of technology.

3.1. Impedances to Technology Development

According to Olson[5], there can only be two reasons why some countries are rich and others are poor: (a) differences in factor endowments (namely, land, labour, capital and technology), or (b) differences in environment. Olson concludes that, of the two, it is the environment that is crucial. Considering the vastly different economic wealth of neighbouring countries with similar endowments, (United States and Mexico, South and North Koreas, or former West and East Germany), wealth and poverty cannot be the result of differences in factor endowments but due to faults in political policies and institutions. According to Olson, economic factors like land, labour, capital and even technology are relatively unimportant, not even material. So, though poor technology is the basic reason why India is poor, the basic issue is not inadequate technology development but poor technology environment.

For instance, South Korea was no better than India thirty years ago. Now it is one of the advanced countries of the world. All that progress was engineered primarily by buying technology. Olson estimates that for every dollar paid out by South Korea for importing technology, the country's GDP increased by 60 dollars. So, he concludes (a) the kind of technology needed for the enrichment of a poor country is purchasable in the international market and (b) the cost of such purchase is minuscule compared to the wealth generated as a consequence. India too has purchased considerable amounts of technology but has not utilised it as productively as South Korea has done.

It may be argued that South Korea has done better because she was richer and had more capital. That is not true. In the 1960s, when

---

5. Mancur Olson Jr., Big bills on the sidewalk: Why some countries are rich and others are poor, *The Journal of Economic Perspectives*, 1996.

South Korea set out on the growth path, she was no richer than India. Yet, South Korea progressed faster because she managed to attract foreign capital far better than India did. As Olson explains,

> "Intrinsically, the more profitable avenues would have been exhausted in rich countries leaving behind only less profitable ones. On the other hand, in poor countries many profitable avenues would have remained unexploited. So, poor countries offer much better pickings for capitalists than do rich ones. Therefore, the natural flow of capital is always from rich countries to poor ones, not the other way around. . . left to the market, capital will flow across borders until the returns to capital become the same in both places - until the extra profits of poor countries equal extra costs of entering such markets. So, poor countries may have little capital of their own but should have little difficulty in attracting capital *provided their culture does not discourage inflow of foreign capital.*

That, however, is not the case in chronically poor countries like India. In India, as in all poor countries, the barrier to inflow of capital is not inside the rich countries; it lies right here at home. Or, the barrier is not the economics of rich countries but the nature of Indian culture.

It may be argued that poor countries are poor because their people are unskilled. It sounds reasonable to argue that people in developed countries are more capable, better skilled, better educated, better trained and so on. According to Olson, that argument too is not tenable. He points out that immigrants from poor countries outperform natives of rich countries. That is true whether they seek employment, or become entrepreneurs themselves. For instance, whether in United States or in Britain, the Indian immigrant community is wealthier or earns more than natives do. So, India has *a set of more talented people than United States has,* but loses them all due to brain drain. Brain drain too is not an economic problem but a cultural one. If Indian culture permitted her to pay her engineers as well as she pays vendors of soap, she would suffer no brain drain. In the words of Donald Christiansen[6]:

---

6. Christiansen, Donald, Engineering Excellence: Cultural and Organisational Factors, New York, 1987, IEEE Press.

A country that trains its engineers and technologists well, then rewards them with both real and psychic income, should have little trouble competing in a world economy that thrives on trading high quality, high tech products over international boundaries.

Thus, we notice that technology is purchasable, capital is available, and the supply of high quality labour is more than the demand.

That leaves only one more factor of production, namely, land and mineral wealth. It is true that there is greater pressure on land in India than in the USA. But many other countries like Japan, Holland, Belgium, England have even higher population densities. Yet they are all much richer than we are. In any case, land accounts for no more than two or three per cent of a nation's wealth. So differences in endowment in land, even arable land is not crucial. In any case, the cost of potato chips in the market is twenty-fifty times the cost of cultivating potatoes. Weight for weight, even a spoon costs ten times more than the iron ore from which it is made. Hence, wealth is derived not so much from agriculture or from minerals but by processing them into high value products. Or, land is a predominant wealth only in an agricultural society and not in a modern one. That is why Singapore is wealthy in spite of having no source of raw materials and India is poor even though she has resources in plenty.

3.2. Economies of Scale and Bottlenecks

In his analysis of the growth of the United States, Denison estimates that Economies of Scale contributed towards 19 per cent of the total. That was twice as much as capital did. Evidently, the managerial ability to handle larger and larger system is an important factor in economic growth. That is an area where India is indeed weak.

India is a large country and large scale is inherent to all its activities. Yet, the pace is slow, much slower than that of much smaller countries. The excuse is given that the pace cannot but be slow because the large size inevitably introduces inertia. Hence, instead of being an advantage, large scale has turned out to be a disadvantage in India. Fig. 3.1 explains these phenomena graphically. As the curves on the left panel show, economy of scale results when the cost increases less rapidly than size does – the curve is then convex towards the upper side. Diseconomies of scale result when cost increases faster than size; the curve is then convex towards the bottom side. Often, the situation is as shown on the right panel – a combination of both diseconomy of scale and economy of scale. That combination too is of two types. Initially, the cost can increase rapidly and economy of scale establishes itself later on. That is the American achievement. They think big; they are willing to wait till the market builds up to an economic size. State policy makes the opposite happen in India. Small scale industries get so many tax incentives and are allowed to evade so many taxes, that it is NOT profitable for them to expand to a globally competitive size. As a corollary, there is no incentive to invest in R&D and keep pace with global advances in technology. That is a double jeopardy – the country loses out both by poor technology and lack of economies of scale.

Figure 3.1

Economy of Scale, Diseconomy of Scale

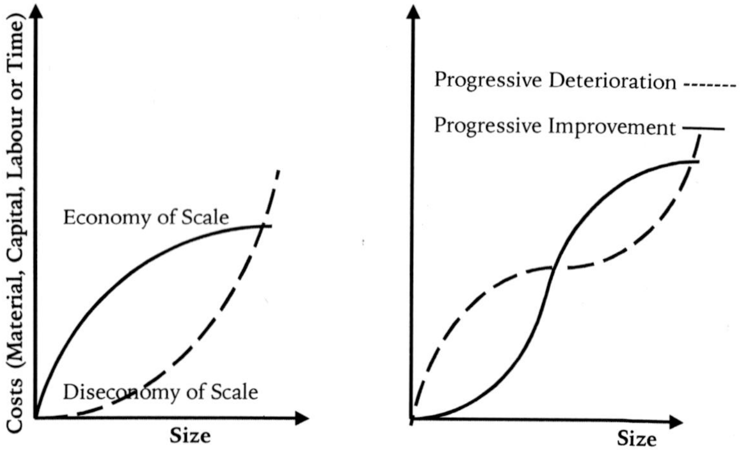

When a system is expanded, the addition could act either as a bottleneck or as a lubricant. In small systems, bottlenecks get identified fast but not so in large complex bureaucracies where there are so many points of delay and obstruction that one more does not get noticed, nor appear unusual. Cost conscious private industry is sensitive to delays and impediments; unwieldy bureaucracies are not.

In their case, delay is actually an addiction – most bureaucrats would be unhappy if the power to impede and delay is taken away from them.

This is a cultural issue. In India, there is insufficient awareness that growth has two elements, material increase and the time taken to achieve it. If time of implementation is halved, for the same increase, growth will be doubled. In India, delays and impedances are seen as a source of power, not as a loss of face. Indian officials see both monetary or psychological profit in impedance. So diseconomy of scale prevails. Or, economy of scale will take root in India if the penalties are so imposed that they cause either monetary or psychological injury on those who impede, and act as bottlenecks and not as lubricants and rewards are granted on those who act like lubricants. In India, there is currently so much fascination for impedance that few people are consciously aware of the extent they practice it, or how it erupts in every kind of transactions. That is particularly true in any issue that concerns technology innovation – the most critical factor in economic growth.

3.2.1 *Slums and Rural-Urban Migration*

Slum infested urbanisation is another example of this phenomenon and a major impediment to both rapid growth and quality of life. Fig. 3.2 compares the variation of cost of urbanisation with city size (indicated in Fig. 2.2) with the curve of Fig. 3.1, which depicts how economy of scale can turn into diseconomy of scale when size increases. That feature of deteriorating economies of scale with increase in size is typical of most construction in the country, whether that be the construction of roads, buildings or any other.

Typically, 25-30 per cent of investment for growth is accounted by construction. So, any diseconomy of scale will seriously impede growth prospects. Many countries have built attractive cities; we are unable to do so. Even Delhi the richest and the most pampered city in the country, has nearly 40 per cent of the population condemned to live in appalling slums. The problem is NOT financial – it would cost far less to house them elsewhere. The problem is cultural – the insistence of concentrating investment in congested, expensive megacities to the exclusion of more economical locations, the insensitivity to human degradation and the unwillingness to do anything about it. That is a major hindrance, impedance to both rapid growth and rational development.

Figure 3.2

Urbanisation : Diseconomy of Scale Follows Economy of Scale

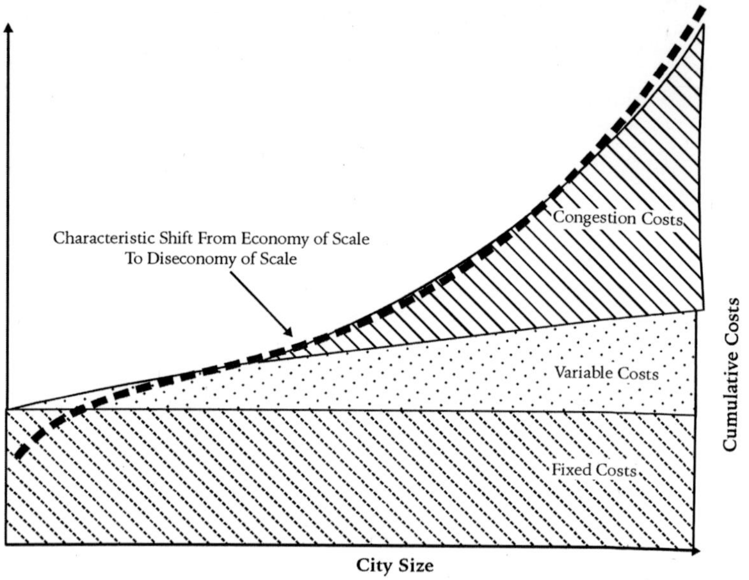

Who imposed these constraints? We imposed them ourselves! These three constraints cannot be basic because there are many beautiful uncongested cities in Europe and elsewhere. So, it should be possible to develop cities without taking recourse to slums. Paraphrasing Sherlock Holmes, once the impossible is eliminated, whatever remains, however improbable, must be the solution. So, when the option of cities is eliminated as impossible, the choice that remains is the improbable one of shifting development to rural areas. That is the only location where land is cheap enough to be affordable even for the poor.

According to current wisdom, slum clearance is an impossibility. That is why even the World Bank has reconciled itself to funding merely "slum improvement" schemes. That pessimism results from the constrained vision that looks only inside congested cities but not beyond. In that scenario, rural-urban migration and natural increase of population will combine to accelerate urban growth beyond control. It is the prevailing view, that as the space in and around cities is limited, and cities are bound to expand, slums are not only unavoidable but will also increase inexorably.

There are three self-imposed constraints here:

a. Rural-urban migration is necessary.

b. Space must be found only inside congested cities.

c. Reverse urban-rural migration is impossible.

Table 3.1

Two Views About Slums

Conventional Wisdom	*Visionary Alternative*
Slums are natural, they are inevitable	Slums are created artificially, needlessly
Space is scarce; so, only a minimal space should be allowed even for the rich	Only when the rich get large spaces can the poor hope to get their due
Rural-urban migration is inevitable	Rural-urban migration is unnecessary
Capital creates jobs	Employers create jobs
Rural poor will migrate to cities only	Rural poor follow wherever employers go
Employers like only CBDs	Basically, employers seek connectivity only
Cities alone can supply large connectivity	Dedicated bus lanes linking a loop of villages can provide similar connectivity
Business must be at the city centre and residences far off at the periphery	Businesses can be distributed around the loop and located close to residences
Space is scarce, hence expensive. So, poor can have slums only	Space is in surplus; so, land prices can be made low enough for the poor to afford

Rural-migration results because the poor need jobs and can get them only in large congested cities. When employment becomes available locally, few villagers will migrate and rural-urban migration will come under control. People may even drift away from cities when job prospects become better in rural areas. So, the cure for cancerous growth of cities lies in generating employment in rural areas.

3.3. Fear of Technology-Induced Unemployment

Fear of unemployment is a major impediment to acceptance of technology change. As a rule, technology reduces employment in three ways:

a. Technology reduces labour per unit of product.

b. Technology increases wages, and hence cuts the demand for labour.

c. Technology makes skills obsolete.

At the same time, technology opens out new opportunities, and more rewarding ones too. However, dislocation is unavoidable. It requires considerable grit to accept the attendant risk of not finding alternative employment. Dictatorships can force people to accept the resultant hardships but not democracies. That is the argument frequently given to justify India's slow pace of progress compared to that of China and other East Asian Tigers.

It might be recalled that in Denison's analysis, better allocation of resources accounted for a significant 19 per cent of US growth. It is not unlikely that India too will grow significantly faster if employers are allowed the freedom to allocate human resources efficiently. Unfortunately, state policy is fashioned otherwise in India. The government goes to great lengths to help the less competent and employ them in superior positions and does so at the expense of the talented. That policy is a direct impediment in so far as it prevents optimum allocation of human resource. Indirectly, it impedes both education and the application of technology, the two major driving forces of economic growth. Until a solution is found to this problem, the country will not be able to grow fast.

As the late J. R. D. Tata used to say, it is easier in India to get rid of a wife than an employee. It is a fundamental principle of fluid mechanics that there can be no flow where there is no exit. Therefore, rigid labour laws that prevent removal of unwanted labour are an impediment to progress.

It is not an accident that in the profession of computers, selection by merit prevails, the policy of hire and fire is accepted without demur, and even with enthusiasm while, in traditional fields, labour clings to the concept of permanent employment with promotions based on seniority rather than on merit. It may therefore be worthwhile to divide the economy into two sections – a traditional non-competitive part and a modern, globally competitive section. Instead of having the same rule for every case, the law may be framed differently for these two sections of the economy.

Employment in the field of computers is much more remunerative than elsewhere and rightly so. That excess remuneration has two components – compensation for the risk of sudden loss of employment and the market premium for relatively rare skills. In all government agencies, the policy is exactly the opposite. Those who are engaged on a temporary basis, and hence, suffer from insecurity, are actually paid less and are denied most perquisites too. Those with seniority but no skills are remunerated better than those who are skilled and competent. There is a lesson here for formulating a national income policy. If the culture of computer industry spreads all over, a major impediment to rapid growth will be removed.

3.4. A Law for Employment Growth

The problem of employment guarantee becomes manageable and organised labour's resistance to efficient allocation of human resources can be minimised if both wages and the labour demand increase simultaneously. Wages will increase automatically when (a) new technologies are inducted because of inevitable shortage of labour with new skills and (b) there is economic growth.

Then, number employed = Total wage bill divided by wage rate

Growth rate of employment = Growth rate of GNP – Growth rate of wages

The first is a tautology; the second one too is also essentially a tautology because, in general, the total wage bill of a nation is very nearly a constant proportion of the GNP. Therefore, the numbers employed will increase, if and only if, GNP increases faster than wage rate. Employment shrinks because this simple arithmetic is often overlooked, and organised labour extracts wage increases faster than the growth rate of the economy. That indeed was the error committed by the last Pay Commission: Because wage increases exceeded the growth rate of government finances, downsizing of the government has now become necessary.

3.5. Wage Policy and Employment Growth

There are two Indias – the India of the organised sector and the India of the informal sector. Relative to the organised sector, government employees are probably underpaid, but taking the country's economy as a whole, they (and every one else in the organised sector) are grossly overpaid as the following comparison will make it clear. In the US, the Chairman of the Federal Reserve Board – a position at times described as more powerful than that of the President even – is paid $130,000 a year, about four times the country's per capita income. India's per capita income is, currently, around Rs. 25,000 a year. Even petty clerks in the government earn more than Rs. 100,000 a year and hence, in terms of the country's capacity to pay are better paid than the America's Federal Board Chairman. Thus, In India, even lowly government jobs catapult a person to the top of the economic ladder. Obviously, many cannot have that privilege and hence, few new jobs can be created. That situation is unavoidable so long as such jobs are overpaid in terms of the country's per capita income. That is another reason why technology change, and consequent loss of employment, is viewed with horror in India. That is why, organised labour insists that jobs be protected at all costs.

It is not an accident that the Planning Commission is talking of downsizing the government while at the same time holding out hope for a momentous eight per cent growth rate. Rapid growth and downsizing are self-contradictory. That anomaly is the consequence of having a salary structure out of step with Indian realities, with Indian per capita incomes. So long as this disparity persists, employment will not grow, and economic growth will get stunted.

3.6. Limitations in Technology Management

3.6.1. Appropriate Technology

True to the Gandhian spirit, many people in the country favour appropriate technology, more accurately described as traditional craft technology. While it has its uses, it has its limitations too. For instance,

a. A bullock cart cannot provide the same quantity or quality of service as a motorised vehicle.

b. It does also pollute – relative to the quantity of service provided, its biological pollution is high, overall more polluting than a motor vehicle.

c. Relative to quantity of service, its capital/running costs are high.

d. It cannot generate high incomes.

3.6.2. Social Activism

A particularly severe controversy concerns irrigation by dams. A study conducted by the National Council of Applied Economic Research has shown that small dams, irrigating 2000 hectares and less, cost about six times more per hectare than large dams irrigating excess of 100,000 hectares. As a thumb rule, to store a given amount of water, a 100 metre high dam will submerge ten times less land than a 10 metre high one. The taller dam is therefore likely to displace ten times less number of people, destroy ten times less forest and cause ten times less environmental stress. There is a romantic view that water harvesting is a good substitute for dams. That may supplement but not supplant dams. Also, dams would better be as high as possible. For instance, Bhakra dam has been built so high that it takes nearly three years in-flow to fill it. There are three reasons why such large storages are preferred. Firstly, our monsoons are so fickle that storage of several years flow is needed as an insurance against monsoon failure. Second, in our tropical climate, evaporation losses alone account for 1.2-1.5 metres per year. Hence, deeper storage reduces effectively the proportion of water lost due to evaporation. Thirdly, dams have a finite life due to siltation. Obviously, a deeper one will have a larger life than a shallow one. Our great-grandchildren's great-grandchildren will thank the designers of Bhakra for their foresight in building such a tall dam.

Table 3.2 depicts the contrarian views of social activists and technologists. Without in any way belittling the concerns advocated by social activists, it must be stated that social activists are among the most significant impediments to rational development. If ecologists had been active at the time Bhakra was being built, and most of Bilaspur town was submerged, that dam would never have been built, there would have been no Green Revolution, and millions would have perished of malnutrition if not by outright starvation. It is even debatable whether their methods will bring prosperity to the people whose cause they claim to espouse – they are more likely to perpetuate their present dismal poverty.

Table 3.2

The Adversarial Relationship Between Social Activists and Technologists

Social Activists	*Engineers and Administrators*
Insist on zero-cost solutions	There is no free lunch
Single issue activity	Should consider all ramifications
Not responsible for resultant problems	Responsible for all consequences
No hesitation to break the law	Constrained to act within the law
Offer impractical solutions	Must make their designs work
Opposed to innovation	Experiment with technology
Seek to avoid poverty	Try to generate wealth
Have high communications skills	No communication skills

3.6.3. Preference for Imports

Except where it is entirely unavoidable, Indian administrators (whether in the public or in the private sector) fear to try local designs. They consider that well-worn imported designs alone are risk free. As a result, Indian designs face a Catch-22 situation. They will not be accepted unless they have been in use, and they cannot be in use until they are tried out! So, except when foreign technology is not available at all (as in defence, atomic energy and space), Indian designs do not get a chance to prove their worth. Private industry too is no different. They want swadeshi *only for manufacturing operations but not for technology*. For several reasons, that is a bad bargain. First, there is an opportunity cost - the Indian design might be superior. Second, imported designs too bear considerable risk. Precisely because they are well worn, they are liable to be obsolete, and not saleable in competitive foreign markets. Third, the policy gives ample scope for foreign firms to form cartels and overcharge. Fourth, there is a strategic risk. Several times in the past, United States (and other Western countries) have denied valuable spares for equipment already sold and have even reneged on committed contracts.

3.6.4. Resistance to Innovation

A peculiarity of technology is that, like vegetables, it must *always* be fresh; otherwise, it is unprofitable. If Indian manufacturers had attempted to *improve their technology continuously*, their technology needs would probably have been within the capability of the Indian scientific community. In any case, over a period of years, the needed expertise would have been built up. As Indian industrialists flog every know-how purchase to its death, there is a long time gap between technology renewals. So, the technology gap becomes too wide to bridge even if talented engineers are available. In other words, India offers little or no scope for 'Sam Pitrodas' because Indian administrators have little interest in improving on imported technology.

The Ambassador car is still ubiquitous in India. It started as the 1958 model of Morris Oxford. In forty years, the vehicle has not changed in essentials even though automobile technology has gone through several revolutions in the meanwhile. In post-war Japan, the story was different. Datsun of Japan procured the identical technology from Morris Motors and at the same time too. Unlike in India, Datsun modified the received design step by step. Over the years, the changes accumulated to such an extent that the vehicle became unrecognisably new one with no remnant of the original Morris Oxford left. In contrast, the Indian model has remained frozen for forty years. Advances that have been occurred in the mean time have been so substantial that the gap between the Ambassador and a modern car is unbridgeable. So, the company has had no option but go shopping abroad once again for new technology. Such repetitive import is a bane of Indian technology.

3.6.5. Overcharging by Foreign Suppliers

Predatory MNCs often trade on India's weakness for imports and attempt to destroy any Indian technology that can prove a threat to their own hegemony. Such predatory tactics are not rare; they are, in fact, quite common[7]. At the same time, MNCs are known to dump

7. The following three examples illustrate the point.

- In 1991, several European suppliers demanded around Rs. 1500 million to supply a communication system for the Indian Navy. At this stage, the navy approached US manufacturers with whom, for political reasons, India had had no contacts at all for years. Apparently, never expecting the Indian government to go to Americans, the French neglected to prime the US manufacturers about the deal. Hence, unlike European manufacturers, the Americans quoted a fair price – Rs. 150 million.
- In another instance, India's aircraft carrier, INS Vikrant was in need of a re-fit for a guidance equipment for landing aircraft. The price quoted by a French firm was Rs. 9.5 million. Finally, IIT Delhi developed the same at a cost Rs. one million only.
- Recently, an American firm quoted Rs. 7.5 million for a piece of railway electronic equipment, but when IIT Delhi succeeded in developing a local version, the price was brought down nearly 80 per cent to Rs. 1.7 million.

their goods at throwaway prices to under cut Indian technology with a view to kill competition. While it would be unfair to tar all foreign firms, it would be unwise not to protect the country from such threats.

In spite of such experiences, it is the official policy in the Department of Telecommunications (and in others too) not to procure any equipment unless it has been used for a minimum of two years. In this connection, the following Irish folk tale about a sailor shipwrecked on a desert island is worth recounting.

> A sailor shipwrecked on an uninhabited island prays to his guardian angel to let him have at least a baby for a companion. Much impressed at that unusual thought, the angel leaves a baby by his side in a sack while he was asleep. The sailor wakes up, sees something wriggling in the sack, *suspicious of anything new,* and as a matter of abundant caution, drives a knife into the sack before opening it.
>
> Look into the mirror. Do we see that sailor is there?

3.7. Lack of Scientific Spirit

Few people in the country, even among scientists and technologists have any clear conception of the nature of the scientific spirit and the discipline and techniques that go with it. That lacuna is particularly acute among the teaching community and is the cause of misdirecting students. That is yet another reason, why India is unable to exploit its technical capabilities to the full.

Thomas Kuhn[8] has explained how Western science has remained ahead of all others, and has maintained that lead successfully for several centuries. That success he attributes to certain features of Western intellectual culture. Just like scholars the world over, Western scientists too believe in received wisdom. They too accept certain theories to be absolutely true. But unlike other, they do not stop there. As Karl Popper[9] has explained, they consider the purpose of science is to disprove - not prove - theories. That they do by pushing the frontiers of the accepted paradigm farther and farther. For that purpose, they set, and attempt to solve, newer and newer

---

8. Thomas S. Kuhn, Structure of Scientific Revolutions, University of Chicago Press, 1970.
9. Karl R. Popper, The Nature of Scientific Discovery, New York, 1959.

puzzles. In that process, sooner or later, anomalies occur where the paradigm fails to predict results accurately. When it becomes impossible to explain such anomalies, a second process takes over. A concerted attempt is made to discover a new paradigm that performs more satisfactorily than the old one. When a better paradigm is found, a third step follows. The old paradigm is consigned to the dustbin, and the new one becomes the received wisdom. This third step is therefore a scientific revolution, a revolution that is no less ruthless than any political one. For instance, no one uses Newton's laws of motion in space science and has been completely replaced by the Theory of Relativity. Likewise, valve radio is dead as dodo. In Western science, once a paradigm fails to deliver, it is discarded without pity. That is the essence of scientific spirit.

For the scientist one flaw is enough to reject the paradigm for all time. To the person of faith one incident is enough to confirm that belief for ever. The true scientist is ever engaged in finding what is wrong with received wisdom, and discards received knowledge the moment it is found to be flawed. The person of faith is ever trying to reinforce the faith, and discards any evidence that goes contrary to the beliefs handed down from the past. The scientist has no compunction to sacrifice one's own faith, even to kill one's own brain-child the moment something better becomes available. The essence of faith is continued devotion irrespective of evidence to the contrary. The education system in India has not as yet rid the country of the culture of faith, nor inculcated that of science.

3.8. Impedance to Rational Education

India has a number of world class institutions, like the IITs and the IIMs for instance. It has also the largest number of world's illiterates. There is much educated unemployment and large-scale under-employment. Though there are 800 or more engineering colleges (nobody knows how many), youngsters of adequate calibre are not available. The really outstanding ones migrate and are lost to the country forever. Vocational education has not taken off at all and that shows up in the poor quality of engineering products produced in the country. Much remains to be done to improve both the quality and quantity of education in the country and at all levels and there are many obstacles to be faced at each step.

3.8.1. School Education

In terms of per capita income, Indian teachers are among the best paid in the world and in many cases, the most pampered too. Salaries are so high relative to available resources that, in many states, as much as 98 per cent of the school budget is spent on salaries. So, there is a gross mismatch between the allocation of finance between wages and academic activities. Single-teacher primary schools are predominant. For various reasons, many teachers are suspected to be chronic absentees. Rote learning is the rule rather than the exception. Many students dropout within a year or two to remain illiterate for life. Schools and school teachers are highly politicised. Major obstacles to the rectification of these errors are:

a. Resource allocation policy is a deterrent. Distributing teachers to every hamlet, even if that means single-teacher school, prevents most rural children from having access to quality education. Financial allocation is skewed grossly on the side of wages and next to nothing for other academic expenses. Finance is not the constraint – its maldistribution is.

b. The negative policy concerning the teaching of English are driving everyone, who can afford it, to go to private schools thereby increasing the disparity between the rich and the poor.

c. Remote control from state capitals, and non-allocation of authority to govern local schools to panchayats has resulted in poor discipline.

d. There is next to no investment on modern tools of education technology.

3.8.2. Vocational Education

Vocational education is the step-child of the education system. The situation is unlikely to improve because:

a. The responsibility is distributed between the Ministries of Education and of Labour but there is no competition between the two.

b. Industries are lukewarm to the idea of supporting this kind of education.

c. At the lucrative end (computer training for instance), vocational education is dominated by expensive commercial institutions precluding the possibility of poor children acquiring such skills.

d. There is little social recognition for the value of vocational skills. As the experience of computer training shows, that is because of relatively poor career prospects and emoluments for vocational skills.

e. Academic institutions are NOT geared to provide quality vocational training in all its myriad forms.

3.8.3. *University Education*

Irrelevance is the major problem at this level. In the middle of the Nineteenth century, cardinal Newman espoused the idea that the purpose of the university was to produce gentlemen – not productive citizens. In the twentieth century, Nobel Prize winner Henri Bergson propounded the idea that the highest knowledge was the one that had no practical use whatever. Such concepts still rule the academia and there is uneasiness about the demand for profitable education. On the other hand, the Finance Ministry has concluded that the private benefit from university education is so high that it is a "non-merit" good not deserving of much public support. University education in India is quantitatively low by Indian standards, and often of poor quality. Progress is probelematical for the following reasons:

a. University education is highly politicised. Teachers form a powerful lobby. Colleges are started and run on commercial lines by powerful local politicians and the government is helpless against the depradations of both.

b. There is no contact whatever between the employers and the academia.

c. Recruitment and promotion are both politicised and caste-based. Both ways, quality suffers.

d. Admission by entrance tests does not select the most deserving candidates.

e. Seniority rule largely precludes recognition of merit.

f. University bureaucracy and policy making are both painfully slow, too slow to keep pace with rapid advancements of knowledge.

g. There is no system of winding down outdated courses.

h. Heavy diversion of research funds towards government laboratories has denuded universities of research funds.

i. Research has ceased to be an attraction for bright students.

j. Brain drain has denuded the nation of high quality talent.

All these problems are well known; there is nothing new. They are being repeated ad nauseum in every gathering of academics. So, the real obstacle is the inability of the system to accept the inevitable cost associated with viable solutions or even experiment with them. Absence of seriousness and integrity are the two major obstacles to improving education in the country.

4. REALISING TECHNOLOGY VISION

Vision, as already explained is quantitative, not qualitative. We have identified our Vision in terms of Quality of Life that will be decidedly better than the world average. In the light of Denison's analysis, we may conclude that (a) technology, (b) education, (c) economies of scale and (d) efficient allocation of resources as the main factors in maximising economic growth. Capital is deliberately excluded because once these four elements are well developed, capital will naturally get attracted. In any case, the contribution made by capital to a modern economy is but a small fraction of what these four factors do.

4.1. Objectives of Technology Development

As shown in Table 4.1, management of technology and administration of a government department call for entirely different, at times, contradictory cultures.

Indian technology output is less than its potential because these differences are not appreciated nor addressed adequately. In the light of these differences, and earlier discussions, a set of objectives of managing technology are listed in Box 4.1. The issues identified are brain drain, import bias, career insecurity, competitiveness, economic justice, and ecology. The first three require correctives. The others can be expected to materialise when the first three issues are tackled.

Table 4.1

A Comparison of Administrators and Technology Managers

Government Administrators	Technology Managers
Must follow rules/ precedence strictly	Expected to innovate all the time
Hierarchical; authority is determined by the position held	Culture of peer system; professional reputation determines influence
Adequate if nationally competitive	Must be globally competitive
Command little value abroad	Command a world market for expertise
Seniority, experience paramount	Productive mainly in young age
Subservient to the organisation	Individualistic; elitist
Good administrators are extroverts	Good scientists are often introverts
Personality critical for success	Scholarship critical for success
Tasks are specific, must be done and persons may be interchanged	Task matched to personal expertise; technology can be exchanged
Transfers are routine; deemed useful	Transfers are rare, deemed harmful

4.2. Remedying Defects

4.2.1. Brain Drain

Brain drain can be treated as the consequence of Ricardo's Law of Comparative Advantage: The situation is best explained in terms of an example. In India, it costs about Rs. 400,000 to produce an

Box 4.1

Vision Objectives of Technology Development

Brain Drain: India will generate such attractive career opportunities that the country will import, not export, talented engineers.

Import Bias: Self-reliance will be realised not by rejecting foreign technology but by trading technologies, acquiring them through exchange with indigenous ones and not by outright purchase.

Career Insecurity: The natural displacement of labour by technology will be remedied not by reducing productivity but by stimulating employment multiplication.

Competitiveness: Indian technology will be so competitive internationally that there will be no need to protect Indian goods and services.

Economic Justice: The threat of increasing income disparities will be met by minimising poverty, not by reducing wealth.

Ecology: In all cases, technology will be developed or acquired in keeping with the requirements of good ecology.

engineer in an IIT and about Rs. 50,000 for a PC system. So, one IIT engineer equals eight PCs. In the US, training an engineer, costs a $120,000 while a PC can be had for about $1000. So, an engineer there is worth a 120 PCs. Then, in a trade between the two countries, it would be *mutually profitable* to exchange one Indian engineer for 30 PCs. That is because, India will then get in place of one engineer 30 PCs, whereas producing it locally, only eight PCs would have been produced for the same price - a nearly four times price advantage. It is four times advantageous for the US also because, they will now have to pay only 30 PCs to get one engineer whereas to produce one themselves it would have cost them the equivalent of 120 PCs. Thus, it appears there is a mutual advantage for both countries if India exports engineers to the US in exchange for PCs. Unfortunately, the lifetime productivity of an IIT engineer far exceeds that of a PC. So, it is ultimately a bad bargain for India. However, such brain drain will remain unavoidable so long as India places a low value on engineers and a relatively high value on machines.

Although this explanation of comparative advantage has been couched in financial terms, in reality, the fulfilment of all Maslow Needs must be taken into account. R&D and technology innovation operate at the highest Maslow level of self-actualisation. That will not be realised until all lower order needs are properly fulfilled. In the Indian situation, salaries are relatively high and so is security. The Indian government is commendably generous in funding projects too. However, it is utterly niggardly in rewarding people psychically. It has a blind spot particularly when it comes to professional travel – an important consideration for all R&D specialists. So, the lower physical and security needs pose are quite well looked after, but the higher order status and autonomy needs are not addressed at all in the Indian milieu.

For scientists, status is determined by the recognition given by world-renowned scholars. Even in old days, a *pundit* was respected only when his ability was acknowledged by experts in Banaras. These days, researchers and designers need similar recognition by experts gathered in international conferences. Attending such conferences is considered so important that the National Science Foundation is known to return a project proposal if too little had been budgeted for travel. Its philosophy is that a work worth doing is worth disseminating and that it is best judged by a gathering of experts. In India, such travel is considered a waste and provided only under humiliating conditions.

Teachers' reputations are made by their students. At present, few youngsters are willing to take up research. That will be remedied only when research becomes as attractive a career as jobs in industry.

Administrators, including lowly clerical staff, rule scientists with an iron hand and allow next to no autonomy. Lack of opportunities for social intercourse with reputed researchers the world over, absence of autonomy and poor remuneration are the three major causes of brain drain. The following reforms are likely to reverse the trend:

a. Every time a scientist has a paper accepted in a reputed, refereed international journal, a travel grant will be given as a reward to attend an international conference.

b. R&D project investigators will have the powers of a Head of Department to authorise expenditure out of those project funds without seeking approval from any other authority.

c. Research assistantships should be instituted in large numbers with remuneration competitive with industry but only on contracts for a period of five to six years.

All these are intrinsically performance-based rewards. They are not permanent. Incidentally, in the 1980s, when Mr. Pickering was US Ambassador to India, a proposal was considered to establish a placement system for Indian academics and scientists for summer jobs in American industry. That would have given regular opportunities for competent Indian researchers to gain real world experience and would have been a help to United States too. Such an arrangement would have given competent Indian youth the best of both worlds. Unfortunately, for political reasons, the Ministry of Education rejected the proposal. As the relationship between the two countries has improved, such a scheme may now be acceptable. That could be another way of retaining talented youth within the country – at any rate for nine months in the year.

4.2.2. Import Bias

In India, when an official's work is evaluated, errors of commission and not errors of omission are questioned. There is no audit of opportunity costs - profits lost due to "risks not taken". So, whenever an Indian comes up with a new idea, the cautious reaction is to ask, "Who has used it before?" and "If the idea is so good why is it nobody abroad has tried it out before?" As a corollary, officials search for current limitations, not look for future prospects. This culture breeds "Technology Checkers", not "Technology Acceptors" as a matter of course. Table 4.2 brings out the difference between these technology acceptors and technology checkers. It is self-explanatory.

This policy creates a no-win situation for indigenous innovation and is an open sesame for imported technology. The bias against indigenous development is now official. Many government departments have a rule that no equipment may be procured unless it has been used elsewhere for two years.

Table 4.2

A Comparison of Technology Checkers with Acceptors

Technology Checker	*Technology Acceptor*
Authorised to procure only that which is currently the best.	Will procure what will ultimately be the best.
Buys off the shelf products; does not support technology development.	Tries out new designs; offers feedback to improve product performance.
Has to live with it even if it proves unsatisfactory.	Gets products on trial; returns them cost free if unsatisfactory.
Pays full price up-front.	Pays only after the product is proved satisfactory.
Career in jeopardy if product proves unsatisfactory.	Career in jeopardy if an opportunity to induct a novel product is overlooked.
Cautious. Will take no risks and buy only proven products even if the technology is old.	Adventurous. Will experiment with new technology.
Will resist change	Will welcome change.

4.2.3. Career Insecurity

Rapid changes in technology continuously make obsolete skills and expertise causing enormous tension and resistance to technology innovation. Fortunately, unlike in the case of scientific discoveries, technology developments can normally be anticipated several years ahead – far better than economic trends can be predicted. So, there is scope to train a person in anticipation of technological change and not wait till the person actually becomes obsolete. Such retraining can be a fundamental right of an employee and not a discretionary favour of the employer.

At times, there is no option but to take recourse to Voluntary Retirement Schemes. At present, VRS schemes make no distinction between those that are still needed by the organisation and those that are redundant. So, the administration uses its own discretion to accept or reject any offer for VRS causing considerable bitterness and ill will. The following rule-based system may avoid these difficulties:

a. Every organisation is bound to state at the beginning of each year the areas of expected technological obsolescence and the nature of the new skills required to match the technology change.

b. The organisation is also bound to name the employees that are under threat of technological change.

c. All affected employees will have the option to acquire the prescribed new skills at no cost to themselves, or alternately, opt for VRS.

d. Further, any employee who is overlooked for promotion, or even denied a posting of his choice in preference to a person junior in service, will have the right to opt for VRS.

e. No other person will have the right to opt for VRS.

f. Once these regulations come into force, all organisations are free to allocate their personnel as best as they think fit.

While these rules may solve technology-induced obsolescence and the problem of long-term economic downsizing, it may not work equally well for unpredictable market fluctuations in the demand for the workforce.

4.3. Technical Education

Next to technology, education is the most potent force of economic and social development and for technology development too. In India, there are currently over 800 engineering colleges and many more are being added. Most of them are expensive but the quality is poor. Table 4.3 compares some features of IITs with those of the MIT, United States. The main difference between the two lies in endowments – MIT is rich and can afford to subsidise education for needy students. Indian institutions have no such resource, not even IITs. In brief:

Table. 4.3

University Financing – A Comparison

Item	*MIT, Cambridge, USA*	*IITs*
Salaries	5000 perchis	30,000 perchis
R&D Income	60%	10%
Fees Income	13%	20%
Endowments	23%	2%
Fees Rate	600 perchis	3000 perchis

perchi = National Per Capita average hourly income

a. Technical education is costly and affordable only by the very rich unless heavily subsidised.

b. Such subsidies may not be available from the government, or it may be inadvisable to be dependent on the state.

c. That leaves no option but to depend on business to secure enough endowments to make education widely affordable.

d. Business will offer such endowments only when it sees value in it. Hence, universities should tune the education to business needs.

e. Such attunement will benefit universities too because that will ground their theoretical studies to the actual state of the physical world.

4.3.1. Science and Technology Entrepreneur Parks

In this connection, the idea of landgrant universities may be considered. In the nineteenth century, United States established a number of "land grant" universities with large land grants. The produce from that land supported agricultural research and education. Similarly, engineering universities may now be established with land granted for Science and Technology Entrepreneur Parks, the rent from which may meet most of the cost of technical education. That is one way of bringing down student fees to 15 per cent of the total.

The Department of Science and Technology, Government of India has established Science and Technology Entrepreneurship Parks (STEP) in a number of engineering colleges. Funds are provided jointly by the DST and by Financial Institutions (IDBI, ICICI & IFCI) with the aim of (a) nurturing innovation and S&T based entrepreneurship and (b) fostering linkages between academic institutions and industry. The STEPs provide basic services and offer guidance to budding as well as existing entrepreneurs. So far, 13 STEPs have been established in and around academic institutions of excellence spread all over the country. The programme has so far resulted in setting up of more than 600 new enterprises employing a capital of about Rs. 50 crores. These units have a turnover of nearly 88 crores and provide direct employment for about 5000 persons. Further, skill development and other programmes have generated employment for another 6000 persons.

These are impressive results. However, they fade into insignificance compared to experience elsewhere – Tsinghua University in Beijing claims to generates all by itself US$ 200 million a year.

As an alternative to STEP, several electronics parks have come up in recent years. Unlike STEP, which is linked to an academic institution, the Electronics Parks (at times called Hi-Tec Cities) are independent systems and cost a hundred times more. They are also much closer to industry. They emulate international standards of construction, total commercial orientation. They are located in expensive congested cities. So, their costs are high. So far, they have shown little interest in basic research or on education in its true sense.

Box 4.2 describes the features of one major park of the Rensselaer Polytechnic Institute (RPI) in the United States for comparison. The RPI lays as much emphasis on the environment as on technological services. It is as much a case of habitat development as one of establishing industrial services. It seeks to attract very small entrepreneurs with fewer than ten employees as zealously as it pursues large multi-nationals. Few STEPs in India can claim to have a Master Plan let alone a vision for an environmentally attractive habitat. The Technology Parks in RPI and other universities are huge; Indian attempts are puny in comparison and are unlikely to be commercially viable.

BOX 4.2

The Rensselaer Technology Park

The Rensselaer Technology Park (Rensselaer Polytechnic Institute) is the owner/developer/operator of multi-tenant rental space in the Park which extends over 1250 contiguous acres with 450 acres of commercial space, 150 acres for housing, 150 acres of river frontage for parks and conference facilities and remaining 500 acres left as nature reserve. The Park has a road network built to highway specifications and all underground utility services, including: fibre-optic cabling, power from two separate sources internally looped, telephone, natural gas, public water and sanitary and storm sewers. Buildings have been designed as one story, highly flexible/adaptable space to accommodate technology enterprises ranging from the sophisticated needs of computer environments and research labs to the provision of conventional office and manufacturing space. Development of the Park is guided by a Master Plan and regulated by Covenants and Development Standards. The intention is to assure standards of development that are characterised by quality and consistency without imposing cumbersome bureaucracy. The standards address such things as density and open space requirements, building setbacks, parking requirements, drainage, waste disposal, noise, air quality, landscaping, building design and materials specifications, etc. It is the policy of the university that *parcels will only be available on a land lease basis. Land will not be sold.*

There is also an Incubator Program designed to help launch new ventures, which will typically "graduate" in two to three years. Rentals progressively increase with duration of occupation to deter lessees from overstaying.

As the Box item tells, the RPI is highly concerned about a pleasant garden environment. That may appear an unwarranted luxury for a poor country like India. There are two reasons why that view is wrong. During a visit to Delhi, the Lord Mayor of London was asked by Indian businessmen how the City of London manages to attract investment as well as it does. His reply was that it was because the streets in London are cleaned six times a day! Modern investors are put off by dirt and squalour. When they can enjoy a high quality of life elsewhere, investors and technologists see no reason to come to places that are at best untidy and at worst repulsive. So, for a STEP to attract business and particularly foreign investment, it must pay as much attention to aesthetics as to technical services.

4.3.2. Incubators

RPI has made a provision for both STEP and for Technology Incubators. Basically, STEP supports new technology industries that may or may not be based on innovation. STEP is a for-profit commercial venture as far as the university is concerned even if those profits are used only for the advancement of education. Incubators are different. They are meant to support innovations and nurse them till they become commercially viable. An industry established in a STEP may continue indefinitely, but the lease in an Incubator is for short periods only, typically not more than three years, rarely if ever, more than five years. So, there is a planned turnover in Incubators that is absent in STEPs. The Mission Statement adopted recently by the Department of Science and Technology and the Asia-Pacific Centre for Transfer of Technology (an arm of the UNDP) is given in Box 4.3.

BOX 4.3

Mission Statement for Incubators

Establishing Technology Business Incubators either independently or in reputed academic institutions and R&D centres,

Instituting policy frameworks, administrative systems and statutes to promote innovation and knowledge-driven businesses,

Networking knowledge centres, industries and governments, both nationally and internationally, to promote entrepreneurs,

Obtaining appropriate financial support from governments, private investors and from multi-lateral agencies,

Creating awareness of incubation concepts among the community, the state and business organisations,

Sponsoring appropriate programmes for exchange of experiences among experts on Incubators from various countries,

And ensuring equity for all stakeholders as also rapid improvement in the quality of life for humanity at large.

4.4. Education in Support of Technology Development

The true raw material of technology development is talented human resource. Much of national talent is lost to the country because that is not identified early enough and is not properly nurtured in a conducive and, even more critically, in a competitive environment. Further, success in any field, particularly in science and technology requires innate talent, matched to the requirements of each case. Obviously, with the best will in the world, one cannot make Lata Mangeshkar a tennis champion nor Tendulkar into a Tagore nor teach Arundhati Roy elementary principles of hydrology.

Empowering poor children to enter universities is a difficult problem. The issues and remedies may be illustrated by taking the case of Dr. A. P. J. Kalam. He started in life with every possible handicap imaginable. Though not illiterate, his parents were unschooled and poor. They belonged to a community of artisans that did not set much store on bookish learning and on any type of formal education. They also lived in a remote corner of the country with next to no educational facilities. At the same time, Dr. Kalam did enjoy several advantages:

a. He was intelligent with mathematical skills far above his peers.
b. Though not educated, his parents were wise and inculcated in him high cultural values.
c. His family was willing even to pawn jewels to support his education.
d. He had an outstanding teacher in Sri Shivasubramania Iyer who recognised his talents *at the elementary stage itself*, and went out of his way to persuade his parents to sacrifice their short-term gain to let him study in the middle school.
e. He had in him a desire to excel, to succeed.
f. He had the opportunity to work in ISRO where the work was of the highest quality and where everyone was driven to excel and succeed.

These advantages outweighed his handicaps. Similar factors will be found to be the case with many others who achieved great success against odds. The state should take special steps to help such talented children – right from childhood stage. For that purpose, the following policy may be considered:

a. Provide good quality nutrition to mothers and children.
b. Identify talent in a tender age (That is the main reason for the phenomenal success of the Chinese in all endeavours).
c. Provide a competitive environment to help such talented people hone each other's skills to the sharpest possible level of brilliance.
d. Select the best available teachers, the best intellectually, emotionally and culturally. (Teachers have to be the best because they are the intellectual seed of the next generation.)

e. Make school education affordable[10].

Some may object to selection of teachers on merit and not on the basis of caste and the like. Such persons will do well to consider "Which will help the poor more – teachers like Sri Shivasubramania Iyer or the kind that is being appointed on political grounds? More than the rich, the poor require, and deserve, the most outstanding teachers.

4.4.1. Identifying Talented Children

Talent requires competition to excel. That is why, all over the world, every country provides special support to a few, select institutions. For instance, Britain has Oxford and Cambridge, Japan – Tokyo University, France – Ecole Polytechnics, and in the US, of the several thousand university institutions, barely twenty are nationally prestigious. Likewise, India too should have a clear-cut policy of identifying and supporting a few select institutions of national importance. That is, a special provision should be made to identify the most talented 10,000-20,000 students each year. That should account for virtually all outstanding youngsters in the country.

In India, it is a common practice to hold centrally conducted written examinations to admit students to prestigious institutions. Written tests with secret question papers, and open to all, have several disadvantages. They cannot match the large variety of backgrounds the children come from. However well the questions are designed, somebody or other will complain that the questions were either too difficult or out of syllabus or inappropriate. Physical management, distribution of question papers, collecting answer books, valuing them, and maintaining secrecy are all difficult, if not impossible. Above all, secrecy is threatening.

Admission rate in centrally conducted entrance examination can be as little as one in fifty or even one in hundred. That way, error

---

10. Dr. S. Radhakrishnan, in his Education Commission Report, has suggested compensating poor parents for the pecuniary loss they suffer when they send their children to school. On that basis, one adult member in the family may be given daily wage employment for each day the child attends school at, say, two-thirds the minimal wage – the reminder being treated as fees. It is estimated that this will cost the exchequer no more than Rs. 10,000-20,000 crores a year.

rate (both Type I and Type II) will be unavoidably high. Multi-stage selection will minimise such errors. Hence, it should be worth making selections to university level courses in several stages as below:

a. All selection examinations will have open questions disclosed beforehand (no secrecy!) and set at a level only talented minds can answer.

b. Students' own teachers will conduct a preliminary test and shortlist a number depending on the numbers that qualified in earlier years.

c. The tests will be held at four stages – at the end of the primary, the middle, the secondary and the higher secondary levels for admission to select prestigious institutions at the next higher level.

d. In order to help late developers, lateral entry will be made available at each level.

e. The admitting institution will test the knowledge of the shortlisted candidates in depth and not in breadth – in the field of their own choice, as in the case of the Mastermind quiz on the BBC.

f. Each admitting institution will admit students only out of the shortlist, which will be no more than two-three times the numbers admitted.

This system empowers those who have taught the children to make the shortlist. That will increase seriousness down the line. It also ensures they select the best because, if they play favourites, the number they can shortlist in the future will get reduced. At the preliminary selection level, questions are open; so the tension is minimum. At the final selection stage, questions are both open and open-ended but the tension is still low because the candidates themselves choose the area where they like to be tested. That will separate those who think from those who mug up – the kind that come on top these days and are of little use for technology innovation.

The administrative and financial burdens will be very low under this scheme. As the examinations are highly decentralised, students from backward regions will have as good a chance as those from cities. Multi-stage selection ensures that the numbers taper off gradually and not abruptly as in the current system of one-shot entrance examinations. Lateral entry offers extra opportunities for those who miss out at any stage for any reason whatever.

Figure 4.1

Proposed Multi-stage Talent Search

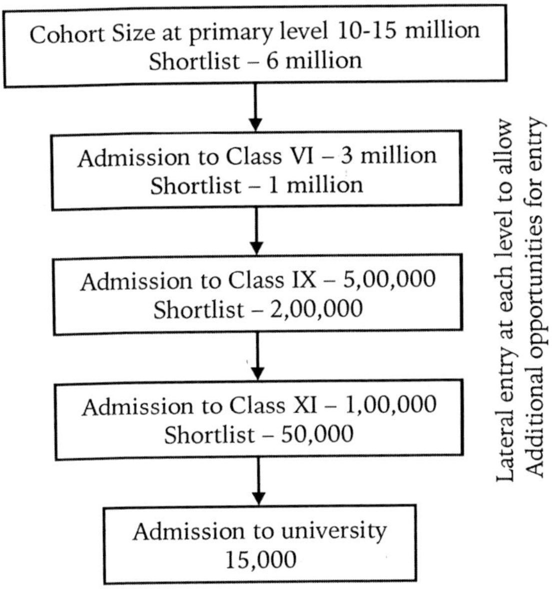

4.4.2. *Empowering the R&D Laboratories and Academic Institutions*

Professor C. V. Raman, India's only Nobel Laureate in science used to be much concerned about the diversion of resources from universities to government research laboratories. As matters stand, it is not possible to undo what has already happened. However, there should be no objection to treat those laboratories as Deemed University and empower them to teach graduate courses. That is not ideal, as they may not like to take on undergraduate students. Yet, as Deemed Universities, they will be able to offer technical facilities and instruction far better than most university institutions.

One further reform is needed to empower these institutions. Status is very important for teachers and researchers. They cannot have a high status unless the institutions in which they work are prestigious. Those institutions will have prestige only when they are autonomous and free from political and other outside interference and control. The IITs are as good as they are mainly because they enjoy considerable autonomy. We need to institutionalise them and even more autonomy for all educational and research institutions.

For that purpose, we may consider installing two autonomous boards for each institution. One will be the Board of Trustees composed of those who provide the capital. They oversee the future development of the institution, operate the capital budget, and will also select the CEO, COO and the CFO of the institution. A second body, the Board of Governors will be composed of reputed academics headed by the CEO and assisted by the COO and the CFO. This Board will have autonomous jurisdiction over academic and research affairs and operate the recurring budget. Such an arrangement has worked well elsewhere. It is the best way of satisfying the autonomy needs of the academic and research staff without the fund providers losing managerial control.

4.5. Vocational Education

Usually, the ratio between engineers and technicians is 1:3 but in India, the two are almost equal. That forces many engineers to perform tasks that can be done better by technicians. The problem lies with the poor state of vocational training in the country. As a remedy to the problems of vocational education listed in Section 3.8.2, the following programme may be attempted:

a. Vocational education is split into two parts and offered as a sandwich of (i) hands-on three-year apprenticeship training under master craftsmen in industry and (ii) academic courses after the elementary school stage.

b. Employers asked to offer at least one apprenticeship for every ten employees with a stipend equal to, say, half the minimum wage or pay the equivalent as a cess.

c. Master Craftsmen identified and empowered to impart vocational training with suitable incentives.

This system will be better than formal vocational schools where it is quite impossible to get adequate trainers nor materials for students to work with. This also inherently matches the skill output to the strength and specific needs of all businesses.

In engineering and medicine, it is common for specialists to have several assistants who provide vocational support. For that reason, those who undergo vocational training should be several times more in numbers than those who undergo purely academic education. In India, the ratio is reversed. In Germany, even those who clean windows and walls get at least a week's training before they are put on the job. In India, persons start off as vice-chancellors without even a day's training. Vocational training does not command much respect, does not have a high status. This situation may be remedied to a certain extent if advanced technician-training courses were eligible for a degree, like say, Bachelor of Technical Arts. At the same time, it is true that computer courses are vocational in nature and yet are highly popular – even if they do not lead to a degree. That is because they lead not only to well-paid jobs but white collar ones too. That is another cultural inhibition – inordinately high value attached to white collar jobs. Until that bias goes, vocational education will not be valued as much as it is valuable to the economy.

4.5.1 Elementary Education

All progress starts with elementary education, one of the most poorly managed sections of Indian economy. That is the result of a basic conceptual flaw – the policy is to take schools to where children reside and not take children to where quality schools can be located. That has led to proliferation of single teacher schools, which are neither properly equipped nor monitored. It is better to take children some distance to good schools rather than take bad schools to the neighbourhood of each and every child.

Every village can be imagined to have eight neighbouring villages in the eight directions of the compass. These eight villages and the one in the middle form a cluster of nine villages, and one school in the middle can serve children from all nine villages if only arrangements are made for children to travel no farther than the next village. In such a case, we can have around 60,000 large schools with as many as nine teachers each instead of the present system of over 500,000 schools, mostly single teacher ones. Such consolidation offers substantial economies of scale in terms of cost of management and cost of delivery of quality. (At any rate, there could be one Hi-Q central school per panchayat.)

The second flaw concerns allocation of resources – over 98 per cent on salaries. A rule that every time teacher's salaries are raised, half of that increase will be statutorily made available for educational infrastructure will make a significant difference to quality of education.

We have had earlier food-for-work schemes. Professor Radhakrishnan's suggestion is the opposite: work-for-educating the child. It is an idea worth exploring and may work if it is decentralised and managed through the schools themselves. As suggested in the previous section, a family member is guaranteed employment at, say, two-thirds of the minimum daily wage every day the child attends school. The remaining one third may be retained by the school to meet its non-wage costs. In effect, the government gives work contracts to schools. If the work is not done up to specifications or child does not perform satisfactorily, the school is bound to return what it has taken. This is a tightly performance-controlled scheme that could help both the school and the maintenance of civil works of the community. Conceptually, it is similar to an engineering college managing a STEP and earning an income out of it.

There is enormous interest in the learning of English. That is opposed not only on academic grounds but for political reasons too. Most existing teachers are not qualified to teach English and they fear for their careers if English is given importance. As a consequence, the rich-poor divide is widening. Rich children learn English and monopolise high paid jobs and the poor are condemned to low paid ones. If the government does not want to antagonise existing teachers, it can at least encourage private initiative to provide supplementary courses in English and support it to the extent that they will be affordable by poor families.

Computer literacy too is a matter of importance, particularly for a nation that hopes to earn foreign exchange mainly in that field. Unless, a school has a minimum of ten to twenty PCs, the computer laboratory will not be economical to maintain and sustain. That is another reason why it is best to concentrate elementary education in 50,000-60,000 big schools. In order to make such a change palatable, existing schools may not be closed down, but future expansion may be concentrated in select schools where both English teaching and computer training of high quality will be made available.

In Section 4.4.1, it was suggested that bright children might be streamed and educated in special schools, the way Chinese do with much success. That will be objected on principles of socialism. That is a deeply flawed argument. Whatever happens, only 2000 children can join the IITs. At present, the selection is made in one stroke. Poor children are suddenly confronted by rich well-trained children and get hopelessly outclassed because only those who can afford private coaching can get to IITs. In a multi-stage screening system, they will start competing among their own peers and gradually hone their skills and have a fair chance to succeed on merits. The government too can help and offer high quality training because the numbers become manageable. So, the so-called social justice argument against streaming actually does irremediable harm to the poor.

This idea is similar to the Navodaya school concept but will benefit many more. It will need one quality school (not necessarily residential) for, say, every 100,000 population and need not necessarily be run by the government.

4.6. Realising the Technology Vision

The ideas suggested here are indicated in Fig. 4.2 and may be summarised as:

The government's contributions are:

a. Empowering poor parents to afford to educate children.

b. Clustering schools to obtain economies of scale.

c. Improving allocation of resources by linking budget for academic infrastructure to salary budget.

d. Offering substantial psychic income to talented scientists and engineers, and

e. Establishing a safety net to cope with unavoidable technological obsolescence.

Figure 4.2

Realising Technology Vision

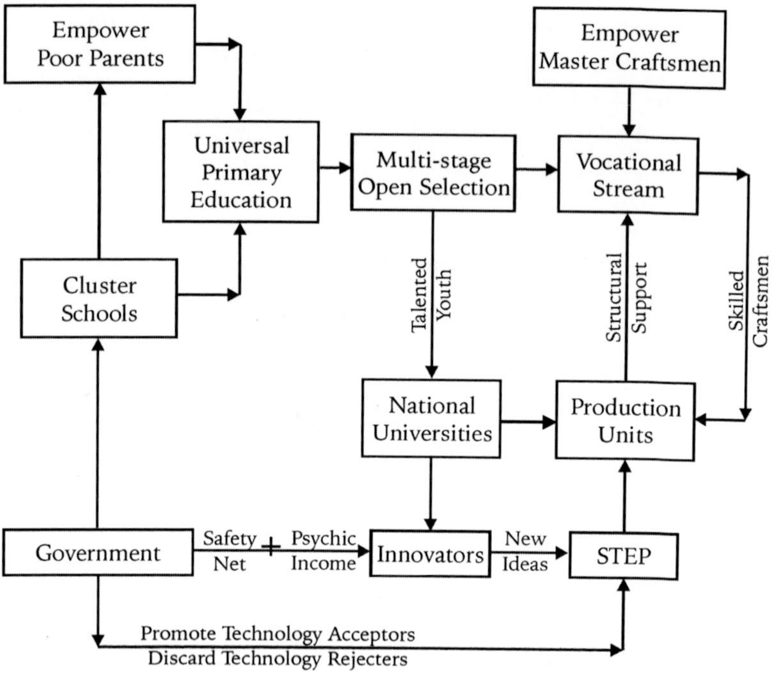

In this visionary set-up, reputed engineering colleges will establish Science and Technology Parks, large enough in size and equipped well enough to attract business to be economically viable. The STEP will not only be a link with industry, it will be a source of income too. Incubators too will be co-located but largely subsidised by the state. Likewise, businesses will offer infrastructure support and the services of their master craftsmen to raise the level of vocational education. Above all, the government will reform its rewards and penalties system to recognise those who help technology innovation and penalise those who obstruct technology change.

5. VISIONARY INFRASTRUCTURE

It is now widely accepted that infrastructure has become the Achilles Heel of India's development. Poor technology practices, concentration of resources in expensive and non-optimum locations and non-utilisation of optimum economies of scale are the reasons why the country appears so poor even though the people are relatively better off – slum dwellers have colour TV and two-wheelers but no toilets and no water.

As for the infrastructure inputs needed for fulfilling Maslow Needs the following eight stand out:

> Reliable water supply, domestic fuel, space for shelter, connectivity, waste disposal and transport/telecom connectivity, social services health and education), markets.

Incidentally, when these services are installed, a large amount of employment gets created both directly and indirectly. Directly, because these are all labour intensive services; indirectly because, the presence of these services will attract industry and commerce. In other words, these are employment multipliers. All these are dependent also on the way the habitat is designed and managed. A new habitat holds promise when:

a. The location has already a population of viable size.

b. There is ample space for expansion.

c. There are no bottlenecks to choke further development.

d. There is a large city in the vicinity.

As Fig. 2.2 explains, there is an optimum range of sizes for habitat – costs are high both when the size is too small and when it is excessive. It is practically infeasible to make large cities small. Hence, for the future, it is best to select some small habitations and expand them to an optimum size.

Expanding small towns is problematic. A habitat does not take off unless it has a minimum quantity and quality of infrastructure, but that is not economically viable until the habitat has already grown to a fairly large size. In that Catch-22 situation, the Indian practice is to wait till the demand picks up some how, and then add the infrastructure. By that time, it is usually too late. Irreparable damage would have been done already. Too little free space would be available for much needed additions to infrastructure, and even if there is space, encroachments would have eaten them up beyond cure.

Several attempts have been made to develop satellite towns and to create Growth Centres by acquiring large chunks of land in the vicinity of large cities and preparing a layout that would be an improvement on the old city. That top-down approach with little participation from intended stakeholders has rarely succeeded. In those developments, the aim has usually been to maximise profit, right at the outset by sale of land, not to maximise the revenue yield of the development. As a rule, investors hesitate to risk going to such new towns where few infrastructure facilities would be available. Consequent delays eat away expected profits leaving little scope for further expansion. Little money too will be available for maintenance, making the city less attractive than what it could have been.

If large cities and towns are ruled out as being overcrowded already, and even small towns are damaged already, investing urban infrastructure in rural areas remains the only possibility. However, rural areas are handicapped by their small size even more than the towns are. However, they have plenty of land; in particular, nearly 15 per cent of the rural land is uncultivable and hence has little commercial value. In most parts of the country, space available is large enough also to make the habitat self sufficient in water through local rainwater harvesting – an important consideration for a country where few habitations boast of adequate drinking water. Local waste recycling and disposal is also a technical possibility – yet another worthy consideration because there is practically no town or city in the country which is clean and free of filth. However, small population size remains a critical problem.

5.1. The Rurban Plan

Suppose a loop of villages is linked by ring road with a high-speed bus lane on which frequent services are run. That is a simple artifice, yet powerful enough to integrate the tiny markets of individual villages into one large one connecting tens of thousands of people immediately with potential to connect several hundred thousand ultimately, and thereby, transform that loop of villages into a virtual city.

Left to themselves, villages are more likely to shrink than to grow. The moment the loop of villages is provided transport connectivity (and as a corollary, telecom connectivity too), they acquire a growth potential like any city in the country. Then, with little or no prodding, the population around the loop is likely to grow four to five times within a generation. Such a habitat that combines rural ambience with the connectivity of a medium-sized town may be called a Rurban habitat.

Most "growth centres" and satellite towns remain moribund only because they were afflicted with a peculiar vicious circle syndrome. They could not grow economically until they had reached a minimum threshold level of infrastructure, and they could not attain that threshold until the economy grew! Establishing transport connectivity with a ring road, linking a loop of villages neatly breaks that vicious circle at a comparatively lower cost. The circular bus lane is a viable solution to the otherwise intractable problem of attracting entrepreneurs to rural areas.

5.2. Empowering Rural Areas to Compete with Cities

Urban amenities come in the form of four types of services:

a. Domestic services – residential space, piped water, electricity, telecommunications, and sanitation. They should be available within each dwelling.

b. Primary services like bus stops, grocery shops, dispensaries, children's playgrounds. They may be described as tele-ineffective services because they are of little use if they are not within walking distance.

c. Secondary services like schools, police stations, fault repair services, railway stations, fire-fighting services, hospitals for medical emergencies. They are needed only rarely but when needed are always required urgently. They may be called security services. These need not be close at hand (the infrequency of demand – and its regularity too – makes it impossible or unnecessary to locate them in every neighbourhood) but must be accessible immediately as and when demanded. That means high quality local transport and telecommunication links.

d. Tertiary services like airports, referral hospitals, wholesale markets, international gateways. These are even more rarely demanded than security services are. Further, unlike security services, it is unusual for them to be needed urgently. In general, they can be planned well in advance. If access times are measured in tens of minutes for secondary services, that can be in hours for tertiary services. So, they need not be located in every city. Several adjacent cities can share these services, the way Frankfurt, Dusseldorf and Bonn do. Hence, while security services need rapid local transport, tertiary services require high-speed inter-city links.

Zero net rural-urban migration is a mark of completed development. That will happen if villages provide access to a full range of services as listed above the way cities do. It is not important for a village to have every service inside, not even a primary school is critical, but the village must provide access – it must be well connected to a complete range of good quality services, at all four levels indicated in the previous section. That is what a Rurban habitat seeks to do.

Rural ambience has its own advantages particularly the following three:

a. Dwellings with ample open space either in the form of a courtyard or as a garden and hence, a low Floor Space Ratio.
b. Public spaces are relatively large, that is, proportion of open space is high.
c. Work place located within walking distance from the home.

Rural ambience offers high quality environment but little capacity for services. Cities offer a wide range of services but at the cost of poor ecology. The Rurban habitat can offer both good ecology and a full range of services.

5.3. Features of the Rurban Habitat

It may be argued that the same result could have been obtained by connecting together a group of villages in a star fashion or by a rectangular grid of bus lanes. That is no doubt a possibility but not an efficient one. Fig. 5.1 explains why. In the diagram, two alternatives are shown. One is a rectangular grid of main roads spaced two kilometres apart and representing an idealised city of size 10 km by 6 km, that is a city 60 sq. km in area. The other is a circular loop two kilometres wide and having the same area of 60 km as before. In both cases, no point is more than a km away from an arterial road. As the figures show, the rectangular pattern requires eight main roads 60 km long but the circular one needs only one single road 30 km in length.

Figure 5.1

Optimum City Shape

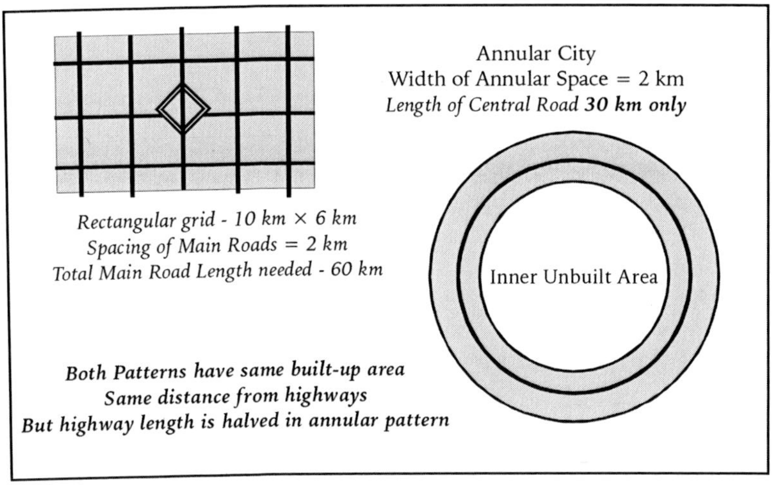

That is, the length of the main roads, and therefore, all other infrastructure like water lines, telecommunication cables, power lines, drains are also halved in length. That is substantial economy. There is much more. In the rectangular grid pattern (that goes for the star pattern too), the central region is the only location that can be efficiently connected to all parts of the city. That naturally leads to the evolution of a Central Business District (CBD). The CBD can grow only by making the central region more and more congested and by forcing employees who work there to reside farther and farther away along the periphery of the city. That forces hundreds of thousands to commute to work every day imposing a heavy load on transport infrastructure. In course of time, expensive road re-development involving flyovers, metros and the like become necessary.

The circular loop is very different in character. All points along the loop are equally well connected to one another. In the rectangular or radial city, the central region alone is the best option for the business district. In the loop arrangement, all points are equally good. That makes it possible for the business district to distribute itself all around. That alone will eliminate congestion with all its attendant problems.

There is yet another incidental benefit. It is now possible to offer each and every employer a package deal where space is provided both for business and for housing employees within walking distance of each other. Ideally, that will eliminate all commuting; realistically, commuting can be expected to be reduced to a fraction of what it would be otherwise.

There is a bonus on top of these benefits. In the conventional pattern, commuting is highly asymmetrical. In the mornings, almost all movement is towards the city centre and in the evenings the other way. In the circular design, there is no preferred direction any time; the traffic load is evenly distributed between clockwise or anti-clockwise movement. That virtually doubles the capacity of both roads and of buses too. Combined with the halving of road length and the intrinsic reduction in the need to commute, the traffic load can be reduced to a tenth of what it is currently to serve the same size of population. That is no mean benefit because almost all urban problems – whether they are economic, social or even political or cultural – have at their root the financial cost of maintaining high capacity transport, and the stress and strain of daily commuting.

The reduction in congestion that is inherent to the Circularly Distributed Business District (CDBD) offers yet another advantage. Congestion imposes a premium on space, raises land prices to astronomical levels. That leads to a vicious circle: as prices are high, highly congested high rise buildings become necessary. When such buildings sprout up, congestion increases even further leading to a vicious circle of congestion, high prices, even more congestion and so on and on. On the other hand, where there is no congestion, land prices are low. So, the circular loop with its distributed business district eliminates that vicious circle too.

Thus, the Rurban Habitat not only combines rural ambience with urban services but also minimises costs in a number of ways, and not merely financially but socially and ecologically too.

5.3.1. The Connectivity Issue

Connectivity has two elements: one, the numbers that are connected; two, how quickly they get connected. Typically, in large cities, it can take upwards of an hour to reach the CBD. So, let us define connectivity as the number of people that can reach the CBD within an hour's time. Then, consider a loop of villages linked together by a circular road having dedicated bus lanes so that buses can travel unimpeded at high speeds. Then, every point on this circle is connected to every other on the route. Typically, that will connect nearly a hundred thousand people immediately and many more in due course of time. If the round trip takes no more than an hour, no two points on the route will be more than 30 minutes apart – an acceptable length of time to connect physically. Or, each and every point on this circular route becomes a possible location for a market with a connectivity of several hundred thousand. In other words, merely by connecting a loop of villages by a fast bus lane, we have sown the seed for a virtual city.

Thus, a well connected loop of villages becomes a Rurban Habitat, that not only combines rural ambience with urban services but also minimises costs in a number of ways, and not merely financially but socially, ecologically too.

5.4. Implementing the Rurban Habitat

5.4.1. Acquiring Land

Availability of land is probably the greatest comparative advantage of rural areas. However, land acquisition is always a painful and politically hazardous process. The cash compensation that is offered is always a matter for dispute and discontent too. That problem can be virtually eliminated by offering farmers compensation not in a lump sum but as an annuity, an annuity equal to twice the current price of whatever they grow. That will give them grain price-indexed income, which after accounting for costs of cultivation, will be three times what they get at present. In addition, they can be given a share in the prosperity that will result from Rurbanisation by offering them 10-20 square metres of shopping space for each hectare of land they surrender. Lump sum compensation suffers from two infirmities: one, large amounts of capital have to be found up front and that is not easy to procure. Two, farmers have to convert that capital into regular income and they are not expert in doing so.

In effect, lump sum compensation involves two wasteful conversions – (a) the state converting farmer's regular income into an equivalent capital and (b) farmers converting that capital into regular income. Compensating farmers with an annuity obviates both types of inefficient conversions. Not surprisingly, Indian farmers have warmly welcomed this idea wherever this suggestion has been made.

5.4.2. Rurban Habitat as a Collection of Employers' Campuses

It is a common experience that, wherever employers manage their own campuses, they do ensure exceptionally fine ambience. Apparently, a peculiar competitive pride among employers induces them to devote much of their resources (and personal attention too) to the maintenance of the space they directly control. It is worth exploiting that spirit and encourage employers to establish and maintain habitats for housing their employees (either individually or collectively).

5.4.3. Comparative Advantage of Rural Areas

Of the eight infrastructure inputs required for fulfilling Maslow needs, cities are poorly equipped to offer three of them, namely, water, space and waste disposal. On the other hand, in each of these three cases, villages have a comparative advantage. As Fig. 5.2 indicates, rural areas can combine water harvesting, water recycling, sewage treatment, biogas generation, manuring and watering of energy farms and recharging ground water in a way it would be quite impossible in congested cities.

Of the eight amenities listed above, transport connectivity is truly the only handicap of rural areas. Even in this case, though cities are effective, they are by no means efficient. Urban transport is extremely costly in money, and even more so ecologically and socially. In any case, rurbanisation by ringing a loop of villages is a good solution for that problem. It provides villagers the same order of connectivity that urban dwellers enjoy.

Figure 5.2

Biogas Generation and Quadruple Re-use of Water

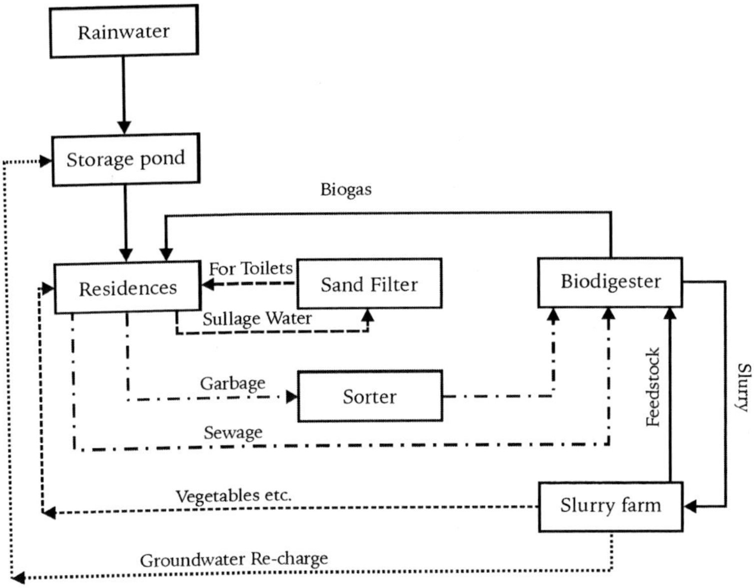

Table 4.1. Seven Ways Rurbanisation Minimises Costs of Urbanisation

1. Cheaper Land
2. Virtual Elimination of Daily Commuting to Work
3. Local Rainwater Harvesting, Waste Disposal
4. Halving the Length of Roads and Other Infrastructure
5. Leasing Land minimises capital costs and eliminates wastage
6. Minimises busy hour rush
7. Habitat Development can be largely left in the hands of Private Businessmen

5.5. Planning for the Future

In particular, connectivity (both transport and telecommunications) are the precursors of development. Unfortunately, we make no prior provision for the space needed for the required order of connectivity.

We let congestion becomes unbearable and then are left with no option but attempt highly expensive solutions like flyovers and metros.

Indian planners have, in the past, failed to make provision for future growth beyond the immediate scheme under consideration. In particular, insufficient reservation of space for future expansion has been the Achilles Heel of Indian planning. The country is likely to stabilise at a population of 1.7-1.8 billion of which, ultimately, around 1.5 billion may reside in urban areas. If space for that order of urban living is not set apart now, we will be paying an extortionate price later on. Even after paying such a price, we can neither the habitat not the connectivity of roads may come up to mark.

So far no thought has been given for reserving adequate space for the ultimate needs of roads, railways, airports, and above all, housing and commerce has never been reserved adequately for future use. Past failure to do so has retarded current progress and made it extremely expensive. If no lessons are learnt even now, and no provision is made for the future, we may manage eight per cent growth in nominal terms but not in Purchasing Power – particularly the Purchasing Power for infrastructure and housing.

Indian planning is also deeply flawed for the reason, it has allowed cities to grow cancerously and has made no attempt whatever to limit their size within desirable limits. As Fig. 4.1 shows, if the size becomes very large, congestion sets in, expensive solutions like flyovers, metros, high rise buildings become necessary. Commuting becomes an unbearable burden both in distances to be travelled, even more in the times to be wasted in crawling through crowded highways. It has been explained already that once a city exceeds a population size of three to five hundred thousand, it needs not one but several Central Business Districts that add to cost and not necessarily to convenience. For that reason, it is best to limit the Rurban habitats to a population size of three to five hundred thousand. That can be managed if the ring road has a circumference of about 30 kilometres and the habitat extends no more than 500 to 600 metres on either side – all points within walking distance from the ring road. However, it is crucial that the ring road be kept free of all encroachments so that traffic moves freely and fast. For that reason, it must be the inescapable rule that no structure will open directly on to the ring road, and that entry to and exit from the ring road should be controlled points only, the way it is on motorways the world over.

As a thumb rule, a kilometre of 50 metre wide tract must be reserved for future highways for every 20-25 sq.km. area. Space should be reserved also for future establishment of at least one airport capable of taking jumbo jets for every 5-10 million population. Space should even now be set apart for housing 70 per cent of the population in prospective urban habitats along with parking space at the rate of one vehicle per family. Our economic progress has been choked because these provisions have never been made.

Rural ambience is obtained through non-congestion, urban quality through good connectivity. Why not combine both and devise a *Rurban* habitat that is characterised by a mix of non-congestion and good connectivity? These two features may be quantified and specified as follows.

Non-congestion for Rural Ambience: (a) Floor Space Ratio of buildings not more than 0.5. (b) Ratio of open spaces to total area not less than 0.5. (c) Setback of buildings from major highways roads not less than 50 metres. (d) Average occupancy in public transport not more than 0.5.

Connectivity for Urban Quality: (a) Half to one hour, or less, access time to a full range of security services by local transport. (b) A minimum of a fifty local transport services per day on any route. (c) All dwellings and commercial buildings to be within 500 metres of a bus stop or suburban railway station. (d) High speed links with adjacent cities to connect to a complete set of tertiary services.

5.6. Importance of Keeping Supply in Excess of Demand

It has been repeatedly emphasised that correct economy of scale is a critical factor in economic growth. In that respect, India's development policy has been much flawed and leading to a chronic problem. Due to financial stringency and administrative complexity, the common practice is to wait for demand to become overwhelmingly expensive before attempting any expansion. That is a self-defeating policy that, ultimately, costs much more than any savings that might have been anticipated. Fig 5.3 explains graphically what happens when supply is short of demand – prices would normally shoot up due to scarcity. Normally, when prices increase, more investment would be attracted and supply should increase. That does not happen in India because prices are controlled and are not allowed to be determined by the market. For that reason, much needed maintenance and replacement is postponed, if not given up altogether. So, a lower price is obtained at the cost of quality – and corruption too.

Figure 5.3

Importance of Supply Exceeding Demand

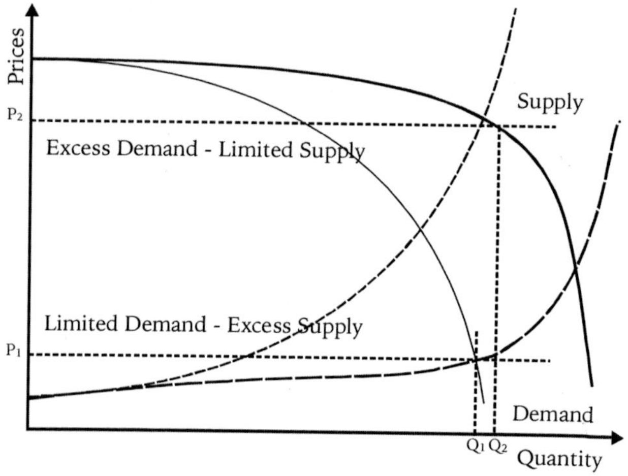

Limited Supply can send price sky-rocketing from P1 to P2 even when demand increase marginally from Q1 to Q2

Only when supply is maintained in excess of demand, will the prices be low. When prices are low, demand will grow automatically and will continue to do so, until supply remain in surplus and till the full potential demand is exhausted.

China and India exemplify two opposite approaches. China installs large infrastructure well ahead of demand. That keeps prices low, ecology high and leads to rapid growth. In India, infrastructure is kept deliberately short of supply. For instance, air travel is increasing seven per cent a year and should double in ten years. Yet, there are no signs of the government planning the capacity of airports and other related infrastructure. They will do so only when the services get completely choked. That increases costs, stifles growth and destroys ecology.

Here is another cultural facet of India that has restricted the pace of development.

6. CONCLUSION

There are many components for a vision. This presentation has chosen two of them: (a) empowering the economy to compete in world markets by trading on high quality, high tech products over international boundaries; (b) empowering people to access a full range of Maslow Needs.

As indicated in the Summary, it is best to plan for a vision by working backwards. Earlier American experience shows that nearly two-thirds of its remarkable economic growth was attributable to technology. Currently, Indian industry is more or less completely dependent on imported technology. Science and Technology Entrepreneurship Parks (STEP) and Technology Incubators have been suggested as the cure for this malady. As talent is the raw material of technology innovation, and education is the means of developing talent, education gets naturally chosen as the second driving force.

Education has three main components: starting with the primary level, it branches off into vocational training for one stream and education for R&D as the ultimate goal in the other stream. The latter naturally dovetails with the STEP system and hence, it is the practice world over to keep STEP as an adjunct of engineering universities. The mutual advantage between the two is not confined to technology development alone; if large enough, STEP can become such a substantial source of income for an engineering university that engineering education can be made affordable by even the poor.

Vocational education has really not taken off in India. It is suggested that such training must be adopted by industry by making it a sandwich program with students spending half the time working in industry and the other half learning basic concepts in special schools. That has several advantages including the fact that no school by itself can provide training in the myriad skills needed by industry.

The poor still shy away from educating children. Dr. Radhakrishnan's proposal of offering Work for Educating Children has been commended for empowering the poor to educate their children. It has been strongly urged that single-teacher schools is a waste of both money and manpower. So, it is best to combine eight or nine schools together into a large viable unit and in such a way that a child has to travel no farther than the next village to attend school.

Technology development needs high quality talent and training. As matters stand, the poor cannot afford the cost of such education and hence all the talent among the poor is lost to the country. The crux of the problem lies in the way engineering students are admitted – by an entrance examination that requires extensive and expensive coaching. As a remedy, multilevel selection, after the fifth, eighth, tenth and twelfth standards has been suggested. Such a system can be devised to provide the same chance to the poor as the rich have.

The hierarchy of Maslow Needs is the other face of the chosen Vision. Originally, these needs were identified as psychological for individuals. However, there are a variety of public goods that people as a society need. For instance, water and electricity are societal services at the lowest physical Maslow level. Likewise, space for shelter and health services are components of the second security level. Education and connectivity come next for status and autonomy needs respectively. To these we can add, waste disposal and non-congested environment as an ecological need. All these are problems of infrastructure design. That makes infrastructure as the primary driving force for the fulfilment of Maslow Needs for the building of a modern society.

A novel proposal has been made as an economical solution to the vexed problem of infrastructure, a field in which, the country has little expertise and less money to invest. The basic problem has been identified to be the policy of expanding cities without limit, however expensive that may be ecologically, socially or even financially. Indian cities are like a tiger on which political leaders, bureaucrats and businessmen have got on – and they cannot get off. As matters stand, there is no way of converting Indian cities into a civilised habitat where the rich and poor can live together in decency. Even smaller towns offer little scope for modernisation.

For that reason, a detailed scheme has been suggested to empower rural areas to provide municipal and other services as well as cities do but at a fraction of the cost – socially, ecologically and financially too. Basically, the idea is to link a loop of villages by a modern ring road around with high speed frequent bus services. That combines the tiny markets of individual villages into a single large one, large enough to make a variety of modern services viable. The ring road offers many advantages including the fact it cuts into half the lengths of all infrastructure, thanks to a peculiar feature of its topology. Hence, the installation of high quality transport makes it possible to market the space alongside the ring road as a superior location for the future expansion of both industries and services.

Two other proposals add to the power of this kind of design, called here the Rurban habitat. One is to offer farmers who spare their land for Rurban development not lump sum compensation but an annuity linked to the value of what they have been producing. That gives them grain price-indexed income that can be three times what they earn now and yet cost barely a fee of one rupee per square foot per year to businessmen ultimately.

The second suggestion is to offer residential space and employment space as single package within walking distance of each other. That will virtually eliminate daily commuting to work – socially, ecologically and financially – the most expensive component of urban living. All in all, the Rurban concept can be expected to cut down urban infrastructure costs by 60-70 per cent.

What is presented here is an integrated approach to economic development at affordable prices.

15

Telecom Sector in India: Vision 2020

MANAS BHATTACHARYYA

Introduction

The purpose of this paper is to construct a vision of Indian Telecom Sector for the year 2020, i.e., about two decades from now. Development being a continuous process, the choice of the year 2020 is just an arbitrary division of time, a pre-defined time horizon to take stock of what is likely to be achieved.

Pre-portrayal of a stage of development in future requires understanding of the process of change, the dynamics that set law of motion. In attempting to do so, the present paper deciphers the recent past.

Process of change is often volatile and responsive to intervention and global circumstances impacting it. In such an inherently dynamic situation it is convenient to assume that cross-country experiences incubate the most recent seeds of change. This is because countries at various stages of development encapsulate developmental experiences that occur with the passage of time.

The present paper isolates the agents of change based on international experiences and situates India in this development continuum. The agents of change, as observed from international perspective, have been broadly categorized into economic structure, competition policy and technology. Economic reforms and liberalization have driven telecom sector through several transmission channels of which these three categories are of major significance.

The paper, as it unfolds, is divided into six sections. Section 1 gives a brief account of the era of competition that was heralded in

Indian telecom sector and the results achieved. Analysis of the results, particularly comparison with other major countries intrigued further discussions on economic structure, synergy between telecom and IT, competition policy and technology in sections 2,3,4 and 5, respectively. Logical extension of the arguments, as they developed, extended to a vision for 2020 in each of these sections. The paper concludes in section 6.

The current policy configurations of India's telecom sector have been listed in the Appendix.

1. Reforms and Performance

India, like many other countries of the world, have adopted a gradual approach to telecom sector reform through selective privatization and managed competition in different segments of the telecom market. To begin with, India introduced private competition in value-added services in 1992 followed by opening up of cellular and basic services for local area to private competition. The Telecom Regulatory Authority of India (TRAI) was constituted in 1997 as an independent regulator in this sector. Competition was also introduced in National Long Distance (NLD) and International Long Distance (ILD) telephony at the start of the current decade[1].

The current policy stance affecting telecom sector in India is presented in the Appendix. Two State-owned public sector incumbents with a large existing subscriber base dominate the fixed line service. As on December 31, 2001, the two Public Sector Enterprises (PSEs), BSNL and MTNL[2] owned 34.73 million Direct

---

1. Government divested 25 per cent strategic stake of Videsh Sanchar Nigam Limited (VSNL), a public sector monopoly incumbent in ILD telephony to Tata Group in the private sector out of 52.97 per cent equity held by the Government. This was followed by opening up of ILD business to private players from April 1, 2002, terminating VSNL monopoly two years ahead of schedule, VSNL, *16th Annual Report, 2001-2002, p.5.*

2. Till 1986, telecommunication was a public utility owned by the Government of India. Mahanagar Telephone Nigam Limited (MTNL) was created in 1986 as a PSE to take out telecommunication services from the Government entirely in the cities of Delhi and Mumbai. It was in the same year that VSNL was created in the ILD segment. Bharat Sanchar Nigam Limted (BSNL) was formed as a PSE on October 1, 2000 as a telecom service provider in all other places. Both these incumbents inherited the entire pre-existing subscriber base with the Government.

Exchange Lines (DELs) against 0.45 million privately owned DELs. These two PSEs were allowed belated entry into the cellular segment in the beginning of the present decade. Consequently, their cellular subscriber base is tiny compared to the private operators. Out of 7.3 million cellular subscribers in the country in June 2002, they had only 0.2 million subscribers[3].

Despite asymmetry in initial market endowments between public sector incumbents and private operators, the act of opening up of the market unleashed dynamism that was hitherto latent in the sector. This is evident from a number of performance indicators. In terms of overall size of main telephone lines in operation, India ranked 14th in the world in 1995. The rank improved to 7th position in 2001 (Table 1).

Network expansion in India was accompanied by an increase in productivity of telecom staff measured in terms of ratio of number of main telephone lines in operation to total number of full time telecom staff (Table 2).

One way of looking at the welfare gains to subscribers is to watch the trend in prices for telecom services, whether such prices came down in the competitive regime. What consumer ultimately pays includes rental as well as telecom tariffs.

Because of complications involved in summarizing differential rates applicable to peak and non-peak hours, a convenient proxy for the change in telecom prices could be constructed in terms of observed trend in revenue earned from telephone services at constant prices, expressed as a ratio of number of main telephone lines in operation. Table 2 shows a significant decline in this ratio since 1995 in Indian fixed line segment. It may be noted that the National Telecom Policy was announced in May 1994. Steps were intensified to introduce private competition in the basic and cellular services thereafter. The beginning of the declining trend in per line revenue at constant prices coincided with the period, which witnessed emergence of competitive pressure in the sector.

---

3 *tele.net*, New Delhi, Vol.3, Issue no. 7, July 2002, pp. 54-55.

Table 1

Top 14 Countries in the World in terms of Number of Main Telephone Lines in Operation

Country	No. of lines in 1995('000)	Ranks (1995)	No. of lines in 2001('000)	Ranks (2001)
USA	159,735.2	1	190,000.0	1
Japan	62,292.0	2	76,000.0	3
Germany	42,000.0	3	52,280.0	4
China	40,705.7	4	179,034.0	2
France	32,400	5	34,032.9	9
UK	29,411.4	6	34,710.0	8
Russia	25,018.9	7	35,700.0	6
Italy	24,845.0	8	27,303.0	10
Korea, Rep.	18,600.0	9	22,724.7	11
Canada	17,567.0	10	20,319.3	12
Spain	15,095.4	11	17,427.0	14
Brazil	13,263.0	12	37,430.8	5
Turkey	13,215.7	13	18,900.9	13
India	11,978.0	14	34,732.1	7

Source: World Telecommunication Development Report 2002, ITU.

Table 3 shows the long run trend in supply and demand of DELs. The number of DELs in operation (i.e., main line in operation) has been taken as supply whereas demand has been computed by adding the number of subscribers in the waiting list to the number of DELs in operation. However, it needs to be kept in mind that the number in the waiting list, in certain cases, is unlikely to reflect potential demand for telecom services in the economy. The market potential may be much more than what is revealed through waiting list because the number in the waiting list reveals demand registered in those areas where telecommunication facilities are available and reasonable expectations exist for demand to be fulfilled. In the areas where telecom infrastructure is not adequate, demand may not get registered at all and remain suppressed.

Table 2

Trend in Productivity and Price

Year	*Number of main telephone lines in operation per full-time telecom staff*	*Telephone service revenue at constant prices (CPI: 1995 =100) per main telephone line in operation (Rs. '000)*
1991	15.58	9.13
1992	17.65	10.25
1993	20.32	11.04
1994	23.38	10.17
1995	28.45	9.23
1996	33.90	6.12
1997	41.89	5.62
1998	50.93	4.92
1999	62.97	4.24

Source: Computed from the data published in the Year-book of Statistics: Telecommunication Services, 1991-2000, ITU.

Table 3

DEL: Supply and Demand (millions)

Year ending March 31	*Direct Exchange Lines (DELs)*	*Waiting List*	*Demand*
1981	2.15	0.45	2.6
1983	2.47	0.66	3.13
1985	2.90	0.84	3.74
1987	3.49	1.12	4.61
1989	4.17	1.42	5.59
1991	5.07	1.96	7.03
1993	6.80	2.85	9.65
1995	9.80	2.15	11.95
1997	14.54	2.89	17.43
1999	21.59	1.98	23.57
2001	32.44	2.92	35.36

Source: Indian Telecommunication Statistics 2002, Ministry of Communications, Government of India.

The figure below shows an interesting phenomenon. Total demand tends to exceed supply by a margin, which does not get narrowed down as supply expands. It shows that market for fixed line is supply constrained and demand tends to increase as supply expands. The figure also reveals that there is significant growth in supply of DEL in the Nineties, the eventful decade of sectoral reforms. The growth momentum is sustained in the current decade with a positive supply gap.

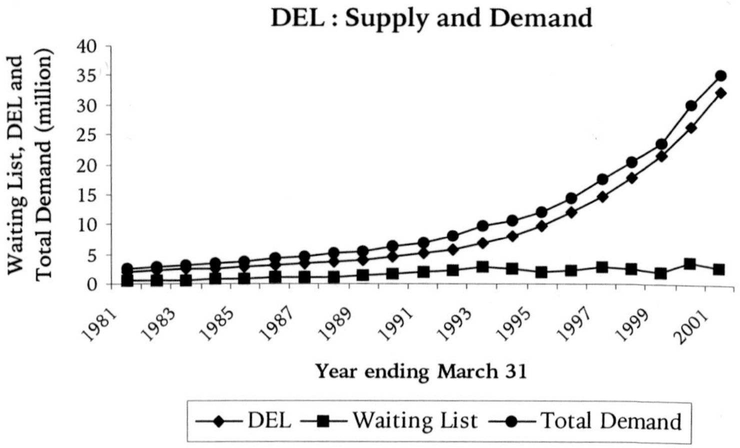

Table 4 indicates tele-density for the countries included in Table 1 as measured in terms of number of main lines per 100 inhabitants.

Above Table indicates that despite phenomenal achievement in terms of network expansion, the size of the population is responsible for India's low tele-density[4]. A comparison between Table 1 and Table 4 reveals that countries with smaller network sizes than India are having much higher tele-densities. However, in terms of total tele-density, i.e., the sum of fixed-lines and mobile subscribers per 100 inhabitants, India's comparative ranking in the

4. It may be noted that tele-density being an average, does not throw light on the distribution of telephones across various income categories. If distribution is skewed, tele-density may not be an appropriate indicator of tele-accessibility of the poor.

world improved from 160 in 1990 to 145 in 2000, an improvement by 15 positions[5]. Nevertheless, closing the digital divide in terms of tele-density remains a daunting task.

Table 4

Number of Main Telephone Lines per 100 Inhabitants

Country	*1995*	*2001*
USA	60.73	66.45
Japan	49.61	59.69
Germany	51.33	63.48
China	3.30	13.81
France	56.01	57.35
UK	50.18	57.78
Russia	16.91	24.33
Italy	43.33	47.06
Korea, Rep.	41.24	47.60
Canada	59.85	65.51
Spain	38.50	43.11
Brazil	8.51	21.69
Turkey	21.44	28.52
India	1.29	3.38

Source: World Telecommunication Development Report 2002, ITU.

The present paper estimates that in order to attain the network size of USA in 2001, India has to expand its number of operational telephone lines at a Compound Annual Growth Rate (CAGR) of 23.44 per cent between 2002 and 2020. The corresponding growth rates to reach China and Japan's levels are 23.06 per cent and 17.63 per cent, respectively. Even that is not going to mean much in terms of tele-densities in comparison to most of the countries cited in Table 4. Assuming no change in India's size of population (i.e., assuming population size to remain at 2001 level of 1.03 billion), India's tele-density will be 18.48 lines per 100 people even if India's network size reaches the

5. ITU, *World Telecommunication Development Report 2002*, Geneva, 2002, p.56.

level of USA. Considering the fact that India's DEL grew at a CAGR of 19.4 per cent during 1995-2000, significant effort would be needed to step up growth rate above 23 per cent.

Understanding telecom growth prospect would require understanding of the sources of growth — what accounts for cross-country differences in growth experiences. Countries do differ among themselves in respect of their economic structure, sectoral policies and technological changes. Assuming these three to be key drivers of growth, it can be said that 'Vision 2020' of Indian telecom sector will be shaped in an important way by the evolving economic structure, sectoral reforms including competition policy and technology trend.

2. Economic Structure

It has been observed that 'growth in the number of new telephone subscribers has far exceeded the growth in the global economy' in the last twenty years[6]. This shows that aggregate growth alone does not determine telecom expansion and there may be need to look at composition of growth as well. However, influence of economic structure on telecom expansion (or for that matter on achievable level of tele-density) does not find explicit consideration in today's literature on telecom economics as much as the other two factors, i.e., competition and technology. One plausible reason could be because of the importance that has been attached to income gap as a factor explaining digital divide. Moreover, income gap, by itself subsumes differences in certain structural characteristics and therefore, diverts the focus of attention from structural gap to income gap[7]. Proponents of 'income determinism' may stop short of addressing structural factors because of their primary concern regarding income transfer between the developed to the developing countries as the only way to address the problems of digital divide. Structural issues, on the other hand,

6. *Ibid.*, p.1.

7. There is a two-way relationship between telecommunications and economic development. The relationship that operates through telecom expansion causing economic growth is known as Jipp's Law, after Professor A. Jipp, who was one of the first to write about it. The relationship is described in terms of a 'Jipp Curve', see for discussion, *ibid.*, p.64.

are more pertinent to the believers of 'leapfrogging' capabilities of the countries who are on the wrong side of the divide[8]. It is for them that the present paper goes on to prove that the effectiveness of direct promotion of telecommunications as a complementary policy to overall macroeconomic reforms will be determined in an important way by how structural issues in the economy are addressed.

In the first place, it is noteworthy that there are countries with per capita income less than that of India but with higher tele-density. As for instance, Bolivia had per capita income of US $2380 in 2000[9] compared to US $2390 for India. Bolivia's tele-density[10] was 6.05 in that year against 3.20 for India. Moldova had a tele-density of 13.33 with a per capita income of US $2240. Georgia, with a per capita income of US $2470 had a much higher tele-density of 13.86. Though Ecuador had a little higher per capita income of US $2920 compared to India, tele-density was significantly higher at 10.00. It was also noted that these countries had either more equitable income distribution than India (measured in terms of percentage of population living on less than $2 a day) or had a higher weightage of value added by the service sector in the Gross Domestic Product (GDP) or both.

A comparative picture of India *vis-à-vis* these countries in respect of the two aforesaid characteristics are presented in Table 5.

In order to examine the generality with which such relationships manifest in a larger sample of countries, tele-density was regressed on percentage of population living on less than $2 a day and per capita income over a cross-section of 77 countries[11] for the year 2000 to yield the following results:

Tele-density = 9.63 – 0.1563** (Percentage of population living on less than $2 a day) + 0.0019**(Per capita income)

$R^2 = 0.82$;

** : Significant at 1 per cent.

---

8. See for instance, Negroponte, N., 'The Third Shall be First: The Net Leverages Latecomers in the Developing World', *Wired Magazine*, January 1998.
9. PPP income, i.e., income measured in terms of Purchasing Power Parity.
10. Number of main telephone lines in operation per 100 inhabitants.
11. There were 77 countries, for which required data was available.

Table 5

Structural Characteristics and Tele-density, 2000

Country	*Tele-density (per 100 inhabitants)*	*Per capita income ($ PPP)*	*Percentage of population living on less than $2 a day*	*Value added by the service sector in the Gross Domestic Product (GDP) (%)*
Moldova	13.33	2240	38.4	53
Bolivia	6.05	2380	51.4	48
India	3.20	2390	41.4	46
Georgia	13.86	2470	Less than 2	52
Ecuador	10.00	2920	52.3	64

Source: (i) Year-book of Statistics, 1991-2000, ITU;
(ii) World Development Report 2002.

The result shows that income distribution has a much larger coefficient than per capita income and therefore emphasizes the fact that telecom development strategy should have substantial equity component built into it.

To assess the significance of service sector in telecom development, tele-density has been regressed on percentage contribution of value added by the service sector in GDP over a cross-section of 115 countries for the year 2000. The following result was obtained:

Tele-density = – 31.54 + 0.9267** (Percentage contribution of value added by the service sector in GDP)

$R^2 = 0.48$;

**: Significant at 1 per cent.

The result indicates a strong association between service sector growth and telecom development implying that future telecom expansion will depend significantly on the proliferation of services in the economy.

As a matter of strategy, it can be said that targeted intervention through access promotion can be potentially instrumental in delivering growth with equity. Access promotion means expansion of telecommunication and therefore will cause growth to occur[12]. Consequently, a broad based access promotion strategy would lead to more equitable growth.

The first step towards broad based access promotion in India was initiated in the Eighties when Public Call Offices (PCOs) were given private franchises for both domestic and long distance services. Total number of PCOs grew from 0.2 million in 1993 to 0.9 million in 2001. The Eighth Plan (1992-97) targeted at provision of *Panchayat*[13] phones in 360,000 villages. Thrust on Universal Service Obligation (USO) as a part of broad based telecommunication development strategy[14] began with the National Telecom Policy of 1994 and was reinforced as one of the objectives of the New Telecom Policy 1999 (NTP-99). The licenses for the basic services, for which open tenders were invited in January 1995, contained an obligatory provision in the agreement for the private operators to provide 10 per cent of the DELs as Village Public Telephone (VPT). NTP-99 targeted complete rural coverage by the end of 2002 providing Village Public Telephones[15] in all the 0.6 million villages with emphasis on 'availability, accessibility and affordability'[16]. By the end of January 2001, 0.4 million villages have been covered. Share of rural areas in total number of DELs in the country stood at about 22.6 per cent in January 2002, increasing from 21.4 per cent in March 2001[17]. The trend is suggestive of potential scope of expansion of telecommunication in the rural sector.

---

12. It was empirically evident that countries having more than expected number of telephones or a higher tele-density (given their income levels) experienced higher growth than the countries with lower than expected number of telephones or tele-densities. See, The World Bank Group, *Information and Communication technologies: A World Bank Group Strategy*, Washington D.C., 2002, p.6. If more telephones equal growth, countries can leapfrog several percentage points growth through direct telecom promotion.
13. Local self-government body consisting of elected representatives at village level.
14. USO is now common in many countries seeking promotion of rural telephony. The modalities differ in matters of details.
15. VPT is a community telephone facility.
16. NTP 99 also envisaged provision of Internet access to all district headquarters by 2000.
17. Government of India, Ministry of Communications & Information Technology, Department of Telecommunications, *Annual Report, 2001-2002*.

Though USO is mandatory for the basic service operators, other service providers are also allowed to participate in it subject to technical feasibility. The subsidy element of the USO will be financed from a fund generated through Universal Service Levy (USL), i.e., levy of certain percentage of license fees charged from different service providers. As a follow up of NTP 99 and subsequent recommendations of the TRAI, The Universal Service Support Policy (USSP) came into effect from April 1, 2002 and the Department of Telecommunications (DOT) issued detailed guidelines for implementation[18]. Apart from expansion of VPTs, the guidelines also envisaged upgradation of VPTs to Public Telecom and Information Centers (PTICs) to provide data transmission facilities and installation of high speed PTICs (HPTICs) in the Short Distance Charging Areas (SDCAs) with broadband access. Allocation of subsidy will be to the bidder quoting lowest amount of subsidy, chosen through a multi-layered bidding process, subject to a ceiling of the benchmark cost estimated by the DOT on the basis of efficiency criteria[19].

So far, the public sector incumbents have spearheaded expansion of rural telephony with very little contribution by the private sector. By the end of December 31, 2001, out of 0.4 million villages, the private operators covered only 718 villages and the rest was by the public sector.

Private sector presence is prolific in Public Call Offices (PCOs) and Internet Kiosks in the cities and towns[20]. However, there are certain pilot projects in the rural sector working to evolve cost

---

18. Department of telecommunications of the Ministry of Communications & Information Technology is the policy making arm of the Government of India in the area of telecom development.

19. Chilean experience is a frequently quoted success story of leveraging US $40 million of private funding 'on the basis of just over US $2 million of public subsidy', see for discussion, The World Bank Group, *Information and Communication Technologies: A World Bank Group Strategy*, Washington D.C., 2002, p.11 and Bjorn Wellenius, *Extending Telecommunications Service to Rural Areas – The Chilean Experience*, The World Bank Group, February 1997. Early pilot results showed that in output-based contracts for rural services Peru succeeded in mobilizing private investment equivalent to double the amount of subsidy provided, for details see Cannock Geoffrey, *Telecom Subsidies*, The World Bank Group, Private Sector and Infrastructure Network, June 2001.

20. MTNL also commercially launched 25 Internet kiosks each in Delhi and Mumbai. Government of India, Ministry of Communications & Information Technology, Department of Telecommunications, *Annual Report, 2001-2002*, p. 64.

effective wireless technological solutions in partnership with local service providers. Many such projects have developed applications based on local content and software in Indian languages and user-friendly icons for illiterate people[21].

Telecommunications have emerged as a springboard of ICT applications with economy-wide ramifications. There are plenty of anecdotal evidences[22] to show that telecom is improving life chances across the strata of the society tiding over the 'divide'. A whole range of information based industry and applications have come up creating new sources of employment and earning with welfare enhancing consequences for the wealthy and the poor. As a meta-technology, ICT has caused rapid innovations to occur in all other areas of material sciences. As a fabric of information society, ICT has improved access in the fields of education, healthcare, governance and all aspects of business services. It has also improved the abilities of the poor to manage risks and mitigate vulnerabilities through provision of timely information.

Vision 2020 is a vision of information society and knowledge economy built on the edifice of ICT. In India, the aggressive expansion of public sector telecommunications infrastructure in hitherto uncharted territories of geographically remote locations would unleash latent economic energies and market forces, which will erode the very foundation of perceived lack of profitability of rural investment among the private investors. Once this is achieved, Vision 2020 will be a vision of wealthier and more equal society full of creativity, innovation and competition.

---

21. CorDect is one such technology. See, Noronha, Frederic, *Internet for all: Indian villagers to get access at prices they can afford*, www.tenet.res.in; also by the same author, *Web kiosks for India's villagers*, www.tenet.res.in; 'Communications Revolution set to transform 1000 Tamil villages', *Infomy*, February 15, 2001; 'India Online', *Nature*, January 24, 2002. It has been reported that 'In Southern India, skilled Internet users download information about weather, agriculture and fishing and broadcast it over the radio'. ITU, *World Telecommunication Development Report 2002*, Geneva, 2002, *op. cit.*, p.34.

22. See for example, *Life at Work in the Information Economy*, World Employment Report 2001, ILO, Geneva; Dasgupta, S., Somik Lall and David Wheeler, *Policy Reform, Economic Growth and the Digital Divide: An Econometric Analysis*, Working Paper No. 2567, World Bank, March, 28, 2001; Sood, Aditya Dev, 'How to Wire Rural India, Problems and Possibilities of Digital Development', *Economic and Political Weekly*, October 27, 2001.

3. Telecom and IT

The vision of telecommunications in 2020 is a vision of information society, built on an edifice where IT and telecommunications merge. Rapid technological convergence has already implied a symbiotic overlap between the development strategies of IT and telecommunications. Part of today's IT is 'telecom writ large', it flourishes on the telecom-network and in turn permits modern day telecommunications to use sophisticated IT-software. Hardware is a common platform for both IT and telecom.

There is a legacy vision derived from export-success of India's software that has given rise to optimism regarding India's growing pre-eminence in global IT canvas. Such a vision builds on a much larger vision of all-round development of IT that pervades wide cross-section of Indian economy and society. Deeper analysis shows that there is need for a comprehensive IT development strategy to ensure India's durable presence in the global software market. As discussion in the subsequent paragraphs will show, 'enclave' type development of software with exclusive focus on export can not bring about desired benefits if such a strategy ignores the linkages between export and the domestic market. Vision 2020, therefore, is a much larger vision.

First, it is to be appreciated that foreign exchange contribution of software export net of import of hardware is roughly fifty per cent[23]. Net foreign exchange contribution will increase if India is able to develop a strong base of hardware.

Second, scrutiny of the structure of India's software export *vis-à-vis* the emerging dynamics of the global market reveals that India has marginal presence in the fastest growing segment of the global IT market consisting of software packages and software products[24]. India's close competitors, on the other hand, have achieved greater success through diversification of exports with software packages[25].

---

23. Joseph K.J. and K.N. Harilal, 'Structure and Growth of India's IT Exports, Implications of an Export Oriented Growth Strategy', *Economic and Political Weekly*, August 25, 2001, p.3267.

24. *Ibid.*, p.3265.

25. Chakraborty Chandana and C. Jayachandran, 'Software Sector: Trends and Constraints', *Economic and Political Weekly*, August 25, 2001, p.3258.

There is, therefore, need for India to climb value chain with more innovative software products in the international market. This is possible when India is able to broad-base the development of IT with a strong and large domestic market supporting innovation and its diffusion along with the growth of component manufacturing base. Appropriate synergy between the domestic and export market will be key to enduring success of Indian IT sector in overseas market and development of state-of-the art telecom infrastructure is a prerequisite to both.

Finally, development of human resources through IT education, training and skill development is fundamental to the whole process.

Two important indicators of IT penetration in Indian market are Internet use and availability of Personal Computers (PCs). There has been significant expansion in both during the last decade (Table 6).

Table 6

Growth in Availability of Personal Computers and Estimated Number of Internet Users

Year	*Estimated Number of Internet Users*	*Availability of Personal Computers*
1992	1,000	410,000
1993	2,000	560,000
1994	10,000	800,000
1995	250,000	1,200,000
1996	450,000	1,500,000
1997	700,000	2,000,000
1998	1,400,000	2,700,000
1999	2,800,000	3,300,000
2000	5,00,0000	4,600,000

Note: Data for 1991 on Internet users is not available. The series start from 1992 because data on both is available from this year.

Source: Year-book of Statistics, 1991-2000, ITU.

Despite impressive growth in the number of Internet users and availability of PCs, India remains on the wrong side of the divide (Table 7). Number of users of Internet is still a negligible fraction of India's total population. Per capita availability of PC is also very low.

Table 7

Internet Penetration and PC Availability, 2001

Countries falling in different income categories	*Internet users per 10,000 inhabitants*	*PCs per 100 inhabitants*
Low income countries	62.21	0.59
Of which		
India	**68.16**	**0.58**
Lower middle income countries	264.94	2.45
Upper middle income countries	992.66	8.24
High income countries	3992.87	37.31

Source: ITU, World Telecommunication Development Report 2002.

Internet kiosks, telekiosks, telecottages and cybercafes have emerged in important roles in expanding community access to ICT popularizing IT among the masses and promoting domestic market. However, their expansion crucially hinges on the growth of telecommunications infrastructure. In India, a spectrum of technologies has been unleashed to connect remote villages, which includes Wireless in Local Loop (WLL), wireless-cum-wired technology developed by C-DOT[26], radio systems, switching systems of different capacities integrated with underground cables, CorDect and medium capacity satellite systems. Besides, a number of small-scale ICT initiatives is already at work in different parts of the country (Box 1). It is envisaged that with the growth of telecom infrastructure such examples would multiply and create an information society in not so distant a future.

26. The Government of India promoted center for the Development of Telematics (C-DOT) in 1984 to develop indigenous digital switches. C-DOT also designed 'Rural Automatic Exchange' (RAX) and manufactured small meters, which became popular with the PCOs. See Noronha Frederic, *Internet for all: Indian villagers to get access at prices they can afford*, www.tenet.res.in.

BOX 1

Harbingers of Information Society

SARI: Sustainable Access in Rural India (SARI) is a joint initiative between MIT Media Lab, Center for International Development at Harvard, IIT Chennai and the I-Gyan Foundation. The project is located in northern Madurai district of Chennai. It seeks to provide voice and Internet connections in 1000 villages with the use of CorDect system. Apart from provision of a kiosk in each village, connections will be provided in schools, colleges and primary health centers. The project also provides for interest free loans and easy installments for purchase of computers and training support to technical personnel. Continuous evaluation of the socio-economic impact of the project is a part of the initiative[27].

n-Logue: 'n-Logue' is a company incubated by a group of professionals in IIT Chennai under private initiative. The company offers wireless equipment, multimedia computer equipped with software in Indian language and other accessories to set up cost effective Internet kiosks in partnership with local service providers. Such kiosks are coming up in Madhya Pradesh, Rajasthan and Tamil Nadu[28].

M.S. Swaminathan Research Foundation: This project is located in Pondicherry of South India. Village Knowledge Centers have been established under this project with dedicated web sites of locally relevant information. The Foundation also disseminates knowledge and information through wireless radios to rural communities[29].

The Warana Wired Village Project: This is a collaborative project between the Central and the state government, located on the banks of river Warana in Maharashtra. It operates distributive accounts system for the Warana sugarcane cooperative.

The Gyandoot Project: A joint initiative of the district collector of Dhar district of Madhya Pradesh and the District Rural Development Agency (DRDA). More than thirty Community Information Centers (known as 'Soochanalaya'), one for a group of villages, have been set up to provide information on market rates of agricultural products, land records, education, health, *Panchayat* related matters, governance issues, issue of certificates and registering complaints. E-mail facilities in Hindi are available. Majority of these Centers are own and run by the village communities with costs borne by the Panchayats. Others are privately run and bank financed[30].

Contd....

---

27. 'Communications Revolution set to transform 1000 Tamil villages', *Infomy*, February 15, 2001 cited in www.tenet.res.in.

28. Noronha Frederic, *Web kiosks for India's villagers*, www.tenet.res.in.

29. ILO, 2001, p.193.

30. Kothari, Brij, Avinash Pandey and Amita Chudgar, 'Gyandoot: Can it be the harbinger of knowledge?' *India Infrastructure Report 2002, Governance issues for Commercialization*, 3i Network, OUP 2002, pp.198-205.

...Contd...

Tarahaat.com: This is a commercial project promoted by a Delhi based NGO, 'Development Alternative'. The project provides online information centers for rural communities with interactive and graphic interface in some places at North India.

Hole-in-the-wall initiative: A pilot project launched by the NIIT, a software company, in urban slums by providing unmanned computers. Through continuous video monitoring it was found that despite language difficulties, boys and girls from the neighbourhood developed access skills in web surfing and graphic designs even without formal training.

Indiagriline: This is an online network of trading, contract management, banking, retailing etc. promoted by EID Parry, a company dealing in food products[31].

School Net India: An initiative of the Infrastructure Leasing and Financial Services (IL&FS) to develop online multilingual content and CD-ROMs as supplementary teaching aid in classrooms.

SEWA: Self-Employed Women's Association (SEWA) is an NGO, which organizes poor and self-employed women. SEWA has promoted online global marketing of the products turned out by their members[32].

Source: Sood, 2001 and other sources.

The list of anecdotes included in the Box is by no means exhaustive. With progress of connectivity such examples will multiply bringing in its train benefits of an information economy and society. According to one estimate, 600,000 jobs have been created in cyberkiosks in India in addition to possible employment due to spillover effects[33].

Employment benefit of ICT occurs across wide range of skill spectrum. Apart from growth of employment and income at firm level due to ICT induced productivity growth in a large number of industries, a whole range of ICT enabled activities and services has started booming. Some such examples include operations like data entry, preparation and maintenance of database, revenue accounting, preparation of payroll, processing of insurance claims, human resource services, call center operations, running of customer support centers, medical transcription, content development and animation, web site services, software development, hardware repair

---

31. www.indiagriline.com.
32. ILO, 2001, p. 195.
33. *Ibid.*, p. 318.

and maintenance, systems engineering, systems design and integration etc. The process of job creation and productivity growth is expected to bring about market expansion supporting growth of domestic hardware and software industries broadening the base of ICT development. This, in turn, will induce R&D spontaneity enabling India to transit from the status of an importer of sub-assemblies of IT and telecom hardware to a higher state of development endowed with strong domestic manufacturing base of sophisticated hardware and software products booming from indigenous ideas, innovation and comparative advantage. A modern telecommunication infrastructure will accelerate this process through provision of high-speed communication links. In the global IT market, India will be a major player at the higher end of value chain based on perfect synergy between the domestic and overseas market.

As in the past, State will play an important role in this development – both as a proactive policy maker and also by taking a position in the market. Major policy thrust of the Government to promote IT was through provision of Technology Park, fiscal incentives, simplification of administrative rules and procedures, promotion of institutional finance including venture capital and liberalization of foreign equity participation. In the area of software, policies to encourage global presence included market support, overseas campaign for export promotion, quality certification, information security management and R&D support. Indian IT companies have been allowed to issue ADR/GDR-linked stock options to employees under favourable tax treatment. Approval mechanism has been simplified under automatic route permitting overseas business acquisition through ADR/GDR route. The IT Action Plan on Hardware envisaged extending Export Oriented Unit (EOU) status to hardware manufacturing units and deemed export status to telecom manufacturers.

Traditionally, State has been the most important source of demand for IT industry[34] in India. The trend continues even today and government spending on IT is a key driver of domestic demand

34. Evans, Peter B., 'Indian Informatics in the 1980s: The Changing Character of State Involvement', *World Development*, Vol.20, No.1, January 1992, p.2.

for IT products. One reason is that the government has significant market presence in many goods and services. The other reason is that the government is consciously promoting the use of IT in activities within its domain of activities. To undertake development of IT as a thrust area, a separate 'Ministry of Information Technology' was formed in October 1999. Recently, Ministry of Communications and Ministry of IT have been merged to form a single 'Ministry of Communications & IT'.

Apart from encouraging use of IT in research and scientific areas, the government has also taken major initiative to computerize work of various ministries and departments. Ministries and departments have come up with their websites with all the relevant details. Though computerization of many more areas within the government are under implementation, significant results have already been achieved in computerization of railway reservation, allocation of Permanent Account Number (PAN) for income tax payers, processing of passport application, conduct of public examination, custom clearance, Regional Transport Offices, schemes under implementation by the NGOs, vigilance information, VSAT-based money orders under the Department of Post, Supreme Court, land records, Parliament questions, debates and deliberations[35]. Different ministries have been advised to earmark two to three per cent of the budget on IT.

Many state governments have also declared IT policies and computerized records, certificates, registration of deeds, issue of licences, various payments systems etc.

Computerisation is also spreading very fast in the field offices of the government, financial and educational institutions. According to one estimate, 12,000 out of 45,000 bank branches have implemented major computerization[36].

Legislative framework has been put in place with the enactment of the Information Technology Act 2000 recognising digital signature as means of authentication of government certificates. The

---

35. These are only some examples. More details of computerization in the Central and the state governments are available in the web site of the Ministry of Information Technology. See www.mit.gov.in.

36. www.nasscom.org.

act imparts legitimacy to contract through electronic means unless otherwise agreed. Indian Copyright Act of 1957 and its amendment in 1994 outlaw software piracy.

The foundation of digital democracy has been laid to usher in an era of e-governance, transparency and e-accountability. A recent study shows that the number of Indians using Internet for accessing government services and products as a proportion to total number of Internet users has increased from 22 per cent last year to 31 per cent this year[37].

Growing legitimacy of IT-based transactions in government has started catalyzing the use of IT in private market and expanding the domain of e-business and e-commerce reducing transaction costs significantly and increasing productivity.

In time to come, the battle against digital divide will be won and ICT will be leveraged to benefit the poor. Apart from higher earnings associated with productivity gains and job creation, benefits for the poor will also result from risk mitigation and reduction in vulnerability due to timely availability of information on weather and market, guidance on improved farm practices and elimination of exploitation by the intermediaries. There will be general improvement in the quality of life of the poor through more responsive governance, improved delivery in the social sector programmes, better quality of public services and more effective public expenditure with more efficient targeting and monitoring. E-education and e-medicine will surmount all the access barriers to reach the remote and isolated locations.

There has been substantial depletion in the stock of IT personnel in India through migration into USA and Europe. There is need to replete this stock and plan for increased availability of skilled manpower to meet the future demand. Education, training and skill development will meet the demand for skilled manpower of the industry and at the same time keep the cost of IT education, servicing and maintenance within reasonable limit. Trained manpower will also be an important source of demand for IT

---

37. 'More Indians using Net to deal with Govt', *The Times of India*, November 9, 2002, p.1.

products and services. The government has taken steps to increase the teaching facilities to double the number of technology students and sponsored training institutes like Indian Institute of Information Technology and Management at Allahabad, Bangalore, Kolkata and Hyderabad in addition to Indian Institute of Technology and Management at Gwalior. Initiative has also been launched to upgrade existing regional engineering colleges, give active support to the polytechnics and colleges and encourage private participation in training in the field of IT. A society[38] has been formed to extend accreditation to institutions at non-formal sector for certain courses, and network services[39] have been launched to link academic and research communities.

Software in local languages is being increasingly available. Computers have also been specially designed for use in the mass market[40].

Vision 2020 is a vision of IT for the masses. All round development of digital literacy would put Indian society in complete command over the ICT tools. Available indications suggest that IT education is gaining popularity[41]. Perceived utility of ICT as enabler of business processes would continue to enhance market for IT education. Education will spur innovation, productivity and entrepreneurship. A knowledge society will be formed with participation from the rich and the poor, men and women, young and old, organized and unorganized, Government and the governed.

4. Competition Policy

Countries often differed in pattern of sequencing and the speed of liberalization. Competition has been controlled within limit by state policy through licensing of limited number of market players in certain segments, granting thereby a period of exclusivity to the

38. Known as DOEACC.
39. ERNET.
40. 'Simputer', a pocket book sized icon-based computer is one such example.
41. In a backward semi-arid sparsely populated district of Rajasthan, more than 100 computer-training centers have been opened under the franchise of popular brand names to operate on commercial basis. Despite total absence of reliable connectivity in the district, enrolment in these centers is high indicating popularity of IT courses. See, Sood, 2001.

operators. Heterogeneity of routes to sectoral reforms, as seen from the examples of some of the Asian countries, classified into different combination of policies and approaches to telecom reform, are presented below[42]:

1. Competition in the fixed line segment with state-owned incumbents: China, India and Korea.
2. Privatization of state-owned incumbents but deferred competition through exclusivity granted to private investors: Hong Kong, Indonesia, Malaysia, Pakistan and Singapore.
3. Simultaneous introduction of privatization and competition: Japan and Sri Lanka.
4. Opening up of local market to competition first: Hong Kong, India and Singapore.
5. Opening up of competition in the international services first: Korea, Malaysia and the Philippines.
6. Introduction of second domestic long distance carrier first: China.
7. The sector ministry exercises regulatory functions: China, Indonesia, Japan, Korea, Malaysia, Taiwan and Thailand.
8. Separate regulator with the responsibility for interconnection lying with the dominant operator while regulator is responsible for arbitration of disputes: Hong Kong, Pakistan and Philippines.

In most countries, restricting the number of licensees or imposing geographic limitations has limited competition. In India, for instance, competition in cellular telephony was allowed in a duopoly mode. This was gradually increased to licensing of four operators in each of the four metros and thirteen circles. Basic service in India is still limited to one private operator competing with state-owned incumbents in the circles. Though private sector has been licensed and they are laying infrastructure, metros are still in the grip of public sector monopoly and it will take a while

---

42. Taken from Fink Carsten, Mattoo Aditya and Randeep Rathindran, *Liberalising Basic Telecommunications: The Asian Experience*, The World Bank, Development Research Group, Washington, DC, November 2001.

before private competition takes place. Differences in modes of privatization have been observed in other countries. In Thailand, private entry was allowed through Build Operate and Transfer (BOT) mode while the network was controlled by the state. In Vietnam, network was publicly managed with foreign operators participating in provision of training, equipment and supervision through Business Cooperation Contracts (BCCs). China did not allow private entry in the telecom sector and limited competition between state-owned entities of the ministries. Many countries in Asia restricted foreign equity participation. For example, China, India, Indonesia, Korea, Malaysia, the Philippines and Thailand limited foreign equity below 50 per cent[43].

It is interesting to note that competing technological standards have also limited competitions. Countries are divided in their technical options for mobile networks. While Europe predominantly opted for Global System for Mobile communications (GSM) technology and USA for Code Division Multiple Access (CDMA), within Asia, China, India, Indonesia and Malaysia have opted for GSM in cellular mobile network, whereas Hong Kong, Korea, the Philippines, Singapore and Thailand have opted for CDMA[44].

However, several countries are now opting for more than one standards. For example, in USA, 'Companies like AT&T and Cingular are increasingly moving to GSM'[45]. 'China is going with some CDMA as well.'[46] India is using CDMA in Wireless in Local Loop (WLL). Multiple technological standards fragment market rendering base stations purchased from one company unworkable with switches bought from another company, potentially limiting the scope of exploitation of economies of scale that could accrue in a multi-vendor environment[47].

The way multiple technological standards may confuse

---

43. ITU, *World Telecommunication Development Report 2002*, Geneva, 2002, p.5.
44. *Ibid.*, p.6. India has opted for CDMA in WLL.
45. Interview with Ian Goetz, published in *tele.net*, Vol. No.3, issue no. 4, April 2002, p.32.
46. *Ibid., op.cit.*, p.31.
47. *Ibid.*, p.31.

regulatory stance leading to market failures can be seen from the recent experiences of several vendors while trying to launch 3G in Europe. European Union has mandated a single technological standard called 'Wideband CDMA' (W-CDMA) for 3G coverage. Some of the companies that sought to launch 3G services in September 2002 (deadline stipulated in the licenses for the launch of services) faced the difficulties that networks and handsets of different vendors could not work with each other. 'CDMA2000', another standard for 3G, which is working successfully in Asia and USA could not be adopted in Europe because European operators did not have freedom to use 'CDMA2000' as per their licensing restrictions[48].

Which competition policies worked better than others? Literature cites certain developmental experiences to draw conclusions from 'before and after' and 'with or without' evaluations. The purpose here is to cite these references. In the absence of more detailed information, examination of the validity of such conclusions is not intended here.

Competition with Privatization

World over, there is an observable trend of growing number of state-owned telecom incumbents being privatized. In 2000, from among the member countries of the ITU, those with fully or partially privatized incumbents outnumbered countries with fully state-owned operators[49]. It has been observed that 'countries with a privately owned incumbent operator account for 85 per cent of the world market by revenue. Those with fully state-owned operators, in mobile as well as fixed lines, account for just two per cent.'[50]

It has been suggested that privatization with competition works better than privatization without competition. For example, Chile started privatization in 1988 but did not limit competition through grant of exclusivity period or licensing obligations. Argentina, on the other hand, privatized in 1990, but granted seven-year exclusivity

48. 3G telecoms: Let Europe's operators free, *The Economist*, September 28th – October 4th 2002, p.15.

49. ITU, *World Telecommunication Development Report 2002*, Geneva, 2002, p.40.

50. *Ibid.*, p.2.

period, which was subsequently extended by three years. Moreover, Argentina imposed licensing obligation in terms of stipulated growth rate of 6.5 per cent. In the decade following privatization, Chile far exceeded Argentina in terms of network growth. Moreover, starting with half of the tele-density, Chile surpassed Argentina in ten years' time[51].

The issue of granting a 'period of shared exclusivity' versus 'allowing more extensive market entry' has been discussed in the literature. Experience of UK has been cited in this context. Telecom expansion was reportedly much more rapid in the United Kingdom (i) after the expiry of exclusivity period from 1982-90, that was granted to Mercury, the second operator and (ii) after cable TV operators were permitted to offer tele-services[52]. Therefore, it was concluded that open competition was better than duopoly. Both USA and Canada lost in terms of their mobile tele-density rankings in the world in the Nineties. Two reasons which have been cited for this are: (i) persistence with regional duopoly for too long, and (ii) slow transition from analog to digital systems[53].

Notwithstanding the merits of the above conclusions whatsoever, it can be argued that privatisation of existing state-owned incumbent operator is not the only way to promote private investment. Opening up of new services not preoccupied by state monopoly can attract private investors, provided regulatory policies do not inhibit growth of private markets in such areas. Growth of private mobile operators in India is a case in point. However, it is necessary for the regulatory authority to ensure that state incumbent does not inhibit growth of competition[54]. Operationalisation of these ideas is not without hazards. A conflict of common occurrence relates to interconnection

---

51. *Ibid.*, p.42.
52. *Ibid.*, p.45.
53. *Ibid.*, pp.54-55.
54. Dasgupta, *et.al.* find econometric evidence to support that 'difference in competition policies have much greater impact on Internet intensity than differences in income'. Here, competition is measured in terms of World Bank's rating index, which captures to what extent state inhibits a competitive private sector. The results suggest positive impact of competition. The study also finds favourable impact of competition on mobile penetration. See, Dasgupta, S., Somik Lall and David Wheeler, *Policy Reform, Economic Growth and the Digital Divide: An Econometric Analysis*, Working Paper No. 2567, World Bank, March, 28, 2001.

issues. Interconnection between state-owned fixed line incumbent network and private mobile network has been a bone of contention in many countries. '...incumbent telecommunication operator, which often holds a monopoly...can set the price, typically at a high multiple of the actual cost'[55].

Independent Regulator?

Sound regulation is a pre-requisite to healthy competition. Therefore, issue of competition cannot be divorced from the issue of regulation. The autonomy that a regulator enjoys from government control has often been given primacy over many other factors in determining a regulator's ability to discharge regulatory role in an impartial manner. In reality, however, it is difficult to perceive independent regulation as synonymous with impartial regulation. There are examples of effective regulation under regulatory functions being performed by the government departments. Similarly, there are instances of 'independent regulators that have been captured by market players'[56].

What about non-sector specific regulation? New Zealand experimented with non-sector specific regulation relying on Competition Commission of the country. This led to protracted litigations and disputes on interconnection and network access issues slowing down the progress of the sector. Finally, New Zealand enacted 'Telecommunication Act' in December 2000 and created a Telecommunication Commission within the Competition Commission[57].

In India, TRAI Act was amended in January 2000, to remove some of the shortcomings observed earlier. The legislation aimed at, *inter alia*, protection of interests of service providers and consumers of telecom sector. With this amendment, recommendatory functions were separated from enforcement functions. A separate Telecom Disputes Settlement and Appellate Tribunal (TDSAT) was set up with both original and appellate jurisdiction. It became mandatory for the Central Government to

55. ITU, *World Telecommunication Development Report 2002*, Geneva, 2002, *op. cit.*, p. 29.

56. *Ibid., op.cit.*, p.49.

57. *Ibid.*, p.50.

seek prior recommendations of the TRAI before introduction of new services. TRAI's power to issue directions was restricted to only its enforcement functions. Direct appeal to the Supreme Court of India against an order of TRAI was provided for. Thus, neutrality of Indian telecom regulatory regime was ensured through reliance on multiple agencies for conflict resolution[58]. TRAI had a proven record of maintaining neutrality. It had challenged several decisions of the Government of India[59].

In tune with the international development and evolution of technology, the Communication Convergence Bill 2001 was introduced in the Parliament and is under consideration of the Standing Committee of Parliament on Telecom and IT. 'The Bill aims at promoting, facilitating and developing, in an orderly manner, the carriage and content of communications (including broadcasting, telecommunications and multimedia), to facilitate development of a national infrastructure for an information-based society, and to enable access thereto. It also seeks to provide a choice of services to the people with a view to promoting plurality of news, views and information'[60]. Thus, regulatory regime in 2020 will be overarching, based on convergence, which apart from paving the way to a full-grown information society will enhance growth and productivity of telecommunications and IT through exploitation of economies of scope and coverage.

Competition Without Privatization

Interestingly, there are other models of competition without privatization. China Telecom, one of the world's major Public Telecommunication Operators (PTOs) is still fully state-owned. Both China and Vietnam followed similar policies of competition without privatization. Competition has been allowed between ministries of the governments. Participation of foreign investors has

---

58. Galal Ahmed and Bharat Nauriyal, *Regulation of Telecom in Developing Countries: Outcomes, Incentives and Commitment*, The World Bank, August 1995.
59. See for such instances, *Sanctity of Contract and Rule of Law in Indian Power, Telecom and Infrastructure Sectors*, Conference document presented by Independent Power Producers Association of India, 12-13 September, 2001, New Delhi, pp. 175-177.
60. Government of India, Ministry of Communications & Information Technology, Department of Telecommunications, *Annual Report, 2001-2002*.

been allowed through joint ventures. Both these countries have been very high achievers in terms of progress of telecom sector[61]. 'The key underlying factor is the will of the state to invest in, and prioritize, telecommunication development'.[62]

There have been instances of repeated market failures arising out of imprudent investment decisions of the private operators. In Norway, license to provide 3G mobile services purchased for US $22 million was returned unused. Investment worth several billion dollars were sunk and lost in the Iridium Global Mobile Personal Communications by Satellite (GMPCS) network project. Global Crossing went bankrupt with debts over US $12 billion for a project of construction of 160,000 km fiber optic network[63]. One view is that too many competitors deciding 'to build enormous networks for which there was little demand' were responsible for such crashes[64]. Market failures of such magnitudes create backlash in the industry and can potentially risk a global crisis. Such failures, if not avoided, would prove too costly in terms of lost investment in a country like India. A calibrated approach through managed competition holds assurances for the investors of a reasonable time period for consolidation and therefore, seems to be a wiser strategy to follow.

Despite differences in competition regimes across the countries, the global trend is towards growing privatization and competition. India, with her commitment to reforms is already a part of this process. From the perspective of business organisation, as the global experience suggests, this process is likely to undergo an alternate cycle of differentiation and convergence. Convergent nature of technology may, by itself dictate mergers and acquisitions between companies in certain cases. Network operators and service providers will have to merge with content developers to add value to their services. This is likely to create temporary oligopoly in the market till competition intensifies with the emergence of more

---

61. ITU, *World Telecommunication Development Report 2002*, Geneva, 2002, p.52.
62. *Ibid., op.cit.*, p.53.
63. *Ibid.*, p.59.
64. The great telecoms crash, *The Economist*, July 20th – 26th 2002, p.11.

firms offering multiple services[65]. India in 2020 will see competition among big firms offering innovative value-added services to capture market through creation of new digital needs and priorities. Regulatory environment will mature to allow maximum flexibility and freedoms to encourage innovation and expansion, consistent with this process of evolution.

5. Technology Trend

Broadly speaking, technologies of mobile telecommunications and Internet are going to set the contours of further technological progress in the current decade and the next. The most recent initiative aims at convergence of voice and data received from multiple sources, both web based and real time video streams in mobile handheld devices. Global satellite systems, mobile handsets and calling cards have made virtual presence possible almost everywhere and anywhere overcoming the barriers of distance, topography and remoteness.

There has been phenomenal growth in mobile subscribers in the world in the Nineties, increasing from 11 million in 1990 to 941 million by the end of 2001. In 1991, less than one per cent of the world population had a mobile phone. The proportion has grown to the vicinity of one phone per every six people by the end of 2001. Similarly, one-third of the total number of countries of the world

---

65. There can be horizontal mergers like mergers between telecom operators and cable operators. Similarly, there can be vertical mergers between mobile telecom operators and content providers. Mergers and acquisitions can also occur with the aim of reaping the benefits of economies of scale. In Indian telecom sector, there are instances of mergers between operators in contiguous license territories. It has been indicated that in 2001, only 7 groups were controlling nearly 90 per cent of the market shares in terms of cellular subscribers against 20 players, who were awarded licenses in 1995-96. See for details, Garg, Lokesh and Venu Madhav, Mergers and Acquisitions in the Indian Telecom Sector, *India Infrastructure Report 2002: Governance Issues for Commercialisation*, 3i Network, Oxford, 2002. A number of examples on U.S. market can be found in Balaji, N., *The Indian Telecom Sector: Basic Telecom & Cellular Services*, Indian Institute of Management, Lucknow, available at file://c:\windows\temp\Indian telecom experience - IIML study.htm. In the context of recent telecom crash in the world market, a view has been expressed that such crisis may 'cause the pendulum to swing back too far in favour of the former monopolies. In the short term, they are likely to attract investment, to pick up the assets of bankrupt rivals, and to lead the way in consolidating the industry. This will provide some welcome stability. But it would be wrong to grant the former monopolies any regulatory concessions now that would protect them from competitors in future.' The great telecoms crash, *The Economist*, July 20th-26th, 2002, *op. cit.*, p.11. Hence, mergers and acquisitions are also likely occur in the process of market consolidation.

had cellular network in 1991. The ratio rose to over 90 per cent by end-2001[66]. Considering that the fixed telephone lines numbered just over a billion in this year, it is likely that mobile phones would surpass fixed line in 2002. It is interesting to observe that China has surpassed USA to become the largest mobile market of the world. In Africa, mobile subscribers outnumber fixed line subscribers in more than half the countries[67]. Mobile telephony has emerged as the major growth driver in this sector. But for expansion in mobile network, there would have been hardly any growth in telecommunications in many countries. In developed countries, mobile phones have complemented fixed lines whereas in many developing countries with low-level fixed line penetration, mobile has already surpassed fixed lines[68], filling up supply gaps created due to inadequate growth in the latter. It has been observed that 'the ability of a country to grow its mobile network to the point where it overtakes the fixed-line network is not a function of its wealth...the crossover point can come as low as a fixed teledensity of 0.4 (for instance, in Malwai) to as high as 75 (the case of Luxembourg) and at any point in between'[69].

There are three important economic implications of mobile explosion for the developing countries. First, by offering a viable techno-economic alternative it is helping in improving telecom penetration bypassing shortages of fixed lines. Consequently, it is bringing along with it all concomitant economic benefits of enhanced telecom accessibility. Second, it is promoting a better entrepreneurial culture and supporting employment generation through proliferation of kiosks[70]. Third, there has been a shift in investment burden from state to private sector and the consumers[71].

Cellular mobile telephones subscribers in India increased from 77 thousand in 1995 to 3.6 million in 2000. By March 2002, it has grown to 6.4 million. Cellular subscribers in proportion to total

66. ITU, *World Telecommunication Development Report 2002*, Geneva, 2002, p.13.
67. *Ibid.*, p.6.
68. *Ibid.*, p.7.
69. *Ibid.*, *op. cit.*, p.65.
70. *Ibid.*, p.15.
71. Mobile telecom expansion does not need to wait for state to lay copper lines. While private service providers lay the base station, consumers purchase mobile stations, i.e., handsets. *ibid.*, p.15.

number of telephone subscribers (basic plus cellular) has increased from 0.6 per cent in 1995 to 14.6 per cent in 2002. This is still lower than the average of 24.6 per cent achieved by the low-income countries in 2001. The corresponding ratio for lower middle-income countries is 41.8 per cent, 52.8 per cent for upper middle-income countries and 50.2 per cent for high-income countries. India is yet to experience mobile explosion of the scale other countries have seen. One would expect a rapid growth in mobile telephony in coming decades. India has also achieved significant quality upgradation of its network in the Nineties. Digital lines in proportion to total number of main telephone lines have increased from 87 per cent in 1995 to 99.8 per cent in 1999.

Like mobile, the last decade witnessed phenomenal growth in Internet usage. In 2001, 95 per cent of the countries were connected to Internet compared to 15 per cent in 1990. There are about half a billion Internet users in the world in 2001 with subscribers numbering an estimated 230 million[72]. It is also interesting to note that in 1995 Internet users in developed countries were seven times more than the number of Internet users in the developing countries. In 2001, this gap has narrowed down to less than four times.

Initial stance of technology supporting expansion of Internet dictated revenue model based on convergence between telecom and Internet. Internet is accessed predominantly through dial up in old telephone lines. This has resulted in unequal distribution of benefits between the dotcom operators and the telecom operators. It has been observed that while dotcom operators 'are failing to make money on the Internet, telecom operators are. The reason is that they control the pipes over which Internet traffic runs'[73]. 'Incumbent telecom operators tend to be among the largest Internet Service Providers (ISPs) in their countries'[74]. There are three important implications of this development. First, it inhibits growth of content development as an independent specialized activity because revenue-share of the content developers depends on the first claim on revenue by the infrastructure providers. Second, technical

72. *Ibid.*, p.7.

73. *Ibid.*, p.7.

74. *Ibid.*, p.8.

capabilities of telephone lines constrain development of Internet infrastructure and conditions speed of download. Third, developing countries are faced with major bottlenecks in the spread of Internet due to shortage of telephone lines and high telephone charges. Technological answers to these problems have already emerged in the forms of Integrated Services Digital Networks (ISDN), wireless solutions and upgraded cable television networks enabling high-speed Internet access without clogging telephone lines. Use of VSAT technology for Internet connectivity can also greatly enhance the speed of data transmission[75]. In the present decade and the next, one would hope to see faster expansion and consolidation of these technologies ushering in Internet revolution. Broadband access technologies, which include Digital Subscriber Lines (DSL) and cable modem, permit faster download and graphic-intensive Internet applications. However, diffusion of this technology is so far minimal, particularly in the developing countries. Commercial exploitation of Internet crucially hinges on the spread of broadband technology. The issue that confronts developing world is how to create demand for broadband applications at the first instance. At the early stage, government can play an important role to promote broadband usage in e-education, e-governance, e-medicine to stimulate its demand[76].

Another convergent trend that has emerged is the use of Internet as carriers of voice. Consequently, 'increasing share of voice traffic shifted to the Internet, to be carried as Voice over Internet Protocol (VoIP)'[77].

At the uppermost end of the convergent technology spectrum have already emerged Third Generation (3G) mobile devices with the capability of access to mobile data and voice[78]. More than US $100 billion have been spent by the industry since 2000 to acquire

---

75. VSAT stands for 'Very Small Aparture Terminals', which 'are miniature earth stations, used for transmission of data, video, or voice via satellite'. The Nepalese Government has allowed ISPs to use VSATs for establishing their own connectivity leading to remarkable gain in speed from 320 kbps to over 5 mbps within six months. *ibid.*, p.30.

76. *Ibid.*, p.31.

77. *Ibid., op.cit.*, p.46.

78. Data-like applications on mobile devices have already started taking off in developed and developing countries. *ibid.*, p.9.

3G license and spectrum. However, a full-grown market is yet to develop to assure investors' return. Technical and commercial consolidation is expected to take quite some time. By 2020, one would expect 3G to be within reach of wider section of Indian population.

The pace at which 3G is going to proliferate in India will depend upon, *inter alia,* the market demand for higher bandwidth data. There is a view that perhaps the present demand for high speed data (greater than 64 kbps) can be met cost effectively with General Packet Radio Service (GPRS). While pent up demand for emerging data-needs can be met by using 2G systems like Short Message Service (SMS), GPRS etc., the drive for 3G in Indian market can come from 'corporate roaming traffic via international visitors'[79].

Substantial work needs to be done in developing 3G relevant contents so as to expand its market. Initiative has already been launched in these areas. For example, Sonera (formerly Telecom Finland) has already launched information portal for mobile phones including Internet localisation services[80]. Future work in this area will be in the form of adding more value to the new services.

Advanced plans are necessary to develop vibrant industries for 3G applications. This may call for investments. A synchronized growth of user industry and 3G technologies would ensure that pay-off period in investment is minimized. Developing knowledge-based industry to provide mobile applications would reduce uncertainties regarding return from private investment in 3G technologies.

As a preparatory groundwork to usher in 3G, it is essential to demarcate areas where massive harmonization efforts would be needed. This would entail upgrading hardware and software for high bandwidth multimedia services. Harmonization would also be needed between the two emerging varieties of CDMA, i.e., wideband CDMA that also supports fixed network and CDMA-2000. Since it is likely that both these solutions would ultimately support fixed

---

79. Interview with Ian Goetz, published in *tele.net*, Vol. No.3, issue no. 4, April 2002, pp.30 - 31.

80. Such services give information like 'which gas stations are nearby'. Finland is a pioneer in cellular telephony. ITU, *World Telecommunication Development Report 2002*, Geneva, 2002, p.19.

and mobile applications, a marriage of the two would prevent technological fragmentation of the market.

There is need to develop deeper understanding of the evolution of new end-users in the market for the mobile multimedia services. Multimedia service providers will emerge as important shareholders in the network value chain. Countries should envision new partners, new entities, and new stakeholders in the business models. Multimedia portals will be important components of such business models.

There is need for further work to match regulatory perspectives emerging as a part of the convergence regime with the requirements of 3G. Another important area of work will involve further thought over efficient billing model — a transition from time dependent billing model to content dependent billing[81].

The revenue model in the telecommunications sector is going to change significantly in times to come. In many cases PTOs have started offering free Internet to augment revenue from telephone lines[82]. In the Philippines, a global leader in SMS use in mobile handsets, revenue from SMS contributed a growing share of mobile revenue. SMS proved to be much cheaper than voice call[83].

6. Conclusions

LDCs are experiencing fastest growth in telecom network. In the mid-Nineties, growth in total telephone subscribers per 100 inhabitants of the LDCs surpassed that of the developed countries. In 2001, LDCs surpassed emerging countries, achieving the distinction of fastest among the three[84]. Given the relationship between telecom expansion and growth, there is hope for narrowing down of digital-divide, provided, LDCs are able to sustain growth momentum in the long run. The vision is no doubt

81. For detailed discussions see various reports of UMTS Forum, London.
82. ITU, *World Telecommunication Development Report 2002*, Geneva, 2002, p.11.
83. *Ibid.*, p.10.
84. ITU classification of LDCs, emerging countries and developed countries has been referred to. *ibid.*, p.17.

optimistic. It has been cited that some twenty years ago, Tokyo had more telephones than the whole of African continent whereas today, Africa has more than twice the number of main telephone lines than that of Tokyo[85]. It is but natural that markets in high-income countries saturate while expansion in developing countries continues unabated.

One notable break with the past is that with the opening up of the developing economies and widespread sectoral reforms, catching up process has become faster. Developing countries with liberal policies have much better opportunity to leapfrog than before. Mobile experience of the low-income countries bears testimony to this process. India is a participant in this global process. There is tremendous appetite to absorb new technology. At the higher end of the market, India will mimic the most sophisticated telecom technology of the world and face all types of uncertainties that are associated with any new technology anywhere in the world. It will take time for the market for new technologies to consolidate. 'Market maturing' will be a continuous process at some of the segments of telecom sector. This holds good even today. Today's market does not guarantee 'reliable revenue stream' to investors in new technology like VoIP, bradband and 3G since they lack an existing client base[86]. Side by side, a process of diffusion will continue unhindered in respect of established technology in the mass market.

What will be the Telecom Scenario in India in 2020?

To look forward, from now on, the growth momentum in the expansion of fixed line network is likely to be sustained. This is the current phase of expansion developing countries are passing through. In 2000, three out of four fixed lines were installed in developing countries. China alone installed more fixed lines in 2000 (35 million) than the entire developed world in 1999 and 2000[87].

Once fixed line market is matured, mobile will crossover fixed line market. India is still much below the crossover point even by

85. *Ibid.*, p.17.
86. *Ibid.*, p.59.
87. *Ibid.*, p. 68.

the standard of the low-income countries. A mobile revolution is in the offing in India.

The next points of crossover will be between data and voice[88], and between mobile and fixed-line Internet[89]. This is going to take some time because this is yet to occur even in high-income countries. The process of technical consolidation and system integration of different competing standards in a single platform will by itself take some time. The process of commercial consolidation will start thereafter.

In order to guess the time frame over which such technological and commercial cycles may run their courses in future, it may be of interest to look at the past experiences. Going by the history, commercialisation of cellular mobile telecommunication services began in late Seventies, when Japan took the lead in 1979. Many developed countries have reached saturation point only now though developing countries are far from it. Similarly, market for Internet in the developing countries is yet to mature though the service commenced in late 1960s, when USA took the lead in 1969. As rightly observed, 'But for both these innovations, the full extent of their impact on businesses and consumers is probably still to come. E-commerce, for instance, is still in relative infancy and is expected to boom in coming years as "old economy" firms re-orient their business processes around it. Similarly, the true potential of a mobile phone, as an integrated communications, entertainment and positioning device, is only beginning to be realized'[90].

If past trend were any guide, it would be reasonable to hope that by 2020 India would complete transition into digital switching and transmission, VoIP, broadband and 3G. Though there would always be a small niche market in India, which would catch up with the cutting age of the technology, consolidation and expansion of

---

88. Increasing demand for data should not lead to a conclusion that voice services will not attract innovation any longer. It has been held that in a miniature handheld device, information can be received only in the form of voice. Lot of developments is in the offing in the area of voice recognition, integration between voice and text and *vice versa*. See, Interview with Ian Goetz, published in *tele.net*, Vol. No.3, issue no. 4, April 2002, p. 32.

89. This point has already been reached in Japan. ITU, *World Telecommunication Development Report 2002*, Geneva, 2002, p.73.

90. *Ibid.*, *op.cit.*, p.72.

evolving technologies across the length and the breadth of the country will follow with a lag.

Future vision of telecom is a vision of IT. Telecom will be the springboard of future expansion of IT heralding in an information society. ICT will spread among the masses and will spur innovation, entrepreneurship and growth. An expanding domestic market will deepen the synergy between the domestic and the export market and strengthen India's presence in the high-value segment of the global trade and investment. ICT benefits will spread among all, the rich and the poor, the young and the old, the men and the women, the organized and the unorganized and the government and the governed.

APPENDIX

Indian Telecom Sector: Recent Policies

1. All the villages shall be covered by telecom facility by the end of 2002.
2. The Communication Convergence Bill 2001 introduced in the Parliament on August 31, 2001 is presently before the Standing Committee of Parliament on Telecom and IT.
3. National Long Distance Service (NLD) is opened for unrestricted entry.
4. The International Long Distance Services (ILDS) have been opened to competition.
5. The basic services are open to competition.
6. In addition to the existing three, fourth cellular operator, one each in four metros and thirteen circles, has been permitted. The cellular operators have been permitted to provide all types of mobile services including voice and non-voice messages, data services and PCOs, utilizing any type of network equipment, including circuit and/or package switches that meet certain required standards.
7. Policies allowing private participation have been announced as per the New Telecom Policy (NTP), 1999 in several new services, which include Global Mobile Personal Communication by Satellite (GMPCS) Service, digital Public Mobile Radio

Trunked Service (PMRTS), Voice Mail/ Audiotex/Unified Messaging Service.

8. Wireless in Local Loop (WLL) has been introduced for providing telephone connections in urban, semi-urban and rural areas promptly.
9. Two telecom PSUs, VSNL and HTL have been disinvested.
10. Steps are being taken to fulfill Universal Service Obligation (USO), its funding and administration.
11. A decision to permit Mobile Community Phone Service has been announced.
12. Multiple Fixed Service Providers (FSPs) licensing guidelines were announced.
13. Internet Service Providers (ISPs) have been allowed to set up International Internet Gateways, both Satellite and Landing stations for submarine optical fiber cables.
14. Two categories of infrastructure providers have been allowed to provide end-to-end bandwidth and dark fiber, right of way, towers, duct space etc.
15. Guidelines have been issued by the Government to open up Internet telephony (IP).

Investment Policy Framework

1. Foreign Direct Investment of up to 100 per cent permitted for the following:
    - Manufacturing of telecom equipment
    - Internet service (not providing international gateways)
    - Infrastructure providers (Category I)
    - E-mail service
    - Voice mail service
    - Call Centers and IT enabled services
2. Foreign Direct Investment of up to 74 per cent permitted for the following:
    - Internet service (providing international gateways)

- Infrastructure providers (Category II)
- Radio paging services

3. Foreign Direct Investment of up to 49 per cent permitted for the following:
   - National long distance service
   - Basic telephone service
   - Cellular mobile service
   - Other value added service
4. Additional foreign investment through holding/investment company.
5. Automatic approval for technology fee up to US $2 million, royalty up to five per cent for domestic sales and eight per cent for exports in telecom manufacturing (higher amount through specific approvals).
6. Full repatriability of dividend income and capital invested in the telecom sector.
7. Fiscal incentives and concessions for the telecom sector:
   - Amortization of license fee.
   - Tax holiday.
   - Rebate on subscription to shares/debentures.
   - Scope for tax exemption on financing through venture capital.
   - Import duty rates reduced for various telecom equipment.

Source: (i) *Annual Report*, 2001-2002 and (ii) Indian Telecommunication Statistics 2002 (Policy Framework, Status and Trends), both published by the Department of Telecommunications, Ministry of Communications & IT, Government of India.

16

Transport: Vision 2020

MAHESH KAPOOR

TRANSPORT AND ECONOMIC DEVELOPMENT

Introduction

Twentieth century revolution in transport has made us aware of the relationship of immobility with poverty, with transport innovations influencing most profoundly the pace and growth of economic development. Obstacles to movement restrict the market, increase production cost and raise prices beyond competitive reach of the consumer.

The total world of transportation is not only too large but of great scope, diversity and complexity. Transport comes into play for everything and remains an essential part of everything, remaining as various as life itself. The great difference between modes is obvious enough but the more subtle differences that exist between groups and classes can be even more important in their consequences.

Modes of Transport

For nearly a hundred years, the railways remained the dominant mode for land transport and continues to remain the land carrier that can carry anything anywhere the rail tracks go and do it at a cost lower than other types of land or air transportation. Today, other modes have developed providing transport more effectively and efficiently. Pipelines for the movement of liquids, aircraft for high speed long distance travel and trucks offering speed, flexibility and door to door service for short and medium levels provide better alternatives. All these have effected the market share and role of different modes of transport.

The fluctuations in demand for transport services can be rapid, both in volume and in direction. There could be an almost chronic imbalance between supply and demand in many services, at any rate, over the short term. This causes both pricing and operating problems. It is sometimes a question of too little or too much. Unlike many other sectors of the economy, transport can neither be stored nor traded and to meet the peak demands of traffic, extra capacity needs to be created, which necessarily idles in the non-peak periods.

The shrinking of the world paradoxically increase transport volume and demand with more exchange of goods. Enterprises which are efficient and flexible, which move with the changing times and provide appropriate technologies and remain commercial in their attitude, will survive and continue to have an important role to play.

Investment by State and Private Sector Participation

A transportation network makes the markets more competitive while the system widens the opportunities for suppliers and buyers and improves the allocation process of goods and services. The supply of transport is a mix bag of public and private entities. The highways are provided by the state while most of the vehicles using them are private. Airports, provided by the government with aircraft both in the private and public sector. Most ports have been developed by the state while ships using it could be public or private owned. Railways, is the only exception, which provides the way and the vehicles as one integrated entity.

Where profits can be made, responses of the private firms are high, subsidies on the other hand tend to continue with vested interest and through political pressure. Subsidized services pursue objectives that often differ from the aims of economic efficiency and transport services are sometimes used for redistribution of income from the general tax payer to the user of subsidized transport operation.

Government comes a great deal into transport affairs and is inevitably closely involved in questions of infrastructure and space. Provision of transport infrastructure calls for state intervention to ensure long term economic development.

As there is no effective way of reducing risks in fixed infrastructure, only the state is in a position to cover the risks. Investments that require long term finance like building of roads, ports, railways, have a high degree of market failure in these activities and have to remain the responsibility of the state. To bring in private sector participation for investments in infrastructure presents the policy makers a task to create an entirely new system of incentives, risk and profit sharing.

GROWTH OF TRANSPORT NETWORK AND DEMAND

Transport Network and Systems

India's transport system is one of the largest in the world serving the land mass of 3.3 million square km and a population of over one billion. The network for the services comprise mainly of roads, railways and air services. The 6000 km coast line has 12 major and over 150 minor ports. While the ministry of Railways is responsible for running of the rail system, the highways are the joint responsibility of the Central Ministry of Road Transport and Highways (for National Highways) and the state governments (State Highways, District and Rural roads). The Ministry of Civil Aviation looks after Airports and the Ministry of Urban Development responsible for Urban Transport.

The growth in the network of transport and the demand for transport services in the last 50 years has been quite significant as can be seen from the figures given in Table 1. Currently, about 800 billion tonne kms of freight and 2300 billion passenger kms[1] is handled by the transport system, with the total transport demand growing at around 10 per cent a year in the last 10 years. The modal growth rates have varied with road transport and air services growing at a much higher rate than the railways.

---

1. Estimated by Planning Commission. World Bank Estimates (Report May 2002) mention 870 billion tkms and 2450 billion pkms.

Table 1

Profile of Transport Sector

S.No.	Item		1950-51	1960-61	1970-71	1980-81	1990-91	1995-96	1996-97	1997-98	1998-99	1999-2000
1	RAILWAYS											
1.1	Route Length	Kms.	53596	56247	59790	61240	62367	62915	62725	62495	62809	62759
1.2	Electrified Route Length	Kms.	388	748	3706	5345	9968	12306	13018	13490	13765	14261
1.3	Throughout											
1.3.1	Freight Traffic (Total)	M. Tonnes	93	156.2	196.5	220	341.4	405.5	409.02	429.4	420.9	478.2
1.3.2	Net Tonne (Kms.)	B.T.Kms.	44.12	87.68	127.36	158.47	242.7	273.52	279.99	286.77	284.27	308.04
1.3.3	Passenger Originating	Million	1284	1594	2431	3613	3858	4018	4153	4348	4411	4585
1.3.4	Passengers Kms.	Million	66517	77665	118120	208558	295644	341999	357013	379897	403884	430666
2	ROADS											
2.1	Total of	000 Kms.	400	525	915	1485	2350	3320	2466	2540	2616	2695
	which NHs.	000 Kms.	22	24	24	32	33.7	34.5	34.6	38.52	49.58	52.01
2.2	%age of village with 100+ population connected with all weather roads	Percent	NA	NA	NA	29	45.8	85.7				
2.3	Surfaced Length	000 Kms.	156	234	398	684	1113	1517	1394	1422	1450	1479
3	ROAD TRANSPORT											
3.1	No. of Goods Vehicles	In'000	82	168	343	554	1356	1785	2260	2529	2858	3229
3.2	No. of Passengers Buses	In'000	34	57	94	162	331	449	488	535	594	659

(Contd...)

(...Contd...)

S.No. Item		1950 -51	1960 -61	1970 -71	1980 -81	1990 -91	1995 -96	1996 -97	1997 -98	1998 -99	1999 -2000
4 MAJOR PORTS											
4.1 No. of major ports	Numbers	5	9	10	10	11	11	11	11	11	11
4.2 Traffic handled	M. Tonnes	19.38	33.12	55.58	80.27	151.67	215.34	227.26	251.66	251.72	271.87
5 MINOR PORTS											
5.1 Traffic handled	M. Tonnes	NA	NA	6.69	6.73	11.27	24.36	24.93	38.61	36.31	62.52
6 CIVIL AVIATION											
6.1 Indian Airlines											
(i) Available tonnes	Km Million	NA	113	208	663	927	1046	1075	1094	1123	1121
(ii) Revenue Tonne	Kms. Million	NA	83	161	420	699	723	698	701	709	740
6.2 Air India											
(i) Available Tonne	Km Million	NA	NA	515	1623	2260	2610	2452	2294	2394	2238
(ii) Revenue Tonne	Km Million	NA	NA	275	980	1381	1619	1485	1454	1474	1457
6.3 No. of Airports and Civil Enclaves	Number	NA	NA	NA	84	117	120	120	120	122	122
7. INLAND WATER TRANSPORT											
7.1 Length of Navigable Waterways	Kms.	14544	14544	14544	14544	14544	14544	14544	14646	14646	14646

Railways which had a market share of 88 per cent of freight and 68 per cent of the passenger business in land transport in 1950-51 has come down to about 40 per cent of freight and about 20 per cent of passenger market share in 1999-2000 while road transport has moved from 12 per cent to 60 per cent in freight and from 32 per cent to 80 per cent in the passenger business in the same period.[2]

Loss of Market Share by Railways

Over the years, while rail freight traffic continued to increase albeit at a slower pace, the more disturbing feature was the continuous loss in the market share. In a situation of less supply of transport and a high priority to the bulk traffic, the more cumbersome 'smalls' and wagon load traffic was gradually discouraged and the railway's unit of movement became a train load. This improved productivity, and the wagon fleet reduced substantially despite an increase in traffic. (Wagon fleet came down from 400946 in 1980-81 to 222147 in 2000-01, while the freight went up from 196 mt to 474 mt in the same period) Bulk traffic also started moving on high capacity trucks while pipelines siphoned off the high tariff traffic petroleum products. Meanwhile, to balance budgets and increase resources while keeping passenger fares low, the freight rates continued to be increased. Today, on PPP terms, the tariff per tonne km on Indian Railways is about the highest in the world. If the Railways is to survive it must cut subsidies (including treating passenger fares as the holy cow), reduce freight rates and invest in capacity building activities and cut out non-core activities and reduce its staff costs.

Investment in the Sector

Investments made in the transport sector in the last 50 years is given in Table 2. Public investment in transport as a percentage of total expenditure has been declining almost steadily since the early 1960s when transport investment was allocated about 23.1 per cent of the total plan funds. It declined to 16 per cent till the mid 1970s and has been close to 12 per cent in the 1980s and 1990s.

2. While Railway data is available for pkms and tkms those for the roads are estimates. Road data for example for the year 2000 varies from 540 to 1000 btkms and 2000 to 4000 pkms.

Table 2

Expenditure in the Transport Sector 1951-2002

(Rs. Crore)

	Ist Plan (1951-56)	IInd Plan (1956-61)	IIIrd Plan (1961-66)	Annual Plan (1966-69)	IVth Plan (1969-74)	Vth Plan (1974-79)	Annual Plan (1979-84)	VIth Plan (1980-85)	VIIth Plan (1985-90)	Annual Plan (1990-92)	VIIIth Plan (1992-97)	IXth Plan (1997-2002)
Sector	*Exp.*	*Exp.*	*Exp.*	*Exp.*	*Exp.*	*Exp.*	*Exp.*	*Exp.*	*Exp.*	*Exp.*	*Exp.*	*Anti. Exp*
Railways	217	723	1326	509	934	2063	714	6585	16549	10208	32302	46405
Roads & Bridges	147	242	440	309	862	1701	467	3887	6335	3656	16095	47600
Road Transport			27	55	128	503	143	1276	2151	986	3538	5933
Ports	28	33	93	53	249	488	57	725	1513	668	2302	5331
Shipping	19	53	40	32	155	469	147	468	720	939	3033	2909
IWT			4	6	11	16	6	63	188	57	152	280
LH&LS			4	2	6	9	2	*	*	4	25	58
Civil Aviation	23	49	49	66	177	294	132	957	1948	1055	7249	6958
Other Transport									72	118	244	1851
Transport Total	434	1100	1983	1032	2522	5543	1668	13961	29476	17691	64940	117325
Tpt as %age of Total Plan	22.05	23.54	23.12	15.58	15.98	14.06		13.00	13.51	14.12	12.88	

Note: * Included under Ports Sector

From V Plan, Rlys outlays and expenditure include outlays financed from depreciation reserve fund.

From IV plan, outlays for metro transport projects also included.

Road transport does not include investments by the private sector in road vehicles.

Considering the developing nature of the country and the state of its transport system plagued with deficiencies, it seems justified to devote a larger proportion of the total resources to the development of this basic infrastructure.

The shortage of funds affected the roads to an extent that almost the entire National Highway system was deficient in pavement thickness while over 17000 kms of the 52000 km National Highway Network continued to be single lane. Fortunately, recent actions have given a fillip to the National Highways and both the Central and some state governments have begun reversing the declining trend and the low level of funding for this sector. Funding for the two main road agencies, MORTH (Ministry of Road Transport and Highways) and NHAI (National Highway Authority of India) has been consistently increased over the past few years, the most important development being the implementation of a Central Road Fund (CRF), fully adopted in 1999, giving the fund on annual income of Rs. 50 billion. The CRF bring a new resource through a tariff of one rupee on each litre of petrol and high-speed diesel.

Railway's internal resource generation increased with the budgetary support coming down. In the Third Plan the budgetary support was as high as 75 per cent but then it came down to 15 per cent by the 1980s and in order to keep the out lays high, Railways resorted to market borrowings.

The experience with market borrowings through IRFC has landed Railways in a debt trap. The payments to IRFC on 10 years borrowing has over shot dividend payments to general exchequer. There is already a net outflow form IR to the general exchequer and a similar situation in respect of IRFC was reached during 1995-96 and repeats are imminent.

Urbanization

India's urban population according to the 2001 census was 285 million or 27.8 per cent of the country's total population of 1027 million. The growth since 1951 is given in Table 3.

Growing urbanization is a natural phenomenon and despite all its implications has beneficial effects on economic growth. Measures proposed or taken to decelerate urbanization or decongest the existing metropolises have not had much success and therefore, pragmatism suggests that urbanization be treated as a catalyst for economic development and efforts be made to facilitate, securing full benefits out of this inevitable process.

Table 3

India's Rural/Urban Population Growth

Year	*Population (in million)*			
	Total	*Rural*	*Urban*	*Urban Population Share (%)*
1951	369.09	306.65	62.44	17.29
1961	439.23	360.29	78.94	17.57
1971	548.16	438.17	109.99	19.91
1981	685.18	526.18	159.00	23.31
1991	844.32	627.14	217.18	25.72
2001	1027.01	741.66	285.36	27.78

One of the most daunting problems faced by the cities in the developing world is that of urban transport and failure to provide facilities increases trip times and costs both for passenger and goods traffic. A transport plan cannot be sensibly conceived without a plan for land use. Planning of transport must go hand in hand with land use planning and each city must involve itself, utilizing its resources for housing, sewerage, health, education and transport.

While the rate of urbanization in India compared to other countries in the world has been quite modest (see Annexure 1), the increase in absolute terms from 62 million in 1951 to 285 million in 2001 has been phenomenal. An unwelcome feature has been the concentration of population in metropolitan and cities having a population of more than a million. The number of cities with a million plus population increased from 5 in 1951 to 35 in 2001. (List of these cities with populations is given in Annexure 2). While three cities have population of over 12 million, ten others have populations varying from 2.1 to 5.4 million.

The growth of cities has been haphazard, growing around a compact central core with industrialization and migration bringing about rapid change in the peripheral land use, resulting in urban sprawl. No organized, viable and significant public transport system is available in the cities, except the four jumbo cities of Mumbai, Kolkata, Chennai and Delhi. Buses and rail transport system are the main stay of public transport in these cities. Kolkata is the first city to have a metro system and New Delhi is on its way to provide a metropolitan transport system with rail tracks on the surface, elevated and underground. By 2005, a network of 62 kms in Phase-I of the project would provide on extensive system of urban transport in the city.

Lack of adequate public transport has resulted in a rapid increase in private ownership of vehicles, particularly two wheelers with consequent effects on pollution both noise and air. In most cities two wheelers comprise more than 70 per cent of total motor vehicles.

Many agencies, at the central, state and local levels are involved in providing urban transport infrastructure and services. Roads by PWDs and to an extent by Municipal Corporations, Bus Services a combination of Public and Private operators, while suburban rail services are run by IR.

Despite all the attention and actions, urban transport in Indian cities is in a bad shape. Increased vehicle population have led to congested roads, slower speeds, increased fuel consumption and accidents on roads.

There is a great potential to open the bus services through contracting or franchising arrangements for many cities in the country. The private buses is a major input to providing services in Delhi, with running of chartered buses meeting a specific demand for schools and office complexes. To encourage people to leave the private vehicles and move to public transport, there is also a great potential for providing air conditioned buses on many routes in major cities. Operated in the private sector, these buses could levy fares based on the market potential and need not be forced to charge lower tariffs that often result in also poor service.

Over the years, the demand for traffic has outpaced the rate of investment in urban transport infrastructure. Both the Central and the state government have been unable to mobilize resources required by increasing fares or reducing subsidies. Lack of funds have not only affected additional facilities but maintenance of existing assets.

Roads

The growth of road transport has arisen from the proliferation of the road network in the last 50 years, from 400,000 kms in 1951 to 3,300,000 by 2000 as detailed below:

National Highways	52,000 kms
State Highways	1,28,000 kms
District Roads, Other Roads and Village Roads	29,20,000* kms
Urban Roads	200,000 kms

Note: * Including about 900000 kms of earth tracks constructed under Jawahar Rozgar Yojana programme.

However, only 4 per cent of the National Highways have four lane (or more) 66 per cent are two lane while 30 per cent is still one lane and the state highways have 1 per cent four lane, 19 per cent two lane and 80 per cent, single lane.

National highway running through the length and breadth of the country connect ports, state capitals, industrial and tourist centres while the state highways link district headquarters and important cities within the state.

The growth of traffic has been far greater than the growth of the highways, as a result the main arteries face capacity saturation. About 40 per cent of the road traffic moves on the National Highways and another 40 per cent on the state highways. These highways constitute about 6 per cent of the total road length and call for capacity argumentation on an urgent basis.

Recent initiatives by the government has increased activity in this area and under the National Highway Development Programme, the Golden Quadrangle, 6000 kms in length connecting Delhi-Mumbai-Chennai-Kolkata-Delhi and the 7300 kms north-south and east-west corridors, connecting Srinagar to Kanyakumari and Silchar to Porbandar have been taken up on priority.

The National Highways are planned to grow to about 75,000 kms in the next 20 years, with four laning (or more) of all lengths where the passenger car units are more than 350,000 and two lanes for the remaining stretches.

For the high density routes around metro and other cities, the need for expressways has been identified. Several sections of the

National Highways are riddled with encroachments and ribbon development where widening of roads may not be a cost-effective solution. 10,000 kms of expressways are proposed to be constructed by the year 2020. Some expressways like Mumbai-Pune, Bangalore-Mysore are already operational.

The highways under the NHAI have brought in fast clearances of projects and are developing rapidly. It has also led to mechanization in road building to match the targets of completion. The funding for the National Highways has been put on a firm footing and the NHAI itself is looking at various other ways to add resources including laying a network of telecom along its route as the work goes on of upgrading the highways.

Road Transport

Road freight and passenger traffic have had a tremendous growth in the last 50 years. Although no reliable data is available of the actual traffic carried, several estimates have been made by different agencies often revealing wide variations. This is one of the major gaps in the transport data compilation and with road transport being the predominant mode, a system to compile data needs early consideration. The Indian Road Congress in their report have indicated data for road traffic and modal share as given in Table 4.

Table 4

Growth of Road Traffic and Modal Shares

	1950-51	*1960-61*	*1970-71*	*1980-81*	*1990-91*	*1999-00*
Passenger kms (Billion)						
Rail	66	78	118	209	296	428
Road	23	57	169	407	859	1659
Total	89	135	287	616	1155	2087
Freight kms (Billion)						
Rail	44	88	127	159	243	302
Road	5	27	77	145	503	800
Total	**49**	**115**	**204**	**304**	**746**	**1102**

These are quite different from estimates of Planning Commission given at page 3. Some other estimates of road traffic are also given in Anenxures 3 & 4.

The population of goods vehicles has grown from 9,63,000 in 1985-86 to 26,00,000 in 1999-2000. Light commercial vehicles increased at a faster rate than the heavy goods vehicles.

An over all growth of all motor vehicles is detailed in Table 5.

Table 5

Motor Vehicles Population Increase

(000)

Category of Vehicles	*1951*	*1998*
Car, jeeps, taxies	160	5,000
Two wheelers	30	255,000
Buses	30	520
Trucks	8	2,050
Other vehicles	@	4,930

@ Included in Trucks.

Freight movement on roads is almost entirely in the private sector with more than 75 per cent of the truck operators having less than 5 trucks. Only 6 per cent of the transport companies have 20 trucks or more (CIRT Pune 1998). Even large transport companies resort to hiring of trucks from the small truck operators.

Road passenger transport originally started in the private sector and later through nationalization of passenger transport in varying degrees by states, public sector was introduced. In 1980-81 the private sector had 55 per cent of the total number of buses, which through a delibrate policy of several state governments has now increased to 77 per cent of the bus fleet at present.

The State Road Transport Undertaking (SRTUs) had a fleet of 1,16,000 vehicles on 31.3.1999. While the physical performance of the SRTUs have shown a consistent improvement, the revenues and expenditure have been such as to report losses consistently. Annexures 5 & 6 detail the financial and physical performance of SRTUs in the country. The losses on SRTUs will gradually make more and more private operators come in this area and the states may get out of this business in future.

Rural Roads

A key component of rural development is the provision of roads for connectivity, access being important for social and economic well being. Families residing on roadside enjoy better standards of health, have higher education opportunities, smaller sized families and higher ownership of assets, compared to those families living in remote villages.

Policy makers have given rural roads an important place in the planning process and several schemes at different times, including the Minimum Needs Programme, National Rural Employment Programme, Command Area Agency, Employment Assurance Scheme etc. have all contributed towards development of rural roads. Some of the schemes have been merged into the Jawahar Rozgar Yojana (JRY).

The concentration under these schemes was to provide earth tracks within the village while connectivity through all weather roads has still a long way to go.

Present status of accessibility of villages by all weather roads is given in Table 6.

Table 6

Connectivity of Villages with Roads

Population category	*Total No. of villages*	*Number of villages connected by 1980*	*Number of villages connected by 1985*	*Number of villages connected by 1990*	*Number of villages connected by 1995*	*Number of villages connected by 2000*
1500 and above	71623	37950 (53%)	49495 (69%)	59722 (83%)	65704 (92%)	71000 (99%)
1000-1500	58229	21970 (38%)	28732 (49%)	35362 (61%)	44120 (76%)	52000 (89%)
Less than 1000	459465	107324 (23%)	142020 (31%)	166311 (36%)	173837 (38%)	200000 (43%)
Total	589317	167244 (28%)	220247 (37%)	261395 (44%)	283661 (48%)	323000 (55%)

Note: Figures within brackets give the percentage of villages in each population category to the total number of villages in that category. The basis for population is 1981 census.

Source: Planning Commission. Last column gives quick estimates.

There are, however, regional imbalances in the connectivity of villages. States like U.P., MP, Bihar, Orissa and Rajasthan and many hill states have low levels of village connectivity. Another issue is that of maintenance of these roads. A neglect in maintenance is self defeating as assets fall into disuse. One of the reasons for the slow progress in connectivity was the insistence to provide all weather roads, rather than having roads that get washed every year (if they were ever constructed in the first place).

The government has given a further push to rural road development by allocating 50 per cent of the additional duty of Rs. 1.00 per litre on diesel exclusively for village connectivity. The Pradhan Mantri Gram Sadak Yojana (PMGSY) has been launched in December 2000 by the Ministry of Rural Development to achieve an all weather road access to villages with population above 1000 by 2003 and for villages with population between 500 and 1000 by 2007.

Of the 825647 habitations requiring connection under the PMGSY, those still unconnected are 162576. (Source Ministry of Rural Development)

Inland Water Transport (IWT)

The economic advantage of Inland Water Transport is well established, being a cheaper mode for transportation of bulk commodities particularly on longer hauls and between pairs of points located on the water front. However, despite 14500 kms of rivers and canals and three major waterways, the Ganga, the Brahmputra and the West Coast Canal, totaling 2716 km, being declared National Waterways, the traffic carried on this subsector is only 1.5 billion tonne km a year (less than 0.2 per cent of the total inland cargo market). At present, only about 5200 kms of major rivers and 485 kms of canals are suitable for mechanized crafts with bulk of the rivers and canals suitable only for country boats.

LOOKING AHEAD

Concerns

While the progress made in the transport sector has been significant, it has not been able to meet the growing demand, particularly in the last decade when the economic reforms triggered an uprecendented growth of Gross Domestic Product (GDP) by 6 - 6.5 per cent. The coming years may have higher growth rates of 8 - 10 per cent and with it the consequent increase in transport demand. The tackling of the existing deficiencies coupled with those coming with a higher economic growth rate, will bring a new dimension.

The existing issues and concerns, the unfinished tasks, the congestion and constraints in movement leading to higher transport costs will be some of the challenges to face as we look at transport requirements by 2020.

That the volumes of demand will be very high with a increase for both railways and road transport, requiring not only massive investments but other actions, covering pricing policies, customer focus, terminal management, safety, transit times, organizational and other changes to provide adequate and efficient services for meeting the demand will be a main concern.

Expectations

- Improvement in the transport networks.
- Increase in productivity and economic efficiency in the field of transport.
- Improvement in quality of transport.
- Better frequency of services.
- Enhancement of comfort levels and provision of facilities for the disadvantaged persons.
- Control of environmental pollution and improving quality of the environment.
- Control of noise nuisance and limiting degradation of the landscape.
- Increase in mobility – for the commuter, for work journeys and for recreation.
- Improvement of rural transport and providing accessibility.
- Reducing transport transit times in general and at initial loading and terminal points.
- Better use of energy.

- Better and more humane cities with adequate urban transport.
- Reduction in accidents and improved safety.
- Improved customer service.
- Diminition of trade obstructions.

Issues for transport planning and thinking

- The increased transport demand for passenger and freight services.
- Increase in transport of finished products rather than bulk movement of unfinished goods.
- Customized transportation requirements with 'made to order' products increasing.
- Own vehicle travel.
- More transportation of long distances by Air, faster and bigger ships.
- Multi modal transport and supply chain management.
- Terminal Management.
- Logistic service providers to manage supply chains.
- Increased containerization.
- Better roads, expressways, heavy-haul vehicles.
- Globalisation, regional links, global trade and economy.
- A web based society that may reduce travel for business and work.
- Borderless transport across states with less or no proper work aided by IT.
- Maintenance of assets.
- Changes in technology.
- Increased Financial Resources.
- Cost based pricing, reduction if not elimination of subsidies. A framework for integrated transport policy.

Transport Demand in 2020

Given the past rate of growth and anticipated GDP growth of 8 per cent, the freight traffic growing at an annual rate of 8 per cent is likely to reach 5490 billion tonne kms in the year 2020. The World Bank in their recent report have indicated a growth rate of 10 per cent in the coming years. If a 10 per cent growth is visualized, the traffic demand would reach 10,056 billion tonne kms. It may be safe to assume that freight traffic is likely to be in the range of 5000 to 7000 billion tonne kms against 1100 btkms in 2000. At the lower end of the range and assuming Railways have a market share of 20 per cent in 2020, the rail freight traffic will be 1000 btkms against 308 btkms in 1999-2000, a more than three fold increase in freight traffic.

Similarly, the passenger traffic is likely to grow to 11,763 billion pkms in 2020 when projected on the basis of past trends and to 10,082 billion pkms when correlated with population growth. The passenger traffic demand thus is likely to grow more than four times in the next 20 years. The different segments in passenger traffic and the distribution between different modes is discussed separately for long distance, medium distance, short distance and commuter traffic.

Freight Traffic

Some of the main trends in freight traffic would be the change in the energy industry and in heavy production. The total of manufactured products to bulk cargo will rise, with liquid bulk suitable for pipelines. General merchandise will have a much wider spread of points of origin and ultimate delivery and in much smaller consignments favouring smaller carrying units. Increased value of consignments will put a higher premium on speed of transit also to reduce inventories. A continous and a close control on the transit will become essential. General merchandise will need to be integrated with the manufacturer's other problems of marketing and distribution. The chain of distribution grouped together and called logistics of business will call for a higher degree of focus on customer services.

These changes, together with the impact of other factors like energy efficiency, environmental pollution technological changes in each mode will require relooking at the market to identify the strengths that a mode may have and then provide matching services to meet the demand and increase its market share.

The main segments of freight traffic have movement of bulk goods and finished products for both long and short distances, and distributional traffic. Railways have a strength in the movement of bulk goods including for very short distance where merry-go-round services are brought in play. Finished goods requiring higher flexibility and better transit times have gradually been moving to the roads, more particularly, as Railways moved towards making train load as the unit of movement with continued increase in freight tariffs. As a consequence, even long distance freight traffic of finished goods started moving by roads. The high tariffs on rail also made investments in pipelines for movement of petroleum products more attractive.

Passenger Traffic

Long distance passenger traffic in the country is presently served by railways and air services. The demand for air services may grow at a faster rate, with speeds being an important criteria in favour of air travel. Even today, between the two cities of Mumbai and Delhi, there are more people who travel by air than those on railways (all classes of rail travel put together) (See Annexure 7). The big competition for this segment of the market between air and rail travel will bring in many changes. There will be no point in increasing speeds on railways to attract this traffic as the cost of high speeds will make rail traffic reach levels when it will be not competitive. Overnight sleeper class travel would continue to be railways strength. So long as booking, reservations, comfort and other customer services are kept at satisfactory levels, railways would have a sizeable share of the total long distance passenger market.

In the range of medium distances, say upto 500 kms, with four lane highways, connecting the country and with expressways coming up close to the main metro cities and ownership of cars increasing, the bulk of the passenger travel may start moving towards 'own vehicle travel'. This is a phenomenon noticed all over the world. The railways with their fast intercity services will have an edge over air travel for this segment of traffic. The advantage of the high speed in the air may be offset by time consuming and off-centre terminals, making the medium distance passenger transport a big market for the railways, so long as it is safe, has a good frequency of service and reasonable comfort, penetrating into the city centres. Larger number of intercity services on frequent fixed time intervals between pairs of points will need to be the pattern. The future train sets would have higher levels of comfort, audio visual entertainment, telephone connections and developed to provide facilities like in aircrafts. This segment of the market will have a big role for bus services, particularly for such places where there are no rail connections. This market would also have luxury, deluxe buses plying between cities giving railways a stiff competition.

Short distance traffic is best suited by road transport, save at places when volumes increase to very high levels and rail based mass rapid transport is the best alternative. Suburban rail services and urban transport services are akin in its operation and need, except that the intra city services is the concern of the city specific, while suburban services are run by railways. These have been dealt under Urban Transport.

Globalisation

Radical changes in the realm of transport and communications has sandwiched time and distance, shrinking the world into a global village. Stimulated by the best means of information, flows of trade, investment and finance, have broken the barriers of state policies to gain admission to different countries and participate in global economic activities. With the forces of science and technology moving ahead, the distances of time and space would shrink further. Satellites, computers and fibre optics would create the reality of a global electronic village, reducing business and travel for work, perhaps, even reduce the shift from the rural to urban areas.

Borders between the countries would become more porous and differences between domestic and international issues would get blurred. Capital would move around the world much faster and technology and technical know how would become more easily available without waiting for governments to sanction or permit them.

Movement in the region will grow with a concerted effort made to develop highways and railways of international importance and to facilitate crossing of goods and vehicles at borders. Large emerging markets of countries like China, India and Indonesia is already attracting the interest of international business and manufacturing processes distributed over several countries making transport, of the final packaged product at the consuming point a major logistic exercise, helped by computerized information on markets and costs.

Globalisation of economies, a universal phenomenon has resulted in the integration of national economies at the regional and sub-regional levels. The production system, increasingly characterized by a new division of labour spread across national boundaries, making economies interdependent. A liberalized regime of trade and transport helped by electronic documentation and streamlined custom procedures have expanded the scope for international trade in goods and services, increasing demand for movement within and across national boundaries.

All this implies increased competition, which in turn calls for a more efficient means of transportation to reduce travel time and cost. Global trade demands 'just-in-time' and reliable delivery ensuring quality of cargo. While hitherto maritime transport has been the main facilitator of globalisation, land transport has started to play an important role.

The Asian Highways and the Trans Asian Railways has commitments of all the countries in the region to open up routes that would facilitate intra-Asian trade and link and integrate with the markets in Central Asia, CIS Countries, Europe and North America through land-cum sea links. Some studies have shown that transit times using land-cum sea routes could be 7 to 10 days shorter compared to the sea route.

With the advent of the container, multi-modal transport will play a greater role with logistic service providers, all the time looking at the time and cost advantage in the supply chain. One of the main benefits of looking at systems to meet international quality is the big rub off effect it has on the movement of domestic transport.

Terminal Management

The total volumes of freight traffic would need a new concept in terminal management. The terminals of the future would need to have both rail and road interface as well the facilities to deal with containers. The clubbing of small consignments for dispatch and on receipt for distribution, will be of paramount importance. Even the heavy duty trucks will not be able to go to the city centres and collection and distribution of truck traffic (contemplated at present through Transport Nagars) will be through these terminals with smaller and light vehicles doing the distribution in the city. There terminals could be operated by the public sector, or as a joint venture or by the private sector. The establishment of Container Corporation (CONCOR) has shown the way for moving piece meal traffic efficiently and providing customer satisfaction. Aided by information technology to give an account of the location of the cargo in real time, with simple and reduced documentation, these new terminals will be managed as independent entities and run on commercial principles to bring both efficiency and profits. Already railways have floated the idea of inviting private sector in the setting up of privately owned and operated goods terminals. The new terminals will have facilities to handle multi-modal transport with rail and road links, adequate werehousing, state of the art handling systems and IT backup for logistic services.

The role of multi-modal transport will increase as it combines the strength of the various modes of transport. Containerization is the most important element in multi-modal transport as it combines the flexibility of road, the reliability of rail, the economy of shipping and the speed of air transport.

The future terminals would need to be developed using the hub and spokes concept to consolidate and distribute traffic.

Technology

Notwithstanding the fundamental importance of users and markets, and of service regulation in the development of individual transport enterprises, it is the wonders of transport technology that catch the public interest. It is the fascinations of actual operations that absorb many of the providers. The periodical technical revolutions over the years has been of vast importance in the development of transport, with the big break through coming often from the industries outside transport. While railways have been responsible for a good measure of development, in other modes, there is little technological development by the carrier. The supply industries has produced the ideas and the equipment. The suppliers of airfields, roads and ports have found the greatest reduction in "unit costs per movement".

Transport technology is of special significance in transport planning both for logistics and usage. The changes in technology by upgrading and uprating meet the fast increasing requirements of transportation, bringing economy and efficiency, energy conservation and expedition in mobility.

The main concerns will be to have maintenance free equipment, providing safety on railways and highways, in handling systems, in reducing pollution, using IT for processing data and computers for improved designs.

The progress in transport technology during the last several decades all over the world has been both starting and phenomenal. In many of the world systems, in view of the enormous strides taken by both road motor transport and civil aviation, railways have lost a significant share of the market, while a mode like inland water transport has became un-economic and non profitable.

The future technology changes would have software and logistical improvements and system changes to improve productivity. Advance information and communications technologies and tailoring new materials to meet prescribed requirements will have a major impact.

The highways will show much technological change on the next two decades by way of a new generation of express ways, modernization of construction practices and better traffic management. The need is also to catch up on years of under maintenance, especially in view of the heavier loads anticipated and for adoption of new technologies in maintenance.

Integrated Transport Policy

Transport planning cannot be a disjointed effort and has to view the totality of demand, cost, supply, return and in each mode, the relative levels of efficiency and productivity. This would involve economic costing and physical planning in the context of the overall systems requirements. A choice between different modes of transport with its quantitative and qualitative limitations are often not entirely interchangeable. The liberalization of the economy recognizes the need for an efficient transport system, providing an adequate and reliable transport infrastructure. An overall and integrated policy, therefore, needs to be in place to encourage competitive pricing and coordination between different modes.

The Planning Commission has recently (October 2001) provided such a policy framework detailing objectives, direction of growth, expansion of the network, modernization and technology upgradation role of the private sector, improving financial resources and capability, defining areas of concern in each mode of transport. This framework would be of great relevance in developing the transport needs for the future.

Maintenance of Assets

With the transport network increasing significantly, particularly the roads, maintenance will be the biggest challenge. It will be necessary to maintain these assets by adequate and timely maintenance. At present the maintenance of the highways suffer from under funding and outdated maintenance methods and organization. As maintenance of the roads go down, vehicle operating cost go up. A very important factor is the overloading of vehicles. Studies have revealed that the damaging effect of an overloaded vehicle to the pavement increases expotentially to the power of four when the axle load exceed the load for which it is designed. Overloading of vehicle will need close monitoring. The construction of the highways has presently brought in new equipment through the contractors who are building the National Highways and Expressways using mechanized means which will be available for better maintenance. Whether National Highways, state highways or rural roads, an organization for systematic maintenance will have to be brought in position.

The maintenance of roads would require a coordinated institutional framework involving the government institutions, the contracting industry, the equipment industry and the consulting organizations.

Likewise for the Railways, adequate funding must be provided to the Depreciation Reserve Fund which caters to renewals and replacement of overaged assets. Presently a sum of Rs. 15,000 crores as a special funding for safety works on railways has been provided to wipe off the arrears of track renewals, upgrading and rebuilding of bridges and replacement of rolling stock. It should not be necessary for special funds but a regular inflow of adequate funds for this purpose must be provided on a year to year basis.

ENERGY AND ENVIRONMENT

The importance of an adequate transportation and communication network has been appreciated afresh. However, creation and continued utilization required substantial recurrent use and absorption of natural resources of land and various kinds of energy. The use and abuse of the transport infrastructure leads to severe pollution of air, land and water causing degeneration of the environment. Transport planning must strive for an ecological balance.

The transport sector is one of the major consumers of energy and the road transport sector fully dependent on liquid fuel. The massive increase in the number of vehicles will not only consume more fuel but also cause pollution. Both technology and regulation will be necessary to have more fuel-efficient engines which are less polluting. Transport also involves broader environmental issues. Land intrusion and congestion are some of the areas of conflict between transport and environment. It would be essential to cover environmental concerns at the planning stage itself to reduce the negative impact of the growth in the transport sector.

There are several organizations campaigning for the protection of environment, ecology etc. and a growing public awareness on these issues. The long term consequences for the development of transport enterprises will not be neglible and the transport sector will have to pay far more regard to subject of noise, fumes and spoiling the landscape in future.

On this count, the more energy efficient and less polluting mode, railways, will have an edge and a scoring point to improve its market share in the transport business.

Data Base

Despite recommendations of various committees, the traffic flow and cost data is not collected in a systematic and regular way. There is no reliable information on the quantum of traffic carried by road transport either for freight or for passengers. Several estimates have been made by different agencies and the variations between them often as high as 100 per cent. For the most dominant mode of transport, lack of this important data affects the planning process adversely. With the growing use of computers and advancement in information technology, a concerted drive would be necessary in this direction. The check posts and barriers in some cases are inevitable, and these could be used for capturing the data on a regular and systematic basis. Help from several institutes of transport training and research could be sought in developing such a system.

Also, lack of good processed data leads to inadequate maintenance management and costly decisions.

There is need to improve the costing information on railways, which would help in concentrating on the market segments that are profitable and also to identify clearly the loss making services and the quantum of loss, so that the decision to retain, or the price to be paid by the agency wanting the services to run or to contract it to enterprises who could run it better by reducing losses or predetermined terms for running of such services, could be taken.

Financial Investments and Pricing

To meet the transport needs of the future, investment requirements will increase to levels three to four times higher in real terms form the present levels. The financing of this level will be a massive task. While the government will continue to be a major source of funds for infrastructure, internal generation of resources by the sector itself will have to increase. Pricing of transport services and reduction in the costs will have to play a much bigger role than in the past. A larger role of the private sector is also visualized.

In a maze of subsidies and social service obligations, public sector transport has lost the importance of commercial operations. Subsidies must be direct and explicit and a redistribution of income through the transport sector not attempted[3].

Quick and corrective action is required – particularly in the case of railways where the decade of the 1990s has been a financial disaster. With an increasingly competitive environment in the world, and changes in government policy, railways will have to become a commercial entity, making investments only in such projects that give returns to cover the cost of funds in the market, regardless of

3. More than 20 years ago the National Transport Policy Committee said "we do not visualize in our scheme of things any need for a general subsidy for transport".

whether they are raised directly by the railways or through the Central Government. It is also not important whether a transport entity is a wing of the government, a public sector enterprise or a private venture, it must be commercial in its attitude and operations.

Public transport organizations have stayed too long with the cost plus tariff policies (although often not even covering costs) without much emphasis on reduction of costs. Cross subsidization by freight of losing passenger services on the railways, for example, has made IR's freight tariffs one of the highest in the world, driving out the business from rail to roads. With the four laning of the 'Golden quadrilateral' and the North South and East West connection, the roads will offer even a higher competition and unless railways wake up to this reality, it will be in serious trouble.

While the Central Road Fund (CRF) has become the main lever for development of roads, making toll roads, private sector participation in expressways and a rational user charge to the road user be necessary for the development and maintenance of roads. Investments in vehicles is mostly in the private sector except for State Road Transport undertakings which is fast coming down and being replaced by the private sector.

Development of new Airports must be taken up with private sector participation and while some of the minor ports have been developed by the private sector, there is need to involve the user and the private sector in providing handling systems at the major ports.

Innovative methods would be required in each subsector of transport to find ways and means of increasing resources for investment and to reduce costs and increase profitability to plow back the resources for growth and improvements in the services.

Roads and Road Transport

Road transport will continue to be the dominant mode in the sector. By 2020 the Golden Quadrilateral of Delhi-Mumbai-Chennai-Kolkata-Delhi and the link from Srinagar to Kanyakumari and Silchar to Porbandar will have four (or more) lanes of the National Highways and close to the metro cities some 5000-10000 kms of expressways. The volume of traffic would have of grown five times over present levels, with as much increase in the number of vehicles and HSD consumption. This will pose a serious challenge in the operations of movement.

The CRF will continue to be the main source of funding but other areas for increasing resources must be tapped, more importantly to tackle the problem of maintenance.

Action will have to be taken to reduce the time losses at borders/ barriers/check posts. Some of these are inevitable but through use of IT the flows could be smoothened.

Collection and compilation of data for road transport is another weakness which will have to be tackled.

Some of the other areas for attention would include:

- Ribbon development and problem of encroachments.
- The door to door service on road transport would under go a change with multi-axle vehicles being used and its entry restricted in the cities. Long distance movement through Transport Nagars (new terminals) and further distribution through light commercial vehicles.
- Over loading of vehicles would need to be monitored closely.
- With increased passenger travel on the highways, there would be a need to develop road side amenities.
- Improved safety on the roads, through technological inputs in vehicles, designs and traffic engineering and through education and training.
- Encouraging private sector participation and toll roads.
- Review road user taxes and charges for raising additional revenue.
- Ensure adequate capacity for manufacturing trucks and buses and reducing the growth rate of population of two wheeler in cities through better public transport.

Urban Transport

Increased population and ongoing rapid urbanisation is likely to take India's urban population to around 540 million in the next two decades and the cities with population of a million plus close to 70. At the rate we have been going, the two wheeler ownership rate in

Class I cities (population over 100,000) may grow from 102 per 1000 population to 393 per thousand population by 2021[4] and cars from 14 to 48 by the same year. To contain this explosion of personal vehicle movement in cities, a very heavy dose of investment in public transport services will become necessary.

A policy framework supported by institutional arrangements to implement must accord explicit priority to mass transport over personalized motor transport with all new facilities in urban infrastructure created and designed to primarily meet this priority.

In the long term, rail based mass transport system would appear to be the only answer to the problems of urban transport in the metropolitan cities of India. Where the flexibility of land use is possible, electrified surface rail transport can be adopted. The technical options are however limited in case of highly developed and congested areas. A choice of underground or elevated systems will have to be considered in such situations. This system is also best suited from the point of view of conservation of liquid fuels and environmental preservation. On medium density corridors, systems like electric trolley buses or CNG operated buses may be best suited.

Since the task in Urban Transport in the coming years will be a major one with nearly 70 cities with population of a million plus, specific plans for each city would need to be taken up by the city authorities starting with the provision of bus services, developing intermediate public transport and identifying corridors for future growth, including reserving land for such activity.

No single solution will be applicable to all cities and each city will have to develop its own system taking the developmental characteristics and geography of the specific city into consideration. A judicious mix of two or more modes may need to be adopted, depending on the total transportation capacities required to meet the demand.

There is need for an integrated approach in land use planning and planning for infrastructure especially transport to tackle the problem of urbanization. Transport can be a very effective tool to shape the growth of a city.

---

4. Theme paper prepared by institute of Urban Transport (June 2002).

For the metropolitan cities, where specific urban development organizations exist, they should develop rail based mass transport systems. A plan should be drawn out to collect resources through property tax, from establishment owners, through special funds, from road users, including a levy on fuel for the specific purpose of developing urban transport and to this fund add assistance from the State and Centre. A scheme with all three contributing equally could be considered as a matter of policy.

The lack of financial resources is the single most important constraint in the way of undertaking any meaningful planning programme of metropolitan transport development, projects being highly capital intensive and have long gestation periods. Several schemes prepared for many cities continue to remain on paper. While in most countries, urban transport investments and operations are funded by the federal and local governments and through some private investments, it has not worked well so far in India. There is now a general acceptance that rail based urban transport facilities could be created on the basis of cost sharing between the Central and state governments and projects in Mumbai and Chennai are examples of success. Delhi metro project has also developed on the concept of cost sharing.

Once funding is taken care of on principle, a corporate structure could be adopted and this could be achieved through special purpose vehicles. The Delhi metro model could well be used by other cities. Property likely to be developed as a consequence of the project itself could give commercial return and help in the investment for both building and running the metro. A constitutional amendment to shift rail based urban transport system to the concurrent list would be necessary if state governments have to discharge their obligations.

The basic problem has been that urban transport is not yet recognized as the responsibility of the city and ends being the secondary responsibility of several agencies in the state and at the centre. City being the beneficiary as well as the victim (when there is no efficient transport system) must carry the primary responsibility. The city can involve itself at an early stage and integrate housing and other developmental plans keeping the transport plan in mind and more importantly reserve land for future traffic corridors which when available on surface can bring down cost of projects very significantly.

State governments and Central government can assist through funding, providing technical guidance, and a joint dedicated and cooperative effort can deliver the goods.

There is an alternative to the growth of cities. With technological inputs in IT, it may well be possible to let office and office type jobs be done in and close to the villages and not requiring migration of population. This will also reduce the pressure on housing in cities. The suburban habitat will combine the transport and telecom connectivity of a city with the spaciousness of a village.

Rural Roads

Several schemes, together with high priority accorded to the main idea of providing accessibility in the rural areas, will help improve the economy in backward areas and reduce migration from the villages to the cities. The fast developing information technology in the rural areas is likely to change the entire pattern of growth. Also with the plans already in place, by 2020, it would have achieved its objective of reaching the last man in the farthest village.

While the roads are likely to be in place the main area of concern will be the maintenance of these roads. Institutional arrangements will have to be put in place together with the regular funding for this activity. Unless this is done, the assets created may not last long.

Railways

Even with a reduced market share, both in freight and passenger traffic, the demand for rail transport in 2020 will be more than three times the level of freight tariff carried now and more than double the passenger traffic. This massive increase will warrant a heavy investment in capacity building on the railways. Railways will continue to be a dominant mode for moment of bulk (pipelines may take the traffic of petroleum products) and must strive to retain and increase its share in the business of finished products atleast over long distances. A more energy efficient and less polluting mode than road transport, railways initiatives through a focus on the customer, offering reduced freight tariffs and custom built services to suit specific needs.

In the passenger business, railways will lose some share in the long distance travel to airlines and should deliberately curtail its loss making short distance commuter type traffic and traffic on branch lines. This will bring in sharp focus the railways big role in medium distance intercity traffic with journeys upto 5-6 hours, where the door to door timings for such distance would compare favourably with airtravel. The services are presently met by Shatabdi type train services which need to be increased with higher frequency between pairs of such points. In this segment of the market, however, the own vehicle travel is likely to have the biggest share with highways and expressways coming and the population of people owning vehicles growing.

Some of the areas of concerns and key issues for the railways would be:

Capacity

- Increase capacity on the quadrilateral by additional tracks making these corridors with quadruple lines and provide capacity ahead of demand.
- Improve asset reliability, using technology to have maintenance free rolling stock.
- Reduce speed differential between passenger and freight trains.
- Run freight trains at 100 kmph acquire new rolling stock fit to run at 100 kmph and retrofit existing stock.

Increase Market Share

- Innovate and increase market share with a focus on the customer through better customer service using freight operation information systems, make provision of siding attractive through user friendly rules and operations.
- Reduce freight tariffs.
- Adjust passenger fares and make it cost based.
- Improve costing to charge realistic tariffs.
- Improve customer services and focus on customers' needs. Railways must be run as a market driven commercial enterprise.
- Have a proper pricing policy.

- Customer driven services integrated logistics, reliable and guaranteed transit times, tracking systems with customer friendly interface.
- Increase market share through market research and offering new products and services.
- Develop terminals on a hub and spokes concept to handle wagon load traffic and use IT for consolidation and efficiency.

Investment and Costs

- Stop uneconomic investments.
- Re-examine and review all on going projects and stop those that are unrenumerative.

  (The white paper on projects issued by the Ministry of Railways in July 1998 stated that for completing the already sanctioned projects Rs. 35,000 crores will be needed and of these, projects costing over Rs. 23,000 crores were non-viable. These non-viable projects not only have unsustainable capital costs but when completed have perpetual operating losses).
- Concentrate on core business of running trains.
- Take off peripheral activities – booking, reservations, terminal management etc. from main stream – use public or joint venture or private entities (CONCOR experiment is a big success).
- Review rate of electrification and gauge conversion projects.
- Invest only on projects that give a return.
- Reduce man power.
- Upgrade skills of the manpower.
- Introduce technology to reduce accidents caused by human error and to improve productivity, restructure loss making branch operation by giving it to the agencies that want such services to be run and give it on contract at the lowest costs for operation.
- Encourage private sector investment – make 'own your wagons' attractive for the investor.
- Provide funds for renewals and replacements.

Airports and Air Services

Shipping, once the main mode for movement between countries, has now given way to airlines and perhaps by 2020, passenger traffic in space will get established. International travel to and from India, with the growth in economy and due to globalisation will increase at a very fast pace.

Long distance domestic travel by air has also been growing at a very fast rate and it has already made inroads in the market share of the domestic long distance travel. As mentioned earlier, even today, more people travel by air between Delhi and Mumbai than by all classes of rail travel. It is perhaps true of other long distance pairs of points in the country. With the entry of private air lines, this mode is developing fast and will provide competition to the once dominant long distance rail travel.

Medium and short distance travel would have a market only in inaccessible areas like the north east. In other areas, rail intercity services and travel by personal vehicles will be more dominant.

Airports for international travel have reached traffic at levels where augmentation is necessary. The four major airports need to be developed to international standards which can be done with private sector participation.

With increased international travel more airports would need to cater to this traffic and more airports cleared for international flights.

Ports

Traffic at the ports have been increasing rapidly and one major port of the standard of Singapore or Colombo will have to be developed to meet the growing needs particularly of traffic in containers. A modern port with the facilities to deal with large container ships, with fast clearance by rail and road transport to meet the needs of the inland container depots, and other main terminals will be one of the major tasks this sector. Existing ports would also need modernization and argumentation of capacity, while private sector participation in developing minor ports for coastal movements and special customer traffic could add to the overall port capacity.

IWT

The development of waterway got an impetus with the setting up of the Inland Waterways Authority of India (IWAI) in 1986 and has been entrusted with the task of maintenance and regulation of national waterways in the country. There is a great potential to increase the cargo movement on the national and other waterways and reduce fuel consumption and costs. While the sector has been given a boost at the policy level on promotion of IWT, it needs a thrust at the operational and executive level. With the proposal to connect the rivers with a network of canals there will be an opportunity to plan and provide for channels that will enable the movement of cargo through inland water transport systems.

VISION 2020

- A well developed network of roads and railways, with adequate capacities to handle the transport demand.
- A network of 70,000 kms of National Highways with the golden quadrangle of Delhi-Mumbai-Chennai-Kolkata-Delhi and the north-south link between Srinagar and Kanyakumari and the east-west link from Silchar to Porbandar with four or more lanes and the rest of the network on two lanes, the state highways connecting districts with at least two-way lanes would be in position.
- The rural roads providing accessibility to the last man in the farthest village for the growth of the economy and telecommunications available to avoid the villager having to move to the cities for work.
- Technological progress to provide vehicles which are pollution free and fuel efficient.
- Reduction in the two wheeler population in the cities with an efficient public transport system.
- The railways provided with capacity ahead of demand on the system and on its main corridors to carry out three fold increase in traffic.
- Focus on the customer with better and customized service, reduction in freight tariffs, elimination (atleast reduction) of

the uneconomic services and subsidies, comfort and safety in travel and generating resources to expand and improve services.

- Reduction in costs and a commercial attitude to get return on the investments, and elimination of investments in non-paying projects.
- Adequate capacities at airports and harbours to provide efficient service. Airports of international standard for passenger and cargo handling and modern handling system on ports to reduce delays in berthing. A gateway port of the type at Singapore and Colombo to deal with the growing traffic.
- Having institutional arrangements in place with adequate funds for proper maintenance specially of roads, where an expanded network, will make the maintenance tasks important and big.
- A reasonable urban transport service in all the major metropolises and in all cities with population of a million plus with systems to monitor and provide continued increase in services to meet the demand.
- The envisaged connection of the tributaries of the rivers through a network of canals will provide an opportunity and an impetus to increase the potential and growth of IWT.
- Modern terminals, with IT backup to provide a quick service and be an integral part of the logistics of reliable and guaranteed transit times.
- Quick flow at barriers and borders, again IT aided, also to help in compiling reliable data on the flow of traffic.
- Generation of internal sources in each mode, an effective system to collect user charges in conformity with costs, and a net return on the operations through cost based tariffs. Increased private sector participation.
- Available routes on highways and railways in the region to promote international trade.
- A coordinated growth in all modes of transport within the framework of an integrated transport policy with institutions and organisation in the sector where control and responsibility are at the working level and structures that have morale, elan, imagination and leadership.

Annexure 1

Share of Urban Population in Selected Countries
(Per cent of Total)

Country	*Year*	
	1980	*1999*
Argentina	83	90
Australia	86	85
Belgium	95	97
Brazil	66	81
Canada	76	77
Chile	81	85
China	20	32
Egypt	44	45
Germany	83	87
India	23	28
Indonesia	22	40
Iran	50	61
Japan	76	79
Malaysia	42	57
Pakistan	28	36
Spain	73	77
Sweden	83	83
U.K.	89	89
U.S.A.	74	77
Zambia	40	40

Source: World Bank – World Development Report.

Annexure 2

Urban Agglomerations/Cities having Population of more than One Million in 2001

Urban Agglomeration/City	Civic Status	Population in 2002 (in million)
1. Greater Mumbai	UA	16.37
2. Kolkata	UA	13.22
3. Delhi	UA	12.79
4. Chennai	UA	6.42
5. Bangalore	UA	5.69
6. Hyderabad	UA	5.53
7. Ahemdabad	UA	4.52
8. Pune	UA	3.75
9. Surat	UA	2.81
10. Kanpur	UA	2.69
11. Jaipur	M. Corp.	2.32
12. Lucknow	UA	2.27
13. Nagpur	UA	2.12
14. Patna	UA	1.71
15. Indore	UA	1.64
16. Vadodara	UA	1.49
17. Bhopal	UA	1.45
18. Coimbatore	UA	1.45
19. Ludhiana	M. Corp.	1.39
20. Kochi	UA	1.35
21. Visakhapatnam	UA	1.33
22. Agra	UA	1.32
23. Varanasi	UA	1.21
24. Madurai	UA	1.19
25. Meerut	UA	1.17
26. Nashik	UA	1.15
27. Jabalpur	UA	1.12
28. Jamshedpur	UA	1.10
29. Asansol	UA	1.09
30. Dhanbad	UA	1.06
31. Faridabad	M. Corp.	1.05
32. Allahabad	UA	1.05
33. Amritsar	UA	1.01
34. Vijayawada	UA	1.01
35. Rajkot	UA	1.00
TOTAL		**107.88**

Source: Census of India.

Annexure 3

Estimated Road Traffic Movement in 2000

Study	*Pass Traffic (billion pkms)*	*Freight Traffic (billion tkms)*
RITES Study 1998	1880	1136
Lucknow Plan 1984	2152	1004
MOST: Study on estimation of total Road Transport in the year 2000	3000-4000	600-1000
Vehicle Fleet Modernization Study (1988)	2300-3800	800-1030
Steering Committee on Respective Planning for Transport (1988)	2400-4000	540-900
India Infrastructure Report	3000	800

Annexure 4

Assessment of Freight and Passenger Traffic by Road

	Year 1995	*Year 2000*	*Year 2005*	*Year 2010*
A. Freight Traffic				
Trucks				
i. Vehilce km (billion)	72	108	154	215
ii. Tonne km (billion)	400	650	1000	1500
B. Passenger Traffic				
Buses				
i. Vehicle km (billion)	22	31	44	61
ii. Pass km (billion)	860	1248	1771	2440
Cars				
i. Vehicle km (billion)	27	42	69	106
ii. Pass km (billion)	41	64	103	159
Two-wheelers				
i. Vehicle km (billion)	69	108	167	250
ii. Pass km (billion)	83	130	200	300
Total Pass km (billion)	984	1442	2074	2899
Say	**1000**	**1450**	**2100**	**2900**

Assumptions

A few modest assumptions have been made in arriving at a decadal traffic projection. These can be enumerated.

Freight Traffic

Trucks

i. Average pay load 5.5 tonnes in 1995 and increasing by 0.1 tonne a year.

ii. Average annual utilization in 1995 taken as 40,000 km and increasing by 400 km a year.

iii. Average annual growth in truck population adopted as:

7.5 per cent during 1995-2000

6.5 per cent during 2000-2005

6.0 per cent during 2005-2010

Passenger Traffic

Buses

i. Average occupancy 40

ii. Average annual utilization at 40,000 km per year in 1995 and increasing by 400 km a year

iii. Average annual growth in number of buses adopted as:

7.0 per cent during 1995-2000

6.5 per cent during 2000-2005

6.0 per cent during 2005-2010

Cars

i. Average occupancy 1.5

ii. Average annual utilization 7,000 km in 1995 and increasing by 100 km a year

iii. Average annual growth in number of cars adopted as:

8.0 per cent during 1995-2000

8.5 per cent during 2000-2005

8.0 per cent during 2005-2010

Two-Wheelers

i. Average occupancy 1.2

ii. Average utilization 3,500 km

iii. Average annual growth in number of two-wheelers adopted as:

9.5 per cent during 1995-2000

9.0 per cent during 2000-2005

8.5 per cent during 2005-2010

Source: Asian Transport Journal, December 1998.

Annexure 5

Financial Performance of State Road Transport Undertakings

(Rs. Crore)

Item	*1992 -93*	*1993 -94*	*1994 -95*	*1995 -96*	*1996 -97*	*1997 -98*	*1998 -99*	*1999 -2000*
1. Gross Receipts	6643	7602	8221	9006	9494	11125	11984	13685
i) Operating Revenue	6202	7190	7805	8478	8909	10490	11351	12953
ii) Misc. Receipts	446	412	416	527	585	635	633	732
2. Total Expend.	7008	7914	8580	9607	10511	12495	13577	15571
i) Operating Expd.	4943	5594	6202	6967	7680	9278	10075	11809
ii) Dep. Res. Fund	756	616	624	699	705	821	877	871
iii) Taxes	916	1061	1113	1220	1308	1433	1558	1705
iv) Int.	308	317	287	313	365	441	479	567
v) Misc. Exp	265	321	370	402	485	522	588	618
3) Net Profit/Loss (1-2)	-344	-312	-375	-594	-1055	-1593	-1886	
4. Internal resources (3+2ii)	232	201	249	105	-342	-549	-716	-1015
5. Term loan re-payments/ adjustments	302	362	308	403	315	526	317	473
6. Contribution to the Plan (4-5)	-70	-102	-59	-299	-665	-1075	-1033	-1488

Annexure 6

Statewise Physical Performance of SRTUs (2001-2002) (Latest Estimates)

Name of SRTUs	*Fleet Utilisation % of Buses on Road*	*Vehicle Prod. Revneue Earning KM per bus held per day*	*Bus Staff Ratio on fleet operated*	*Staff Prod. Revenue Earning KM per worker per day*	*Fuel Efficiency Km per litre.*
Andhra Pradesh	99	315	6.8	44	5.07
Arunachal Pradesh	68	136	5.2	23.9	2.94
Assam	51	96	31.0	6	4.0
Bihar	12	29	29.4	8.3	4.1
D.T.C. (Delhi)	80	183	10.4	34.7	3.85
Goa (Kadamba)	77	203	6.7	40	4.2
Gujarat	88	327	7.0	51.7	5.3
Haryana	95	308	6.0	54.4	4.44
Himachal Pradesh	97	222	5.4	42.1	3.52
Jammu & Kashmir	65	76	4.1	17.9	3.9
Karnataka					
KSRTC	95	341	5.7	59	4.83
NWKRTC	95	333	6.0	52.5	5.01
BMTC	97	217	5.7	38.2	4.46
NEKRTC	92	325	5.5	53.7	4.87
Kerala	80	273	7.0	45	4.0
Madhya Pradesh	81	227	6.0	35.5	4.1
Maharashtra	94	292	6.8	44	4.67
Manipur	10	6	17.0	31	3.5
Meghalaya	39	60	17.1	9.1	3.5
Mizoram	54	60	5.0	6.2	3.15
Nagland	63	63	11.7	13.1	3.5
Orissa	32	253	7.7	37	4.1
Punjab Roadways	84	222	4.2	46.4	4.25
PEPSU RTC	95	262	5.0	52.2	4.37
Rajasthan	92	310	6.1	58.2	4.85
Sikkim	80	61	3.2	18.8	3.25
Tamil Nadu	92	376	8.0	50.1	4.29
Tripura	50	81	18.2	8.9	3.55
Uttar Pradesh	93	266	6.2	41.6	4.85
Calcutta STC	70	133	11.3	16.9	3.55
North Bengal STC	65	158	10.5	24.2	3.9
South Bengal STC	74	193	7.9	33.2	3.85
All India Average	**90**	**290**	**7.2**	**45.4**	**4.61**

Annexure 7

Passenger Travel by Rail and by Air between Delhi and Mumbai

Rail Traffic

Train	*No. of passengers carried (all classes) daily between Delhi-Mumbai (August 2002)*
Rajdhani	546
August Kranti	353
Frontier Mail	258
Paschim Express	198
Swaraj Express	105
Janata Express and Dehradun Express	75
Total	**1535**

Air Lines

	No. of Flights each way	*Daily Passengers Carried*	*Load factor*
Indian Airlines	9	605	52%
Jet Airways	10	727	57%
Sahara	5	318	57%
	Total	**1650**	

Note: (Excl. Passengers carried by Air India. Traffic on Jet & Sahara estimated on load factor of 57 per cent)

Total Traffic = 1650 + 1535 = 3185

Airlines 52 per cent

Railways 48 per cent

Bibliography

Anand, V., (2002), International Logistic Solutions, *IRT Journal*, June.

Annual Report and Accounts, Indian Railways.

Gupta, D.P., (1998), Perspective of Modernization of Road Development in India, *AT Journal*, December.

Gupta, D.P., (2001), Perspective on Rural Roads in India, *RITES Journal*, September.

India's Transport Sector: The Challenges Ahead, World Bank, May 2002.

Integrated Transport Policy – Planning Commission, October 2001.

Poulose, A.V., (1998), Financing Metro Rails and Metropolitan Commuter Networks, *Asian Transport Journal*, December.

Ray, S.K., (1995), Transport Planning for Developing Countries, Prentice Hall of India, New Delhi.

Report of the National Transport Policy Committee, Planning Commission, May 1980.

Rahmatullah, Dr. M., (1998) Asian Transport Linkages and State and Institutional Involvement – *Asian Transport Journal*, June.

Report of the Export Group on Indian Railways – Rakesh Mohan Committee, July 2001.

Road Development Plan, Indian Road Congress, November 2000.

Ray, S.K., (2002), Planning, Growth and the Economy, Prentice Hall of India, October.

Sharma, R.C., (2001), Need for National Urban Transport Policy, *Urban Transport Journal*, December.

Shanti Narain, Indian Railways Programme for the Century.

Thoopal, R.K., (2000), Vision 2010 Indian Railways, February.

Thomson J. Michael, (1983), Towards Better Urban Transport Planning in Developing Countries.

Vankataraman, N. and Harbhanjan Singh, (2001), Planning for National Arterial Highways in India, RITES Journal, April.

Wilson Reginald, The Development of Transport Enterprises under Different Economic and Political Conditions – EDI World Bank.

17

Water Policy and Action Plan for India 2020

An Alternative

G. N. KATHPALIA & RAKESH KAPOOR

Need for an Alternative Water Policy

1.1 Water is the very basis of life and is the foundation for human survival and development. Sustainable and equitable use of water over millennia has been ensured by cultural adaptation to water availability through water conservation technologies, agricultural systems and cropping patterns adapted to different climatic zones and conservation-based life styles. But in the last few decades the consequences of population growth, industrialisation and urbanisation, and the associated consumerist culture, have interfered with the natural hydrological cycle of rainfall, soil moisture, groundwater, surface water and storage of all sizes. This has led to overuse, abuse and pollution of our vital water resources and has disturbed the quality and the natural cleansing capacity of water.

Water is one of the most crucial elements in our national developmental planning for the 21st century. The proper management of our limited water resources will be essential to ensure food security for our growing population and to eliminate poverty. It will be essential also to avoid the growing conflicts and the possibility of social unrest in the country in future due to water scarcity.

1.2 To minimise the negative impacts of the overuse and misuse of water and to ensure that our precious water resources are used optimally in removing poverty and achieving economic and human development, it is necessary that we have a water policy which recognises and adequately addresses the challenges we face and are going to face in the twenty-first century. A national water policy for the twenty-first century has to recognise water as a national resource for the purpose of national development goals and planning, although the management of water has to be done in a decentralised way in partnership between local communities and the concerned state governments. The policy should provide broad guidelines, and should be flexible enough to suit the various conditions in each watershed and river basin, such as the agro-climatic zone, location of polluting and other industries, the location of towns and population density. Different regions of the country, endowed differently with water in the form of precipitation, surface flows and ground water, need their own region-specific water policy, which can be based on broad guidelines elaborated below.

The earlier National Water Policy was adopted in September 1987 and a revised policy has been adopted by the National Water Resources Council in April 2002. In the last few years a number of problems/challenges have emerged in the development and management of water resources. On the one hand the water crisis (of its reduced availability per head and deteriorating quality) has grown and on the other hand local initiatives in water conservation have started to respond to the challenge. Strengthening these initiatives requires the strengthening of the water rights of the community, rejuvenation of the traditional techniques in conservation and management, recognition of water as a common property resource and not merely a commodity subject to market forces. The implications of the 73rd and 74th Amendment too need to be considered. These were some of the factors that led to the revision of the National Water Policy (1987).

The Vision: Key Elements of the Alternative Policy

1.3 Centralised and distant decision-making, indifferent or poorly responsive to the ecological, socio-economic and cultural circumstances of different regions, has led to increased incapacity to deal with drought and water scarcity. Dealing with drought and water scarcity has therefore become an urgent policy objective, to be guided by the principles of conservation, protection of water quality, sustainability and equitable access. Dealing effectively with drought and water scarcity requires that local water resources are harnessed, conserved and used in the most optimum manner. This, in turn, requires that water users and communities themselves have a central role in the overall management of local and regional water resources, with higher levels of government playing a suitable supportive and regulatory role in providing appropriate inputs of information, technical help and financial resources.

1.4 People-centered and managed watershed development in India's rainfed areas has to be accorded the highest priority in order to contribute to the vital national goals of employment generation, food production and food security. The production of food grains has increased from around 50 million tonnes in the fifties to about 200 million tonnes by the year 2000 but this will have to be raised to around 300 million tonnes by the year 2020. Out of a total culturable area of 195 mha in the country, the net area under cultivation has remained stagnant at 142 mha[1] (irrigated area 54 mha—which may go up to a maximum of 65 mha by 2020—and the remaining 141 mha being rainfed area) for the past two decades (see Table 1 below). Another 42 mha of potentially culturable land exists in the form of wasteland and fallow land while 11 mha of culturable land exists as orchards and tree-covered land. This 53 mha of culturable land needs urgent attention for watershed development and for the production of fuel, fodder, timber and food. Overall, a total rainfed area of 141 mha at present needs more attention for watershed development. This is expected to come down to 110 mha in 2050, as per the projections made in Table 1.

1.5 Domestic and industrial water needs have largely been concentrated in or near the principal cities at the cost of the basic needs of rural society. The demand of water for thermal power generation and other industrial use is also increasing substantially. Besides taking care of urban and rural needs, maintaining the life of river systems and other water bodies should be an important objective of planning. This includes maintaining minimum water flows, prevention of pollution from industry and agriculture and control of riverbed sand extraction to ensure the maintenance of aquatic life and other ecological factors. As a result, water, a limited resource, will be under greater demand pressure in future. This underscores the need for utmost efficiency in water utilisation and public awareness of the importance of its conservation.

1. This may go down to 140 mha in the future.

Table 1

Land Area of India by Usage (mha): Current and Projections for 2020 and 2050

Usage	*Area Reported (1995-96)*	*Projections for 2020*	*Projections for 2050*
Culturable area	195**	190	185
Net irrigated area	(54)	(65)	(85)
Non-irrigated/rainfed area	(130)	(110)	(80)
Area covered by trees*	(11)	(15)	(20)
Forest area	69	66	65
Non-agricultural use (urban, roads, etc.)	22	30	36
Barren	19	19	19
Total area reported	305	305	305

Source: CWC for current land area; projections by authors.

*: This includes orchards and areas with low tree density, which are not classified forests and which yield fruits or NTFP, primarily for local use.

**: Out of this, area actually under cultivation is 142 mha and this is expected to go down to 140 mha in the future.

1.6 Water quality has to be a very important aspect of water policy. The best way to ensure water quality is the prevention of pollution of water bodies and introduction of the "polluter pays principle". In addition, improvements in existing strategies and the innovation of new techniques resting on a strong science and technology base will be needed to eliminate the pollution of surface and ground water resources, to improve water quality and to step up the recycling and re-use of water. Realising the importance and the pressure of demand on fresh water, it has to be treated as an essential part of the environment for sustaining all life forms.

2. ALTERNATIVE WATER POLICY FOR INDIA 2020

2.1 Information System and Water Resources Assessment

2.1.1 A national information system that builds itself on micro-watershed level databases and integrates with the state and national levels is required. This database should contain information on rainfall, ground water, surface water availability and also water use for different purposes along with its quality. Successful community action for water conservation and use as well as details of traditional water conservation and use systems should also be contained in the database, which should be constantly upgraded. The GIS format will be most appropriate for this database and for making it available in the public domain. It should be available in a user-friendly format and should be available for public access through the Internet.

2.1.2 Uniform standards for coding, classification, processing and methods/procedures for data should be adopted. Advances in information technology must be introduced to create a modern information system promoting free exchange of data among the various agencies like the Ministries of Water Resources (MoWR), Agriculture, Environment and Forests, Urban Development and Rural Development in GoI and similar departments at the state level. MoWR may be the nodal agency for this purpose. Similarly, access to this information at district, panchayat and community levels is also important. Special efforts should be made to develop and continuously upgrade the capability to collect, process, use and disseminate reliable data in the desired time frame. At present, comprehensive data is being collected from about 2000 sites. This needs to be increased to about 30,000 in the next five years to coincide with the number of watersheds (average size of 10,000 ha).

Apart from data regarding water availability and its use, the system should also include comprehensive and reliable projections of future demand, availability and its quality. The depth to which groundwater extraction is advisable/allowed along with quality in each watershed area should be publicly available. Both surface water and ground water should be regularly monitored for quality. A phased programme should be undertaken for improvements in water quality. The data generated by this exercise should be available in the public domain through the Internet.

Assessment

2.1.3 It has been estimated that out of the total precipitation of around 400 million hectare metres in the country, the surface water availability is about 187 million hectare metres. Out of this, about 50 per cent can be put to consumptive beneficial use because of topographical, ecological and other constrains. In addition, there is a ground water potential of about 43 million hectare metres. The availability of water is highly uneven in both space and time. Precipitation is mainly confined to about three or four months (5 to 60 rainy days) in the year and varies from 100 mm in the western parts of Rajasthan to over 10000 mm at Cherrapunji in Meghalaya. Some parts of south India are more fortunate with the northeast monsoon in addition. Many rivers and underground aquifers often cut across state boundaries. Water as a resource is one and indivisible, as such rainfall, river waters, surface ponds and lakes and ground water are all part of one system; water is a part of a larger ecological system. Development of ground water must take India's great hydro geological diversity into account. Great caution needs to be exercised especially in hard rock regions that constitute a major part of India's land area. There should be a reassessment every ten years on a scientific basis of all forms of water, taking into consideration the quality of the water available for various uses.

2.2 Demand Management, Conservation and Efficiency of Utilisation

The efficiency of utilisation in all the diverse uses of water should be improved and an awareness of water as a scarce resource should be fostered. Conservation consciousness should be promoted through education, regulation, incentives and disincentives in the following ways in different sectors.

Domestic Sector

- Introduction of domestic water saving devices
- Water meters on all consumers/groups of consumers
- Progressive water tariff structure
- Auditing of water balance on each distribution system
- Sewage and other domestic use to be piped out separately.[2]

2. The domestic effluent may be segregated, so that the wastewater from the water closet and wash hand basin is conveyed to a sewage treatment plant, and the wastewater from bathing and from the kitchen is collected from relatively small settlements, treated suitably and utilised for flushing toilets in the same settlement.

Industrial Sector

- Progressive water tariff.
- Water recycling facilities.
- Treated urban sewage water for cooling and other processes.

Agriculture Sector

- Water rates on volumetric basis to WUAs should be pegged at an appropriate level to yield enough revenue for maintenance costs.
- Treated sewage water for non-edible crops.
- Saline water for tolerant crops.
- Improvement in irrigation practices and reduction of water losses.
- Pressure irrigation systems to be introduced.

River Management for each Basin

- Afforestation and soil conservation.
- Livestock management.
- Treatment before disposal of sewage.
- Prevention of pollution from agriculture use through use of biofertilisers and biopesticides.

2.3 Integrated Planning for Maximising Water Usability

2.3.1 Utilisation of water within a river basin should be planned in an integrated manner taking into account the following types of integration:

- Between rainfall, surface water and ground water.
- Between different sectoral uses and environmental requirements.
- Between structures i.e. water harvesting structures for use of water and recharge of ground water to the high dams on the main rivers.
- Between water to be supplied from the bigger structures to the smaller structures when required during drought/lean period.

- Between institutions at the community level, NGOs and the government.
- Between different types of land use (agriculture, forestry, wetlands, non-agricultural uses, flood buffer zone) keeping in mind the requirement of water for different uses.

Besides such integrated planning, conservation through demand management, recycling and reuse after treatment, improving irrigation efficiency and then desalination of brackish or seawater and inter-basin transfers can be considered, among the steps needed to increase the availability of utilisable water.

All individual development projects and proposals should be formulated and considered within the framework of such an overall plan for a basin or a sub-basin so that the best possible combination of options can be made and sustained. There should be an integrated and multi-disciplinary approach to the planning and implementation of projects. This should *inter alia* include catchment area treatment and management, environmental and ecological aspects, the rehabilitation of affected people and command area development. Co-ordinated development of surface water and ground water and their conjunctive use should be envisaged right from the project planning stage and should form an essential part of the project. Over exploitation of ground water should be avoided near the coast to prevent ingress of sea water into sweet water aquifers.

2.3.2 At the planning stage, decisions should be taken after according opportunity to the respective Gram Sabhas to voice their concerns and if their submissions are rejected, the reasons should be duly recorded and publicised. The management of the water resources for diverse uses should be done by adopting a participatory approach: by involving not only the various governmental agencies but also the users and other stakeholders in an effective and decisive way in various aspects of planning, design, development and management of the water resources schemes. Necessary legal and institutional changes should be made at various levels to ensure the implementation of the above objectives. WUAs and the local bodies such as municipalities and gram panchayats should particularly be involved in the operation, maintenance and the management of water infrastructures/facilities at appropriate levels progressively with a view to eventually transfer the management of such facilities to the user groups/local bodies.

2.3.3 The study of the impact of a project during construction and later, on human lives, settlements, occupations, socio-economic environment and other aspects should be an essential component of project planning. All projects that seek to conserve/impound water or generate power should make the Environmental Impact Assessment (EIA), the Social Impact Assessment (SIA) and Cost Benefit Analysis open for public scrutiny and should examine alternate options before coming to a conclusion about the most appropriate strategy. Environmental Management Plan (EMP) and compensatory actions should also be considered and should be open to public discussion to ensure public participation in implementation and subsequent maintenance.

2.3.4 Economic development activities including agricultural, industrial and urban areas should be planned with due regard to the constraints imposed by the water availability. There should be water zoning of the country and the economic activities should be guided and regulated in accordance with such zoning. Relief works undertaken for providing employment to drought stricken populations should be for drought proofing like water harvesting with watershed management.

2.4 Water Allocation for Various Uses

Sectoral Allocation: The water allocation amongst the basin states should be guided by a national perspective with due regard to water resources availability and requirement within each state and the river basin. Necessary guidelines should be formulated accordingly for allocation of water amongst the basin states[3]. In planning operation systems, water allocation priorities should broadly be as below, but governed on the basis of local conditions and requirements:

---

3. In 1991 the annual per capita availability of water was 2731 cubic metres. In 2020 this is expected to be just over 2000 cubic metres and by 2050, 1403 cubic metres (Indian Water Resources Society, *Water: Vision 2050*, 1999). The allocation of water for each hydrological zone should be based on the principle of providing at least 1000 cubic metres per capita per annum (for all uses). The surplus water over and above this amount can be allocated by mutual agreement between different hydrological zones.

i) Drinking and domestic use.

ii) Sustaining livelihoods.

iii) Sustaining environment, maintaining river systems and acquatic life.

iv) Irrigation and hydro-power.

v) Thermal power and industries.

vi) Recreation and religious uses.

vii) Navigation.

The first three uses have the highest priority but within these, the allocation of water should be decided by the people at the watershed level. For allocation to other uses where bulk supplies are required and where supply to the first three categories is affected, people's agreement would be necessary.

2.5 Domestic Use

Adequate drinking water facilities should be provided to the entire population both in urban and in rural areas. Irrigation and multipurpose projects should invariably include a drinking water component, but these should only supplement locally developed sources of drinking water. Drinking water needs of human beings and animals should be the first charge on any available water. The community should have the first right to use rainfall directly, store and recharge groundwater wherever possible. The rights over water should not be restricted to only those who own land. Water should be allocated on per head basis and not on the basis of land area and heavy water consuming crops should not be allowed by consensus/ agreement. Some existing models are notable in this regard. For instance, Ralegaon Sidhi and the Pani Panchayat model developed by Gram Gaurav Pratishthan. In Bangladesh, the Grameen Bank gives credit for development of shallow tubewells for groundwater development to landless people, and the groundwater is then sold to landowners.

The standard with regard to water allocated per capita for domestic use should be 30 to 60 litres per day. It may vary according to rainfall zones i.e. less in Rajasthan and more in Assam, but should be the same for rural and urban areas. Sanitation requirement, however, should be considered separately.

2.6 River Life, Pollution and Environment

2.6.1 A minimum good quality water flow should be ensured at all times as required for the life of the river and for sustaining livelihoods. This should include the allocation of water for various purposes including conserving the environment, preventing groundwater salinity and sea water intrusion, supporting livelihood based on aquatic life and other uses of water, recreation, and cultural activities like bathing and festivities. The requirement of water for these various purposes should be calculated scientifically. To begin with at least 50 per cent of the lean period flow before the structure was built (average of one to two months) over and above the committed use should be allowed to go downstream of all existing and new structures. Implementation of this would be possible only with the help of all communities involved with proper monitoring and also by allocating this quantity on a priority from new reservoirs.

2.6.2 In project planning, implementation and operation, the preservation of the quality of the environment and the ecological balance should be a primary consideration. The adverse impact, if any, on the environment should be minimised and should be off-set by adequate compensatory measures. Effluents should be treated to acceptable levels and standards before discharging them in natural streams and other water bodies. Details of all effluents generated by each industry or urban area should be available to the public. The standards of treatment and the achievement levels by each effluent discharger should also be available to the public. The responsibility of making this available to the public will be with the pollution control board and with the local government bodies.

2.6.3 Necessary legislation should be made for the preservation of the existing water bodies by preventing encroachment and deterioration of water quality. An annual list of defaulters in this regard with the extent of area under encroachment will be prepared and published by the pollution control board so that social and legal pressure can be brought to bear on the defaulters.

2.6.4 Traditional and natural wetlands and water bodies like tanks, *jheels, chors* and village ponds, etc. have been badly neglected in the last few decades. These structures should be restored, maintained and used properly and these water bodies should not be allowed to be encroached upon for any other land use.

2.7 Watershed Areas Management

2.7.1 Watershed management and minor irrigation projects would be most suitable for drought prone, tribal and hill areas, which should be allowed and encouraged to be developed by the local communities, with technical and financial help from the government and NGOs. Special efforts should be made to investigate and formulate projects either in, or for the benefit of, areas inhabited by tribal or other specially disadvantaged groups such as scheduled castes and scheduled tribes. A lower cost-benefit ratio should be acceptable for such areas in view of the advantages that reach such sections. The management of these projects should be with the local communities, through Watershed Management Associations/WUAs.

2.7.2 The planning of projects in hilly areas should take into account the need to provide assured drinking water, possibilities of mini hydro-power development and the proper approach to irrigation in such areas. In the context of physical features and constraints such as steep slopes, rapid run-off, the incidence of soil erosion and the eco-fragility of the area, the benefit-cost ratio of projects in such areas should be acceptable even at a lower rate.

2.7.3 The people of these areas face a rapid decline in their standard of living as natural resource base become degraded and loses its ability to recover. Increasing number of environmental refugees migrate to other lands, which are then also endangered by over use. The programme should be such that first, they focus on the positive synergies between poverty reduction, economic efficiency, and environmental protection. Second, the projects are developed with the beneficiaries rather than for them. Third, they are based on an integrated approach to natural resource planning and management in consonance with an Environment Action Plan.

2.8 Irrigation and Hydropower

2.8.1 Irrigation planning, either in an individual project or in a basin, as a whole should take into account the irrigability of land, cost effective irrigation options possible from all available sources (including traditional ones). Wherever water is scarce, if economically advantageous, deficit irrigation may be practiced. The irrigation intensity should be such as to extend the benefits of irrigation to as large a number of farm families as possible, keeping in view the need to maximise production and providing minimum sustainable income above the poverty level. Water intensive crops such as sugar cane and paddy should be strongly discouraged in the areas of water scarcity. Irrigation efficiency in irrigation projects should be improved from the present average of 35 per cent to the maximum achievable, which is approximately 60 per cent.

2.8.2 Water allocation in an irrigation system should be done with due regard to equity and social justice. Disparities in the availability of water between head-reach and tail-end farms and between large and small farms should be obviated by adoption of a rotational water distribution system and supply of water on a volumetric basis to WUAs subject to certain ceilings. WUAs should have an important role to play in managing distribution, maintenance and recovery of service charges.

2.8.3 Canal irrigated areas have created some water-logged areas which need to be drained out to make the land fit for agriculture and other purposes. First, attempt should be to avoid the supply of excess water and then wherever possible, bio-drainage, and vertical drainage should be preferred rather than surface drainage. The quality of surface drainage water should be improved so as to make it reusable for various purposes. The basic idea should be to store the water after proper treatment, so that water can be reused usefully rather than flow to the sea during the monsoon without use. A combination of drainage arrangements should be adopted to use the least amount of land and which can also be properly maintained at least cost on a regular basis.

2.8.4 Prioritisation of minor/major/medium projects: The prioritisation of projects basin-wise and state-wise is needed. Due to the extreme paucity of funds, projects should be prioritised in such a way that those on-going projects where over 20 per cent of the project cost has already been incurred should be completed first. In basins where most water resources available have already been developed, the emphasis should be on the modernising and up-gradation of existing systems in an integrated manner. However, in basins where much development work remains, the emphasis should be on complete investigation and planning in an integrated manner. Economic criteria should not be ignored in sanctioning projects except in some special cases where development has been poor because of paucity of water potential and there is no other alternate means of economic development.

2.8.5 Redefinition of major, medium and minor projects: So far the utilisation of potential created on an irrigation project is one of the main criteria for its performance. The potential given in the project report is based on a certain assumed cropping pattern. But in actual practice these cropping patterns keep on changing on the basis of demand and market price from year to year. The actual potential is also different at the time of completion of the project due to land availability and the soil condition at site being different from those given in the project report. Often there is an over-estimate of potential, so as to indicate a better B/C ratio and Rate of Return. In some cases, in actual practice, the use of water also shifts from agriculture to industrial or other uses. In spite of all efforts by the Planning Commission and the known reduction in the actual potential of irrigation, this is not reflected accurately in the figures, which gives a wrong picture of the gap between potential and utilisation. Besides, there is also the need to reduce the gap by more efficient use of and better distribution of water in the field. In agriculture, the efficient use of water should also be judged through the economic value of the product per unit of water used.

The present system of categorisation is based on irrigated area, and the irrigation potential is based on an assumed cropping pattern, which keeps on changing over time. The focus, however, should be on overall water use. In certain projects, it may be power generation, drinking water or flood control, which may be the major component, rather than irrigation. Thus, instead of being based on the area irrigated or height of the dam, projects should now be categorised on the basis of live storage capacity. Projects above 100 MCM would be categorised as major, between 10 and 100 MCM would be medium, and those below 10 MCM would be minor. Projects smaller than 1 MCM would be categorised as micro. For run of the river schemes, the volume of water diverted in a year would determine the categorisation of the project as major, medium, minor or micro.

2.9 Industry and Thermal Power

Most of the thermal power houses and industries with heavy use of water should be located on the coast. They should be encouraged to use sea water/desalinated water, adopt processes with minimum use of water, recycle, reuse and discharge only treated and cooled water into the sea to maintain its ecology.

2.10 Navigation

In order to save energy and reduce our dependence on petroleum products, the major portion of which are imported, navigational transport in rivers is essential. This will require that minimum flow and depth in specific reaches of the river is assured.

2.11 Groundwater Management

2.11.1 The first right to groundwater should be to the concerned community and not to an individual on land-ownership basis. In areas with scarcity of water, the respective community organisations should have the right to inspect and monitor the use of groundwater by private landowners to ensure that groundwater beyond permissible limits is not being withdrawn. Diversion of groundwater to urban areas or for industrial use without consent of the gram sabha/village community should also not be permitted. In canal-irrigated areas, groundwater planning should be integrated with the water supplied through the canal system so as to avoid water-logging and also utilise public or private funds of the community and local management talent.

2.11.2 Development of groundwater resources should be so regulated as not to exceed the recharging possibilities, as also to ensure social equity. The detrimental environmental consequences of over-exploitation of groundwater need to be effectively prevented by legislation and its enforcement by local government bodies, RWAs and gram sabhas, who will have to play a vital role in this. To give teeth to their actions the Central and state governments should enact suitable legislation and notify the permissible water depths to which ground water depletion will be permitted for each region/block/gram sabha/watershed after identifying the special problems of each area. Groundwater recharge projects should be developed and implemented with community participation for augmenting the available supplies. There should be a reassessment of groundwater quantity and quality every five years.

2.11.3 The Government should transfer the authority for regulating groundwater use to the lowest level, the Gram Sabha. In this case the Government should have the responsibility of laying down the rules and regulations and then monitoring the implementation. In case of default the Gram Sabha should be penalised and would in turn be authorised to collect it from individuals or groups as necessary.

2.11.4 In order to discourage excessive use of ground water, the electricity and diesel should be supplied at the market rate and should not be subsidised. However, it should be ensured that the electricity is supplied for 12-16 hours per day without interruption. This would also encourage use of other means of energy. In case subsidies are to be given to the marginal and poor farmers, these should be designed and targeted in such a way that the subsidies reach only the targeted beneficiaries and not the better-off farmers.

2.11.5 Over-exploitation of groundwater should be avoided near the coast to prevent ingress of sea water and also from excessive saline layers of aquifers.

2.12 Flood Management and Drainage

2.12.1 Insurance against floods and droughts requires local action as well as national coordination. It is essential to realise that floods and their negative consequences can only be managed, they cannot be 'controlled'. The seasonal floods in most parts of India are largely a consequence of the concentration of heavy rainfall within a period of few days/weeks during the monsoon months and low flows for most part of the year. The flood management policy should recognise this fact and should begin with the premise that people are prepared to live with the floods in ways that are least disruptive and harmful for them.

A number of systematic measures, that include the adoption of suitable policies, operational and managerial steps, disaster preparedness, flood forecasting, ecological measures and international river water sharing agreements should be taken urgently to deal with floods in such a way that their intensity is moderated and the negative consequences on flood-prone populations are minimised. The planning for flood management should be done in a holistic manner so that the needs during the non-flood season are also taken care of.

2.12.2 *Measures for Flood Management*

i) There should be a master plan for flood control and management for each flood-prone basin. An integrated river basin water policy for states sharing a river basin should be evolved. Such groups of states should co-operate, make use of computerised information systems and undertake joint measures for information sharing, flood forecasting, management, and operation of reservoirs, etc.

ii) In those instances where flood control is one of the key purposes of multi-purpose dams, it should be ensured that the dam intercepts significantly at least 33 per cent of the catchment/drainage above the affected area. Wherever dams and reservoirs exist or contemplated for multipurpose benefits, flood management should be integrated among its purposes. In highly flood prone areas, flood management should be given overriding consideration in reservoir regulation policy, even at the cost of sacrificing some irrigation or power benefits.

iii) While physical flood protection works like embankments and dykes may be necessary in some areas, increased emphasis should be laid on non-physical measures such as flood forecasting and warning, flood-plain zoning and flood proofing, for the minimization of losses, so as to reduce the recurring expenditure on flood relief. An extensive network for flood forecasting should be established for timely warning to settlements and economic activity areas in the flood plain zones in order to keep people in a state of preparedness and to minimise the loss of life and property on account of floods. The working of the existing flood forecasting and warning network in flood prone regions should be reviewed and strengthened. Its working should be updated so as to correspond with latest technology and to render real time information/warning coupled with a decisive support system, comprising simulation models, policies of operation of structures based on historical data, to develop the likely scenario in the flood plains.

iv) Land-use regulation should be integrated with flood plain zoning to avoid inappropriate land-use in flood-plains and other flood-prone areas and consequent higher damages and relief costs in the long run. Flood prone areas should be demarcated at different probability levels and appropriate development measures and economic activities should be devised for flood prone and non-flood prone areas (as recommended by the Rashtriya Barh Aayog).

v) Unauthorised and unabated encroachment in the flood plains and riverbeds as also cultivation of riverbeds/drainage courses during the flood period should be prevented. The land, however, may be leased for agricultural purposes during the non-flood months.

vi) Watershed management through extensive soil conservation measures, such as check dams, contour trenches etc., preservation of forests, increasing the forest cover, etc. should be promoted to reduce the intensity of floods. The traditional flood management systems of the area should be revitalised, maintained and suitably upgraded. The traditional method of building houses on stilts, for instance, should be revived and encouraged. Thus the government policy should build on people's resolve to live with floods and should aim at dealing with floods so as to minimise losses and hardship while obtaining certain benefits.

vii) Construction of embankments should be considered only after careful detailed studies and investigations as a part of a package. Regular and adequate maintenance of embankments should be ensured with the involvement of people. Where embankments have been made, arrangements for adequate drainage of the area behind them should be made through appropriately located sluices. Development works such as roads, railways and housing construction should take into account natural waterways and adequate natural drainage should be provided without creating an aflux upstream.

2.12.3 Drainage

Draining out water becomes necessary for the following purposes:

- To get rid of bad quality water from sewage and industrially used water. This can be avoided by treating the water and reusing it.

- To recover land area from water logged and salinity, which can be made fit for various uses. Wetland and other water bodies, both natural and man made, should be used, without reclaiming it for land use without water. These can be used for aquaculture, recharge of ground water, maintaining ecology as in mangrove or rain forests, etc.
- To get rid of excess water during monsoon season due to sudden heavy rainfall. If natural depression, wetlands, tanks, can be properly maintained and even more created to absorb water and retain it during wet season and land with water, used for various economic purpose. This way flood intensity could be moderated and water dose not flow to the sea unused.

2.13 Resettlement and Rehabilitation

Although optimal management of water is best achieved through a sound micro watershed development programme, sometimes it would be necessary to construct large storages. The consequent resettlement and rehabilitation of people should be governed by a national policy. Under this policy the project-affected persons (PAPs) should be entitled to rehabilitation that precedes the project completion and compensation where payable, should be both for appropriation of property as well as for livelihood.

2.13.1 Land for land in respect of agriculturists should be the preferred option in those regions and states where land for resettlement is or can be made available. In some cases, where allotting land for land is not possible due to small holdings throughout the command, following alternative measures should be taken:

- Annuity for a certain number of years, where the amount of annuity and the number of years for which it is to be paid may be worked out on the basis of factors like skill level, value of loss of livelihood, and number of remaining years of active working life.
- A suitable job in the development project itself, where the skill and job profile match or person's skill can be upgraded by suitable training and only where the job is expected to be of a permanent nature, and is not merely created for the purpose of rehabilitation.

2.13.2 The compensation awarded to PAPs should match market rates, even if this means that the cost of Resettlement and Rehabilitation (R&R) as percentage of the total project cost goes up.

2.13.3 The definition of PAPs should be such as to cover all the people who are actually affected by the project[4]. The definition should include, besides the persons displaced due to the dam reservoir, borrow area or mine etc., the persons displaced due to the project colony, the canal system or any other 'development' during the project construction. Tribals or others, who may not have legal titles to the land, but who are nevertheless land-owners in terms of customary laws, should also be considered as PAPs. Persons, such as downstream fisher-folk, washermen, etc. whose livelihood is affected due to a project, should be compensated suitably.

2.13.4 All water and power development projects should ensure that the benefits of the project go to the local people first. For example, water supply and electric connections should be provided on priority to all local people who are affected.

2.13.5 A separate R&R cell or wing should be created within the project management structure to be staffed with social scientists (sociologists, anthropologists, economists) and extension/community workers, besides engineers. This cell should focus on bringing about attitudinal change among the project managers and government officials towards the problems of the PAPs. The Central or state governments or corporations which are repeatedly involved in R&R activities should set up a cadre of persons (from both engineering and social science backgrounds) trained in R&R activities.

2.13.6 The concerned government should appoint an independent agency (outside the project implementation) to monitor the R&R activities at regular intervals for the whole duration of the development project. Representatives of local people/reputed NGOs should be associated/Co-opted as a part of this agency to inspire confidence among the affected people. They should visit the sites/villages for redressing the grievances rather than wait for complaints.

---

4. According to the NWDT Award, for instance, an oustee meant "any person who, since at least one year prior to the date of publication of notification u/s 4 of the Land Acquisition Act, has been ordinarily residing or cultivating land or carrying on any trade, occupation or calling or working for gain in the area likely to be submerged permanently or temporarily."

3. ACTION PROGRAMME AND IMPLEMENTATION SCHEDULE

3.1. Partnership with Communities in Water Resources Management

3.1.1 The management of water resources for diverse uses should be done by adopting a participatory approach; by involving the user communities, through community based organisations, in the various aspects of planning, design, development and management of water resources. Necessary legal and institutional changes should be made at various levels for this purpose. Water Users Associations and local bodies such as municipalities and gram panchayats should particularly be involved progressively at appropriate levels in the operation, maintenance and the management of water infrastructures/facilities with a view to eventually transfer the management of such facilities to the community based organisations/ Local bodies. The number and different types of community based organisations required in the country is given in Table 2 below. A list of operational aspects relating to establishing and sustaining community organisations is given at Annexure 1.

It is evident from this table that nearly 6.7 lakh community level organisations are required at present and about 7.1 lakh such organisations will be required by 2020 in the country as a whole to ensure participation of all local level communities in the management of land and water resources.

3.1.2 Since all water resources have a common property character, private participation in planning, development and management of water resource projects must be subjected to careful social scrutiny based on well-developed mechanisms of accountability and regulation. Where local communities or public utilities are neither able to invest nor able to efficiently manage water delivery systems, corporate sector participation can be invited. All agreements/ contracts must be cleared by the local community, whose water resources are being tapped on the principle of prior informed consent based on recognition of water rights of local communities. Private sector participation may help in introducing innovative ideas, generating financial resources and introducing modern management practices in improving service efficiency and accountability to users. However communities need to be involved in decisions related to technology choice, and prices of services. For urban projects various combinations of private sector participation, in building, owning, operating, leasing and transferring of water resources facilities, may be considered. However at no point should water be reduced to a commodity, with access determined by purchasing power and not as a common resource to be equally shared.

Table 2

Number of Community Based Organisations (CBOs) for Management of Water Resources at the Local Level

Sl. No.	*Type of Land Area/Population*	*Land Area (mha) and Corresponding Number of CBOs Required (lakhs)*		
		1995-96	*2020*	*2050*
1.	Net Irrigated Area	54	65	85
2.	Number of WUAs required @ one WUA/500 ha	1.08	1.30	1.70
3.	Area that needs watershed management	141	1.25	100
4.	Number of WMAs required @ one WMA/500 ha	2.82	2.50	2.00
5.	Forest Area	69	66	65
6.	Number of Joint Forest Management (JFM) committees required @ one JFM committee/500 ha	1.38	1.32	1.30
7.	Urban population	350 million	500 million	700 million
8.	Number of RWAs/NUGs required @ one RWA/500 households	1.40	2.00	2.80
9.	Total number of community organisations required	6.68	7.12	7.80

3.1.3 The involvement and participation of beneficiaries and other stakeholders should be mandatory at every stage of project conception, planning, implementation, operation and maintenance. Consultations with the gram sabha should be held before projects are taken up in the area of each gram sabha. If the decision is to go against the recommendation of the gram sabha, it should be mandatory for the government agency concerned to state the reasons why the recommendation is being over-ruled. This information should be available in the public domain. Formation of water users associations and other community based organisations should be mandatory as this will facilitate accountability and maintenance of the distribution system, discipline and recovery of charges.

3.2. Changes in the Institutional Structure[5]

3.2.1 Water in each river basin including rainfall, groundwater and surface water with storages in various structures, wetlands, etc. of all sizes can be used many times over for various purposes if planned, developed, operated and managed in an integrated manner. For this, it is necessary to set up a water resources department in each state with wings for each river basin in the state (see attached Chart 1 for the ministry of water resources at the Centre and Chart 3 for the state water resources department). For an interstate river these River Basin Organisations (RBOs) can be set up jointly by the concerned states by agreement among themselves (see Chart 2 on RBOs). These would be advisory and could act on the authority delegated by the states. A RBO should have two wings: a River Basin Assembly (RBA) consisting of representatives from each state starting from the lowest watershed with a federated system, and another wing consisting of a multidisciplinary team of professionals taken from various departments of each state and fresh recruits in disciplines where such experts are not available from departments. The RBA representatives should represent all interests like:

- Watershed Associations.
- Water Users Associations in irrigated areas.
- Associations of forest users and pastoral people.
- Resident Welfare Association representatives as users of drinking and/or domestic water including those from urban areas.

5. The rationale for and the nature of changes needed in the institutional structures for water resources management have been discussed by the authors in a separate paper titled "Institutional Structural Changes in the Water Sector".

- Large industries.
- Small and tiny industries.
- Other users such as fishermen, washermen, potters etc.

3.2.2 Where interstate disputes are not resolved by themselves or by RBO, these could be referred by states to a single or a team of arbitrators to give the verdict, which should be accepted by all under a legal provision. This system would lead to quicker decision and help to reduce the politicisation of the issue and avoid time-consuming judicial process.

3.3 Implementation of Watershed Projects

3.3.1 A total land area of 141 mha is to be covered under this programme (see Table 1 above). There is no precise record/information with regard to the land area taken up and completed under various watershed management schemes by various agencies. However, it is estimated that about 40-50 mha has been tackled by government agencies and NGOs through outside financial help, thus, the balance 80-90 mha has still to be managed by various agencies. The Planning Commission has drawn up a programme of covering 63 mha in the next 25 years. There is no adequate arrangement for the maintenance and management of the watershed work already done by the government agencies, as the people were not fully involved in carrying out this work. Such works may have to be repaired or re-done through community level organisations. Table 2 (above) gives an idea of the large number of WMAs that are needed for people-centred watershed development and management activities in the country.

3.3.2 At present various departments and ministries like rural development, forest and agriculture etc. are looking after this programme through special programmes imposed from the Centre, which are not always suitable for local conditions. A nodal agency like the Rural Development ministry needs to co-ordinate and monitor the work and funds released, with the freedom to choose the technology as per local conditions, with full involvement of the gram sabha from the planning stage itself so that maintenance and operation can be done by them with authority and responsibility.

There are several land-based programmes being serviced by different ministries of the Government of India. The important land-based programmes are: Drought Prone Area Programme (DPAP) and Desert Development Programme (DDP), National Watershed Development Project for Rainfed Areas (NWDPRA), Integrated Watershed Development Programme (IWDP), soil conservation in the catchments of river valley projects and flood prone rivers. However, despite efforts in the past, progress has not met expectations. The MoA has restructured NWDPRA providing for decentralisation for procedures, flexibility in choice of technology and provision for active involvement of the watershed community in the planning, implementation and evaluation of the programme so that it becomes sustainable. The states of Karnataka, Maharashtra, Orissa and Rajasthan have already established a separate nodal department for implementing all the GOI and the state government watershed and soil conservation programmes.

3.3.3 At present not many NGOs are involved in watershed management. They should be persuaded, motivated and trained to take up this work, so that the total work can be completed in a shorter period. Adequate legal and administrative action would have to be taken to encourage gram sabhas and NGOs to get involved in this work. Technical help can be provided by the government and also by technically competent NGOs at a reasonable cost.

3.4 Legal Changes

On a number of policy issues relating to the management of water resources which have been suggested herein, necessary legislation should be passed by the Parliament and by state governments to enable the changes to be implemented in practice. Appropriate and enabling legislation will have to be passed particularly with respect to the following policy and operational aspects:

a) Setting up of river boards, both within states and interstate, to plan in an integrated way for the development of water resources within a river basin: The necessary legislation should provide for the two-tier constitution of river boards, consisting of the river basin assembly and a supporting technical body. River basin organisations within states can be set up by Government Orders under existing legislation itself.

b) Enabling full and effective participation of the farmers and rural and urban communities in the task of managing water resources: The existing legislative framework, which provides overriding control over water resources to the state, should be modified to provide usufruct rights to local communities and a pivotal role in the management of water resources at the local level. The exact modalities of how such water users associations, watershed associations and resident welfare associations in urban areas will interact with panchayats and urban local self government bodies will have to be worked out. In the southern and western states of India, the panchayat system is working reasonably well, so a separate committee under the gram panchayat consisting of the actual users/ beneficiaries of water could be formed to deal with watershed management and irrigation management at the minor levels. In the northern and eastern states it may be necessary to set up separate WMAs and WUAs who could cooperate with panchayats but not under them, as the latter are not functioning properly.

c) Regulation of groundwater so as to prevent and stop the overuse and depletion of groundwater in many areas: The existing law provides for control and ownership of groundwater by the landowner. This should be modified by transferring at least the management of groundwater to the gram sabha and the RWA. The overuse of groundwater should be stopped and regulated by the respective gram sabhas/RWAs, with higher levels of government providing the necessary information, framing rules for regulation and monitoring the situation.

d) Provision of accurate and up to date information on water resources in the public domain in a user-friendly form: This is essential for the rational and integrated planning of water resources in the country, for involving local communities in the task of management of water resources and for smooth resolution of water related conflicts between different parties. The Official Secrets Act and the attitudes and practices relating to its interpretation should be modified in order that information on water resources in the country is freely available.

3.5 Project Implementation

3.5.1 There should be a system to monitor the performance of the project and socio-economic impact of the project. Such a monitoring process should take the community into confidence by involving them at every stage. All data gathered for this should be made available in the public domain. A close monitoring of the projects to identify bottlenecks and to adopt timely measures to obviate time and cost overruns should form part of project planning and execution.

3.5.2 In the first four decades after Independence, due to the absence of expertise and the required skills not being available in the private sector, the expertise and skill for investigation, planning, feasibility reports, detailed designs, and even departmental construction were developed in the government sector. Since a number of projects were taken up in various states, most of the major states had developed this expertise along with research and model testing. Now the tempo of work has slowed down and the required expertise has also developed with the private sector, which can move from project to project in different states, or even take up projects outside India. The private sector can operate with less manpower and better utilisation of expertise. Such tasks can now be given out on contract to private sector firms (through competitive bidding) who are in a better position to keep themselves up-to-date with the latest technology and with least cost.

3.6 Financing Projects and Water Service Charges

3.6.1 Government financing of water projects is getting reduced due to other priorities and this situation is likely to continue for a long time. It has increasingly become evident that government alone cannot provide the funds needed for the financing of water projects. Local communities on the one hand and the corporate sector on the other have an important role to play in the better development and utilisation of water resources. The government should facilitate this by putting in place a suitable legal and administrative environment.

3.6.2 At present, government investment is in major, medium and minor irrigation projects, besides domestic water supply, while watershed development has been done both by the government and the private sector. The capital cost is not recovered and even the operational and maintenance cost is only partially recovered for government projects. Private investment is mainly in groundwater development for irrigation and industrial purposes and the investors also fully bear the cost of operation and maintenance. However, electricity to agriculture sector is highly subsidised, leading to an overuse and wastage of groundwater. This situation will have to be rectified and the subsidies reduced and, ultimately removed if there is to be viable investment of the private sector in groundwater development.

3.6.3 As a matter of principle, in government projects the full cost of operation and maintenance along with the 50 per cent cost of the capital should be recovered. The water charges should be increased gradually to reach that level within the next 10 years. In the case of private sector investment, suitable means like commercial use of land or other means can be found to compensate for less recovery in the early stages of operation of the projects. In areas where sanitation services have been provided by the government, the water user charges should be substantially enhanced (to double the existing charges or so) in order to recover the capital cost and to generate the funds for maintenance, extension and modernisation of the sewage disposal system.

3.6.4 The energy pricing should be done at market rates for electricity and diesel (used for groundwater exploitation) and the surface water rates should be comparable so that it induces conservation of water and creates a sense of value of water. Recently, under the Uttar Pradesh Water Sector Restructuring Project, the World Bank and the Government of Uttar Pradesh have entered into an agreement to set up an autonomous regulatory body to fix service charges for all types of uses of water. This kind of regulatory body to fix tariffs for the different uses of water should be set up in all states.

3.6.5 The water may be sold on volume basis to WUAs, RWAs and other groups so that recovery points and administrative cost can be reduced. This will reduce chances of theft and better distribution by local groups and agencies. This would also require transfer of authority and responsibility to them and in some existing projects even transfer of funds.

3.6.6 Adequate emphasis needs to be given to the physical and financial sustainability of existing facilities. There is, therefore, a need to ensure that the water charges for various uses should be fixed in such a way that they cover at least the operation and maintenance charges of providing the service and a part of the capital cost. The water charges could be increased gradually. These rates should be linked directly to the quality of service provided. The subsidy on water rates to the disadvantaged and poorer sections of the society should be well targeted and transparent.

3.7 Maintenance and Modernisation

Performance Improvement

3.7.1 There is an urgent need for a paradigm shift in the management of water resources sector. From the present emphasis on the creation and expansion of water resources infrastructure for diverse uses, there is now a need to give greater emphasis to performance improvement of the existing water resource facilities. Therefore, allocation of funds under the water resources sector should be re-prioritised to ensure that the needs for development as well as operation and maintenance of the facilities are met along with the funds allocated to other activities under the sector. Structures and systems created through massive investments should be maintained in good health. Appropriate annual provisions should be made for this purpose in the budget. There should be a regular monitoring of the structures and systems and necessary rehabilitation and modernisation programmes should be undertaken.

Safety

3.7.2 There should be proper organisational arrangements at the national and state levels for ensuring the safety of storage dams and other water related structures consisting of specialists in investigation, design, construction, hydrology, geology, etc. Dam safety legislation should be enacted to ensure proper inspection, maintenance and surveillance of the existing dams and also to ensure proper planning, investigation, design, construction and safety of new dams. The guidelines on the subject should be kept under constant review and periodically updated and reformulated. There should be a system of continuous surveillance and regular visits by experts.

3.8 Action Programme and Important Implementation Aspects

The implementation of this water policy requires administrative, organisational, legal and project implementation action. Since it requires decentralisation of authority to states, districts, blocks and gram sabha organisations and the people themselves, besides co-operation among the various departments and ministries concerned, it should be discussed widely among water sector professionals, NGOs, community organisations and all concerned officials within the government, in the next one to two years, especially with a view to finalise the action programme.

New Organisational Structures

3.8.1 A National body of experts should be set up by the Central government to midwife the process of setting up the first few RBOs (out of a total of about 20 to be set up) and to lay down the rules and regulations for their functioning. This body may be initially constituted for a period of two to three years during which the first five RBOs may be set up, and may suggest ways in which all the possible RBOs may be set up and made operational within a decade. The first five RBOs may be set up within states and may include at least two river basins in the North and two in the South. Subsequently, RBOs may be set up for interstate rivers and for one river basin that goes beyond national boundaries.

Once the policy measures and the action programme outlined here are agreed upon, it would be necessary to switch over to the new administrative organisations. This would have to be a gradual process so that at least by the end of five years, all intrastate and interstate RBOs would have been set up. A Water Resources Department should be set up in each state in two years along with a few intrastate RBOs. At the state level, the nodal ministries/departments should be identified for water resources (MoWR), watershed development (MoRD), irrigation (Irrigation Department) domestic water supply (Public Health Department), and pollution control (State Pollution Control Board). Similar action should be taken at the Central level.

Legal Changes

3.8.2 These have been discussed above in section 4 and should bc carried out within the next five years so as to remove the hurdles for implementing the new water policy, with the involvement of NGOs and people's organisations. Groundwater regulation is another priority area that needs to be finalised within the next five years.

Project Implementation

38.3 The first task should be to set up an information organisation with the co-operation of all the departments who are already collecting information. This information collection, starting at the lowest level, should be computerised and made available to the public on the Internet, with the MoWR being the nodal agency for this purpose. This should begin at the lowest level and for this purpose the number of full-fledged information centres should be increased from about 2,000 to 30,000 in the next five years. Various departments at present collect limited data at many more places but not at agreed locations, which need to be consolidated. This organisation would also have to revise and update the assessment of water resources in various forms, which should be completed in first 10 years and then revised every 10 years.

The environmental and rehabilitation aspects have not been up to the mark, particularly in terms of implementation in the existing projects and those under construction. All these projects should be reviewed and action taken for completion in the next five to 10 years.

Domestic Water Supply

3.8.4 A target of providing water to everybody within next five years, particularly in all the rural areas and especially where the quality of water is not up to the mark, should be fixed. However, after this, certain areas would still come up where the quality has deteriorated and as such would have to be given a new source of supply or better treatment of the water available. This, of course, would have to bc a continuous process and should be monitored all the time. For sanitation in urban areas the target should be to provide it to all in the next 15 years. Wherever possible, two separate pipeline networks, one for sewage and one for kitchen and bath water should be provided so as to reduce treatment costs and to be able to recycle the water. Rooftop rainwater should also be stored separately for use or for groundwater recharge.

Watershed Areas

3.8.5 As indicated earlier, this sector requires more urgent and intensive attention, both for integrated development of land and water and for improvement in the economic condition of the population. Watershed management is required in the culturable land of about 141 mha that is rainfed at present. This has to be managed by people with the help of NGOs and the government for integrated development of land, water and biomass. Some of these areas have already been covered by watershed management or by Joint Forest Management but these would have to be reviewed in order to achieve the above objectives. The rural development ministry at the Centre and in the states should be the nodal agency for this purpose.

Pollution of Water

3.8.6 Special attention has to be paid to the water from agricultural lands, which are difficult to treat as there is no single point of pollution and as such prevention is the best answer. For this purpose, bio-fertilisers, bio-pesticides and organic farming should be encouraged, in order to reduce the use of chemicals, which could be done gradually but substantially over the next two decades. Treatment of water from industries and sewage should be implemented within the next 10 years. All this water could also be reused and recycled for various purposes.

Irrigation

3.8.7 Far too many projects are under construction at the present moment and it would be necessary to provide funds on priority for those on which more than 20 per cent of expenditure or physical progress has been made for completion in the next 5-10 years with practically no new projects to be taken up during these years. Some of the existing projects would need to be modernised, which should be the next priority and completed within the next 15 years. The third priority should be to complete all hydro and irrigation project within each basin by the year 2025. An agreement with Nepal for the purposes of hydropower generation and flood moderation should be pursued vigorously for all common rive basins.

Water Service Charges

3.8.8 Water charges need to be increased gradually to cover at least O&M expenditure, both in irrigation and domestic water supply and subsidies should be eliminated over a period of 10 years. Transfer of management and authority to local organisations would be necessary to achieve this objective.

3.9 Research and Training

3.9.1 For effective and economical management of our water resources, the frontiers of knowledge need to be pushed forward in several directions by intensifying research efforts in various areas, including the following:

- Hydro-meteorology.
- Assessment of water resources.
- Groundwater hydrology and recharge.
- Water quality, recycling and reuse.
- Prevention of salinity ingress.
- Prevention of water-logging and soil salinity.
- Water harvesting in rural areas in an integral manner.
- Water harvesting and groundwater recharge in urban areas.
- Economical and easy to operate and maintain designs for water resource projects.
- Seismology and seismic design, safety and longevity of structures.
- Sedimentation of reservoirs.
- River morphology and hydraulics.
- Soils and materials research; construction material and technology (with particular reference to roller compacted concrete, fibre reinforced concrete, new methodologies in tunnelling technologies, instrumentation, advanced numerical analysis, etc.)
- Use of remote sensing techniques.
- Better water management practices and improvements in operational technologies.

- Use of sea water resources.
- Risk analysis and disaster management.
- Crops and cropping systems.
- Design of less consumptive use in domestic appliances.
- Sewage treatment on smaller scales and reuse of water after treatment.

3.9.2 Since the over all thrust of the new national water policy is towards people's participation at all stages, the highest priority should be accorded to the training of those who are to manage the water resources at all levels. The training must sensitise all partners to the demands of a people's planning approach to water resource development. Training should also ensure the technical empowerment of all local institutions and communities who are to plan for, develop and manage water resources. These include panchayats, gram sabhas, NGOs, watershed associations, WUAs, RWAs, etc. It should cover training in information systems, sectoral planning, project planning and formulation, project management, operation of projects and their physical structures and systems and the management of the water distribution systems. The training should have a strong component on attitudinal and behavioural change.

ANNEXURE 1

Action Programme for Establishing and Sustaining Community Based Organisations (CBOs)

- The CBOs should have a legal status and should be recognised fully by the concerned administrative authorities.
- Government officials/NGOs may help to set up Community Based Organisations but should not themselves be members of the CBO. They may advise the CBO from the outside and may even be present in their meetings, but should not have voting/decision-making rights.
- NGOs with the requisite competence should be asked to come forward, motivate and train the potential leaders and competent individuals from the community or smaller NGOs. To facilitate and support the work of the NGOs, the concerned nodal departments/ministries (Ministry of Rural Areas for WMAs, Irrigation department for WUAs, Forest department for JFM committees, Ministry of Urban Areas for RWAs/Neighbourhood User Groups) should play a suitable role.
- Since each area has its own local problems and priorities, there should be no restriction through a centralised scheme for the type of project to be prepared. Only broad guidelines should be indicated by the government within which the community based organisation can prepare the project.
- Potential leaders (five to six candidates) in each unit should be identified and trained further for leadership roles, care being taken not to include contractors.
- Technical NGOs and government departments should help the CBOs in preparing required projects aimed at the integrated management of land, water and biomass and the provision of livelihood for all, for funding by various agencies.
- Contribution to the creation of physical assets, in the form of labour, material or cash, should be at least 10-20 per cent in the initial stages and should gradually, over the years, be increased to 50 per cent.

- After project approval and funding, the work should be implemented only by the CBO. For this purpose a committee should be formed to supervise the project implementation.
- Operation, maintenance and management should be done by the CBO concerned, for which the cost should be recovered from the beneficiaries or members.
- Monitoring of works should also be done by fund providers and also by government to safeguard natural resources and ensure proper use of funds. Post-project monitoring should also be done to ensure that the project benefits reach all members of the community and are not cornered by the powerful local elite or upper classes or castes.

CHART 1

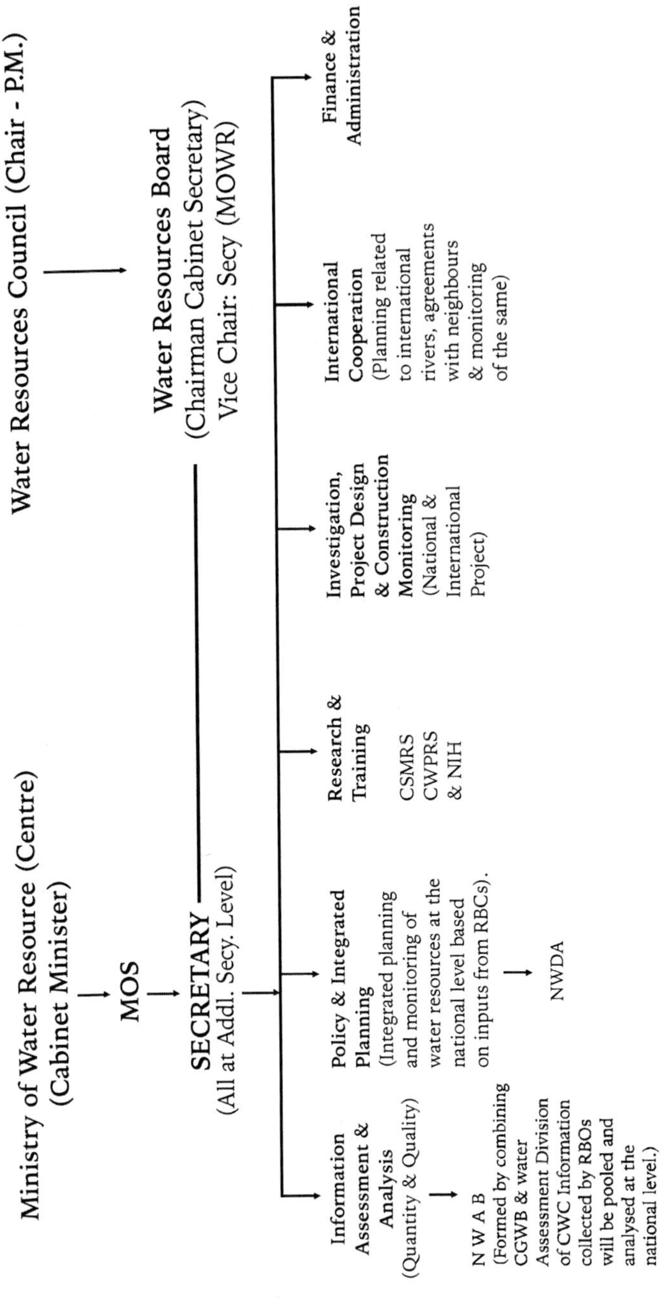
Ministry of Water Resource (Centre)
(Cabinet Minister)
MOS
SECRETARY
(All at Addl. Secy. Level)
Water Resources Council (Chair - P.M.)
Water Resources Board
(Chairman Cabinet Secretary)
Vice Chair: Secy (MOWR)
Information Assessment & Analysis (Quantity & Quality)
N W A B
(Formed by combining CGWB & water Assessment Division of CWC Information collected by RBOs will be pooled and analysed at the national level.)
Policy & Integrated Planning
(Integrated planning and monitoring of water resources at the national level based on inputs from RBCs).
NWDA
Research & Training
CSMRS
CWPRS
& NIH
Investigation, Project Design & Construction Monitoring
(National & International Project)
International Cooperation
(Planning related to international rivers, agreements with neighbours & monitoring of the same)
Finance & Administration

CHART 2

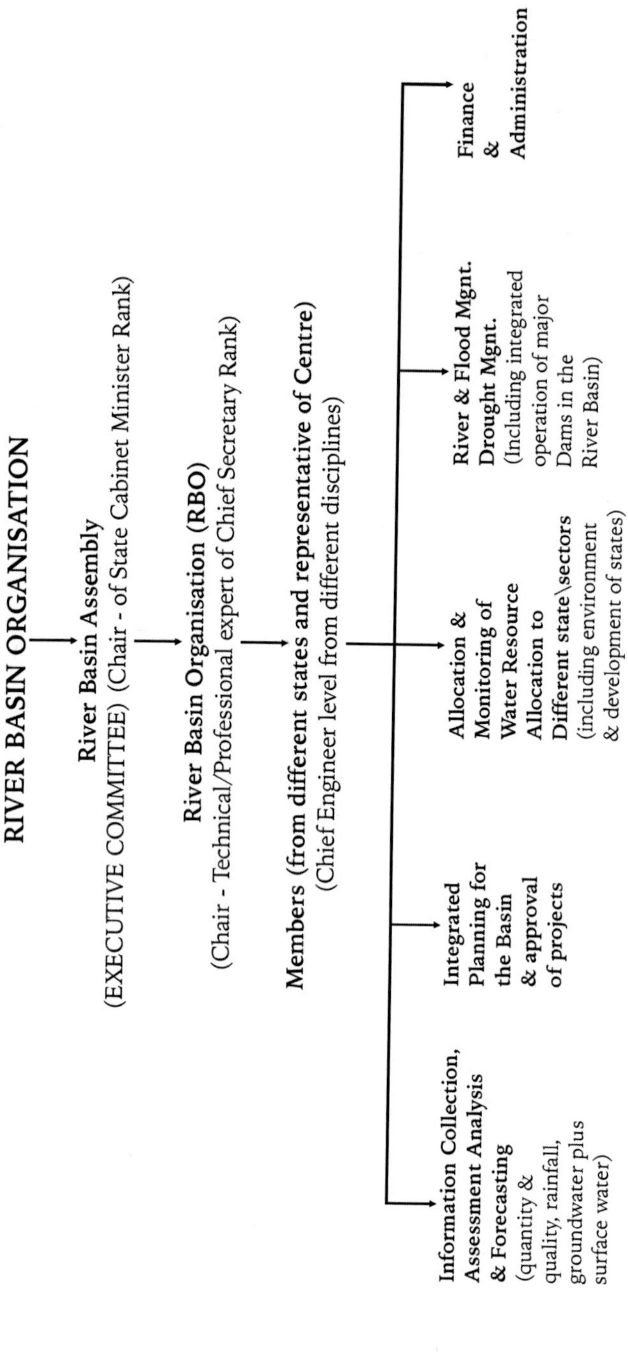
RIVER BASIN ORGANISATION
River Basin Assembly
(EXECUTIVE COMMITTEE) (Chair - of State Cabinet Minister Rank)
River Basin Organisation (RBO)
(Chair - Technical/Professional expert of Chief Secretary Rank)
Members (from different states and representative of Centre)
(Chief Engineer level from different disciplines)
Information Collection, Assessment Analysis & Forecasting (quantity & quality, rainfall, groundwater plus surface water)
Integrated Planning for the Basin & approval of projects
Allocation & Monitoring of Water Resource Allocation to Different state\sectors (including environment & development of states)
River & Flood Mgnt. Drought Mgnt. (Including integrated operation of major Dams in the River Basin)
Finance & Administration

CHART 3

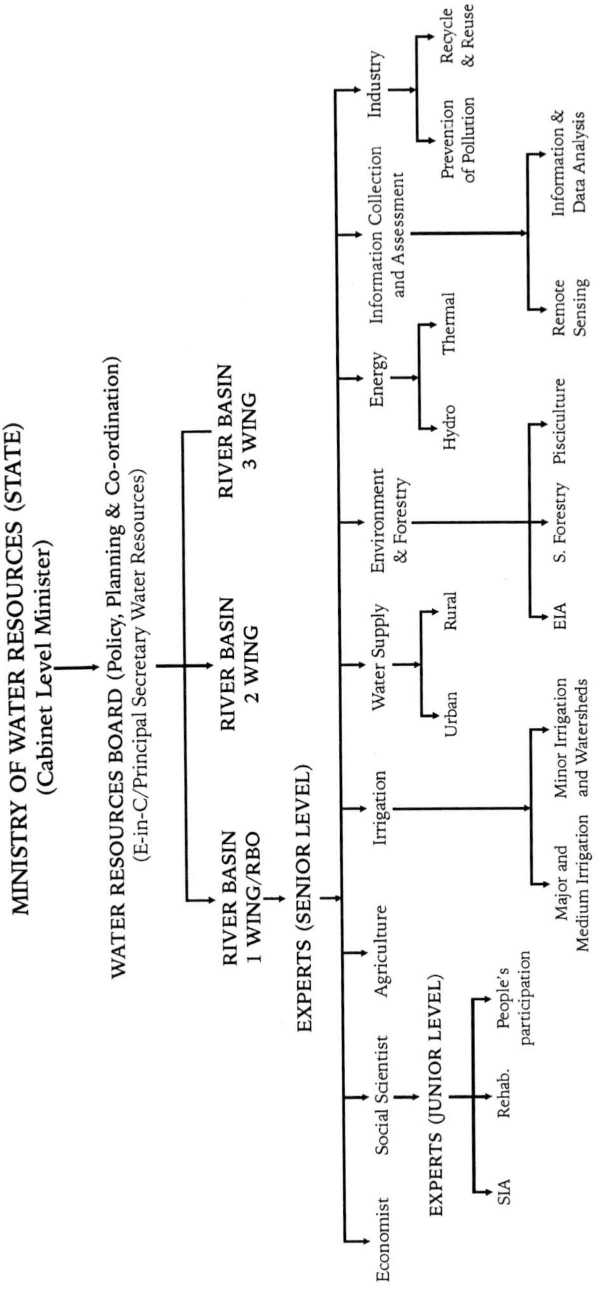
MINISTRY OF WATER RESOURCES (STATE)
(Cabinet Level Minister)
WATER RESOURCES BOARD (Policy, Planning & Co-ordination)
(E-in-C/Principal Secretary Water Resources)
RIVER BASIN 1 WING/RBO
RIVER BASIN 2 WING
RIVER BASIN 3 WING
EXPERTS (SENIOR LEVEL)
Economist
Social Scientist
Agriculture
Irrigation
Water Supply
Environment & Forestry
Energy
Information Collection and Assessment
Industry
EXPERTS (JUNIOR LEVEL)
SIA
Rehab.
People's participation
Major and Medium Irrigation
Minor Irrigation and Watersheds
Urban
Rural
EIA
S. Forestry
Pisciculture
Hydro
Thermal
Remote Sensing
Information & Data Analysis
Prevention of Pollution
Recycle & Reuse

ANNEXURE 2

Action Plan Schedule for Implementation of Policy Measures

2002 2003 2004 2005 2006 2007 2008 2009 2010 2011 2012 2013 2014 2015 2016-26

	Policy Implementation Aspect	
1.	Public discussion on policy and Action Plan	1 to 2
2.	Setting up WRD/Ministry in each state	2 to 3
3.	Finalise state water policies & set up RBOs within states	2 to 3
4.	Setting up inter-state RBOs	2 to 5
5.	Administrative and legal changes required	2 to 5
6.	Information and Assessment Organisation	2 to 6
7.	Groundwater regulation	2 to 6
8.	Review and implementation of R&R in existing projects	2 to 5
9.	Review and implementation of EIAs in existing projects	2 to 10
10.	Domestic water supply provided to all	1 to 5
11.	Sanitation provided to all	1 to 15
12.	Watershed management in 130 mha (net)	1 to 15
13.	Completion of priority projects under construction including CAD	1 to 10
14.	New irrigation area projects (21 mha) completed	10 to 25 years and beyond
15.	Modernisation and rehabilitation of old projects	1 to 25
16.	Pollution control and prevention in existing projects	1 to 15
17.	Increase water charges gradually to cover O&M costs	1 to 10
18.	Agreement with Nepal on Power, Floods, Envt. R&R	2 to 6
19.	Completion of Nepal projects	5 to 25

18

Sustainability of India's Material Resources: Vision 2020

R. K. PACHAURI & POOJA MEHROTRA

Introduction

Economic growth the world over has been driven by energy, whether in the form of primary sources (such as finite resources—for example, coal and oil and gas, or renewables, wood, hydro) or its converted form, electricity. The pattern of their utilization of inputs for driving various industries has impacted our natural resources—the air, water, land, forests, and biodiversity. Signs of this impact, in case of India, as also in other countries, have led to substantial efforts in rethinking our development path. For future growth to be sustainable, it needs to be resource-efficient and environmentally accountable, requiring a long-term vision while planning for the immediate and long-term future. This has been the drive for rethinking India's future. Vision 2020 exercise undertaken by the Planning Commission, Government of India, is a right step in that direction.

It is well known that various sectors in the economy such as the agricultural, domestic and commercial sectors, municipal services, transport services, the mining industry, manufacturing industries, and the power industry are most heavily dependent on finite resources. They have the maximum impact on the environment. Apart from dependence on finite resources, most of these sectors are dependent on energy. In this paper we would restrict our detailed discussion to the power sector, coal, oil and gas, and renewable energy; and discuss the impact of their development on air, water, land, forest, and biodiversity. The strategy to achieve an alternative sustainable scenario with respect to the sectors are not discussed in detail but are included in Annex 1.

Power Industry

In India, like in any other country, power consumption is expected to rise with economic growth and social development. At the same time, high environmental costs in the form of water and air pollution, soil erosion, deforestation, loss of biological diversity, etc. associated with increased resource extraction and power generation, pose a threat to ecological security and human health. This section will investigate ways to achieve sustainable growth in the power industry by 2020.

The power industry in India has registered significant progress since the inception of the economic planning process in 1951. Installed capacity grew from about 1360 MW in 1947 to about 101 630 MW by 31 March 2001. (Figure 1 shows the growth in installed capacity and the change in fuel mix from 1970/71 to 1998/99.) Development of infrastructure in rural areas has also received due emphasis: about 85 per cent of the villages have access to grid electricity, though fraught with problems of erratic supply and low voltage. Despite the significant progress, this sector is associated with poor performance, and serious social and environmental issues.

Figure 1

Total Installed Capacity and Fuel Mix

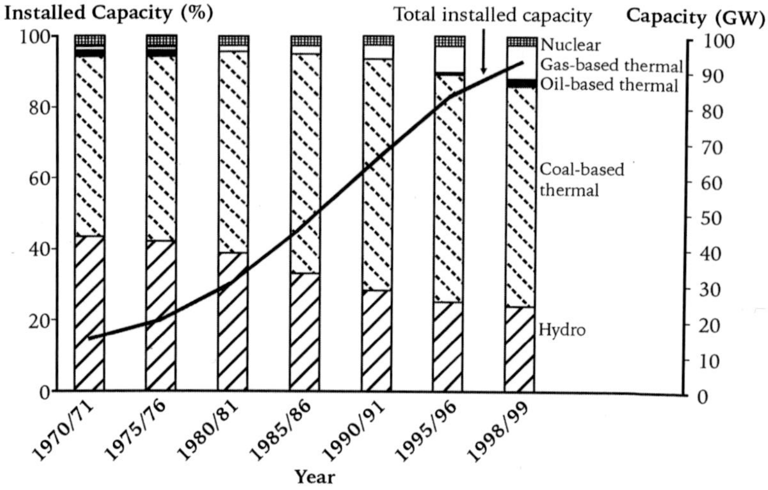

Source: TEDDY, various years.

Performance Issues

Several reasons are often cited for the poor performance of power sector, some of which are outlined as follows:

- Poor financial condition of the SEBs (state electricity boards) are due to a) unremunerative tariff structure—subsidized domestic and agricultural consumption (which accounts for almost 50 per cent of the total), b) poor billing and collections, c) growing preference of the industrial sector (major contributor to the revenues of SEBs) for captive generation because of high cost and poor power quality, and d) high T&D (transmission and distribution) losses—due to pilferage and theft of electricity, weak and inadequate sub-transmission and distribution systems, large-scale rural electrification programme involving long low-tension lines, and inadequate investment in upgrading and maintenance.
- Financial constraints leading to poor plant maintenance, adversely affecting plant availability and system efficiency.
- Insufficient generation of resources on an installed capacity basis and lack of the right kind of capacity to meet demand. Declining share of hydro electricity has adversely affected the performance of thermal plants in some regions.
- Inadequate transmission capacity to link different regions.

Environmental and Social Issues

In addition to the above performance issues, there are serious environmental and social issues with power sector development. Coal-based thermal power constitutes 62 per cent of total power generation, accounting for almost 75 per cent of the total coal used. High ash content of Indian coal results not only in poor performance of thermal power stations and their high O&M (operation and maintenance) costs, but also production of seven to eight times more ash than in European countries. In addition, there is pollution from suspended solids and oil including grease present in the effluent and the discharge of water at high temperature from thermal power plants. Solid waste in the form of fly ash, the land required for its disposal, percolation of hazardous elements to groundwater through ash ponds, and greater incidence of pulmonary diseases in the vicinity of the dumps due to air-borne ash, are some of the major problems in this regard.

In contrast, large-scale dislocation of people, submergence of valuable resources including forests, loss of estuaries and endangered species, adverse impacts on downstream hydrology, and siltation rendering dams ineffective in a short period are problems associated with hydropower. On the positive side, multipurpose hydro projects facilitate better management of water resources by storing water in times of surplus and dispensing with it in times of scarcity. Dams prevent or control devastating floods and catastrophic droughts as seen in river valley projects.

Nuclear power is associated with fears of radioactive leakage/ accidents, disposal of radioactive waste, and decommissioning of power plants. However, in the wake of rising concerns about global warming, it is perhaps a greener option—the Uranium Information Centre claims that in 1997, 3,49,350 MW_e of nuclear energy generated worldwide prevented 2,270 million tonnes of CO_2 emissions. Interestingly, India's reserves of nuclear fuels are sufficient to generate more than 3,00,000 MW_e (CEA 1997), and it has achieved expertise and maturity in nuclear technology.

Business-as-usual Scenario

Based on the assumptions (see Annex 3), the aggregate future demand and fuel mix (assuming different load factors) for power sector have been calculated and are indicated in Table 1 and 2, while the demand for coal, oil, and gas are shown in Table 3.

Table 1

Projected Power Demand (TWh) of Various Sectors in the BAU Scenario

Year	*Industry*	*Transport*	*Agriculture*	*Commercial*	*Residential*	*Total*
1997	137	7	89	47	48	329
2020	570	22	202	262	165	1221

Note: Future demand from the agriculture, industry, transport (railways), and commercial sectors is estimated on the basis of past trends in electricity intensities and their relationship with sectoral GDP. For the residential sector, demand projection is based on an assessment of the changing fuel mix on account of the upward movement along the energy ladder and improvements in rural electrification. Projections are based on restricted consumption data: the inherent unmet demand has not been taken into account.

Table 2

Fuel Mix: Installed Capacity and Generation in the BAU Scenario

Year		Fuel mix (%)				
		Thermal	Hydro	Nuclear	Renewables	Hydro (imports)
	Installed capacity (GW)					
1997	90	71.3	24.4	2.5	1.3	0.4
2020	292	70.1	13.8	4.5	6.4	5.3
	Generation (TWh)					
1997	426	79.0	17.5	2.4	0.8	0.3
2020	1550	81.2	7.7	4.5	3.2	3.5

Table 3

Demand for Fossil Fuels for Power Generation in the BAU Scenario

Year	Coal (million tonnes)		Oil	Gas
	Domestic	Imported	(million tonnes)	(billion cubic metres)
1997	230	0	3	8
2020	375	147	15	27

There are several concerns if we consider the BAU (business-as-usual) scenario. These are:

- High level of electricity intensity is unsustainable as countries with per capita income comparable to that projected for India have achieved lower electricity intensity levels.
- T&D losses, assumed to decrease, are still high in comparison with those in the developed countries. These losses, both commercial and technical, result in poor cost recovery and unproductive energy generation.
- Poor financial performance hinders the sector's ability to import such cleaner alternatives as hydro and natural gas, which could be used for power generation. Despite its abundant potential in the region, imported hydropower meets a small fraction of the total demand while dependence on imported coal rises, which in turn results in further deterioration of environmental quality due to SPM (suspended particulate matter) and fly ash.

- Increase in the share of thermal energy and a drop in the share of hydropower will adversely affect the availability of peak power leading to grid imbalance, which will be more acute in the eastern and western regions where the share of hydropower is limited.
- Despite their abundance, renewable energy sources account for only three per cent of the generation requirement.

These concerns in the BAU scenario obviously call for a look at new directions, innovations, and strategies that might lead to a sustainable alternative. These are discussed as follows (see Annex 4 for various assumptions).

Directions, Innovations and Strategies

Short-term Strategies

Renovation and Modernization (R&M) of Power Plants

R&M can, in certain cases, effectively increase a power plant's capacity at one-fourth the cost of new generation. This, in turn, reduces the emissions of pollutants and GHGs (greenhouse gases) apart from increasing capacity and reducing fuel consumption. While promotion schemes may be needed today, these could be phased out once competition in generation is introduced.

T&D Improvement

The present T&D losses need to be reduced to about eight per cent. There is a need to establish norms and use performance-based regulation to induce T&D companies to make the required investments.

National Grid

A national grid system will reduce the current imbalance in power generation and consumption between regions and promote optimal use of power resources by facilitating inter-regional exchange of surplus energy, both seasonal and off-peak. The Centre's plan of developing a national grid system should be expedited using the regulatory bodies to evolve suitable incentives.

Cleaner and More Efficient Generation Technologies

Technological change will be driven by environmental factors, which, in turn, would reduce capital and operating costs and resource intensities. In the long run, competition driving the development and use of a more diverse set of energy resources and supply chains, with competitive pressure on prices, will usher in state-of-the-art technologies. In the short run, research priorities should focus on the commercialization of clean-coal technologies, coal being the major energy resource in India with the potential of providing long-term security of supply.

Medium-term Strategies

Renewable Energy

Renewable sources of energy have immense potential, particularly as decentralized energy sources in remote rural or hilly areas, where extension of the grid may not be economically viable. Market reforms will enable renewables to compete with conventional energy. Economic pricing that reflects the true opportunity costs of resources will correct the bias towards conventional sources. In the short term, it will be necessary to provide financial incentives such as subsidies/ cross-subsidies. Subsidies should be determined by market-based competitive bidding, which will provide an in-built mechanism for restricting subsidies and offer incentives to producers to continually improve generation efficiency. Strategies will include incentives for RD&D (research, development and demonstration) of RETs (renewable energy technologies), market development, and mandatory procurement of a prescribed minimum of renewable energy in each state determined by the regulators.

Cogeneration

Cogeneration, with 70 per cent–90 per cent efficiency of energy utilization (as opposed to 35 per cent in a conventional power generating system), saves fuel and reduces fuel gas emissions in India. Cogeneration potential in India exceeding 20,000 MW could be significant in bridging the supply–demand gap. It would also be economically competitive. Bagasse-based cogeneration of electricity is already competitive. Appropriate institutional arrangements for purchasing such electricity are required, besides increasing awareness amongst other industries of the potential of cogeneration.

Hydropower

The public sector would play a dominant role in hydropower development in the foreseeable future. Capacity building in the public sector along with expediting the implementation of the National Hydro Policy, 1998 (which includes such incentives as time-of-the-day pricing) is, therefore, urgent. Pumped storage potential can also be used where found economical. Issues related to land acquisition, resettlement, and rehabilitation of people should receive high priority and compensation packages should be designed in consultation with affected people at the project investigation stage. This would help in speedier completion of such projects and also promote equity.

Public Sector Management

Organization and management of the public sector need to be improved in keeping with its significant role in hydro and nuclear power as well as in transmission in the future.

Long-term Strategies

Structure of the Industry

- Opening the power sector will improve its viability, arrest the inefficient generation and use of power, and encourage the use of non-conventional energy by correcting the underpricing of conventional sources.
- Efficiency gains need to be achieved by creating conditions for markets to function efficiently.
- Competition will have to be introduced in phases since immediate opening up of retail markets to competition will not be possible given the short supply of power and weak social security systems.

Imports

- The hydro potential of Bhutan and Nepal needs to be developed further to enhance import of hydropower.
- Imports of cleaner fuels need to be promoted. Import of coal, especially for blending with domestic coal, will reduce the ash content of coal used in power generation. Import of natural

gas should be considered on environmental grounds and also because gas-based generation is competitive with other fuels, especially at sites far from coal-bearing areas. (Iran and Central Asian countries to the west and Bangladesh and Myanmar to the east of India are rich in gas resources).

- Diversifying the import-mix will spread the risk of price increase in imported fuels.

Thus, a greater emphasis on regional economic cooperation is called for. India also needs to participate actively in the development of the SAARC grid. This requires restoration of financial viability of the power sector in India and in some other countries of the region.

Measures to Control Pollution

- Given the share of coal-based power, it is necessary to encourage and ensure reduction of emissions through superior technology at the process (FBC [fluidized bed combustion], IGCC [integrated gasification combined cycle], and CFBC [circulating fluidized bed combustion]) and end-of-the-pipe level (high-efficiency ESPs [electrostatic precipitators], flue gas desulphurization systems, DeNOx systems, and effluent treatment plants).
- Enforcement mechanisms need to be strengthened and such economic instruments as pollution charges employed to ensure compliance.
- Fly ash management requires fiscal, regulatory, and institutional measures for improving mining techniques, discouraging dumping, and encouraging its dry collection and utilization in cement, bricks, mine fills, etc. State governments in some cases have announced sales tax concessions on fly ash products (bricks and cement [Bhanumathidas and Kalidas 1998]). Orissa government has banned clay for brick manufacturing within 70 km of thermal power stations.
- Bioremediation for fly ash management needs to be promoted.

Emerging Sustainable Alternative Scenario

The following are the demand and impact states under a sustainable alternative scenario:

Demand

Efficiency improvements in various sectors through strategies outlined in Annex 1 could reduce power demand by over 7 per cent (Table 4). This, coupled with lower T&D losses, will reduce the generation requirement. Demand is met through the same set of fuels as in the BAU scenario but the relative shares of the fuels are different as necessitated by the unsustainable BAU scenario. The share of total thermal power (oil, gas, and coal) in generation would decrease from 81.2 per cent to 66.8 per cent with the share of gas increasing slightly, and that of coal and oil decreasing. The share of domestic coal would increase and that of imported coal significantly decrease (from 25.1 per cent to 5.7 per cent). The declining share of total thermal is compensated by increase in the share of hydro (from 7.7 per cent to 13.3 per cent), nuclear (from 4.5 per cent to 9.3 per cent), renewables (from 3.2 per cent to 5 per cent), and hydro imports (from 3.5 per cent to 5.6 per cent) (Table 5). In case of generation from renewables, the share of small hydro projects would increase and the share of biomass significantly decrease (Table 6).

Table 4

Sectoral Power Demand (TWh) Projections: the BAU versus Alternative Scenario (2020)

Scenario	*Industry*	*Transport*	*Agriculture*	*Commercial*	*Residential*	*Total*
BAU	570	22	202	262	165	1221
Alternative	510	45	181	235	163	1134

Table 5

Fuel Mix in Generation (TWh): the BAU versus Alternative Scenario

	Coal							
Scenario	*Domestic*	*Imported*	*Oil*	*Gas*	*Hydro*	*Nuclear*	*Renewables*	*Hydro imports*
1997	278	23	1	34	75	10	4	1
2020: BAU	638	389	70	162	119	70	49	54
	(41.2%)	(25.1%)	(4.5%)	(10.4%)	(7.7%)	(4.5%)	(3.2%)	(3.5%)
2020: Alternative	646	78	41	146	181	127	68	76
	(47.4%)	(5.7%)	(3%)	(10.7%)	(13.3%)	(9.3%)	(5%)	(5.6%)

Table 6

Generation from Renewables (TWh): the BAU versus Alternative Scenario

Scenario	*Wind*	*Solar*	*Small hydro*	*Biomass*
1997	2.9	0.00128	0.2	0.5
2020: BAU	20.9	4.6	5.9	18.0
	(42.4%)	(9.2%)	(12.0%)	(36.4%)
2020: Alternative	28.3	6.2	12.7	21.1
	(41.4%)	(9.0%)	(18.6%)	(30.9%)

Impact on Resources and Environment

Under the new scenario, demand for coal, oil, and gas is reduced (Table 7). Reduced generation requirement, improved fuel mix, superior generation technology, and more efficient equipment to control emission of pollutants (ESPs are assumed to operate at the designed efficiency of 99.5 per cent) will have a positive impact on the environment (Table 8).

Table 7

Fuel Demand: the BAU versus Alternative Scenario (2020)

	Coal (million tonnes)		*Oil*	*Gas*
Scenario	*Domestic*	*Imported*	*(million tonnes)*	*(billion cubic metres)*
BAU	375	147	15	27
Alternative	359	30	8	24

Table 8

Emissions (million tonnes) of Pollutants: the BAU versus Alternative Scenario (2020)

Scenario	*SPM*	*NOx*	*SO_2*
BAU	6.1	3.3	3.4
Alternative	0.4	2.0	2.4

COAL

Coal being the primary source of commercial energy in India, meets about 56 per cent of industrial energy requirements. Table 9 gives the data for the coal reserves in India by category and by depth. With current mining technologies, reserves up to a depth of 300 metre are being successfully exploited. However, the exploitation of reserves for depth range 300 to 600 metre needs to be stabilized. Exploitation of reserves beyond 600 metre depth does not appear feasible.

Table 9

Coal Reserves (billion tonnes): 2001

Depth (metre)	*Proved*	*Indicated*	*Inferred*	*Total*
< 600	82.74	89.41	33.85	206.01
600–1200	1.67	9.13	4.17	14.97
Grand total	**84.41**	**98.54**	**38.02**	**220.98**
Coking	16.39	12.90	1.25	30.54
Non-coking	67.61	85.57	36.37	189.55
Tertiary	0.41	0.08	0.40	0.89
Total	**84.41**	**98.55**	**38.02**	**220.98**

	Proved reserves	*Net proved reserves*[a]	*Net recoverable reserves*[b]
Coking	14.0	12.1	4.4
Non-coking	53.0	41.7	27.9
Total	**67.0**	**55.8**	**26.3**

Note: Net proved and recoverable reserves (billion tonne) up to a depth of 600 metre was estimated by Committee on Integrated Coal Policy 1996, at total reserves of 200 billion tonne in 1995 (latest study).

a: Net proved reserves are estimated after accounting for depleted reserves.

b: Net recoverable reserves are estimated based on depth, technology, surface features, etc.

Coal production increased from about 35 million tonnes in 1951 to 310 million tonnes in 2000/2001: an annual average growth rate of 4.46 per cent. After nationalization of coal mines, enhanced investment, increased share from opencast mining, increased emoluments and welfare amenities for coal workers, etc. resulted in large increases in production. The share of inferior-grade non-coking coal in the production mix has increased significantly, whereas that of superior grade non-coking coal, which was 80 per cent in 1980, declined to 40 per cent by 1997-98.

The power sector is the largest consumer, followed by the industrial sector—the major consumers being steel, cement, and brick-manufacturing units. Due to the limited availability of indigenous coking coal and its deteriorating quality, low-ash coking coal is imported for blending with indigenous coal and used in integrated steel plants. Imports of coking coal have been rising continuously over the last 15 years, and stood at more than 10 million tonnes in 1999-2000. The imports of non-coking coal have been marginal but, due to poor quality of indigenous coal supplies and with lowering of import duty, cement manufacturers, some other industries, and power plants along the southern and western coasts, now import about 15 million tonnes of coal annually.

The concerns in the coal sector are as follows:

- Requirement of adequate funds to develop the production capacity to meet future requirements. This would require private sector participation.
- Need to step up exploration investments.
- Inefficiency and the absence of a competitive market due to the present pricing regime and existing structure of the coal industry.
- High production costs due to low levels of technology in underground mines, surplus staff, and low productivity. Opencast operations have not kept pace with modern technologies except in a few mines. In some cases, opencast operations extend beyond an economical depth, increasing production cost.
- Increase in price of coal due to increase in royalty and other charges at pithead and rail freight resulting in domestic coal facing stiff competition from imported coal and other fuels, which are relatively more environment-friendly.
- Coal quality has resulted in the steel and cement sectors increasing the share of imported coal and other industries, e.g. glass, ceramics, and refractories, shifting to other fuels. The power sector plans to increase imports especially in areas far from the coalfields.

- Rehabilitation of land degraded due to subsidence, excavated pits, overburdens, and spoil dumps or fire has not been satisfactory in almost all the coal mining areas.
- Land acquisition is a major issue in new projects.
- Impacts on land, water, air, and forest resources—a few coal mining areas have already been identified as critically polluted.

Business-as-usual Scenario

Considering the business-as-usual scenario, the demand of coal for power generation and other industries is given in Table 10. This demand cannot be fully met from indigenous production due to inadequacy of proved coal reserves and environmental and social impacts. Continuing exploration will result in some of the reserves under 'indicated' and 'inferred' categories moving to the 'proved' category which will be available for projectization. Production from many of the existing mines will decline. Assuming accretion to proved reserves in the future, the production in 2020 will be 450 million tonnes. This would imply large quantities of imports to meet the projected demand. Moreover, such demand will lead to significant impacts on land, forest, air, and water resources. Besides, the acquisition of land for mining will displace many. People who live around coal mines are affected by the mining in different ways and to varying degrees. Those who lose their land and other productive assets on which their livelihoods depend, such as owners, tenants, and farm labour, may experience a decline in their standard of living.

Table 10

Projected Demand (million tonnes) for Coal: the BAU Scenario

Year	*Power sector*	*Industries*	*Brick and other end-users*	*Total*
1997	230	53	28	311
2020	522	108	58	688

Note: The demand for other industries is based on the projected production of steel or hot metal and cement. The demand for brick manufacture and other end-uses is based on current trends and efficiency improvements in coal consumption.

The BAU scenario, however, raises the following concerns:

- Environmental and social impacts of mining are deterrents to large-scale increase in production. Land acquisition would require an acceptable rehabilitation/resettlement package.
- Substantial investments to develop coal resources would require private sector participation (difficult under the present policy regime) due to declining budgetary support from the government and the inability of the companies to raise adequate financial resources internally.
- Movement of such large quantities of coal is not feasible with the already saturated rail network (both passenger and freight traffic) experiencing low levels of investments in capacity addition.

Directions, Innovations and Strategies

In order to address the above concerns, the coal industry must commit to the following while meeting the future demand:

- Enhanced exploration.
- Adoption of best practices to improve coal quality, productivity, and safety and to protect the environment.
- Adoption of environment-friendly technologies including coal gasification, beneficiation, and liquefaction for value addition to domestic coal.
- More efficient use of energy.
- Environmental protection including rehabilitation of affected land and preservation of biological diversity.
- An acceptable rehabilitation and resettlement policy for displaced people.

These can be achieved through suitable legislation and policy, technology, and fiscal measures, as indicated below.

Short-term Strategies

Legislative and Policy Measures

The following initiatives should be adopted.

- Promoting private sector investment for growth of the industry.

- Opening up exploration to the private sector as being practised for other minerals.
- Retention of Coal India's current structure and ownership is incompatible with complete liberalization of the sector.
- Greater autonomy to subsidiary coal companies, options being (a) privatization of individual subsidiary companies or parts of their operation (loss-making companies need a different approach) and (b) partial divestments to create public–private sector partnerships.
- Closing down of uneconomic mines and reduction in surplus manpower.
- Ban on mining in ecologically fragile or sensitive areas rich in biodiversity.

Technology

The following initiatives should be undertaken:

- Adoption of modern technologies in mining operations for increased safety, production, and productivity—in-pit crushers, surface miners for opencast mines, and continuous miners for underground mines and coal-handling plants.
- Beneficiation of coal produced from opencast to improve and maintain consistent quality.

Fiscal Measures

Application of market-based instruments and other fiscal measures to promote eco-friendly technologies in mining operations, utilization of washery rejects for power generation at the pithead, efficient use of mine water by recycling, i.e. after treatment, and complete rehabilitation of affected land areas for economic benefits to the local community are urgently called for.

Medium-term Strategies

Legislative and Policy Measures

The following measures should be initiated:

- Improving rail and port infrastructure to augment the offtake from Korba, Ib Valley, Talcher, and North Karanpura coalfields.

- Planning the use of wasteland generated by mining. Some form of a reclamation trust fund or a performance guarantee bond should be established and this should be a prerequisite to the grant of a mining lease.
- Government owning the responsibility of rehabilitation of old abandoned mine sites. This could be financed by levying cess on coal production.
- Formulating mine closure policies. The government should publish detailed guidelines on decommissioning of mine sites and a programme to monitor compliance with those guidelines.
- Amendments in various labour laws including contract labour laws.

Long-term Strategies

Legislative and Policy Measures

- Formulation of a comprehensive rehabilitation and resettlement policy.

Technology

- Promotion of coal gasification and liquefaction technologies in anticipation of rising prices of oil in the international market. This will add value to domestic coal and is important from the viewpoint of energy security. A research programme could be initiated to establish the feasibility and techno-economic viability of gasification of large reserves of superior grade non-coking coal in Raniganj coalfield.
- Exploitation of coalbed methane reserves. A programme has been taken up to establish the potential and also the technical feasibility in Jharia and Raniganj coalfields.

Emerging Sustainable Alternative Scenario

The demand for coal (Table 11) under the alternative scenario could be reduced because of the following measures (see Annex 1 and 'Power industry' section):

- Substitution of coal by natural gas or LNG (Liquefied Natural Gas) for electricity generation.

- Adoption of cleaner and more efficient technologies in electricity generation—coal-based integrated gasification combined cycle, and super critical technology.
- Substitution of domestic coal (which is both more expensive and of poor quality) in the steel and cement industries by imported coal to the extent of 50 per cent.

Table 11

Projected Demand (million tonnes) for Coal: the BAU and Alternative Scenario (2020)

Scenario	*Domestic coal*	*Power sector Imported coal*	*Total*	*Industries /steel/cement Domestic coal*	*Brick-making and other end -uses*	*Grand total*
BAU	375	147	522	108	58	688
Alternative	359	30	389	97	52	538

OIL AND GAS

India has a prognosticated hydrocarbon resource base of 21 billion tonnes with an additional 9 billion tonnes from deep-water areas. However, only 6.8 billion tonnes of geological reserves have been established through exploration, leaving two-thirds of the area unexplored. The balance recoverable reserves, as on 1 April 2000, stood at 658 million tonnes of oil and 628 BCM (billion cubic metres) of gas (MoPNG 2000).

Crude

Domestic availability of crude has not kept pace with demand (Figure 2). Imports of crude have resulted in a substantial drain on our reserves of foreign exchange, necessitating increased domestic exploration. To boost domestic oil and gas production, the Government announced the NELP (New Exploration and Licensing Policy) in 1997, offering blocks on attractive terms to operators. Two biding rounds have been conducted under the NELP framework, with 25 blocks being awarded under the first round and 23 under the second round. Altogether, the second round would witness investments to the tune of 780 million dollars in three phases, with the first phase investments at 290 million dollars. The Government plans to offer the third round of NELP by the end of the current fiscal year.

Figure 2

Availability (million tonnes) of Crude

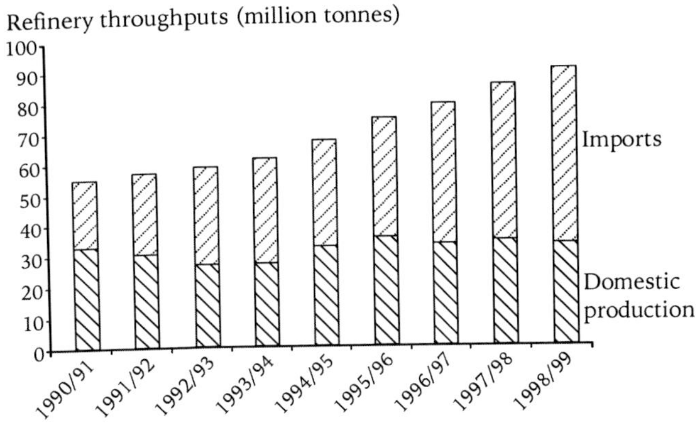

Source: Ministry of Petroleum and Natural Gas (MoPNG) web site <http://petroleum.nic.in>

Petroleum Products

The total consumption of petroleum products in 1999/2000 stood at 96.29 million tonnes. Sales by national oil companies accounted for 94 per cent of the total sales, the rest being accounted for by private parties. High-speed diesel sales accounted for about 42 per cent of the volume, followed by fuel oil (12 per cent), SKO (11 per cent), naphtha (8 per cent), LPG and motor spirit (6 per cent each), and aviation turbine fuel (2 per cent).

The 6 per cent growth rate in demand for petroleum products over the last decade was arrested in 2000/2001. Aggregate PSU (public sector unit) sales for 2000/2001 at 90.2 million tonnes were marginally lower by 0.5 per cent than those in the preceding year. In the retail trade category, only motor spirit witnessed a growth with demand increasing by 12 per cent over the preceding year, while SKO consumption came down by 0.4 per cent and high-speed diesel by 2.7 per cent. The slowdown in demand is attributed to factors ranging from a fall in agricultural demand to a continuing economic slowdown.

Natural Gas

Gas production was 28.4 BCM in 1999/2000. The three main gas producing basins—the Western offshore region, the Cambay basin in Gujarat, and Upper Assam region—are in the mature phase of exploration. As per the projections of the Sub-Group on Utilisation of Natural Gas constituted under the Hydrocarbon Vision 2025, domestic gas availability is expected to decline to about 16 BCM by 2011/2012.

On the other hand, the demand for natural gas has been growing rapidly with gas sales increasing at 7.2 per cent annually over the last decade. The demand for gas accrues from preference of gas in power generation and fertilizer production. Gas sales[1] in 1999/2000 aggregated 23.8 BCM. Non-energy sector accounted for 45 per cent of off-take of natural gas, power 38 per cent, industry 11 per cent, captive use/LPG shrinkage 4 per cent, and agriculture and domestic sectors 1 per cent each (MoPNG 2000). With domestic gas production expected to decline, rising gas demand would have to be met largely from imported gas.

Oil: Business-as-Usual Scenario

Demand

Despite the current slowdown in consumption of petroleum products, long-term forecasts retain a 5 per cent growth rate. The demand for oil (Table 12), which extrapolates present trends and practices, reveals that the transport sector continues to drive the demand. Oil demand for non-energy uses, e.g., feedstock, industrial consumables (greases, waxes, lubricants, etc.), and bituminous carpeting, and by industries is also high.

Table 12

Projected Oil Demand (million tonnes) by Sector: the BAU Scenario

Year	*Industries*	*Non-energy*	*Transport*	*Agriculture*	*Commercial*	*Domestic*	*Power*	*Total*
1997	12	13	39	1	2	14	3	83
2020	42	40	105	2	15	26	15	245

1. Production net of flaring and offtakes by ONGC.

Supply

Domestic crude production is expected to fall short of the target as revealed by the mid-term review of the Ninth Five-Year Plan. Increase in domestic refining capacity has resulted in increased crude imports: 80 million tonnes are expected in 2001/2002. The Group on India Hydrocarbon Vision 2025 has developed a long-term strategy for the development of the hydrocarbons sector. Its recommendations for enhancing domestic output include (1) 100 per cent exploration coverage of Indian sedimentary basins by 2025, (2) extensive exploration in frontier and deep-water areas, (3) offering attractive fiscal terms, and (4) acquisition of acreages abroad for exploration and production. The subgroup on long-term external policy for the hydrocarbons sector including oil security estimated that domestic crude production could rise to 50 million tonnes by 2010 and to 80 million tonnes by 2020, implying that the bulk of incremental demand would need to be met through imports (Table 13).

Table 13

Projected Demand and Supply (million tonnes) of Crude Oil: the BAU Scenario

Year	*Demand*	*Refinery throughput*	*Domestic production*	*Imports*
1997	83	69	34	35
2020	245	258	80	178

Note: Assumption: refinery fuel and loss at 5 per cent and no product imports.

Concern: Oil Security

Oil security is an important issue. Since the bulk of India's oil imports are from the Middle East and are likely to remain so, India will be vulnerable to any supply disruptions arising from political instability in the region.

Natural Gas: Business-as-usual Scenario

Demand

Power generation and fertilizer production account for the bulk of gas demand. In addition, industrial gas use, excluding gas used as feedstock for fertilizers, has been increasing rapidly over the last decade, registering an annual growth rate of over 20 per cent. Even after moderating estimates of industrial gas requirements for the forecast period, gas use by industries would account for a significant portion of the total gas demand. Table 14 gives sectoral gas demand projections.

Table 14

Projected Demand of Gas (billion cubic metres) by Sector: the BAU Scenario

Year	Industries	Non-energy	Transport	Domestic	Power	Total
1997	3.7	9.4	0.1	0.2	8.1	21.5
2020	20.8	21.8	0.5	0.6	27.1	70.8

Supply

Gas availability has to be analysed in the context of both domestic gas production and gas imports through pipelines or LNG terminals.

Domestic Sources

Natural Gas

Production of domestic gas, based on the estimates of the subgroup on the development and utilization of natural gas under the Hydrocarbon Vision 2025 group, is estimated at 14 BCM by 2020. These are conservative estimates based on the rate at which existing fields are being depleted and assume that no new discoveries are made. The projected import requirements will, however, change, depending on the discovery and exploitation of new gas fields.

Coal-bed Methane

Considerable headway has been made with regards to exploitation of CBM (coal-bed methane) resources. A conservative estimate places reserves at about 850 BCM, with the Gondwana basin accounting for 837 BCM and the tertiary basins, 13 BCM. Seven CBM blocks were put on offer in April 2001—two in Jharkhand (Bokaro and North Karanpura), three in Madhya Pradesh (East and West Sohagpur and Satpura), one each in Rajasthan (Barmer) and West Bengal (Raniganj). Exploitation of these would be structured on a revised model contract, which is a modified version of the NELP. Unlike the traditional profit-sharing contract, these blocks are being offered under a production-linked programme. Estimated 'in place' reserves of these blocks are about 478 BCM.

The exploration programme, as charted by the Directorate General of Hydrocarbons, envisages a minimum of eight years for exploration, pilot assessment, and market confirmation (DGH 1999), followed by a development phase of five years. Preliminary estimates indicate a production potential of 17 BCM from the blocks on offer. Even if a fourth of this potential is realized by 2020, domestic CBM production could be expected to be about 4.4 BCM.

Gas Hydrates

Production of gas from hydrate-sealed traps is somewhat sustainable as the reduction of pressure caused by production can initiate a breakdown of hydrates and a recharging of the trap with gas. However, unlike CBM, gas production from hydrates is not a commercially proven technology as yet and, given the very preliminary stage of efforts, gas production from hydrates has been excluded from possible supply sources in this analysis.

Gas Imports

Pipelines

Imports are likely to fructify from (1) an eastern route from Bangladesh and (2) a western route from Iran. Unocal is keen on exporting gas from the Bibiyana gas field (estimated reserves of 170 BCM) in Bangladesh to India. The company plans to develop a 0.5-billion-cubic-feet-per-day (5-BCM-a-year) pipeline from Bangladesh, traversing West Bengal, Bihar, and Uttar Pradesh, to link up with the existing HBJ trunk pipeline system.

On the west coast, gas imports are being envisaged from the South Pars field in Iran, via Pakistan. The Indian government has held several rounds of negotiations with the National Iranian Oil Company. Both offshore and onshore routes are under consideration, though Iran and Pakistan are both in favour of the latter, as the offshore option could turn out to be considerably more expensive than the 2 billion-cubic-feet-per-day (20 BCM-a-year), 4.5 billion dollars onshore route. The Indian government had reservations about the onland route based on the perceptions of problems with security of supplies. However, the Indian stand appears to be more open now. Accordingly, feasibility studies have been initiated for both the onshore and offshore routes. NIOC (National Iranian Oil Company) has engaged Australia's BHP to conduct a feasibility study for the onshore route, while the feasibility of the offshore route is to be analysed by Snamprogetti of Italy.

Although, there are uncertainties regarding these projects at present, it is expected that these pipelines would be operational by 2020.

Terminals for LNG

While a number of LNG terminals have been proposed along India's coastline, only a couple of them are at relatively advanced stages of development. Promoters are currently facing problems on account of the long-term take-or-pay agreements required for LNG supply. SEBs, the likely anchor load customers, are in poor financial health. Many states have initiated reforms in the power sector and it is expected that by 2020 current problems would be overcome. However, actual materialization of capacity will be demand-driven.

Concerns

Table 15 summarizes the demand and supply for gas. Against a potential LNG import capacity of 62 BCM (43 million tonnes a year) by 2020, imports of only 25 BCM (20 million tonnes a year) are required. However, if the pipelines from Iran and Bangladesh do not materialize, LNG import requirement will rise to 52 BCM (38 million tonnes a year) by 2020.

Directions and Strategies

Oil security is likely to be a major issue given that India's reliance on the Gulf for imports is expected to increase. The increasing traffic through the straits of Hormuz also makes the supplies vulnerable to any disruption due to political instability of the region. While oil imports are likely to be concentrated from the Middle East, gas can be sourced from many countries across the world, e.g., Australia, Indonesia, Malaysia and Bangladesh.

Table 15

Demand and Supply for Gas (billion cubic metres): the BAU Scenario

Year	Demand	Domestic sources		Supply		Imports	
		Natural gas	CBM	Total	Required	By pipelines	As LNG
1997	21.5	21.5		21.5	—	—	—
2020	70.8	14.1	4.4	18.5	52.3	25.3	27.0 (19.8 million tonnes)

In the long term, therefore, the fuel mix of the country should be restructured to reflect a larger share of gas and other alternative energy sources *vis-à-vis* oil, while, at the same time, increasing domestic production of oil and gas and facilitating demand management through appropriate policies. The following are the suggested strategies:

Short-term Strategies

- Establish a regulatory framework to enthuse investors.
- Ensure commitment to ongoing reforms.
- Invite exploration bids on more attractive fiscal terms.
- Correct demand imbalances through rational product prices.
- Search for equity oil abroad/gas imports.

Medium-term Strategies

- Sustain production levels through enhanced oil recovery schemes.
- Launch a focused foreign policy and diplomatic initiatives to build equity oil base.

Long-term Strategies

- Complete basin analysis for sedimentary basins (which could be funded by the Oil Industry Development Board).
- Encourage indigenous R&D in the exploration of CBM and gas hydrates.

Emerging Sustainable Alternative Scenario

Demand

Based on the assumptions (see Annex 5), the demand for oil and gas under the alternative scenario is presented in Table 16.

Table 16

Projected Demand for Oil (million tonnes) and Gas (billion cubic metres) by Sector in the Base Case and the Alternative Case

Year	Scenario	Industries	Non-Energy	Transport	Agricultural	Commercial	Domestic	Power	Total
Oil									
1997	BAU	12	13	39	1	2	14	3	83
2020	BAU	42	40	105	2	15	26	15	245
	Alternative	38	36	72	2	13	25	8	195
Gas									
1997	BAU	3.7	9.4	0.1	—	—	0.2	8.1	21.5
2020	BAU	20.8	21.8	0.5	—	—	0.6	27	70.8
	Alternative	18.6	20.4	0.9	—	—	0.5	24.3	64.7

Environmental Impact

The alternative scenario is environmentally more benign. The reduction in oil demand for transport together with a higher penetration of cleaner technologies, e.g., ULSD (ultra-low-sulphur diesel) or CNG (compressed natural gas), battery-operated vehicles, and four-stroke engines, and a shift from road to rail transport will reduce the emissions of SPM from the transport sector. Such reductions will improve the air quality in cities that have witnessed rapidly rising numbers of motorized vehicles.

RENEWABLE ENERGY

Development and implementation of ecologically safe, risk-free, and renewable sources of energy would help reshape the energy industry and infrastructure. Greater reliance on renewable energy sources has enormous economic, social, and environmental benefits for India. India became the fifth country in wind power utilization in the last decade, with more than 95 per cent investment by the private sector. Other renewable energy technologies, e.g. solar photovoltaic, solar thermal, and small hydro, also picked up pace. Though government policies have established an investment framework for the propagation of renewable energy, it still faces many barriers—technology availability and performance, consumer decision-making, market organization, financing, taxes, energy policy, and regulatory issues. Some of these will shrink as technologies gain acceptance and market share and others are likely to persist unless they are lowered through further policy interventions.

Business-as-usual and Alternative Scenarios

Renewable energy sources have large-scale potential applications in the domestic sector and the power industry. Projections of the extent of spread of these technologies are provided in Table 17.

Table 17

The Spread of Renewable Energy: the BAU and Alternative Scenarios

Year	*Scenario (million)*	*Biogas plants (solar home system + lantern) (million)**	*Solar photovoltaic heating system Collector area* (million square metres)*	*Domestic sector Solar water*	*Power industry (TWh)*			
					Wind	*Solar hydro*	*Small*	*Biomass*
1997	BAU	2.5	0.2	0.123	2.9	0.00128	0.2	0.5
2020	BAU	3.9	2.01	1.101	20.9	4.6	5.9	18.0
	Alternative	5.7	3.60	3.062	28.3	6.2	12.7	21.1

* BAU scenario assumption: increase of 80,000 systems per year; Alternate scenario assumption: enhancement in the increase by 5 per cent. This cannot be altered much, as the current market for solar home systems is estimated to a maximum of 4.5 million units (18,000 villages and 100 household per village, and one to two systems per household); although the resource changes by changing the 18,000 villages and household number estimation.

The projections are achievable from the resource point of view, but would require a proper institutional and policy framework aided by adequate infrastructure, namely power evacuation and manufacturing capability.

Directions, Innovations and Strategies

The following are the policy interventions required in this regard:

- Policies should be integrated into market transformation strategies, addressing the needs for both 'technology push' and 'demand pull'. Moreover, policies should evolve over time as some barriers are overcome and others become more prominent.
- Successful market transformation requires national policies and programmes which in turn depend on the participation of state and local authorities, and action at the regional and local levels.
- International agencies such as the Global Environment Facility and other multilateral agencies can play a key role in financing national efforts as well as in supporting capacity and institution-building. International cooperation should be expanded whereever appropriate.
- The private sector should be involved in policy development since it plays a key role in its implementation. Policy-makers can work with companies that are actively developing, producing, or investing in high-efficiency renewable source of energy to develop and implement progressive policies and programmes that will lead to a more sustainable energy future.

A summary of the proposed interventions is given in Table 18.

AIR

The major sources of air pollution are motor vehicles, industries, thermal power plants, and domestic fuels. It would be useful to study the impact of the sectors on the air quality and then consider strategies that would lead to an alternative scenario with better air quality.

Business-as-usual Scenario

Domestic and Commercial Sectors

Fuel combustion from domestic sources is a major source of indoor air pollution with about three-quarters of all Indian households using unprocessed biomass as the primary fuel, mostly for cooking (Census of India 1991). Emissions from traditional fuels

Table 18

Directions, Innovations and Strategies for Renewable Energy

Directions	*Innovations and strategies*	*Action by*	*Time frame*
Grid-connected renewable energy technologies			
Increase the share of renewable energy sources	Minimum procurement legislation (certain minimum quantity of electricity to beprocured through renewables)	Central and state governments	Short term
Improve performance	Introduction of performance-linked incentives Frameworks for large-sized projects State-of-the-art power evacuation network	Central and state governments Central and state electricity regulators Private sector	Short term
Reduce capital cost	Propagation of indigenous R&D Private sector	Central and state governments medium term	Short to
Promote new technologies, e.g. solar, thermal	Policy framework demonstration projects research, development, and demonstration of selected technologies	Central and state governments	Short term
Off-grid and decentralized renewable energy technologies			
Increase the share of solar water-heating systems	Building by-laws	Central and state governments	Short term
Ensure availability of credit	Energy services companies Micro-credit facilities	Central, state, and local governments NGOs, private sector	Short term
Develop maintenance infrastructure	Entrepreneurship development	Central, state, and local governments NGOs, private sector	Short term
Reduce capital cost	Indigenization of R&D and product development	Central and state governments	Short term
Promote new technologies, e.g. solar pond	Policy framework demonstration projects research, development, and demonstration of selected technologies	Central and state governments	Short term

in the residential sector are estimated under the BAU scenario (Table 19). Urbanization and economic development will result in a shift towards cleaner gaseous fuel, and emissions from the residential sector will decrease. However, due to their significant health impacts, adequate measures need to be taken to reduce indoor air pollution.

Transport Sector

Transport is the major source of air pollution in many cities with road transport being the predominant source. The critical issues of this sector include increasing number of vehicles (annual growth of 10 per cent or more), outdated engine technology and old vehicles, fuel quality, and inadequate traffic planning. Emissions of major pollutants are estimated for urban areas under the BAU scenario (Table 19) based on the projections of the number of vehicles, which considered the population growth and economic development.

Manufacturing Industry

Air pollution in terms of SPM loads has been analysed for some of the resource-intensive and highly polluting industries: copper, aluminium, steel, cement, fertilizers, textiles, and PVC (poly vinyl chloride) (Table 19). Emission loads have been worked out on the basis of emission load per unit of output from these industries (WHO 1993). The extent of installed pollution control systems in these industries has been estimated by the CPCB on the basis of regular surveys (CPCB 1996). In the BAU scenario, it is assumed that due to strict environmental regulations, all industrial units would have installed adequate pollution control devices. The critical issues of this industry include low efficiency of resource use, fuel quality, and lacunae in environmental governance (which is overly dependent on command-and-control type of environmental management).

Power Industry

Thermal generation contributes substantially to the total emission load and since bulk of the thermal power generation is coal- and gas-based, projections are based on these two categories (Table 19). The critical issues in this sector include process technology, fuel quality (with coal-based power generation having severe adverse impacts due to 30 per cent–45 per cent ash content and nuclear power generation associated with issues of radiation and disposal of radioactive wastes), and pollution control measures (with some of the older thermal power plants using such low-efficiency control devices as mechanical dust collectors and those with electrostatic precipitators having operational problems leading to overall reduction in efficiency).

Table 19

Estimated Emissions (million tonnes) from Various Sectors

Year	*Sector*	*Carbon monoxide*	*Hydro-carbons*	*Oxides of nitrogen*	*Suspended particulate matter*	*Sulphur dioxide*
1997	Domestic and	7.08			1.00	
2020	commercial	5.19			0.7	
1997	Transport	4.25	0.02	0.18	0.03	0.04
2020		17.13	0.07	0.57	0.09	0.13
1997	Manufacturing				0.98	
2020					1.93	
1997	Power			1.73	11.92	1.34
2020				3.27	6.1	3.44

Note: For the power industry, BAU scenario: all coal-based power plants would have installed ESPs (electrostatic precipitators) to limit SPM emissions; emissions from the transport sector include urban passenger transport only; emissions from the manufacturing industries sector comprise suspended particulate matter from seven industrial sectors.

Directions and Strategies by Sector

Domestic and Commercial Sectors

Short- and Medium-term Strategies

Improved Ventilation of Kitchens

Although new rural housing units can be designed to ensure better ventilation, this may not be feasible in small and crowded areas, especially in urban slums where it becomes important to promote awareness of the dangers related to indoor air pollution so that people may try to adopt ways of minimizing exposure through better kitchen management and infant protection.

Improved Stoves

Improved stoves reduce indoor air pollution by burning less fuel and providing better ventilation due to the chimneys in the improved design. The stoves are also inexpensive. User participation and improved design for higher efficiency and longer life will make them more popular.

Long-term Strategy

Cleaner Fuels: Moving up the Energy Ladder

Use of cleaner fuels, e.g. liquid or gaseous petroleum products (e.g. kerosene and LPG) and processed biomass fuels (e.g. biogas and producer gas), comprise effective long-term interventions. A faster transition from solid fuels to cleaner liquid or gaseous fuels requires appropriate policy interventions. A reliable, affordable, and secure supply of liquid and gaseous petroleum products is necessary to meet the cooking energy demands. Subsidies on kerosene are often misdirected and fail to reach the poor. Despite a preference for commercial fuels amongst households that can afford these, supply constraints often restrict their actual availability and use. Steps should, therefore, be taken to increase the availability of LPG and kerosene to meet the demand for cooking.

Transport Sector

Short-term Strategies

Controlling the Emissions from Each Vehicle

- Strict emission norms for new vehicles.
- Well-enforced I/M (inspection and maintenance) programme and phasing out or replacing old vehicles. This can be achieved through fiscal incentives or disincentives and government's dictates. Also, the new emission norms should be progressively tightened and their strict enforcement ensured.
- Improved fuel quality. The specifications for gasoline and diesel will have to be revised and perhaps brought in line with the European specifications. Studies carried out in the United States by the auto and oil industries indicate that low-sulphur fuel can reduce SO_2 and particle emissions (WHO 1993).
- Better infrastructure for the sale of such alternative fuels as CNG should be provided.

Fiscal Strategy

- Rationalization of fuel prices and removal of subsidies in kerosene

Short- and Medium-term Strategies

Controlling the Number of Vehicles on the Road

There is a need to curb the rate at which new vehicles are added to the fleet and to promote a shift towards the use of public transport. This may be achieved through adopting the following measures:

- Increased use of mass transit by making public transport better—extending its coverage, reducing waiting time and travel time, making the service more reliable, coordinating transfers, and making available park-and-ride facilities (short-term). The capacity of public transport can be augmented by leveraging private investment (medium-term).
- Disincentives for the use of private automobiles—increased parking charges, parking restrictions and area licensing, a surcharge on motor vehicles and fuels, and fuel rationing (medium- and long-term).
- Incentives for carpooling, commuter bus services (short-term).

Other Transport Management Measures

- Management measures—bans and restrictions, high-occupancy-vehicle lanes, clearing encroachments on roads, etc.
- Engineering measures—provision of cycle tracks, pedestrian walkways, proper maintenance of roads, etc.
- Control measures—traffic signal synchronization, appropriate signage, etc.

Manufacturing Industry

Short-term Strategies

- Mandatory efficiency standards for upcoming process industries will force new plants to adopt the latest technologies.
- Appropriate sites for industries—issues of suitable sites for industries need to be addressed, industries relocated, if

necessary, from non-conforming areas to conforming areas (short-term), and integrated regional environmental quality management plans that take into account the carrying capacity of the ecosystem developed and implemented (medium-term).

- Voluntary agreements on energy efficiency by industry associations on behalf of their members will also reduce consumption.

Short- and Medium-term Strategies

- Recycling and re-use of secondary materials.
- Mandatory energy labelling of equipment for promoting energy efficiency.
- Promotion of clean technology and waste minimization measures.
- Development and installation of appropriate pollution control devices for small-scale industries. Provision of fiscal incentives for pollution control measures.
- Strict enforcement of pollution control measures and effective implementation of environmental law—transparency in environmental management system and capacity-building in pollution control boards.
- Promotion of cogeneration.

Power Industry

The following strategies are suggested:

Short-term Strategies

- Adoption and proper functioning of end-of-the-pipe control options—high-efficiency ESPs and low NOx burners.
- Adoption of load-based standards for SO_2 and NOx.
- Strict enforcement of existing regulations.
- Supply of beneficiated coal to thermal power plants located beyond 1000 km from a pit-head as well as those located in urban, sensitive, or critically polluted areas.

Short- and Medium-term Strategy

- Promotion of renewable forms of energy including hydro.

Short- to Long-term Strategies

- Adoption of clean technology options at the process stage—clean-coal technologies.
- Shift to cleaner fuels such as natural gas.
- Provision of economic incentives—electricity pricing encourages such demand-side management options as using more efficient energy appliances. In the case of wind energy, the current investment-oriented incentives should gradually make way for generation-oriented incentives. Incentives should be provided for the management of fly ash. The success of market-based incentives as effective options in controlling emissions has been demonstrated in other countries, e.g. pollution charges for NOx emissions in Sweden and allowance trading for SO_2 emissions in USA.

Emerging Sustainable Alternative Scenario

The strategies and directions listed before will lead to a more sustainable alternative scenario, as indicated in Table 20.

Table 20

Estimated Emissions (million tonnes) from Various Sectors: Alternative Scenario (2020)

Sector	*Carbon monoxide*	*Hydro-carbons*	*Oxides of nitrogen*	*Suspended particulate matter*	*Sulphur dioxide*
Domestic and commercial	3.67			0.5	
Transport	9.6	0.04	0.37		0.070
Manufacturing				1.93	
Power			2.0	0.4	2.4

Note: Power industry: besides technological improvements resulting in efficient use of energy, more stringent steps would be taken to curtail environmental emissions.

Manufacturing industry: use of state-of-the-art pollution control equipment and compliance by all units with stricter emission norms.

Other Directions and Strategies

Besides the sectoral strategies discussed earlier, there are other directions and strategies that cut across sectors and deserve due consideration for the management of air quality. Some of these are as follows.

Short-term Strategies

Development and Maintenance of a Credible Database for Air Quality Management

- Air quality monitoring should be strengthened and data on air quality should be used to check compliance with standards, to inform the public, and to help policy-makers in formulating measures to control air pollution or to evaluate the measures that have already been implemented.
- Emissions inventories and dispersion models for identifying the sources, estimating the quantities of pollutants, and relating them to ambient pollutant concentrations need to be updated and refined. This would help to evaluate the impacts of changes in the characteristics of emission sources and of the strategies to control air pollution.

Capacity Building and Information Sharing

Training and education of the various stakeholders (industry, government agencies, local bodies, and the public) play an important role in combating pollution problems. Greater transparency in matters related to pollution control and sharing information with the public are also required.

Enforcement

There should be strict enforcement of legislation both in letter and spirit. Also, appropriate fiscal punitive measures should be imposed on defaulters.

Short- and Medium-term Strategies

Urban Planning with Focus on the Environment

Accelerated development of priority towns around big cities should be ensured for the dispersal of economic activities, industries, and immigrants. Regional development plans need to be developed and implemented that incorporate policies relating to population distribution, transport and communications, tax structure, physical and social infrastructure, regional land use, the environment, and eco-development. Integrated regional management plans for environmental quality that take into account the carrying capacity of the ecosystem are required.

Institutions and Regulations

The roles and responsibilities of each relevant institution should be clearly defined, loopholes covered, and strong institutional links established through effective communication.

Internalizing the Cost of Environmental Degradation

Internalizing the cost of environmental degradation in the production and service sectors will indicate to society the real cost of a product. By making it mandatory, the government would, in effect send a signal that it does not promote development that adversely effects the environment. The environmental costs included in the price of a product could then be used in improving not only air quality but also the overall quality of life.

Long-term strategy

Development and Maintenance of a Credible Database for Air Quality Management

An integrated study of air quality monitoring, exposure assessments, and epidemiological studies should be conducted to set more reliable air quality standards and suitable emission norms.

WATER

Sectoral Pressures

Agriculture

The agricultural sector accounts for over 95 per cent of the total water consumption. Subsidized/free supply of power and water has resulted in overexploitation and inefficient use. Inefficient use of canal water and groundwater accompanied by neglect of drainage has resulted in waterlogging and salinity. Other environmental problems of intensive agriculture that have emerged include degradation of soils and water from unbalanced and excessive use of chemical fertilizers and pesticides. Leaching of chemicals (particularly nitrates) from fertilizers affects the quality of public water supply and eutrophication causes excessive algal growth, which kills fish.

Domestic

The domestic sector accounts for about 4.2 per cent of the total consumption. However, in some 36 per cent of Indian cities, the daily per capita supply even now is less than 100 litres and in another 46 per cent that gets the basic supply of 135 litres, it is erratic or with inadequate pressure. The quality of water too has been deteriorating. Only 70 per cent of the population in Class 1 cities (those with a population of 100 000 or more) has access to basic sanitation services. Wastewater treatment efficiency, even in Class 1 cities, is only 30 per cent (CPCB 2000a). The remaining untreated sewage from the urban areas finds its way into water bodies, making the water unfit for drinking or even to use for bathing and, at the same time, affecting ecological health.

Manufacturing

The manufacturing sector accounts for 0.3 per cent of the total water demand but has generated significant and increasing quantity of wastewater—about 70 million litres a day in 1947 to 3000 million litres a day in 1997. About 45 per cent of the total pollutant load in the industry is derived from the processing of industrial chemicals. In 1997, there were 851 defaulting GPIs (grossly polluting industries) with pollutant discharge more than 100 kg of BOD (biological oxygen demand) a day along the rivers and lakes—228 have been closed and there are now 34 defaulters (CPCB 2000b).

Power

Water in the power sector is required for steam generation and disposal of fly ash. Due to the high ash content of Indian coal, along with the system of wet collection of fly ash, almost 45 per cent of the sector's water requirement is accounted for by slurry preparation. Wet collection also causes percolation of hazardous elements to groundwater from ash ponds.

Critical Issues

Availability Versus Use

Large variations in the availability of water result in some regions facing shortages. In 1991, per capita availability in the 20 basins was more than 1700 cubic metres in four, 1000–1700 in nine, 500 to 1000 in five, and less than 500 in two (Chitale 1992). Only 35 per cent of the total available run-off of 1952 BCM (billion cubic metres) is used (CWC 1993, CGWB 1995) due to lack of proper storage facilities and increasing public opposition to hydro projects. Transfer of water from across basins has not been adequately explored leading to poor utilization of available resources.

Furthermore, in the case of large- and medium-sized irrigation projects, the entire potential was used up to the mid-1950s; the figure dropped to 90 per cent in 1993/94 (CWC 1996). Moreover, government investments concentrate only on initiation of new projects and ensuring efficient exploitation of completed projects is accorded low priority.

Micro-level storage structures, e.g. on-farm storage through water harvesting, have not been developed fully. The share of tank irrigation in the net irrigated area, for instance, declined steadily from 20 per cent in 1958/59 to about 5 per cent in 1997.

Availability Versus Demand

A demand of 555 BCM against the availability of 1086 BCM indicates a state of surplus but uneven spatial as well as temporal distribution result in many regions facing water scarcity—for example the Western plains, the Kachchh region, and some pockets in the Northern Plains.

Overexploitation of Groundwater

The share of groundwater in urban and agricultural consumption has increased substantially (Saleth 1996). Severe shortage of water supplied for domestic purposes in urban areas has resulted in groundwater being drawn from boreholes. The share of groundwater in the net irrigated area has increased from a third in 1965/66 to over half at present to either supplement surface deliveries of water or to provide irrigation water when limited or no surface supplies are available. Groundwater overdraft beyond certain recharge capacities poses serious threats—a long-term decline in water levels, with associated adverse consequences such as land subsidence, deterioration of water quality in aquifers, and ingress of saline water in coastal aquifers.

Resource Degradation

Water quality of Indian rivers has degraded considerably due to inadequate collection and inefficient treatment of domestic wastewater in Class 1 cities and discharge of highly complex waste from industries. Groundwater sources too are undergoing severe degradation due to chemical contamination, mainly from fertilizers, industrial wastes, and municipal solid wastes as well as biological contamination, particularly in the form of human waste in dug wells.

Poor Conservation of Resource

Government policy has provided little incentive to encourage efficient use. Evapotranspiration losses are 42 per cent, and distribution losses of treated water 25 per cent–40 per cent. Wastage in irrigation occurs to the extent of 45 per cent by seepage through unlined channels and about 15 per cent due to excess application. Losses in storage are estimated at 15 per cent (MoWR 1999). Industrial output per unit of water withdrawal is only $5 per cubic metre as compared to $20, $25, and $32 for Argentina, Japan and Sweden, respectively (Chopra and Sen 1992). Even in the domestic sector, areas with high per capita water availability are known for poor water utilization. Poor water tariff structure also provides little incentives for conservation.

Water Pricing

The price for water use in different sectors is fixed by the state governments and varies from state to state. For agriculture and domestic consumption alike, recovery through water rates does not cover even the working expenses of providing the services. The subsidy regime has led to inadequate financial allocations to the sector (even for O&M). Inefficient service institutions, in turn, have led to poor and unreliable service, making the users dissatisfied and unwilling to pay. Large-scale and poorly targeted subsidies and incentives send wrong signals to the market, causing wasteful use of resources and suboptimal choices by consumers. Further, in the case of agriculture, water rates are not based on the quantities used, which offers little incentive for efficient use, apart from leading to inappropriate cropping pattern in some regions. High resource cost for industries, on the other hand, cross-subsidizes the water consumed in the domestic sector.

Inefficiency at the supply end is also a related issue. The cost of supply—capital and recurring—often reflects inefficiencies in generation and supply in the form of technology used, project design, over-capitalization, overstaffing, high administrative costs, and time and cost overruns. These translate into poor quality of service and, therefore, unwillingness to pay.

Institutional Set-up

Separate planning and implementation of surface water and groundwater development programmes, and for the various sectors using water, discourage unitary analysis of water and its use as a single resource, and results in duplication and ambiguity of functions. Thus, while the CPCB (Central Pollution Control Board) and the state pollution control boards focus on pollution from industrial and domestic sources, agricultural pollution tends to be overlooked. Central and state groundwater boards have their own separate observation wells for monitoring water tables but do not share the data among themselves, and doubt each others' databases.

Water being a state subject, the states are empowered to enact laws or frame policies, but only few have set up organizations for planning/allocating water for various purposes. The National Water Policy (1987/2002) had recommended the creation of multidisciplinary units in different states for water management and proposed participation of beneficiaries in water management and water price rationalization among others. The states are required to move in this direction.

Weaknesses in Current Legal Framework

Absence of appropriate laws, inadequate provisions in the existing legislative framework, and weaknesses in implementation of environmental laws, result in unsustainable use. Surface water is treated as state property leading to conflicts and litigation with individuals asserting that they lose their rights to the state when irrigation projects are developed. The legal framework on groundwater promotes neither equity nor sustainability by allowing landowners to withdraw water beneath their lands. Groundwater authorities attempt to regulate groundwater withdrawals through licensing but do not define any limits for withdrawals. Inadequacy of resources with the monitoring agencies leads to weak enforcement, especially in the small-scale sector.

Business-as-usual Scenario

The cumulative water requirement from different sectors in the BAU scenario is shown in Table 21 and water pollution in Table 22.

Table 21

Projected Total Water Demand (billion cubic metres): the BAU Scenario

Year	Irrigation	Urban	Domestic Rural	Total	Manufacturing	Power	Total
1997	528.85	13.62	9.89	23.52	1.60	1.39	555.36
2020	734.98	24.75	11.4	36.2	3.94	3.14	778.26

Note: Assumptions for estimating the demand

Agricultural sector: Cropping intensity increase up to 144 per cent and with 48 per cent of the gross cropped area under irrigation. Irrigation will continue to be the predominant end-use: its share will reduce marginally from 95.2 per cent in 1997 to 94.5 per cent in 2019.

Domestic sector: A per capita daily supply of 135 and 40 litres in the urban and rural areas, respectively.

Manufacturing sector: A rise in the sector's share in total consumption from the present 0.29 per cent to 0.67 per cent by 2047.

Power sector: Based on water requirements per unit of electricity generated and the sector's share of water requirements is projected to increase from 0.25 per cent to 0.75 per cent. The water requirements for steam generation and fly ash disposal are projected to grow at 4.73 per cent and 0.51 per cent, respectively, from a current annual level of 0.742 BCM and 0.645 BCM, the slower growth in the case of ash collection representing a shift towards dry collection.

Table 22

Projected Pollution Levels (million tonnes of BOD): the BAU Scenario

Year	*Domestic BOD*		*Industrial BOD*
	Urban	*Rural*	
1997	3.75	3.70	0.4
2020	5.95	4.29	0.014

Note: The projected BOD load from the urban domestic sector assumes an overall wastewater collection efficiency of 70 per cent in 2019 from the present level of 60 per cent. Wastewater treatment facilities in urban areas are projected to be augmented by 40 per cent by 2019. Projections for water pollution for the industrial sector assume that all production units have facilities to control pollution in accordance with the CPCB's year-wise analysis of the polluting units and strict compliance due to stringent environmental regulations.

Directions and Strategies: Sectoral Level

Agriculture

The following strategies are suggested:

Short-term Strategy

- Policy-level reforms in the structure of subsidy and pricing in the water, power, and fertilizers sectors.
- Economic use of irrigation water and increasing water application efficiency by encouraging sprinkler and drip-irrigation systems.

Short- and Medium-term Strategy

Improvement in fertilizer application efficiency, integrated with the use of biofertilizers, to check the degradation of existing resources due to contamination with nitrates.

Medium-term Strategies

- Institutional changes in terms of operational autonomy in the irrigation sector.
- Promotion of traditional modes of irrigation and adoption of the watershed approach.

- Conjunctive use of surface water and groundwater (this will also help by ensuring better drainage in canal command area, thereby checking waterlogging and salinity).
- Utilization of treated wastewater from domestic and industrial sources for irrigation.

Domestic

Critical areas in domestic sectors include an increase in the coverage and quality of water supply and basic sanitation services. Inefficiencies in the distribution and treatment of water supplies and lacunae in the existing policy structure, need to be tackled by administrative and functional decentralization of service providers and upgrading infrastructure facilities. These will be facilitated through various strategies as discussed below:

Short-term Strategy

Water pricing mechanisms that ensure economic viability of operations and encourage resource conservation practices.

Short- and Medium-term Strategies

- Participation of the private sector in one or more stages of the water supply process.
- Upgrading operational and financial infrastructure for an improved service quality and increased system efficiency.
- Propagation and encouragement of practices to minimize, recycle, and reuse treated wastewater.

Wastewater treatment capacity needs to be enhanced by introduction of such low-cost and effective waste treatment facilities as UASBR (upflow anaerobic sludge blanket reactor), duckweed ponds, and horizontal filters. These technologies offer numerous advantages—negligible energy consumption, useful by-products (manure and biogas), and lower O&M costs.

Manufacturing

Short-term Strategies

- Instituting a system of policies and practices that encourage water conservation at all levels. Legislation needs to be strengthened and backed by economic incentives and subsidies that encourage water-saving technologies and installation of devices to control water pollution.

- Adopting cleaner and less water-intensive technologies for efficient use.

Short- and Medium-term Strategies

- Plugging the shortcomings in the existing command-and-control regime to ensure thorough compliance in terms of quantity and quality of wastewater discharged.
- Putting in place a mandatory system for monitoring and recording the quantity of water consumed and the quality of effluent discharged. Such environmental management tools as performance benchmarking, ISO 14,000 standards, and environmental rating serve to improve not only environmental performance but also international image and competitiveness of the Indian industry.

Medium- and Long-term Strategy

- Encouraging R&D efforts in using and conserving water, especially in accordance with local capabilities and requirements.

Power

Short- and Medium-term Strategies

- Encouraging technological options that conserve water by minimizing its use in steam generation, cooling towers, and ash disposal.
- Other prominent measures that reduce the quantity of ash and thus that of water in handling and disposing ash include better quality of coal, dry ash collection, and alternative cleaner fuels and clean technologies for power generation.

Directions and Strategies: National Level

Integrated River Basin Approach

A basin-based approach to water management will ensure that different aspects—water allocation, pollution control, protection of water resources, and mobilization of financial resources—are not dealt with in an isolated manner, thereby providing requisite directions for the overall development process and land-use planning. Appropriate legislation will be required to set up planning units such as river basin authorities, which will act as autonomous institutions with policy formulation, planning, financial, and regulatory powers. The administrative mechanisms of these authorities need to be defined and operationalized in coordination with relevant state government departments, the Central Government, and representatives from the community, ensuring that the delegation of authority from the existing departments is consistent and avoids overlapping. The basin authorities must be empowered adequately with a view to achieve financial self-sufficiency in the long run.

Community Management

Community participation in the development and management of water resources will facilitate effective redressal of problems of the affected people within their own social and regional domains. NGOs can provide an important link between the community and government institutions and can offer services in capacity building of the relevant stakeholders, R&D for low-cost and effective water supply and sanitation facilities, and timely enforcement of policies.

Market-based Instruments

Market-based instruments including appropriate water-pricing policies will encourage resource conservation and provide additional financial support for the fund-starved municipal service providers. These could include water charges levied on both extraction of water and its pollution by public and private entities, unit costs increasing in tandem with consumption, water subsidies/rebates for those public and private bodies that attempt to treat it well before discharging it. Attempts at rationalizing water tariffs in any sector must go hand in hand with improvements in the efficiency of supply and the quality of service. Contamination of the existing water resources should be checked by the use of economic instruments such as charges on pollution beyond the permissible limits.

A Balanced Approach to Water Management

The approach to water management at the project, sector, or national level needs to focus on all the related issues of importance in a balanced way. In the agricultural sector, for instance, it is essential that pricing of all inputs—power, fertilizers, and water—takes into account the likely implications on cropping patterns and the use of those inputs. Project planning and operation of systems need to be based on water allocation criteria, which should broadly follow the order: drinking water, irrigation, hydropower, navigation, and industrial and other uses. At the national level, such policy decisions as those related to resource pricing need to integrate the issues relating to sectoral shares of water demand and efficiency of use.

Increasing Resource Availability

With utilizable surface water about 35 per cent of the total available run-off, augmenting the available resources becomes necessary. The need is to develop surface irrigation sources, harvest rainwater, and prevent run-off by building appropriate water-harvesting structures in the lower reaches especially during June–November when the rivers generally carry water in excess of 90 per cent. The concept of watershed development has to be adopted more rigorously, which effectively contributes to the revival of local traditional water control works.

Inter-basin transfer proposals need to be explored for making more water available in water-stressed basins. The National Water Development Agency envisages the utilization of 200–250 BCM of water by such transfers. Preliminary studies also highlight the possibility of using about 160 BCM through artificial recharge (MoWR 1999). Detailed feasibility studies need to be carried out to study the potential for increasing utilizable water resources.

Emerging Sustainable Alternative Scenario

Sectoral interventions along with reforms in pricing, regulatory, and other policies at the national level will significantly improve the efficiency of resource-use and lead to the more sustainable alternative scenario (Tables 23 and 24). Institutional reforms at the national level can be expected to further improve the scenario.

Table 23

Projected Total Water Demand (billion cubic metres): the BAU and Alternative Scenario (2020)

Scenario	*Irrigation*	*Domestic*	*Manufacturing*	*Power*	*Total*
BAU	734.98	36.2	3.94	3.14	778.26
Alternative	620.14	34.32	3.53	1.88	659.8

Table 24

Projected BOD Load (million tonnes) from Urban Areas and Industries : the BAU and Alternative Scenario (2020)

Scenario	*BOD from urban areas (million tonnes)*	*BOD from manufacturing sector (million tonnes)*
BAU	5.95	0.014
Alternative	4.92	0.011

Note: By expanding the existing sewerage network to increase the collection efficiency, upgrading treatment capacities, and using other efficient and low-cost technologies, the urban BOD load reduces. More efficient technologies for treating wastewater and stringent legislation results in reduction in BOD load from the manufacturing sector.

LAND, FORESTS AND BIODIVERSITY

Competing uses of land for forestry, agriculture, pastures, human settlements, and industries exert pressure on the finite land resource influencing land-use patterns and sometimes causing degradation. Changes in land use and land cover, and land degradation, have adverse impacts on forest resources and biodiversity. Given that they are intertwined in various ways, there is a need for treatment of land, forests, pastures, and biodiversity as an integrated resource.

Land Degradation

Status

India supports approximately 16 per cent of the world's population and 20 per cent of its livestock on 2.5 per cent of its geographical area. This pressure on land has led to its deterioration—soil erosion, waterlogging, salinization, nutrient depletion, lowering of groundwater tables, and soil pollution—largely caused by human interventions. Water erosion accounts for 45.3 per cent of the total land area, chemical deterioration 4.2 per cent, wind erosion 4.1 per cent, physical deterioration 3.5 per cent, and 5.5 per cent is not fit for agriculture and this is likely to continue—land under soil erosion rising from 166.0 million hectares (MHa) in 1997 to 189.0 MHa in 2019; water-logging, 12.7 to 22.3 MHa; and salinity, 11.0 to 15.1 MHa (Narayan and Ram Babu 1983).

According to the data provided by the National Remote Sensing Agency and Forest Survey of India based on satellite imagery, 80 MHa of 142 MHa under cultivation is substantially degraded and about 40 MHa of 75 MHa under the forest department has a canopy density cover less than 40 per cent (Gadgil 1993). Nearly 11 MHa of pasturelands is substantially degraded, thus a total of 131 MHa representing about 40 per cent of the country's landmass, has a productivity below its potential. However, according to the Wastelands Atlas of India 2000 (1:50 000 scale map), the total wastelands area covered in 584 districts is 63.85 million which accounts for 20.17 per cent of the total geographical area. It is this figure of about 64 MHa that has been used in the projections.

Concerns

- Soil erosion has led to loss of topsoil and terrain deformation. Siltation, an off-site effect of erosion, is reducing the reservoir storage capacity by 1 per cent to 2 per cent annually.
- Human-induced waterlogging is resulting in a rise in the water table.
- Salinization is likely to render more land unfit for biomass production, especially in the irrigated areas in Uttar Pradesh, Haryana, Punjab, Rajasthan and Karnataka.
- Most regions have a net negative balance of nutrients and suffer from a gradual depletion in the level of organic matter, a trend that is likely to continue. Maintaining the nutrient balance and preventing nutrient deficiencies is a major concern given that the required demand for food production will have to be met through increased intensity of cropping (Sehgal and Abrol 1994).

- Over-extraction far exceeding recharge in areas where groundwater is mostly used for industrial and agricultural purposes, has led to progressive lowering of water table affecting the economy of water in use and the environment.
- Improper and indiscriminate use of agrochemicals and untreated sewage sludge and municipal wastes have led to the pollution of soil and water with toxic substances and heavy metals.

Directions, Innovations, and Strategies to Combat Land Degradation

The following strategies are suggested:

Short-term Strategies

- Assessment of land degradation: Assessment of the nature and extent of degradation using scientifically sound criteria, indicators, and techniques will help plan appropriate reclamation measures. The SOTER (Soil and Terrain) database and GLASOD (Global Assessment of Human-induced Soil Degradation) can be helpful along with rapid inventorying using remote-sensing techniques and GIS (geographical information system).
- Improvement of degraded land: There is a need for adopting location-specific soil and water conservation measures to arrest further deterioration and for following practices that suit local conditions to restore the productivity of degraded lands. A multi-level stakeholder approach for the planning process is essential to obtain socially balanced results in which both the economic and ecological objectives are given due weightage. This requires data about the properties of the land, different types of land-use options and their effect on the resilience of ecosystems, and technology transfer and training of farmers, especially small and marginal farmers.

Short- and Medium-term Strategies

- **Revamping Agricultural Extension**: 'Lab[oratory]-to-land' concept should be put into practice by providing land-users multidisciplinary technical information and viable land-use options and alternatives identified for various agro-ecological and socio-economic units. Crop combinations/rotations, suitable for different agro-ecological regions (as suggested by the Indian Council of Agricultural Research) need to be advocated for better land management.

- **Waste Management**: Domestic and municipal wastes, sludge, pesticides, industrial wastes, etc. need to be used with caution to avoid polluting the soil with heavy metals and other toxic substances.

Medium-term Strategies

- Nutrient deficiency monitoring: Projected increase in cropping intensity and consequent nutrient depletion make it necessary to develop a system of monitoring mechanism for soil nutrients. Fertilizer use will need to be optimized (Annexe 1, see section on agriculture).
- Land and water management: Effective management and rational utilization of land and water resources for optimum production with minimum hazard to resources is possible treating natural watershed as a unit. In rainfed areas, *in situ* soil and moisture conservation on mini-watershed basis, irrespective of the ownership of land, should be a major thrust area for increasing productivity.
- Discouraging shifting cultivation with short fallow periods: Shifting cultivation, a traditional practice responsible for large-scale land degradation due to shortened fallow cycle, should be discouraged and alternatives provided.

Land Use

Business-as-usual Scenario

The current and projected land-use pattern is presented in Table 25.

Pressure on forests and grazing lands will continue to increase, given that the increase in human and livestock population will pace the growth in forests and pasture land. This calls for a review of land-use patterns.

Table 25

Land use (million hectares) in India: the BAU Scenario

Year	*Agriculture*	*Forest and tree cover*	*Pastures*	*Human settlements, industries, etc.*	*Scrub, wasteland, fallow, and remote land*
1997	142	71	11	21	64
2020	142	74.1	11	26.2	56.7

Note: The totals will not add up to the reporting area of 305 million hectares because forest and tree cover includes forest cover and miscellaneous tree crops and groves as well as agro-forestry (plantation on land included under agriculture) and strip plantations on land included under human settlements, industries, etc.

Assumptions: Net sown area will remain unchanged as required increase in agricultural production can be met through increase in cropping intensity. Given the absence of initiatives to enhance pastures and grazing land, this area will remain unchanged. The area under human settlements and industries etc. will increase to accommodate the growing population and to keep pace with industrialization.

Directions, Innovations, and Strategies for Sustainable Land Use

The following strategies are suggested:

Short-term Strategies

Integrate policies for land use, grazing and fodder, and fuelwood to ensure consistency in the management of land and forest resources. An efficient and effective administrative structure for prescribing and regulating land use would be essential.

Medium- and Long-term Strategies

- Create a national land use commission under the stewardship of the Planning Commission. This land use commission could enforce the policy set out in National Land Use Policy: outlines and action points and associated legislation published in 1988 by the National Land Use and Conservation Board, Department of Agriculture and Co-operation, Ministry of Agriculture. This commission could also address most of the land-related issues with support from the AIS&LUS (All-India Soil and Land Use Survey), the NBSS&LUS (National Bureau of Soil Survey and Land Use Planning), and the FSI (Forest Survey of India).
- Adopt a holistic approach to land management: Land management should combine technologies and policies to

integrate ecological, socio-economic, and political principles taking into account intra- as well as inter-generational equity.

- Adopt a multi-level stakeholder approach: All communities and land users should be involved in technology development for leveraging local experience and knowledge and ensuring maximum involvement and hence, success of any intervention. Negotiated participatory approach should be adopted.
- Develop and utilise a land-use capability classification: Land capability classification developed by the US Department of Agriculture, modified to suit Indian conditions, should be adopted to ensure efficient resource allocation. This would require completion of land and soil surveys underway and the development of an inventory of land resources on the basis of land-use classification. This, along with scientifically sound practices, will address land degradation problems and maintain land quality for sustainable use.
- Revisit the issue of land tenure and land titles: Property rights of land is an important issue with 'ownership vs. user rights' and 'private *vs.* communal ownership' being main concerns. Issues of land reforms and conferring ownership rights to small and marginal farmers, women, and tenants need to be addressed. Land titling policy is a user-enabling incentive at the national level. Clear property rights or security of tenure, developed in participation with local land users, will be an important incentive for long-term investments in the technologies and systems necessary for sustainable land use. Land tenure regime should be clear, flexible, and secure. Checking the fragmentation of land holdings by providing security of land rights and land tenure is a major challenge in the agricultural sector.

Long-term Strategies

Focus on education, training, research, and technology development: there is a need to focus on evolving resource conservation technologies and practices and on analysing the conditions and principles of sustainable land use. Efficient use of marginal lands needs to be encouraged and areas of untapped potential developed to ensure optimal utilization.

Alternative Scenario

In the alternative scenario, if one were to adopt the prescription in the National Forest Policy (1988) of bringing 30 per cent of the country's reporting area under tree cover by 2047 (see section on Forests), this will lead to an increase in the area under 'forests and tree cover' from 74 MHa in the BAU scenario to about 83.4 MHa. There is also a decrease in the area under 'scrub, wasteland, fallow, remote land' from 56.7 MHa in 2020 under the BAU scenario to 50.6 MHa under the alternative scenario. The area under other sections remains constant.

Forests

Business-as-usual Scenario

Area Under Forest and Tree Cover

Table 26 gives the estimates of area under forest and tree cover in the current and BAU scenario. The projections assume a marginal increase in forest cover due to improvement in some of the forest area currently under scrub. Also, the composition of forests will change in favour of dense forests, primarily because of improvement in crown density of open forests. Tree cover is expected to increase due to expansion of agroforestry and strip plantation as well as plantation on current fallow land.

Table 26

Forest and Tree Cover (million hectares): the BAU Scenario

Year	*Dense forests*	*Open forests*	*Miscellaneous tree crop and groves*	*Agro forestry*	*Strip plantations*	*New areas*	*Total forest and tree cover*
1997	37	26	4	3	1	0	71
2020	39.1	25	4	4	1	1	74.1

Demand for Wood and Pressure on Forests

At present, 40 per cent of the commercial demand for timber and less than 20 per cent of the demand for fuelwood are being met by sustainable supply from forests (Table 27). Paucity of funds and other resources will lead to an inadequate emphasis on superior quality planting material and improved practices resulting in marginal increase in wood yield of forests. The future demand for both commercial timber and fuelwood will, therefore, not be met sustainably from the wood produced from forest and tree cover; even though people's preferences will move up the energy ladder with the availability of a range of substitutes for fuelwood.

Table 27

Area Under Forest and Tree Cover (million hectares) and Sustainable Production and Demand of Timber and Fuelwood (million cubic metres): the BAU Scenario

Year	*Area under forest and tree cover*	*Timber*		*Fuelwood*	
		Production	*Demand*	*Production*	*Demand*
1997	71	26	64	53	260
2020	74.1	41.5	149	64.4	148.3

Grazing Pressure on Forests

In India, an average of 42 animals graze on a hectare of land, compared to the threshold level of five (Sahay 1999). Thus, nearly a third of the fodder requirement is met from forest resources in the form of grazing and cut fodder for stall-feeding (MoEF 1999). An estimated 100 million cow units graze in forests annually against a sustainable level of 31 million. Additionally, graziers collect 175–200 million tonnes of green fodder annually. Grazing affects approximately 78 per cent of India's forests (FSI) and occurs even in protected areas (MoEF 1999). Over-grazing and over-extraction of green fodder lead to forest degradation through decreased vegetative regeneration and, through compaction of soil, to reduced infiltration and vulnerability to erosion. In the BAU scenario, inadequacy of grazing land will be more acute (0.019 hectare per livestock head in 2020 as compared to 0.024 in 1997) and forests will continue to be used for grazing extensively.

Directions, Innovations and Strategies to Manage the Pressure on Forests

Combating the pressure on forests would require demand-side management with respect to wood and fodder and supply-side management with respect to enhancing wood yield in forests and increasing the supply of fodder.

Short-term Strategies

Management of Open Forests through Plantation Forestry and Joint Forest Management

'Open forests' representing 26 MHa are degraded (FSI 1998). The following may be noted in this regard:

- 15 MHa of this can be managed under the Joint Forest Management (JFM) programme and the remaining used for commercial timber production. Nearly 10 MHa is already under the JFM leaving 5 MHa to be covered.
- 4.2 MHa of scrub (less than 10 per cent cover) can be brought under plantations and 4 MHa currently under culturable waste and permanent fallow could be used for raising trees. This would imply an increase to about 83.4 MHa under tree cover by 2020.
- Plantation forestry requires the participation of communities, NGOs, and the private and corporate sectors.

Information Management

Information availability and transparency are important in developing any forestry policy. State forest departments and the Ministry of Environment and Forests should collect, analyse, and communicate forestry information on a regular basis.

Short- and Medium-term Strategies

Management of Dense Forests through the PA (protected area) Network and through Conservation Forestry

Of the 37 MHa of dense forests in 1997,

- We may develop 18.7 MHa as PAs that may be kept aside for conservation. The current area under PAs being 15.6 MHa, it must be increased by 3.1 MHa by 2020.
- And we may manage the remaining dense forest area sustainably for meeting local requirements and for conservation forestry.

Expansion of Agroforestry and Strip Plantations

There is a need to increase the area under agroforestry and farm forestry on agricultural lands by planting trees along farm boundaries and in homesteads in a manner that does not affect crop production adversely bring an estimated 4 MHa net sown area for growing tree crops. Strategies for promoting agroforestry should focus on,

- Removing legal barriers, bringing about market reforms, fostering farmer–industry linkages, and enhancing the overall profitability of farm forestry. Legal restrictions on land-ownership and on the harvesting and transport of timber products need to be rationalized. Proposed provisions for the revision of norms for timber extraction and transport are inadequate.
- Timber pricing by forest corporations should reflect the scarcity value of timber.
- Farmer–industry linkages need to be strengthened by a free flow of information between the producers and consumers on demand, supply, and pricing of timber products. Further, farmers should receive support from research and extension.

Also, we need to bring about 1 MHa along roadsides, canals banks, etc. under strip plantations and enrich about 4 MHa currently under miscellaneous trees through plantations.

Demand-side Management: Wood Resources

- Improved efficiency in use: R&D and import of technology, with the government playing the role of a facilitator, could address the urgent need to improve the technology used by the forest-based industries, particularly paper. Financial assistance, say soft loans to the industries, would promote efficient technologies.
- Development of alternatives and substitutes: Only 14 per cent of the paper consumed is recovered due to paucity of funds with the government and municipal bodies, lack of policies on the collection and utilization of waste paper and incentives for the informal network, diversion of recovered paper, and ignorance of its potential. This has resulted in import of waste paper but supply through imports is likely to dry up (Chemprojects 1999). The strategy should aim at improving the recovery of waste

paper to over 33 per cent through measures such as segregation of waste paper at source (household level), strengthening the informal network of waste paper collection through price incentives, preventing diversion of waste paper, etc. (Sharma, Beukering, and Ramaswamy 1999). Similarly, developing alternatives to fuelwood can produce desirable outcomes and, hence, the strategy should focus on an integrated energy programme augmenting such alternative fuel systems as LPG (liquefied petroleum gas) and kerosene.

- Management of pasture and fodder: Limiting livestock population through selective breeding and pasture and fodder management could mitigate the pressure on land and forests.

Medium-term Strategies

Livestock Management

- Double work output of 80 per cent of the work animal force (nondescript animals) by breeding them with selected Indian draught breeds so as to halve their requirement. Proper breeding of indigenous cattle with improved breeds for increasing both milk yield and draught power is required.
- Earmark funding for specific livestock breeding programmes, in which the Indian Veterinary Research Institute, Bareilly, and the National Dairy Research Institute, Karnal, will have the key role.

Short- and medium-term strategies

- Formulate and implement a national policy on livestock population and the creation of forage resources.
- Carry out a detailed assessment of fodder requirement, at the national and regional levels, on the basis of which regional allocation for production of fodder can be undertaken with proper financial and technical support from the appropriate ministries is required. The Indian Grassland and Fodder Research Institute, Jhansi, has a distinct role to play in this regard.
- Encourage stall-feeding to control grazing, incentives to farmers to include green fodder in crop rotation, and use of crop residue as fodder. Fodder could also be grown on land under agroforestry and JFM.

Medium- and Long-term Strategies

Technological Advancements for Increased Forest Productivity

Superior genetic stock is a prerequisite for correcting the poor annual productivity of Indian forests (1.36 cubic metres/hectare compared to the world average of 2.1). Annual productivity of clonally propagated eucalyptus plantation could be 20 to 40 cubic metres/hectare compared to four to five in traditionally raised plantations. Improvement in growth and productivity through superior quality planting stock, especially in industrial plantations and agroforestry, will enhance the sustainable supply of wood.

Emerging Sustainable Alternative Scenario

Forest management strategies as already described, could lead to an increase in total forest and tree cover (83.4 MHa) and increased sustainable supply of timber (123.2 million cubic metres) and fuelwood (about 91.8 million cubic metres). Due to the difficulty in quantifying the impact of substitution on demand, the demand for timber is at the same level both in the BAU and alternative scenario at 149 million cubic metres. The unsatisfied demand for timber could be met through imports and the use of substitutes. In the case of fuelwood, despite increased supplies, the demand of fuelwood will decline and stabilize at about 76 million cubic metres with the provision of more efficient substitutes, e.g. LPG.

Strategies towards increasing the supply of fodder from agricultural and forest lands and limiting livestock population growth through selective breeding will result in a livestock population pegged at 585 million in 2019. It is envisaged, however, that livestock populations will stabilize at these levels. While it may not be possible to increase area under pastures, fodder supply could be enhanced from farm lands, farm forests, and JFM areas. Stall-feeding could be encouraged along with controlling grazing in forests. Reduced demands on forests for grazing in the long term coupled with wood demand optimization and strategic forest management will mitigate the pressure on forest resources. This, in turn, will have a positive impact on the country's biodiversity.

Biodiversity

India's biodiversity is being gradually decimated. Maintaining viable populations of species, whether plant or animal, is crucial in biodiversity conservation requiring the conservation of important ecosystems, habitats and the ecological processes of which they are part. According to IUCN, the World Conservation Union, five per cent of a country's area should comprise PAs. India has almost achieved this target and given the intense pressures on land and forests, there is only a limited scope to increase the area under parks and sanctuaries. Currently, the PA network does not adequately cover some important biomes and species of conservation significance. It is, therefore, recommended that the area under parks and sanctuaries be increased to 160 national parks and 698 sanctuaries accounting for 18.7 MHa as suggested by Rodgers, Panwar, and Mathur (2000). This coverage will provide a 'better distribution of protected areas with less gaps in the protection of biogeographic zones, biomes and species and fewer spatial or geographic gaps in the pattern of PA coverage' (Rodgers, Panwar, and Mathur 2000).

Since the number of protected areas cannot be increased substantially, the next question is of size of the reserves. Ideally, an effective conservation area should be large enough to ensure that all target species have genetically viable population sizes and that ecological processes are maintained. In general, therefore, the thumb rule is to have areas as large as possible to maintain viable population sizes and if not, do with what one has and manage the area intensively. This can be done, for example, by ensuring genetic viability by the creation of corridors, translocation and restocking, ensuring effective conservation of the surrounding reserve and protected forests including buffers. Further, the portions of dense forests other than PAs, are also important for maintaining the extant biodiversity, a significant proportion of which lies outside the PA network.

Directions, Innovations and Strategies

Short-term Strategies

Controlling Wildlife Trade

The following steps will help tighten the enforcement of the existing wildlife law (MoEF 1994):

- Setting up a central task force to be designated as the Directorate of Prevention of Crime against wildlife, comprising an intelligence unit, a legal cell, an investigation wing, and an operations cell to carry out undercover operations; creating special courts in each state for wildlife crimes.

- Creating a central wildlife crime databank to collect and analyse data on wildlife trade.
- Activating state forest vigilance cells and creating legal cells within each state forest department, and
- Forming an enforcement cell by the state chief wildlife wardens.

Enhancing Enforcement

Project authorities fund the Environmental Impact Assessments of their projects, some of which have potentially adverse effects (e.g. mining and power plants). This undermines the objectivity of impact assessment thereby clearing many projects that despoil forest tracts. Further, clearance to projects that may damage the environment is sometimes obtained in contravention of the Forest and Wildlife (Protection) Act. This calls for setting up an independent panel of experts to review all the EIAs so as to provide objectivity to the process.

Creation of New Conservation Reserves

New types of legally recognized reserves should be created, where sustainable utilization and community involvement is the norm. Community reserves will protect landscapes, ecosystems, and species traditionally or culturally conserved by local communities (Kothari and Bhatt 1998). Conservation reserves can either be additional to the current PA network or may act as a buffer around the existing ones and are to be created on government land alone. Local communities could help in managing such areas to meet their *bona fide* livelihood needs, perhaps through ecotourism. The inclusion of these categories within the Wildlife (Protection) Act, currently on the anvil, must be expedited.

Conservation Forestry

Divisional working plans need to be more sensitive to issues of biodiversity conservation. A new working plan code being drafted to guide the development of working plans should incorporate the following concerns:

- Biannual census of large mammals using scientific census techniques and of water birds for important wetlands.

- Updated information on vegetation communities and floral inventories with cooperation of the Botanical Survey of India, Zoological Survey of India, and universities.
- Identification of important habitats (e.g. caves, dens, sandbanks, salt licks, areas of unique plant species assemblages, and wetlands) and their management.
- Compartment histories inclusive of all wildlife data.
- Simple regular monitoring and maintaining records of sightings and observation of flora and fauna by forest guards and foresters.

It is also suggested that each state must identify forests, grasslands, wetlands, and other areas of importance for biodiversity and include those on forest lands within protection working circles (where silviculture is not allowed). These can also be designated as wildlife ranges where wildlife range officers report to the territorial divisional forest officers. This will ensure that biodiversity conservation is not merely restricted to the wildlife wing of the forest departments but becomes a regular feature of forest management.

Integration of Rural Development with Biodiversity Concerns

Creation of a forest area development agency to operate along the lines of the District Rural Development Agency, headed by the forest department, is a progressive step. The chief development officers in forest areas should be from the forest department as in Andhra Pradesh.

Short- and Medium-term Strategies

Biodiversity Policy and Legislation

- A national biodiversity strategy and action plan is being prepared. Once finalized, it needs to be implemented within a fixed time frame with the setting up of institutions to oversee its implementation. The Indian Biodiversity (Conservation and Regulation) Bill needs to be considerably amended before its passage by Parliament, given its many lacunae.
- Current policy environment suffers from lack of coordination and communication between different departments and agencies, the activities of which impinge on natural resources.

There is a need to incorporate biodiversity, forestry, and land-use considerations in development planning itself. At the district level, a coordination committee headed by the district collector and involving the forest department and other relevant agencies including the District Rural Development Agency needs to be created to oversee the impact of different projects on natural resources.

- To ensure that all development activities and actions relating to the utilization, production, or management of natural resources are evaluated before implementation, it is necessary to create an environmental cell in all the departments connected with the management of air, water, land, and biodiversity.

Mapping of Forest types, Protected Areas, Natural Forests, etc.

This will provide a way for determining possible corridors, habitat contiguity, and buffer zones and facilitate biodiversity conservation. Further, vegetation mapping according to forest types needs to be done. The FSI data need to show the disaggregated changes in area according to forest types and natural forest areas.

Preservation Plots

Uttar Pradesh and Uttaranchal have forest preservation plots for assessing change conserving and protecting vegetation as well as for assessing ecological changes over a period of time. These plots need to be demarcated and actively maintained.

Landscape-level Planning

For large ecosystems of value, landscape-level plans are needed as in Uttar Pradesh and Uttaranchal where the forest departments have already prepared three landscape-level plans, one each for Corbett, Dudhwa, and the Nanda Devi national parks.

Involving the Private Sector

The private sector needs to be involved much more in such biodiversity projects as the development of forest areas for tourism or in the setting up of nature parks and interpretation centres or in bioprospecting agreements. There must be, however, priority to local communities.

Involving the Local Community

- Community biodiversity registers must be developed before issues of ownership of resources and equitable sharing of benefits are sorted. The government needs to issue clear guidelines for managing bioprospecting agreements.
- In PAs, there can be several ways of involving local communities or at least mitigating some of their hardships (MoEF 1994).
    - Reserving up to 50 per cent of available posts (e.g. wildlife guards and forest watchers).
    - Employing them in collecting snake venom, building anti-poaching awareness groups, and other local activities.
    - Capturing and training elephants who devastate standing crops to reduce conflicts.
    - Initiating timely schemes of compensation for those who lose their cattle to wildlife.

Short- to Long-term Strategies

Population Surveys and Assessments and Creating Databases

The Ministry of Environment and Forests through the Botanical Survey of India and the Zoological Survey of India, could play a guiding role by preparing a list of priority issues and areas for circulation to relevant institutions, based on a countrywide consultation of experts. Funding for these prioritized projects could be stepped up to ensure that research focuses on these issues. The Ministry of Environment and Forests must set up a database perhaps by making use of the Global Biodiversity Information Facility.

In situ Conservation

Good management of the extant populations in the wild is essential for their survival; these may include facilitating gene flow through corridors, introduction of new genetic stock, and translocation. Large-scale manipulations of the extant populations—translocations etc.—could be popularized.

Captive Breeding and Species Reintroduction

Captive breeding and species reintroduction will maintain viable and healthy genetic captive stocks in conservation facilities and can provide animals for possible reintroduction to the wild at a later stage or for supplementing current populations with new stock. *In situ* measures are, however, preferred, since in most cases it is cheaper to protect populations in their natural habitat than to reintroduce captive-bred ones. Limitations of space, finances, and facilities for captive breeding make species prioritization a primary concern. Zoos may need to restrict their efforts to a few species that can benefit from captive breeding initiatives, such as small-bodied species of Chiroptera, Rodentia, and Insectivora. Mini zoos and deer parks can act as a sink for the surplus, hybrid, aged, and infirm animals.

Ex situ *Techniques for Plants*

Gene banks—seeds, pollen, embryo, tissue, cells, and DNA—are alternatives to conservation of complete organisms requiring minimal space. Seed storage under controlled conditions can be used for short-/medium-/long-term storage. Tissue culture offers advantages over traditional methods in conserving vegetatively propagated plants, species with seeds that do not germinate readily, species with long vegetative period prior to seed set, and sterile individuals with useful traits. Cryopreservation is useful for long-term germplasm storage.

Medium-term Strategy

There is a need to involve the local community: eco-tourism and recreation forestry are being tried as income-earning options for local communities. These need to be formalized and included in the relevant policies, to be preceded by in-depth studies to determine the feasibility and the costs and benefits of such projects to all stakeholders.

CONCLUSION

The short term, medium term, and long term strategies are required to be followed for promoting sustainability of India's material resources. This would require policy changes, involve larger issues of implementation, and call for a change in governance.

Annex 1

Strategy to Achieve an Alternative Sustainable Scenario for Agriculture, Domestic and Commercial Sectors, Municipal Services, Transport Services, Mining Industry, and Manufacturing Industries

Agriculture

Directions	*Innovations and strategies*	*Action by*	*Time frame*
Irrigation			
Canal water pricing	Water price to reflect the scarcity and value of water	State governments	
	• Increase the price of canal water in a phased manner from 25 per cent of O&M to full recovery of O&M costs		Medium to long term
	• Increase capital costs gradually		Long term
Rationalizing power tariffs and related issues	• Increase power tariff at least to equal the average price charged by private power suppliers in the agricultural sector	State governments	Short term
	• Promote metered supply		
	• Ensure reliable and steady supply: privatize state electricity boards		
Decentralized management of canal irrigation	Promote decentralized management • Implement the Irrigation Act in all states • Promote water users associations through fiscal and non-fiscal incentives • Provide a grant to cover the setting up costs • Give a formal legal status to water users associations • Define property rights Define the organizational structure of the water users associations	State governments in collaboration with NGOs	Short to long term

(Contd...)

(...Contd...)

Directions	*Innovations and strategies*	*Action by*	*Time frame*
Promotion of conjunctive irrigation	Integrate tube well schemes with canal irrigation by digging tube wells along the drainage lines	State governments	Medium term
Sprinkler and drip irrigation	• Extend the existing scheme of providing financial incentives for installation charges to all states	State governments and agriculture extension	Short to medium term
	• Promote awareness and provide technical knowledge to farmers through agriculture extension services	services, corporate sector, research institutes	Medium to long term
	• Improve the technology (R&D)		
Waste water utilization	Initiate R&D on the utilization of waste water	Ministry of Water Resources, Ministry of Science & Technology, Ministry of Agriculture, municipal corporations	Medium to long term
Fertilizer pricing	• Remove price distortions between the three major nutrients, namely nitrogen, phosphorous, and potassium • Decontrol prices of urea in phases; bring it on par with the import price: increase the price initially by at least 25 per cent and increase by up to 10 per cent every two years to remove the subsidy entirely	Ministry of Chemicals and Fertilizers	Short to medium term
Integrated nutrient management and fertilizer losses	Education and awareness about integrated nutrient management and management practices	National biofertilizer development centre, regional biofertilizer development centres, agriculture departments, farm information centres, NGOs	Short to medium term
	Increase production of biofertilizers	State governments	Short to Medium term
	Initiate R&D to increase the efficiency of biofertilizer systems	Research institutes, corporate sector	Continuous process

(Contd...)

(...Contd...)

Directions	*Innovations and strategies*	*Action by*	*Time frame*
Pesticides			
Promotion of integrated pest management	Allocate at least half of the plant protection budget to integrated pest management	State governments	Short term
	Promote education and awareness through farmers' field schools	Agriculture departments, farm information centres, NGOs	Short to medium term
Production of biopesticides	Set up more production units Exempt the product from sales tax	State governments and the industry	Short to medium term
Quality control	Set up more quality control laboratories in each state private laboratories	State governments, medium term	Short to
R&D	Improve formulations, increase the efficiency of biopesticides, initiate network for identifying new genes and molecules	Department of Biotechnology, Ministry of Science & Technology, Indian Council of Agricultural Research, other research institutes	Short, medium, and long term
Transgenic varieties for resistance to pests and diseases	Facilitate early release of *Bt* cotton	Indian Council of Agricultural Research, Department of Biotechnology, Ministry of Environment & Forests	Short term
	Initiate work on other crops	Research Institutes	Medium term
Mapping of areas with high residual levels in the soil	All-India Coordinated Research Project on Pesticide Residue to estimate pesticide residues in soils	Indian Council of Agricultural Research	Medium term

(Contd...)

(...Contd...)

Municipal Services

Directions	*Innovations and strategies*	*Action by*	*Time frame*
For holistic municipal reforms			
Financial reforms	• Designing fiscal instruments to broaden the financial resource base for infrastructure	State governments, municipal corporations	Medium term
	• Reforms in the intergovernmental transfers of funds to municipalities	State governments	Short term
Institutional restructuring	• Functional decentralization of municipalities to facilitate increased approachability and transparency *vis-à-vis* communities.	Municipal corporations	Medium term
	• Increasing community participation in local governance and residents welfare associations, community-based organizations	Municipal corporations	Long term
Capacity-building in municipalities performance	Developing inherent capabilities of municipal officials to manage and monitor services	Research institutes, NGOs	Medium term
Targeting improvement	• Developing framework for performance measurement and benchmarking of municipal services	Research institutes	Short term
	• Linking budgetary allocations with continual performance improvements	State governments, municipal corporations	Medium term
For water supply			
Improving functional and operational efficiencies	• Private sector participation in different stages of water supply system	State governments, municipal corporations	Medium term
	• Private sector participation in distribution to be identified as a priority area		Short term

(Contd...)

(...Contd...)

Directions	*Innovations and strategies*	*Action by*	*Time frame*
Upgrading the existing infrastructure	• Equipping the urban water utilities with state-of-the-art operation and performance monitoring systems	State governments, research institutes	Medium term
	• Financial resource mobilization		Short term
	• Technical collaboration with international consultants	State governments, donor agencies	Medium term
	• Improved management by minimizing losses using such tools as water audits and resource conservation methods	Research institutes, NGOs, and municipal corporations	Short term
Increase economic viability of operations	Design of appropriate water pricing mechanism justifying the costs of treatment and supply	Municipal corporations	Short term
For municipal solid waste management			
Minimizing waste generation at source	Changes in lifestyle habits by awareness generation activities, targeting higher- and middle-income groups	NGOs and funding organizations	Long term
Scientific management of waste	• Segregation at source and door-to-door collection system • Composting at neighbourhood level in a decentralized way • Harnessing the potential value of recyclables by formalizing the network of ragpickers	RWAs[a], NGOs, CBOs[b], and municipal corporations	Short term
Enhancing the technical and managerial capabilities for efficient waste management	• Involving the private sector at both micro and macro levels	Municipal corporations, state governments	Medium term
	• Providing fiscal incentives to attract private sector participation		Short term
Improved technology for collection and treatment	• Designing waste collection systems to avoid multiple handling	Research institutes	Medium term
	• Enhancing use of such efficient technologies as aerobic composting, anaerobic digestion, and sanitary landfill for decentralized waste treatment	NGOs and municipal corporations	Short term

(Contd...)

(...Contd...)

Directions	*Innovations and strategies*	*Action by*	*Time frame*
Institutional and regulatory reforms	• Introducing structural changes within the municipal corporation for improvements in performance	Municipal corporations, state governments	Medium term
	• Involving greater community participation in local governance	NGOs, CBOs	Short term
	• Effective implementation of Municipal Solid Waste (Management and Handling) Rules, 1999	CPCB[c]/SPCBs[d]	Short term
	• Use of market forces, mandatory standards, and voluntary initiatives for effective waste management	State governments, MoEF[e], private sector	Medium/ long term
For waste water management			
Minimizing pollution loads from waste water discharge	• Expanded sewerage network to increase waste water collection efficiency	Municipal corporations and funding organizations	Medium/ long term
	• Augmentation of waste water treatment capacities	Community, NGOs	Medium term
	• Reduction in water consumption, recycling, and reuse of the treated waste water		
Reinforcing the institutional mechanisms	• Integration of policy interventions with other municipal sectors, particularly solid waste management	Municipal corporations, state governments	Long term
	• Training and capacity-building of municipal officials in the use of improved technology	Research institutes	Short term
	• Formulation of appropriate taxing/fee mechanisms for waste water collection and treatment	Municipal corporations, state governments	Short term

a: Resident welfare associations
b: Community-based organizations
c: Central Pollution Control Board
d: State Pollution Control Boards
e: Ministry of Environment and Forests

(Contd...)

(...Contd...)

Transport Services

Directions	*Innovations and strategies*	*Action by*	*Time frame*
Check the decline in the share of the railways	Increase productivity by improving technology	Indian Railways	Long term
	Increase capacity on high-density corridors	Indian Railways and Union government	Short term
	Promote multimodalism with private sector participation	Indian Railways	Medium term
	Check investment on non-remunerative routes	Indian Railways	Short term
Promote inland waterways	Encourage greater use of inland waterways fleet through mechanization and provide navigational aids	Inland Waterways Authority of India	Medium term
	Leverage investments from the private sector for fleet expansion	Ministry of Surface Transport	Medium term
Promote coastal shipping	Introduce a coastal shipping act to simplify customs procedures for coastal shipping	Ministry of Surface Transport	Medium term
	Charge concessional rates for coastal vessels	Major ports	Short term
	Encourage the development of minor ports to provide cheaper services to coastal vessels	State governments	Long term
Promote pipeline transportation	Provide infrastructure status to pipeline transport to enable funds to be leveraged at lower interest rates	Union government	Short term
Improve road network	Facilitate private investment by mitigating risks and uncertainties	Ministry of Surface Transport and Financial institutions	Short term
Encourage multi-axle vehicles	Offer financial incentives	Ministry of Finance	Short term
	Introduce changes in the Motor Vehicles Act 1988	Ministry of Surface Transport	Short term
Increase the railway energy efficiency	Promote rail electrification	Indian Railways	Medium term
	Introduce energy-efficient technologies and management practices	Indian Railways	Long term

(Contd...)

(...Contd...)

Directions	*Innovations and strategies*	*Action by*	*Time frame*
Reduce travel demand	Integrate land-use and transport planning	Local governments and Land-use authorities	Long term
	Develop a robust real estate market	Local governments and Land-use authorities	Medium term
Increase share of public transport	Augment capacity of public transport by leveraging private investment	State road transport undertakings	Medium term
	Discourage use of personal vehicles	Local and state governments	Long term
	Improve quality of public transport	State road transport undertakings	Short term
Improve vehicle technology and fuel quality	Introduce a phased programme of emissions standards	Ministry of Surface Transport, Ministry of Industries, and Ministry of Petroleum and Natural Gas	Medium term
	Introduce a phased programme for introducing automobile and cleaner fuel technologies	Ministry of Petroleum and Natural Gas	Short term
	Introduce inspection and maintenance programme for in-use vehicles	Ministry of Surface Transport	Short term

(Contd...)

(...Contd...)

Mining Industry

Directions	*Innovations and strategies*	*Action by*	*Time frame*
Ban on mining in ecologically fragile or sensitive and rich areas, rehabilitation of old abandoned mine sites	Prepare a schedule of lands where mining will not be permitted	Central and state governments	Short term biologically
	Levy a cess on mineral production to finance the work	Central and state governments	Medium term
Formulation of mine closure policy	Prepare detailed guidelines on mine closure	Central and state governments	Short term
Rehabilitation of degraded land in ongoing and planned mines	Make it mandatory for mine operators to furnish performance guarantee bonds before mining lease is granted or renewed	Central and state governments, mine operators	Medium term
Environmental protection in areas where small- and medium-scale mining operations are carried out	• Prepare a policy document • Follow the 'polluter pays' principle	• Central and state governments • Central Pollution Control Board and state pollution control boards, mine operators	Short term
Promotion of waste utilization	Prepare an action plan on technology options and fiscal measures needed to promote waste utilization	Central and state governments, industry, industry associations, Central Pollution Control Board, and state pollution control boards	Short term
Environmental protection of mining areas	• Develop environmental indicators for different activities • Encourage companies to obtain environmental certification	• Central and state governments, industry • Central Pollution Control Board and state pollution control boards	Short term
Ocean mining	Develop a policy paper on ocean mining for implementation	Central government	Short term

(Contd...)

(...Contd...)

Manufacturing Industries

Directions	*Innovations and strategies*	*Action by*	*Time frame*
Promote energy-efficient technologies	Mandatory energy efficiency norms for upcoming process industries	Central government with support from industry associations	Short term
Modernize or upgrade small-scale industries	Development of clean technologies for small-scale industries	Research institutes with support from Central and state governments	Short to medium term
Promote conservation of primary raw materials	Promotion of recycling and use of secondary materials	Industry, Central and state governments, municipal corporations, NGOs	Short to medium term
Ensure effective environmental governance	Better implementation of environmental laws	Central and state pollution control boards, central government, courts	Short to medium term
Improve energy efficiency	Voluntary agreements on energy efficiency	Industry and the relevant industry associations, government, research institutes	Short term
Promote the market for energy-efficient products	Mandatory energy labelling of equipment	Bureau of Indian Standards, research institutions, universities, equipment manufacturers and relevant associations, government, NGOs	Short to medium term
Create demand for energy-efficient products	Public procurement policies for energy-efficient products	Central and state governments, municipal corporations, public-sector undertakings	Short term
Develop new technologies	Enhanced research, development, and demonstration efforts	Research institutes, universities, industry, government	Medium to long term

(Contd...)

(...Contd...)

Domestic and Commercial Sectors

Directions	*Innovations and strategies*	*Action by*	*Time frame*
Discourage energy wastage	Gradually phase out subsidies on conventional energy	Central and state governments	Long term
Promote renewable energy technologies by providing a level playing field	Provide soft loans to renewable energy technologies; subsidize solar cookers	Ministry of Non-Conventional Energy Sources, state governments	Medium term
	Tailor pricing policies to favour efficient technologies	Central and state governments	Long term
Adopt integrated and rational energy pricing	Devise methodologies to internalize indirect costs and benefits	Central and state governments	Medium to long term
Improve the efficiency of use	Enforce stringent efficiency standards	Energy Conservation Bill	Short to Medium term
	Make energy labelling mandatory		
	Increase the budget for R&D	Central government	Short to Medium term
Enhance the adoption of improved cook-stoves	Identify appropriate target groups	Ministry of Non-Conventional Energy Sources, NGOs	Short term
	Invest in R&D of cook-stove design		Medium term
	Formulate and implement action-bound programmes for dissemination and adoption of cook-stoves		Short to Medium term
Ensure a reliable and long-term supply of conventional fuels	Adopt holistic planning to encompass fuels and all sectors	Planning Commission, Ministry of Coal, and Ministry of Petroleum and Natural Gas	
Use alternative technologies	Initiate R&D for processed biomass fuels	Ministry of Non-Conventional Energy Sources	Long term
	Enhance marketing efforts and community sharing for adoption of bio-gasifiers	NGOs	Medium to long term
	Create awareness of the benefits of biogas plants	NGOs	Short to Medium term

Annex 2

References

Bhanumathidas, N. and Kalidas, N. (1998), Programmes and policies of fly ash utilisation in India, p. 32 [Proceedings of the International Conference on Fly Ash Disposal and Utilisation, New Delhi, 20–22 January 1998, organized by the Central Board of Irrigation and Power and Fly Ash Mission, TIFAC].

Census of India. (1991), Housing and amenities New Delhi: Registrar General and Census Commissioner, Ministry of Home Affairs, p. 371.

CEA. (1997), *Fourth National Power Plan 1997–2012*, p. 42 New Delhi: Central Electricity Authority, p. 346.

CGWB. (1995), Groundwater resources of India New Delhi: Central Groundwater Board.

Chemprojects. (1999), Study on forest industry Chemprojects Design and Engineering Pvt. Ltd Report submitted to Ministry of Environment and Forests, Government of India, New Delhi.

Chitale, M. A. (1992), Population and water resources of India In *The Inevitable Billion Plus: science, population and development*, pp. 111–127, edited by V. Gowarikar Pune: Unmesh Communications, p. 452.

Chopra, R. and Sen, D. (1992), Natural bounty and artificial scarcity: water resources In *The Inevitable Billion Plus: science, population and development*, edited by V. Gowarikar Pune: Unmesh Communications, p. 452.

CPCB. (1996), Annual Report 1995/96 New Delhi: Central Pollution Control Board, p. 165.

CPCB. (2000a), Status of water supply and waste water generation collection, treatment and disposal in Class 1 cities Delhi: Central Pollution Control Board, p. 51.

CPCB. (2000b), *Parivesh* [newsletter] Delhi: Central Pollution Control Board, p. 26.

CWC. (1993), Reassessment of water resources potential of India New Delhi: Central Water Commission

CWC. (1996), Water and related statistics information system directorate: performance overview and management improvement organization New Delhi: Ministry of Water Resources, p. 314.

DGH. (1999), Petroleum exploration and production activities in India, 1998/99 New Delhi: Ministry of Petroleum and Natural Gas, Directorate General of Hydrocarbons, p. 70.

FSI. (1998), The State of Forests Report 1997 Dehra Dun: Forest Survey of India, p. 72.

Gadgil, M. (1993), Biodiversity and India's degraded lands *Ambio* 22, pp. 167–172

Kothari, A. and Bhatt, S. (1998), Protected areas in India: proposal for an expanded system of categories Pune: Kalpavriksh, p. 23.

MoEF. (1994), Report of the committee on prevention of illegal trade in wildlife and wildlife products New Delhi: Ministry of Environment and Forests, p. 68.

MoEF. (1999), National Forestry Action Programme, vol. 1 New Delhi: Ministry of Environment and Forests, p. 179.

MoPNG. (2000), Basic statistics on Indian petroleum and natural gas 1999/2000 New Delhi: Ministry of Petroleum and Natural Gas.

MoWR. (1999), Water resources development plan of India: policy and issues New Delhi: Ministry of Water Resources, p. 26.

Narayan, V. V. D. and Ram, Babu. (1983), Estimation of soil erosion in India *Journal of Irrigation and Drainage Engineering* 109, pp. 419–434.

Rodgers, W. A., Panwar, H. S. and Mathur, V. B. (2000), Wildlife Protected Area Network in India: a Review (Executive Summary) Dehra Dun: Wildlife Institute of India, p. 44.

Sahay, K. B. (1999), Problem of livestock population New Delhi: Indian Institute of Technology.

Saleth, R. M. (1996), Water Institutions in India: economics, law and policy New Delhi: Commonwealth Publishers, p. 299.

Sehgal, J. and Abrol, I. (1994), Soil degradation in India: status and impact New Delhi: National Bureau of Soil Survey and Land Use Planning. p. 80.

Sharma, V. K., Beukering, P. and Ramaswamy, K. V. (1999), International trade and recycling in developing countries: the case of waste paper trade in India London: Executive Summary of the Final Report, IIED.

WHO. (1993), Assessment of sources of air, water and land pollution: a guide to rapid source inventory techniques and their use in formulating environmental control strategies Geneva: World Health Organization. p. 208.

Annex 3

Assumptions for 2019 used in Developing the BAU Scenario for Power Sector

Parameter	*BAU scenario*
Demand*	**Aggregation of projected sectoral electricity consumption**
T&D losses (%)	20
Fuel mix	
Hydro	Based on annual accretion between the period beginning the 8th Plan and ending the 9th Plan
Nuclear	Official targets for plants cleared by CEA; those sanctioned and ongoing and new plants for the11th Plan deferred until 2019
Nuclear plant load factor (%)	60
Renewables	Official targets for plants cleared by CEA; those sanctioned and ongoing and new plants for the11th Plan deferred until 2019
Renewables plant load factor (%)	Wind: 25, Solar: 25, SHP (small hydro projects): 20, Biomass: 60
Imports of hydro-power	Half the potential of projects in the pipeline (constituting 15 per cent of hydro potential in both Nepal and Bhutan) available. Domestic electricity demand (1997–2019) growing annually at 8 per cent in Nepal and 10 per cent in Bhutan
Thermal	Residual
Thermal plant load factor (%)	68.5
Oil-based thermal	Official targets for plants cleared by CEA; those sanctioned and ongoing and new plants for the 11th Plan deferred until 2019
Domestic coal -based	Constrained by domestic availability of 368 million tonnes (after catering to the need of other industries)
Imported coal-based	Residual
Gas-based thermal	Official targets for plants cleared by CEA, those sanctioned and ongoing and new plants for the11th Plan deferred until 2019
Thermal efficiency (%)	36
Pollution control mechanisms	ESP installation: 100 per cent, ESP efficiency: 95 per cent, FGD installation: 0 per cent Low NO_x combustion: capacity addition beyond 1997, NO_x emission reduction factor: 30 per cent
Ash content (%) in coal used for power generation: 37	
Sulphur content in coal (%): Domestic = 0.35, Imported = 0.5	
Fly ash management	
Dry collection of ash (%)	70
Utilization of ash	**Cement**: share of pozzolana cement in total cement: 40 per cent Fly ash content in pozzolana cement: 20 per cent **Bricks**: share of bricks using fly ash in total bricks: 20 per cent Fly ash in bricks: 25 per cent

* Electricity demand in the BAU scenario (2019): Agriculture = 195 TWh; Commercial sector: 243 TWh; Residential sector: 156.3 TWh; and Manufacturing sector: 535 TWh.

Annex 4

Assumptions for 2019 used in Developing the Alternative Scenario

Parameter	*Alternative scenario*
Demand*	**Aggregation of projected sectoral electricity consumption**
T&D losses (%)	15
Fuel mix	
Hydro	Official targets for the 11th Plan deferred until 2019
Nuclear	Installed capacity of 20 000 MW (based on the target of 20 000 MW by 2020 set by the Nuclear Power Corporation)
Nuclear plant load factor (%)	65
Renewables	Availability based on a current assessment of exploitable potential
Renewables plant load factor (%)	Wind: 30, Solar: 25, SHP (small hydro projects): 25, Biomass: 60
Imports of hydro-power	Higher potential materialization of 20 per cent in both countries. Demand assumptions same as those for the base case (2019).
Thermal	Residual
Thermal plant load factor (%)	75
Oil-based thermal	Based on materialization of sanctioned and ongoing plants
Domestic coal -based	Constrained by domestic availability of 352 million tonnes (after catering to the needs of other industries)
Imported coal-based	25 per cent of domestic coal blended with imported coal
Gas-based thermal	Residual
Thermal efficiency (%)	38
Pollution control mechanisms	ESP installation: 100 per cent, ESP efficiency: 99.5 per cent, FGD installation: 0 per cent
	Low NO_x combustion: 100 per cent, NO_x emission reduction factor: 30 per cent
Ash content (%) in coal used for power generation: 34	
Sulphur content in coal (%): Domestic = 0.35, Imported = 0.5	
Fly ash management	
Dry collection of ash (%)	100
Utilization of ash	**Cement**: share of pozzolana cement in total cement: 65 per cent; Fly ash content in pozzolana cement: 40 per cent
	Bricks: share of bricks using fly ash in total bricks: 30 per cent; Fly ash in bricks: 25 per cent

* Electricity demand in BAU scenario: Agriculture = 175 TWh; Commercial sector: 219 TWh; Residential sector: 155.0 TWh; and Manufacturing sector: 482 TWh

Annex 5

Assumptions

The alternative scenario envisages reduced resource requirements through a combination of interventions, e.g. technological developments, governance measures, and market-based instruments (Annex 1).

In addition, it prescribes the use of fossil fuels in accordance with their availability. Though gas is preferred on environmental considerations, its domestic resources are limited. In addition, prices of imported gas are subject to fluctuations as they are linked to international oil prices. Domestic coal production, on the other hand, is expected to be constrained, necessitating coal imports as well.

Given a choice of importing gas versus coal, gas imports are preferable given that gas is a relatively 'green' fuel. A shift from coal to gas will also help diversify the fuel mix. Accordingly, the balance energy requirements under the alternative scenario are met through gas imports. However, some quantities of coal would continue to be imported for use in steel and cement industries (coking coal) and for blending in power generation.

Assumptions for the Transport Sector

The transport sector accounts for the bulk of reductions in oil demand that accrue from reversing the current preference for road to rail for freight movement, according priority to inland waterways and coastal shipping, improvements in energy efficiency, higher penetration of mass transport systems and use of cleaner fuels—ULSD (ultra low sulphur diesel) or CNG (compressed natural gas) in urban transport, etc. (Annex 1).

Assumptions for the Power Sector

Demand for oil and gas in the BAU scenario is estimated on the basis of proposed additions in capacity as considered by the Central Electricity Authority in its long-term planning exercise. While all categories of projects are considered for gas-based power generation, oil-based thermal capacity is restricted to the existing capacity plus sanctioned and ongoing projects. The pessimistic outlook on oil-based generation draws support from the volatility in oil prices.

Under the alternative scenario, detailed assessments have been undertaken for non-fossil fuel based generation—hydro, nuclear, and hydro imports. For thermal sources, oil-based capacity remains capped at current plus the sanctioned and ongoing projects. Given the constraints in coal production, coal availability for power generation is restricted. Coal imports are considered as well, however, these are primarily for blending and in coastal locations far away from coal bearing areas. Gas-based capacity accounts for the rest of the thermal capacity.

Assumptions for Other Sectors

Demand for oil and gas in other sectors has been based on an international cross-sectional analysis. Oil intensity plotted against per capita income levels in different countries indicated that the intensity was lower in the developed economies (higher per capita income levels) than that in the developing economies. The analysis, based on the expected increase in per capita income levels in India, indicated that it would be possible to reduce oil intensity by 18 per cent in 2020. However, more conservative estimate of a 10 per cent reduction by 2020 has been employed for this analysis. Similar reduction levels were also assumed for the intensity of gas use.

19

India's Trade in 2020

A Mapping of Relevant Factors

NAGESH KUMAR

Introduction

India's trade has generally grown at a faster rate compared to the growth of GDP over the past two decades. With the liberalization since 1991 in particular, the importance of international trade in India's economy has grown considerably. As a result, the ratio of international trade to GDP has gone up from 14 per cent in 1980 to nearly 20 per cent towards the end of the decade of 1990s. Given the trends of globalization and liberalization, the openness of Indian economy is expected to grow further in the coming two decades. The more exact magnitude of India's trade in 2020 and its proportion to India's national income would be determined by a variety of factors. Many of these factors are in the nature of external shocks and are beyond the control of national policy making. One illustration is the recent surge in the crude oil prices in the international market to unprecedented levels that have impacted the country's imports in a significant manner. In addition, the implementation of various WTO agreements are likely to affect India's trade. India's trade is also likely to be affected by various bilateral/regional preferential trade arrangements that have been concluded and those that might take shape in the coming years.

An earlier version of the paper was presented at the Fifth Meeting of the Committee on Vision 2020 for India, Planning Commission, on 8 February, 2001. I benefited from discussions with Dr V. R. Panchamukhi, and from comments of Dr S.P. Gupta and other participants at the meeting. The usual disclaimer applies.

This paper attempts to provide a mapping of different factors that are likely to shape the patterns and magnitudes of India's imports and exports over the coming two decades. These factors are classified into three, namely:

1) Factors affecting the demand for India's exports of goods and services.

2) Factors affecting the supply of India's exports of goods and services, and

3) Factors affecting the demand for India's imports.

The supply of imports may be assumed to be elastic and hence is not discussed.

The structure of the paper is as follows. Section 1 maps out various factors affecting demand for India's exports. Section 2 gives factors affecting supply of India's exports. Section 3 lists the factors that are likely to affect demand for India's imports. Section 4 briefly summarizes emerging patterns of India's comparative advantage in exports of good and services. Section 5 makes some concluding remarks.

1. FACTORS AFFECTING THE DEMAND FOR EXPORTS

There is a multitude of factors that are likely to affect the demand for India's exports of goods and services as seen below.

1.1 Growth Performance of World Economy and Key Trading Regions

The growth rates of the world economy and world trade do influence the overall demand for India's exports. For instance, the rates of stagnation in the growth rate of world trade in the period since 1996 have affected the growth of India's exports. Some broad correspondence between the growth rates of world trade and Indian exports is evident from Figure 1. Depending upon the intensities of India's trade relations, the growth prospects in these specific regions may also affect the demand for India's exports. The regions which may be particularly important for India's exports include North America, the European Union, Middle East, East and Southeast Asia and South Asia. Therefore, it will be important to watch the growth outlook and projections for these regions.

Figure 1

Growth Rates of World Trade and India's Exports Over the 1990s

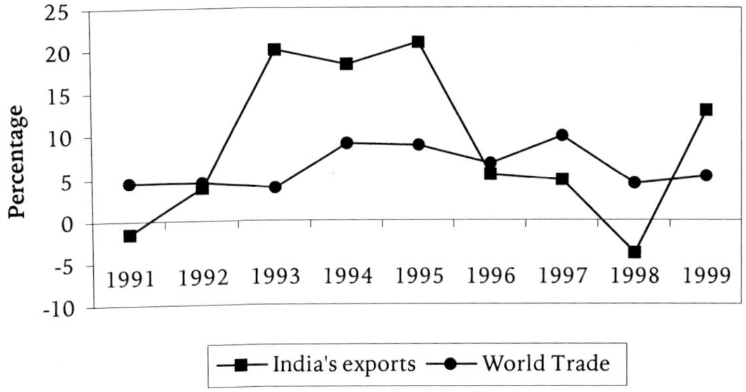

Source: RIS on the basis of WEO Database of the IMF

1.1.1. *World Output and Trade at the Turn of the Century and the Outlook*

The world economy in 2000 seems to have fully recovered from the slow down of 1998-1999 on account of the East Asian crisis. The estimated world output growth of 4.8 per cent in 2000 is highest since 1988 and of world trade at 12.4 per cent is highest of the past 25 years (Table 1, Figure 1). The impressive recovery of the world economy and world trade in the early part of 2000 generated optimism all around as countries expected to benefit from favourable spillovers in the form of rise in demand for their exports. However, the optimism has proved to be short lived. It has been partly tarnished somewhat by the crude oil prices hitting the roof in the third quarter of 2000 and adversely affecting the outlook of many regions besides raising the threats of inflation in different parts of the world. Furthermore and more importantly, the emerging trends confirm that a trend of slow down was set in the US economy in the third quarter of the 2000. Hence, fears of a hard landing of the

US economy in 2001 have continued to grow. A scenario of hard landing of the US economy in 2001 is thus likely to short-circuit the rebound of the world economy of 1999-2000, even though the major European Union economies are improving their performance. The Japanese economy continues to remain sluggish.

The slow down of the US economy has a compounded effect on the growth of the world economy by adversely affecting the demand for the products of partner countries as well. As a result the growth rate of world output is likely to slow down in 2001 from the levels reached in 2000 to 3.2. The world economy is expected to pick up moderately to 3.9 per cent in 2002. The effect of the impending slow down is more severe on the growth rate of world trade which is likely to reduce by nearly half from the rate achieved in 2000 to around 6.5 per cent in 2001 and 2001. In the light of recent trends, the outlook for the world economy and trade growth over the next ten years could be taken at three and six per cent respectively.

Table 1

Annual Growth Rates of World Output and World Trade

(Percentage p.a.)

	1991	*1992*	*1993*	*1994*	*1995*	*1996*	*1997*	*1998*	*1999*	*2000*	*2001*[p]	*2002*[p]
World Real GDP	1.5	2	2.3	3.7	3.6	4.1	4.1	2.6	3.5	4.8	3.2	3.9
World Trade in goods and services	4.5	4.5	3.8	9	8.9	6.7	9.8	4.3	5.3	12.4	6.7	6.5

p: projected. IMF WEO Projections 04/01.
Source: RIS on the basis of WEO Database of the IMF.

Table 2 summarizes the growth rates of output in key regions of the world and projections for the coming years.

1.2 WTO Agreements

Since the implementation of the Final Act of the Uruguay Round in 1995, the WTO Agreements have become important factors in determining the patterns of world trade. Their full impact is not yet obvious as many provisions of these agreements are yet to be implemented because of the transition period provided. Most of the remaining provisions of the WTO agreements would be implemented in the coming five years. Therefore, the patterns of trade in 2020 would have to be speculated keeping in mind the impact of full implementation of the WTO agreements. Some of the agreements which are likely to affect India's exports are as following:

Table 2

Growth Outlook in India's Major Trade Partners

Region/country				*WB/GEP Projections (12/00)*		*IMF/WEO Projections (05/01)*	
	1998	*1999*	*2000*	*2001*	*2002*	*2001*	*2002*
World	2.6	3.5	4.8	3.4	3.2	3.2	3.9
United States	4.4	4.2	5.0	3.2	2.9	1.5	2.5
European Union	2.7	2.6	3.4	3.2	2.8	2.4	2.8
Japan	-2.5	0.8	1.7	2.1	2.2	0.6	1.5
Developing Countries	3.5	3.8	5.8	5.0	4.8	5.0	5.6
Developing Asia	4.1	6.1	6.9			5.9	6.3
East Asia 5*	-8.2	6.7	6.9	5.5	5.1	3.4#	4.7#
South Asia	5.6	5.7	6.4	5.5	5.5	5.6	5.9
Middle East		0.8	5.4			2.9	4.6
Latin America and the Caribbean	2.0	0.2	4.1	4.1	4.3	3.7	4.4
Sub-Saharan Africa	2.0	2.3	3.0	3.4	3.7	4.2	4.4

*: Indonesia, South Korea, Malaysia, the Philippines, and Thailand.

#: ASEAN-4.

Source: RIS based on World Bank (2001), IMF (2001).

1.2.1 Agreement on Textiles and Clothing

The Agreement on Textiles and Clothing (ATC) proposes to phase out the MFA quotas imposed by the developed countries on the imports of textiles and clothing from developing countries over a period of 10 years ending on 31st December, 2004. Given the fact that India has substantially fulfilled her quota for the products coming under MFA, it may appear that the phasing out of these quotas would help in the expansion of exports. However, the impact of the phase out is likely to be a mixed bag. This is because with MFA phase out, Indian exporters would be competing directly with other exporters of textiles and garments such as China, Korea, Taiwan, Pakistan, Thailand, Turkey, Mexico, Hong Kong, Indonesia, Macau, Philippines, Sri Lanka, Bangladesh, among others. Therefore, while ATC provides an opportunity to Indian exporters to expand their exports of textiles and garments by removing the quota restrictions, it also poses a challenge of increased international competition. Some of them will enjoy preferential access to the importing countries due to their least developed country (LDC) status such as Bangladesh.

There are apprehensions on the full benefits of phase out being available to developing countries. As such, the schedule of the phase-out has been back-loaded over a ten-year long phase-out period. The industrialized countries may use other protectionist measures such as anti-dumping to prevent market access after the phase-out of quotas. A large number of textiles and clothing products already face tariffs in the range of 15 to 30 per cent in the Quad countries (World Bank, 2000). Some attempts of restricting them with anti-dumping duties have already been made against these exports including those from India.

Another factor that will affect the competitiveness of Indian exports of textiles and garments in the post-MFA regime is the availability of trade preferences to emerging competitors of India. For instance, Mediterranean countries such as Turkey, Cyprus and Malta and Central and Eastern European countries enjoy free trade agreement with the European Union ahead of their full membership. The Caribbean countries enjoy a similar preferential access to the United States market under the Caribbean Basin Initiative (CBI). Mexico enjoys a privileged access to the North American Market as a member of NAFTA. These trade preferences have already resulted into diversion of trade in textiles and clothing to these countries. For instance, Mexican exports of clothing to the United States have grown at the rate of 27 and 15 per cent in 1998 and 1999, respectively, with the growth rate of exports to Canada in these years being 30 per cent and 26 per cent, respectively. Similarly, exports of clothing from Bulgaria, Hungary, Poland, Romania, Turkey to the European Union in 1998 have grown at 26 per cent, 14 per cent, 11 per cent, 23 per cent and 11 per cent, respectively (WTO, 2000).

The ability of Indian exporters to take advantage of phase out of the MFA quotas by 2004 will depend upon a number of factors such as their ability to enhance overall international competitiveness with productivity and efficiency improvements, quality control, ability to quickly come up with new designs, ability to respond to changes in consumer preferences rapidly and the ability to move up the value chain by building brand names and acquiring channels of distribution to more than outweigh the advantages of her competitors. The reservation of the garment industry for small-scale sector has affected capital investment, modernization and automation in the sector in the country. Although the small sector operation has imparted flexibility, it has prevented exploitation of economies of scale and scope by the Indian industry. The new Textiles Policy takes care of some of the concerns. It remains to be seen if the Indian industry will be able to exploit the opportunities provided by the increased market access with the MFA phase-out.

1.2.2. Agreement on Agriculture (AoA)

The AoA proposes to liberalize the international trade in agriculture by restricting the agricultural subsidies provided by governments to the farmers, reduction in export subsidies in agriculture, removal of Quantitative Restriction (QRs) and establishment of tariff rate quotas applicable to trade in agricultural commodities. In general, India's obligations under AoA are limited, given the low level of agricultural subsidies compared to EU and the US. It is believed that implementation of the AoA commitments by industrialized countries will benefit countries like India in terms of market access for some agricultural commodities. However, the implementation of the commitments on the part of industrialized countries so far does not provide any room for optimism. The extent of subsidies given by industrialized countries have actually increased over the past few years as acknowledged by OECD reports. It is possible that in the coming years the provisions of the Agreement are implemented in letter and in spirit. The likely effect of the full implementation on India's trade is difficult to be speculated. However, one can have an idea about the likely scenario from efficiency indicators and incentive structure. Given the lower than world prices of rice, wheat, maize, sorghum, chickpea and cotton in India, their exports may expand under the liberalised trade in agriculture. Hence, the area under cultivation for these crops may increase since profitability and effective incentives will get tilted in favour of these crops. The same is true for pearl millet, pigeonpea and soya bean. However, production of oilseeds e.g. groundnut, rapeseed, mustard and sunflower, and pulses may be adversely affected in a free-trade scenario, given the lower world prices. Thus, the import dependence in edible oils and pulses may increase.

1.2.3. Anti-dumping Regulations

The Indian exports of a number of commodities have been subjected to anti-dumping regulations by some of our important trading partners such as the United States and the European Union. The onslaught of the anti-dumping measures on Indian exports is likely to increase in future with the growing competitiveness of Indian products. In order to minimize their disruptive effect of these regulations on India's exports, the industry and government will have to strengthen the machinery to counter such actions (Panchamukhi, 2000).

1.2.4. Tariff Negotiations and New Trade Round

Although the average tariff rates in the industrialized countries are low, they have high peak tariffs for certain products, some of which are of export interest to India such as textiles and garments, and agricultural commodities (see Table 3). Market access for these products could be facilitated by our ability to secure reduction in these tariffs in the industrialized countries through future tariff negotiations in the WTO framework.

1.2.5. Trade Preferences for the Least Developed Countries

One emerging development in the WTO system has been the tendency to divide the developing countries with the offer of special trade preferences for the least developed countries. A sizeable proportion of India's exports still comprise labour and resource intensive goods that are also exported by some of the least developed countries. If successful these preferences have the prospects of diverting trade from India to the least developed countries. The potential of these trade preferences for adversely affecting India's exports needs to be kept in mind.

Table 3

Distribution of Tariff Peaks by Product Groups in Quad Countries

Product group	*Total*	No. of Items					No. of peaks	Share in
		12-19%	22-29%	32-99%	100-299%	>=300%	*Total*	*Total (%)*
European Union								
Agricultural and fishery products (1-24)	2779	544	331	313	31	2	1221	97.7
Mineral products, fuels (25-27)	257	0	0	0	0	0	0	0
Leather, textiles, clothing (41-43,50-64)	1565	6	0	0	0	0	6	0.5
Industrial products (28-96)	7771	27	7	8	0	0	42	3.3
ALL PRODUCTS (1-96)	10807	571	338	341	31	2	1263	100
Japan								
Agricultural and fishery products	1897	204	299	111	81	65	[illegible]	35.1
Mineral products, fuels	194	0	0	0	0	0	[illegible]	0
Leather, textiles, clothing	2410	42	39	15	28	7	131	14.7
Industrial products	6880	44	39	15	28	7	133	14.9
ALL PRODUCTS	8971	248	338	126	109	72	893	100
USA								
Agricultural and fishery products	1779	138	70	99	15	11	333	36.6
Mineral products, fuels	183	0	0	0	0	0	0	0
Leather, textiles, clothing	1814	374	110	40	0	0	524	57.4

(Contd...)

(...Contd...)

Product group	*Total*	*No. of Items*					*No. of peaks*	*Share in*
		12-19%	*22-29%*	*32-99%*	*100-299%*	*>=300%*	*Total*	*Total (%)*
Industrial products	8123	407	127	45	0	0	579	63.4
ALL PRODUCTS	10085	545	197	144	15	11	912	100
Canada								
Agricultural and fishery products	1429	65	10	16	68	0	159	27.4
Mineral products, fuels	187	5	0	0	0	0	5	0.9
Leather, textiles, clothing	1209	320	27	0	0	0	347	60.1
Industrial products	6791	374	39	0	0	0	413	71.6
ALL PRODUCTS	8407	444	49	16	68	0	577	100

N.B. HS Chapters are given in parentheses.

Source: RIS based on UNCTAD/WTO (2000) *The Post-Uruguay Round Tariff Environment For Developing Country Exports: Tariff Peaks and Tariff Escalation*, UNCTAD, Geneva (TD/B/COM.1/14/Rev.1; 28 January, 2000)

1.3 China's Accession to WTO

One of the important events of the coming years for the world trade may be the entry of China into the WTO regime. China signed an agreement with the US for its entry into the WTO in November 1999. It has subsequently been negotiating such agreements with other WTO members. The accession of China to the WTO and hence the MFN status that it will receive from other WTO countries may have some implications for the competitiveness of India's exports. This is because India and China compete in the international market for a number of labour intensive and matured technology goods such as textiles and garments, leather goods, light engineering products, chemicals and pharmaceuticals, among others. China has already been giving tough competition to Indian exports in many commodities and markets. There is a view that the accession to WTO may further strengthen China's competitiveness and hence may affect the Indian exports adversely. There is another view that the accession of China to WTO would force it to follow WTO norms and procedures, etc. and will bring their trade policy under international surveillance. State subsidies will be regulated and hence it will make it more difficult for the Chinese exporters to dump their products in the world market. The exact impact of the accession of China to the WTO on India's export prospects will depend upon these counteracting effects. It is important to analyze the effects of Chinese accession to WTO on the competitiveness of Indian exports.

1.4. Preferential Trade Arrangements/Free Trade Arrangements in Rest of the World

The last decade and a half has seen the proliferation of regional trading arrangements in different parts of the world. The major trading blocks that have emerged over the years include the European Union, NAFTA, Mercosur, AFTA, COMESA, among others. Besides these free trade and common market agreements, a number of other countries have become integrated with the trading blocks through a variety of preferential or free trade arrangements. For instance, European Union has extended free trade agreement treatment to a number of Central Eastern European Union and Mediterranean countries in anticipation of full membership to these countries in the EU. These arrangements could also act to divert trade away from India especially in the labour intensive goods, as indicated earlier in the case of textiles and clothing.

1.5. Regional/Bilateral Free Trade Arrangements

India has taken several steps to liberalize trade with her trading partners in the South Asia region on regional as well as bilateral basis. These steps include participation to SAARC Preferential Trading Arrangements (SAPTA) that came into being in December 1995. Under this Agreement, India has exchanged trade concessions with the SAARC member countries for nearly 3000 commodities in the first three rounds of negotiations. The fourth round of these negotiations is in the process. It is expected that the process of trade liberalization in the framework of SAARC will culminate into a South Asia Free Trade Agreement (SAFTA), although, it may take some time to take shape, given the current impasse in the SAARC process. Besides SAPTA, India has recently signed a bilateral free trade agreement with Sri Lanka. India already has bilateral free trade agreement with Nepal and Bhutan. A bilateral free trade agreement is being contemplated with Bangladesh as well. There are other attempts of regional/sub-regional economic integration which may also come into being in the coming decade, for instance, BIMST-EC (Bangladesh, India, Myanmar, Sri Lanka and Thailand Economic Cooperation) which has been formed recently may adopt a preferential trading arrangement between the member countries. Although India is also a founder member of the Indian Ocean Rim Association for Regional Cooperation (IOR-ARC), a preferential trading arrangement is not contemplated as the Association has adopted the concept of open regionalism on the lines of APEC.

All these attempts at free trade with the regional partners may open the markets for Indian goods further in the countries concerned. It is evident that the share of South Asian countries in India's exports has increased from 2.73 to 4.9 over the period 1990 to 1999. The recent initiatives in regional/bilateral trade liberalization may help to divert some trade of the countries concerned from their other trading partners in favour of India given the supply capabilities.

2. FACTORS AFFECTING THE SUPPLY OF EXPORTS

It is widely believed that the major factors constraining India's exports lie not in the lack of demand but more in the supply side constraints. Most of the supply side factors need to be addressed as a part of the policy towards trade. Some of the factors that constrain the volume and composition of India's exports are as follows:

2.1 Infrastructural Bottlenecks

It is widely accepted that India's export potential remains considerably unfulfilled because of infrastructure bottlenecks such as power shortages, port handling facilities, delays in transportation which in turn are due to poor transport links within the country and poor communication facilities. The inability of Indian exporters in meeting supply schedules costs dearly in terms of image of India as a reliable source of supply. Not only that, the availability of the infrastructure services is inadequate but the efficiency and quality of the delivery of what is available is highly uneven. The ability of the government in removing these constraints in the coming years will also determine the supply side of Indian exports.

2.2 Growth of Domestic Demand

A rapid growth of domestic demand may also affect India's ability to export at least in certain products, for instance, in tea where the rapid growth of domestic demand is expected to reduce the export surplus in the coming years. It may also apply to a number of other agricultural commodities such as rice, cotton, among others.

2.3 Inflows of Export-oriented Foreign Direct Investment

Multinational Enterprises (MNEs) have played an important role in the rapid growth of manufactured exports from the East and South-East Asian countries. This is because the South East and East Asian countries were able to attract export platform investments from US and Japanese MNEs in the 1970s and 1980s. The export platform or export-oriented investment arises in the process of relocation of production by MNEs abroad in order to maintain their international competitiveness in the face of rising wages and other costs in their home countries. In Malaysia and Indonesia, for instance, 70 per cent of the projects involving FDI have been export-oriented. In China, the share of foreign owned firms in exports has risen from five per cent in 1988 to 40 per cent by 1997. In contrast, the share of foreign affiliates in India's exports is marginal at five to seven per cent (Kumar and Siddharthan, 1997, for a review of evidence from different countries). Therefore, India has not been able to exploit the potential of MNEs for export-oriented production. MNEs can play an important role in promotion of India's manufacture exports with relocation of export platform production in the country with their access to global marketing networks, best practice technology and organizational know-how. To some extent, therefore, India's ability to attract export-oriented FDI will determine the magnitude of India's exports in 2020. The studies have shown that export-oriented FDI inflows are of special type and are determined by different factors than other types of FDI (Kumar, 1994). The studies also find differences in the nature and determinants of export platform investments that are geared to MNEs' home markets and those targeting the third countries (Kumar, 1998). India may make an effort to target the export platform investments of both types by sharpening her bundle of resource endowments and created assets in the light of determinants identified by these studies.

2.5 Technological Upgrading and Movement along with the Value Chain

The Indian export structure has been highly dominated by simple and undifferentiated products, where the main competitive advantage lies in cheap labour, low levels of skills and simple technologies compared to that of China and South East Asian countries except for recent growth of pharmaceuticals and software services (Lall, 1999). Not only these products are slow moving, the export structure is highly vulnerable to competition. India's competitiveness has also been adversely affected by the failure to diversify the commodity composition of our exports. In fact, the commodity concentration of India's exports has increased with a nine per cent rise in the share of top six groups of exports in total and exports between 1987-1988 to 1998-99 (Kumar, 2000a). In comparison to India, Southeast and East Asian countries have rapidly diversified their export structure in favour of technologically advanced goods. For instance, share of technologically advanced goods (differentiated and science based goods) in India's manufactured exports rose marginally to about eight per cent by the mid-1990s over 5.6 per cent in the mid-1970s; in China, this proportion increased from 8.8 per cent to 23 per cent over the 1987-95 period, and for Malaysia from 12 per cent to 57 per cent over the 1980 to 1995 (Pigato et al. 1997). The markets for low technology undifferentiated goods are highly price competitive and margins are kept under pressure by constant competition by entry of new low wage countries.

Paying Attention to R&D Activity

The failure to diversify the export structure in favour of technologically more demanding products has been due to the relative neglect of R&D activity by the Indian industry, among other factors. The R&D activity of enterprises helps them in strengthening their international competitiveness with productivity improvements and product innovations. Not only has the proportion of national resources devoted to science and technology come down from a peak of 0.98 per cent attained in 1988 to 0.66 per cent by 1997, the R&D intensities in most industries have also declined in the 1990s (Kumar and Aggarwal, 2000). Studies have shown that export competitiveness in technology intensive industries can not be secured on the basis of import of technology alone (Kumar and Siddharthan, 1994). Therefore, technological upgrading of India's exports will not be possible without a considerable emphasis paid by the corporate sector to in-house R&D activity aimed at efficiency seeking process innovations and new product developments. The government needs to review, strengthen and consolidate the incentive structure for corporate R&D activity in the country. In particular, there is need to examine the desirability of more direct incentives to R&D activity which have been adopted by the advanced industrialized countries to further the international competitiveness of national enterprises as a part of strategic trade policy.

Building Indigenous Brands

Furthermore, the importance of building indigenous brands and their following globally through advertisement in the global media for international competitiveness can not be over emphasized. The ability to market a product under own brand name alone allows realization of value addition more fully. Otherwise, Indian companies will continue to produce and export undifferentiated simple technology and standardized products that are sold cheap and have low margins. Here again, there is imperative for assisting the industry in building their own indigenous brands. This could include funding of brand promotion expenses and incentives given to products sold under indigenous brand names.

Overseas Presence

Establishment of foreign presence in the globalizing world economy and hence, the ability to develop and supervise marketing network and provide after sales services has become an important aspect of overall competitiveness. The Indian enterprises should make aggressive use of overseas Mergers and Aquisitions (M&As) abroad as a part of their strategy to gain competitiveness, access to markets, brand names and marketing networks. A few Indian companies have strengthened their presence in respective markets with acquisitions and overseas investm... These include Tata Tea that has taken over T... overseas it an instant access to globally re... ...ents successfully. networks and world-wi... ...etley in the UK and with production activi... ...cognized brand names, marketing be able t... ...ue presence. By integrating its Indian ...ties with Tetley's marketing network, Tata Tea will ...to realize the value addition in different phases of value chain in the tea industry more completely. Companies like Ranbaxy in pharmaceuticals and Titan Industries in brand name sensitive segment of watches have adopted overseas investment route with significant success. More Indian companies need to follow these channels for strengthening their presence abroad.

Efficiency Seeking Corporate Restructuring

Finally, an efficiency seeking restructuring and consolidation of Indian industry could also help them to reap economies of scale, scope and specialization and in the process strengthening their international competitiveness. The liberalization of the economy has already provoked some restructuring in the Indian corporate sector focusing on core competencies of the enterprises through M&As (for instance, Tata Steel selling its cement plants, Raymonds selling its cement and steel divisions, Birla companies consolidating their cement capacities, etc.). Subject to the competition policy, this trend is a desirable one and will contribute to the efficiency improvement.

2.6 WTO Regime

Some of the WTO Agreements also have the provisions that are likely to affect the supply of India's exports as discussed below.

2.6.1. *TRIPs Agreement*

The Agreement on Trade Related Intellectual Property System (TRIPs) attempts to harmonize the intellectual property protection regime across the world. In particular, India will have to adopt product patents for chemicals, pharmaceuticals and food processing industries besides extending the term of the patents to 20 years by 1.1.2005. In the transition period till 2005, a mail box mechanism has been set-up and the applicants for product patents are granted exclusive market rights. Very few Indian companies are capable to sustaining product innovations in pharmaceutical industries given huge research, development and commercialization costs. Therefore, TRIPs Agreement is likely to lead to an international division of labour in pharmaceutical industries where countries like India with limited capability of product innovations will specialize in off-the-patent generic products markets and more advanced countries on innovation based new drugs. The markets for generics are highly competitive and price elastic. In order to be able to move up the value chain and upgrade their profile in the international markets, Indian pharmaceutical companies will need to develop some market niches and build product innovations capability in those areas. Some leading companies have begun to conduct R&D activity for product innovations and to develop New Drug Delivery Systems (NDDS).

2.6.2. *Phase out of QRs and Dividend Balancing under TRIMs*

A number of companies especially MNE subsidiaries were prompted to export in the previous trade regime by the need to earn import licenses or by dividend balancing condition imposed on 22 consumer goods industries. With the removal of QRs and the dividend balancing requirements to fulfil India's commitments under WTO Agreements, those exports will not be necessary any more. Hence, export-orientation of some companies may come down.

2.6.3. Agreement on Sanitary and Phytosanitary (SPS) Measures

The Agreement on Sanitary and Phytosanitary (SPS) Measures aims at uniform standards for the protection of human, animal and plant life or health. The Agreement provides a transition period to developing countries for complying with the provisions. SPS measures are likely to affect India's ability to export high-value food products and perishables. Thus, there is no alternative but to align standards in accordance with international norms.

2.7. Supply Constraints on Exports of Knowledge-based Services

India has emerged as a significant supplier of certain knowledge intensive services such as custom software and other IT enabled services over the past few years. Software exports over the past five years have grown at a compound annual growth rate of over 50 per cent (Kumar, 2000b). Sustainability of such a rapid growth of these exports is critically dependent upon our ability to increase the supply of engineering manpower (also see Wood and Calandrino, 2000). The growing scarcity of the engineering talent in the recent years is compounded by growing brain drain. In response to the growing scarcities of trained manpower for their IT industry, many countries have relaxed their immigration policies allowing their companies to recruit Indian engineers. However, currently some of these workers who emigrated are returning back because of slow down of the US economy. This, however, is a temporary phase.

The rapid rise of software industry has suddenly caused general scarcity of engineers in all disciplines leading to a sharp rise in their salaries. The engineering industry in the country is finding it difficult to find an adequate number of engineers for their requirement. The impact of rising salaries on the competitiveness of the engineering and other industries that compete for the engineering talent with the software industry is not clear but is likely to be significant.

Side by side the growing scarcity of engineering and IT trained manpower, India's educational system is churning out masses of conventional science and social science graduates who can not find adequate job opportunities. There is an immediate need for re-engineering the educational system geared for the presence times. IT education should be integrated in school and college curricula and traditional disciplines such as fine arts which could feed the growing needs for Computer Aided Design personnel. Some steps have been taken recently to augment the supply of engineering manpower as a part of the IT Action Plan which includes expanding the capacity of IITs and upgradation of REC to the IIT levels. Some new institutes of IT have been set up besides promotion of private sector training. It remains to be seen how far this expansion can be achieved without affecting the quality of the education.

2.8. Exchange Rates Alignments

The competitiveness of India's exports is also likely to be affected by the alignments in the exchange rates. The future trends in the parities of not only the major currencies such as dollar, euro and yen but also currencies of India's major competitors in specific product/market segments will affect the competitiveness of India's exports.

3. FACTORS AFFECTING THE DEMAND FOR IMPORTS

The demand for India's imports will be largely determined by the overall growth of the economy, the changing patterns of growth and the ongoing process of trade liberalization.

3.1 India's Growth Performance

The magnitude of imports to a large extent is linked to the size of the economy. The changing pattern of the economy in favour of tradable goods in future may also affect the overall import requirements for the country. The import to GDP ratio has increased from an average of 7.7 per cent for the 1980s to 10 per cent in the 1990s as a result of increasing import dependence of the Indian economy in the wake of trade liberalization and changing patterns of development. It is of interest to speculate on the projected growth rate of the economy in the next two decades and emerging patterns of demand and import intensity of the economy.

3.2.1 *Trade Liberalization*

As a result of the trade liberalization attempted since July 1991 maximum tariff rates applicable in India have come down from a peak of 355 per cent in 1990-91 to 50.8 per cent by the year 1998-99. The average weighted tariff rate has come down from 87 per cent to 20 per cent from the same period. The non-tariff measures for most of the commodities have also been phased from 1st April 2001. The process of trade liberalization is still not completed. It is expected that the tariff rates will be lowered further in the coming years in the context of regional and bilateral preferential trade arrangements as well as future WTO negotiations. Given the fact that demand for many of the items of imports is price elastic, the future tariff reductions may lead to higher imports. In particular, consumer goods imports may be highly sensitive to liberalization.

3.2 Crude Prices

The year 2000 witnessed extreme volatility in the crude oil prices that hit the roof at $ 35 per barrel in September 2000 from about $ 12 per barrel a year ago. Although these prices have since declined to a level of $ 26 per barrel, they have hardly stabilized. OPEC has decided to cut the oil output by 1.5 million barrels a day in an effort to raise the prices in mid-January 2001. It has been estimated that $ 1 per barrel variation in the international prices of crude results in $ 500 million change in India's oil import bill on an annualized basis at the current level of imports. Given the determination of OPEC to keep the prices at high levels by cutting production, the oil prices may rule around $ 25 per barrel in the coming years, although international organizations are more optimistic (World Bank 2000; IMF 2000). The volatility of oil prices is a highly destabilizing factor for the Indian economy.

3.3 Industrial Restructuring and Rationalization

The process of liberalization is likely to provoke a trend of efficiency seeking restructuring of Indian industry where some of the indigenous intermediate inputs may be substituted by imported materials to enhance the overall efficiency and competitiveness of the manufacturing process. This rationalization of production may lead to increased demand for imports of a number of products at the cost of local production.

4. EMERGING PATTERNS OF COMPARATIVE ADVANTAGE IN GOODS AND SERVICES

A look at the export profile of India over the past two decades brings out products where it has improved its share of the world market and others where it has lost the markets. Table 4 summarizes the patterns emerging from the analysis of changes in India's share in world markets. It comes out that other than textiles and garments industry, metals and gems and jewellary, chemicals and allied sectors are the only groups of manufactures where India has strengthened its presence in the world market. In almost all engineering and capital goods industries, Indian presence has either been stagnant or has declined. It would be useful to consolidate India's presence in the chemical industry with a coordinated plan to become key players in specific niche areas and strengthen the competitiveness with further process and product innovations. India also has a potential to develop into a leading player in the large market of generic pharmaceuticals. Some Indian companies have positioned themselves as leading and most cost effective producers of some common generic drugs which are in public domain. As observed earlier, we need to consolidate our presence in this sector further and also make some headway in highly lucrative proprietary drugs business that is dominated by MNEs with product innovations.

Poor attention paid to technology development is one of the factors responsible for India's declining presence in the engineering industries. In particular, IT hardware is one area where India should focus because of its long term growth potential. Countries such as Korea, Taiwan, Singapore, Malaysia, Thailand and China have positioned themselves as significant players in the IT hardware and peripherals markets. While India has lost its position in IT hardware, it has emerged as a most important player in the IT software market, as seen below.

Table 4

India's Share in World Exports, 1980-98

(percentage share)

Code Group	*Commodity Division/Group*	*1980*	*1985*	*1990*	*1995*	*1998*
	A. COMMODITIES WITH INCREASING SHARES					
03	Fish, crustaceans and molluscs and preparations	2	2.4	1.6	2.1	2.5
042	Rice	3.7	5.6	6.4	18.6	10.4
06	Sugar, sugar preparations and honey	0.3	0	0.1	0.8	0.4
071	Coffee and coffee substitutes	2.1	1.9	1.7	2.8	2.7
08	Feeding stuff for animals	1.6	1.5	2.2	3.4	4.3
22	Oilseeds and oleaginous fruit	0.3	0.3	0.8	1.2	1.6
51	Organic chemicals	0.1	0.1	0.3	0.7	0.9
52	Inorganic chemicals	0.2	0.1	0.2	0.2	0.4
53	Dyeing, tanning and colouring materials	0.8	0.8	1.2	1.1	1.3
54	Medicinal and pharmaceutical products	0.8	0.8	1.2	1	1
57	Explosives and pyrotechnic products	0.1	0.1	0.2	0.3	0.7
58	Artificial resins, plastic materials, cellulose esters & ethers	0	0	0	0.1	0.1
59	Chemical materials and products n.e.s. 0	0.2	0.2	0.4	0.6	
65	Textile yarn, fabrics, made-up articles	2.3	2.1	2.1	2.6	3.3
667	Pearls, precious and semi-precious stones	3.1	9.6	9.8	12	10.7
67	Iron and steel	0.1	0.1	0.3	0.6	0.8
84	Articles of apparel and clothing accessories	1.8	2.3	2.3	2.5	2.3
	Other exports	0.2	0.1	0.3	0.3	0.3
	Total exports	0.4	0.5	0.5	0.6	0.6
	B. COMMODITIES WITH DECLINING OR STATIC SHARES					
01	Meat and meat preparations	0.4	0.4	0.2	0.4	0.4
05	Vegetables and fruits	1.1	1.4	0.8	1	1
074	Tea and mate	27.7	26.2	22.1	14.3	16.4
075	Spices	14.5	19.3	7.7	9.5	11.2
12	Tobacco and tobacco manufactures	4.4	1.8	0.8	0.5	1

(Contd...)

(...Contd...)

Code Group	Commodity Division/Group	1980	1985	1990	1995	1998
28	Metalliferous ores and metal scrap	1.5	2.4	2.1	1.5	1.4
55	Essential oils and perfume materials soap, cleansing etc	1.1	0.7	1.1	0.5	0.4
61	Leather, leather manufactures & dressed fur skins	6.8	8.3	6.3	3.1	2.9
69	Manufactures of metals n.e.s.	0.6	0.4	0.5	0.5	0.6
71	Power-generating machinery and equipment	0.2	0.2	0.2	0.1	0.2
72	Machinery specialized for particular industries	0.1	0.2	0.2	0.1	0.2
73	Metal-working machinery	0.2	0.4	0.2	0.2	0.2
74	General industrial machinery & equipment & machine parts thereof	0.1	0.1	0.1	0.1	0.1
75	Office machinery and ADP equipment	0	0.1	0.1	0.1	0.1
76	Telecommunication and sound recording and reproducing apparatus and equipment	0	0	0	0.1	0
77	Electrical machinery, apparatus and appliances	0.2	0.2	0.1	0.1	0.1
78	Road vehicles (including air cushion vehicles)	0.2	0.1	0.1	0.2	0.1
79	Other transport equipment	0.1	0.1	0	0	0

Source: Compiled on the basis of Government of India, *Economic Surveys*, various years.

Software and IT Services[1]: A New Field of Comparative Advantage for India

The rise of the IT software and services industry (henceforth software industry) over the 1990s represents one of the most spectacular achievements for the Indian economy. As shown in Table 5, the Indian software industry has grown at a phenomenal compound annual rate of over 50 per cent over the 1990s from a total revenue of US$ 175 million in 1989/90 to a $ 8.7 billion industry by 2000/01. Furthermore, the industry has earned 70 per cent of its revenue (totaling $ 6.3 billion) from exports.

1. This section draws upon Kumar (2000b).

Table 5

Indian Software Industry Revenues and Exports

(US $ million)

Year	*Total*	*Domestic*	*Exports*
1989/90	197	97	100
1994/95	835	350	485
1995/96	1224	490	734
1996/97	1755	670	1085
1997/98	2700	950	1750
1998/99	3900	1250	2650
1999/2000	5700	1700	4000
2000/1[P]	8750	2450	6300
Compound Annual Growth Rate			
1994/99	56.3%	46.05%	60.71%

Notes: [P] projected;

Figure 2

Revenues and Exports of Indian Software Industry

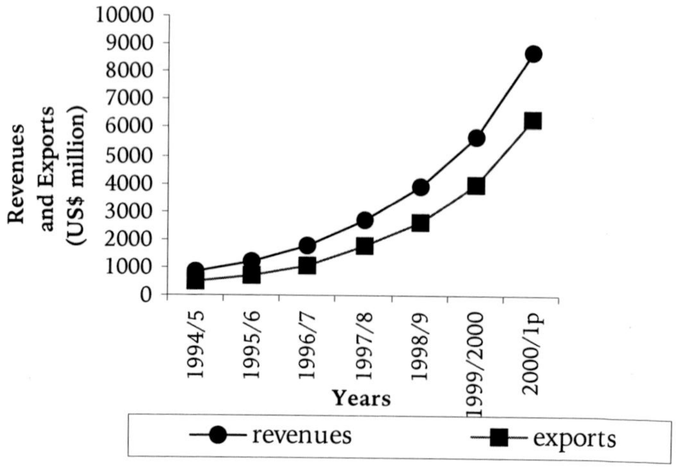

Source: Table 5.

Growth Rates and Share in the Global Industry

The growth rates of revenues and of exports in US$ terms are summarized in Table 6 and Fig. 3. It is clear that except for 1996/7, the annual export growth rate has been higher than 50 per cent. The growth rate of overall revenue has been lower than that of exports except for 1996/7 on account of a somewhat slower rate of growth of the domestic software market. However, the growth rates of overall revenues and of exports have tended to converge over the past couple of years as a result of the growth rates of the domestic software market also picking up.

Table 6

Growth Rates of Magnitudes of Software Revenue and Exports

	1994/95	1995/96	1996/97	1997/98	1998/99	1999/2000
Growth Rate of Revenue in US$		34.61	56.14	53.85	44.44	48.65
Growth Rate of Exports in US$	54.46	51.34	47.82	61.29	51.43	50.94

Source: Based on Table 5.

Figure 3

Growth Rates of Software Revenue and Exports

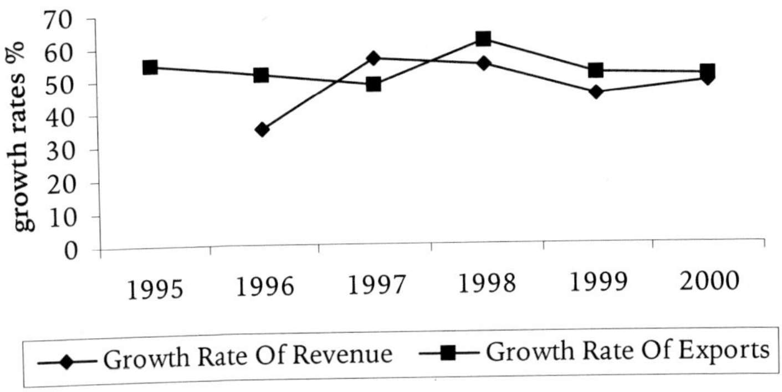

Source: Based on Table 6.

To put the above growth performance in an international perspective, the Indian software industry would account for roughly one to one and a half per cent of the US$ 400 billion global software industry. However, India's share in the global market for customized software that is outsourced across borders is significant at 18.5 per cent in 1999 compared to 11.9 per cent in 1991. The growth rate of the Indian software industry has been substantially higher than the global software industry. Apparently, India is the only country in the world to register a growth rate of around 50 per cent in the software industry.

Future Outlook

The performance of the Indian software industry over the past few years has generated tremendous optimism. Nasscom had commissioned McKinsey to provide a vision document for the year 2008 for the Indian software industry that was released in late 1999. Nasscom-McKinsey Report presents a bold vision for an industry with US$85 billion revenue by 2008 of which $50 billion would come from exports. The McKinsey Report bases its projections on the basis of a few assumptions. These include that the global IT-services market will grow from $327 billion in 1997 to $1010 billion by 2008 at a cumulative annual growth rate of 10.8 per cent at which it has been growing. Secondly, Indian exports account for marginal shares of total spending on IT services in world's major markets in 1997, hence the potential for a rise in their share by 2008 given the faster growth rates of the industry in India. Finally, that Indian software industry will be able to sustain its existing competitive advantages and build further. For instance, leading Indian companies will develop into multinational companies to anchor Indian capability with worldwide brand recognition. On the basis of these assumptions, the Nasscom-Mckinsey Report predicts that it would be possible for Indian software industry to export $50 billion worth of software services and products as shown in Table 7. This target has also been adopted by the National Taskforce on IT and Software Development (NTITSD) set up by the Prime Minister in 1998.

As is clear from the Table 7, the Report's targets put a big thrust on products and on IT-enabled services in terms of the composition of Indian exports by 2008 with a proportionate decline in the share of services in exports. The McKinsey Report's analysis expects Indian companies to be able to exploit opportunities in enterprise software (ERP/EAS) and mobile computing and embedded software, given their ability to develop quality software products for the domestic market. It finds that a big potential exists for India in the large and expanding market of what is termed as IT-enabled services which could fetch $15 billion in export earnings by 2008 compared to just $145 million in 1999. These services include several business activities of large corporations that can be relocated overseas facilitated by the development of satellite communication links. These cover broadly the back-office operations such as accounting, insurance claims processing, legal databases, content development/ animation, payrolls and logistics management, call centres, medical transcriptions, etc. The back-office management and other IT-enabled services generate global revenues of $ 75 billion and are recording a 20 per cent growth rate per annum. Call centre services is already a large industry with global revenues of $ 200 billion and is growing at an annual rate of 23 per cent. Most companies in service industries such as finance and banking and transport among others, use call centres to provide an interface to clients on a 24-hour basis. India's large pool of English speaking computer-literate graduates could help her to tap a share of these service industries. The government has already begun to take note of the potential of these services and has taken steps to provide the necessary communications infrastructure. Already a number of large MNEs, such as GE Capital, British Airways, Bechtel and Healthscribe, among others, have started seting up their call centres or back-office operations in India.

The current slow down of the IT industry in the US may tamper some of the assumptions that underpin these projections. Yet, the point remains that software and IT-enabled services do represent an area where India has a comparative advantage. The realization of these projections and the potential of the country in these sectors will depend on the ability of the country to respond to such emerging challenges as growing skill shortages, rising wages and competition from other countries. Given the strong push some other countries like China, the Philippines, are giving to the industry, there is no room for complacency though. India should use her first mover advantage effectively to upgrade her profile in high value added and upper-end services and in shrink wrapped packaged software before the onslaught of competition from other countries begins to bite.

Table 7

Export Targets of Nasscom-McKinsey Report for 2008

(US$ billion)

Segment	Actual 1998/9	Target 2008
IT Services	2.13(80.6)	23(46)
Software Products	0.209(7.9)	8(16)
IT-enabled Services	0.145(5.5)	15(30)
E-business	0.159(6.0)	4(8)
Total	2.65(100)	50(100)

Source: Kumar (2000b) based on Nasscom-McKinsey Report and Nasscom (2000a).

5. CONCLUDING REMARKS

Projecting the magnitude of India's imports and exports in the year 2020 is not an easy task given the fact that a large number of factors external to the national economic policy operate and affect a country's trade in a significant manner. In the foregoing, we have provided an inventory of some of the important factors –internal as well as external— that may have a bearing on the magnitude and patterns of trade flows in 2020. Given the uncertainties involved in projecting the trade figures, it may be more appropriate to set targets for specific items of India's exports by 2020 that seem feasible and desirable given the local capabilities, resources and competitiveness, likely world demand scenario, emerging competition, and other relevant factors. Then we may work backwards to delineate the necessary conditions that will be required to be fulfilled to achieve those targets. The target setting also has the advantage of giving to the industry a mission to accomplish in a given time frame. The government may also facilitate the process of achieving the targets with strategic interventions in the realm of trade, investment and technology policies (see Kumar 2001). It may also target export-oriented FDI flows from MNEs more effectively and participate actively in the multilateral trade negotiations to secure Indian interests and make the playing field less uneven.

References

IMF (2000), *World Economic Outlook: October 2000*, Washington, DC: International Monetary Fund.

Kumar, Nagesh (1994a), 'Determinants of Export-Orientation of Foreign Production by U.S. Multinationals: An Inter Country Analysis', *Journal of International Business Studies* 25(1): pp. 141-156.

———. and Siddharthan, N. S. (1994), 'Technology, Firm Size and Export Behaviour in Developing Countries: the case of Indian Enterprises', *Journal of Development Studies* 31(2), pp. 289-309.

———. and Siddharthan, N. S. (1997), *Technology, Market Structure and Internationalization: Issues and Policies for Developing Countries*. London and New York: Routledge.

———. (1998), 'Multinational Enterprises, Regional Economic Integration, and Export-Platform Production in the Host Countries: An Empirical Analysis for the US and Japanese Corporations', *Weltwirtschaftliches Archiv*, 134(3): pp. 450-483.

———. (2000a), *Indian Economy Under Reforms: An Assessment of Economic and Social Impact*, New Delhi: Bookwell and RIS.

———. (2000b), 'Developing Countries in International Division of Labour in Software and Service Industry: Lessons from Indian Experience', Background Paper for *World Employment Report 2001*, Geneva: ILO.

———. (2001), 'WTO Regime, Host Country Policies and Global Patterns of MNE Activity: Recent Quantitative Studies and India's Strategic Response' *Economic and Political Weekly*, 36(1) 6 January, pp. 39-50.

———. and Agarwal Aradhna (2000), Liberalization, Outward Orientation and In-house R&D Activity of Multinational and Local Firms: A Quantitative Exploration for Indian Manufacturing, RIS Discussion Paper # 7, New Delhi.

Lall, Sanjaya (1999), 'India's Manufactured Exports: Comparative Structure and Prospects', *World Development* 27(10): 1769-86.

Panchamukhi, V. R. (2000), World Trade Organization and India: Challenges and Perspectives, RIS Discussion Paper # 01/2000.

Pigato, Miria et al. (1997), *South Asia's Integration into the World Economy*, Washington, DC: The World Bank.

Wood, Adrian and Michele, Calandrino (2000), 'When Other Giant Awakens: Trade and Human Resources in India', *Economic and Political Weekly*, 35(52-3), 30 December, 4677-94.

World Bank (2000), *Global Economic Prospects and the Developing Countries*, Washington, DC: The World Bank.

WTO (2000), *International Trade Statistics 2000*, Geneva: World Trade Organization.

20

The Financial Sector: Vision 2020

ROHIT SARKAR

I. Introduction

A financial system, which is inherently strong, functionally diverse and displays efficiency and flexibility, is critical to our national objectives of creating a market-driven, productive and competitive economy. A mature system supports higher levels of investment and promotes growth in the economy with its depth and coverage. The financial system in India comprises of financial institutions, financial markets, financial instruments and services. The Indian financial system is characterised by its two major segments - an organised sector and a traditional sector that is also known as informal credit market. Financial intermediation in the organised sector is conducted by a large number of financial institutions which are business organisations providing financial services to the community. Financial institutions whose activities may be either specialised or may overlap are further classified as banking and non-banking entities. The Reserve Bank of India (RBI) as the main regulator of credit is the apex institution in the financial system. Other important financial institutions are the commercial banks (in the public and private sector), cooperative banks, regional rural banks and development banks. Non-bank financial institutions include finance and leasing companies and other institutions like LIC, GIC, UTI, Mutual funds, Provident Funds, Post Office Banks etc.

The banking system is, by far, the most dominant segment of the financial sector, accounting as it does, for over 80 per cent of the funds flowing through the financial sector. The aggregate deposits of the scheduled commercial banks (SCBs) rose from Rs. 5,05,599 crore in March 1997 to Rs. 11,03,360 crore in March 2002 representing a rise of 17 per cent. During the same period, the credit portfolio (food and non-food) of SCBs grew from Rs. 2,78,401 crore to Rs.5,89,723 crore, i.e. by 16 per cent. The net profits of SCBs witnessed a noticeable upturn from Rs. 6,403 crore in 2000-01 to Rs.11,572 crore in 2001-02. The extent and coverage of the banking system can be gauged from the fact that the number of branches of SCBs grew from 8045 in 1969 to 66,186 in June 2002. While rural branches constituted 49 per cent of the total in 2002, semi-urban branches accounted for 22 per cent, urban branches accounted for 16 per cent and metropolitan branches accounted for 13 per cent.

As regards the capital market, the resource mobilization from the primary market by non-government public limited companies has declined in the recent past from the high levels witnessed between 1992-93 and 1996-97. Resource mobilization of these companies in the public issues market stood at Rs. 5,692 crore in 2001-02 registering an increase of 16.4 per cent over the amount mobilized during the previous year. The public issues market has been dominated by debt issues both in the private and public sectors in the recent past. In recent years, private placement has emerged as an important vehicle for raising resources by banks, financial institutions and public and private sector companies. Such placements continued to dominate the primary market although the pace of growth of the private placement market has slackened during the last two years. Resource mobilization by mutual funds is an important activity in the capital markets. Although there has been a decline in the net resource mobilization by mutual funds to the extent of 28 per cent during 2001-02, according to SEBI, outstanding net assets of all mutual funds stood at Rs.1,00,594 crore as at end-March 2002. The strong potential of the capital market as an area of resource mobilization needs no emphasis and this segment of the financial sector would continue to play a significant role in the future.

Reforms

The quantum of resources required to be mobilised, as the economy grows in complexity and generates new demands, places the financial sector in a vital position for promoting efficiency and momentum. It intermediates in the flow of funds from those who want to save a part of their income to those who want to invest in productive assets. The efficiency of intermediation depends on the width, depth and diversity of the financial system. Till about two decades ago, a large part of household savings was either invested directly in physical assets or put in bank deposits and small savings schemes of the Government. Since the late Eighties, however, equity markets started playing an important role. Other markets such as the medium to long-term debt market and short term money market remained relatively segmented and underdeveloped. In the past decades, the Government and its subsidiary institutions and agencies had an overwhelming and all encompassing role with extensive system of controls, rules, regulations and procedures, which directly or indirectly affected the development of these markets.

The financial system comprising of a network of institutions, instruments and markets suffered from lack of flexibility in intermediary behaviour and segmentation of various markets and sets of financial intermediaries. Well-developed markets should be inter-connected to facilitate the demand-supply imbalances in one market overflowing into related markets, thereby dampening shocks and disturbances. The inter connection also ensures that interest rates and returns in any market reflect the broad demand-supply conditions in the overall market of savings. But such adjustment of interest rates is delayed when the intermediaries lack flexibility. On account of the historical role of the Government in controlling and directing a large part of the financial activity, such adjustments were slow and the problem needed to be addressed urgently if the financial sector had to keep pace with the reforms in the real sector.

World wide experience confirms that the countries with well-developed and market-oriented financial systems have grown faster and more steadily than those with weaker and closely regulated systems. The financial sector, in general and banking system in particular, in many of the developing countries have been plagued by various systemic problems which necessitated drastic structural changes as also a re-orientation of approach in order to develop a more efficient and well functioning financial system.

The Indian financial system has been no exception in this respect and the problems encountered in the way of efficient functioning necessitated the financial sector reforms. Recognising the critical nature of the financial sector prompted the Government to set up two Committees on the Financial System (Narasimham Committees) in

1991 and 1998 to examine all aspects relating to the structure, organisation, functions and procedures of the financial system. The deliberations of the Committees were guided by the demands that would be placed on the financial system by the economic reforms talking place in the real sectors of the economy and by the need to introduce greater competition through autonomy and private sector participation in the financial sector. Despite the fact that the bulk of the banks were and are likely to remain in the public sector, and therefore, with virtually zero risk of failure, the health and financial credibility of the banking sector was an issue of paramount importance to the Committees.

The Committees proposed reforms in the financial sector to bring about operational flexibility and functional autonomy, for overall efficiency, productivity and profitability. In the banking sector, in particular, the measures have been taken, aimed at restoring viability of the banking system, bringing about an internationally accepted level of accounting and disclosure standards and introducing capital adequacy norms in a phased manner. Most of the measures suggested by the Committees have been accepted by the Government. Interest rates have been deregulated over a period of time, branch-licensing procedures have been liberalised and Statutory Liquidity Ratio (SLR) and Cash Reserve Ratio (CRR) have been reduced. The entry barriers for foreign banks and new private sector banks have been lowered as part of the medium term strategy to improve the financial and operational health of the banking system by introducing an element of competition into it. A Board for Financial Supervision has been set up within the Reserve Bank of India and it has introduced a new system of off-site surveillance even while revamping the system of on-site surveillance. The financial sector reforms have been pursued vigorously and the results of the first set of reforms have brought about improved efficiency and transparency in the financial sector. It is well recognized that reforms in the financial sector are an ongoing process to meet the challenges thrown up on account of the integration of financial markets, both within the country and worldwide.

Future Direction of Reforms

If the financial sector reforms are viewed in a broad perspective, it would be evident that the first phase of reforms focussed on modification of the policy framework, improvement in financial health of the entities and creation of a competitive environment. The second phase of reforms target the three inter-related issues, *viz.*, (i) strengthening the foundations of the banking system; (ii) streamlining procedures, upgrading technology and human resource development; and (iii) structural changes in the system. These would cover aspects of banking policy, and focus on institutional, supervisory and legislative dimensions.

Although significant steps have been taken in reforming the financial sector, some areas require greater focus. One area of concern relates to the ability of the financial sector in its present structure to make available investible resources to the potential investors in the forms and tenors that will be required by them in the coming years, that is, as equity, long term debt and medium and short-term debt. If this does not happen, there could simultaneously exist excess demand and excess supply in different segments of the financial markets. In such a situation the segment facing the highest level of excess demand would prove to the binding constraint to investment activity and effectively determine the actual level of investment in the economy. Such problems could be resolved through movement of funds between various types of financial institutions and instruments and also by portfolio reallocation by the savers in response to differential movements in the returns in the alternative financial instruments. In this context, it is very important to identify the emerging structure of investment demand, particularly from the private sector, in order to reorient the functioning of the financial sector accordingly, so that investment in areas of national importance flows smoothly.

A major area that needs to be focused in the context of the country's development policy is investment in infrastructure. Financing of infrastructure projects is a specialized activity and would continue to be of critical importance in the future. A sound and efficient infrastructure is a *sine qua non* for sustainable economic development. A deficient infrastructure can be a major impediment in a country's economic growth particularly when the economy is on the upswing. A growing economy needs supporting infrastructure at all levels, be it adequate and reasonably priced power, efficient communication and transportation facilities or a thriving energy sector. Such infrastructure development has a multiplier effect on economic growth, which cannot be overlooked.

Infrastructure services have generally been provided by the public sector all over the world for a large part of the twentieth century as most of these services have an element of public good in them. It was only in the closing years of the century that private financing of infrastructure made substantial progress. It may be relevant to point out that infrastructure was largely privately financed in the nineteenth century. The twenty-first century would, therefore, be more like the nineteenth than the twentieth century.

This trend has been visible in India as well where financing of infrastructure was till recently a Government activity. This has been so because infrastructure services are difficult to price so as to fully cover all costs, thereby making it unattractive for private sector participation. Also, the provisions of infrastructure usually involve high upfront costs and long payback periods and the private investor is often unable to provide the large initial capital required and is not capable of obtaining matching long-term finance. Finally cross-subsidization, which forms an important part of infrastructure provision, is easier done by public sector than the private.

However, there has been a paradigm shift in funding of infrastructure from the Government to the private sector mainly due to budgetary constraints in making available funds to meet the huge requirements of the infrastructure sector. The other contributing factors for the diminishing role of the Government have been the dissatisfaction with the performance of state provided infrastructure, more efficient utilization of resources by the private sector and greater Government emphasis on allocation of budgetary resources to social service sectors such as health and education. The Government's role is perceived as the ability to provide a stable and conducive macroeconomic environment and carry out necessary regulatory reforms, which in turn would facilitate private sector investments in the infrastructure sector.

The Government continues to play the role of a facilitator and the development of infrastructure really becomes an exercise in public-private partnership. The fact that funding for infrastructure has to increasingly come from the private sector has now been widely recognized and the focus of the debate has been on best practices in reform strategies, regulatory frameworks and risk mitigation techniques. The Government has the challenging task of providing fair, predictable and sustainable framework for private sector participation in infrastructure that will deliver better services with greater efficiency. It has been observed globally that project finance to developing countries flows in where there is a relatively stable macro-economic environment. However, there are certain other conditions, which must be present. These include regulatory reforms and opening markets to competition and private investment. Liberalized financial markets, promoting the deepening and widening of local markets, wider use of risk management and other financial products, improved legal frameworks and accounting standards and privatization programmes are some of the other aspects which favourably impact on infrastructure project finance.

Infrastructure projects are characterised by large capital costs and long gestation periods. The assets of these projects are not easily transferable and the services provided are non-tradable in nature. These projects are typically vulnerable to regulatory and political changes and are also dependent on supportive infrastructure. There are also politically sensitive issues like tariffs and relocation and rehabilitation of people. For these reasons, the infrastructure projects carry a relatively higher risk profile and, therefore, this funding is different from the traditional balance sheet financing. The characteristics and complex nature of infrastructure projects call for proper risks assessment and mitigation mechanisms. The financing of infrastructure projects is largely cash flow based and not asset based. In fact, in some sectors like telecom, roads, bridges etc. the tangible assets may not even provide adequate cover for the loans. These projects are financed through Special Purpose Vehicles by way of non-recourse/limited recourse financing structures. The approach to such projects is to properly identify and allocate various elements of project risks to the entities participating in the project. The role of sponsors is normally limited to bringing in the contracted equity/ contingent equity contribution.

The non-recourse financing of infrastructure projects necessitates exhaustive due-diligence process on the part of the funding agencies to ascertain that the project cash flows are adequate to cover the debt service obligations. Risk analysis and risk mitigation mechanisms, therefore, constitute a critical part of the due-diligence exercise. These risks can broadly be classified into various types, *viz.*, construction risk, operation risk, political risk, force majeure risk, market risk and payment risk. The success of project financing depends in a large measure on good risk management. There are various mechanisms for mitigating these risks such as execution of appropriate contracts, performance guarantees, liquidated damages, purchase/sale contracts, cash support agreements, insurance coverage etc. Financial structuring has to be such that it would help a project withstand a wide variety of risks, both expected and unexpected.

The complexity of the transactions and large funding requirements demand an innovative approach towards financial structuring and the use of a variety of financial instruments. The involvement of project finance lenders in some projects is quite intense, who often take a blend of debt and equity positions in these ventures. Such a blended role includes broad representation and tiered returns and levels of security for various tranches of participation. In India, such financing is usually undertaken by the specialized term lending agencies like IL&FS, IDFC, ICICI and IDBI. Commercial banks rarely take equity positions in projects. Infrastructure financing necessarily requires the commitment of long-term funds, both as equity and long-term debt. In the past, since the infrastructure sector was predominantly catered to by public investment, the need to develop appropriate financing mechanisms was not felt. As a result, the Indian financial sector is heavily biased towards short and medium term debt, whether it is the commercial banking sector or the financial institutions. This position needs to be changed and the availability of equity and long-term debt to the private sector has to be increased substantially.

The traditional approach to financing is inadequate to match the risk-return profile and payback periods of infrastructure projects. Financial institutions and banks are constrained by the time profile of their own liabilities. Consequently, they are limited in their capacity to finance long gestation projects. The Government and RBI are seized of these problems and important steps have been taken to facilitate financing of infrastructure sector like removing the ceiling on a single term loan by commercial banks and relaxing the exposure norms for financing such projects. The modalities of financing in so far as appropriate appraisal, supervision and monitoring mechanism at the operating level are concerned have been spelt out by RBI in addition to the proper exposure and maturity norms at the policy level.

Banks and financial institutions on their part need to lay down internal exposure norms for the infrastructure sector as a whole as also for each sector in the infrastructure area from the risk management point of view. Another important aspect to be viewed is asset-liability management and appropriate policy needs to be formulated for the asset-liability mismatch, which is likely to occur as the resources of banks are essentially short term in nature whereas the maturity requirement for funding of infrastructure projects extends up to 15 to 20 years. There is also need to develop a secondary debt market so that there is liquidity and recycling of funds.

The debt market which is central to infrastructure financing, comprises basically these segments, *viz.*, Government securities market which is the oldest and most dominant; PSU Bonds Market, which is basically a development since the late Eighties; and Corporate Securities Market, which is growing fast after liberalization. The major focus in the development of debt markets has been the Government securities market because apart from it constituting the principal segment of the debt market, it has a role in setting benchmarks in the financial markets as a whole. The reforms in the debt market have taken the shape of bringing about various structural and institutional changes. The Treasury bill market has been streamlined and with the strengthening the dealers system, retailing in Government securities has been promoted. To widen the participation in the debt market including Government securities, Foreign Institutional Investors (FIIs) have also been permitted to operate. Although significant progress has been made, a number of rigidities persist and certain issues still need to be tackled. The actions required for this purpose are in areas relating to legal, technological, regulatory and market microstructure, retailing, risk management, standardization etc.

An extremely important issue in infrastructure financing is the availability of funds. The funding is required to be met by the private sector from various commercial sources including banks and financial institutions. According to the India Infrastructure Report, the level of investment in infrastructure needed to be increased from 5.5 per cent of GDP to about seven per cent by 2000-01 and eight per cent by 2005-06 to attain a GDP growth of seven per cent by 2000-01 and eight per cent by 2005-06. The funding requirements of various sectors in the infrastructure area aggregate to about Rs.12,00,000 crore by the year 2005-06. The estimated availability of financing from Indian financial institutions and banks for infrastructure is expected to be about Rs.1,20,000 crore. Financing of Infrastructure sector will thus be a major responsibility of the banks and financial institutions in the years to come. However, this would still leave a large funding gap, which would have to be met through other sources, *viz.*, bilateral/multilateral/Government funding.

Other possible sources for such financing could be institutional, such as pension, provident and insurance funds that have the advantage of providing a better maturity match for infrastructure financing. But in India, the investment patterns of these funds are highly regulated with a bias towards investment in Government securities. There is need to deregulate these long-term fund sources and formulate prudential norms for such financing. To begin with, participation of pension, provident funds etc. can be to a limited extent in projects appraised by the all India financial institutions. These funds could also be allowed to deposit in banks for long periods, subject to banks using them exclusively for infrastructure financing. Banks could also be permitted to float 10 to 15 year tax-free bonds to raise long-term resources specifically for financing of infrastructure projects.

A financial technique that has been successfully used in infrastructure financing in several developed countries is securitisation. This is a process through which illiquid assets are transferred into a more liquid form of assets and distributed to a broad range of investors through the capital markets. The lending institution's assets are removed from its balance sheet and are instead funded by investors through a negotiable financial instrument. The security is backed by the expected cash flow from the assets. Securitisation facilitate better asset-liability management for the lender by reducing market risks resulting from interest rate mismatches. From the point of view of the financial system as a whole, securitisation increases the number of debt instruments in the market thereby providing additional liquidity. It also facilities unbundling, better allocation and management of project risks. It has the effect of widening the market by attracting new players on account of superior quality assets being available. However, suitable prudential norms must be in place and adhered to, for the process to function smoothly. The RBI encourages banks and financial institutions to securitise the receivables, repackage and offer them to investors at various stages of the infrastructure project.

One of the specific proposals circulated by RBI to banks for hedging liquidity risk and interest rate risk is the concept of Take-Out Financing facility and market making in project debentures, say after a pre-determined period of five years to give comfort to commercial banks which are willing to deploy their funds in infrastructure. However, the RBI would need to monitor the extent of such facilities in relation to the balance sheets of the parties. In any case, the provision of a "liquidity back stop" by the RBI for supporting market making at the end of the pre-determined period has implications for monetary management.

The current Government policy on external commercial borrowings allows considerable flexibility in the case of power and other infrastructure projects. But the use of external financing of infrastructure is being inhibited by the inability to hedge long term exchange risk under current regulations of the RBI. Several measures are being taken to deepen the forward market in foreign exchange but there is a limited forward supply beyond one year. In some cases, long-term currency swaps have been used, though in a limited way and market participants also run a swap book subject to prudential limits. Of course, the exchange risk issue does not inhibit external financing where there is a natural hedge such as in export-oriented units or where there are foreign exchange receivables.

Government support to infrastructure financing, which is the traditional route, can take several forms. Central and state governments have underwritten the major sources of risk in some infrastructure projects through various kinds of guarantees. The capital that the private sector provides to such derisked projects is analogous to lending to the Government with a risk premium added for any residual risks in the projects. Income tax incentives are often provided to infrastructure projects or to the investors in such a project. Limited tax breaks or tax holidays are methods used in this regard. Governments also use the mechanism of directed credit to infrastructure but this is essentially a pre-liberalisation phenomenon. Other methods like negative license fee and various forms of credit enhancement have been used in different countries to develop infrastructure projects.

These areas of Government intervention in the form of subsidy and credit enhancement would exist as the public sector will continue to have a major role in the infrastructure sector even as its share declines and gives way to private investments, principally in the areas of power generation, telecommunications initially and in roads, civil aviation and urban infrastructure thereafter.

In the new paradigm, with the private sector entering into infrastructure services and private capital having to be accessed on competitive terms, the regulatory framework assumes great importance. Such a framework must provide for transparency, clarity of obligations between the participants in the infrastructure projects and should reduce the layering of approvals to bring about a greater degree of certainty in obtaining them within a definite time frame. The rules of the game should not be changed too frequently and without notice, to enable the participants to have reasonable planning horizons. In such an atmosphere, the private sector would be encouraged to participate in infrastructure financing more effectively and the Government need not step in with direct or indirect support to such an extent that the private project really becomes a privately managed but publicly funded enterprise.

Even in a more general sense, for any investment activity to take off, the availability of equity is the starting point and with this end in view, a serious thought needs to be given to the domestic capital markets. While the secondary market is quite well developed, it is the primary market which remains dormant making the equity raising exercise by both new as well as existing companies difficult. While attracting foreign equity to bridge this gap is possible to some extent, there is a strong case for developing a vibrant primary market and instilling confidence amongst the small investors. This can be brought about by ensuring that the transparency and disclosure norms of SEBI are strictly complied with and defaulters are penalised. Further, the tendency to list new issues on the major stock exchanges should be checked and an alternative route of listing on the OTCEI should be encouraged, of course after energising this organisation. With the pricing of shares being left to the respective company boards, institutional improvements in the market are needed to ensure that share pricing is reflective of the intrinsic worth of the company and its potential. The involvement of mutual funds in the primary issues market needs to be encouraged, as this is essential for the healthy growth of industry and revival of investor confidence.

As far as long-term debt is concerned, at present the Government monopolises practically all forms of long term funds, such as insurance, pension and provident funds. With the desired shift in investment responsibilities, it has become necessary for the Government to vacate some of this space for the private sector. Conditions should also be created whereby savers are attracted towards investing in long-term debt instruments. One way is to make much more concerted efforts for the creation of a debt market, for, in the absence of such a market, practically all debt investments are held to maturity and this illiquidity reduces the attractiveness of debt instruments particularly those of longer maturity. Until the secondary debt market becomes sufficiently active so as to absorb debt instruments of various maturities, there is a case for the Central Government to move its debt portfolio towards the shorter end of the maturity spectrum, which would increase liquidity in the debt market. This would be consistent with the recommendation for the Centre to vacate more space in SLR placements in favour of the states and PSEs.

The insurance sector has been an important source of low cost funds of long-term maturities all over the world. In the Indian context, however, the insurance companies, particularly in life insurance, apart from covering risk are also committed to repayment of the principal with interest although with long maturities and thereby tend to act as investment funds. One of the reasons that this has happened is that the average premium charged by the insurance companies in India tends to be relatively high due to obsolete and rigid actuarial practices and inefficient operations. There is pressing need to reorient the insurance sector in a manner that it fulfills its principal mandate of providing risk cover. The opening up of the insurance sector to private participation, including banks in August 2000 has been able to instill an element of competition which would in turn promote efficiency and professionalism and enhance consumer choice through product innovation.

The Insurance Regulatory and Development Authority (IRDA) is vested with the power to regulate and develop the insurance and reinsurance business. The IRDA has prescribed stringent licensing criteria and solvency margins, with guidelines for investment of the larger part of resources in Government securities and other approved investments (including infrastructure) and exposure norms for other investments. The liberalisation of the insurance sector impacts the functioning of the financial system through the inter-linkages with the existing financial institutions and financial products. However, a critical issue to be addressed is increasing the insurance penetration to make it comparable to the other emerging market economies, including enhanced coverage of the rural sector.

Banking System

An area of concern which impacts on investment is the relatively high interest rate structure that prevails in the country. Interest rates are no doubt related to inflation in a trend sense but this relationship is primarily with respect to the rates received by the savers. With a decrease in inflationary expectations in the economy the nominal deposit rates should be amenable to reduction without materially affecting the expected real returns to the savers. The Government would have to clearly signal an anti-inflationary stance in a credible manner and also the actual rate of inflation would need to be brought down to its target level and maintained there for a sufficient period of time for inflationary expectations to be adjusted downwards. A beginning has been made by reducing the interest rates on small savings schemes run by the Government as well as on bank deposits. However interest rates paid by borrowers are also dependent on the level of efficiency of the financial system. The spread between the deposit and lending rates in India is high by international standards and reflects both the constraints faced by and the relatively low level of efficiency in the financial intermediation system. Although in recent years there has been considerable liberalisation in the banking sector with tightening of prudential norms and accounting practices which have led to an improvement in the health of the banking sector, there are some areas of concern which need to be examined.

The banking industry has a high level of non-performing assets (NPAs) to contend with. High NPAs raise the cost of bank operations and thereby the spread and efforts need to be made to bring these down. However, a balance has to be drawn between the reduction in

NPAs on one hand and ensuring adequate supply of credit to the economy on the other. Excessive pressure on banks to reduce NPAs is likely to lend to a high degree of selectivity in the credit disbursal process and consequently, a reduction of the total level of credit as dictated by the growth of deposits. The rate of reduction of NPAs will therefore have to be fairly gradual keeping in mind the notional lending risks associated with the Indian economy and the speed at which debt recovery and settlement processes operate. In addition, the factors other than NPAs which affect the level of spread required for the viability of banks would need to be considered in the context of national priorities and policy objectives. To achieve this, action has to be taken on strengthening and professionalising the internal control and review procedures of banks and financial institutions with a view to ensuring autonomy with accountability. Also, the process of judicial review and implementation of debt recovery processes and decisions need to be given further impetus and the role of the states is critical in this regard. In this context, the Securitisation and Reconstruction of Financial Assets and Enforcement of Security Interest Act 2002 will go a long way in allowing the banks to take control of the assets of willful defaulters without going through cumbersome and time-consuming litigation.

The ability of the banks to increase their loan portfolio is not only determined by a growth in their deposits, but also by the need to conform with prudential norms relating to capital adequacy. Once a bank has reached a level of advances commensurate with the capital adequacy norms, any increase in loan assets has to be preceded by a proportionate increase in capital. This can be achieved either by tapping the market or by the Government providing the capital in case of public sector banks. It was earlier difficult for public sector banks to raise fresh equity from the market unless the Government subscribed to the issue in order to maintain its majority share. This was limiting the options for some banks to enter the market. With the Government's decision to bring down its stake in banks to 33 per cent, this immediate bottleneck will be removed. The Government is also seized with the need to find remedial measures to improve the health of weak banks, which have poor bottom lines and high costs, principally staff costs. The Government has recapitalised some of the weak banks and restructuring exercises have been undertaken to bring about a turnaround in their health.

Another point of policy intervention by the Government in the operation of the banking system has been the Statutory Liquidity Ratio (SLR) through which banks are compelled to hold Government and public sector securities. The negative effects of SLR have been mitigated to a considerable extent in recent years, both by progressive reduction in SLR rates and by having market-determined rates of interest on public debt instead of rates prescribed by Government. However, in the absence of an active debt market in Government securities, the SLR is characterised by a certain degree of illiquidity with the banks and an interest rate on public debt, which is not determined in a truly competitive market. On the whole, however, the SLR is desirable, both as a prudential measure and in view of the need to generate debt resources for the Government.

Priority sector lending by banks in another area which needs examination. The role that priority sector lending has played in making credit available to sectors which are of national importance in terms of their effects on employment and poverty alleviation, such as agriculture and Small Scale Industries (SSIs) which have strong externalities, cannot be over emphasised. However, there is a case for reviewing the system of directed lending in so far as development of specialised institutions not only on a sectoral basis but also on a regional basis is concerned. In this context, institutions such as NABARD, SIDBI, Local Area Banks (LABs) Regional Rural Banks (RRBs) and cooperative financial institutions need to be strengthened and professionalised and linkages between themselves and with the commercial banking sector established on a firmer and more formal footing. The institutional structure of branch networks which are critical for effective implementation of priority sector lending should, however, not be diluted even with greater autonomy and private participation in pubic sector banks. Micro-credit, which has been a focus in India and has proved successful in social sector lending needs to be pursued much more vigorously.

With the advent of liberalisation and greater integration of the financial architecture globally, major challenges face the financial sector and it is critical that the necessary skills are acquired and upgraded to meet the new demands. Globalisation has brought about fierce competitive pressures on Indian banks from international banks. In order to compete with the new entrants effectively, Indian commercial banks need to possess matching financial muscle, and size has therefore assumed criticality. However, in the days of 'virtual' banking, the size of a bank measured by its branch network may not be as important as the size of its balance sheet. Indian banks would therefore have to acquire a competitive size. Mergers and Acquisitions (M&A) route provides a quick step forward in this direction offering opportunities to share synergies and reduce the cost of product development and delivery. There are, however, legal and social constraints to these moves at present but it is possible that market compulsions will soon force their removal. A beginning has already been made in the area of private sector banking.

There has been a paradigm shift in Indian banking with the absorption of the latest technology and the need to meet the client's expectations in a customised manner. However, the race for customers could lead to adverse selection. To succeed in the changed environment, banks would need highly efficient assets and liabilities management systems to take care of the need to identify, anticipate, manage and mitigate risks which are known today as well as those which may appear in relation to the products of the future. Growing disintermediation and competition will also put pressure on bank spreads and even fee based and service generated incomes will come under pressure. The way out seems to be compensation through higher turnover without compromising on asset quality, as well as product innovation, which would include relationship banking to a significant degree.

A very important challenge before Indian banking will be to manage the different segments of the economy. Banking services have to be delivered in keeping with the different levels of economic prosperity enjoyed by the population in rural, semi-urban, urban and metropolitan areas, and their relative needs. Providing high technology driven banking in the metros on the one hand and ensuring availability of basic banking services in the rural areas on the other, form the two ends of the spectrum and banks need to manage both equally competently.

Issues in Integration

At present the structure of the financial sector is such that while the different sub-sectors are highly stratified within the subsectors, particularly those which do not any more belong to the State sector, there is a high proliferation of constituents of varying levels of size and efficiency. These sub-sectors are commercial banking, investment banking, development banking, asset management, securities trading and distribution, insurance and NBFCs. The current trend worldwide and the present debate within the country, suggests that the end of stratification between sectors and consolidation within subsectors would be inevitable. Deregulation of the sector and the lowering of entry barriers would speed up this process. Unification in the shape of cross-over between banking and insurance and the emergence of bancassurance has begun and shades of universal banking are already evident and the larger of the constituents are expected to adopt this strategy. However, regional and niche players will continue to be relevant.

The wide area covered by the financial sector in terms of an array of products and geographical reach makes regulation critical and both institutional regulation and self-regulation assume importance. The regulatory system today is far more conscious and better equipped, institutionally and legally, to demand and enforce necessary disclosures and compliance with laid norms for protection of the users of the system as well as the credibility and efficacy of the system itself. The aim would be to achieve international standards in this area within the shortest possible time frame.

An area which requires considerable streamlining is the lack of free flow of information within the financial system regarding the credit worthiness of borrowers and solvency of institutions. The high level of NPAs can in some measure be traced to this lacuna. Unless information sharing and early warning systems are instituted, the dangers to the financial system will get multiplied as the level of complexity of financial transactions in the economy increases. The institutionalisation of such an information system has been recognized as a high priority area requiring legislative action to make it credible. The setting up of the Credit Information Bureau is a beginning in this process.

In the field of technology-based banking, information technology and electronic funds transfer system have emerged as the twin pillars of modern banking development. Products offered by banks have moved way beyond conventional banking and access to these services have become round the clock. This, indeed, is a revolution in Indian banking but some systemic changes are urgently required. Cyber laws and other procedures which are commensurate with modern technology-based banking have to be put in place immediately and sufficient regulatory mechanism has to be instituted so that the fast strides in banking automation does not go on undesirable lines.

Corporate governance in banks and financial institutions has assumed great importance in India and there is still some ground to cover for making all banking institutions safe, sound and efficient. It is necessary that institutions, which form a part of the financial system, have internal management, governance and accountability structures, which measure up to the highest standards. Some of the issues which need to be debated are those of compatibility of corporate governance with public ownership of banks and making the system accountable to economic institutions and regulators. It is also imperative that there is complete alignment between the goals of the management of the banks and the goals of shareholders.

The various steps taken by the Government to meet the challenges of a complex financial architecture have ensured that a new face of the Indian financial sector is emerging to culminate into a strong, transparent and resilient system. The situation, however, is quite dynamic and there would be changes, which we are unable to anticipate now. It is clear, however, that the financial sector players of the future will emerge larger in size, technologically better equipped and stronger in capital base. The regulatory as well as the self-regulatory mechanisms will match up to the best worldwide thereby ensuring that the health of the Indian financial system is not only preserved but improved upon and its ability to withstand shocks, which are inevitable with global integration, remains strong.

21

Vision of Peace in 2020

JASJIT SINGH

"Ours is the great design of promoting peace and progress all over the world."

-Jawaharlal Nehru*

Peace is a fundamental precondition for human development. There has been a view that human development will lead to peace. But the weight of historical evidence confirms that it is the state of peace and an assured sense of security that allows human development to be effectively nurtured and sustained. The vision for 2020, therefore, must seek to establish durable peace, both internally as well as in the external environment. The new millennium offers unprecedented opportunities to put in place concepts and policies which would ensure durable peace and security so that human development can be pursued unhindered by violence and the threat of violence. At the same time, new as well as many of the old inherited challenges face us. The most critical of these is the challenge of the mindset and belief systems of the past. The strong tendency to interpret the future in terms of the past needs to change although within the context of the lessons learnt from the past experiences. We need to remember that to prepare for peace is the most effectual means of preserving peace.

Challenges to peace are numerous. For example, society has always been involved in violence, war preparedness and contributing the means and manpower for war. War, however, had been historically treated as an exclusive undertaking of the military. But

* During the Inaugural address at the Asian Relations Conference, New Delhi, March 23, 1947.

during the past 200 years, society has been made increasingly inclusive to war (and conflict). Society became the target in war under the Clausewitzian concept of targeting and destroying the "will of the nation." Strategic bombing and nuclear weapons have added an apocalyptic dimension to the (indiscriminate) targeting of population centres and innocent human beings. At the same time, the proportion of civilian casualties in wars has increased dramatically. Equally disturbing but more debilitating is the expansion of violence inside society for political ends, with or without external linkages. This is one of the most serious problems of peace and security since it not only undermines national and international security, but also threatens social peace. It is against this general background that we need to look at the issues of peace and stability in the coming decades. Before we embark on an assessment of the future needs it is important to make a quick review of the past.

The Great Experiment

Taken in its totality, the progress of independent India can be described as the "great experiment" and perhaps the most ambitious one in human history. India had been predominantly an agrarian society. However, at the time of its independence it could not feed itself. For the next twenty years we existed in circumstances that at one time came to be known as a "ship-to-mouth existence" symbolising our dependence on food assistance from foreign countries, especially the United States. Indian society had become rigidly stratified over the centuries with deep fissures and discrimination being practiced. The people as such had no say in the their governance, and poverty characterised the general condition of the population. Population was essentially rural-based with a life expectancy even by 1950-51 of a mere 32 years. The literacy rate was a shade above 18 per cent for the country at that time (with female literacy below 9 per cent). India generated a lordly amount of 6.6 GW of domestic electricity which was to rise to 331.6 GW by 1992-93. There was virtually no industry of consequence in the country in spite of valiant attempts made by a few Indian entrepreneurs and the transfer of what had become "sunset" industries in the UK like the textile mills in mid-20th century. Some industry perforce had to be located in India after World War II started. The importance of this has to be judged not so much comparing ourselves with some other country although there would be many lessons in that approach. But the real significance rests with examining the historical context in which we had reached where we were by the time of independence.

The two centuries prior to our independence constituted the period in human history when the Industrial Revolution transformed the world and equations between major countries. At the beginning of the 18th century India accounted for nearly a quarter of the world's manufacturing output. Only China had a higher share of the world output. (See Fig. 1). It was this sustained capability over the previous centuries that attracted foreign invaders to India. And the British (or for that matter the Portuguese and the French) were no different. The combination of Industrial Revolution and the expansion of colonialism led to the bulk of the world losing out on the benefits of industrialisation which were mostly limited to the metropolitan powers of Europe. This basic equation has not changed except that the colonising powers are broadly grouped as 'developed' while the

Figure 1

World Manufacturing Output (in %)

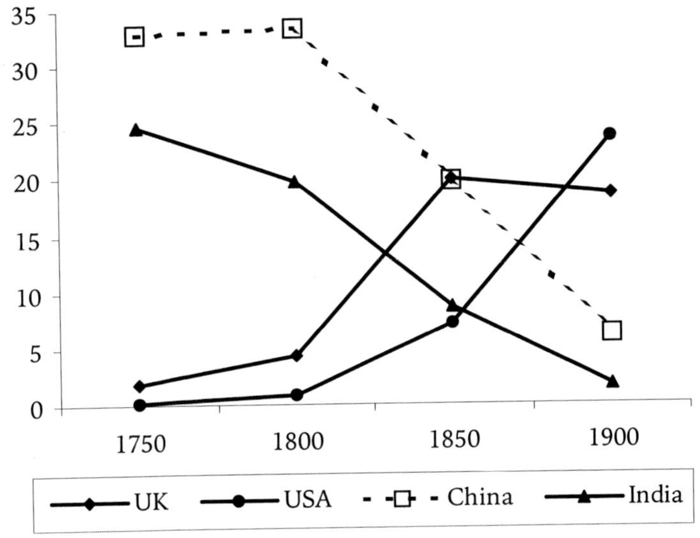

colonised regions are the present world's 'developing' countries. India stood out because of the comparatively much higher level of economic base of production and international trade. Traditional methods of manufacturing started to become obsolete and India, like many other countries regressed into becoming a provider of raw materials. The process led to the de-industrialisation of India during the two centuries under colonial rule. The secondary impact was the virtual decimation of the middle class and the trading communities except for small-scale 'kirana' traders. This only intensified the gap between the rulers and the ruled.

The impact of this de-industrialisation has not been adequately assessed or understood especially by the younger generations who have no personal memories of the earlier years. For example, one major impact of this process was to denude Indian society of an industrial base and narrowing of the trading capacities from the earlier international levels to mostly localised village level trading capacity. The industry started to come up around the time of independence but had to remain confined to small-scale sectors. It was only by the 1980s that industry started to grow into medium and large-scale sectors outside the public sector which of necessity had to establish the larger industrial units. With a gross domestic saving rate of less than 10 per cent and an economy which rested on food shortages, there was little scope for market principles to operate during the early years.

It is the process of change that India has been going through during the past half-century that constitutes this great experiment, that of transforming a weak agrarian economy into a modern multi-dimensional economic enterprise, to transform a traditional stratified society into an egalitarian society, above all to manage the great transformation and people's empowerment through consultative politics. It is inevitable that a billion people on the move in social, economic, technological and political terms would also generate turbulence. Domestically, it is this turbulence that has to be managed in such a way that it does not retard the forward movement. In addition, the external dimension of challenges to peace and security have to be addressed. Domestic peace, however, by itself is a necessary component of broader peace both because it provides the confidence as well as the internal strength and ability to deal with external challenges successfully. This is the meaning of peace and this gives an indication of the challenges to peace and stability in future.

Great Expectations

The greatest global challenge that faces the international community in general and our country today is that of the current transnational revolution of rising expectations. The future international order, peace, and security will substantively depend on the progress of this revolution and the way international community, states, and societies interrelate to it. If we look at major departure points in intrastate balance of power and societal equations, we find that the present revolution, in fact, is the fifth such revolution related to the structures of society and state in modern world dominated by western civilisation.

The *first* revolution, of which the Thirty Years War was the manifestation, and which finally came to an end at the Peace of Westphalia (1648 AD) was, in a way the struggle between the aristocracy against the clergy. The struggle was finally resolved by the separation of the State and Church (in the Occidental Civilisation). The *second* revolution manifested in the French Revolution, resulted from the socio-economic mobility (as a result of the fruits of the Industrial Revolution) seeking to alter the intrastate and societal balance of power. The upwardly mobile segments of society, the merchants, industrialists, capitalists - the bourgeoisie, sought a greater role in the distribution of power and status. While the first revolution altered the basis of the state, the second also sought to alter the basis of state as well as transform the society. The *third* revolution manifested in the shape of a violent implosion following the halting of imperial expansion and resulted in the totality of First World War. The third revolution, as we know, was proletarian versus the bourgeoisie to bring about distributive justice in the socio-economic field. Ironically, it was the capitalist system that started to provide the welfare state that Marxism had held out at the prime hope for mankind. The *fourth,* the revolution of decolonisation, sought political equality in a struggle between the colonised and the imperial metropolitan powers, and a concurrent struggle for redistribution of (of economic and political) power within these states and societies took place, often with violence and repression. The Second World War had given this struggle a great boost because the war itself altered the power equations of the dominant international order.

All the four revolutions were identifiable struggles and closely connected with restructuring of state power, society and international political architecture in association with violent upheavals and major, general wars involving all significant actors. The alteration of the interstate balance of power after the Peace of Westphalia, Congress of Vienna, Paris Conference, and Yalta meeting was also contemporaneous with the intrastate balance of politico-economic power.

We need to recognise that the world has been in the middle of a *fifth* revolution for nearly two decades now. This is the revolution of rising expectations, propelled by an impetus for upward socio-economic mobility and an increasing gap between expectations and satisfaction. A second revolution, that of information and communications has concurrently intensified the revolution of rising expectations by raising aspirations of people world-wide of the potential and desirability of a quality of life which otherwise may not be (and in developing countries lagging behind in human development is not) available in real life. Four decades ago formal education was a pre-requisite for awareness and hence, the understanding of the possibilities of what may be available. The information-communications revolution, especially with the spread of satellite-based audio-visual information has completely altered this equation between awareness and formal education. Like the earlier revolutions, its manifestation also happens to coincide with the culmination of another great international conflict, the Cold War. In fact, the revolution received a marked boost as the Cold War ended. Not the least amongst the reasons was the expectation of the global "peace dividends" and a sense of release and freedom from existing tensions and confrontations.

Human expectations inevitably keep growing with human progress. In fact, a divergence between expectations and actuality is necessary to provide the driving force for human endeavour. The rate of growth not only defines the productivity, but the gap in the rates of growth has a powerful influence on human responses. But if the expectations start rising at a rate far exceeding the rate at which achievement and satisfaction of those expectations rises, social turbulence would start to increase. (See Figure 2). Any further increase in the expectations actuality gap would correspondingly increase instability in the socio-political order with a deleterious effect on the economic activities. At some point a pattern of dynamic instability could set in, which then, results in a socio-political upheaval.

Figure 2

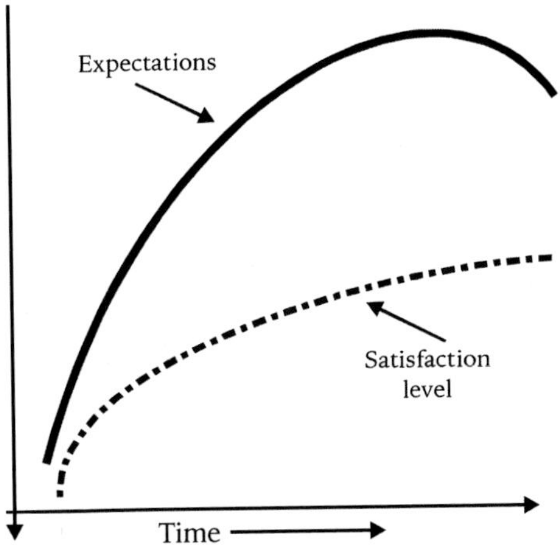

In essence, this is a global phenomenon and challenge. Hence, this is not a problem that can be addressed at the national level alone. Globalisation of trade, information flows, especially through satellite communication systems have not only shrunk the globe, but has rapidly increased the awareness and aspirations of people. There are structural and situational limits to the rate of growth of achievements, especially in the developing world. And the real problem may be that we have yet to achieve adequate consciousness of the ongoing revolution. So far, attention has been focused essentially on the effects of this revolution rather than its true dimensions. But increasing ethnonationalism, religio-political radicalism, erosion of state control over economic, social, and even political-administrative activities of a modern state (Cambodia and Somalia stand out as stark examples), corruption, societal violence and conflicts, erection of trade and tariff barriers, and other forms of protectionism and cartel building are only symptoms of the real problem.

It may be hypothesised that the rate of growth of expectations can be kept depressed through tight control over information flows (and/or authoritarian suppression) on one side and an ideological rationalisation on the other. This was the case with the Soviet Union of Stalin and Brezhnev. However, as information flows increased rapidly, increasing the levels of awareness, expectations shot up almost in an exponential growth pattern. The actuality inevitably lagged behind. It was this phenomenon that Mikhail Gorbachev tried to manage through a harmonisation of ideology and policy to keep the expectations-actuality gap within manageable limits. It is also this rapidly increasing gap that resulted in the continuing politicoeconomic and social crises and turbulence that has far outlived the Soviet Union and the Communist party.

In some respects, the fifth revolution was spawned by the fourth revolution which had created strong expectancies. It was felt that with decolonisation, national governments would automatically bring equality, social justice and economic prosperity. Jawaharlal Nehru's famous speech on the theme of "tryst with destiny" when India became independent on August 15, 1947 is symptomatic. The spread of education and communications has rapidly increased awareness. Given the diverse inherent problems, national governments in developing countries would have found it extremely difficult to meet the aspirations of people even if expectations had not begun to rise so dramatically under the influence of the information revolution since the 1970s. At the same time rising prosperity (or reducing poverty) also led to rising inequities among the people while newly found prosperity also created new sense of vulnerability. As people moved out of abject poverty, they started to have something to lose. The big differences between the India at the turn of the century and that of five decades earlier is that the people are no longer willing to accept poverty. And means are getting compromised for the expected ends.

The problem is of the rapidly widening gap between expectations and satisfaction levels, especially when the latter has been loosing its historical roots of family life, spiritual solace, and traditional cultural moral/ethical values. In most cases, particularly in developing countries without participatory political systems, this gap is at the root of contemporary turbulence. Iran in the 1970s was typical. The inability of the state system to narrow and control the increasing achievement-expectation, fulfilment-aspiration gap is rapidly leading to action for change. The thrust towards democracy (and participatory politics), the return of religion in politics, ethnonationalism representing the disillusionment faultline with existing state nationalism, are all symptomatic of the new revolution, high levels of disillusionment and frustrations. Nearly two-thirds of India's population is below the age of 35 years; and this may be treated as representative. With such high concentration of youth, expectation-achievement equation assumes another dimension. The transition from disillusionment and frustration to violence for the youth comes early and quickly. All the militants/terrorists in Punjab, Kashmir, Assam, Sri Lanka, and other places are young, mostly between 15-25 years of age, and educated to varying degrees. The two hundred thousand *karsevaks* who demolished the Babri Mosque at Ayodhya on December 6, 1992 belonged to the same age group. While secular liberal democratic systems are better equipped to vector this revolution, it nevertheless poses special challenges to them. That is why the need for "renewal" is felt even within the United States and Japan.

The most serious challenge for (international and national/ societal) peace and security in future is the management of the revolution of rising expectations. This is essentially a socio-economic human developmental (including that of gainful employment) problem to which politics must provide the direction. On the other hand, democracy (which more often than not manifests itself in competitive if not combative politics) and free market economy (relying on competitive activity) will need to address this issue. The challenge will be how to maintain competitiveness for efficiency and selectivity while maintaining co-operation for social and distributive justice. In the overall analysis, it needs to be remembered that revolutions are highly destructive without appropriate ideological vectoring and a goal. The present revolution is being hijacked by ethno-religious ideologies. Political leadership and statesmanship will have to define the vision and ideology to provide direction to this revolution. These would have to be continuously reviewed and sustained.

Conceptual Framework for Peace and Security

Conventional wisdom in most parts of the world has tended to treat national security as synonymous with national defence. The reality, which is being increasingly appreciated, is that the former covers a much broader spectrum of challenges, threats and responses as compared to the latter, which being a subset of national security in its comprehensive framework, relates to military security essentially from external threats. At the same time, it has to be noted that military capability also constitutes the ultimate instrument in application of force when and where required in the pursuit of national security. In India, the broader concept of national security may be seen to have its roots in the struggle for independence itself, and well articulated and operationalised in the early years of India's history as an independent nation state. Nehru's concept of an "area of peace" extending all around India, the pursuit of the policy of non-alignment in a global system that was characterised by adversarial bloc confrontation with the resultant coldwar politics, and the emphasis on development even at the cost of defence throughout the 1950s are representative of the comprehensive approach to national security. The basic approach also emphasised that India's security issues cannot be isolated from the geostrategic environment and geopolitical realities of the international system.

National Security

In this context, therefore, it would be useful to attempt a definition of national security so as to formulate the framework of national strategy to achieve it. According to Morton Berkowitz and P.G. Bock, "national security can be most fruitfully defined as the ability of a nation to protect its internal values from external threats". However, this definition falls short of a comprehensive approach to national security. Views on exact definitions will no doubt differ, but we may adopt a broad concept of national security as the protection and preservation of the core values and vital interests critical to the nation state from external and internal challenges and threats. The framework of strategy, therefore, must seek to identify the core values as the very foundations of the state and society as it is sought to be sustained. Secondly, it is important to define the vital national interests that require to be protected. The former starts to constitute the national ideology while the latter start to define the goals and objectives so essential to the well being and sustenance of the state and its ideology.

At the same time it is necessary to note that although external and internal security issues are substantially different in nature, they often interact or are interrelated. Many issues affecting internal security may stem from external political, economic or military pressures. Similarly, domestic insecurity and, perhaps, what is even more relevant, perceptions of domestic vulnerabilities would influence our ability to deal with external challenges while providing incentive to inimical powers to apply pressures. As it is, a nation bedevilled with internal unrest facing chronic economic crises, or political turmoil cannot deal effectively with external threats. Objective and reasonably accurate assessments of security threats are not easily achieved; and the balancing of priorities between the external and internal dimensions of security poses the greatest dilemma and challenge. An underestimation of an external threat with a correspondingly lower military preparedness to permit greater resources to be allocated to development in order to enhance domestic security could lead to the erosion of national security if an attack does take place. This indeed, was the experience of India in the first 15 years of its independent existence culminating in the 1962 debacle. On the other hand, the exaggeration of an external threat and the correspondingly higher military preparedness could, at one level, lead to countermeasures by the potential adversary, thus escalating the threat environment to a higher plane, and at another, demand excessive resources eroding the developmental processes within the State and possibly creating conditions inimical to domestic security. The history of Iran during the 1970s under the Shah's rule and thereafter is representative of this phenomenon. The answer lies in viewing defence and development as concurrent goals to be sought in an objective balance rather than in a mutually exclusive paradigm.

Internal security problems, especially in a newly emerged independent but developing country like India essentially grow out of the laborious processes of nation state building. At the root of the problem lies the issue of economic disparities and social inequities. The dynamics of development, industrialisation and modernisation promise on the one side, to reduce the scope and extent of these disparities and inequities. On the other side, they also tend to generate turbulence in society which, if not contained within manageable proportions, could start serious erosion of internal security. Use of force remains an essential instrument to manage turbulence and challenges to territorial integrity. But force must remain the last and ultimate instrument of the state to be used with great care. Its highest utility arises from its value as a deterrent. And the success of deterrence lies in the military capabilities not having to be used. A developing nation like India, by definition, is a society in transition, and a nation on the move. And like any object in transition, it should be expected to create waves of turbulence. Expansion of education, civic amenities and communications tends to raise aspirations. These aspirations can mostly be met only through socio-economic development and empowerment. However, a significant differential between economic growth and population growth is required to be achieved if these aspirations are to be fulfilled to at least some reasonable degree. Failure to meet these aspirations rapidly leads to disillusionment and cynicism.

Economic disparities tend to generate pressures for subnational, linguistic and communal groups to seek betterment of their lot through search for advancement of their own lot, at times at the cost of other groups in society. Ethnicity is grasped more tenaciously in a society in transition towards modernisation especially where centuries old traditional value systems (like joint family system) rapidly give way to more nuclear families and impersonal relationships. While at the personal plane, ethnicity may provide a reassuring anchor in a climate of turbulence and uncertainty, at the community and societal level it tends to encourage divisive tendencies. Against the background of inherited social inequities, cohesion in society becomes vulnerable to conflicting pressures. While the essential means to resolve the socio-economic contradictions is a political system with a wide decisionmaking base, the stability of that political system becomes a crucial element in the paradigm for national security. The erosion of social cohesion tends to get reflected in partisan politics. The inevitable existence of external pressures tends to have a further debilitating effect on political stability. In a nascent nation state, the maturity of the political institutions is crucial to political stability. The alternative is the shift towards overcentralisation of power, narrowing the decision-making base to an everreducing select elite till the system turns authoritarian and then totalitarian.

A notional representation of national security is depicted in Figure 3. The innermost ring represents the core values and vital interests that a state seeks to protect, preserve and promote. Beyond the outermost ring are the multi-dimensional multifarious challenges and threats that impinge ultimately on this core through more visible components represented in the figure in terms of the middle ring. The core values are derived from the vision and ideology that a nation defines/chooses for itself. Geopolitical and other factors also define the vital interests of states. Often these values and interests are in competition and conflict with those of another state as indeed is the case between India and Pakistan. For example, India set about establishing its nation state on the idea that every human being is equal. Hence democracy, adult franchise, secularism, social justice, etc. as the main components of the Constitution. Pakistan, on the other hand, set about creating a state on the basis of religion and discrimination where women would have different rights, and non-Muslims would be denied an equal

Figure 3

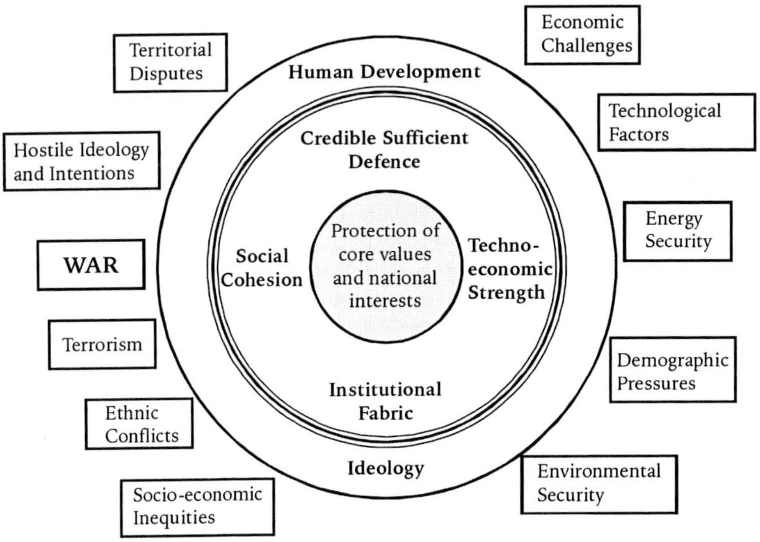

status. At its simplest level the innermost core would require a protective ring of capabilities related to the maintenance of social cohesion and building up of techno-economic strength. These cannot be achieved except through the creation and strengthening of the institutional fabric of the society and state. Crucial in this paradigm is also the factor of military capabilities although they must be kept at the minimum sufficient level to provide credible deterrence against challenges/treats to the innermost core.

The turbulence and erosion of the political institutions, especially if they tend to overcentralise political power, permeates into the institutional and administrative (including diplomatic and judicial) infrastructure with a deleterious effect on socio-economic growth. The negative trends in all the key elements discussed above tend to create a vicious circle of ever increasing insecurities. A positive growth in the key elements of the security paradigm would tend to enhance national security in its comprehensive form; negative trends would tend to increase the vulnerabilities. The key fundamental constituent of a framework for national strategy, therefore, is to impart a positive impetus to the national security paradigm. Within this paradigm, each of the segments of national security plays a stabilising role and provides for State security. But national security can be provided for only by a dynamic and positive paradigm as a whole.

Conceptual Framework

The prime objective of a national security doctrine is the preservation of the core values of the nation. In very general terms these values may be interpreted as the 'way of life' but more substantive identification is needed. The core values of the Indian nation derive their strength from its culture and civilisation. But their greatest manifestation, perhaps, is seen in the fundamentals of the struggle for freedom which led to the establishment of the Indian nation state. The very existence, legitimacy and consolidation of the Indian nation state has its foundations in the values and principles on which the struggle to create the nation state was based. Any weakening of these values endangers the legitimacy of the nation state; and every reinforcement of these values strengthens national security in its comprehensive sense. The importance of some of these values becomes even greater when seen in the historical sense. The struggle for independence in India may be seen to have ultimately bifurcated along two separate, disparate and conflictual lines: one which led to the establishment of the Indian nation state, and the other to the creation of Pakistan. This, incidentally, is also substantially responsible for the sense of mutual insecurity, distrust and threat between the two countries.

The Indian struggle for freedom recognised the realities of the contradictions, stresses and strains that inhere in a plural and heterogeneous society. The only way to reduce the centrifugal and conflictual pressures was to accommodate them in an essentially egalitarian, liberal democracy and a secular society. The fact that democratic values and secularism had been an integral part of indigenous Indian culture and civilisation was an additional reinforcing factor. Given India's regional diversity, the only logical approach to unity and strength lay in a federal polity. It was, therefore, logical for the pioneers of the struggle for freedom to work for a sovereign State on the basis of democracy, secularism and federalism. And when a section of the people and their political leaders insisted on denying these values as the basis of the new nation state, and instead substituted religion as the foundation of the Indian political leadership reluctantly agreed to the partition of India and creation of Pakistan rather than compromise these basic values.

A single fundamental idea defines the conceptual framework for India's security, that is, 'the idea of equality of human beings'. This is derived from the vision of a classless caste-less egalitarian society and in turn leads to a number of core values, the most prominent being that of democracy, secularism and federalism. Erosion of any or all of these values in any form for whatever reason erodes the legitimacy of the Indian nation state and hence poses threats to its security. It was for this reason that these values were so carefully enshrined in the Constitution of the young nation by its founding fathers. Strengthening of these values and upholding the Constitution which gives form and substance to these values, thus, becomes the primary component of the strategy for national security.

Conceptually, the framework of India's security requires it to be structured on two more fundamental criteria: that of optimum freedom of action to protect and advance national interests, and secondly, that of a paradigm of national power. It is also apparent that these two are deeply interlinked and interrelated. The problem perhaps lies in the fact that the first, having been practised as an article of faith in dealing with international issues, is better understood by most in terms of non-alignment in a world of alliance systems and bipolar power blocs, but the latter is not well understood.

Non-alignment is a strategy to preserve national freedom of action and response in the prevailing international order so as to nurture and enhance national interest and power. Non-alignment is a vital prerequisite for nation state building especially for a country with tremendous power potential resources like India. It is instructive to remember that the spectacular growth of the USA and Russia in terms of the (traditional) denominators of relative power of the States took place mainly outside the prevailing zones of influence in the fields of international power.

Freedom of action to select policy options is not only necessary to safeguard national interests, but in a bipolar world order which was inherently unstable, it became an essential catalyst to help move the international world order towards a stable multipolar or balance of power system. Attempts to achieve this in India have so far been based more on reactive responses rather than on a coherent concept of national power. It is, thus, the last of the five fundamentals of the framework of security — that of national power — which the Indian nation has probably found most difficult to comprehend.

Comprehensive national power (especially intellectual power) is a critical constituent for building and conducting international relations. And while moral force is an integral component, the spectrum of total national power goes far beyond it. Also, in international relations it is not so much a question of what we believe; but perhaps, more relevant are the belief systems of all the other actors in the conduct of international relations which have to be taken into account. The developed industrialised nations firmly believe in the concept of national power as a major instrument in the framework of security and in dealing with international issues. Power basically provides the means to create and safeguard an environment for the development and growth of the individual and the society constituting the State. Power is more than capability to act: it provides refuge from the inequities and uncertainties of the ordinary world and society; and its relationship with ideology, to a large extent, can be one of mutual reinforcement.

Change and transformation in the world are brought about essentially by the exercise of power. Mahatma Gandhi looked at national freedom as the means of providing the power to do things for the nation. Thus, if the national objective of a developing country is to remove poverty, power to make the changes to achieve this becomes essential. Toward this end structural changes need to be brought about not only at the national level, but also at the international level. National comprehensive power is necessary if the country is to ensure an environment of peace in which to pursue human development unhindered by negative impulses. The structural relationship of specific local changes to the larger framework is important and power provides not only the means but also the linkages between the various levels of change. For example, if land reforms have to be introduced and implemented successfully at the village level, some structural changes at the state and national level become necessary; and power becomes important and relevant in bringing about the requisite structural changes. Similarly, it becomes an essential instrument in bringing about changes in the international system in order to further the national interests.

Power has also been defined in international relations as "the capacity of a nation to use its tangible and intangible resources in such a way as to affect the behaviour of other nations". Therefore, the developing countries essentially need to increase their relative power to obtain a tilt in favour of the developing world. National power, thus, must be seen not from the antiquated concept of power in the 19th century Europe, but in its proper perspective at the turn of the century. In a world order of increasing interdependencies, the relative power of nations will increasingly govern and direct the terms of the interdependencies, and therefore, the future of nations as well as the global order.

However, two points need emphasis here: the anatomy of national power must be seen in its totality (not merely in relation to military power) in comprehensive terms, and the relational aspects of power. While military power is a critical component a nation's capabilities to pursue its policy options, it is no longer the only or even the main element among the many constituents of national power. In fact, throughout history, it is the intellectual power of the state that knits all elements of national power into a comprehensive whole.

In sum and substance, therefore, the conceptual framework for a strategy for India's security must rest on five fundamentals: democracy, secularism, federalism, freedom of action, and national (intellectual, economic, social, political and military) power.

Structural Trends

There are a number of structural trends spanning the coming two decades that India's security (at its most comprehensive level) will have to take into account. These could be clubbed together as those where a degree of certainty prevails regarding their persistence and those which are more extensively affected by uncertainty and hence have a higher quantum of variables. The following list is neither exhaustive nor definitive and should be viewed as representative with regard to the factors that we need to influence/manage in order to ensure a durable and predictable environment of peace and security.

There are many factors that are likely to consistently influence our environment during the next 20-25 years:

(i) The twin revolutions (of rising expectations and information-communication) would continue to persist.

(ii) The basic territorial disputes are unlikely to be resolved during this time frame.[1] We must continue our efforts to resolve the territorial disputes at an early date. However, our medium term objective should be to ensure stability and peace and tranquillity on the frontiers with adequate insurance measures for possible reversal.

(iii) The fundamental ideological conflict between Pakistan and India is unlikely to be resolved without a major socia-political change in Pakistan. Such change would create its own dynamics and possibly unprecedented challenges especially if that change is accompanied by instability.

(iv) Religious extremism and radical politics would continue to have an adverse impact on our core values.

---

1. While normally referred to as "border disputes" most of the disputes concerning our frontiers in reality are *territorial disputes*. Since territorial integrity and sovereignty are involved in such cases, they are more complex and difficult to resolve than purely border disputes.

(v) Transnational terrorism as a form of war through other means for political and strategic goals is likely to dominate for the coming decades as a major threat to peace and security.

(vi) The challenge of economic security will increase in scope and complexity. For example, competition for energy could generate serious tensions along the energy fault-lines (between the demand heartland of Japan, China and India and the resource periphery around this heartland). Most estimates indicate that the output of crude oil would peak around 2030 AD. The coming decade, therefore, is likely to witness intensification of geopolitics of energy and significant changes in the equations between producers and consumers as well as among major consumers.

(vii) Public information would play increasing influence in shaping beliefs and hence would be a major factor affecting prospects of peace and peaceful change.

Strategic Uncertainties

Compared to the more identifiable trends, there are a large number of strategic uncertainties that Indian policy will have to contend with in future. The most important factor in this process would be the need for long-term perspective in assessments, planning and strategy formulation so that short-term decisions can be situated in long-term goals and objectives. Some of the strategic uncertainties likely to impact our macro policymaking and prospects of peace and which we would need to manage and vector toward more favourable direction and outcome are outlined in the following paragraphs.

India's Socio-economic Growth and Development

This has to be seen in the context of increasing rates of economic growth during the past three decades and the consequent impact on reducing absolute levels of poverty and improving the quality of life of a large segment of Indian population (compared with the earlier generation). As it is the revolution of rising expectations is impacting our society in a major way. But a potential set back to rising levels of prosperity could almost certainly lead to major upheavals. The continuing social and political turmoil in Indonesia consequent to the economic crisis of 1997 is symptomatic. It needs to be remembered that most revolutions in human history have occurred not when there was acute poverty but during periods of relative prosperity (or its decline after a period of rising prosperity) when the reality and/or perceptions of disparities and inequities intensified.

The International Order

The international order is in a state of transition and its evolution will have a profound impact on the prospects of peace and prosperity. Contrary to conventional wisdom the reality is that new centres of power (with some old ones regaining their position) have been emerging in the past two decades or so. This defines the true contours of the emerging international order. The nature of this evolution is such that the world order can best be described as *polycentric.* There are certain characteristics of this polycentric order that also define the nature of the international geopolitical architecture. These may be summed up as follows:

- Substantive asymmetry of power, capability, and willingness to exercise that capability already exists among the leading centres of power in today's world. This imposes concurrent pressures for competition and co-operation among states especially the leading centres of power.
- Co-operation and competition is increasingly issue based and driven by national interests. States may co-operate in economic matters and yet differ strongly on strategic goals.
- Uncertainty and fluidity in international affairs is accentuated by the information revolution which no longer allows governments the luxury of long reaction time, or the predictability available in earlier times.
- As we advance into the 21st century, the following half-a-dozen primary centres of power and capability are likely to influence politico-military and economic dimensions of the new international order:
  (1) United States of America is the most complete power and has maximised its influence through military, political and economic alliances/partnerships. However, the power of some other states has been rising in comparative terms.

(2) China is growing rapidly across the board and will soon represent the second most powerful centre of power in the world. Its political system is likely to continue along the current vector making China the most powerful corporate authoritarian state in human history.

(3) Japan has established itself as a techno-economic super power. But it hesitates to convert this into political influence and is very shy about exercising its military power.

(4) The European Union (with France and Germany at its core) coming together in increasing ways and co-ordinating its policies is emerging as a major centre of power. However, while individual countries are likely to co-ordinate their policies with alliance policies and interests, significant autonomy in national policy choices is likely to continue in the coming decades.

(5) India as the world's largest democracy is now on the move in economic and technological terms. It has successfully progressed in what can only be described as the human history's most ambitious experiment of transforming a traditional society into a modern one, of transforming an agrarian-based economy into a comprehensive industry-service sector-agricultural economy, rapidly increasing social mobility transforming the country into a class-less society, and so on, all through processes of consultative politics. The World Bank estimates that India will possess the fourth largest economy in the world by 2020. It has a resilient democratic system which has, if anything, gained in strength during the past half century. The country has overcome the fundamental deficiencies in agriculture (where it remained dependent on import of food grains for two decades after independence) although nearly 87 per cent people lived on agriculture in 1950. India emerged into independence in 1947 after 200 years of de-industrialisation (see Figure 1). But since independence India has made rapid strides and now has the world's second largest pool of highly competent

scientific and technological expertise while its software strength is likely to play a major role in the coming years. India's economic growth, not as dramatic as that of China or the East Asia "Tigers" has, nevertheless, shown increasing rate of growth in every decade since the late 1960s.

(6) Russia has been seriously weakened by the collapse and break up of the Soviet Union and the continuing economic vulnerability and political-social crisis. The Red Army is struggling to retain its basic capabilities. But it still possesses a huge nuclear arsenal and the basics around which it could rebuild a powerful state. Above all, it retains the images of a former super power that could exercise influence in many areas.

- The centre of gravity of the emerging international order and strategic affairs is increasingly shifting to the Asian landmass (and contiguous island territories). The 21st century is likely to be Asia-centred due to some of the reasons outlined below:

  1. Asian landmass is where the most far-reaching social, economic and political changes are taking place. How these countries manage change will largely influence the course of world events in the coming decades.
  2. The region still has extensive un-resolved disputes extending from issues of sovereignty to ideological issues which are often constructed on religious extremism.
  3. By 2015, seven out of ten largest economies would be Asian countries (including three out of the four top being Asian, the other country being the United States with its deep and extensive interests in Asia).
  4. Seven out of nine[2] nuclear weapon states are located in Asia (including the United States which has strategically shifted forward into the Asian contiguous oceans, has deployed nuclear weapons in Asia, and will remain an "Asian" power).

---

2. China, North Korea, Pakistan, India, Israel, Russia, and the United States

5. World's energy "demand heartland" composed of Japan, Koreas, China and India is in Asia. And so is the energy "resource periphery" extending from Siberia, Central Asia, Persian Gulf, North Indian Ocean, South China Sea, and East China Sea. Future needs and availability of energy resource base are likely to further emphasise the Asia-centred world order while enhancing the role of major centres of power.

China's Future Policies

China would not only remain the primary strategic challenge (in political-diplomatic, techno-economic, and ultimately, in military terms), but it would be in a position to cause serious damage to our vital interests unless we are adequately prepared. China, which is already the strongest military power in Asia, would have moved rapidly in further accretion of techno-economic strength. Its military modernisation is moving ahead vigorously. It already has increasing access to Western sources of military technology. More important, it now has access to Soviet/Russian military technology without which it could not have transformed the quality of its military technology on a large scale. Increasing Chinese power and the transformation of the international strategic landscape has opened up opportunities for China to move forward into the strategic vacuum created as a consequence of the Soviet collapse. If Russian recovery remains at a low pace, the emerging "strategic partnership" between China and Russia could strengthen, posing new challenges to our security. China-US relationship will be crucial to peace and security in Asia. This relationship appears to contain the seeds of a new cold war and confrontation. Polarisation of such relationship will pose new challenges and choices for countries on the periphery of China (many of which also now contain the world's reserves of oil and gas). It is highly unlikely that the United States would, in future, act against China, especially in Asia, and particularly in military terms. Its own compulsions may lead to the United States pursuing an ambivalent policy toward China. China's southward drive, especially into Myanmar, has longterm strategic implications for us. For example, the terrain and altitude limitations that China faces on the Sino-Indian borders may not be applicable to Chinese military posture in the Indo-Myanmar sector, especially as China continues to develop the strategic infrastructure in Myanmar. Tibet will continue to be a source of concern to Chinese leadership because it perceives serious vulnerabilities in this area. For the same reason, China repeatedly seeks assurances from India that it recognises China's sovereignty over Tibet. Any turmoil in Tibet in future has the potential of seriously eroding China-India relations (as much as they did after 1959). Domestically, China has its own vulnerabilities to resolve which could make it over-react externally. The special place of the PLA in the national power structure also needs notice. Unfortunately, unlike other countries, there is little transparency in China's policies and postures, especially in the military dimension. In the absence of transparency, and China's rapidly growing strength along with its demonstration and readiness to use assertive force (as the missile firings abeam Taiwan showed) are likely to generate a worse-case scenario approach in defence planning by other countries. This runs the risk of becoming a self-fulfilling prophecy. It is essential to note that China's evolution will depend not only upon China itself, but also upon the way other states deal with China through these years of transition and change. This is why India would need to pursue the course of building closer co-operative relationship and stabilise the frontiers with China within a policy framework of 'co-operate and ensure'.

Impact of globalisation could generate serious imbalances and domestic disparities with far reaching effects on domestic peace.

Strategic Priority?

The nature of challenges that we are likely to face and the need to successfully meet them requires that human development in all its dimensions continues to remain our highest strategic priority for the foreseeable future. As noted earlier, peace is an imperative and a pre-requisite for human development if we are to successfully sustain our core values and safeguard our vital interests in the coming decades.

It is reasonable to assume that there will be strong tendency toward polarisation of the polycentric international system over time leading to multipolarity, and possibly, even bipolarity again, although the poles in either case would be significantly different in the past. But any form of polarity (which the US and Chinese policies appear to be heading for) in the international system intrinsically contains an implicit phenomenon of hegemonism and hegemonic framework of interstate relations. While this may reflect the traditional concept of power, it also remains contradictory to the goals of democratisation of the international system.

India's interest would be served well by the perpetuation of non-hegemonic polycentrism rather than any form of polarisation in the international order. This would allow for greater room for manoeuvre to serve our core national interests. India, therefore, may be expected to continue pressing for polycentrism in the international system as the fundamental strategy in the coming years. This would also be consistent with the philosophy and policy of non-alignment (with its roots going back to Indian political thinking before World War II) that it has pursued since independence. Its stand that the UN must continue to play its rightful role in a more democratised world, and consequent need for restructuring and reform of the UN as opposed to the tinkering through ad-hoc additions to the Security Council are premised on the same basic logic. In a parallel process the leading powers of the world are already seeking to ensure that no single power assumes a dominant position. The question that remains is whether some of the older centres of power will be willing to concede and adjust to polycentrism?

India, as one of the key country of Asia (and geographically at the centre of the energy resource circle) with its geo-strategic importance is likely to play significant role in Asian affairs. Peace and stability in the Persian Gulf/Central Asian region, peaceful transition to democratic non-aligned polities, assured continuous access to oil and gas at affordable prices, and co-operative relationship among countries of the region and beyond are some of these interests, besides the safety and well-being of more than 3 million Indian expatriates in the Arab states of the Persian Gulf.

Peace in search of human development must not only be durable, but also seek harmony between peace and security at different levels — international (global and regional), national, and societal levels, not to talk of the level of the individual. Interstate security has been characterised for far too long by the sovereign statecentred, egocentric, and *competitive* paradigm of security which is inherently destabilizing. This paradigm has historically relied on generating insecurity and exploiting vulnerability (as in nuclear deterrence) to seek one's own security. A major paradigm shift to a cooperative security is fundamental to durable peace and security. This requires not only a conceptual framework, especially for remoulding the mind to change the very way we think about security matters, but also concrete feasible actions to reshape the security environment where human development must remain the prime strategic objective. This, however, requires co-operation by the adversary.

India has consistently sought co-operative security in preference for (unilateral or alliance-based) competitive security which seems to have marked the policies of Pakistan and even China in the early years. Organising the Asian Relations Conference of March 1947 even before the country became formally independent, Panchsheel, the principle and strategy of non-alignment (as distinct from the movement), Tashkent Declaration, the 1972 Simla Agreement, Delhi Declaration of 1988, bilateral agreements with China in 1993 and 1996 to maintain peace and tranquillity on the basis of "mutual and equal security," the Lahore Declaration of 1999, and the Vision Statement (between the United States and India) are but some of the examples that the country has followed for more than five decades. The vision for 2020 must seek peace as a strategic priority based on the principle of harmony within the country and co-operative security in international arena.

22

Governance and People's Participation: Vision 2020

H. RAMACHANDRAN

Introduction

In the last decade of the 20th century, the need for good governance has been an important and recurring theme in the literature dealing with human development - both research and popular. There is now a growing body of evidence, which shows that the quality of governance is related to differentials in growth and development. However, much of this literature deals with improving the performance of short term normal government functions such as increasing efficiency of public services, accountability of bureaucracy and enhancing transparency in decision making but ignore the larger and critical role of governments geared to the national future. Governance needs to be seen not merely in terms of managing resources and people during the tenure of a government but its ability to take a long-term view not only of the nation but nation in the global context.

Attributes of good governance must be determined by the nation's vision of the larger social and economic goal(s) and the value system it wants to promote. While a consensus among political parties on the former is more easily achieved and therefore, possible to insulate it from the government of the day, to reach such a consensus in the case the latter is extremely difficult. It is, however, possible to move towards a minimal common agenda across the spectrum of political thinking on a value system that would be promoted.

The goals and value systems tend to be dynamic and change more often at a sedate pace resulting in a sense of continuity thus enabling the society at large to adjust more easily with those changes. Along with such changes in goals, therefore, the system of governance, the institutions as well as attributes of good governance also changes. It is necessary, however, to note that (i) the changes that have swept most nations in the last quarter of the 20th century have been rapid and decision making at all levels have become more complex and dependent on a whole range of factors that are outside the control of decision makers and (ii) that a substantial part of the governance concern must pertain to long term view. A system of governance that has performed well in the past would also require to be changed due to larger changes that take place both within the nation and across nations. What should continue as central to governance, are the people.

As noted earlier, the latter part of the 20th century was an era of radical transformations, some brought about by internal compulsions and the way in which the country was governed and partly due to technological change and the global context. These changes have reduced predictability of the future. As Akio Morita, former president of SONY said, the only way to predict the future is to create it. But creating future requires vision as well as commitment.

A working definition of governance could be "processes, systems and structures that guide the social, economic and political relationships". The relationships could be viewed between government and market, government and citizen, government and private sector and Voluntary Organisations, elected and appointed officials, levels of governments (Union, state and local), and between legislative and executive structures.

A widely prevalent perception of state of governance in India has been summarised as, "Those in the government, continue to feel that that they are doing a fine job and nothing could be better. The citizen clearly feels otherwise. This mismatch in the perceptions of the people and the government is made worse by the credibility gap that exists between the citizen and the government. By now, the general feeling outside the government is that the government is huge, it lacks direction, it is unmanageable, is wasteful and it is uncaring of the citizen. The government on its part keeps on reasserting itself with new policy prescriptions from time to time in a bid to 'win friends and influence people'. A stage has been reached when the people take with a pinch of salt whatever the Government says or claims" (Gupta 2001).

Central to the theme of achieving economic and social development is the quality of Governance. The common and oft repeated attributes of good governance include participation, rule of law, transparency, responsiveness, consensus based, equity concerns, effectiveness, accountable and strategic vision. Governance, therefore, is larger than government and envisages a role for private sector, civil society and citizens at large. Improvement in governance cannot be limited to reforms within government but would need to encompass a wider arena including civil society. Thus, people and civil society institutions themselves form an important link in the governance chain. Notwithstanding several shortcomings and limitation in different models, the experiences across the world show the emergence of self-instituted civil society as an independent social partner which has thoroughly modified governance system. However, increasing role of market, civil societies and non-government organisations cannot compensate the inadequacies of governance, even though their role is crucial in shaping the quality of governance. Government is the focal point for instituting good governance, as all other institutions function within the overall institutional framework provided by the government. An incremental approach to quality of governance cannot meet the emerging challenge of rapid transformation.

In order to develop a vision of governance, it is necessary to map out the social goals in a time perspective. For operational purposes these goals may be stated as:

> Through accelerated social and economic development, by harnessing advances in science and technology and through related concerns for sustainability, by 2020 India will banish poverty and hunger, provide an enabling environment for near full employment through multiple livelihood opportunities and improve living standards qualitatively and quantitatively, while leap-frogging up the ladder of Human Development Index. There will be significant improvements in environmental hygiene, sanitation, health and nutrition. Decentralizing decision making, strengthening local institutions and empowering them will sensitize them of their rights, responsibilities, entitlements and contributions to overall sustainable development. Sustained attention towards conservation of the natural resource base will improve productivity, enhance income and maintain ecological balance and promote environmental safety. India, with its committed democracy would provide a leadership role in this regard.

If we expand on this vision, by 2020, no family will lack basic needs of food, clean water, clothing and shelter. Every citizen would have opportunities to learn and develop skills and the country would have a quality-and-productivity-conscious workforce that would command commensurate returns to lead a respectable life. The vulnerable segments - the old, the physically disabled, mentally challenged, and children would be able to lead a secure life with dignity. Need of the every segment of the life-cycle of our citizens would be addressed – the child hood, adolescent, youth, middle-aged and the old. Values would be promoted toward creating an egalitarian society. The pattern of development would rapidly reduce the urban-rural duality and build a rural urban continuum in living standards and infrastructure.

Governance, Decentralisation and People's Participation

All political power in democracy stems from people. Central, therefore, to governance is empowerment of people by increasing their control over governance. The irony of a discourse on empowerment of people is because "As the colonial state had consciously distanced itself from the people, and as that distance did not significantly narrow in the post-independent era, tradition of consultation of and participation by the people did not develop. Accessibility of government to the common people and their sensitivity to people's need had progressively declined" (Iyer 2001). "Over the decades, after having inherited very substantial powers from it's colonial legacy, the State apparatus has steadily amassed functions — and more powers. The new developmental State has been bestowed a vast number of new responsibilities and vastly extended financial powers. Although the exercise of these powers is not untrammelled, there are a number of checks and balances imposed by the democratic system — the labyrinthine and obscure processes through which decisions are taken, over-regulation in many spheres of public life, the weakness of democratic institutions, and the sheer monopoly which vests with the State, creates sufficient ground for arbitrary exercise of this power. This has led to two very major problems in the governance structures, inefficiency and corruption" (Srivastava 2001).

A culture of dependency on government for almost every thing developed over the last few decades needs to be broken. One of the important components of the solution to the crisis of resource distribution lies in the involvement of people through appropriate institutions at the local level. It is only in recent years that a consciousness of the importance 'stakeholder participation' and 'share holder participation' have begun to emerge. From a situation of extreme of state control the pendulum has started moving back in the other direction — towards the user communities and people. Devolution to local bodies has emerged as a major plank of governance reform, both in the Centre and the States. According to the Human Development Report 1993, where decentralisation has taken place, it has often been quite successful, encouraging local participation, increasing accountability of local officials, reducing costs and increasing efficiency.

As Iyer (2001) notes, Project Affected Persons (PAPs), with the assistance of some NGOs have become more conscious of their rights — both their fundamental rights as citizens and their traditional rights of use of river waters, forest produce and other natural resources. It is by now evident to all but the most diehard proponents of centralism is that in this increasingly worsening scenario of water scarcity, centralised and inefficient systems of water management will not work. Civil society (in the sense of the people concerned, i.e., beneficiaries and those who are likely to be adversely affected and the community in general) plays little or no role in the planning and implementation of such projects. For example, the Irrigation Acts vest the management and control of waters in the hands of the state, and project planning and implementation are largely internal activities of the state. In the absence of institutional arrangements for consultation and grievance-redressal, the process of displacement, resettlement and rehabilitation often generate serious dissatisfactions leading in some cases to conflicts.

> Up-till early to middle of the last century, there existed throughout India, numerous water harvesting structures and small irrigation schemes, and systems of community involvement around these. Since the responsibility for the operation and the maintenance of these structures lay with the community, the close involvement of people in the management of water resources was ensured. The situation changed completely during the latter part of the last century. The community-managed structures went into disuse and decline and the state assumed complete monopoly of water supply and management, even at the local level.
>
> **(Contd...)**

(...Contd...)

As a World Bank study points out, India's policy clearly contradicts these elements. "First, water is provided free of cost (up to 40 litre per capita per day), and users do not contribute to the capital cost associated with higher level of services. Second, ownership of rural water supply installation is not transferred to communities... Communities do not have any control over 'what', 'when', 'where' and 'how' installations are provided. Lastly, mechanisms for communicating feedback from users to water agencies are poorly developed, with few offices to which to report defunct installations. In general, water agencies are not responsive to even this limited feedback" (World Bank, 1999b).

As Kundu (2002) observes, in the urban context community participation dates back to early Seventies largely limited to a few pockets and to creation of local infrastructure.

Involving Community in Infrastructure Development

Community participation in urban development projects has a history dating back to the early Seventies when Urban Basic Service Programme was launched by the Central government with assistance from UNICEF. The projects covered only a few slums in select number of cities. There was no perspective for building a network to cover all the slums even within the selected cities and, consequently, the solutions pursued were local in nature. Attempts were made to do social mobilisation by creating community groups and involving these in implementation of the project at the grassroots level. Community was, thus, viewed merely as an agent, providing support to state sponsored development activities to ensure better implementation, in the initial experiments of community participation.

In subsequent years it was realised that community involvement not only results in effective implementation of the projects but also leads to better designing and substantial reduction in operational costs. Following this, community was often involved not just for project implementation and supervision of work but also in designing the project. All these initiatives notwithstanding, community participation remained a state sponsored activity until the late Seventies.

Community participation as a component of development strategy gained currency in the Eighties as a consequence of failure of public agencies and growing deficiency in the level of basic amenities. It was argued that the community can help not only in social mobilisation but also in raising financial resources that the local authorities need very badly. In many cases, it became possible to have substantial reduction in project cost as the prospective beneficiaries provided their labour free or at a wage rate much below that in the market. Further, the pressure of peer group under participatory arrangement resulted in better monitoring, more productive engagement of the beneficiaries in the project and better recovery of development loans sanctioned to

(Contd...)

(...Contd...)

individuals. The community was mobilised not merely for making contributions in terms of ideas and labour but also for sharing a part of the capital and current expenditure. Only, there was demand for making credit available outside the formal institutional structure, which was beyond the access of the slum communities. In several cases, attempts were made to build mechanisms at community level to ensure timely repayment of loans.

The most innovative form of community participation in infrastructural projects, which has been hailed as a major achievement in the Nineties, is the neighbourhood and slum networking schemes, launched with substantial financial support from the state or Central government (Kundu 2002).

While the need and the rationale for people's involvement in local resources management is increasingly accepted by the government, and some efforts in this direction have been made on the ground, legal provisions and effective institutional structures to facilitate such involvement is yet to be put in place. Thus, Reddy (2000) succinctly notes: "while participatory development is propagated on a large scale, one hardly finds any legislative, policy or political support for it."

Simultaneously, the government sponsored initiatives for people's participation have come into several programmes: Water Users Association in irrigation projects, Watershed Association in watershed management, JFM committees in forest areas, VEC in Primary education and SHG in micro-credit and Resident Welfare Associations (RWAs) or Neighbourhood User Groups (NUGs) in urban areas.

"People's participation has become a standard rhetoric in India today. Different actors interpret it differently. One view is that participation means getting people to agree to and go along with a project already been designed for them or to get support of a few leaders.... The important question is participation for whose benefit and on what terms? ...It must be, therefore, understood as a process by which the people are able to identify their own needs and share in the design, implementation and evaluation of the participatory action. Thus, various elements of participation are decision making at various stages, control and management of funds and resources, share in usufruct and final produce and certainly of benefits." (Mid Term Appraisal of the Ninth Five-Year Plan (Planning Commission, 2000)

Institutional Framework for Decentralisation - The Panchayat

Two major policy shifts took place in India in the 90s - one dealing with the economic restructuring and the second concerning decentralisation of political power, through the 73rd and the 74th Amendments to the Constitution of India. The factors that culminated in these two policy shifts were different - the former brought about by compulsions of balance of payment and the latter by increasing inefficiency and costs of delivery systems of development programmes. This basic difference in the factors that led to the two reform processes of globalisation and decentralisation resulted in an artificial distinction between issues relating to national governance and those of local governance.

The 73rd and the 74th Amendments to the Constitution of India, enacted in 1992, lay down ground rules with basic structural framework for decentralised governance at district and lower levels which can sustain themselves against external interference and emerge as effective and strong people's institutions. The Amendments mandate that every state shall establish a three-tier system of Panchayat, at the village, intermediate (with some exceptions) and district levels. The Panchayat will consist of persons elected directly from the territorial constituencies, all members of the Panchayat shall have the right to vote in the meetings, a fixed tenure of five years, (if dissolved, election must be conducted within a period of six months of the dissolution), each state will constitute a State Election and a Finance commission to review the finances of the Panchayat and recommend principles on the basis of which the taxes could be appropriated by or assigned to various tiers of the Panchayat and the state. The primary role of the Panchayat will be in the area of development planning and implementation of programmes of economic development and social justice. The Eleventh and the Twelfth Schedules of the Constitution lists 29 and 18 functional areas to be transferred to the rural and urban elected local bodies, respectively.

In this backdrop, the emerging literature tends to reduce the issues of decentralisation into one of simple redistribution of administrative power and financial resources among different governing units and viewing them as a question of turf. It can also be viewed as an attempt by higher levels of governments to get rid of trivial local issues and concentrating on larger national issues. In such a case, it is necessary to ask whether the decentralisation merely directs people towards local issues and deflect their discontent from the larger structural questions of political and economic organisation.

Distribution of Power between Various Tiers of Governance

The devolution of power between the Union and the states is more or less clear and constitutionally derived, and the encroachments are minimal. The elected heads of government - the Prime Minister of the Government of India, and the Chief Ministers of various states are recognised as the chief political executive. The control of the state bureaucracy vests with the states and it cannot by-pass the state governments – the formal lines of command are well defined. The friction that appears is largely a result of the demands for greater autonomy from the states, which has accentuated over the years with different political combinations getting elected to the Union and state governments. This clarity is lost when we consider the emerging intra-state arrangements. The functions, power and authority at the sub-state levels are invariably derived not through statutes and can be withdrawn at any time at the pleasure of the state governments. Even in those states, which are considered rather progressive, in terms of their efforts to decentralise, we can find several instances, where, devolved power/authority, has been withdrawn. One exception to this general trend is the state of Kerala, where an ordinance was passed barring the state government from taking back official notification on the subjects devolved; this could only by done through legislation.

The bureaucracy at the district and lower level comes under the direct control of the state government, rather than that of the local bodies. Unless the political and administrative arrangements between the state and sub-state levels are broadly comparable to those between the Union and the state governments, effective decentralisation cannot take place.

Decentralisation - The Process of Learning by Doing

Many events relating to decentralisation are taking place after the 73rd and the 74th Constitutional Amendment. The action has shifted to the states, and the Union government is continuing to prod the states along the path of decentralisation. How various states are responding and at what speed they are implementing the Panchayati Raj as envisaged in the Constitutional Amendment is of interest not only to the politicians, researchers and bureaucrats, but also, more importantly, to the masses and therefore, the nation. Implementation of the provisions of the Constitution Amendments could either be done after a detailed blueprint of all actions are developed at the state level, or with a combination of details of major actions and adhoc responses to emerging field level questions. Almost all the states have chosen the latter approach.

> Following the new Constitutional mandate to the PRIs, issues of administrative decentralisation was referred by the Government of Uttar Pradesh to a committee chaired by J. L. Bajaj. The Bajaj Committee in its report on decentralisation of administration (1995) recommended a modest set of proposals compared to what is already in place in several states. The response of the state government to the recommendations of the Bajaj Committee was initially cautious and implementation was slow. Subsequently a High Powered Committee (HPC) also examined the report. Government line departments have also naturally been slow to decentralise. It took nearly five years after the amended state legislation for thirty-two government departments to issue instructions for devolving powers and functions to PRIs. But almost in all cases, the administrative control of the officers concerned still remains by and large with the line departments.

In response to the field level needs for participatory approach, a number of informal but state sponsored groups appeared. Some of these, as noted earlier, are Water Users Association in irrigation projects, SHG in micro credit and Resident Welfare Associations (RWAs). The need for such forums did exist when the Panchayat institutions were not in place. The need for such parallel forums along with the functional Panchayat institutions has to be reviewed, since their continuance would undermine and erode the legitimate role of Panchayat. Similarly, the concept of development funds allocated to Members of Parliament and Members of Legislative Assembly is a contradiction in the context of Panchayat Institutions and needs to be revisited. These parallel structures and arrangements, often state sponsored and patronised will have to be brought within the ambit of Panchayat institutions – perhaps in the form of standing committees for which there is a provision in the Act.

Despite reservations for weaker sections and women in Panchayat, because of the wide inequity in control and access to resources across class, caste and gender, people's participation is stymied and skewed. Unless this distortion is corrected people's participation would remain notional. It is in this aspect of meaningful participation of weaker segments of the population where Voluntary Sector should play a significant role.

Almost a decade after the 74th Amendment, which provides for mandatory District Planning Committees, only some states have taken steps to constitute them. However, in some states such as Kerala, West Bengal and Madhya Pradesh, decentralised development planning has progressed substantially. The People's Campaign for the Ninth Plan gave the plan priorities to Kerala State Planning Board. Gram Panchayat level plans have been made. The state government has issued guidelines for an evaluation of the plans of local bodies for the financial year. It has constituted expert committees at block, municipal and district levels for this purpose. Block level committees process Gram Panchayat plans and the district level committees process those of blocks and districts. The state level expert committees approve the evaluation reports of municipalities and before they are forwarded to the district planning committees. The people's campaign for the Ninth Plan is an ambitious exercise launched by the government and is being touted as a model to be followed by other states. The Gram Sabha itself exerts peer pressure and also acts as a social auditor. Once the roots of the system become stronger and deeper, the direction will be difficult to reverse. There have, however, been many critics, calling it a democracy of the mob, an anarchy and plans devoid of technical input.

> In Madhya Pradesh, the district governments have taken charge. District Planning Committees met on April 1, 1999 at all district headquarters, with the newly acquired powers to review, supervise and monitor the state government's schemes related to their districts. These committees consisting of 15-25 members, at least four-fifths of who are elected Panchayat representatives, are required to meet at least once a month.

There is still a great deal of ambivalence about the status of the PRIs and some level of uncertainty regarding the mode of functioning, with multi-layered control at various levels, without clear political directions of the government of the day. In the context of an untried arrangement of local autonomy, to a large extent, what is happening in the arena of decentralisation within various states is adhoc – compelled by events of marco-economic policy shifts and the compulsions of emerging pressures for empowerment from below. As various states respond to increasing pressures from the grassroots for empowerment, a whole range of legal battles between the district and lower level elected bodies on the one hand, and that of the state government and its executives, on the other, are being fought in various courts.

> In Haryana, Zilla Parishad members have threatened to resign enmasse, in protest against the government failure to enforce Zilla Parishad Act effectively. Similarly, in Orissa and Maharashtra, presidents of Zilla Parishad have demonstrated over the powerless status of the Panchayat bodies. In Andhra Pradesh, Mandal Parishad chiefs resent curbs on their power, after the state government appointed nodal officers by-passing the elected bodies through the janmabhoomi scheme. In Karnataka, the Forum for Village Republics (Gram Ganarajya Vedike) a group of volunteers launched a state-wide campaign for the empowerment of the Gram Sabha. In Karnataka, women members of the Bangalore Rural Zilla Panchayat thretened to boycott its meetings if they were not allowed to speak in future.

Despite, such two-step-forward-one-step-backward movement, by now there are new rural local bodies with over two million elected members and about 60,000 in the urban/municipal government. Although the design and impact of the decentralized system differs from state to state, the essence of the new bodies are that they have a right to live. Election commission has been set up in the states. The changes so far are far-reaching in nature – there is little prospect of the past being repeated, where at some time 40 per cent of the local bodies were found to be superceded and even large municipal corporations had no elected bodies for over 20 years (Sivaramakrishnan, 1999).

While there are states that have gone in for field level actions for decentralisation, there are others who have constituted committees to work out a blueprint of such actions. For example, Uttar Pradesh has constituted a state level policy cell to make Panchayat system, simple, transparent and effective. In Rajasthan, the state has announced that it will set up a Rural Development Service and a Rural Engineering Service to helps PRIs to render better services.

Direct Democracy - From Panchayat to Gram Sabha

The Gram Sabha is an institution which seeks to place direct political power in the hands of people, without the mediation of elected representatives. It ushers in major change from representative to direct democracy. Some states have gone on to empower not only the elected local governments but also their electorates by providing a larger role for the Gram Sabha. However, as Dror (2001) observes, "Direct democracy can work reasonably well in small communities, where the voters have personal experience of most issues, provided that this is combined with suitable deliberative processes and professional explanation of complex issues".

> The Union Food Ministry has brought the Revamped Public Distribution System under the control of Panchayat Raj Institutions. The new guidelines issued by the Ministry advise the state governments to make arrangements for displaying the list the of beneficiaries from poor households in fair price shops and at the offices of the Gram Panchayat. Gram Panchayat have been advised to form Fair Price Shop Committees, and the Gram Sabha will review the reports of the committees.In Madhya Pradesh, state government has issued directives to hold meetings of the Gram Sabha in all Panchayat. Patwari's presence in Gram Panchayat meeting has been made compulsory, and they are expected to attend to the meetings with all records to answer people's queries. In Rajasthan, the government has decided to make it mandatory for the general body meeting of the Gram Panchayat to be held at least four times a year. The dates have also been fixed.

Financial Devolution

Without financial devolution, decentralisation has no meaning. As mandated by the Amendments to the Constitution, State Finance Commissions were constituted by the states. Many State Finance Commissions have submitted their reports. Some of these have been tabled in the State Legislative Assemblies and a few states have accepted the recommendations. These Commissions address issues of sharing of resources between the state government and the PRIs, including other instruments of augmenting resources of the PRIs such as powers to levy tax, access to control over use of natural resources such as minerals, forest products, etc. The state governments as well as PRIs are also addressing the issue through other means such as reduction of personnel through privatisation, issue of secured redeemable bonds, user charges for services, etc. Besides, the Government of India decided to allow direct lending to Gram Panchayat, Self Help Groups and NGOs for providing roads, drinking water, primary schools, etc. A two member team of the World Bank in fact visited Ahmedabad to discuss a proposal seeking assistance to meet financial requirements of urban local bodies for augmenting infrastructure.

There is enough empirical evidence that the people are quite capable of participating in governance. Experience has also demonstrated that it is best to avoid detailed instructions from the top; that the people know and can prioritise their needs and they will readily contribute and supplement resources, if the projects are beneficial and developed by them. Even Land Survey is now being conducted the PRIs and they are also maintaining land records. Many Gram Panchayat have started maintaining a register of bio-diversity. But this does not mean that they are fully equipped to take part in governance. Information and knowledge base of the general population have to be enhanced. Creating informed people is not a task that can be performed by governments, since that could end up in political marketing. There is a need to raise the knowledge base of political class as much as there is a need for increasing knowledge base of the general masses.

People's Participation and Social Change

Many state governments utilised the opportunity while enacting the Panchayat Raj Act, to usher in social change by various provisions in the Act for contesting Panchayat elections. Besides reservation for the socially deprived sections and women, some have introduced provisions to promote small family norms people with more than two children are barred from contesting elections. Such two-child norm, in the case of Municipal Corporation of Delhi, also applies to nominated members. Section 12 of the Karnataka Panchayat Raj Act lays down that only those who have latrines in their houses can contest Panchayat elections. High courts have upheld many such provisions. Though the spirit behind such a rider is good, in reality it prevents poor people from contesting the poll.

In Kerala, over 12,000 elected PRI members were disqualified for not submitting accounts of their election expenses within the stipulated time. In Punjab, the Panchayat have started working as agents of social reforms through resolutions to avoid wasteful expenditure on rituals. Violators are fined and socially boycotted, it is taking the form of a movement in parts of the Punjab. On the other hand, in the neighbouring state of Haryana, Panchayat continue to order death sentence for inter-caste marriages and elopement. Nyaya Panchayat are slated to be formed in Karnataka, which will be a five member body and no member of PRI can be a member of the Nyaya Panchayat. The Nyaya Panchayat will look into petty offences and problems within its territorial jurisdiction and it will not have powers to punish the culprits, but only impose a fine. Rules have been framed, but they will not override the Indian Penal Code.

Corruption, Transparency and Accountability

The issues of corruption, transparency and accountability are not only related with each other, but need to be addressed at all levels, simultaneously, in order to be meaningful. The issues are also becoming complex with decentralisation of decision making and devolution of administrative and financial power. These issues are sought to be addressed through various instruments.

"To ensure that public servants behave as public servants, and this includes all of them, namely, the political administrators, the civil servants, members of judiciary and the elected representatives of the people, they will have to be subjected to full accountability not only for misfeasance but also for nonfeasance. And this will have to be ensured strictly, even ruthlessly. Some of the pillars of democracy lack accountability while they seek accountability of others. This will have to be rationalized. I have no doubt in my mind that the next 20 years will witness the strengthening of the process of accountability not only of the limbs of governance but even the Press and the Media, the Controller and Auditor General, members of the judiciary and the components of civil society." (Gupta 2001).

In his address to the National Development Council meeting held on February 19, 1999, the Prime Minister stated: "People often perceive the bureaucracy as an agent of exploitation rather than a provider of service. Corruption has become a low-risk and high-reward activity. Frequent and arbitrary transfers combined with limited tenures are harming the work ethics and lowering the morale of honest officers. While expecting discipline and diligence from the administration, the political executives should self-critically review its own performance. Unless we do this, we can not regain credibility in the eyes of the people who have elected us to serve them."

In the broader context, it is realised that accountability should go hand in hand with necessary authority and responsibility, appropriate delegation of powers, and making every unit of government a discrete entity for the performance of its assigned tasks. At the national level, the agenda in this regard includes enactment of Right to Information Act. Pending the enactment, several actions are on the anvil, such as easy access to information regarding procedures, awards of tenders/ contracts, government performance relating to expenditure on programmes and schemes and criteria of selection of beneficiaries of government programmes being easily made available to the public. Legally, people can get extracts from Panchayat documents, photocopies, etc., at a prescribed charge. Computerisation in government departments/organisations are getting scaled up not only to promote efficiency at all levels of government, specially at the level of citizen interface, but also to increase transparency and reduce corruption.

However, it is important that till such time that physical and economic access to technology-based information system is substantially expanded, traditional forms of information would continue to be improved so that in the name of modernisation weaker sections are not excluded in sharing of rapidly expanding knowledge and information base. While an expanded system of acquisition of knowledge and information is a pre-requisite, for it is insufficient to ensure wider people's participation, it must also be realised that participation is not an event such as attending community meetings but is a process, which has to be embedded in the social ethos. It is, therefore, necessary to promote a whole range of opportunities besides Panchayat institutions, which are limited to participation in political arena and local development efforts.

> In Kerala, the state government intends to bring about necessary changes in the rules in order to make public auditing of all plan accounts possible. There are also suggestions to exclude contractors from plan implementation as far as possible, with village committees of the beneficiaries taking up developmental projects. In cases of complaints, the voters will have the right to examine all documents. Rules relating to government contracts will, however, need amendment. Similar experiments in the District Primary Education Programmes, where school buildings are constructed by the community with necessary technical supervision have been successfully completed in many parts of the country.

Increasing Awareness, Conflicts and Judicial Recourse

Increasing level and spread of awareness about the rights of the citizens has led to increasing legal actions, both individual and of public interest, demanding compensation for negligence on the part of governments.

The ongoing processes of decentralisation have also articulated a number of latent conflicts. The decentralisation process envisaged greater decision making powers to be vested with the elected bodies at local levels and the bureaucracy is little inclined to work with non-officials at that level. Thus, one set of conflicts arise between the bureaucracy and the elected representatives of the PRIs. Duplication of authority and lack of clear demarcation between political leadership and officials, with each standing on personal prestige and ego are found to be responsible for such situations, resulting in neglect of work and waste of money.

There are tensions at the local level, the village community being divided on caste, class and political lines. In order to reduce the problems arising out of such conflicts, in Uttar Pradesh, the defeated candidates (who finish second in the polls) have been made special invitees to all Panchayat Committee meetings. In order to empower socially deprived section, reservations for women, scheduled castes and tribes were mandated. Some states also introduced reservations for other backward castes. Both in Bihar and in Tamil Nadu, High courts quashed such reservations. In Panchayat of Rajasthan, over sixty no-confidence motions were moved against women belonging to weaker sections.

The third kind of conflict arises out of use of local resources, say land, by commercial enterprises.

> The Orissa High court has asked the state government not to evict residents of a village for the proposed Tata Steel plant at Gopalpur. The directives came in the wake of petitions filed by the village Panchayat president and the Orissa Unit of People's Union for Civil Liberties. A Gram Panchayat in Himachal Pradesh, has decided to file a petition in the High Court against state government's decision to privatise the golf course in its area. Similarly, we have had Zilla Parishad opposing power plant, as in the case of Cogentrix thermal plant in Karnataka, wherein the state government had observed that such issues were beyond the jurisdiction of the district bodies. On the other hand, we have successful struggle of the people of Querim in

(Contd...)

(...Contd...)

Goa, armed with its new found powers under the Goa Panchayati Raj Act, against the US multinational corporation Du Pont's plan to set up a Nylon plant in their area. In the Gram Sabha meeting held on July 17, 1997, it was resolved to refuse permission to the project as it was bound to cause pollution in the villages of the area and also affect population within a belt of 10 kilometres from the proposed site.

The fourth kind of conflict arises out of the disparate financial arrangements, devolution of powers and differential development programmes between the urban and rural entities.

The Bangalore Urban Zilla Panchayat in Karnataka decided to challenge the amended section 205 of the Karnataka Panchayat Raj Act, which deprives taluk Panchayat of their right over the entire proceeds of the stamp duty cess collected in their respective jurisdiction. The amended section enabled the government to pool together the three per cent cess on stamp duty collected all over the state and distribute it among taluk Panchayat on the basis of their population. This has affected the taluk Panchayat in urban areas, which collected huge amount through the cess, which they now have to share with their rural counterparts, which hardly contributed to the kitty.

Similar, urban-rural dichotomy could be seen when the question of amalgamation of villages in town and the resultant loss of development benefits of anti-poverty programmes to the amalgamated villages occur. About 45,000 residents of 18 villages included in the expanded municipal limits of the twin cities of Cuttack and Bhubaneswar have expressed apprehensions over the continuation of the poverty alleviation and rural development schemes. The Gram Panchayat presidents and the Panchayat Committees were not consulted on the issue, and neither was there any assured infrastructure benefit of urbanisation. The village population is also concerned with higher stamp duty on transfer of immovable property. In Tamil Nadu, 45 of the 67 town panchayat have sought rural status, which will benefit them through centrally sponsored schemes to the tune of Rs. 500,000 to 10,00,000. In Karanataka, we have the complaints of Gram Panchayat presidents in Bangalore Urban district, of neglect by the Zilla Parishad.

Concluding Observations

- Given the continental dimensions and the range of diversities in physical, human and cultural traits, the progress of Independent India has been described as the "Great experiment" and perhaps the most ambitious in human history (Jasjit Singh 2001). However, in the context of rapid transformation across nations, there is an urgency to hasten the reform process and improve governance of the nation. Such reforms would not be confined by a minimalist approach of curbing corruption, improving delivery of service and crating a transparent and accountable bureaucracy but include, putting in place, structure and processes to address long term critical choices to place the nation in a position that it merits in the global community. In a democratic set-up, the sustenance of a bold agenda of reform requires political will at the highest level of government to withstand the pressures of vested interest and sustained pressure by the people. Such pressures would have to be exercised by the civil society.

- The nation would improve its capacity to shape the future rather than wait to be shaped by it. "Ongoing global transformations need guidance, to avoid very negative looming consequences and realise very positive potentials. Markets, civil society etc., however important, cannot provide the needed guidance; normatively and realistically only governance can do so.... Governance should be moral, knowledge-intense, future committed, consent-based, highly energetic but selective, deep thinking, holistic, learning, pluralistic and decisive ... in order, to adequately fulfil crucial future-building tasks, politics must be revitalised. Democracy must be refocused and governance must be radically redesigned. At the heart of the idea of good governance is some rolling back of the state and providing more space for civil society" (Dror 2001).
- It will strive to improve the quality of legislation so that the common people could more easily follow the import of legislation, move from over governed to better governed state and help to remove redundant layers in government functioning through streamlining of processes and systems as well as increasingly deconstructing the power centres.
- Participation and decentralisation share a symbiotic relationship. Some level of gap between people's expectation of their role in decision making and the real world situation may work as a propeller and impetus for greater decentralisation but persistent large gaps could only alienate people from government and pave the way for large discontent.

- While, to start with the process of decentralisation and empowerment of people was initiated from the top rather than from the pressures from the grassroots, over a time, pressures from below have started building up. Given the high stakes provided for the country's future, the fact that (from a relatively uncertain and slow-moving situation) a paradigm shift is being effected throughout the system of governance. Politically, the importance of the PRIs is that they are closest to the people and would command the influence if they performed well. This may, however, lead to over-politicisation of societies, which if sleepy would have little energy for transforming society and if over active would raise demands, which could only be met through redistribution – a zero-sum game (Beteille, 1999).
- These changes have tended to produce a kind of tense social and political equilibrium, which needs to be addressed jointly and collectively, at various levels of government apparatus, the politicians, bureaucrats, the non-governmental organisations and the media. While the bureaucracy, in general, and the established political power do offer some resistance to the ongoing changes, there is no dearth of elements in each of these segments, which have positive attitude towards decentralisation, as a value in it self. A much more active role from a combination of non-governmental organisations and such positive elements from the bureaucracy and the political executive would be necessary to build up the pressure from below.
- It is important that decentralisation design provide for ordinary people to express their views and see them translated into future policy; that it enables citizens to participate in policy formulation and not merely pre-selected choices. The decentralisation process could and should be viewed as an attempt to create a new framework of governance towards fundamental restructuring of society. An analysis of on going processes in India lead us to believe that this is what is emerging, although only a short stretch of the long road to decentralisation has been traversed. Given the low literacy level, particularly among women and the highly stratified

society, the route will be bumpy. The ultimate objective is the empowerment of people and to bring the reins of the power closer to them. Since such an empowerment is perceived to result in dis-empowerment of the existing power structure, there is, and will be, many hiccups on the way as evidenced by a spate of litigation between the 'old players' and the 'new players'.

- The Union and the state governments would essentially play a strategic role in the development of policies and plans relating to the development of physical and human resources and facilitate arenas of people's forum for wider participation in policy choices. By 2020 the Government of India would not only put in place a policy framework for a transparent and responsive (to people's needs) government but also nurture an environment where citizens will play a leading role in decision making and developmental activities, establish a robust mechanism for public scrutiny of government functioning and build an ethos of public service and collective well being.
- An active citizenry and effective participation can only be achieved by enabling access to all citizens (IT for e.g.). It is necessary to establish specific systems and procedures for storage, dissemination and updation of information and ensure that the disadvantaged segments have both economic and physical access to the information base.

The mid term review of the Ninth Plan lists eight aspects of governance that would need to be addressed to improve governance: stability of tenure (of civil servants), transparency and corruption, reduction in size and scale of civil services, professionalism in performance, effective implementation of development programmes, accountability to people, improving quality of life through greater attention to environment, decentralisation and redefining role of government. Each tier of government would play a role that is appropriate to that level.